Political Power in the U.S.S.R.
1917–1947

Political Power in the U.S.S.R. ☆ 1917-1947

The Theory and Structure of Government in the Soviet State

JULIAN TOWSTER

Assistant Professor of Political Science, University of Chicago

With an Introduction by Quincy Wright

NEW YORK

OXFORD UNIVERSITY PRESS

1948

TO THE MEMORY OF MY PARENTS

Preface

In a world of nation-states in which the Soviet Union, as one of the two super-powers, plays a dominant role, the nature of political power in the U.S.S.R. becomes a matter of universal import. This study attempts to survey the development of the theory and structure of government in the Soviet state over the three decades of its existence. It traces the evolution of the basic principles of government, describes the structural arrangements of power, analyzes the relative role of the diverse social, political, and ideological forces in Soviet politics, and evaluates past and prospective trends in terms of liberty and authority, political control, administrative efficiency, and capacity for change.

Three aims were consciously pursued by the author in the matter of presentation: (1) to offer ample detail and documentation, (2) to treat the topics in evolutionary fashion, and (3) to give adequate emphasis to theory. The first aim is dictated not only by the controversial character of the subject, but by the obvious lacunae in existing information on public administration in the U.S.S.R., and the desirability of aiding further researches on specific problems through suggestive footnotes and bibliography based primarily on original sources. In this connection, abundant direct quotation was employed as the best mode of illustrating Soviet thinking on vital political questions.

An evolutionary treatment of the subject appeared desirable in view of the constant stream of change in the Soviet Union and the value of a study of developmental stages for an understanding of the essence and spirit of its existing institutions. As for theory, despite the flexibility of its application and its frequent divergence from practice, it plays a far greater role in political architecture and social engineering in the U.S.S.R. than is generally realized. Hence the attention given to it throughout the study.

The author has also striven for objectivity in the sincere belief that it is the only axe which it is proper for a scholar to grind and the approach through which he serves best the interests of his profession and

of his fellow citizens as well. For any errors of fact or interpretation, substance or form, the author assumes full responsibility.

To the extent to which academic pursuits are stimulated by the work of
others, I deem this an appropriate occasion to mention in particular such
former teachers or present colleagues as the late Professor Samuel N.
Harper of the University of Chicago, Professors Harold D. Lasswell and
Frederick L. Schuman, now of Yale University and Williams College
respectively, and Professors Charles E. Merriam and Quincy Wright of
the University of Chicago. I have likewise benefited from my contacts
with Professor Geroid T. Robinson, Director of the Russian Institute
at Columbia University.

To Professor Wright I am grateful for a number of valuable suggestions in the execution of this study. I am also indebted, and hereby
express my appreciation, to: the Social Science Research Council, for a
fellowship which made possible the completion of this book and to
the Library of Congress for extending to me its excellent research facilities
over a number of years.

JULIAN TOWSTER

University of Chicago
February 1948

Introduction

Broadcasting a month after the outbreak of World War II and six weeks after the Hitler-Stalin Pact had been concluded, Winston Churchill declined to forecast the action of Russia. 'It is a riddle wrapped in a mystery inside an enigma,' he said, but suggested that the key might be found in 'Russia's national interests.'

Experience since the end of World War II has made it clear that the interests of the Soviet Union cannot be deduced only from a study of the history of Russia. Marxist-Leninist ideology; the constitutional and administrative structure of the Soviet government; the peculiarities of the monolithic Communist Party; the revolutionary background of the present leaders; their experience in conducting foreign policy during the past quarter of a century; their interpretation of the impact of the United Nations, the atom bomb, and other social and technological inventions; and the ideas to which their propaganda have committed them and their people during that period — all of these and other factors must be weighed and appraised to solve the enigma.

As the difficulty of solving the enigma has increased, the importance of finding a solution has also increased. It is doubtless true that the United States must, irrespective of Soviet intentions, pursue a policy designed in the short run to preserve such an equilibrium of power that Russia could not, if she wanted, initiate aggression with any hope of success, and in the long run so to strengthen the United Nations that its law will inspire confidence and develop a general sense of security. Both of these aspects of American policy could, however, be pursued with more assurance, with more precision in details, and with less danger that the short-run maneuvering interfere with the long-run goal if more were known of Soviet policy.

There has been no lack of literature on the subject. Correspondents formerly in Russia and now safely on this side of the iron curtain have produced books of the 'now-it-can-be-told' variety. Observers friendly and unfriendly to the Communist experiment have told their story. The Soviet press, the Soviet laws, the Soviet statistics, and the Soviet actions have been reported and analyzed. Officials with experience in Moscow have summarized their impressions, and scholars with a broad background in Russian character and institutions, in the social sciences, and in history have presented their data and conclusions.

The present volume, however, is different in the breadth of its synthesis. Mr. Towster brings to his task a broad knowledge of Russian history, a detailed examination of Soviet official documents and official pronouncements of the Communist Party, and an understanding of Marxist-Leninist ideology based upon study of the original sources in the Russian language. For years he had the opportunity as an official of the Office of Strategic Services and of the Department of State to check his background knowledge with current policy. The objectivity of his conclusions, drawn from this unparalleled knowledge of the field, has been recognized in official as well as in scholarly circles.

Throughout the volume Communist ideology, Russian conditions, Soviet constitutionalism, Party structure, and official policy are related to one another and the changing character of all is repeatedly emphasized. 'One of the chief points of difference [from other governments] is revealed in the continual stream of change in the implements and mechanisms of the Soviet state.' These changes have occurred not only in the political constitution of the state, but also in the role of the Party and the army; in the position of women, of youth, of the nationalities, and of the church; in the relative weight accorded to Russian traditions and to Communist ideology; in the relative influence of peasant, workman, intelligentsia, and other social groups; in the types of economic incentive employed; and in the relationship of liberty and authority. These changes have not always been in the same direction. They have manifested continuing attention of those in control to exigencies and to experience in a process of trial and error.

Soviet constitutionalism still relegates the government of laws to the future, and is today a government of men directing a monolithic party and a totalitarian state which, while ostensibly laboring for the welfare of the people, has put external security first and has substituted psychological rewards for a rising standard of living. Nevertheless the evidence here presented of change and flexibility should warn against grim predictions of the inevitable consequences of such a government. The wealth of detail in the book, presented with a singular objectivity of attitude and a careful balance of judgment, suggests that the Soviet government has been less enigmatic, more human, and less rigid than the superficial stereotypes often represent it.

The author presents his conclusions on the various points clearly and concisely. 'The generalization,' he says, 'seems justified that more liberal practices might grow during periods of substantial external security and internal prosperity, while the dictatorial and centralist aspects would become accentuated in periods of actual or fancied threats from outside and material straits within.' To check such generalizations the reader has available the wealth of detail on which they are based and also copious references to literature and documents if he wishes to convince himself by further research.

This book does not trace Soviet foreign policy in the past, nor does it attempt to predict what that policy is going to be in the future. It, however, presents facts and generalizations about Soviet ideas, conditions, institutions, and politics which should assist the discerning reader to formulate judgments on this problem so momentous to the peace of the world and the future of civilization.

QUINCY WRIGHT

Contents

PART II
THE STRUCTURE AND OPERATION OF GOVERNMENT

Part I

The Principles of the Constitutional Order

Chapter I · The Concept of State and Law

1. THE NEW EMPHASIS IN SOVIET THEORY

(1) THE INTERRELATION OF THEORY AND PRACTICE

So great is the stress placed upon the interrelation of theory and practice in the Soviet state [1] that an understanding of its operative constitutional order would lack coherence without due attention to avowed theory.

Marxism as the Exclusive Ideology. The only theory considered safe and scientific is the Marxian explanation of socio-political phenomena, first expounded by Marx and Engels and subsequently applied and developed by Lenin and Stalin. Depending upon the particular contribution stressed, the teachings of this theory are called Marxism, Leninism, Stalinism, Marxism-Leninism, or Leninism-Stalinism. Compact and all-embracing, this theory is the proclaimed *Weltanschauung* or world view of the Party and the alleged foundation upon which the new Soviet society has been built.[2] Hence, knowledge of its teachings is an absolute requirement for all who aspire to any position of confidence or responsibility in the Soviet state — above all, to the cadres of governmental or Party institutions.[3] In view of developments abroad in the past decade and a half, such knowledge is deemed especially important, and the determinism of the historical process inherent in the Marxian philosophy of history is held not to exclude the realization of the force played by will and ideas in the evolution of social life.[4]

---

1. 'It is known that theory, if it is really theory, gives practical people strength and orientation, a clarity of perspective, confidence at work, faith in the victory of our cause.' (Stalin, *Voprosy Leninizma*, pp. 299–300.)
2. Vyshinsky, 'The Marxian Teaching concerning Law and State,' pp. 11–12.
3. Stalin, *Report on the Work of the Central Committee to the Eighteenth Congress of the C.P.S.U.(B.)*, pp. 62–3.
4. 'It [Marxism-Leninism] teaches that "the method of production of material life conditions the social, political and spiritual processes of life in general," that the ideas dominant in society are the ideas of the class which is dominant in this society. But this gives no reasons for underestimating the role and significance of ideas, political views, theories and science in the development of society. To the contrary, Marxism-Leninism accords

3

Theory as a Guide to Action. Indeed, Marxism is activism incarnate.[5] It takes its cue from Marx's dictum that 'the philosophers have only *interpreted* the world in various ways, but the thing to do is to *change* it.'[6]

(2) THE ADAPTABILITY OF MARXIAN THEORY

Creative Marxism. As a theory of action, Marxism cannot stay frozen. While most of its basic postulates may remain true, some may age with time, others may require changes in emphasis and application, and new truths may be discovered.[7] As early as August 1917, at the Sixth Party Congress, Stalin made the statement: 'One must discard the antiquated idea that only Europe can show us the road. There is such a thing as dogmatic Marxism and creative Marxism. I stand on the latter ground.'[8]

Changing Theory the Norm of the Present. 'Creative Marxism' — that is, theory subject to revision and rejuvenation in consonance with estimates of conditions — has become the current watchword of the Soviet Union. In theory no less than in practice, those who guide the destinies of the Soviet state reserve the freedom of alteration and innovation in accordance with shifts and turns in the environment.

2. THE MARXIAN–SOVIET VIEW OF STATE AND LAW

(1) THE CONCEPTION OF THE STATE

Marxism alone is held to have offered a scientific explanation of the state by showing the historicity of the institution and thus removing the ground from under all mechanistic and idealistic conceptions concerning it.[9]

---

them a tremendous significance, underscoring the principle of interaction of economics and ideology.' (Vyshinsky, 'Lenin and Stalin on State and Law,' p. 44.) Cf. 'Theory becomes a material force, as soon as it takes hold of the masses.' (Marx, quoted ibid. p. 45.) 'Without a revolutionary theory, there can be no revolutionary movement.' (Lenin, *Sochinenia* [Works] IV, p. 380. These works will be referred to hereafter as Lenin, with the given volume indicated.)

5. This view is extensively developed in Mitin, 'The Marxist-Leninist Theory Is Not a Dogma, but a Guide to Action,' pp. 64–82.

6. Ibid. p. 65.

7. See 'Short History of the Communist Party,' *Bol'shevik*, No. 19 (1938), pp. 90–91. 'We do not at all look upon the theory of Marx as something finished and untouchable; to the contrary we are convinced that it only laid down the cornerstones of that science, which the Socialists *must* push forward in all directions if they do not want to remain behind life.' (Lenin, II, p. 492.)

8. Mitin, op. cit. p. 67.

9. Vyshinsky, in *Bol'shevik*, No. 12 (1938), p. 28. 'Marxism has also in these questions given an orderly system of views and principles, not only explaining, in reliance on the

Origin and Essence of the State. The cardinal, summary statement of the origin, essence, and destiny of the state, around which most of the later expositions revolve, was given by Engels as follows:

> The state, therefore, has not existed from all eternity. There have been societies which have managed without it, which had no notion of the state or state power. At a definite stage of economic development, which necessarily involved the cleavage of society into classes, the state became a necessity because of this cleavage. We are now rapidly approaching a stage in the development of production at which the existence of these classes has not only ceased to be a necessity, but becomes a positive hindrance to production. They will fall as inevitably as they once arose. The state inevitably falls with them. The society which organizes production anew on the basis of free and equal association of the producers will put the whole state machinery where it will then belong — into the museum of antiquities, next to the spinning wheel and the bronze ax.[10]

Thus, the origin of the state is laid to the appearance of classes in human society. The state as an institution was born on the ruins of the gentile order, when early invention brought about the development of new, improved means of production with the sequels of the division of labor, the institution of private property in goods and means of production, the appearance of trade and exchange of products, and the coming into being of new social formations — possessing and non-possessing classes — with the state emerging as the instrument of institutionalized domination of the former.[11] The conquest theory of state origin — the specific question whether and to what extent the state as an instrument of rule and subordination came about as a direct result of intertribal war with the victors establishing themselves as rulers — is not discussed extensively by Marxian writers. Such a question would be secondary in any event, since conquest and subjection of one group by another are not visualized as having been an economic possibility or desideratum as long as man was unable to produce more than he could live on. It was only when new and better tools made surplus production and exchange possible, creating the potentiality of some men living on the surplus produced by others, that the *raison*

---

works of Morgan, McKennon, M. M. Kovalevsky, and others, the historical origin of the state and its class nature, but also indicating the perspectives of development of the state, its transformations in the hands of the proletariat, and, finally, defining the conditions of disappearance or withering away or, as Marx and Engels said, the going to sleep of the state.' (Vyshinsky, *Sov. Gos. i Pr.* No. 1 [1939], p. 49.)

10. Engels, *The Origin of the Family, Private Property and the State*, p. 158.
11. Vyshinsky, *Sovetskoe Gosudarstvennoe Pravo* (referred to hereafter as *S.G.P.*), pp. 10–11. For an extensive development of this view see Engels, *The Origin of the Family, Private Property and the State, passim;* Lenin, XXIV, pp. 362–77; and Strachey, *The Theory and Practice of Socialism*, ch. XVII.

d'être for conquest was supplied.[12] Hence, the Marxian thesis of state origin is felt to be sustained.

Since 'the state arose from the need to hold class antagonisms in check,' and its very existence is seen as proof that 'the class antagonisms *cannot* be objectively reconciled . . . *are* irreconcilable,' the state is regarded as 'an organ of class *domination*, an organ of *oppression* of one class by another.'[13] Rooted in the material life of individuals, the state is visualized as a machine, a mechanism, an instrument of coercion maintained by the class dominant in society for the preservation of its privileged position, regardless of the form it takes or its incidental beneficent activities.[14] Throughout the ages, the essence of the state has been violence, and its purpose the protection of the interests of the ruling class, 'the creation of "order" which legalizes and perpetuates this oppression by moderating the collisions between classes.' Only in a few cases in history was the state ever able to pose as a real mediator between classes.[15]

Rejection of Extra-Class Conceptions of the State. Such, in Marxian-Soviet theory, is the general nature of the state. From the point of view of this theory, therefore, it is deliberate deceit or idealistic folly to regard the state as some 'categorical imperative' standing above classes as an expression and guardian of general human interests common to all within the state.[16] It was Engels himself who disposed of the Hegelian concepts of the state as 'the reality of the moral idea,' 'the image and reality of reason.'[17] And his followers in the U.S.S.R. have similarly rejected most of the other characterizations of the state current in Western jurisprudence and philosophy, including those expositions (Gumplowicz, Ratzenhofer, et cetera) that view the progression of history in terms of group struggle but lack the specific class interpretation and terminology of Marxism. Especially such conceptions of the state as *Rechtstaat* or *Kulturstaat* (Jel-

---

12. Lenin, xxiv, p. 369; Strachey, op. cit. pp. 178–9.
13. Engels, *The Origin of the Family*, etc. p. 156; Lenin, *State and Revolution*, pp. 8–9.
14. *S.G.P.* pp. 13, 15; Strachey, op. cit. pp. 172–6. Cf. Sir Thomas More, *Utopia*: 'Therefore when I consider and weigh in my mind all their commonwealths, which nowadays anywhere do flourish, so God help me, I can perceive nothing but a certain conspiracy of rich men procuring their own commodities under the name and title of the commonwealth.' (Robinson's trans. p. 159 [rendered in modern English here].) 'The forms of bourgeois states are exceedingly variegated, but their essence is the same: in one way or another all these states are in the last analysis inevitably *a dictatorship of the bourgeoisie*.' (Lenin, *State and Revolution*, p. 31.)
15. Lenin, *State and Revolution*, p. 9; *S.G.P.* pp. 11–12; Engels, *Origin of the Family*, etc. p. 157.
16. *S.G.P.* pp. 12–14, 16.
17. Engels, *Origin of the Family*, etc. p. 155; Lenin, *State and Revolution*, p. 8.

linek, Gumplowicz), definitions of the state as an embodiment of 'Social Contract' (Rousseau), as grounded in or resting on 'Social Solidarity' (Duguit) or *Genossenschaft* (von Gierke), or as identified with some higher law or objective 'legal order' (Krabbe, Kelsen) et cetera, are regarded in Marxian-Soviet political theory as idealizations in complete contradiction to existing reality.[18]

(2) THE CONCEPTION OF LAW

What is said above about the state is held equally applicable to law, since it is a fundamental position of Soviet theory that state and law are inseparable and cannot be studied apart, and that 'law is nothing without an apparatus capable of *forcing* the observance of legal norms.'[19]

Origin and Nature of Law. For Marxists, the origins of law are not veiled in mists. According to Engels:

At a certain, very primitive stage of development of society there appears the need to embrace by a general rule the acts of production, distribution and exchange of products which repeat themselves day in and day out, to take care that the individual should subordinate himself to the general conditions of production and exchange. The rule, first expressed in custom, then becomes *law*.[20]

---

18. *S.G.P.* pp. 17–35.
19. Ibid. p. 7; Lenin, XXI, p. 438. 'Bourgeois jurists: Bergbohm, Gierke, Meyer, Gumplowicz, Jellinek, Ihering, Anton Menger, Krabbe, Duguit, Petrazhitski, Kelsen, Karner, etc., etc. — unable to move a step from the pitiable idealistic conception, define law, each in his own way as "spirit," "idea," "will," "general will," "particular will," "social solidarity," "social function," etc., etc. . . .' (Vyshinsky, 'The Marxian Teaching Concerning Law and State,' p. 13.) The same is said of the outstanding jurists of pre-revolutionary Russia: Chicherin, Gradovsky, Korkunov and Petrazhitsky. (Ibid. See also *S.G.P.* p. 16.) Related, of course, is Engels' statement: '. . . the jurists find [justification in the various legal systems themselves, independently of economic relationships] by summing up that which is more or less common to all these legal systems as *natural law*. However, the standard which is taken to determine what is natural law and what is not is precisely the most abstract expression of law itself, namely, *justice* . . . the development of law for the jurists, and for those who believe them uncritically, is nothing more than the striving to bring human conditions . . . into closer and closer conformity with the ideal of justice, *eternal* justice . . . [But] the conception of eternal justice varies not only according to time and place but also according to persons, and it belongs among those things of which . . . "everyone understands something different." ' (*The Housing Question*, p. 89.)
20. Engels, cited in *Sov. Gos. i Pr.* No. 3 (1939), p. 6. Yet the precise sequence of arrival of state and law upon the historical scene, which of the two was the first born, is not yet made clear. Engels states further that, '*Together with the law there necessarily appear also organs to which [care of] its observance is entrusted, the public power, the state.*' (Ibid.; italics J.T.) Academician Vyshinsky comments on Engels' discussion of the origin of law: 'This remarkable excerpt shows conclusively that right and law as its form are the expression of the general demand which is presented by the class dominant in the given society to all members of this society for the purpose of upholding social

The essence and purpose of law, as understood by Soviet jurists in accordance with Marxian teachings, is given in the following definition by
the accepted text:

> Law is the aggregate of rules of conduct expressing the will of the dominant class
> and established by legislation, as well as of customs and rules of the community
> sanctioned by state power, the application of which is guaranteed by the coercive
> force of the state for the purpose of guarding, strengthening and developing the
> social relations and arrangements advantageous to and desired by the dominant
> class.[21]

Law is based on society, not vice versa. It is rooted in the material conditions of life and, like the state, is part of the 'superstructure' over the
economic structure that conditions its very existence: its substance, form,
and development.[22] Juridical relations are based on economic relations —
legal systems are but reflections of corresponding material arrangements
in production and exchange. Law, thus, is tied to the chariot wheels of
economy. It can neither rise above nor fall below the economic level of a
given society, but must correspond to and is basically co-ordinated with
it.[23] From this basic postulate the conclusion is drawn — and underscored
— that law as an institution is the expression of the will of the class dominant in the given society at and by virtue of the stage it has reached in
material evolution.[24]

---

discipline, *and from the moment of the appearance of the state* for upholding the state
discipline.' (Vyshinsky, 'Marxian Teaching concerning Law and State,' p. 20; italics
J.T.) This would seem to imply that there was law before the state arrived. Cf. Hazard,
'Housecleaning in Soviet Law,' pp. 6–8.

21. *S.G.P.* pp. 52–3. Cf. Malitski, *Sovetskaia Konstitutsia*, p. 8.
22. Vyshinsky, 'Lenin and Stalin on State and Law,' pp. 64–5. The crux of this theory is
found in the following statement by Marx: 'In the social production of their means of
existence men enter into definite, necessary relations which are independent of their will,
productive relationships which correspond to a definite stage of development of their
material productive forces. The aggregate of these productive relationships constitutes
*the economic structure of society, the real basis on which a juridical and political super-
structure arises and to which definite forms of social consciousness correspond.* The mode
of production of the material means of existence conditions the whole process of social,
political and intellectual life.' (Marx, *A Contribution to 'The Critique of Political
Economy,'* Author's Preface, in Burns, *A Handbook of Marxism*, pp. 371–2; italics J.T.)
23. Vyshinsky, in *Bol'shevik*, No. 12 (1938), pp. 20–21. Hence legal institutions and concepts cannot be carried over mechanically from one epoch into another, and Professors
Pashukanis and Krylenko erred in viewing Soviet law as merely bourgeois law carried
over into socialist society. (Ibid.)
24. *S.G.P.* p. 15. Hence, Professor Stuchka, the leading Soviet jurist of the early days, is
severely taken to task for defining law as a system or form of social relations and thereby
missing the fundamental thesis that law is 'the will of the dominant class raised into
law.' (Ibid. p. 25.)

The Future of State and Law. The ultimate future of law and state is not a matter of doubt for Marxists. Being but embodiments of the pattern of command and obedience required in a material environment productive of antagonistic classes, law and state will leave the historical scene when those classes disappear. The state, and with it law as a state-enforceable command, will 'become dormant,' dry up, eventually 'wither away.' [25] But, it is strongly emphasized, now even more than before, this inevitable destiny [26] lies in the dim and distant future, after all states, or at least the most advanced ones of the world, have become socialist.[27] Meanwhile, the road to extinction reserved for the state in Marxian theory is not one of easy and peaceful transition. Since it is a fundamental assumption of this theory that no class ever yields its position of dominance without a struggle, the non-soviet type of state is visualized as destined to go through a period of violent revolution at the hands of the proletarian strata of its population. During this period the prevailing bourgeois state form would be supplanted by the proletarian type.[28] Only then, and not before, does the state in its new form step into a long period of transition toward the classless and stateless society. This brings us to a consideration of the Marxian-Soviet conception of the Soviet state and Soviet law.

---

25. 'As soon as there is no longer any class of society to be held in subjection, as soon as, along with class domination and the struggle for individual existence based on the former anarchy of production, the collisions and excesses arising from these have also been abolished, there is nothing more to be repressed, and a special repressive force, a state, is no longer necessary . . . Government over persons is replaced by the administration of things and the direction of the processes of production. The state is not "abolished," *it withers away.*' (Engels, *Herr Eugen Dühring's Revolution in Science,* pp. 306–7.) 'Finally, only communism renders the state absolutely unnecessary for there is *no one* to be suppressed — "no one" in the sense of a *class,* in the sense of a systematic struggle with a definite section of the population.' (Lenin, *State and Revolution,* p. 75.)

26. Such formulations of the future, Professor Lasswell suggests, gave the Marxian theory a strategic superiority over competing symbolisms, since the theses of classlessness, statelessness, etc., carried an appeal to deep-seated human cravings for omnipotence, effortless happiness, and fraternal equality. (See his *World Politics and Personal Insecurity,* pp. 133–5.)

27. See *infra,* pp. 12–14. 'It is clear that there can be no question of defining the exact moment of the *future* withering away — the more so as it must obviously be a rather lengthy process.' (Lenin, *State and Revolution,* p. 69.) 'The expression "the State *withers* away," is very well chosen, for it indicates both the gradual and the elemental nature of the process.' (Ibid. p. 74.)

28. 'The replacement of the bourgeois by the proletarian state is impossible without a violent revolution. The abolition of the proletarian state, i.e. of all states, is only possible through "withering away."' (Ibid. p. 20.)

3. THE DOCTRINE OF INDISPENSABILITY OF SOVIET AUTHORITY

(1) THE CONCEPTION OF THE SOVIET STATE

It was in accordance with the foregoing first-principle of the Marxian (Soviet) political theory [29] that the first proletarian state in modern times came into being.

Origin of the Soviet State. The Soviet state arose on the ruins of the bourgeois-democratic state form, which followed Tsardom in Russia when the old state apparatus — the army and officialdom — was supplanted by its proletarian counterpart, and the Soviets with their central congresses took the place of the local dumas and of the pre-Parliament and Constituent Assembly. The Soviet state is even described as an entirely new state. Soviet writers insist that, in consonance with Marxian teachings, it was emphasized from the very inception of the Soviet regime that the proletariat has need of a state, of a governmental system of its own making.[30]

Early View of the Soviet State. The essence and purpose of this new state, as conceived for the period following its creation, are given in the following definition:

The new Soviet state is a machine for the suppression of the resistance of the exploiters, for abolition of exploitation, for abolition of the class domination of the exploiters, and for the strengthening of the class domination of the proletariat and its leadership of the rest of the toiling population for the purpose of the complete liquidation of classes in general and the transition towards communism.[31]

---

29. See *The Dictatorship of the Proletariat*, p. 17; Stetsky, *The Constitution of the Socialist State*, pp. 3–4, cited hereafter as Stetsky, *Constitution*.
30. Vyshinsky, 'The Marxian Teaching concerning Law and State,' pp. 29–30; Trainin, 'Communism and the State,' p. 115. Bukharin's advocacy of emphasis on 'hostility in principle to the state' (1916) and his theory of 'blasting' or 'abolition' of the state, were bitterly resented by Lenin and, following the latter, by Stalin, as semi-anarchistic blabber that ignores the whole transition period from capitalism to communism. (*The Dictatorship of the Proletariat*, pp. 21–2.) His proposal to inscribe a provision regarding 'withering away' of the state into the party program (March 1918) was rejected by Lenin as premature and 'distortive of the historical perspective' (Lenin, XXII, 365). And his scheme for such 'withering away' whereby: 'The external compulsive standards will begin to die away: first the army and the fleet, as instruments of the sharpest external compulsion; then the system of punitive and repressive organs; afterward the compulsive nature of work etc.' was laughed out of court by Lenin. Rejoining, Lenin asked contemptuously: 'Is it not the other way around: first "afterward," and then "then" and finally "first"?' (Cited by Vyshinsky in *Bol'shevik*, No. 12 [1938], p. 32.)
31. *S.G.P.* p. 5.

In short, it was a substitution of one class rule by another with the avowed ultimate aim of the elimination of all class rule. Until the possibilities for the fulfilment of this aim were created, however, the proletariat was to be fully conscious of its need of a state — an instrument of rule — to insure its own domination over the former ruling classes and to secure those social-political-economic arrangements that were envisaged as leading to the chosen goal.[32]

The Conception of the Soviet State at the Present Stage. The advent of this ultimate goal — definitive communism — is pictured by Marx as follows:

In a higher phase of communist society, after the enslaving subordination of individuals under division of labour, and therewith also the antithesis between mental and physical labour, has vanished; after labour, from a mere means of life, has itself become the prime necessity of life; after the productive forces have also increased with the all-round development of the individual, and all the springs of co-operative wealth flow more abundantly — only then can the narrow horizon of bourgeois right be fully left behind and society inscribe on its banners: *from each according to his ability, to each according to his needs!* [33]

Somewhere on the road from capitalism to communism there is a road-post termed Socialism — The First Phase of Communism. This is a point in the evolution of the new society when the means of production have been socialized, and when, in the words of Lenin, ' "Equality" seems to

32. See Vyshinsky's articles in *Sov. Gos. i Pr.* No. 1 (1939), pp. 51, 56; *Bol'shevik*, No. 12 (1938), pp. 21, 24; also Trainin, op. cit. p. 110. For a long while various teachings and theories concerning the state, including such as deviated or detracted from the declared nature and purpose of the Soviet state, seem to have been tolerated in greater or lesser measure. For Bukharin, the state was a relation between people, a 'hoop which supports the unity of the exploiters and the exploited' and the Soviet state was 'submerging' or 'dissolving' in its economic basis. (Vyshinsky, in *Sov. Gos. i Pr.* No. 2 [1939], p. 103.) Professor Pashukanis, who climbed to first place among Soviet jurists, taught that: '. . . ethics, law and the state, are the forms of bourgeois society. If the proletariat is forced to use them, it does not mean that there is a possibility of further development of these forms by way of filling them with a socialist content . . . The proletariat must take a sober and critical attitude not only toward the bourgeois state and ethics, but also towards its own proletarian state and ethics . . .' (Pashukanis, *Obshchaia Teoria Prava i Marksizm*, pp. 104–5.) Pashukanis even went so far as to declare that the Soviet state began to wither away on the day it came into existence. (Hazard, op. cit. pp. 11–12.) Other professors, like Reisner, gave idealized or abstract versions of the state as a psychological experience of the people, etc. A relentless struggle has been waged of late years against these and similar views as treasonable or misguided conceptions obfuscating the essence and harmful to the interests of the Soviet state. (See *Sov. Gos. i Pr.* No. 2 [1939], pp. 103–4.)

33. Marx, *Critique of the Gotha Programme*, p. 14. Italics J.T. See also Lenin, *State and Revolution*, pp. 78–9.

reign supreme'; actually this point still spells inequality, since different people, unequal in their abilities, needs, or capacities, are remunerated on the basis of the same principles: '*to* each according to his toil.'[34] And this, it is claimed, is the point now reached by the Soviet Union.[35] About the state at this stage, Lenin said:

And there is no other standard yet than that of 'bourgeois right.' To this extent, therefore, a form of state is still necessary, which, while maintaining public ownership of the means of production, would preserve the equality of labour and equality in the distribution of products.

The state is withering away in so far as there are no longer any capitalists, any classes, and, consequently, no class can be suppressed.

But the state has not yet altogether withered away, since there still remains the protection of 'bourgeois right' which sanctifies actual inequality. For the complete extinction of the state, complete communism is necessary.[36]

The founding fathers had envisioned the victory of socialism as a more or less simultaneous occurrence in the leading countries of the world. Lenin is, therefore, considered to have made a unique contribution to the Marxian science of society in advancing the thesis of the unequal development of capitalism in various countries, which likewise conditions a disproportionate development of possibilities for proletarian revolutions. From this it followed that the social revolution could win first in a few countries or even in one, that socialism could be built in one land.[37] Stalin followed up this thesis and carried it into practical realization in the U.S.S.R. The first Five-Year Plan brought about the socialization of the industrial means of production and extensive collectivization of agriculture. The second brought these processes near completion. Socialism was pronounced built in the main in the U.S.S.R. and was given juridical expression in the new (1936) Fundamental Law of the Land. Not only in designation and aspiration, but in essence, it was said, the Soviet state was now a socialist state. The classless society was declared at hand.[38] And thus, almost inevitably the question of the future of the Soviet state came to the fore.

The Question of the Future of the State under Soviet Communism. Hitherto in Marxian theory classlessness meant statelessness. The prole-

34. Lenin, *State and Revolution,* pp. 75–8.
35. The Constitution of 1936, article 12; *Stalin on the New Soviet Constitution,* pp. 11, 12, cited hereafter as Stalin, *Constitution.*
36. Lenin, *State and Revolution,* p. 78.
37. Iudin, 'The Teachings of Leninism about the Victory of Socialism in One Country,' pp. 35–47, *passim;* Trainin, op. cit. pp. 115–16
38. Vyshinsky, in *Sov. Gos. i Pr.* No. 3 (1939), p. 10.

tarian state was a transitional state.[39] In 1930, however, Stalin pronounced the following dialectic formula:

We are for the withering away of the state. But at the same time we stand for a strengthening of the proletarian dictatorship, which constitutes the most powerful, the mightiest of all governing powers that have ever existed. The highest development of governmental power for the purpose of preparing the conditions *for* the withering away of governmental power, this is the Marxian formula. Is this 'contradictory'? Yes, it is. But this contradiction is life, and it reflects completely the Marxian dialectic.[40]

To this he added early in 1933:

The abolition of classes will be achieved not by extinguishing the class struggle but by intensifying it. The withering away of the state will come not through weakening of governmental power, but through its utmost strengthening, which is necessary in order to put an end to remnants of the dying classes and to organize the defense against the capitalistic encirclement, which is far from being destroyed yet and will not soon be destroyed.[41]

Still, these pronouncements were not immediately taken to mean that the Soviet state will remain even after classes will have been abolished.[42] True, Lenin said that 'for the complete extinction of the state, complete communism is necessary.' But is not Soviet society now moving toward complete communism, when each member of society will be remunerated according to his needs? And, if so, what is to become of the state? Stalin supplied the answer in 1938 in a letter to a perturbed youthful inquirer concerning the finality of the victory of socialism in the U.S.S.R.:

We could say that this victory is final, were our country located on an island, were it not surrounded by a multitude of other, capitalistic countries. But inasmuch as we live not on an island but 'in a system of states,' [Lenin] a considerable number of which are hostile towards the land of socialism, which creates the danger of

---

39. For Marx, Engels, and Lenin the proletarian state was a transitional and temporary, even if lengthy, phenomenon: 'The proletariat needs the state only for a while.' (See Lenin, *State and Revolution*, p. 52.) A number of Soviet jurists, during the earlier period, hewed to this line. '*Its* [*the proletariat's*] *state must be a semi-state*. It must already be suitable for its gradual withering away.' (Gurvich, *Osnovy Sovetskoi Konstitutsii*, p. 33.) Also, Zinoviev stated in December 1925 that while the dictatorship of the proletariat remains, its forms must become 'more and more mild' and that year by year the dictatorship will 'soften down.' (*XIV S'ezd VKP* (*b*). *Stenograficheskii otchet*, pp. 100, 428.)
40. Political Report of the Central Committee to the Sixteenth Congress, C.P.S.U. (B), 27 June 1930, in Stalin, *Voprosy Leninizma*, p. 427.
41. Report of 7 January 1933, ibid. p. 509.
42. Professor Pashukanis went so far as to say that the withering away of the Soviet state would enter a decisive stage in 1937, since classes were expected to have disappeared by the end of the second Five-Year Plan. (See Hazard, op. cit. pp. 11–12.)

intervention and restoration, we say openly and honestly that the victory of socialism in our country is not yet final . . . it is necessary by all means to strengthen and fortify our Red Army, Red Fleet, Red Aviation, Osoaviakhim. It is necessary to keep the entire people in a condition of mobilized preparedness in the face of the danger of military attack, so that no 'accident,' no tricks of our external enemies should catch us unawares . . .[43]

And, finally, to remove all doubt regarding the future, Stalin announced in March 1939:

We are going ahead toward Communism. Will our state remain in the period of Communism also? Yes, it will, unless the capitalist encirclement is liquidated, and unless the danger of foreign military attack has disappeared . . . No, it will not remain and atrophy if the capitalist encirclement is liquidated and a Socialist encirclement takes its place. That is how the question stands with regard to the Socialist state.[44]

Thus, the theory of the future of the state under communism has undergone a fundamental revision. Marx and Engels, it is stated, formulated their conception of the destiny of the socialist state as issuing from the laws of its internal development alone and without consideration of the international situation, since they assumed the simultaneous triumph of socialism everywhere. Stalin, on the other hand, from the experience of over two decades of existence of the Soviet state, reformulated this theory to meet the particular historical conditions of the present and the possible future; that is, on the basis of his assumption that a communist society can be constructed even in one separately taken country in an international milieu of non-communist states.[45]

To summarize, the Soviet state of the present is pictured as on its way from the present or lower phase of communism to the higher phase. No Chinese wall is seen between the two to prevent a gradual, evolutionary transition. There still are remnants of class differences, residues of the old psychology in people's consciences, left-overs of contradictions between urban and rural communities, differences between mental and physical toil, and continuing distribution of the social product according to work done.[46] But most of these heritages from the past are considered well on their way out. An approaching social order is visualized in which these vestiges will have disappeared; where toil will have become a habit, a first necessity instead of a compulsion, and a means to a livelihood; and

43. Stalin's answer to Ivanov, 12 February 1938, in *Vlast' Sovetov,* No. 4 (1938), p. 4.
44. Report . . . to the Eighteenth Congress of the C.P.S.U. (B), pp. 73–4.
45. Ibid. pp. 67–71; Vyshinsky, 'Stalin's Teaching concerning the Socialist State,' pp. 106–8; Trainin, op. cit. pp. 116–17.
46. Trainin, op. cit. p. 110.

where the productive forces of the country will have increased so tremendously as to create the abundant life and permit social reward for work according to one's needs.[47] These forecast changes and the growth of culture and habitual understandings expected to go with them will have created those prerequisites that have always been regarded in Marxian political theory as conditions precedent for the dying of the state.

Still, the Soviet state will remain as long as its encirclement by capitalistic states exists, and, above all, longer than all, will remain those organs of the state that have to deal with this encirclement — with war, foreign trade, and foreign relations. Only the victory of communism on a world scale, it is said, will definitely put the state 'into the museum of antiquities.'[48]

(2) THE CONCEPTION OF SOVIET LAW

Because of the organic connection between state and law, the evolution of views in regard to the Soviet state is paralleled with respect to Soviet law.

Early Definition of Soviet Law. The general definition of law is held applicable to Soviet law throughout most of the elapsed years of existence of the Soviet state. That is, Soviet law was the will of the dominant class, the proletariat, raised into law and serving its interests. The proletariat needed law, it is said, because the complexity of social relations in the transition period of proletarian dictatorship did not admit of repression of the former governing classes by means of extraordinary, administrative measures alone. But the proletariat also needed law as a lever of control, a means and method of regulating social relations in general in its remaking of Soviet society, since, as Lenin wrote, it would be utopian to think 'that people will at once learn to work for the benefit of society *without any norms of law* . . .'[49]

Present Definition of Soviet Law. However, the classless condition of society seen as approaching in the Soviet state renders the general defini-

---

47. Ibid. p. 77.
48. Ibid. pp. 120–24.
49. Vyshinsky, 'Lenin and Stalin on State and Law,' p. 65; 'The Marxian Teaching concerning Law and State,' pp. 21–2, 25–6. Hence, all schematic presentations and specific views formerly propounded by such Soviet jurists as M. Reisner, P. I. Stuchka, E. Pashukanis, N. Krylenko, Volkov, Dotsenko, Ia. A. Berman and Ia. L. Berman, L. Ginsburg and G. Amfiteatrov, in one way or other questioning the proletariat's need of law, or holding that Soviet law is bourgeois in form or substance and is already withering away or destined to do so in the near future, are deprecated and completely repudiated now as wittingly or unwittingly teaching nihilism and harming the Soviet state by attempting to disarm it of a mighty instrument of struggle. (*S.G.P.* pp. 56–62, 77.)

tion of law no longer suitable for it. The newly suggested conclusive definition of Soviet law of the present is as follows:

Socialist law of the epoch of conclusion of socialist construction and the gradual transition from socialism to communism is a system of rules of conduct (norms) established in legislative order by the rule of the toilers and expressing their will, the will of the entire Soviet people, which is led by the working class headed by the Communist Party (Bolsheviks), for the purpose of defending, strengthening, and developing socialistic relations and for the gradual construction of the communist society.[50]

Thus, for the present, the thesis that all law is class law is discarded for the Soviet Union.

View of the Nature of Soviet Law. From its very inception, according to Soviet writers, Soviet law has been socialist law, that is, law called forth to serve in the struggle for socialism. Moreover, because of the close interconnection between the Soviet state and Soviet society, any division of Soviet law into state — that is, public — and private law is rejected.[51] Discarded as well is the classification of law into public in the wider sense and public in the narrower sense. Especially now after the victory of socialism, there can be no juxtaposition of public and private rights and interests in Soviet society. The interests of society, state, and personality are synthesized in a new unity.[52] Hence, all branches of the law are part and parcel of the same uniform law — socialist law. Another distinctive feature of Soviet law, it is emphasized, is its definite imposition of duties in addition to the granting of rights.[53] Corresponding to the still-prevailing unequal rights, it is still unequal law, but its inequalities are said to be increasingly ameliorated and will ultimately vanish with the achievement of the final goal set for itself by Soviet society.

The Question of the Future of Law under Soviet Communism. As in

---

50. Vyshinsky, 'The Eighteenth Congress of the C.P.S.U. (B) and the Tasks of the Science of Socialist Law,' p. 10.

51. See articles by Vyshinsky, Arzhanov, and Trainin in *Sov. Gos. i Pr.* No. 3 (1939), and especially M. Kareva's article, ibid. No. 4 (1939), pp. 14–27.

52. Vyshinsky, 'The Eighteenth Congress of the C.P.S.U. (B) and the Tasks of the Science of Socialist Law,' pp. 24–5. 'The normativists (Kelsen, etc.), too, say that every law is state [public] law. However, one must keep in mind the difference between two types of state. The socialist state expresses the full rule of the Soviet people. The bourgeois state, in all its political forms, stands above society, above the people, is a tool of domination of the exploiters.' (Trainin, 'The Content and System of Public Law,' p. 42, n. 11.)

53. Here reference is made to Marx's dictum: 'Instead of "for the equal right of all" I propose: "for the equal rights and *equal duties of all*" etc. *Equal duties* — for us it is an especially important supplement to the bourgeois-democratic *equal rights,* a supplement taking away from the latter their specifically bourgeois sense.' (Vyshinsky, 'Lenin and Stalin on State and Law,' p. 66.)

the case of the state, the immediate future calls for the further strengthening of Soviet law. The ground for its disappearance will have been prepared internally when the Soviet people will have learned to get along without any special rules calling for certain conduct under threat of punishment — when all will have become accustomed habitually to observe the fundamental rules of communal living without any compulsion whatever.[54] But even under Communism, recently carried over by Soviet writers from the realm of the possible to that of the probable and even the certain, Soviet law will remain, leaving the historical stage only if, when, and as the Soviet state makes its exit.

Thus, the progressively enhanced emphasis on the adaptability of Soviet theory to the exigencies of unfolding history found potent application in the reformulation of views on the state and law. Pleading the impact of external surroundings, Soviet statesmen and theoreticians reversed the conceptions of the future shaped in earlier times and places, answering the vital query whether state and law are 'to be or not to be' in the Soviet social order with emphatic assertions of the present and prospective indispensability of Soviet authority. And this is the view maintained to date. Since any change toward earlier formulations is posited on a problematical mutation in the nature of the international milieu of the Soviet state, this present view gives promise to remain stabilized, enduring — along with other Soviet concepts — as long as that state itself continues to exist.

---

54. Vyshinsky, 'The Marxian Teaching concerning Law and State,' pp. 28, 31, 33.

Chapter II · The Understanding of the Constitution

1. STAGES IN CONSTITUTIONAL DEVELOPMENT

THE Soviet state is functioning at present under its third constitution. The first constitution was adopted for the Russian Socialist Federated Soviet Republic on 10 July 1918, eight months after the assumption of power by the Bolsheviks. As the Fundamental Law for the entire state, it was superseded by the Constitution of the Union of Soviet Socialist Republics, declared as in force on 6 July 1923, and conclusively confirmed on 31 January 1924. The last or present constitution, termed the Stalinist Constitution, was adopted on 5 December 1936.[1] These comprise the main stages in the development of the Soviet constitution.

2. THE NATURE OF THE FUNDAMENTAL LAW

(1) THE INTERRELATION OF CONSTITUTION AND SOCIETY

In the view of Soviet jurisprudence, constitutions are but juridical expressions of the actual correlation of social forces in the state.[2] One must distinguish, in analysis, between the constitution in a substantive material sense and the constitution in a formal sense, that is, between the real force underlying all phenomena of state life and the document in which the nature and attributes of this force are expressed.[3] A true constitution is a reflection of reality. Where there is a divergence between the con-

---

1. For the texts of these constitutions, see respectively *Sobranie Uzakonenii i Rasporiazhenii,* No. 51 (1918), sec. 582, pp. 599–609 (cited hereafter as *S.U.; Sistematicheskoe Sobranie Deistvuiushchikh Zakonov S.S.S.R.,* I, pp. 1–15, cited hereafter as *D.Z.; Konstitutsia Soiuza S.S.R. i Konstitutsii Sovetskikh Sotsialisticheskikh Respublik.*
2. Diablo, *Sudebnaia Okhrana Konstitutsii,* p. 11.
3. Gurvich, *Osnovy Sovetskoi Konstitutsii,* p. 3; Stuchka, *S.S.S.R. i R.S.F.S.R., Sovetskaia Konstitutsia v Voprosakh i Otvetakh,* pp. 6–9. Bourgeois jurisprudence is regarded as lacking bottom in failing to distinguish between the two. Only Lassalle is considered by Soviet jurists to have properly estimated the nature of the constitution (see Diablo,

stitution and the balance of social forces in a state, the constitution is a mere fiction, say the Soviet jurists.[4]

View of the Soviet Constitution as 'Conquered Territory.' With singular unanimity Soviet authorities maintain that there is no divergence between constitution and society in the Soviet state. The Soviet constitution, they declare, is not a program[5] — an ideal presentation of rights and arrangements actually non-existent at present — but 'conquered territory' — a formal description of political, social, and economic arrangements already established in the state.[6] Inseparably connected with the state, the development of the constitution follows that of the state, and alterations in the socio-political environment are reflected in periodic amendments to the constitution. Thus, the constitution is kept up to date as a juridical mirror of changing reality. And the three Soviet constitutions represent major changes in the life of the state and correspond to fundamental transformations in the correlation of forces therein.[7]

Designations of the Constitution. The constitution has been variously designated as Soviet, socialist, federal, proletarian, democratic, and international. These designations derive from the declarations of state theory — describing the fundamental purposes of the Soviet polity — which, unique among constitutions, the Soviet constitution contained in its various stages.[8] They also stem from the basic characteristics of the Soviet constitutional order: the federal territorial-administrative structure, the Soviet governmental form, the socialist nature of the economy, the

op. cit. p. 10; Gurvich, op. cit. pp. 3–5), since his conception of the relation between the constitution and political forces is, in fact, identical with the Soviet view. (See Ferdinand Lassalle, 'Über Verfassungswesen' in his *Gesammelte Reden und Schriften*, pp. 25–61.)

4. Lenin, in keeping with the fundamental Marxian approach to all socio-political phenomena, thought that 'the essence of a constitution lies in the fact that the fundamental laws of the state . . . express the actual correlation of forces in the class struggle. A constitution is a fiction when law and reality part; not a fiction when they meet.' (Lenin, XIV, p. 18.)

5. Though it may have 'the significance of a program of action' for the peoples of other states. (Stalin, *Constitution*, pp. 29–30, *Molotov on the New Soviet Constitution*, p. 17, cited hereafter as Molotov, *Constitution; S.G.P.* p. 122. It is admitted also that to the extent to which the pre-1936 constitutions aimed at Socialism, which is only now deemed established, those constitutions were programs. (Stetsky, *Constitution*, pp. 3–4; Strong, *The New Soviet Constitution*, pp. 65, 66, cited hereafter as Strong, *Constitution*.)

6. Stalin, *Constitution*, pp. 11–12; *S.G.P.* pp. 89, 97, 120; Molotov, *Constitution*, p. 4; Stuchka, op. cit. pp. 7–8; Gurvich, op. cit. p. 7; Malitski, op. cit. p. 457.

7. *S.G.P.* pp. 89–91.

8. Declaration of Rights of the Toiling and Exploited People, *passim;* Constitution of R.S.F.S.R. (1918), article 1; Constitution of U.S.S.R. (1924), Part I. Declaration of Formation of the U.S.S.R.; Constitution of U.S.S.R. (1936), *passim.* See also *S.G.P.* pp. 96–8.

avowed position of dominance of the proletariat in the state — termed 'proletarian dictatorship' — and the role of the Communist Party therein.

Growth of the Constitution. Except during the first eight months of Soviet rule, when the operative constitution was being evolved in the form of a string of declaratory legislative acts, the Soviets have had a single written text embodying the Fundamental Law of the state. But, as in all other states,[9] the written constitution has required legislative supplementation in important particulars and in actual operation has been interwoven with unwritten constitutional customs that have gradually developed within the political power system of the state.[10] Of these, only those norms may eventually find their way into the written instrument that have proved their viability and expediency in constitutional practice.[11]

(2) THE QUESTION OF CONSTITUTIONAL SUPREMACY

The Constitution and Laws. The superiority of the constitution to ordinary laws is generally recognized by Soviet jurists. It is termed the 'Fundamental Law' in every constitutional text and is considered the juridical foundation for all subsequent legislation.[12] Theoretically, therefore, the constitution would be modifiable by neither statutes, decrees, or ordinances, nor, presumably, by treaties.[13] But in practice this theoretical supremacy of the constitution over other juridical norms has been considerably modified.

The Constitution and the 'Proletarian Dictatorship' Principle. In this connection, it should be borne in mind that the Soviet constitution, as the repository of governing principles, is itself limited by the nature and

---

9. Cf. McBain, 'Constitutions,' p. 259.

10. Malitski, op. cit. pp. 9–10; Diablo, op. cit. pp. 18–19, 34–5.

11. 'We resolved not to present at this Congress for your examination statutes adopted at the last session for inclusion in the constitution. We shall wait a while; we shall test them in practice and that which will manifest its capacity to live, which will be in complete agreement with the interests of all the republics, that we shall adopt as an amendment to our constitution at the following Congress.' (Enukidze, Speech before Second Congress of Soviets of the U.S.S.R. on 31 January 1924, cited in Malitski, op. cit. pp. 457–8).

12. Gurvich, op. cit. p. 2; Diablo, op. cit. pp. 6–8, 16–17; S.G.P. pp. 79, 98–9, 109.

13. The relative weight of constitutional versus treaty norms in case of conflict between the two seems to be absent from the discussions of Soviet jurists, though Professor Kotliarevsky maintained that a treaty would supersede previous legislation by the U.S.S.R. or a Union republic. (Kotliarevsky, *S.S.S.R. i Soiuznye Respubliki,* pp. 28–9.) That a treaty cannot create powers not found in the constitution merely because it presupposes the capacity for certain action was recognized implicitly by the fact that it was deemed necessary to include an explicit section in article 49 of the constitution, dealing with the power to proclaim a state of war, in order to implement the Franco-Soviet mutual-assistance pact of 2 May 1935.

content of a higher governing principle of the Soviet state — that of Proletarian Dictatorship. The constitution is a creature, not the creator, of the proletarian dictatorship — which is the acclaimed fountainhead of all power, and is itself called 'the essence of the constitution' in the material sense.[14] Hence, while the proletarian dictatorship is stated to be 'signifying strict order and firm government, acting on the basis of strict principles laid down in the Fundamental Law of the proletarian state, in the Soviet constitution,' it is at the same time declared that *the dictatorship of the proletariat is a power not limited by any laws.*[15] Though the constitution is a primary source of legal norms, it is admittedly not the sole source, since the program and periodic directives of the Communist Party constitute continuous criteria for the functions of the entire body politic.[16]

(3) THE FLEXIBILITY OF THE CONSTITUTION

The outstanding characteristic of the Soviet constitution is its extraordinary elasticity. Though the generally accepted test of the rigidity or flexibility of a constitution [17] is the degree of complexity or facility of its amending process, it is becoming increasingly recognized that a truly valid evaluation requires an inquiry into the actual constitutional practices of the state.[18]

---

14. *S.G.P.* p. 96. Cf. also Diablo, op. cit. p. 41. At one time, Professor Gurvich, a prominent jurist of the early days, spoke of *'the party* about which our constitution [the pre-1936 constitution] is silent, but *which* nevertheless *is the* juridical and *actual essence of this constitution.'* (Gurvich, op. cit. p. 88; italics J.T.) However, since the identification of the Party as synonymous with the proletarian dictatorship has been condemned as misleading (see *infra,* pp. 33–4), Professor Gurvich has repudiated his earlier formulation. His criticism, however, of bourgeois jurisprudence as attempting to stand things on their heads by viewing society as resting on laws and the state on a constitution and not the reverse (Gurvich, op. cit. p. 3) would still be considered a valid Soviet point of view. Diablo, too, maintains that 'Constitutional practice has destroyed the conception of a constitution as of a social contract established for all time and standing above governmental power. No one doubts the fact that constituent functions are governmental functions.' (Diablo, op. cit. p. 21.)

15. *S.G.P.* pp. 50–51. Italics J.T.

16. A writer of the organ of the Attorney Generalship of the U.S.S.R. goes as far as to say that 'The program of the All-Union Communist Party (Bolsheviks) is, thus, the *sole* source, defining the political content of the activities of the entire Soviet state, all of its organs . . .' (L. P. 'Kassatsia v systeme Sovetskago gosudarstva,' *Sotsialisticheskaia Zakonnost,'* No. 5 [May 1938], p. 36; italics J.T. This journal is referred to hereafter as *Sots. Zak.*)

17. This classificatory characterization of constitutions by Lord Bryce has, at least until recently, found ready acceptance in Soviet jurisprudence.

18. McBain, *Encyc. Soc. Sci.,* IV, pp. 260–61; Diablo, op. cit. pp. 18–19.

Causes of the Constitution's Flexibility. There is unanimous agreement among Soviet jurists about the flexible nature of the Soviet constitution.[19] Such flexibility has resulted heretofore from a broad interpretation of the right to exercise constituent functions and a wide leeway in the delegation of powers.[20] But the basic cause of non-rigidity, the *causa causans* flowing from the fundamental nature of the Soviet polity, is the conception of the constitution as a thing to serve, not to be served or worshiped — an instrument constituting at once a juridical crystallization of existing arrangements and a basis for further institutional evolution in the state structure in accordance with changing necessities and altering situations.[21] Thus, before the adoption of the last constitution, the elasticity of the Fundamental Law was given the strength of a principle by Soviet jurists.

Constitutional Elasticity in the Future. The Constitution of 1936 is regarded as consolidating and perfecting state forms. It enhances the constituent process by expressly restricting the amending power to the highest sovereign body and by erecting a higher voting-strength qualification for constituent, as compared with ordinary, legislation. There is little reason to suppose, however, that this will make for greater rigidity of the constitutional order, though it may denote a tendency toward greater stability and stricter observance of the amending process. The prime mover of change in the state, the Communist Party, was, in the words of Molotov, 'always subordinating the forms of state structure to

---

19. Diablo gives the following as reasons for the flexibility of the Soviet constitution: (1) Impossibility of transformation of the constitution in the interests of groups hostile to the 'Proletarian Dictatorship.' (2) Similar impossibility for combinations of opposition parties, since there is but one party. (3) Extensive application of the principle of expediency in the Soviet constitution, rather than bowing before tradition-ridden, outworn state forms, or shibboleths such as 'Supremacy of Law,' etc. (4) The fact that the Soviet constitution is one of a transition period during which social, economic, and political transformations take place, making it necessary that the governing principles embodied in the constitution incessantly change accordingly. (5) Absence of the separation of powers principle — promoter of stability in bourgeois constitutions — from the Soviet constitution, facilitating its amendment by established forms. (Diablo, op. cit. pp. 23–5.) Professor Gurvich assigns as a reason for non-rigidity the constitution's freedom from class compromises. (Gurvich, op. cit. p. 16.)

20. For instances, see Diablo, op. cit. pp. 41–2.

21. See *supra*, p. 19; Gurvich, op. cit. pp. 10–17; Diablo, op. cit., *passim;* Strong, op. cit. pp. 43–5. '[It must] grow and develop, lightly accepting all those changes which are dictated by fast moving life . . . Every minute it must preserve its significance as a working plan, guidance, reflecting the economic interest of the dominant proletariat, not as something abstract, frozen, given for all times and circumstances, but as a practical task, decided differently, dependent upon different historical conditions.' (Gurvich, op. cit. pp. 10–11.) This flexibility was boastfully compared with the rigidity of most bourgeois constitutions, which were seen as class compromises at best. (Ibid., pp. 11–17.)

the fundamental interests of socialism and to the task of strengthening the proletarian dictatorship.' [22] And as Stalin, the principal maker of the last constitution, remarked with regard to the future: 'Naturally, of course, the forms of our state will again change in conformity with the change in the situation at home and abroad.' [23]

3. THE INTERPRETATION AND ALTERATION
OF THE CONSTITUTION

(1) THE POWER TO INTERPRET THE CONSTITUTION

Interpretation under the Constitution of 1918. The power to interpret the constitution was placed in the Central Executive Committee of the Russian Socialist Federated Soviet Republic (R.S.F.S.R.) by the Constitution of 1918, which provided that 'The All-Russian Central Executive Committee shall supervise the observance of the Soviet constitution (article 32).'

Interpretation under the Constitution of 1924. Upon formation of the Union of Soviet Socialist Republics and the adoption of the Union Constitution, identical power was vested in the Central Executive Committee of the U.S.S.R. and its Presidium, while the Supreme Court of the Union was entrusted with 'rendering opinions concerning the constitutionality of decisions of the Union republics, upon demand of the Central Executive Committee of the U.S.S.R. (Articles 30, 43b,c, Constitution of 1924). By the statute defining its functions, the Supreme Court was empowered, upon its own initiative or on request of the Union republics, to make representations to the Presidium of the C.E.C. calling for suspension or annulment of decisions and ordinances of the central organs, i.e. of the Council of People's Commissars and Council of Labor and Defense, and of individual commissariats of the U.S.S.R. on grounds of unconstitutionality. [24] Also, when requested by the Presidium of the C.E.C., the court was required to submit advisory opinions on whether given decisions by the supreme organs of the Union republics and by the Council of People's Commissars of the U.S.S.R. were in accord with the provisions of the constitution. [25] Decisions of the C.E.C. and its Presidium, however, and,

---

22. Molotov, *Constitution,* p. 21.
23. Report . . . to the Eighteenth Congress of the C.P.S.U. (B), p. 73.
24. Statute concerning the Supreme Court U.S.S.R., article 2, section A, par. 'v'. *Vestnik Ts. I.K.* 1923, No. 10, item 311.
25. Ibid. 'b'; Reikhel, *S.S.S.R.,* pp. 123–4; Diablo, op. cit. pp. 94–5; Malitski, op. cit. p. 465.

of course, of the Congress of Soviets were exempt from such jurisdiction.[26]

Thus, barring the process of 'invisible' interpretation of the constitution by all organs of authority — going on in every state in the day-to-day practice of the governmental machinery — the power to interpret the Union constitution rested largely with the Presidium of the C.E.C., with the Supreme Court acting as a sort of auxiliary, consultative body.[27] This was owing not only to the burden of ultimate decision placed in the Presidium, but also to the fact that under various provisions of the first Union Constitution many cases involving the interpretation of the constitution had come directly before the Presidium.[28]

Interpretation under the Constitution of 1936. The Constitution places among matters that are within the jurisdiction of the U.S.S.R., as represented by its highest organs of power and of state administration, 'control over the observance of the Constitution of the U.S.S.R. and the ensurance of conformity of the constitutions of the Union republics with the Constitution of the U.S.S.R.' (article 14d). Specifically, the power to interpret laws in force in the Union — hence, presumably, also of the Fundamental Law — is vested in the Presidium of the Supreme Soviet of the U.S.S.R. (article 49b). At the same time the Procurator (Attorney General) of the Union, now called Procurator General, is entrusted with 'the highest supervision of accurate execution of all laws by all People's commissariats [recently renamed Ministries] and institutions responsible to them, as well as individual officials, and also by citizens of the U.S.S.R.' (article 113).

(2) THE POWER TO AMEND THE CONSTITUTION

Amendment under the First Two Constitutions. As regards the process of amendment, the Constitution of 1918 vested the power of ratifying, supplementing, and amending the constitution in the Congress of Soviets and the Central Executive Committee, specifying that the adoption and

---

26. Professor Malitski bases such exemption on the sovereignty of these organs (Malitski, op. cit. p. 465), though, as Diablo points out, by the letter of the constitution (article 8) the Presidium of the C.E.C. was not a sovereign organ. (Diablo, op. cit. pp. 29–30.)
27. Diablo, op. cit. pp. 94–5.
28. Article 5 requiring Union republics to amend their constitutions in conformance to the Union constitution; article 35 giving the Presidium the power to settle questions in the mutual relations between the Council of People's Commissars and the people's commissariats on the one side and the central executive committees of the Union republics and their respective presidiums on the other; and article 59 allowing the Union republics to suspend ordinances of the U.S.S.R. commissariats if such are palpably in violation of the constitution or laws of the Union or of the Union republic. (See also Diablo, op. cit. ch. v, *passim*.)

amendment of 'fundamental principles' of the Soviet constitution was within the exclusive competence of the Congress of Soviets (articles 49a, 51a).

The Union Constitution of 1924 provided merely that 'the ratification and amendment of the fundamental principles of the present constitution shall be within the exclusive competence of the Congress of Soviets of the U.S.S.R.' (article 2). This was interpreted to mean that the Union Central Executive Committee also had the power of amendment, except that changes in *fundamental* principles of the constitution would require subsequent confirmation by the Congress of Soviets.[29] Neither of these constitutions laid down any special rules or conditions, such as time limits, composition of the amending body, order of initiation and proceedings, special voting-strength requirements, et cetera, that would tend to complicate amendment of the constitution. Amendments were to be carried out by the above-mentioned bodies in regular legislative manner by a simple majority vote.

Non-Rigidity of the Amending Process in Past Constitutional Practice. The Soviet constitutional practice has rendered the amending process even less rigid than formally provided. The need for supplementing the constitution for operative purposes by legislation and interpretation is felt in every constitutional system because of the usual brevity of the instrument. This was even more true in regard to the Soviet constitutions of 1918 and 1924 containing, respectively, 90 and 72 articles. Thus, constitutions inevitably grow through what Jellinek called 'transformations,' or unpremeditated changes in their content brought about by legislative acts detailing and concretizing the general provisions of the constitution, and by interpretations of judicial, legislative, and administrative bodies.[30] In Soviet practice, however, the nature and extent of such transformations in regard to the pre-1936 constitutions have brought about a veritable amendment of the amending process, allowing the Presidium of the C.E.C., the Council of People's Commissars, and the Council of Labor and Defense considerable leeway in ordering important alterations in the governmental structure and in the scheme of division of spheres of competence.[31]

---

29. Stuchka, op. cit. p. 67; Diablo, op. cit. p. 25; italics J.T.
30. Jellinek, *Verfassungsänderung und Verfassungswandlung.*
31. Thus, while the first Union constitution (1923) placed the ratification of international agreements, 'the conduct of all diplomatic relations,' the conclusion of concession agreements, etc., within the competence of the supreme Soviet organs — the Congress of Soviets and the Central Executive Committee — a number of subsequent statutes and decrees have in fact added to the sphere of organs conducting foreign affairs without amending the constitution. This they did by authorizing the Council of People's Com-

The Amending Power under the New Constitution. The new constitution of the U.S.S.R. vests the amending power exclusively within the
Supreme Soviet of the U.S.S.R. and requires a majority of not less than
two thirds of the votes in each of the chambers (article 146). In general
it is a very comprehensive instrument, containing 146 articles. That it
will prove as amendable as the previous constitutions would seem to be
borne out by the fact that since its coming into existence it has been
amended at almost every session of the Supreme Soviet.

(3) OTHER PRACTICES IN CONSTITUTIONAL CHANGE

The Role of the Party in Constitution-Making. There is no mention
anywhere of any required participation of the Communist Party in the
amendment of the constitution. Yet the Party participated in the making
of every constitution and was the initiating source of most of its changes
and amendments, practical as well as formal.[32] Such participation, therefore, though no part of the written constitution, must be considered part
of the unwritten attitude, part of the peculiar system of constitutional
relationships and understandings of the Soviet state.[33] The juridical basis
for such participation since the late 'thirties might be implied from the
constitutional status accorded the Party by the last constitution (article
126). Any such basis in the earlier period, if inferrible at all, would have
to be looked for in the governing principle of Proletarian Dictatorship
— mentioned in every Soviet constitution — within which the Party is
recognized to hold the position of leadership.

Popular Discussion of the Draft of the New Constitution. Constitutions,
as a rule, are not submitted to a direct popular vote for acceptance or rejection.[34] Nor was such submission called for under the provisions of the
Soviet constitutions. Of interest, therefore, is the submission of the draft

missars to approve treaties classified as not calling for ratification, to issue full powers
to plenipotentiaries negotiating such treaties, and to confirm concession treaties, as well
as by empowering the Presidium of the C.E.C. to ratify international agreements in the
interim between C.E.C. sessions, even though these two organs were not 'supreme' by
the terms of the constitution. For other instances of structural-functional changes introduced by statutes and decrees altering the meaning if not the letter of constitutional
articles, see Diablo, op. cit. pp. 28–42.

32. See *S.G.P.* pp. 97, 104, 105, 106, 117, 118. In general, for a history of the making of
Soviet constitutions, see Gurvich, *Istoria Sovetskoi Konstitutsii;* Alymov, 'K Istorii
Sovetskoi Konstitutsii'; Libman, 'O Pervoi Sovetskoi Konstitutsii'; *S.G.P.* pp. 95–7,
103–7, 117–20; *Lenin i Stalin O Sovetskoi Konstitutsii; Istoria Sovetskoi Konstitutsii v
Dekretakh i Postanovleniakh Sovetskago Pravitel'stva* 1917–1936.

33. For a classical exposition of 'constitutional understandings' in general, see Wright, *The
Control of American Foreign Relations,* pp. 7–8, 368–9.

34. McBain, op. cit.

of the Constitution of 1936 for wide popular discussion, which is reported to have involved the distribution of 60 million copies of the draft and its being printed in thousands of newspapers. The projected constitution was studied and discussed everywhere, and 154,000 amendments to it are said to have been suggested by organizations and individuals. The gist of these reached the Constitutional Commission, which integrated them and prepared the final draft for submission to the Eighth Congress of Soviets. On 5 December 1936 the congress, after voting 43 changes in it, adopted the draft as the new constitution of the Union.[35]

The Question of the Future of the Constitution under Soviet Communism. The first two constitutions of the Soviet state are considered constitutions of a period of transition from capitalism to socialism. The present constitution is designated as the constitution of socialism considered established in the U.S.S.R., but not yet of communism, toward which the Soviet state is aiming.[36] Unlike the view formerly held by Soviet jurists, it is now contended that even under communism there will still be a constitution, since the socialist state with its political power structure will remain at least as long as it is surrounded by capitalist states.[37] Only when the latter is no longer a fact and the state and political machinery have gone overboard, will there no longer be any constitution.

In all of its stages, the Soviet constitution has contained provisions purporting to outline the nature and distribution of political power in this new type of polity. From what has been said above, however, it is evident that at no time did the written constitution represent the sole source of derivation or definition of the powers and attributes of the organs of rule. The flexibility of the constitutional instrument, itself largely conditioned by a dynamic balance of forces without as well as within the state, rendered the norms embodied in it into convenient, but neither exclusive nor all-embracing, formulations of the governing arrangements that prevailed from time to time. A comprehensive view of the nature of the political power scheme, therefore, must be sought in a wider context than the formal constitution, that is, in both the constitutional and extra-constitutional structural and conceptual arrangements and understandings that form in their totality the operative constitutional order.

---

35. See Strong, op. cit. ch. III.
36. *S.G.P.* p. 91; Stalin, *Constitution*, pp. 11–12.
37. See *supra*, pp. 12–14.

Chapter III · The Class Principle

1. THE CONCEPT OF PROLETARIAN DICTATORSHIP

(1) VIEW OF THE ESSENCE OF THE DICTATORSHIP

Proletarian Dictatorship as Foundation Stone of the Constitutional Order.
Proletarian dictatorship forms the foundation stone of the Soviet constitutional order. Its open avowal is considered a distinguishing mark of this order, indicative of the realism of Soviet political theory and constitutional legislation.[1] It is the forecast, as being historically inevitable and the prescribed rule of the transition period, the state itself being but the form of the proletarian dictatorship.[2] Structurally, it is a socio-political power system consisting of a central 'directing force' — the Communist Party — and a network of 'levers' and 'belts.' The latter consists of the soviets, trade unions, co-operatives, youth leagues, cultural organizations, et cetera, through which are circulated, carried out, checked, and controlled, policies and functions considered necessary by present or prospective interests and purposes of the toiling strata of the populace.[3]

Coercive and Constructive Sides of the Dictatorship. That by nature the dictatorship partakes of unequivocal violence is readily admitted: 'The scientific concept of dictatorship,' wrote Lenin, 'means nothing else but power based directly on violence, unrestrained by any laws, absolutely unrestricted by any rules.'[4] But its essence in the state is not violence alone, but a higher social organization of the productive forces aiming to establish a society devoid of exploitation of man by man.[5] Hence, it

---

1. *S.G.P.* pp. 132, 147, 148.
2. See *The Dictatorship of the Proletariat,* pp. 39–46, with citations from Marx, Lenin, and Stalin; 'The Program of the Communist Party,' *Source Book on European Governments,* pp. 9, 10, cited hereafter as *Comparty Program, Source Book.*
3. See Stalin, *Problems of Leninism,* pp. 29–33.
4. Lenin, xxv, p. 441; see also p. 436.
5. Lenin, xxiv, pp. 314, 335–6; Stalin, *Problems of Leninism,* pp. 25–6. Stressing only the coercive side of the dictatorship is condemned as one-sided and misleading. (See Stetsky, *Constitution,* p. 42.)

has always been emphasized that the dictatorship of the proletariat, representing rule in the interests of the vast majority of the formerly deprived masses, does not preclude but inaugurates and develops real democracy for them.[6] The dictatorship has its periods, and whether its coercive or constructive side predominates depends upon the tasks envisaged as paramount within each of them.[7]

View of the Role of the Proletariat vis-à-vis *the Other Classes in the Earlier Period.* The setting up of the proletarian dictatorship, it is said, does not connote the end of social struggle. The battle of classes continues.[8] But underlying it are new assumptions of power based upon the newly achieved and further evolving inter-class balance of forces. Stated in one sentence, these assumptions are that 'the dictatorship of the proletariat is the rule of *one* class, which takes into its hand the *entire* apparatus of the new statehood, which *conquers* the bourgeoisie and *neutralizes* the entire petty bourgeoisie, the peasantry, the Babbittry, the intelligentsia.'[9]

---

6. Such statements as 'Proletarian democracy is a million times more democratic than bourgeois democracy' (Lenin, XXIII, p. 350) abound in the writings of Soviet statesmen and jurists, and point to various features and aspects of Soviet rule, especially to the socialization of natural wealth and means of production, as the only valid criteria of genuine democracy.

The following selections contain some of Lenin's most important statements on the subject: XXI, pp. 266, 393, 402–3, 429–31, 439; XXII, pp. 96–7, 158–67, 233–4, 371–4, 462, 465, 526; XXIII, pp. 220–21, 345–51, 440–44; XXIV, pp. 251, 279–307, 375–7, 468–9, 514–15, 517–19, 626–7; XXV, pp. 8–10, 143–4, 469–70; XXVI, pp. 193, 272–4; XXX, pp. 257–61. Stalin's most relevant expressions are given in *Voprosy Leninizma,* pp. 28–9, 30–33, 38–9, 204–5, 355–6, 544–5, and in *Constitution,* pp. 15–16, 23.

7. Stalin, *Voprosy Leninizma,* p. 113.

8. Lenin defined classes as 'large groups of people that are distinctive: by their place in the historically established system of national production; by their relations towards the means of production (in the majority of cases fixed and shaped by laws); by their role in the national organization of labor; consequently, by their methods of obtaining their share of national wealth which they dispose of; and by the size of their share.' (Lenin, XXIV, p. 337; see also XXV, p. 391.)

9. Lenin, XXIV, p. 398. Who comprises the 'proletariat'? Lenin speaks of the proletariat under capitalism as 'an oppressed class, a class deprived of any property in the means of production,' and this definition is accepted by Stalin, who states that: 'The proletariat is a class exploited by the capitalists.' (*Politicheskii Slovar',* p. 451, cited hereafter as *P.S.;* Lenin, XXIV, p. 513. For Lenin's definition of 'worker,' see also *Vsesoiuznaia Kommunisticheskaia Partia (b) v rezoliutsiakh i resheniakh s'ezdov, konferentsii i plenumov T's K. 1898–1935,* II, p. 358, hereafter referred to as *V.K.P. (b) v Rezol.*) In 1925, the Comintern adopted the following definition: 'The proletariat is one of the basic classes of capitalistic society. Deprived of the means of production, selling its labor for hire, the proletariat works mostly in conditions wherein it is unified by the very mechanism of capitalistic production. The conditions of its social existence (the polar contrast between its interests and those of the bourgeoisie, its lack of private property, the collective nature of its toil, finally, the constant growth of its numbers) make the proletariat

The proclaimed political ruler and leader in the state is the proletariat, openly asserting its exclusive status:

This concept [of proletarian dictatorship] has meaning only when one class [the proletariat] knows that it alone takes political power into its own hands and does not deceive either itself or others by talk about popular, elected government, sanctioned by the whole people.[10]

The proletariat's position, however, for vital reasons of initial survival and progressive establishment,[11] rests upon an alliance with the toilers of other classes, especially the peasantry, directed against the formerly dominant classes.[12] It seeks to neutralize and win over to its side the wavering intermediary strata of the population and it strives for the progressive elimination of all classes and the establishment of a completely unified community.[13] Functionally the dictatorship thus exhibits several

---

socially the class-bearer of communistic overthrow.' (*Kommunisticheskii Internatsional v Dokumentakh. Reshenia, tezisy i vozzvaniia kongressov Kominterna i plenumov IKKI.* 1919–1932, p. 496, cited hereafter as *K.I. v Dok.*) The ranks of the proletariat are said to be replenished by newcomers from the petty bourgeoise: ruined peasants, tradesmen, artisans. (*P.S.* p. 451; Gurvich, op. cit. p. 28.) The latest addition to these definitions is that: 'During the period of its dictatorship the proletariat is an entirely new class — the working class, liberated from exploitation and directing the development of society towards communism.' (*P.S.* p. 452.)

10. Lenin, XXVI, p. 286.

11. As a Comintern thesis put it: 'One of the strongest sides of Leninism, guaranteeing victory for Bolshevism in revolution, always consisted in being able to discover a *concrete ally for a given, concrete task* . . . the question of possible allies for the working class in the revolution was considered by Leninism one of the most important tactical problems of present day.' (*K.I. v Dok.* p. 486. See also Lenin, XXVI, p. 460; Stalin, *Problems of Leninism*, pp. 22–5.)

12. 'The dictatorship of the proletariat is a special form of class alliance between the proletariat — the vanguard of the toilers — and the numerous non-proletarian strata of toilers (the petty bourgeoisie, the small proprietors, the peasantry, the intelligentsia, etc.) or the majority of these . . . aiming at . . . the complete suppression of the resistance of the bourgeoisie and of any attempt at restoration on its part . . . it is an alliance between the firm supporters of socialism and its wavering allies and sometimes neutrals.' (Lenin, XXIV, p. 311.)

13. *S.G.P.* p. 133. 'The peasantry, as the petty bourgeoisie in general, *also* under the dictatorship of the proletariat occupies a middle, intermediary position: on the one hand, it is a very considerable (in backward Russia a huge) mass of toilers unifiable by the common interest of toilers to free themselves from the landlord and capitalist; on the other it is: insulated petty owners, proprietors, and merchants. Such an economic position inevitably calls forth hesitations [in choosing] between the proletariat and the bourgeoisie . . . desertions from one side to the other, vacillations, turns, uncertainty, etc. In regard to this class — or to these social elements — the task of the proletariat consists in leadership, in striving to gain influence over them. To lead the vacillating, the unsteady — that is what the proletariat must do.' (Lenin, XXIV, p. 514; see also XXIII, pp. 289–97, 307–30; *K.I. v. Dok.* pp. 25–6, 496–8.)

facets or aspects that Stalin summarized as: '(1) *in regard to the capitalists and landowners,* the exercise of violence unrestricted by law; (2) *in regard to the peasantry,* the leadership of the proletariat; (3) *in regard to society as a whole,* the building of socialism.'[14]

(2) EARLY VIEW OF THE RELATIONSHIP OF PROLETARIAT AND PARTY

The Party as Primary Institutional Expression of the Dictatorship. Institutionally, the primary expression of the dictatorship is the Communist Party, regarded as 'the main guiding force' and 'the instrument' of the proletarian dictatorship.[15] As Stalin said in December 1925:

The dictatorship of the proletariat is not carried out of its own accord, but, primarily, by the Party forces under its [the Party's] direction. Without the direction of the Party, the dictatorship of the proletariat would have been impossible in the contemporary conditions of capitalistic encirclement . . . I want to say only that in all basic questions of our domestic and foreign policy the directing role belonged to the Party. And for that reason only did we have successes in our domestic and foreign policy.[16]

The Question of the Relative Weight of the Proletariat in the System of Authority. Because of the proclaimed role of the proletariat in a vast peasant country, queries repeatedly came to the fore whether the relative weight of the proletariat — numerical and otherwise — was increasing *vis-à-vis* the other classes. More specifically, questions were raised whether the proletariat's position of dominance was being implemented by a continuous increase of the number of workers and communists in Soviet institutions, in the Red Army, and in positions of authority, and by an increase of the percentage of workers in the Party itself.

These were deemed crucial points for the maintenance of the class principle in the governing structure. The enrollment of 200,000 'workers from the bench' into the Party in 1924, following the death of Lenin, was regarded by the Communist leaders as a supreme vote of confidence by the class in its vanguard.[17] 'Our party has become the elective organ of the working class,' declared Stalin at the Thirteenth Party Congress (May 1924), which adopted a resolution stating that 'the RCP [Russian Communist Party] was and remains a workers' party . . . The time is

14. *The Dictatorship of the Proletariat,* p. 54.
15. Stalin, *Foundations of Leninism,* p. 116; *Problems of Leninism,* p. 29. See also *infra,* pp. 119–20.
16. *XIV S'ezd VKP(b),* p. 51.
17. Zinoviev's and Stalin's political and organizational reports. *XIII S'ezd R.K.P.(b),* pp. 49, 246.

approaching when the entire basic mass of the proletariat of our Union will enter the Party.' The congress charged the Central Committee so to direct its efforts 'that the vast majority of Party members should in the near future consist of workers directly employed in production.[18] At the Fourteenth Party Congress (December 1925), members of the Central Committee sought to refute 'ultra-Leftist' assertions at home and abroad that the Russian Communist Party was not a workers' party because of heavy and growing pressure of muzhik interests upon its policies, and Molotov advanced figures to show that the percentage of workers had increased from 37 per cent to 47 per cent among cells' secretaries, from 50 per cent to 71 per cent in the Central Control Commission, and had reached 53 per cent in the Central Committee itself. 'As far as the size of its proletarian part is concerned,' said Molotov, 'such a Central Committee the Party never had before.'[19]

From time to time official Party reports themselves complained of an insufficiency of the 'workers' sector' and Party membership in the Red Army, of a preponderance of non-Party men at the lower levels of Soviet organs, and of considerable fluctuations and replacements of communists in the state apparatus. So far as the first item is concerned, however, the War Commissar's pronouncements successively demonstrated that the percentages of workers and Communists were on the upgrade in the armed forces.[20]

The plaguing problem of the class purity of the dictatorship, and of the Party as its projection, reached its highest point of tensity with the bitter intra-Party debate at the time of the Fifteenth Party Congress (December 1927). Opposition accusations that the working class had entered a stage of 'political twilight' and was 'folding up,' and that the Party had 'moved its class pivot' all along the line, and had become nothing more than 'a bloc of four classes . . . a Russian Kuomintang,' were overwhelmingly condemned and rejected, the congressional resolution concluding that:

The denial of the socialist nature of Soviet institutions, the denial of the possibility of victorious socialist construction in our country, the denial of the policy of alliance

---

18. Ibid. p. 246; *VKP(b) v Rezol.* i, p. 579.

19. *XIV S'ezd VKP(b)*, pp. 80–81. Zinoviev, already in opposition at the time, disputed some of Molotov's figures in a special co-report, voiced his fear that the Party was becoming a 'workers-peasants' party, and demanded that 'the Party must remain a workers' party.' (Ibid. p. 127.)

20. See *XIII S'ezd VKP(b)*, p. 250; *XV S'ezd VKP(b)*, pp. 92–3; and Voroshilov, *Stat'i i Rechi, passim.*

between the working class and the main masses of the peasantry . . . have logically led the opposition to slandering the U.S.S.R. . . . to a denial of the existence of a proletarian dictatorship.[21]

The Party historian, Yaroslavsky, explained that the regulation of the social composition of the Party is a very complex question and that it was not feasible to close the Party doors entirely to peasants; while Stalin pointed specially to the appointment of two metalworkers — Ukhanov and Komarov — as chairmen of the Moscow and Leningrad Soviets, and demanded to know where else in the world metalworkers were nominated as 'Lord-Mayors' of state capitals.[22] The resolution adopted by the congress called attention to the 'October enrollment' by which thousands of workers were again admitted into the Party on the occasion of the tenth anniversary of Soviet rule [October 1927], and declared once more that:

. . . the directing role of the CPSU(B) as the basic lever of the dictatorship can be preserved, guaranteed, and fortified only on the basis of . . . the systematic improvement of the social composition of the Party by way of constant recruitment into the Party of men and women workers of production.[23]

This was a repetition of an essential Party thesis as being still fundamental at the time. There, the explicit and implicit principles of selection of the governing strata discussed above rested until the middle and late 'thirties.

Formulations of the Term 'Dictatorship of the Proletariat.' Equally vital, in the eyes of the Communist leaders, was the question of a correct formulation of the very term 'dictatorship of the proletariat.' As the concept has progressively evolved, it became the established point of view that 'dictatorship of the proletariat' does not mean 'dictatorship of the Party,' or 'dictatorship of the leaders,' and that above all it does not mean 'dictatorship over the proletariat.'[24] The Party, said Stalin, exercises the func-

---

21. *XV S'ezd VKP(b)*, especially pp. 239, 340–41, 373–4; *VKP(b) v Rezol.* II, p. 232.
22. *XV S'ezd VKP(b)*, pp. 65, 340.
23. *VKP(b) v Rezol.* II, p. 231.
24. Stalin, *Problems of Leninism*, ch. v. In the early part of the regime no attempt was made to differentiate clearly between such terms as 'Dictatorship of the Proletariat' and 'Dictatorship of the Party.' Some of the leaders used them interchangeably and even the formal resolution of the Twelfth Party Congress (April 1923) contained the statement that: 'The dictatorship of the working class cannot be secured otherwise than in the form of the dictatorship of its advanced vanguard, i.e. the Communist Party.' (*VKP(b) v Rezol.*, I, p. 483.) In 1924, however, Stalin took exception to this formulation and, objecting to expressions employed by Sorin and Zinoviev, he denounced the use of the term 'dictatorship of the Party' as harmful and misleading. (Stalin, *Problems of Leninism*, ch. v, especially pp. 53–9.)

tion of leadership, but it does so only by taking into account 'the will, the condition, the level of class consciousness' of those who are being led — it leads 'only to the extent that it has the support of the class. For the Party cannot replace or be a substitute for the class.'[25] Hence, since the concept of dictatorship contains the aspect of violence,

> . . . to talk of the dictatorship of the Party as applying to the proletarian class, and to identify it with the dictatorship of the proletariat, is tantamount to saying that in relation to its own class, the Party must be not only a guide, not only a leader and teacher, but must also be a sort of state power employing violence against it . . . which is absurd and absolutely incompatible with Leninism.[26]

In an extensive exposition on the relationships involved, Stalin, frequently citing Lenin, developed the thesis that the basis of the Party's guidance of the class is mutual confidence, to be won by the former through firm and self-sacrificing conduct, close and continuous contact with the masses, and correct policy, strategy, and tactics. The basic method to be pursued was that of persuasion of the majority of the class, with the right and duty to coerce the minority into falling in step with the majority thereafter — persuasion first, coercion afterwards.[27]

(3) REVISION OF THE PROLETARIAN-DICTATORSHIP PRINCIPLE

These problems of yardsticks, measurements, and formulations of class content in the application of the principle of proletarian dictatorship to the architecture of the Soviet state took a new turn in the thirties, in consequence of the socio-economic changes brought about by the Five-Year Plans. Many of the earlier complexities of theory and practice have disap-

---

25. Ibid. pp. 37–8. At the Thirteenth Party Congress he declared: 'The Party exists for the class. In so far as it is tied up with the class, keeps contact with it, enjoys prestige and respect in the non-Party masses, it can exist and develop even if there be bureaucratic deficiencies . . . The Party is part of the class, existing for the class, not for its own self . . . the Party exists for the masses and not vice versa.' (*XIII S'ezd R.K.P.(b)*, pp. 244, 246.)

26. *Problems of Leninism*, p. 40. Professor Korovin and Professor Gurvich, who wrote that 'in the concept of dictatorship of the proletariat there is inevitably included the dictatorship over the proletariat,' as well as other earlier jurists, who made similar statements and identified the Party with the dictatorship, have subsequently withdrawn their views. (See Korovin, *Mezhdunarodnoe Pravo Perekhodnogo Vremeni*, p. 62; Gurvich, op. cit. pp. 57–8; *Sov. Gos.* No. 2 [1934], pp. 141–2, and No. 4 [1935], pp. 171–2.)

27. *Problems of Leninism*, pp. 42–52. 'Confidence of the working class in the Party is not attained at one stroke, and not through the medium of force directed against the working class but by the Party's prolonged work among the masses, by a correct Party policy, by the ability of the Party to convince the masses through their own experience of the correctness of its policy, and by the ability of the Party to gain the support of the working class and to induce the masses of the working class to follow its lead.' (Ibid. p. 44.)

peared, and many of the earlier *sine quae non* have lost their significance. Since socialism was pronounced achieved, with Soviet society substantially unified and remaining class differences in a process of dissolution, the very principle of preferential treatment called for a fundamental revision. This, the Communist leaders proceeded to execute in a number of directions.

Elimination of Workers' Privileges and Relinquishment of the Party's Aspect of Class Exclusiveness. Although, as will be shown later, 'state guidance of society (dictatorship)'[28] was still asserted for the working class, the former differences in franchise between workers and peasants were eliminated in the new constitution (1936), as were other special workers' privileges as well. The intelligentsia was accorded a status of legal equality. But most significant of all was the fact of the Party's relinquishment of the aspect of single-class exclusiveness in designation, appeal, and recruitment.

Creation of the 'Non-Party Bolsheviks' Category and the Practice of a 'Bloc of Communists and Non-Party Men.' The elections to the Supreme Soviet of the U.S.S.R. and the supreme soviets of the Union republics in December 1937 and June 1938 were conducted in the name of a 'bloc of Communists and non-Party men' and hailed at the Eighteenth Party Congress (March 1939) by Stalin and others as 'a magnificent demonstration of that unity of Soviet society and of that amity among the nations of the U.S.S.R. that constitute the characteristic feature of the internal situation of our country.'[29] Common reference and emphasis was no longer on the former designation of the Party as a 'workers' party' and 'vanguard of the proletariat,' but on the more inclusive term used in the constitution itself, 'vanguard of the toilers,' while a new descriptive category to attest supreme loyalty, came into prominence in the political vocabulary — the appellation 'non-Party Bolsheviks.' Speaking to the Congress, Voroshilov announced:

Our army consists more than half of Communists and Komsomols. But also [those of] the part which does not belong to the Party or Komsomol organization — are genuine *non-Party Bolsheviks,* whose life belongs entirely to the Red Army and to their socialist fatherland, to the cause of Lenin-Stalin.[30]

---

28. This new definition of dictatorship was introduced by Stalin in his speech in 1936 on the new constitution. (See Stalin, *Constitution*, p. 13.)

29. Stalin, Report to the Eighteenth Congress of the C.P.S.U.(B), op. cit. pp. 46–7. See also Alekseev, 'The Monolithic Unity of the Soviet People,' pp. 22–5; and Tikhomirov, 'Indestructible is the Might of the Stalinist Bloc of Communists and Non-Party Men,' pp. 27–31.

30. *Pravda,* 15 March 1939, p. 5; italics J.T.

Likewise, Zhdanov, proposing in the name of the Central Committee that admission to the Party be equalized for workers, peasants, and intellectuals, declared:

> Around the Party have grown up numerous cadres of *non-Party Bolsheviks* from among the advanced workers, peasants, and intelligentsia, active and conscientious fighters for the cause of the Party, executants of its line among the masses.[31]

The congress amended the Party rules accordingly, thus granting equal opportunity of access to the primary directing pyramid in the political structure. With these changes and innovations, the concept of proletarian dictatorship concluded another major cycle in its evolution.

The Question of the Future of the Dictatorship and Party under Soviet Communism. At this point it seems pertinent to ask: what of the future? Since the last Party congress declared that with the third Five-Year Plan (1938–42) the Soviet Union had entered a new phase of development, 'the phase of completing the construction of a classless socialist society,' [32] what was to become of the dictatorship and the Party when this phase had run its course? Hitherto in communist theory classlessness meant statelessness, the absence of dictatorship, and non-existence of the Party. 'Socialism,' wrote Lenin, 'means abolition of classes . . . The dictatorship will be unnecessary when classes disappear.' [33] And as for the Party, an early Comintern resolution read: 'The necessity for a political party of the proletariat ceases only with the complete abolition of classes.' [34] In 1938, however, Stalin declared the thesis of statelessness under communism to be conditional and dependent upon the removal of 'capitalist encirclement.' As long as there will be capitalist states surrounding the U.S.S.R., said he, just so long will the Soviet state continue to exist, even with the achievement of communism.[35] Hence, the answer of prominent Soviet theoreticians in the late 'thirties to the above-posed queries was that 'state guidance of society (dictatorship)' will also continue to exist, and will be exercised by 'the foremost people,' that is, 'by the vanguard of the "toilers of the unified communist society" united in the Communist Party — a section of the Communist International.' [36] To what ends? To suppress

---

31. *Pravda,* 20 March 1939, p. 2; italics J.T.
32. *P.S.* pp. 109–10.
33. Lenin, xxiv, p. 53; see also Stalin, in *The Dictatorship of the Proletariat*, p. 86.
34. *K.I. v Dok.* p. 109.
35. See *supra,* pp. 13–14.
36. Vyshinsky, 'The XVIII Congress of the C.P.S.U.(B) and the Tasks of the Science of Socialist Law,' p. 10; Trainin, 'Stalin's Teaching about the Socialist State,' *Sov. Gos. i Pr.* No. 2 (1939), p. 120. The Communist International was declared dissolved in the spring of 1943. (See *N.Y.T.,* 23 May 1943.)

all attempts upon this society practiced or incited from the outside, to admit and indoctrinate in communism new, periphery communities or states joining the Soviet Union, and to elevate communism to higher phases.[37]

Such is the development of the concept of proletarian dictatorship in the Soviet state to date.

2. THE EVOLUTION OF THE SOCIAL STRUCTURE

(1) CLASSES IN PRE-BOLSHEVIK RUSSIA

The Relative Standing of the Social Groups under Tsarism. Of the five social classes established by law in pre-revolutionary Russia — the nobility, the clergy, the merchants, the so-called 'burghers,' and the peasants[38] — the first alone wielded political power. It was composed of the aristocratic large-estate owners and high office holders, of which the Tsar himself was the first representative. Of the potentially ascendant classes, the growing industrial and commercial bourgeoisie and the proletariat (misfits in the legal categories of 'merchants' and 'burghers,' respectively), the bourgeoisie exerted great influence in the economic, but was powerless in the political, sphere.[39] Unique was the position of the intelligentsia, recruited from all classes and reflecting various interests, but never itself attaining the status of a clearly defined social class.[40]

The Ascendancy of the Bourgeoisie before the November Revolution. The war altered the class balance. The call placed upon the bourgeoisie by the autocracy for industrial mobilization enabled it better to organize politically, and, with the fall of Tsardom in March 1917, the bourgeoisie found itself in the saddle. Its rule, however, was not undivided. Not only did the provisional government, formed at that time, itself contain representatives of the other classes, but its power was to a considerable extent

---

37. Trainin, loc. cit.
38. For a description of these classes, see Harper, *The Government of the Soviet Union,* pp. 16–18. In this section, primary attention is given to the theory of the social structure from the standpoint of political power. The numerical strength of the social groups and their share in the political process are treated more fully in Chapter Thirteen.
39. *S.G.P.* pp. 139–40.
40. Yaroslavsky, *O Roli Intelligentsii v S.S.S.R., passim.* See also Harper, op. cit. p. 19, and cf. Lasswell, *World Politics and Personal Insecurity,* pp. 112–13. Lenin fought against attempts to identify the intelligentsia as a class, and the teachings of I. V. Machaisky (pseudonym A. Volsky) that the intelligentsia was a separate class, out to enthrone itself politically and economically, were bitterly condemned and rejected. (See Yaroslavky, op. cit. pp. 12–14, 30–32.)

paralleled by the Soviets, where parties representative of the peasantry and the urban middle class were in the majority. The subsequent bolshevization of the Soviets resulted in sweeping the entire bourgeoisie from power in the November Revolution of the same year.[41] In turn, the state was taken over in the name of the proletariat; the Dictatorship of the Proletariat was proclaimed.

(2) THE EVOLUTION OF SOVIET SOCIAL POLICY

Main Phases of the Dictatorship. According to Stalin, the evolution of the dictatorship to the present covers two main phases: 'first, from the October [November] Revolution to the elimination of the exploiting classes' (1917–32) and 'second, from the elimination of the capitalist elements in town and country to the complete victory of the socialist economic system and the adoption of the new constitution' (1932–37).[42]

The Meaning of the Term 'Workers' and Peasants' Government.' At the beginning of the first phase a 'workers' and peasants' government' was formed. This designation did not connote an equal sharing of state power, for, by its socio-economic position, geographic concentration, superior education, and consciousness of purpose, as well as by the role it played in the revolution, the proletariat alone was deemed fit and deserving to rule and lead in the state.[43] Consequently, it was accorded a constitutionally preferred position over the peasantry, while the propertied classes were entirely disfranchised.[44] The term 'workers and peasants,' it was explained, derived from the fact that it was a basic policy of the new regime to forge and perfect a bond between proletariat and peasantry.[45]

Policies vis-à-vis Possessing Groups before and during the NEP Period. In fulfilment of one of its declared purposes, the dictatorship was executing the suppression of the formerly dominant classes, so that by the end of the civil war (1921) the rural landlords and urban industrial-commercial capitalists had been practically eliminated.[46] The New Economic

---

41. *S.G.P.* pp. 141–7.

42. Stalin, Report at Eighteenth Party Congress, op. cit. pp. 71–3.

43. *Comparty Program, Source Book,* pp. 7–16; Lenin, XXIV, p. 513.

44. See also Stetsky, *Constitution,* pp. 7–8; Strong, *Constitution,* pp. 29–30. Workers were favored by the electoral law granting one deputy to Soviet congresses for every 25,000 city electors as against one for every 125,000 in the case of the rural population. They also enjoyed special privileges in regard to admission and promotion in the Army, Party, etc.

45. Stalin, in *The Dictatorship of the Proletariat,* pp. 90–91.

46. *S.G.P.* pp. 133, 148–50. This principle of suppression was based on the assumption that the overthrown classes, still possessed of superior organizing and administrative skill

Policy (the NEP), inaugurated at that time, represented a halt, a certain let-up, and to some extent a relapse. In the city a peculiar social formation of *nouveaux riches* entrepreneurs and traders, who came to be called 'nepmen,' appeared on the scene, while in the village the *kulaks* or rich peasants remained and prospered. Their status was closely related to the whole complex of problems of policy, strategy, and tactics *vis-à-vis* the peasantry — by far the most important question that confronted Soviet rule for over half the period of its existence.

The Initial Policy toward the Peasantry. The initial policy, pursued before and in the first years after the seizure of power by the Bolsheviks, was that of neutralizing the peasantry as a whole. This was accomplished by the nationalization of the land and the distribution of the large estates, which, more than anything else, secured the loyalty of the vast majority of the peasantry during the critical period of civil war and foreign intervention.[47] But the questions of foreign debts, concessions, agricultural exports, the foreign-trade monopoly — the entire gamut of problems connected with the establishment of trade and diplomatic relations and so intimately affecting the interests of the Russian village — again and again posited the question of the attitudes of the peasantry. The actual or potential threats of the Curzon ultimatum (1923), the Locarno agreements (1925), and the rupture of Anglo-Soviet relations (1927) served to focus the Communist leaders' continuous attention on the pivotal role the peasantry would play in case of a war involving the soviets.[48]

---

and of international connections, would utilize these to attempt restoration or to thwart the Socialist program. The 1917–18 strikes in state institutions, the civil war, the long list of trials of the 'social-revolutionists,' 'the industrial party,' the 'Shakhta' affair, and the 'centers' of 1937–8 — were pointed to in substantiation of this view. (Ibid. pp. 140–50; also Lenin, xxiv, p. 514; Stalin, *Voprosy Leninizma*, pp. 608–11.)

47. Over 150 million hectares of land, which belonged to the state, church, and large-estate owners, were transferred by the Soviet government to poor- and middle-peasant households. (*P.S.* p. 11.)

48. Because of this close relationship between the soviets' foreign and domestic policy, Zinoviev, presenting the political report of the Central Committee to the Thirteenth Party Congress (May 1924), demanded: 'In my opinion we must aim now that no provincial congress of soviets, or even a district congress of soviets, should pass without a detailed report about the work of the Narkomindel. We have entered a phase when the Narkomindel must become one of the most popular commissariats in the village . . . when, unfailingly, we must publish all the most important of our decisions on foreign policy and post them throughout all the rural counties . . . Without the peasants, without their clear understanding of the sum total of our maneuvers in the international arena we shall not be able to move forward at present.' (*XIII S'ezd VKP(b)*, p. 50.) In the succeeding years many heated intra-Party debates raged over the question where, among the different parts of the peasantry, lay the greatest danger of non-support in case of war.

Post-Civil-War Social Policy. As early as 1919, the Party congress made a strong statement for a policy of differentiation in regard to the various strata of the peasantry:

To confuse the middle peasants with the kulaks, to apply to them in any extent the measures which are directed against kulakdom, means to violate in most flagrant fashion not only all the decrees of the Soviet government and its entire policy, but all the basic principles of communism, which point toward an agreement between the proletariat and the middle peasantry for the overthrow of the bourgeoisie . . . Therefore the tactics of the Soviet officials in the village, as well as of the Party states-men, should be reckoned for a prolonged period of collaboration with the middle peasantry . . . The policy of the workers-peasants' government and of the Com-munist Party should, also in the future, be conducted in the same spirit of an agree-ment on the part of the proletariat and the poor peasantry with the middle peasantry.[49]

Then, partly in answer to the ruin and famine preceding it, came the NEP (1921), with its peculiar difficulties and retracing of steps. While seeking to balance the leasing of state enterprises to private entrepreneurs by building up at the same time 'the commanding heights' in the hands of the state (big industry, transport, credit, the foreign-trade monopoly, et cetera, the Party sought to create an economic foundation for its policies in regard to the peasantry through an 'economic bond' between city and village. This it hoped to achieve in a series of successive measures, such as the exchange of goods and products, reduction of the divergence (the so-called 'scissors') between agricultural and industrial prices, efforts to restore heavy industry as a basis for raising the agricultural economy, de-velopment of village co-operatives, wide credits to peasant households, a money in lieu of a products' tax, et cetera.[50] Grave apprehensions were voiced at the Twelfth and Thirteenth Party Congresses (April 1923, May 1924) lest the hold gained by private enterprise in commerce and in rural credit should alienate the sentiments of the peasantry and adversely affect the sought-after 'bond between city and village,' which was regarded by the Party leadership as 'a question of the existence of the proletariat it-self, a question of the life and death of our Republic, a question of the victory of socialism in our country.'[51] These and similar measures were designed to curtail and prevent such development.

The strategy of differentiation in regard to the peasantry received its most comprehensive formulation along with the resolution for indus-

49. *VKP(b) v Rezol.* i, pp. 315–17; see also ibid. p. 322.
50. See the relevant resolutions of the Tenth to Fourteenth Party Conferences and the Eleventh to Fourteenth Party Congresses in *VKP(b) v Rezol.*
51. *VKP(b) v Rezol.* i, pp. 481, 577, 579, 594–610.

trialization taken at the Fourteenth Party Congress (December 1925). This resolution followed from the fundamental decision of the leaders in power that the U.S.S.R. has the wherewithal and should proceed to build socialism without waiting for sustaining revolutions elsewhere, on the ground that success in such an undertaking would in itself constitute the biggest factor for world revolution.[52] The congress painted a class picture of a growing industrial proletariat paralleled by an increase in kulak strength in the village and the growth of a new bourgeoisie in the city, and having as its major political manifestation a struggle between the bourgeoisie and the proletariat for possession of the peasantry. A significant aspect of this struggle was the kulaks' attempts to take hold of the middle-peasant strata and through them subject the Soviets to the kulaks' influence. The Fourteenth Congress took issue with opposition from the Right, which thought the kulak danger magnified, and with opposition from the Left which did not think that it was possible or necessary to win over the middle-peasant strata. Following the lead of the Central Committee majority, the congress heavily stressed the view that, although the poor peasants and farmhands are the proletariat's prop in the village, the central figure of agriculture is the middle peasantry, and that, therefore, no effort must be spared to mold it into a sure and stable ally.[53] The road to socialism in the village lay by way of drawing the mass of the peasantry into co-operatives, for which socialistic development would be guaranteed through the use of the 'commanding heights' in the hands of the state to crowd out the non-socialist elements. In this effort the struggle against the kulaks should be carried on by organizing the poor peasants against them and by strengthening the ties with the middle-peasant strata 'in order to detach the middle peasantry from the kulaks and for the purpose of isolating the kulaks.'[54]

Collectivization and the Liquidation of 'Nepmen' and Kulaks. These were the policies gradually pursued, when, along with directives for composing the Five-Year Plan in 'organizing a broad offensive of socialism on the entire front,' i.e. along with the decision for industrialization, the Fifteenth Party Congress (December 1927) took the crucial decision for collectivizing agriculture through a wide network of state and collective farms.[55] The real drive for collectivization, however, began in 1929 —

---

52. Resolution of the Fourteenth Party Conference (April 1925), *VKP(b) v Rezol.* II, p. 3; *P.S.* p. 634; and Resolution of the Fourteenth Party Congress, *VKP(b) v Rezol.* II, pp. 47–53.

53. *XIV S'ezd VKP(b)*, p. 517.

54. Ibid.

55. *VKP(b) v Rezol.* II, pp. 226, 227–64; *P.S.* p. 464.

'the year of the great turning point' — when Stalin launched the slogan of 'liquidating the kulaks as a class on the basis of total collectivization,' confirmed by the Sixteenth Party Congress in June–July 1930.[56] Reporting to this congress, Stalin declared that the U.S.S.R. had entered the period of socialism, the 'nepmen' and kulaks — the last of the capitalist class — were well on the way out, and collectivization had become a mass phenomenon.[57] The first phase of the dictatorship of the proletariat had ended.

Early in 1932 the directives for the second Five-Year Plan were resolved upon. The relevant resolution of the Seventeenth Party Conference (January–February 1932) proclaimed:

. . . the fundamental political task of the second Five-Year Plan is the final liquidation of capitalistic elements and of classes in general, the complete abolition of the causes which give rise to class distinctions and exploitation and the overcoming of the survivals of capitalism in the economy and in people's consciousness — the transformation of the entire toiling population of the country into conscious and active builders of the classless socialist society.[58]

This was admittedly a large order. And, though Stalin would not claim at the Seventeenth Party Congress — 'the congress of victors' —two years later (January–February 1934) that 'the survivals of capitalism in the economy and in people's consciousness' have been overcome, he was able to state that 'the policy of liquidating the kulaks and of mass collectivization has conquered.'[59] Above all, the Communist leaders felt that the perennial question mark that hung over Soviet policy — both internal and external — the problem of peasant loyalty, was removed. 'Our Soviet peasantry,' declared Stalin, 'has definitely and unalterably come under the red banner of socialism.'[60]

---

56. *VKP(b) v Rezol.* ii, p. 398. At the congress, Stalin justified his timing of the speeded-up drive for industrialization and the order for all-round collectivization in 1929 on the ground that, had the Party listened to the Right opposition led by Bukharin and withheld the offensive at the time, the whole process of Socialist reconstruction would have been ruined and the kulaks would have triumphed. On the other hand, said he, had the Party listened to the Trotsky-Zinoviev Left opposition and begun the offensive in 1926–7 when it was not yet equipped to substitute collective-farm and state-farm production for kulak production, the result would have been utter failure. (*XVI S'ezd VKP(b)*, pp. 76–7.)

57. *XVI S'ezd VKP(b)*, p. 519; *VKP(b) v Rezol.* ii, p. 398.

58. *VKP(b) v Rezol.* ii, p. 487; see also ibid. p. 497.

59. *XVII S'ezd VKP(b)*, p. 28; *VKP(b) v Rezol.* ii, p. 633.

60. Cited in *VKP(b) v Rezol.* ii, p. 633.

(3) THE SOCIAL STRUCTURE AND ITS THEORY AT PRESENT

Basic Changes in the Social Structure. The tremendous sweep of the industrialization and collectivization processes, carried forward under the Five-Year Plans, wrought profound changes in the nature and composition of classes in the state. An official comparative table for 1913 and 1937 gives the relative percentage as follows: [61]

	1913	1937
Workers and Employees	16.7	34.7
Collective farmers, artisans, and handicraftsmen in co-operatives	—	55.5
Individual peasants and unorganized artisans and handicraftsmen	65.1	5.6
Bourgeoisie (landlords, big and petty urban bourgeoisie, merchants, and kulaks) (Of this number kulaks constituted 12.3 per cent)	15.9	—
Rest of the populace (students, army, pensioned people, etc.)	2.3	4.2
Total	100.0	100.0

Accordingly, a decision was taken by the Party, then introduced and adopted by the Seventh Congress of Soviets (January–February 1935) to redefine the constitution in the sense of making it 'conform with the present correlation of class forces in the U.S.S.R.' [62]

Workers and Peasants as the Remaining Classes. Outlining the new class structure, when the new constitution incorporating the suggested changes was being adopted (December 1936), Stalin declared that there were no more antagonistic classes in the state.[63] Soviet society, said he, now consisted of 'two friendly classes: the workers and peasants,' and it was no longer proper to use the term 'proletariat' because the working class was no longer an exploited class, 'bereft of the implements and means of production, but, on the contrary, possesses them in conjunction with the whole people.' Furthermore, the peasantry had become an entirely new peasantry — in its overwhelming majority a 'collective farm peasantry,' basing 'its work and its possessions not on individual labor and backward technique but on collective labor and modern technique.'

The Position of the Intelligentsia. New also was the position of the intelligentsia. Despite the fact that the greater part of the Bolshevik leadership itself — the 'professional revolutionaries' — came from its midst, the intelligentsia was long regarded with singular suspicion. The fact that many of its members were 'defensists' during the First World War, and subsequently took part in sabotage, civil war, and subversive attempts against the Soviet regime, counted heavily, in the eyes of the Communist

61. *S.G.P.* p. 115.
62. *SSSR S'ezd Sovetov VII-i, Postanovlenia*, Moskva, 1935, p. 23.
63. Stalin, *Constitution*, pp. 5–6, 13.

leaders, against a possible rehabilitation of the social position of the intelligentsia. In the summer of 1931, however, Stalin called for a complete
change in attitude toward it.[64] In the meanwhile, a new, assiduously fostered intelligentsia, largely of labor descent, had grown up. In 1936,
Stalin declared the Soviet intelligentsia 80 to 90 per cent derived from
'the working class, the peasantry, and other strata of the toiling population,' now serving the people and for that reason 'an equal member of
society.'[65] This position has been taken ever since and was specifically
reiterated at the last Party congress (March 1939) in the following words:

The remnants of the old intelligentsia were dissolved in the new, Soviet intelligentsia, the intelligentsia of the people. There thus arose a new Soviet intelligentsia,
intimately bound up with the people and, for the most part, ready to serve them faith-
fully and loyally . . . Our new intelligentsia demands a new theory, a theory teaching the necessity for a cordial attitude towards it, solicitude and respect for it, and
co-operation with it in the interests of the working class and the peasantry.[66]

View of the Relative Political Standing of the Social Groups at Present.
As to the question of which class was now wielding power, Stalin declared before the congress that adopted the new constitution that 'precisely these toiling classes [the workers and peasants] are in power, [but]

64. Yaroslavsky, op. cit. pp. 16–27. As early as 1927, Stalin maintained that a process of
differentiation was taking place in the intelligentsia, with hundreds of thousands coming
over to the side of the regime — particularly the technical intelligentsia, which viewed
industrialization as proof of progress, and participation in it as not merely a question of
bread but as 'a cause of their honor, a cause of creativity, which naturally brings them
closer to the working class, to Soviet rule.' (*XV S'ezd VKP(b)*, pp. 61–2.) However,
the 'Shakhty Affair' (1927–8), the 'Prompartia' trial (1930), etc., which followed,
were regarded as proof that 'the most qualified part of the old technical intelligentsia
was infected with the disease of wrecking.' Under such conditions, said Stalin, the only
feasible policy was 'a policy of *destroying* the active wreckers, *dividing* the neutral ones,
and *attracting* those who were loyal.' (Stalin, *Voprosy Leninizma,* pp. 459–60.) For the
last category, he demanded at the Sixteenth Party Congress (1930) 'maximum care and
consideration in regard to the vast majority of specialists and technicians who disavowed
the wreckers,' saying that he had in mind 'not the smooth talkers and posers of the
Ustrialov type, but the really scientific workers, who work at one with the working class
without philosophizing slyly.' (*XVI S'ezd VKP(b)*, p. 86.) Of greater portent in the
evolvement of a reversal of policy toward the intelligentsia was Stalin's statement on
23 June 1931, in which, along with insistence on the task of creating a working-class
industrial-technical intelligentsia, he also emphasized the need 'to change the attitude
toward the engineering-technical forces of the old school, to show them more attention
and care, to attract them more boldly to work,' on the ground that, following the suppression of the capitalistic elements, even those formerly sympathizing with wreckers
had turned toward Soviet rule. (Stalin, *Voprosy Leninizma,* p. 461; see also Stalin,
Report at the Eighteenth Party Congress, op. cit. pp. 74–6.)
65. Stalin, *Constitution,* pp. 8–9.
66. Stalin, Report at the Eighteenth Party Congress, op. cit. p. 76.

that the state guidance of society (dictatorship) belongs to the working class as the advanced class of society.'[67] The constitution itself describes the U.S.S.R. as 'a socialist state of *workers and peasants*' (article 1). At the same time it speaks of the political basis of the state being formed by the soviets of *toilers'* deputies (article 2) and declares that 'all power in the U.S.S.R. belongs to the *toilers* of city and village as represented by the soviets of toilers' deputies' (article 3).[68] In these provisions and allegations no confusion or contradiction was seen. The basis for the continued differentiation between workers and peasants was said to be the still different economic status of the two, the first being attached to 'consistently socialist' enterprises — state-owned property — while the second were bound up with merely 'socialist' enterprises — property belonging to individual collective farms or co-operative associations.[69] The removal of the suffrage and other former inequalities between the workers and peasants in the new constitution was not to be interpreted as a dissolution of the dictatorship. Rather it was to be viewed as the perfection of the alliance between the two classes under the leadership of the former, as 'the expansion of the base of the dictatorship of the working class, and the transformation of the dictatorship into a more flexible and consequently more powerful system of state guidance of society.'[70] The variance in terminology between articles 1, 2, and 3 of the constitution was explained as purposive: to show by article 1 that there still were these two classes in the state; while articles 2 and 3 were to indicate the progress already made toward the obliteration of the dividing lines between the working class and the peasantry, and between these two and the intelligentsia, that is, toward transforming the entire population of the Soviet state into 'toilers.'[71] The emphasis since has been wholly on the continued vanishing of the residues of class differences and on the monolithic unity of Soviet society.

The feature that distinguishes Soviet society today from any capitalist society [said Stalin at the last Party congress (March 1939)] is that it no longer contains antagonistic, hostile classes . . . is free of class conflicts, and presents a picture of friendly collaboration between workers, peasants, and intellectuals. It is this com-

---

67. Stalin, *Constitution*, p. 13.
68. Italics J.T.
69. Molotov, *Constitution*, pp. 28–9; Stetsky, *Constitution*, pp. 18–20.
70. *S.G.P.* p. 151; Stalin, *Constitution*, p. 21; Stetsky, *Constitution*, p. 43.
71. Stetsky, *Constitution*, pp. 20–21; *S.G.P.* pp. 151–2. In his speech on the new constitution Stalin spoke of 'the future society, when there will be no classes any more and when the workers and peasants will become *toilers* of a unified Communist society.' (Stalin, *O Proekte Konstitutsii*, p. 24; italics J.T.)

munity of interest which has formed the basis for the development of such motive forces as the moral and political unity of Soviet society, the mutual friendship of the nations of the U.S.S.R., and Soviet patriotism.[72]

With the adoption of the new constitution the second phase had ended. In the present or third phase of the dictatorship 'the completion' of the construction of a classless society is expected, with the remaining socio-economic categories defined as classes disappearing altogether from the Soviet scene.[73]

3. CLASS AND SOVEREIGNTY [74]

(1) THE LOCUS OF SOVEREIGNTY IN SOVIET SOCIETY — EARLIER VIEW

The Toiling Majority as Possessor of Sovereignty and the Soviets as its Legal Expression. Soviet jurists accept the definition of sovereignty as the supremacy of state power, unlimited internally and independent externally.[75] Most of them do not draw any explicit distinction between political and legal sovereignty. Not without some confusion in terminology and approach, they have by various routes of emphasis and interpretation arrived at the conclusion that, during the greater part of the Soviet regime, political sovereignty resided in the toiling strata of the population (that is, the majority of the people) and found its legal embodiment in the Soviets.[76] Is not this conclusion in conflict with the long-

---

72. Stalin, Report at Eighteenth Party Congress, op. cit. p. 46.
73. *P.S.* pp. 109–10.
74. With singular unanimity Soviet jurists, both of the earlier and present period, regard the concept of sovereignty as having been born, evolved, and applied in the non-Communist world as a convenient cloak concealing the actual lack of a 'general will' and the existence of class rule.
75. *Entsiklopedia Gosudarstva i Prava*, III, pp. 1074–5, cited hereafter as *E.G.i P.; S.G.P.* p. 262; Trainin, 'The Question of Sovereignty,' p. 75, and 'Questions of Sovereignty in the Soviet Federal State,' p. 12.
76. Professor Cheliapov wrote in the *Encyclopedia of State and Law* that the establishment of the dictatorship took the place of 'popular' sovereignty: 'Doing away with the illusory sovereignty of the entire nation, or the entire "people," Soviet constitutions establish the real domination of its *overwhelming toiling majority* over the exploiting minority.' (*E.G.i P.* III, p. 1080; italics J.T.) Professor Gurvich, viewing the soviets as the legal sovereign as early as March–November 1917, stated that, as compared with the claims of representation made by bourgeois parliamentarism, the soviets 'have in mind not the people, a nebulous, indefinite, multicolored mass, but the dominant class: the proletariat and toiling peasantry only. And here there does exist a single common will, because there exists a single common interest.' The Soviet Republic, he said, was in fact a 'republic' — 'a common affair,' the dictatorship, a 'Dictatorship of the Majority' because 'the toiling masses of the Union constitute a majority' and 'here, the people in

standing precept that the dictatorship of the proletariat is the rule of one class? Does it not contradict the long-maintained view that, as law is 'the aggregate of rules of conduct expressing the will of the dominant class,' Soviet law was the will of the proletariat raised into law and serving its interests?[77] The answer suggested by the outstanding Soviet jurists of the present is that there is no conflict, that, owing to the status of the proletariat, its will had in fact become the will of the majority of the people.

View of the Forging of the Majority Will Earlier in the Regime. Quoting Lenin's statement that 'if political power in the state is in the hands of a class whose interests correspond with the interests of the majority then it becomes possible to govern the state really in accordance with the will of the majority,' these jurists maintain that after the seizure of power in Russia the further tasks of the proletariat were: first, to rally its own ranks and, second,

. . . to convince the non-proletarian masses of the toilers that the will of the proletariat encompasses the basic interests of all the toilers, i.e. the majority of the people, that being realized in the political order the will of the proletariat will secure the attainment of these interests.[78]

Although a complicated and dialectical process, the latter task, it is said in retrospect, was carried out. Already in the pre-seizure-of-power period, the Bolsheviks fought under the slogan of 'all power to the soviets' and won over a majority of the toilers to the revolution, the soviets being the expression of this majority. Subsequently, it is said, the working class led the peasantry and, by persuasion and practical deeds, helped it to forge its will towards a struggle for the common cause, so that in the main the wills of the working class and the peasantry corresponded, 'fusing into the general will of the overwhelming majority of the toilers, led by the working class.' In short, before the transformations brought

its *overwhelming laboring majority* is really its own boss and master — is sovereign.' (Gurvich, op. cit. pp. 43, 76–8, 80; italics J.T.) Professor Malitski, characterizing the Soviet Republic as an organization of toilers aiming at a revolutionary dictatorship of the proletariat allied with the peasantry, by implication if not in express terms, placed political sovereignty in 'the toilers' and legal in the Soviets, writing that: 'this class, state rule of the toilers has as its bearer (its social basis) not the people as in the democratic republics, since the concept of "the people" or of "democracy" takes in both the toilers and the bourgeoisie, but exclusively the toilers or the toiling populace and . . . the organs of this rule of the toilers are the soviets, to which the fullness of governmental authority in the center and localities belongs.' (Malitski, op. cit. p. 28; see also Trainin, 'The Question of Sovereignty,' p. 90, and cf. *supra* pp. 29–30.)
77. *S.G.P.* pp. 52–3; Vyshinsky, 'The Marxian Teaching concerning Law and State,' p. 25.
78. *S.G.P.* p. 163.

about in the social structure by the industrialization and collectivization processes, 'the will of the working class and of the peasantry, and also of the toiling Soviet intelligentsia, was the will of the *majority of the people.*' [79]

(2) THE PRESENT VIEW OF THE LOCUS OF SOVEREIGNTY IN SOVIET SOCIETY

The People as Possessor of Sovereignty and the Highest Organs of Power as its Legal Expression. As to the question where the seats of political and legal sovereignty are now, after these transformations have taken place, the answer is supplied that: 'In the U.S.S.R., sovereignty belongs to the multinational Soviet people, which realizes it through its socialist state in the person of its highest organs of power.' [80] Since participation by peasants and intellectuals in the work of the soviets is said to have greatly increased and the new constitution declares that 'All power in the U.S.S.R. belongs to the toilers of city and village as represented by soviets of toilers' deputies' (article 3), the soviets are declared to be 'the only state form in which popular sovereignty can be realized.' [81] In other words, the Soviet state has become a 'popular' state, and no gap exists between state and society, or, as the authoritative public-law text puts it, the will of the working class, the peasantry, and the intelligentsia is now:

. . . *the will of the entire Soviet people* . . . In so far as the exploiters have been liquidated as a class in Soviet society, we can rightly speak of the *unified will* of the Soviet people, of the *popular will* in the genuine, socialist sense of the word and of Soviet rule as its genuine expression.[82]

View of Harmony between the 'Dictatorship' Designation of the Governing System and the New Concept of Sovereignty. Here no contradic-

---

79. Ibid. pp. 164, 165.
80. Ibid. p. 262; see also Trainin, *Sov. Gos. i Pr.* No. 3 (1939), p. 42. The latter part of this formulation was objected to by at least one jurist on the ground that the designation of 'soviets of toilers' deputies' in article 3 of the constitution meant the local as well as the highest organs of power. (See Vladimirov in, *Problemy Sovetskago Prava*, No. 3 [1939], p. 137.) Chapter III of the constitution, on 'The Highest Organs of State Power' — (note the plural) — speaks specifically of the Supreme Soviet as 'the highest organ of state power of the U.S.S.R.,' but deals also with the Presidium of the Supreme Soviet. The accepted public law text, however, refers to the Supreme Soviet as 'the sole bearer of the sovereignty of the Soviet people,' 'the expressor of the sovereignty of the people' (*S.G.P.* pp. 314, 313); and Professor Trainin also speaks of 'the bearer of the sovereignty of the entire Soviet people — the Supreme Soviet of the U.S.S.R.,' while maintaining that article 3 of the constitution secured the sovereignty of the Soviet people. ('The Question of Sovereignty,' p. 90; 'Questions of Sovereignty in the Soviet Federal State,' pp. 14, 20.)
81. *S.G.P.* p. 161; see also ibid. pp. 158–60.
82. *S.G.P.* p. 165.

tion is seen in the present designation of the system of governance as a 'dictatorship of the working class' and the simultaneous assertion of sovereignty in 'the entire Soviet people,' since the two are considered completely identical.[83] And, as we have seen above, to remove all doubts and allow for all angles, the latest definition of Soviet law was brought into accord with the present evaluation of Soviet society. Thus, the Soviet views on sovereignty within the state have been related to the changes in the social structure of the U.S.S.R. and have undergone a development not unlike that of the concept of Proletarian Dictatorship.

We have seen that in the evolution of the doctrine of dictatorship in the Soviet state the principle of preferential treatment gave place to the conception of common concern. Coming on the heels of radical altera- tions in the nature and composition of Soviet society, this change found theoretical reflection in the views on the complection of Soviet rule and the locus of sovereignty at the present stage, and practical expression in the new attitude on civic loyalty, the mode of election to the soviets and the standards of admission and advancement in the Party, army, and state institutions. The Communist leaders are not unaware that wide public recognition of an enlargement of the base of participation in the processes of government would widen the actual popular consensus be- hind the regime, from the need of which no polity is ever completely free. Throughout this evolution, by far the most important consequence of the application of the class principle in the system of rule to date has been the nature and extent of the role it has permitted a single po- litical party to play in the affairs of state. Later, we shall have occasion to look into the conception of this role in some detail.

---

83. Trainin, *Sov. Gos. i Pr.* No. 3 (1939), p. 43. This accords with the explanation rendered by Vyshinsky in meeting criticism that the Soviet Law Institute's definition of law as 'the will of the dominant class' was inappropriate for the 'classless' society so close at hand. 'In these conditions the place of the *class* is taken by the *people,* the toilers,' said Professor Vyshinsky, and 'one cannot speak in such case about "the will of the dominant class" without the reservation that here the will of the class fuses with the will of the people.' He argued, however, that 'in essence state policy of the classless society is a continuation of the policy of the proletariat in a class society. Therefore the definition of law as the expression of the will of the dominant class does not contradict the fact of the absence of a "dominant class" in the classless society.' (*Sov. Gos. i Pr.* No. 3 [1939], pp. 9–10.) This has become the accepted view.

Chapter IV · The Nationality Principle (I)

1. THE SOVIET CONCEPT OF NATIONALITY

(1) THE PLACE OF THE NATIONALITY PROBLEM

The Principle of Nationality in the Political Framework. The principle of nationality is one of the basic pillars of the Soviet structure of political power. An appreciation of its ramifications can be gained from the public references to the Soviet state as: a 'multinational state,' 'a voluntary union of peoples,' 'a voluntary unification of equal Soviet socialist republics,' 'voluntary solidification of the toilers of numerous nationalities into one, Soviet, union state,' 'a voluntary federation of the nationalities of the U.S.S.R.' et cetera.[1]

It is, however, a fundamental tenet of Soviet theory that the nationality problem is not independent and self-sufficient but part and parcel of the question of proletarian dictatorship.[2] From this interrelation derives the complex evolution of the concept of Soviet nationhood.

(2) EARLY MARXIST VIEWS ON THE NATIONAL QUESTION

Marx's Attitude toward Self-Determination. In few fields were the teachings of the founding fathers of Marxism of less conclusive impact upon the theory and practice of their Soviet successors than in that of the nationality question. To begin with, Marx's idea of nationality was rather nebulous, the term 'nation' not infrequently being used by him in the varying and interchangeable senses of 'country,' 'state,' and 'society.'[3] Marx was realistically aware of the presence of 'nations' as inexorable facts, though he did not view the modern nation as an indissoluble cul-

---

1. *S.G.P.* pp. 201, 203, 218–19, 222; Stalin, *Voprosy Leninizma*, p. 188.
2. Stalin, *Marxism and the National and Colonial Question*, pp. 68, 75–6, 114–15, 168, 169, 192, 223–4, cited hereafter as *M.N.C.Q.; Voprosy Leninizma*, pp. 45–6, 172; *K.I. v Dok.* p. 6.
3. See Marx and Engels, *Selected Correspondence*, 1846–1895, p. 7, cited hereafter as *Selected Correspondence;* Bloom, *The World of Nations*, pp. 16–18.

tural-linguistic entity to be defined geographically on the basis of histori-cal-traditional, legal, and strategic motivations. He conceived of it rather as a society whose basis is the integration of a large territory and popula-tion through the media of a modern technology and economy and whose *raison d'être,* continuity, and geographic configuration are, or should be, determined by considerations of an advanced economic order.[4] Not sep-arate statehood as such but large-scale industrialized economies were in the eyes of Marx and Engels prime prerequisites of world progress. Since they believed that only large polities could effectively organize such economies, they opposed as reactionary self-determination for small na-tions and advocated the assimilation of such nations in larger entities. In general, nationalism *per se* cut no figure in their scale of values. While they would not disregard the national question, they never felt that nationalism, particularly in its extreme manifestations, was natural with the class they deemed destined for ascendancy — the proletariat. Unre-servedly, their ideal for mankind was internationalism, in which there would be a place for enlightened patriotism, but not for any narrow nationalism, based on a self-seeking mission or on the glorification of tradition, racial affinity, or state power.[5] Hence, national movements were to be considered on their individual merits and always in the light of their effect on the paramount world interests of the international pro-letariat.[6]

---

4. Marx, *The Civil War in France,* pp. 62, 74; Velikovsky, 'Marx and Engels on the National Question,' p. 43; Bloom, op. cit. pp. 19–21, 204–5.

5. Marx, *The Civil War in France,* pp. 42, 47–8, 62, 69–78; Velikovsky, op. cit. pp. 44, 47, 48; Bloom, op. cit. pp. 33–41, 75–86, 194–201; *Selected Correspondence,* pp. 165, 208, 296, 329–34, 399; Marx and Engels, *The Communist Manifesto, passim.*

6. Thus, despite their condemnation of national oppression, Marx and Engels regarded the national movement of the Austrian Slavs in 1848–9 as contrary to the larger in-terests of the proletariat in Europe at that time. They also opposed national independ-ence for South France, which in their opinion had become the mainstay of feudalism, and counter-revolution in France. By contrast, regarding Tsarist Russia as the strong-hold of reaction in Europe and the chief cause of Prussia's military strangle hold on Germany, they repeatedly supported the struggle for an independent Poland as a means 'to free Europe from Russia as a neighbor' and to subvert the German military regime 'as a preliminary condition for the general emancipation of the European proletariat.' In 1877, however, when Marx thought that a revolutionary situation was developing in Russia itself, he was in favor of the Poles 'lying low' at the moment in order to fore-stall any intervention by Bismarck. Likewise, although Marx once believed that the ascendancy of the English working class would have to precede the emancipation of Ireland, he later arrived at the opposite conclusion and sought to convince the English workers that 'the *national emancipation of Ireland* is no question of abstract justice or human sympathy but the first condition of *their own emancipation.*' At the base of this view lay his conviction that the dissolution of the union between England and Ireland

Marx's Conception of Federalism. These views conditioned also the conception of federalism of Marx and Engels. Considering federation a survival of feudal particularism and a hindrance to economic and cultural development, they opposed it as a matter of general principle. 'The proletariat,' wrote Engels, 'can use only the form of the one and indivisible republic.'[7] They did not, however, rule it out altogether, believing that in special sets of circumstances federation might be a 'step forward,' a link toward integration, serving as a form of transition toward a centralized, unitary state.[8]

This, in brief, was the theoretical heritage in regard to nationality and federalism left by the founders of Marxism. And on this legacy the Soviets made efforts to build, though they found it necessary to depart from it and expand it at a number of points.

(3) THE SOVIET CONCEPTION OF NATIONAL SELF-DETERMINATION

Recognition of the Self-Determination Principle. As far as the general principle of self-determination is concerned, the Russian Communist leaders have a record of positive pronouncements whose origin goes back to the closing decade of the last century, to Lenin's expressions concerning 'the equality of rights of all nationalities.' His demand for recognition of 'the right of self-determination for all nations which form part of the state' was embodied verbatim in point 9 of the program adopted at the Second Party Congress, in 1903.[9]

Self-Determination as the Right of Secession. Later, he endowed the principle with a distinctive meaning when he secured the adoption by a Central Committee consultation, in the summer of 1913, of the thesis that: 'The section of our program (concerning self-determination of nations) cannot be interpreted otherwise than in the sense of *political* self-determination, i.e. the right of secession and formation of an inde-

---

would result in the overthrow of the English aristocracy and hasten the social revolution in England, 'for the time being the most important country for the workers' revolution.' (See *Selected Correspondence*, pp. 95, 144, 228–30, 278–81, 286–90; Velikovsky, op. cit. pp. 43–51; Bloom, op. cit. pp. 36–41.)

7. Lenin, *State and Revolution*, p. 60. See also Marx, *The Civil War in France*, p. 42; Velikovsky, op. cit. p. 48; *S.G.P.* pp. 210–12.

8. *S.G.P.* pp. 210–11; Lenin, *State and Revolution*, pp. 60–62; Velikovsky, op. cit. p. 50. Marx considered federation between Ireland and England desirable and held similar views in regard to such multipeopled territories as the Balkans, etc. (See *Selected Correspondence*, p. 278; Bloom, op. cit. pp. 38ff.)

9. *S.G.P.* p. 204; Lenin, I, p. 451 (1894–6); v, p. 13 (1902), also p. 243 (February 1903); *VKP(b) v Rezol.* I, p. 22 (July–August 1903).

pendent state.'[10] This formulation did not pass without opposition within the Party ranks. Lenin insisted, however, on his definition. Investigating the historical-economic conditions of national movements, he said, one must inevitably come to the conclusion that: 'by self-determination of nations is understood their separation from foreign-national collectives, the formation of an independent national state.'[11] He took issue with the view that self-determination was superfluous under socialism. Maintaining in general that, in the form in which he understood it, it was an inevitable feature of the current historical period, Lenin reiterated his basic contention times without number to drive the point home and overcome all waverings.[12] This conception of the right of nations to self-determination found juridical expressions in certain Soviet decrees and constitutional provisions of the succeeding periods, and it was repeatedly recognized in the formal resolutions of the Party and the Comintern.[13]

Rejection of Nationalism. Whence, it may be asked, such strong support for the idea of national self-realization? Did the Communist leaders turn converts to the ideal of nationalism? Quite the contrary. 'Marxism,' wrote Lenin in 1913, 'cannot be reconciled with any nationalism, even the most "just," "pure," refined, or civilized.' What is required is 'the independence of the proletariat from nationalism.' Hence, said he again and again, socialists 'are enemies of every nationalism.'[14] And in the light of the

10. Lenin, xvi, p. 507 (July 1913); xvii, p. 12; *VKP(b) v Rezol.* i, pp. 215–16 (August 1913).
11. Lenin, xvii, p. 428 (February 1914). See also Stalin *M.N.C.Q.* p. 139; *Voprosy Leninizma,* pp. 44, 48, 471. 'Concretely, this demand of political democracy signifies complete freedom to agitate for secession and to decide the question of secession by a referendum of the seceding nations.' (Lenin, xix, p. 39 [March 1916]; see also ibid. p. 245; xxi, p. 223 [October 1917]; and xxii, p. 178. [January 1918].) 'The will of the nation is determined by way of a referendum or through a nationality constituency.' (Stalin, on 23 November 1917, cited in *S.G.P.* p. 238.)
12. See Lenin, v, p. 243; xvi, p. 521; xvii, pp. 12, 65, 118, 129–59, 168, 220, 326, 361, 427–75; xviii, pp. 206–7; xix, pp. 37–48, 195–235, 239–72, 534–5; xx, pp. 123, 276; xxi, pp. 223–4, 423; xxii, p. 11; xxx, pp. 250–56.
13. See *S.G.P.* pp. 237–9; *VKP(b) v Rezol.* i, pp. 216, 239, 251, 392, 502; *K. I. v Dok.* pp. 22–3, 30–31, 42, 396, 405–6, 487–8, 637, 862. The wild particularistic extremities of the early months of the Soviet regime made all governing such a difficult undertaking that some of the Bolshevik leaders raised the question whether the slogan of self-determination was not 'antiquated,' declaring at the Third Congress of Soviets that 'it is necessary to oppose the decentralizing tendencies that would make an independent republic out of every gubernia.' (*Izvestia,* No. 11, 29 January 1918, p. 3.) As the resolutions referred to in this note show, however, thereafter the Party has continuously followed the principle officially.
14. Lenin, xvi, p. 554; xvii, pp. 65–6, 124, 135, 145, 326, 360, 361, 450, 473–4. [1913–14]. Deriding 'the ulcer of nationalism in all its forms' (xvii, p. 109), Lenin lashed out

Marxist view that modern capitalism and the bourgeoisie are more progressive forces than feudalism and the landed aristocracy, 'the nationalism of the Great Russians' was for a time regarded as particularly obnoxious, as it was considered even more feudal than bourgeois in character.[15] Ultimately, there would be no nationalism of any kind. The proletariat, on attaining power, would prepare the ground for the removal of national oppression and national frictions. And the nations of the earth would draw together, fusing their different cultures and languages into one common culture with one common language, constituting one, unified community of mankind.[16] In the meantime, Lenin thought, national pursuits *per se* were of no concern to Marxists. 'To a struggle against any national oppression,' he announced, 'we say absolutely yes. To a struggle

---

with equal vehemence against the nationalism of the ruling Tsarist aristocracy, of the bourgeoisie and petty bourgeoisie of all nationalities, and of certain Social-Democrats. Characterizing the first as 'rude,' 'reactionary,' 'black-hundred's,' 'coarsely militant,' and 'coercive,' he denounced it for striving 'to incite nationalism, insulate one nationality from another in the state, strengthen their estrangement,' and especially for 'seeking to secure the privileges of one of the nations, condemning all the other nations to a subordinate, unequal or even totally rightless position.' (xvi, pp. 389, 513, 553–4; xvii, pp. 124, 360 [1913, 1914].) But he also decried the second on the ground that, whether 'rude or gentle,' 'militant' or 'subtle,' and 'more or less refined and cloaked,' it in effect pursued the same ends and 'harping above all on "national culture," and stressing that which divides one nation from another, bourgeois nationalism *divides the workers* of different nations and fools them "with national slogans." ' (xvi, p. 389; xvii, pp. 65–6, 124, 135, 138, 220, 360, 361 [1913, 1914].) And he inveighed heavily against the 'social-nationalism,' 'social chauvinism,' 'national-liberalism,' and 'opportunism' of most of the leaders of the Second International and other socialist groups and individuals in Russia and Europe for their 'chauvinistic, patriotic mood,' 'their treason, i.e. their actual going over to the side of the bourgeoisie, their alliance with their governments and general staffs' during World War I, their 'adaptation to bourgeois nationalism, forgetting that the boundaries of nationality or fatherland are historically transient.' (xvii, p. 203; xviii, pp. 67, 101–16, 146–9, 157 [1914, 1915]. See also xvi, pp. 364–5.)

15. Lenin, xvii, pp. 440–41, 473–4. (February 1914.)
16. Lenin, xix, pp. 40, 245 (1916); Stalin, *Voprosy Leninizma*, pp. 423, 426–7, 431–3. (1930.) Communist theorists believe that there already exists a world-historical tendency 'to *assimilate* nations — [a tendency] which is becoming mightier with every passing decade.' (Lenin, xvii, p. 140.) The economic operations of capitalism turn dull, settled, boorish peasants into mobile proletarians whose new conditions of life break up their narrow, specifically national outlook. Hence, the melting pot of America, the mingling of Great Russians and Ukrainians in the mines of South Russia, and similar phenomena elsewhere are regarded as highly progressive manifestations. And Lenin goes so far as to call 'this process of assimilation of nations by capitalism the greatest historical process' and 'one of the greatest propellers [of change] transforming capitalism into socialism,' concluding that, barring coercion or discrimination, the proletariat 'welcomes every assimilation of nations.' (Ibid. pp. 140–46.)

for any national development, *for* a "national culture" in general, we say absolutely no.'[17]

Internationalism as the Soviet Ideal. Not nationalism but international-ism is the theme and desideratum: 'In place of any nationalism Marxism proposes internationalism — the amalgamation of all nations in a supreme unity.'[18] The understanding is that this credo carries a triple appeal: first and foremost, for 'the unity of proletarians of all nations,' welded together in joint associations, pursuing common class aims and sharing in the building of an international culture; second, for the intertwining of the efforts and fates of the workers of advanced countries with the toiling humanity of backward, oppressed peoples and countries;[19] and third, for the sweeping-away of 'every insulation of nations,' in the hope and expectation of complete coalescence in the end — views rooted in the fixed conviction that 'economic considerations as well as the instinct

---

17. Lenin, xvii, p. 146. (October 1913.) One should note here the Communist approach to the question of patriotism. 'Patriotism,' wrote Lenin, 'is a feeling connected precisely with the economic conditions of life of petty proprietors.' As revealed in the position of the middle peasantry — before it was neutralized — and of other elements during the times of the Brest-Litovsk peace, etc., 'the petty-bourgeoisie is the most patriotic as compared with the proletariat and the big bourgeoisie. The last is more international.' That is because by comparison the petty bourgeoisie is less mobile, less tied up with other nations or drawn into the vortex of world trade. (Lenin, xxiii, p. 313; xxiv, pp. 118, 119 [1918, 1919].) The Marxist attitude on patriotism, on defense of the fatherland in war, is not stationary and immutable for all times and cases. It issues 'from an analysis of the concrete historical peculiarities of each individual war.' (Ibid. xix, pp. 41–2, note [March 1916].) Hence, the stand in approval of such defense in the wars of the French Revolution and of Garibaldi, and in disapproval of it in regard to the war of 1914–18. (Ibid.) One of the latest illustrations of this variability of applica-tion to situations is offered by the resolution of the last Comintern Congress (1935), which — along with old-line insistence on educating working people in the spirit of internationalism — required the Communists to demonstrate that 'only the Communist policy defends to the very end the national freedom and independence of the people of one's country.' (*Seventh World Congress of the Communist International. Resolu-tions and Decisions.* Moscow-Leningrad, 1935, p. 26. See also *infra*, pp. 99–102.)
18. Lenin, xvii, p. 145 (October 1913); Stalin, *Voprosy Leninizma,* pp. 205, 206, 587. (1927, 1934.)
19. Lenin, xvi, *pp.* 512, 513, 390, 618; xvii, pp. 12, 66, 135–6, 361, 457, 471–2; xviii, p. 164; xix, pp. 227, 261; xxiv, pp. 96, 660 (1913–19). In this connection one of the cardinal sets of dialectical formulas is introduced: 'People who have not thought this problem through find it "contradictory" that social-democrats of the oppressing nations should insist on "freedom of *secession*" [for the oppressed nations], while social-democrats of the oppressed nations should insist on "freedom of *unification*" [with the former]. But a little contemplation will show that *any other* road to international-ism and the amalgamation of nations, any other road to this goal *from the present* situation does not and cannot exist.' (Ibid. p. 262 [1916]. See also Lenin, xx, p. 276 [1917] and Stalin, *M.N.C.Q.* pp. 197–9.)

and consciousness of internationalism and democracy call for the earliest getting together and fusion of all nations in a socialist society.[20]

Bases of Bolshevik Advocacy of Self-Determination. It is not faith in nationalism, then, that lies behind Bolshevik advocacy of the right of self-determination. Nor is it based on any supposition of the inherent superiority of small states. The reverse is true. Steadfastly asserting that they are opponents of particularism and partisans of centralism, the Russian Communist leaders believe that 'large states and unions between states . . . are more advantageous for the masses and are more conducive to economic development,' and that, what is more, the masses of the population themselves 'know very well from their daily experience the importance of geographic and economic ties, the superiority of a large market and a large state.'[21]

The crux of the Communist assessment of the nationality problem in the current epoch is contained in the following statement:

> Developing capitalism knows two historical tendencies in the nationality question. First, the awakening of a national life and national movement, the struggle against every kind of national oppression, the creation of national states. Second, the development and increasing frequency of all kinds of relations between nations, the breaking down of national fences, the creation of an international unity of capital, of economic life in general, of politics, science, et cetera. Both tendencies constitute the universal law of capitalism.[22]

Better than their teacher-predecessors the Bolshevik leaders have realized, however, the strength and viability of the first tendency and its extraordinary explosive potentialities. 'National and state differences among peoples and countries,' wrote Lenin, 'will continue to exist for a very long time yet, even after the dictatorship of the proletariat will have been established on a world scale.'[23] And it is this realization that constitutes the most important single cause why, unlike their masters Marx and Engels, these leaders have loudly proclaimed their support for the right of self-determination of all nations, large and small.

Other reasons are likewise urged. The proclamation of this right is held necessary in the interests of democracy and freedom. Without it, equality of the rights of nations is considered meaningless. What is more, it is

---

20. Lenin, XIX, pp. 40, 228; XXIV, p. 656 (1916, 1919).
21. Lenin, XVIII, p. 206 (1915); XVII, p. 449 (1914). See also XVII, pp. 220, 326; XVIII, pp. 82, 229, 328; XX, pp. 123, 535; XXI, p. 316 (1914–17).
22. Lenin, XVII, pp. 139–40 (1913); see also Stalin, *Voprosy Leninizma*, p. 48; *M.N.C.Q.* pp. 137–8; *VKP(b) v Rezol.* I, pp. 501–3.
23. Lenin, XXV, p. 227 (1920); see also XIX, p. 267, and Stalin, *Voprosy Leninizma*, pp. 423, 431 (1930); and cf. Bloom, op. cit. pp. 199–202.

thought to be required by the very interests of the socialist revolution, by the needs of proletarian class solidarity.[24] For, while the unification of nations is the goal *ne plus ultra,* there are enormous psycho-political obstacles in the way. Such unification can never be achieved without the removal of mutual suspicions, enmity, and estrangement between nations, which in turn is declared impossible without recognition of the right of self-determination to the point of secession:

> In order to overcome the mistrust of the toiling masses of oppressed countries toward the proletariat of states that oppressed these countries, it is necessary to abolish any and all privileges of any national group whatsoever, to grant complete equality of rights to nations, to recognize the rights of colonies and of juridically unequal nations to state separation . . . On the part of the proletariat of those nations that were oppressing nations, particular caution and particular attention must be exhibited toward the survivals of national feelings in the toiling masses of nations that were oppressed or unequal in rights. Only with such a policy does the creation of conditions for a really durable and voluntary unity of the nationally heterogeneous international proletariat become possible.[25]

Whereas denial of the right of self-determination would play into the hands of the various brands of undesirable nationalism, its defense would have an opposite effect by increasing confidence between peoples and laying the foundation for their amalgamation by mutual consent. Lenin's basic thinking on this point is revealed in the following statements:

> If we demand freedom of secession for . . . *all* oppressed and juridically unequal nations without exception, it is not at all because *we are for their secession, but only* because we are for a *free, voluntary* coming together and fusion, and not for a coercive one. Only for that reason. [1916] The republic of the Russian people must attract to itself other peoples or nationalities not by coercion, but exclusively by a voluntary agreement to establish a common state. [1917] We, on our part, do not want separation at all. We want as large a state as possible, as close a union as possible, the greatest number of nations neighboring on the Great Russians, we want that in the interests of democracy and socialism . . . We want [however] a voluntary amalgamation and that is why we are obliged to recognize the freedom of secession (without freedom to secede amalgamation cannot be called free). [1917][26]

In short, reduced to a simple formula, 'freedom of unification presupposes freedom of separation.' The latter freedom, Lenin believed, would in fact decrease the actual danger of secession.

---

24. Lenin, xvii, pp. 328–9, 361, 442, 448, 450, 465; xviii, pp. 206–7, 228–9; xix, p. 207; *VKP(b) v Rezol.* i, pp. 216, 239 (1913–16).

25. *VKP(b) v Rezol.* i, pp. 295–6 (1919). See also Lenin, xvii, p. 361; xix, pp. 41, 267; xxiv, p. 96 (1916, 1919).

26. Lenin, xix, p. 228; xx, p. 295; xxi, pp. 316–17. See also xvii, pp. 120, 440, 450 (1913–14).

The freer Russia will be, the more decisively our republic will recognize freedom of secession for the non-Great-Russian nations, the stronger will other nations be attracted toward union with us, the less friction will there be, the rarer will be the cases of actual secession, the shorter will be the period during which some of the nations will stay separated, the closer and more lasting will — in the long run — be the fraternal alliance of the proletarian-peasant Russian republic with the republics of any other nation whatever.[27]

Stalin also thought in April 1917 that 'after the overthrow of Tsarism, nine tenths of the nationalities will not wish to secede,' and two decades later (1936) he reiterated his conviction that 'not a single republic would want to secede from the U.S.S.R.'[28]

Lastly, there is also the strategic-political consideration that the proletariat would benefit from the application of the self-determination principle, in its foregoing conception, to small nations and backward peoples, since the strivings of these latter for national independence would weaken imperialism and correspondingly strengthen the proletarian position within states and in the world at large.[29]

Most of these reasons were thought to hold particular force in regard to pre-Bolshevik Russia, with its complex, variegated nationality structure in which a minority of the people, the Great Russians, occupied the center of the state, while the non-Russian nationalities, constituting 57 per cent of the population and inhabiting primarily the borderland regions, were smarting under the most barbarous and oppressive regime in the world. This condition was intensified because some of these distinct nationalities were more developed and cultured than the Great Russians themselves; some in the west and south had kinsmen across the borders enjoying greater national freedom; others in Asia were feeling the impact of bourgeois revolutions and national movements among related peoples in neighboring states; and most of them, full of mutual suspicions and an

27. Lenin, xx, p. 325 (May 1917); see also xvii, p. 448 (1914); xix, pp. 39–40 (1916).
28. Stalin, Marksizm i natsional'no-kolonial'nyi vopros, p. 48; Stalin, Constitution, p. 25.
29. Lenin, xix, pp. 225, 267–70. 'To consider a social revolution thinkable without uprisings by small nations in the colonies and in Europe . . . means to renounce the social revolution.' (xix, p. 269.) 'The dialectics of history is such that small nations, powerless as an independent factor in the struggle with imperialism, play a role as one of the ferments . . . helping the appearance on the scene of a real force against imperialism, namely, the socialist proletariat.' (Ibid.) 'Comrade Chicherin's third mistake is that he speaks too much of national self-determination . . . Our program speaks not of national self-determination — an absolutely vague slogan — but of a better-minted and more clearly defined slogan — the right of nations to political secession . . . But for us at the present moment, when the movement for emancipation has flared up in the colonies, this slogan is a revolutionary slogan.' (Stalin, M.N.C.Q. p. 106 [March 1921]. See also ibid, pp. 112–14; Voprosy Leninizma, pp. 44–5, 48–9.)

understandable hatred for their Russian oppressors, often carried similar antipathies toward the proletarian strata of the various nationalities, thus retarding the development of the solidarity of laboring people that figures so large in Communist ideology.[30]

Subordination of National Self-Determination to Proletarian Interests. From all that has been said above, it is obvious that, while self-determination was accorded loud recognition, it was to be subject and subordinate to considerations of proletarian preferences, a reservation of which the Communist leaders have made no secret. The essential significance of the proletarian demand for recognition of self-determination, wrote Lenin, is that of a protest and struggle against national discrimination and against unfair and coercive influences from without upon a nation's self-determination within. But fulfilment of this demand is primarily a negative duty, while the positive task and concern of the proletariat is further-

---

30. Lenin, xvi, pp. 507, 553; xvii, p. 437; xviii, p. 83; xix, pp. 46, 204; xx, pp. 534, 538; xxi, p. 317; xxii, p. 100 (1913–17); *VKP(b) v Rezol.* i, pp. 216, 239, 251 (1913–17). Before the revolution Lenin exhibited a passionate faith in the psychological efficacy of proletarian recognition of the self-determination principle. In response to fears that because of it Russia would break up into separate republics, he answered that in that case, as in the case of Sweden and Norway, 'more confidence, more bonds' would result, that 'sometimes *more* ties would come about *after* free secession.' (xvii, p. 90.) And, since in his opinion 'the question of state boundaries is for an internationalist a second-rate if not a tenth-rate question' (xxiv, p. 645), he was convinced that 'over boundaries . . . the workers of all lands and all nations will not part company' (xxii, p. 100) and that a democratically organized Russian republic would act as a powerful force of attraction for nations 'by the fact that they would be creating their own socialist world, their own Soviet republics.' (xxii, p. 237.) The highly cultured Finns and Poles would see the advantage of fusion in a socialist society, so that 'the secession of Poland and Finland following the victory of socialism can occur for but a short time,' (xix, p. 228), while the Ukrainians, treated as brothers and equals, would not wish to secede from a republic of soviets (xx, pp. 278, 535). While the experience of the first years of the regime was not lost upon Lenin, he did not abandon faith entirely, still believing at the end of 1919 that their joint struggle would show the Ukrainians and Russians the need of 'a close military and economic union' and demanding of the Russian Communists to show pliability in their differences with Ukrainian colleagues over 'the state independence of the Ukraine, forms of its union with Russia, the national question in general.' (xxiv, pp. 645, 658–60. See also xx, pp. 123, 277, 325, 534, 541.) In 1920, however, Stalin — with the facts of intervention and civil war fresh in his memory — insisted that secession of the border regions was highly undesirable: 'We are in *favor* of the separation of India, Arabia, Egypt, Morocco, and the other colonies from the Entente, for here separation implies the liberation of these oppressed countries from imperialism, thus undermining the position of imperialism and strengthening the position of revolution. We are *against* the separation of the border regions from Russia, since separation would here involve imperialist servitude for the border regions, thus undermining the revolutionary power of Russia and strengthening the position of imperialism.' (*M.N.C.Q.* note 36 and pp. 79–80.)

ance of its own position and interests. Marxists, therefore, are not obliged to support every demand for self-determination or separation. A specific decision may be necessary for each nation according to its economic, political, and cultural situation, as well as to Communist desiderata:

The question of the right of nations to self-determination (i.e. a guarantee by the constitution of the state of a perfectly free and democratic method of deciding the question of secession) should not be confused with the question whether the secession of this or that nation is expedient. This latter question must be decided by the S–D [Social-Democratic, later Communist] Party in each individual case entirely independently, from the viewpoint of the interests of the whole social development and of the interests of the proletariat's class struggle for socialism.[31]

Hence, recognition of the right of self-determination to the point of separation would not preclude propaganda and agitation against secession, and, since this right is an exception to the Communist premise of centralism, it is not to be interpreted broadly.[32] Also,

As regards the question, who is the bearer of the nation's will for secession, the RCP [Russian Communist Party] stands on the historical class point of view, taking into consideration the stage of historical development of the given nation: [i.e. whether it is] on the road from medievalism to bourgeois democracy or from bourgeois democracy to Soviet or proletarian democracy, et cetera.[33]

Theoretically, it is impossible to state in advance whether secession or a position of juridical equality would advance a nation along this scale of historical progress.[34] The important thing for a Marxist to remember

31. *VKP(b) v Rezol.* I, p. 216. See also ibid. p. 239; Lenin, V, pp. 243, 337; XVI, pp. 508–9; XVII, pp. 12–13, 145, 431–2, 439, 453 (1913–17); Stalin, *M.N.C.Q.* p. 64; *K.I. v Dok.* p. 126.

32. See Lenin, XVII, pp. 90, 120, 472 note; XIX, p. 228 (1913–16). In 1913 Stalin also strongly stated that: 'A nation can set itself up as it wishes. It has a right to arrange its life on principles of autonomy. It has a right to enter into federative relations. It has a right to secede entirely. A nation is sovereign and all nations have the same rights.' At the same time he admonished the Party to 'conduct such an agitation and so influence the will of nations that the nations should set themselves up in a form that corresponds the most to the interests of the proletariat.' (*Marksizm i natsional'no-kolonial'nyi vopros*, pp. 14, 39.)

33. *VKP(b) v Rezol.* I, pp. 295–6 (March 1919).

34. Lenin, XVII, p. 439 (1914). The flexibility of these criteria did not save the Bolsheviks from theoretical, no less than practical, complications, especially at the beginning of their rule. Earlier, Lenin himself had tempered his exuberant endorsement of self-determination with the warning that the first Communist concern was 'for the self-determination not of peoples and nations, but of the proletariat within each nation.' (V, pp. 243, 337; XVII, p. 453 [1903, 1914].) Soon after the seizure of power, Stalin ascribed the Soviet-Ukrainian conflict mainly to the fact that 'the Rada issues from the principle of sharing of power between the bourgeoisie on the one hand and the proletariat and peasantry on the other, while the soviets reject such a division, giving

is that he must evaluate every national demand from the class angle, keeping in mind that 'the interests of socialism stand higher than the interests and the right of nations to self-determination,' that the latter is but a segment of the former, and that the part must yield to the whole in case of divergence between the two.[35] And this holds even after the proletariat is established in power. As Stalin said in April 1923:

There are instances when the right to self-determination comes into conflict with another, higher right — the right of the working class, which attained to power to fortify its power. In such cases, it must be stated frankly, the right to self-determination cannot and must not serve as an obstacle to the realization of the right of the working class to its own dictatorship. The first must recede before the second.[36]

2. THE SOVIET CONCEPT OF FEDERALISM

(1) REJECTION OF FEDERATION BEFORE THE REVOLUTION

View of Federation as Hindrance to Economic Development. The above-stated views and criteria largely conditioned also the evolution of the Soviet conception of federalism. From the turn of the century and until after their revolution, the Bolsheviks were against federation as a 'Babbitt ideal,' which does not necessarily spell a greater amount of free-

---

all power to the people, without the bourgeoisie.' (*VTsIK., Sozyv II*, pp. 155–6 [27 December 1917].) Almost simultaneously he called attention to the fact that the Soviet government 'treated entirely impartially even the demands of the bourgeoisie' of Finland to grant that country independence, which the soviets decreed at once. (Ibid. p. 175 [4 January 1918].) Three weeks later, however, Stalin demanded at the Third Congress of Soviets that: 'The principle of self-determination should be limited in such a way as to make it applicable to toilers and not to the bourgeoisie.' (Cited in Bunyan and Fisher, *The Bolshevik Revolution*, p. 394.) And the Congress approved the government's policy as 'based on the principle of self-determination of nations *in the sense of self-determination of the toiling masses* of all nationalities living in Russia.' (Ibid. pp. 396–7; italics J.T.) When it came, however, to the adoption of the new Party program in March 1919, Lenin, now more than ever aware of the fact that politics is the art of the possible only, balked at Bukharin's proposal to substitute 'toilers' for 'nations' in the self-determination formula. 'You wish to recognize that which in reality is not achieved in a single country, except Russia. That is ridiculous.' (xxiv, p. 135 [1919].) 'For us to say that we do not recognize any Finnish nation [for instance], but only toiling masses would be a most nonsensical thing. One cannot refuse to recognize that which exists: it will force itself to be recognized.' (Ibid. p. 138.) Moreover, argued Lenin, 'such a postulate fails to consider the attending difficulties and the tortuous road which differentiation within nations takes' (ibid. p. 137) and would only lend credence to the scarecrow that 'the Bolsheviks wish to set up their order by force.' (Ibid. pp. 138–9.) Thereafter, Lenin's stand was maintained in the Party program.

35. Lenin, xvii, p. 440; xix, pp. 257–8, 261; xxii, p. 198; xxiii, pp. 14, 313. (1914–18.)
36. *XII S'ezd RKP(b)*, p. 597.

dom than a centralized republic and which is undesirable because 'capitalism requires for its development the largest and most centralized states possible,' as does socialism, its expected heir and successor.[37] 'We are against federation on principle, it weakens the economic ties, it is an unfit type for one state,' wrote Lenin in 1913. 'Autonomy,' he continued, 'is our plan for a democratic state.'[38]

Preference for Autonomy within a Centralized State. For nations remaining within a multinational state, wide local self-rule and autonomy in regions distinguished by national composition and mode of living would be best. Not only would centralization — so highly valued and desired — not suffer from such autonomy, but it would in fact be strengthened by it, since 'bureaucratic intervention into *purely* local (regional, national, et cetera) questions is one of the greatest hindrances to economic and political development in general and to *centralism* in serious, major, basic matters in particular.' In short, stated Lenin, in so far as different nations comprise one state, Marxists would never preach federation or decentralization: 'Only in individual, exclusive cases can we advance and actively support demands tending toward . . . the replacement of the complete political unity of the state with the weaker, federal unity, et cetera.'[39]

(2) ACCEPTANCE OF FEDERALISM FOR THE SOVIET STATE

Federation as a Necessity in Particularistic Conditions. Soon after the taking of power, however, the Bolsheviks reversed their position on federalism. As Stalin pointed out later, the weight of national movements turned out to be more serious and the road toward unity of nations more complicated than was foreseen before the War and before the Revolution. In fact, so completely torn from each other were the nationalities of Russia at the time of the November Revolution, that in the circumstances 'federation proved a step forward, from the dispersion of the toiling masses of these nationalities to their coming together and unification.' The Party proposed federation as a means of stopping the wave of sep-

37. Lenin, v, p. 337; xvIII, p. 82; *State and Revolution*, p. 62; xvII, p. 154. [1903–August 1917.] 'The wide and rapid development of the productive forces of capitalism *demands* large, state-solidified and unified territories, which alone would enable the bourgeoisie — and along with it its inevitable antipode, the class of proletarians — to solidify, destroying all the old, medieval, estate-bound, narrowly local, petty-national, denominational, and other partitions.' (xvII, p. 154.)

38. Lenin, xvII, p. 90.

39. Lenin, xvII, pp. 154–6; v, p. 337; see also xvI, p. 509; xvII, pp. 65, 90, 463–4 note; xIX, p. 40 (1903–16); *S.G.P.* pp. 213–14.

aration. It was deemed necessary in order to overcome the lack of confidence of the formerly unprivileged nationalities, and was advanced 'as one of the transitional forms on the road to complete unity.'[40]

Federation as a Step toward Unity. Added, in explanation, was the belief that 'around revolutionary Russia will more and more be grouped individual, different federations of free nations,' the dream that 'the Russian Soviet Republic will sooner or later be surrounded by daughter republics and sister republics, which, uniting, will lay the foundation for a federation first of Europe and then of the whole world.'[41] Abandoning his earlier fears, Lenin saw certain virtues now in federal arrangements:

Even federation, in fact, if it is established within bounds that are reasonable from the economic point of view, if it is based on serious national distinctions that create a real necessity for a certain political apartness — even federation does not in the least contradict democratic centralism. Time and again, given a real democratic order, a federation . . . constitutes only a transitional step to a really democratic centralism. In the example of the Russian Soviet Republic we see most graphically that the federation we are introducing will serve now as the surest step to the most solid unification of the different nationalities of Russia into a single, democratic, centralized Soviet state.[42]

---

40. *S.G.P.* p. 215; *VKP(b) v Rezol.* I, p. 295 (March 1919); Lenin, XXII, p. 372 (March 1918).

41. Lenin, at the Third Congress of Soviets, 31 January 1918 (XXII, p. 224), and Steklov, introducing the first Soviet constitution at the Fifth Congress of Soviets, 10 July 1918. (*Piatyi Vserossiiskii S'ezd Sovetov*, p. 186. These reports are cited hereafter as *V.S.S.* with the number of the congress indicated.) Five years later, introducing the constitution forming the Union at the First Congress of Soviets of the U.S.S.R. (30 December 1922), Stalin also stated: 'Today is a day of triumph for the new Russia, which has . . . transformed the red flag from a Party banner into a state banner, and rallied around that banner the peoples of the Soviet republics in order to unite them into a single state, the Union of Soviet Socialist Republics, the prototype of the future World Soviet Socialist Republic.' (*M.N.C.Q.* p. 130.) This view was embodied in Part I, of the Constitution of 1924.

42. Lenin, XXII, pp. 415–16. (28 March 1918.) Lenin was apparently considerably influenced by Stalin, then Commissar of Nationalities, who saw the American and Swiss federations as historical evolutions 'from independent states — through confederation to federation, while in fact they became unitary states preserving only the forms of federalism.' (*Izvestia*, 3 April 1918), and who evidently had no apprehension that the path of a Soviet federation would differ in this respect. The above-mentioned progression is regarded as an expression of the centralization of state power, which accompanied the centralization of the market induced by the economic changes — big industry, mass production, etc. — of the nineteenth and twentieth centuries. (*S.G.P.* p. 234.) And, as far as the Soviet state was concerned, 'the very forms of federation, which became apparent in the process of Soviet construction,' said Stalin subsequently, 'turned out to be far less inconsistent with the purposes of bringing the toiling masses of the nationalities closer economically than it may have seemed earlier, or even not inconsistent with these aims at all, as practice showed later.' (Cited in *S.G.P.* p. 215.)

Stalin even visualized definite criteria in regard to who could and who could not be subjects of federation. In line with his 1913 definition of a nation — which became standard in Soviet theory — as 'a historically evolved, stable community of language, territory, economic life, and psychological make-up manifested in a community of culture,' [43] he stated in April 1918 that:

Not every part and unit and not every geographic territory should or could be a subject of federation, but only specific regions, which naturally combine in themselves peculiarities of mode of living, a singularity of national composition, and a certain minimal completeness of the economic territory.[44]

(3) EMPHASIS ON CLOSE AND ELASTIC UNION

Acclamation of Flexibility in Forms of Federation. The internal and international difficulties of the early Soviet period, however, made it impossible to follow any definite form of federalism. Elasticity was the rule of necessity. But this very lack of uniformity proved to the Bolsheviks conclusively the full usefulness of the federal principle. Federation was now definitely acclaimed by the Party as the most suitable form of state association for the transition period, guaranteeing the integrity and progress of the Union and its separate parts, allowing for the diversity of living, culture, and conditions of peoples at different levels of development, and contributing toward the collaboration of the participating nations.[45] And, though never expressed in so many words in formal Party resolutions, confederation too was apparently not overlooked as a possible medium for the solution of the national question in certain cases.[46]

43. Stalin, *M.N.C.Q.* p. 8. For an elaborate description of the process of formation of modern nations, see ibid. pp. 88–91, 99–101, 270–72.

44. *Izvestia*, 3 April 1918; *S.G.P.* pp. 215–16. Cf. in this connection Marx's criteria for nation and state building, in Bloom, op. cit. pp. 44–6.

45. Stalin's theses, adopted by the Tenth Party Congress, *VKP(b) v Rezol.* I, pp. 393–4 (1921). 'Soviet autonomy is not a rigid thing fixed once and for all time; it permits of the most varied forms and degrees of development . . . This elasticity makes it possible to embrace all the various types of border regions in Russia.' (Stalin, *M.N.C.Q.* pp. 80–81 [10 October 1920].) 'The experience of Russia in applying various kinds of federation . . . has completely confirmed the full expediency and flexibility of federation as a general form of political union for the Soviet republics.' (*VKP(b) v Rezol.* I, pp. 393–4 [1921].)

46. On 12 June 1920, Stalin wrote to Lenin: 'For nations that were part of old Russia, our (Soviet) type of federation can and should be considered expedient as a road toward international unity. The motives are known: these nationalities either had no statehood of their own in the past or lost it long since, wherefore the Soviet (centralized) type of federation is taken on by them without particular friction. But the same

Stress on Need of a Compact Union. Last but not least, the Communist leaders strongly underscored the principle that, 'recognizing federation as a transitional form to complete unity, it is necessary to aim at a more and more close federal union.' A tightly woven association, they thought, was dictated by the necessities of maintaining the existence of the Soviet republics surrounded by stronger military powers, of restoring production, and of developing and completing the already marked 'tendency to create a single world economy regulated as a unit' in accordance with one general plan.[47]

3. THE IMPLEMENTATION OF THE NATIONALITY PRINCIPLE

(1) THE GRANTS TO THE NATIONALITIES

It was in accordance with this elaborate body of theory that the Soviets sought to erect their governmental practice. For the nationalities, this took the form of recognition of 'freedom of national development,'[48] in the triple shape of political expression, economic equalization, and cultural autonomy.

Political Expression

Guarantee of National Equality. The U.S.S.R. is defined as 'a federal state, formed on the basis of the voluntary association of the Soviet So-

---

cannot be said about those nationalities that did not form part of old Russia, which existed as independent formations, developed their own statehood and which, were they to become Soviet, would in the nature of things have to establish certain state relations (ties) with Soviet Russia. For example, the future Soviet Germany, Poland, Hungary, Finland. These peoples . . . becoming soviet, would hardly agree to establish immediately federative ties with Soviet Russia . . . because they would consider a federation of the soviet type as a form of lessening their state independence, as an attempt on the latter. There is no doubt in my mind that for these nationalities confederation (a union of independent states) would be the most acceptable form of coming together. To say nothing of backward nationalities, e.g. Persia, Turkey . . . I think that the point in your theses concerning transitional forms for bringing together the toilers of different nations should be amended to include (along with federation) *confederation.* Such an amendment would give the theses greater elasticity . . .' (Lenin xxv, note 141.)

47. Lenin's theses, adopted verbatim by the Second Comintern Congress, xxv, p. 287 (June 1920); *K.I. v Dok.* p. 127 (July–August 1920). See also Stalin, *M.N.C.Q.* p. 103.
48. Resolutions of the Tenth Party Congress (March 1921), the Tenth Congress of Soviets of R.S.F.S.R. (26 December 1922), the First Congress of Soviets of U.S.S.R. (30 December 1922), in *M.N.C.Q.* pp. 126–8, 132, 151, 278.

cialist Republics with equal rights' (article 13, Constitution of 1936). The Constitution of 1918 spoke of 'striving to bring about a really free and voluntary, and, therefore, a more complete and lasting union of the laboring classes of all the nationalities of Russia,' declaring the basis of the Soviet Republic to be 'a free union of free nations' (articles 2, 7); while the Constitution of 1924 — in line with the stress on 'voluntary consent and equality of status' for republics and peoples, in Stalin's reports before the Soviet and Party congresses that decided on forming the U.S.S.R. — declared the Union to be 'a voluntary association of peoples enjoying equal rights' (Part I).

The Union is arranged as a graded territorial-administrative pyramid consisting of: Union Republics; Territories, Regions, and Autonomous Republics; Autonomous Regions; National and Administrative Areas; Districts; Cities, and Villages.[49] Equality of status for the nationalities is constitutionally guaranteed by the grant of equal rights and the imposition of equal duties at each level of the pyramid, by a number of special political-structural arrangements, as well as by the provisions for the protection of national minorities throughout the U.S.S.R.[50] And as it came to be constituted, the Union is deemed the result and culmination of the Party's early undertaking to provide opportunities for self-realization to all the peoples of Russia, to help them 'to develop and consolidate their own Soviet state system in forms consistent with the national character' or with 'the national social conditions of these peoples.'[51]

The Union Republic as the Highest Form of National Statehood. The highest form of statehood a national group can attain under Soviet conditions is the Union republic. Its exalted status in the territorial-administrative structure is ascribed to the following attributes: each Union republic

---

49. In 1938 there were in the U.S.S.R.: 11 Union republics, 6 territories and 62 regions, 22 autonomous republics (A.S.S.R.), 9 autonomous regions, and 11 national areas. (See *S.G.P.* pp. 259, 280–81.) As a result of the changes that have occurred since, the national entities comprised at the end of 1945: 16 Union republics, 6 territories and 124 regions, 15 autonomous republics, 9 autonomous regions, and 10 national areas. All the units are divided into districts (*raions*), except for the Baltic republics, which were not completely reorganized administratively and are still divided into *uyezds* and *volosts* as in Imperial Russia. (See Trainin, *Velikoe Sodruzhestvo Narodov SSSR,* pp. 39–41, cited hereafter as *Sodruzhestvo;* Shabad, 'Recent Changes in the Political Geography of the Soviet Union,' and 'Political-Administrative Divisions of the U.S.S.R., 1945.')

50. Constitutions of 1918, 1924, and 1936, article 22, Part I, and article 123, respectively; Stalin, *M.N.C.Q.* pp. 66, 96, 277–8, 285.

51. *M.N.C.Q.* pp. 94, 275 (1921). See also *S.G.P.* p. 282.

has its own constitution, conforming to the federal one, but taking into account the specific features of the republic; its territory cannot be altered without its consent; and it retains the right 'freely to secede from the U.S.S.R.' (articles 16–18, Constitution of 1936; articles 4–6, Constitution of 1924).[52] Considerable stress is placed especially on this last aspect.[53] Additional evidence of the fullness of the Union republic's statehood is seen in the constitutional provision that: 'The sovereignty of the Union republics is restricted only within the limits set forth in article 14 of the Constitution of the U.S.S.R. [enumerating the jurisdiction of the Union]. Outside of these limits each Union republic exercises state power independently' (article 15, Constitution of 1936; article 3, Constitution of 1924, same in substance). The Union republics were to implement this residuary competence through their own governmental organs. Moreover, and this, too, has been emphasized for a long time, from the inception of the U.S.S.R. certain branches of the administration have been expressly reserved for the Union republics. Speaking to the Tenth All-Russian Congress of Soviets, on 26 December 1922, concerning the formation of the Union, Stalin outlined the following scheme:

The principles that must serve as a basis for the composition of the treaty of union should be the following: the Commissariats of Foreign Trade, War and Navy, Foreign Affairs, Ways of Communication, and Post and Telegraph must be fused, i.e. these commissariats should cease to exist within the republics that are entering into the treaty. They shall be formed only at the summit, in the organ of the Union, in the organ of the [entire] Republic, i.e. in the Council of People's Commissars of the Union. The People's Commissariats of Finance, National Economy, Food, Labor and Inspection shall continue within each of the contracting republics, but in such a way as to operate in accordance with the directives of the corresponding commissariats of the Union center . . . Finally, the remaining commissariats: of Internal Affairs, Justice, Education, et cetera — there are six in all — which are directly related to the mode of life, customs, the specific forms of judicial proceedings, and the

52. The Constitution of 1918 contained no specific secession article, but it embodied the 'Declaration of Rights of Toiling and Exploited People' of 31 January 1918, which left 'to the workers and peasants of each nationality the right to make an independent decision at their own plenipotentiary congress of soviets, whether they desire, and if so on what basis, to participate in the federal government.' Preceding it, the 'Declaration of the Rights of the Peoples of Russia' of 15 November 1917 proclaimed 'the free right of the peoples of Russia to self-determination, including secession and the formation of an independent state.' (*S.U.* 1917, No. 2, item 18.)

53. *S.G.P.* pp. 223, 224–5, 269, 270. 'To delete from the constitution the article stipulating the right freely to secede from the U.S.S.R. would mean violating the voluntary character of this union . . . It is true, of course, that not a single republic would want to secede from the U.S.S.R. But this does not prove that we should not record in the constitution the right of the Union republics freely to secede from the U.S.S.R.' (Stalin, *Constitution*, pp. 24–5.)

culture of the peoples forming the republics, these should be left as commissariats independently directed by the central executive committees and councils of people's
commissars of the contracting republics . . . As far as the commissariats [of the
first group] . . . are concerned, in these the sovereignty of the center is complete.
[As for] the following five commissariats . . . to use juridical terms, they operate
according to a divided sovereignty: they obey their own central executive committees
and councils of people's commissars, but predominance on the part of the Center
remains. While in the commissariats that relate to the mode of living and are specifically national in character, full sovereignty remains in the contracting republics.[54]

Despite considerable subsequent shifts in allocation of activities between
these categories, certain fields of function have at all times been specified
as within the sole domain of the Union republics.

The latest advance in the status of the Union republics was introduced
by the reform of 1 February 1944, which gave them the right to enter into
direct relations with foreign states, to conclude agreements and exchange
diplomatic and consular representatives with them, and to create their
own military formations. Accordingly, the constitution of the U.S.S.R.,
and later also the constitutions of the Union republics, were amended to
provide for these rights and to transform the Foreign Affairs and Defense
Commissariats (now Ministries) from all-Union to Union-republic commissariats, thus making foreign policy and military affairs joint spheres of
the Union and the constituent republics.[55]

---

54. *Izvestia*, 27 December 1922, p. 3. See also *VKP(b) v Rezol.* I, p. 539 (June 1923).
These three kinds of commissariats have been variously referred to as follows: the
first as 'fused,' or 'all-Union'; the second as 'federated,' 'joint,' 'mixed,' 'directive,'
'Union-republic'; the third as 'independent,' 'autonomous,' and 'republic' or 'republican.'
While the Union of Soviet Republics was being effected, the Party warned against attempts to regard such as a return to the 'single and indivisible' credo of Imperial Russia.
It called upon its members 'to keep vigilant watch lest the amalgamation of the republics and the fusion of the commissariats should be utilized by chauvinistic Soviet
officials as a screen for their attempts to ignore the economic and cultural needs of the
national republics.' It declared: 'The fusion of the commissariats is a test for the Soviet
apparatus: if this experiment were in practice to betray a great-power [imperialist]
tendency, the Party would be obliged to adopt the most resolute measures against
such a distortion, even to the extent of raising the question of annulling the fusion of
certain commissariats until such time as the Soviet apparatus has been properly re-
educated so that it will give genuinely proletarian and genuinely fraternal attention to
the needs and requirements of the small and backward nationalities.' (Stalin's theses,
and resolution of the Twelfth Party Congress [March–April 1923], *M.N.C.Q.*
pp. 143–4, 284–5.)

55. See *E.B.*, 5, 12, 15, and 23 February 1944. The aims officially indicated for the reform
are: to strengthen the defensive power of the U.S.S.R.; to widen its international connections; and to meet the specific needs of the Union republics for wider activity in the
foreign field, which are an outgrowth of the progress of their national development.
(Ibid; Trainin, *Sodruzhestvo*, pp. 53–5.)

The Position of the Autonomous Republics and Lower Units. The position of the lower rungs of the territorial-administrative ladder is different. Thus, an autonomous republic, though having its own constitution and governmental structure, is fundamentally and admittedly a ward of the Union republic of which it forms a part and which is responsible for its economic and cultural development. Not only does it lack a constitutionally proclaimed right of secession, but its constitution must be confirmed by the Union republic above it, which also has the power of confirmation over its boundaries and district divisions. The autonomous republic has no exclusive competence in any branch of administration or economy, all of its ministries being subordinate both to its own council of ministers and to the corresponding ministries of the Union republic. The decisions and orders of its council of ministers can be suspended by the Council of Ministers and annulled altogether by the Presidium of the Supreme Soviet of the Union republic.[56] And even more circumscribed in power are the other territorial-administrative formations; they lack most of the above-mentioned outer signs of statehood and are subject to the right of the Union republic's Council of Ministers 'to annual decisions and orders of the executive committees of the Soviets of toilers' deputies of territories, regions, and autonomous regions' (article 82, Constitution of 1936).

Elevation of Status for the National Entities. The position of the lower units is not, however, inflexible. As the evolution of the federal union shows, they can rise to higher stages, and they can even reach the highest status — that of a Union republic—provided they are able to meet the following prerequisites, outlined by Stalin in 1936:

In the first place, a republic must be a border republic, which is not surrounded on all sides by other territories of the U.S.S.R.; for if a Union republic has the right to secede from the U.S.S.R., it is necessary that the republic that becomes a Union republic be able logically and realistically to raise the question of its secession from the U.S.S.R. . . . Secondly, it is necessary that the nationality that gives a Soviet republic its name must represent a more or less compact majority of that republic . . . In the third place, such a republic must not be very small in population; it ought to have a population of, say, not less but rather more than one million at least. Why? Because it would be wrong to assume that a small Soviet republic, with a small population and a small army, could count on maintaining its independent state existence.[57]

---

56. *S.G.P.* pp. 284–7.

57. Stalin, *Constitution*, pp. 25–6. While the economic and cultural growth of the autonomous formations would be reflected in their development and in increased independence (*S.G.P.* pp. 256, 283–4), Stalin, with a constant weather eye on possible sources of jealousies between the nationalities, objected to proposals and explanations of elevation to Union-republic status by reference to such growth (see e.g., Stetsky, *Constitution*,

The admission of the Ukrainian and Byelorussian Union Republics to separate representation at the United Nations Conference on International Organization, in May 1945, marks the farthest point of advance in political status for a national entity in the U.S.S.R.[58] It should be pointed out here that whatever the particular level of territorial-administrative autonomy, Soviet writers maintain that fair and ample opportunity is offered therein for the national groups enjoying such to develop their own 'Soviet national statehood.'[59]

Institutions for the Nationalities. The Narkomnats. In addition to the forms of expression stated above, a number of special instrumentalities and devices have been introduced at various times to safeguard the interests and secure the political participation of the numerous nationalities of the state. Among the commissariats established the day after the Bolsheviks' accession to power was one that had no counterpart among the ministries they displaced — the Narkomnats, or People's Commissariat for the Affairs of the Nationalities.[60] Headed by Stalin, it operated as watchdog, organizer, sovietizer, and protector of the nationalities till the time of the formation of the Union (1923), serving, in the words of the official text, as 'the initiator of the entire Soviet legislation on the national question, including the recognition of independent Soviet republics, the formation of autonomous Soviet republics, measures regarding the economic and cultural uplifting of the nationalities, et cetera.'[61] The Narkomnats enlisted local people not only for the furtherance of programs for their national cultures and territorial-administrative autonomy, but for a struggle against designated 'bourgeois-national' movements as well. It also played a prominent part in the civil war, especially by carrying on extensive propaganda to win over the nationalities to the Soviet side and organizing substantial numbers among them for military work.

All of these activities were carried on by the Narkomnats through its nationality departments and in close collaboration with native Communist groups that it helped to form, particularly among the eastern

p. 24), declaring that: 'The transfer of autonomous republics to the category of Union republics must not be motivated by their economic and cultural maturity, just as the retention of a given republic on the list of autonomous republics must not be motivated by its economic and cultural backwardness.' (Stalin, *O Konstitutsii Soiuza SSR,* p. 25.)

58. For the texts of the declarations of the Ukrainian and Byelorussian Republics in regard to their admission to UNCIO, see *E.B.,* Special Supplement, May 1945.

59. *S.G.P.* p. 287; Trainin, in *Sov. Gos.* No. 2 (1938), pp. 104–5.

60. For descriptions or evaluations of the Narkomnats, see S. Dimanshtein, in *E.G.i P.* II, pp. 1171–86; Lenin, XXVII, note 114; Engel', *Osnovy Sovetskoi Konstitutsii,* pp. 133–6; *S.G.P.* pp. 247–8, 307–8.

61. *S.G.P.* p. 247.

peoples of Russia that had had neither proletariat nor Party membership before.[62] By reorganizations successively executed by the Central Executive Committee of the R.S.F.S.R. on 19 May 1920, 26 May 1921, and 27 July 1922, the scope of the commissariat's authority was further broadened and it was converted in part into a deliberative organ of the nationalities. The latter were to delegate representatives to head the corresponding departments of the Narkomnats and all these representatives were to constitute a Council of Nationalities, presided over by the Commissar of Nationalities, assisted by a collegium of nine, to guide the ramified work of the commissariat.[63] Charged, in addition to the functions sketched above, with rendering opinions on pending projects of other commissariats affecting the nationalities and their administrative units, and in fact with the exercise of 'supervision over the execution of the nationality policy of the Soviet government,' the Narkomnats was empowered to have its own representatives not only at the governments of the autonomous regions and republics but also at those of the allied Soviet republics. These were deemed necessary in order to guard the rights and interests of the national minorities, and 'for the purpose of generalizing the experience of carrying out the policy of the Soviet power in the autonomous regions and republics as well as in the treaty republics.'.[64] Thus, the Narkomnats was able to play a decisive role in forging the links that in 1923 resulted in the creation of the U.S.S.R. And in July of that year the Narkomnats' dissolution was decreed on the ground that it had fulfilled 'its basic mission of readying the cause of formation of national republics and regions and unifying them into a union of republics.' Most of its duties and prerogatives passed to a new Council of Nationalities, now a second chamber of the Central Executive Committee of the U.S.S.R.[65]

The Council of Nationalities of the C.E.C. For this newly shaped agency of and for the nationalities, an intensive barrage of theoretical preparation was laid. Taking up the question of a second chamber at the February (1923) plenum of the Party Central Committee, and suggesting it again vaguely in his March (1923) theses for the Twelfth Party Congress, Stalin came out bluntly and emphatically for such an organ at the congress itself, in April 1923:

62. *E.G.i P.* II, pp. 1172–81; Lenin, XXVII, note 114. The Commissar of Nationalities was assisted by a collegium composed of his deputy and nine members.
63. See also Engel', op. cit. pp. 134–5; items III–IX, decree of 27 July 1922.
64. *E.G.i P.* II, p. 1182; *S.G.P.* pp. 247–8; items I, II, XII, decree of 27 July 1922.
65. *S.U.* 1923, No. 66, item 639.

If within the Central Executive Committee of the Union we could create two chambers, one of which would be elected at the Union Congress of Soviets, irrespective of nationality, and the other would be elected by the republics and regions (all the republics being equally represented and all the national regions being equally represented) and endorsed by the Congress of Soviets of the Union of Republics, I think that our supreme institutions would express not only the class interests of all proletarian groups without exception, but also purely national needs. We should have an organ that would reflect the specific interests of the nationalities, peoples, and tribes inhabiting the territories of the Union of Republics. Under the conditions prevailing in our Union, which embraces not less than 140,000,000 people, of which about 65,000,000 are non-Russians, one cannot, in such a state, govern without having before us here, in Moscow, in the supreme organ of government, emissaries of these nationalities who can express not only the interests common to the proletariat as a whole, but also the interests that are particularly, specially, and specifically national. Without this, comrades, it will be impossible to govern. Unless we have this barometer, comrades, unless we have people capable of formulating these specific needs of the various nationalities, it will be impossible to govern.[66]

This urgent statement was intended also as a cardinal answer to arguments that the proposed arrangement would perturb the established system of government. But the espousal of equality of representation met with strong opposition on the part of the Ukrainian Party delegates headed by Rakovsky. These delegates expressed the fear that equal participation of 'all the nationalities' in the second chamber, by the representation of autonomous republics and regions side by side with the constituent republics, would result in the continuance of a voting preponderance on the part of the R.S.F.S.R. and thereby deny the 'guarantee to the separate republics,' for the erection of which the bicameral system was being established. Accordingly they proposed 'that not nationalities but state entities enter the second chamber,' i.e. that it be based exclusively on the four republics that had concluded the treaty of union: the R.S.F.S.R., the Transcaucasian Federation, White Russia (Byelorussia), and the Ukraine.[67]

---

66. *XII S'ezd RKP(b)*, pp. 451–4 and *M.N.C.Q.* pp. 164–5.

67. *XII S'ezd RKP(b)*, pp. 599–600, 603–4; *S.G.P.* p. 308. Echoing earlier opposition harking back to the second half of 1922 and the February plenum (1923), Rakovsky based his chief contention on the argument that, if in the provisionally constituted Union Central Executive Committee 280 out of 360 deputies came from the R.S.F.S.R., the result of the congressional commission's approval of the current scheme would be 'that the R.S.F.S.R. will have in fact 64 or 70 votes, the Ukraine would have 4 votes, White Russia would have 4 votes.' And he concluded by urging a proposal that 'none of the state units composing the second chamber may have more than two fifths of all the votes.' The majority of the commission, however, regarded these expressions as a very strange line of approach having no place in Communist considerations. (Ibid.) In this connection, it may be interesting to point out that, while there were 70 members for the units comprising the R.S.F.S.R. and 30 for those of the Ukraine, White Russia

Stalin — the reporter on the question — vigorously denounced this proposal.[68] And the Party Congress rejected it as without merit, and voted verbatim approval of Stalin's thesis 'that within the system of supreme organs of the Union a special organ be instituted representing on an equality basis all national republics and national regions without exception,' including his suggested addition that 'possible provision [be] made for the representation of all nationalities forming part of these republics.'[69] Subsequently, a consultation of the Party Central Committee with delegates from the national units (9–12 June 1923), designated this organ, as the second chamber of the C.E.C., 'Council of Nationalities,' while the first chamber became the 'Council of the Union.' It expressed the desirability of avoiding overlapping membership in them, and charted the provisions for equality of status between the two chambers, which were embodied in the first Union constitution (1923–4).[70]

The Council of Nationalities of the Supreme Soviet. The considerations that led to the establishment of the Council of Nationalities were held to prevail also at the time of the readjustments in the governmental scheme called forth by the new (1936) constitution, and this organ was retained in the newly created Supreme Soviet. Again countering arguments that a second chamber was cumbersome and superfluous,[71] Stalin stated in December 1936:

---

and Transcaucasia in the first composition of the second chamber (1924), a year later, with the transformation of the Uzbek and Turkmen Republics into Union republics, there were 68 and 63 members (30 and 23 candidates), respectively, for the R.S.F.S.R. and the other Union republics. (*S'ezdy Sovetov S.S.S.R. v postanovleniakh i rezoliutsiakh,* pp. 35–6, 75–7.)

68. *XII S'ezd RKP(b)*, p. 605. He also countered Rakovsky's attempt to insinuate into the question a proposal for simultaneous orientation eastward and westward in the envolvement of the nationality policy. (Ibid. pp. 602–3.) Taking issue on perspectives and retorting that 'generally people face either one way or the other — to face both ways at the same time is impossible,' Stalin answered that 'the Eastern peoples, organically connected with China, with India, connected with them by language, religion, customs, etc., are first in importance for the revolution. The relative weight of these little nationalities stands much higher than the relative weight of the Ukraine.' (Ibid. pp. 603, 605–6.)

69. Point 9 of both the theses (March) and the resolution (April) spoke of a 'special organ representing *all the nationalities* on an equality basis' (italics, J.T.). Since, however, reference in point 10 to this organ as representing 'all the national republics and regions' was felt as weakening the intended sense of inclusiveness in republics having several nationalities, the concretizing clause was added. (Ibid. p. 606; *M.N.C.Q.* pp. 144, 285 [25 April 1923].)

70. *VKP(b) v Rezol.,* I, p. 539.

71. Agreeing with the proposition that parliamentary history demonstrates 'that a second chamber usually degenerates into a center of reaction and a brake upon forward movement,' Stalin contended that that was because second chambers were often endowed

A single-chamber system would be better than a dual-chamber system if the U.S.S.R. were a single national state. But the U.S.S.R., as is well known, is a multinational state. In addition to their common interests, the nationalities of the U.S.S.R. have their special and specific interests connected with their special national features . . . Is it necessary to have a special supreme body that would reflect precisely these specific interests? Undoubtedly, it is necessary. There cannot be any doubt that without such a body it would be impossible to administer such a multinational state as the U.S.S.R.[72]

From this persisting conception of the need for an organ of the nationalities, equality of the chambers followed as a matter of course, and was essentially expressed in the constitutional provisions for procedural and substantive parity between them in the initiation, consideration and passing of legislation, convocation, dissolution, et cetera (articles 11, 21–7, 34, Constitution of 1924; articles 37–41, 45–8, Constitution of 1936). And under the new constitution, the position of the Council of Nationalities as a special organ of the nationalities was further enhanced by a number of steps. To begin with, it was made part of a body in the Soviet hierarchy, over which there is no longer any higher organ, as was previously the case when the Congress of Soviets existed. Also, in perfection of its status, direct election to it and as nearly as possible numerical equality of it with the Council of the Union were introduced; and the representation of the nationalities was stepped up by increasing the number of representatives for the Union republics from eleven to twenty-five, the autonomous republics, from five to eleven, and the autonomous regions from one to five, and by granting one representative for each of the national districts.[73] Thus, the first newly elected Council of Nationalities (12 December 1937) comprised representatives of fifty-four nationalities, and Soviet publicists proudly assert that 'the Council of Nationalities is the only second chamber in the world that is constituted on the basis of the nationality criterion.'[74]

Other Channels for the Expression of Nationality Interests. From time to time forms of assurance of guardianship and expression of the separate interests of the nationalities were sought in numerous other ways. Thus, by constitutional fiat, the number of chairmen in the Central Executive Committee, and subsequently of the vice-chairmen of the Presidium of

with more rights than first ones and were formed undemocratically by co-option from above. Hence 'these minuses will not exist, if equality be established between chambers and the second chamber organized just as democratically as the first.' (*O Konstitutsii Soiuza SSR*, p. 27.)

72. Stalin, *Constitution*, p. 26.

73. Ibid.; Molotov, *Constitution*, p. 20; and cf. article 15, Constitution of 1924 with article 35, Constitution of 1936.

74. *S.G.P.* p. 308.

the Supreme Soviet were to accord with the number of Union republics (article 27, Constitution of 1924; article 48, Constitution of 1936). Like the measures detailed immediately below, this was in implementation of the resolutions of the Twelfth Party Congress (April 1923) and the Fourth Central Committee Consultation (June 1923) 'that the executive organs of the Union be so constructed as to ensure the real participation of the representatives of the republics and the satisfaction of the needs and requirements of the peoples of the Union' and that the Presidium be elected in a manner 'securing the representation of the nationalities, at least the largest of them.' Similarly, the Party's resolutions in 1923 provided 'to construct the commissariats of the Union of Republics in such a way as to enable at least the chief nationalities to have their representatives on the collegiums.'[75] Provisions were enacted whereby, at the request of and upon consultation with a Union republic, the Commissariat for Foreign Affairs would appoint special counselors of diplomatic missions in those countries relations with which were, for reasons of contiguity, et cetera, of particular interest to the given republic.[76] And for a time military formations of separate nationalities were allowed in the Red Army.[77]

The Rooting or 'Naturalization' of Public Institutions in the National Localities. By far the most important series of endeavors aimed at creat-

---

75. See *M.N.C.Q.* pp. 164, 285; *VKP(b) v Rezol.* I, pp. 539–40; *XII S'ezd RKP(b)*, p. 451 (April 1923).

76. C.E.C. decree of 22 May 1925, *S.Z.* 1925, I, p. 530.

77. In June–July 1917 a conference of military organizations of the Party expressed its conviction 'that the formation of national regiments [i.e. of separate nationalities] is in general not in the interests of the toiling masses, although the conference, of course, does not deny the right of each nationality to form such regiments.' (*VKP(b) v Rezol.* I, p. 251.) Soon after the seizure of power, an order was issued by Stalin that 'the free grouping of warriors according to the nationality criteria is permissible within the bounds of a given military unit.' (*E.G.i P.* II, p. 1178.) In May 1918 the collegium of the Narkomnats decided that 'only on the territory of the given nationality (for example, the Ukraine, Bashkiria, Armenia, etc.)' are national military detachments to be allowed, exceptions requiring the sanction of the respective nationality's department at the commissariat, and of its 'National Soviet Socialist Party.' In this way Moslem units, Lettish and Estonian sharpshooters' detachments, etc., took a prominent part in civil-war operations. (Ibid.) In 1923, the Twelfth Party Congress, on Stalin's report, voted 'that practical measures be taken to organize national military units' (*VKP(b) v Rezol.* I, p. 506), and the C. C. consultation that followed resolved to implement this decision by organizing such units in localities with old military cadres, and by creating military schools in other national regions and republics 'in order to prepare a commanding staff from local people, which could later serve as a nucleus for the organization of national military formations.' (Ibid. I, pp. 540–41. See also *infra*, pp. 90–91, 355–7.)

ing channels and possibilities for political expression by the nationalities revolved around the so-called rooting or 'nationalization' and 'naturalization' of the public institutions in the national localities. The cardinal statement on the subject was made in 1920 as follows:

The Soviet government must become no less near and dear to the populace of the border regions of Russia. But to do so the Soviet government must first be comprehensible to them. It is therefore necessary that all Soviet organs in the border regions — the courts, the administration, the economic bodies, the direct organs of government (as also the organs of the Party) — should as far as possible be recruited from among local people acquainted with the customs, life, habits, and language of the native population; that the best people from among the native masses should be got to participate in these institutions; that the local toiling masses should be drawn into every sphere of administration of the country, including military formations, in order that the masses may see that the Soviet government and its organs are the products of their own efforts, the embodiment of their aspirations.[78]

This, it was expected, would in fact aid also the process of Sovietization of the nationalities and the political-administrative integration of their territories.[79] Accordingly, in a stream of successive decisions and pronouncements, measures such as the following were directed: to rear and develop indigenous Communist organizations in the national republics and regions where they were non-existent; gradually, but systematically, to introduce the use of the local languages into the secretarial-administrative work in these territories 'with the obligation on the part of responsible workers to become versed in the local tongues'; and to follow a concerted program of attracting local people to participation in government.[80] Special emphasis was placed on drawing in the native intellectuals as well:

Particularly here in the republics and regions . . . it is necessary, in greater measure than in the central regions, to meet half-way the elements who are revolutionary-democratic or even simply loyal to Soviet rule. The role of the local intelligentsia in the republics and regions is in many respects different from the role of the intelligentsia in the central regions of the Union of Republics. The borderlands are so poor in local intellectual workers that no effort should be spared to attract every one of them to the side of Soviet rule.[81]

---

78. Stalin on 10 October 1920, *M.N.C.Q.* p. 83. See also ibid. pp. 94, 145, 181, 208, 275, 285. That Stalin had been thinking along these lines even much earlier is evident from his appeal 'To the Soviets of Kazan, Ufa,' etc., in April 1918. (See *Istoria Sovetskoi Konstitutsii*, pp. 62–3.)

79. *M.N.C.Q.* p. 84 (1920).

80. *VKP(b) v Rezol.* I, pp 538–40 (June 1923).

81. 'This shortage cannot but hamper both educational and revolutionary constructive work in the border regions. But for this very reason it would be unwise and harmful to alienate the all too few groups of native intellectuals, who perhaps would like to serve

In this connection, the Party leaders resolved to train Communist cadres of officials for the national territorial-administrative units, taking particular care not to carry over into the localities methods of government and administration customary to the center, without appropriate psycho-political adjustment. At the same time they decided to introduce into the various departments of the Party's Central Committee a definite number of nationals — two or three in each — in order to facilitate the Party's work and the proper distribution of Party and Soviet officials in the border regions, as well as 'to allow certain recessions from the accepted norms, which would facilitate the entrance into the Party and the promotion to the leading Party organs of local proletarian and semi-proletarian elements of the national republics and regions.'[82] Not least of all, it was stressed that, wherever members from the Party center work among the more backward nationalities, they must avoid any semblance of dictation, 'under no circumstances permitting anything by way of action or talk that would appear as an assumption of the right to bind, decide, allow, or brush aside, in general to order around, formally relying on the authority of the center.'[83]

The totality of this array of diverse and diffused yet interrelated undertakings comprised the pattern of political expression accorded to the nationalities, constituting one of the three arches of the 'freedom of national development' program in the Soviet state.

---

the masses of the people but are unable to do so, perhaps because, not being Communists, they believe themselves to be surrounded by an atmosphere of mistrust and are afraid of possible measures of repression. The policy of drawing such groups into Soviet work . . . may be successfully applied. For it will hardly be maintained that these intellectual groups are less reliable than, let us say, the counterrevolutionary military experts who, their counterrevolution notwithstanding, were appointed to work at important posts and were subsequently Sovietized.' (Stalin, *M.N.C.Q.* p. 85 [1920].) This attitude toward the native intelligentsia did not, however, signify any substantial abandonment of the policy of class differentiation in the border regions as long as it was practiced generally. (See ibid. p. 276 [1921].)

82. See *VKP(b) v Rezol.* I, pp. 540–41 (June 1923), also p. 394; *M.N.C.Q.* pp. 85, 184, 208, 275. 'This flexibility . . . can be created and developed only *if* we take into account all the complexity and the specific nature of the situation prevailing in our regions and republics; *if* we do not simply engage in transplanting the models that are being created in the central districts, which cannot be transplanted mechanically to the border regions; *if* we do not ignore the nationalistically inclined elements of the population, the nationalistically inclined petty bourgeois; and *if* we learn to draw these elements into the general work of the state.' (*M.N.C.Q.* p. 179 [June 1923].)

83. *VKP(b) v Rezol.* I, p. 538 (June 1923).

Economic Equalization

The Prescription of Material Assistance to the Nationalities. Among the worst aspects of the heritage left them by their imperial predecessors, the Soviet rulers counted the extreme backwardness of numerous nationalities, particularly in the eastern border regions, where nearly thirty million people were, during the early Soviet period, either wholly or partially in a patriarchal-tribal or feudal state, and where neither industry nor industrial wage earners, neither culture nor socio-economic progress were known.[84] To be sure, the Bolsheviks granted them recognition of equality at once. Though fair and necessary, however, that was admittedly but a shell, lacking the material to provide inner substance. 'A new element has been introduced into the national question,' wrote Stalin in May 1921, 'the element of real (and not merely juridical) equalization of nations.' And if that was true as a general proposition, he said, it was particularly true in the Soviet land: 'We have proclaimed equality of legal status and are practicing it; but equality of legal status, although in itself a factor of the greatest importance in the history of the development of the Soviet republics, is still a long way from true equality.'[85] The cultural and economic backwardness of some of the nationalities robs them of the capacity to enjoy the fruits of the rights they gained and 'actual inequality is the basis of all discord and friction.' Hence, real and systematic assistance must be given these nationalities that they may rise from their backward condition to one of actual equality with the more advanced peoples. Accordingly, the task envisaged, especially once the civil war subsided, was to abolish *in toto* the former 'privileges of colonizers' enjoyed by Russians and to 'help the populace of the border regions to emancipate themselves from the survivals of the feudal patriarchal yoke' and join in the construction of a Soviet economic system.[86]

Economic Progress as a Primary Criterion of Equality. In concrete

---

84. *M.N.C.Q.* pp. 81–2, 104, 115–16, 142, 156 (1920–23). These 30 millions, roughly constituting half of the non-Great-Russian population after the deduction of the Ukraine, White Russia, part of Azerbaijan and Armenia, 'which in a more or less degree have passed through the period of industrial capitalism,' consisted mainly of the Turkic peoples of Turkestan, most of Azerbaijan, Daghestan, the Gortsi, Tatars, Bashkirs, Kirghiz, etc. And, if from these were excluded the greater part of Turkestan, the Volga and Crimean Tatar Republics, Bokhara, Khiva, Daghestan, some of the Gortsi, and several other small peoples who have become settled on definite territory, there remained about 10 million Kirghiz, Bashkirs, Chechens, South Turkestanians, Ossets, and Ingushes, dispossessed of arable land by past Russian colonization. (Ibid. pp. 275–7; *VKP(b) v Rezol.* i, pp. 394–6.)

85. *M.N.C.Q.* pp. 115 (May 1921), 155–6 (April 1923).

86. Ibid. pp. 82, 95, 116, 142, 156; see also *K.I. v Dok.* pp. 23, 321.

terms this meant: allotment of suitable land to indigenous peoples pushed out into desert wastes in earlier times; the setting up of agricultural credit, co-operatives, projects, and courses, as well as trade and technical schools; and, most important of all, that 'the Russian proletariat must take every necessary measure to establish centers of industry in the border regions, in the republics that are culturally backward — backward not through any fault of their own, but because they were formerly looked upon as sources of raw materials.'[87] Both in theory and in practice, the Communist leaders heavily stressed the last item and warned that in this sphere also, while the accumulated and growing experience of the Russian people would be of great aid to the nationalities, the economic development of the latter would proceed successfully only if the material conditions, social structure, habits of living, and history even, of each particular nationality were fully considered in concrete applications. The ultimate goal so assiduously pursued and uppermost in the minds of the Communist leaders was to enable the backward peoples of the state to pass directly from their primitive livelihoods to the present phase of Soviet economy, skipping altogether the stage of industrial capitalism. Rapid strides in this direction were mapped out and expected in the Five-Year Plans, and, although always visualized as a long and arduous track, much is held to have been achieved already.[88] Before the recent war comparative statistics pointed to remarkable increases in industry, electrification, collectivized and mechanized agriculture, railroad traffic, and retail trade in the national republics.[89] These results are regarded as adequate proof of

---

87. *M.N.C.Q.* p. 156; see also pp. 207, 276, 277, 283; xii *S'ezd RKP(b)*, p. 600; *VKP (b) v Rezol.* i, p. 540 (1921–3); ii, pp. 247–8, point 10 (1927). 'Certain attempts have already been made in this direction . . . Thus the conditions now exist enabling these republics, which are backward economically and possess no proletariat, to establish with the aid of the Russian proletariat their own centers of industry, small though they may be, in order to create in these centers groups of local proletarians who will serve as a bridge between the Russian proletarians and peasants and the toilers of these republics.' (*M.N.C.Q.* p. 156 [April 1923].)

88. Ibid. pp. 95, 104–5, 152; *S.G.P.* pp. 226–7, 254–5. The successful industrialization of backward Soviet regions is looked upon as definitive proof that a capitalistic stage of development is not an absolute inevitability. (Trainin, in *Sov. Gos. i Pr.* No. 2 [1939], p. 13.) In this connection it is interesting to note that Marx's basic test of the beneficence of political dominion, even that of foreign imperialism, was whether or not its perpetrator was contributing toward the economic and social advance of the subject nation or territory, which he visualized in terms of industrialization — to be followed later by socialization — of introducing a higher system of production and economy, breaking thereby the ages-long stagnation of the backward population. (See Bloom, op. cit. pp. 48–56.)

89. A comparison of industrial production in the Union republics in 1913 and 1936 indicates the following rise: RSFSR, 7.8 times; Ukrainian SSR, 6.9; White Russian SSR,

the sincerity of the Soviet attempt at equalization — in a broad rather than literal sense — of opportunities for the nationalities.

Cultural Autonomy

Many of the arguments for economic equalization were offered also for the third aspect of the national development policy — cultural autonomy.

The Bolshevik Stand on Cultural National Autonomy Prior to the Revolution. Prior to the revolution, 'cultural national autonomy' was rejected by the Party as contrary to the international culture sought by the universal labor movement and as artificially setting working people apart even in the same localities and enterprises. Culture and education, the Party maintained, cannot be torn away from economics and politics. It was absurd, therefore, to reduce the question to one of national culture, as was implied — according to the Bolshevik leaders — in the projects of the Austrian socialists and the Jewish Bund.[90] That there was no intention, however, to discriminate against any nationality is evident from the stand taken at that time by the Communist leaders on the question of a state language. Unquestionably, said Lenin in 1913, a single language is of progressive significance, yet compulsion toward such would only lead in the opposite direction. And while he believed that economic factors can always be expected to bring about the usage of one common language — in this case Russian — he was against the setting up of one state language as being undemocratic in a multinational country like Russia.[91]

The Soviet Design of Cultural Autonomy. Following their establishment in power, the Bolsheviks, still opposing — as more comprehensive — their three-plank program to cultural national autonomy 'as a form of al-

---

15.9; Azerbaijan SSR, 5.4; Georgian SSR, 18.6; Armenian SSR, 12; Turkmen SSR, 7.1; Uzbek SSR, 4.4; Tadzhik SSR, 116; Kazakh SSR, 11.8; and Kirghiz SSR, 95. In the same order, the percentage of peasant households collectivized and mechanized in these republics by 1937 is given as: 92.6, 96.1, 87.5, 86.5, 76.5, 88.7, 95.4, 95, 89.9, 97.5, and 89.1, respectively; while the increase in electrification from 1928 to 1936 ranges from 3.4 times (Azerbaijan) to 31.3 times (Kazakh and Kirghiz Republics). The soviets laid 7,694 kilometers of railroad track in their first two decades, and the rise in freight in 1936 as compared with 1913 was 3 to 5 times in the national republics, and 8 and 17 times, respectively, in the Tadzhik and Kazakh Republics. Likewise, retail trade turnover in the republics is shown to have increased between 6.3 and 8.3 times — 35.5 times in the Tadzhik SSR — under the first two Five-Year Plans. (See 20 *Let Sovetskoi Vlasti, Statisticheskii sbornik,* pp. 97–101.)

90. Lenin, xvi, pp. 390, 618; xvii, pp. 12, 66, 135, 147 (1913); *VKP(b) v Rezol.* I, p. 240 (May 1917); see also *S.G.P.* p. 205.

91. Lenin, xvii, p. 89; xvi, pp. 595–7 (1913).

liance between the center and the border regions of Russia,' took a clear stand not only for autonomous cultural expression, but in favor of sustained aid for such, as part of that program.[92] It was as early as April 1918 that Stalin listed among the prerequisites for turning Soviet rule into popular government in the borderlands 'local schools, local courts, a local administration, local organs of power, local public, political, and educational institutions, with the guarantee of a plenitude of rights for the local language native to the toiling masses of the territory in all spheres of public-political work.'[93] The specific measures visualized at the end of the Civil War were intended to inaugurate universal education, 'to develop a press, schools, theaters, clubs, and cultural and educational institutions generally, functioning in the native language, and . . . organize and develop an extensive system of courses and schools both for general education and for vocational and technical training given in the native languages.'[94] Later, decisions were taken to enact special laws guaranteeing the use of the native tongue in all organs and institutions that served the local populations and national minorities, and punishing 'with all revolutionary sternness' all violation of these rights.[95] By the provisions of the Constitution of 1924, the decrees and regulations of the federal C.E.C., of its Presidium, and the Sovnarkom were printed in the languages generally spoken in the Union republics (article 34). A similar article was included in the Constitution of 1936 in regard to the laws passed by the Supreme Soviet (article 40), provision being made also for conducting court proceedings 'in the language of the Union republic, autonomous republic, or

92. Stalin, *M.N.C.Q.* p. 80 (October 1920). Lenin called for 'particular carefulness in regard to the national feelings of nations that were oppressed (for example, on the part of the Great Russians, Ukrainians, Poles toward Jews, on the part of Tatars toward Bashkirs, etc.); support not only for real equality in rights, but also for the development of the language, the literature of the toiling masses of the formerly oppressed nations.' (xxiv, p. 96 [1919].)

93. Appeal 'To the Soviets of Kazan, Ufa,' etc. *Istoria Sovetskoi Konstitutsii*, pp. 62–3. While cultural aid was broadly understood to be help to backward nations 'to make the transition toward the use of machines, the easing of toil, to democracy, to socialism' (Lenin, xix, p. 228 [1916]), in a more specific sense its reference was to language, folklore, and socio-educational undertakings.

94. *M.N.C.Q.* pp. 83, 85, 94–5, 275; *VKP(b) v Rezol.* i, p. 394 (October 1920, March 1921). 'It is the accomplishment of these tasks that will facilitate the work of socialist construction in the Soviet republics of the East. People talk of model republics in the Soviet East. But what is a model republic? A model republic is one that honestly and conscientiously performs all these tasks, thereby creating an impulsion among the workers and peasants of neighboring colonial and dependent countries toward the movement for emancipation.' (Stalin, speech at the University of the Peoples of the East, 18 May 1925, *M.N.C.Q.* p. 208.)

95. Ibid. pp. 285–6; *VKP(b) v Rezol.* i, p. 506 (April 1923).

autonomous region, persons not knowing this language being ensured full acquaintance with the materials of the case through an interpreter and also the right to speak in court in their own language' (article 110). And gravely frowning upon all theories of superior and inferior races, the Party regarded as particularly objectionable talk of the superiority of the Russian culture and of the inevitability of its victory over the culture of more backward peoples; it viewed such expositions as 'nothing but an attempt to strengthen the dominion of the Great-Russian nationality.'[96]

These views played an important role in the framing of the cultural items of the Five-Year Plan and were further solidified by Stalin's strong restatement of the theoretical position at the Sixteenth Party Congress (1930). It is obvious, said he, that the Soviets have already entered the period of socialism, 'and yet, despite this . . . the national cultures and the national languages are developing and blossoming.' Why? Because the time has not yet come to renounce the policy of fostering the development of the national culture of formerly oppressed peoples. Languages cannot and will not fuse into one common tongue unless and until socialism becomes world-wide.[97] Consequently, 'agitating for one common language within the boundaries of a *single* state, within the boundaries of the U.S.S.R.,' he averred emphatically, amounts in fact to 'striving for the restoration of the *privileges* of the formerly dominant language, namely the *Great-Russian* language,' a condition the Party must oppose with all its might.[98]

It was in line with this set of conceptions that the cultural program for the nationalities was laid down, and tremendous strides are claimed by the Soviets to have been taken in this field, especially under the Five-Year Plans. No nationality, however small, is said to have been forgotten, literacy in the backward regions having been raised from 1 to 2 per cent in 1925 to 80 to 90 per cent in 1937, written literatures promoted and

---

96. *VKP(b) v Rezol.* I, p. 504 (April 1923). 'It was formerly the "accepted idea" that the world has been divided from time immemorial into inferior and superior races . . . One of the most important results of the October Revolution is that it dealt this legend a mortal blow, by showing in practice that the liberated non-European nations, once having been drawn into the channel of Soviet development, are no less capable than the European nations of promoting a *truly* progressive culture and a *truly* progressive civilization.' (Stalin, *M.N.C.Q.* p. 254 [November 1927].)

97. *M.N.C.Q.* pp. 256–7, 264–5. 'The dying away of national languages and their fusion into a single common language is not an *internal state question,* not a question of the victory of socialism in *one* country, but an *international* question, a question of the victory of socialism on an *international* scale.' (Ibid. pp. 265–6.)

98. Ibid. p. 258. See also, *Voprosy Leninizma,* pp. 424–33.

even alphabets created where none existed before.[99] As compared with 1913–14, the student population, the number of books and newspapers published in the languages of the nationalities, theaters, cinemas, et cetera, increased by 1936–7 in unprecedented proportions in the national republics.[100]

These acts and expressions in the domain of culture complete the composite program of grants to the nationalities. If legal equality constituted the bone structure of the national development program, political, economic, and cultural equality, sought through the manifold efforts detailed above, were the vaunted flesh, blood, and breath together comprising a pulsating body of practice and principle.

(2) THE RIGHTS OF THE UNION

Freedom of national development was not, however, to be a one-way affair. Outer limits, based on the conception of the interests of the Union as a whole, formed the obverse side of the triangular grant to the nationalities. Political expression, economic equalization, and cultural autonomy were bound by opposite numbers in the shape of political centralization, economic co-ordination, and cultural concordance.

Political Centralization

The Range of Union Competence. It was always clearly understood that the national statehood of the nationalities within the domain was to be *Soviet* in character and full conformity of the Union republic constitutions with the Constitution of the U.S.S.R. was assured.[101] And paramount

99. *S.G.P.* pp. 209, 255.

100. The number of pupils rose from 7,853,000 in 1914–15 to 27,611,000 in 1936–7, i.e. 3.5 times over the entire U.S.S.R. By republics this increase was: RSFSR, 3.2 times; Ukrainian SSR, 3.1; White Russian SSR, 3.7; Azerbaijan SSR, 7.6; Georgian SSR, 4.2; Armenian SSR, 7.1; Turkmen SSR, 23; Uzbek SSR, 49.4; Tadzhik SSR, 497.5; Kazakh SSR, 8.9; and Kirghiz SSR, 32.4 times. Non-Russian books, published now in 110 languages of the peoples of the U.S.S.R., rose from 6,521,000 in 1913 to 132,851,000 in 1936, while for books published in Russian the figures were 80,218,000 and 438,–220,000, respectively. In 1913 there were 84 non-Russian newspapers as against 775 printed in the Russian language. By 1936 there were 2,965 of the first, printed in 68 languages, and 6,285 of the second. As for theaters, to give a few examples, the numbers increased by 1936 as compared with 1914 — in the White Russian SSR — from 2 to 14; Georgian SSR, from 3 to 40; Armenian SSR, from 0 to 17; Uzbek SSR, from 1 to 37; Tadzhik SSR, from 0 to 6; Kazakh SSR, from 2 to 26; and Kirghiz SSR, from 0 to 5. And similar stupendous climbs are shown for public health undertakings. (For more details, see 20 *Let Sovetskoi Vlasti,* pp. 102–6.)

101. *S.G.P.* pp. 209, 269–70, 287; article 5, Constitution of 1924; article 16, Constitution of 1936. Even the earlier republics of Khorezm, Khiva, and Bukhara were 'Soviet' or

importance was attached to the structural-procedural arrangements for centralized direction of basic polity and policy. The exclusive competence of the Union covers the fields of foreign trade; state security, control of constitutional observance, admission of new republics, and approval of territorial-administrative changes; the all-Union budget, economic plan, monetary and credit system, insurance, loans, and administration of transport, and communications as well as all-Union economic enterprises; legislation on the judicial structure, procedure and codes, citizenship and rights of foreigners, and issuance of all-Union acts of amnesty; and the establishment of basic principles with regard to education, public health, the utilization of land and natural resources, and legislation on toil (article 14, Constitution of 1936. Cf. part II, ch. i, article 1, Constitution of 1924). Before the constitutional reform of 1944, it likewise embraced the fields of defense and foreign relations. The laws of the U.S.S.R., binding throughout the territories of the Union republics, prevail in case of conflict with the laws of the latter (articles 19, 20, Constitution of 1924; articles 19, 38, Constitution of 1936).

Powers and Devices Ensuring Conformance with Central Objectives. While items of joint jurisdiction are carried out by the U.S.S.R. commissariats (now renamed ministries) through the identically named commissariats (Ministries) of the Union republics (article 76, Constitution of 1936; article 54, Constitution of 1924), there are a number of constitutional devices designed to ensure conformance with the central government's objectives and to guard against trespassing upon the wide scope of federal authority outlined above. Thus, the central, all-Union commissariats (Ministries), which exercise their functions throughout the U.S.S.R. either directly or through organs appointed by them, have their representatives attached to and participating in the work of the councils of people's commissars of the Union republics (articles 75, 83, Constitution of 1936; articles 53, 67, Constitution of 1924).[102] By the Constitution of 1924, the former Presidium of the Central Executive Committee U.S.S.R. had the power to suspend and annul orders of the central executive committees

---

'People's Soviet,' though not 'Socialist' in designation. Where the ties are less fully perfected, however, this designation may be absent, as in the case of Outer Mongolia, bearing the title of 'Mongolian People's Republic.'

102. These representatives were to participate 'in a consultative capacity' according to the plan of the first U.S.S.R. constitution (*M.N.C.Q.* p. 135, article 18), but the text adopted provided for 'a consulting or deciding vote as the central executive committees of the Union republics may decide' (article 67). The absence of such provision in the present constitution (article 83) apparently gives them outright the status of full participants.

and councils of people's commissars of the Union republics, and also to suspend orders of the congresses of soviets of the latter, bringing such suspension up for review by the Central Executive Committee of the U.S.S.R. While the central executive committees of the Union republics and their presidiums could appeal to the Presidium C.E.C. of the U.S.S.R. any decree or order of the federal Council of People's Commissars, they could not suspend the execution of such decision (articles 31, 32, 42). Similarly, the Constitution of 1936 gives the Presidium of the Supreme Soviet U.S.S.R. the power to annul and the Council of People's Commissars U.S.S.R. (Council of Ministers) the power to suspend decisions and orders of the councils of people's commissars of the Union republics (articles 69, 49e). And the organs of the State Attorney of the U.S.S.R. perform their functions in the national territorial-administrative units entirely independently of any local organs, being appointed, or confirmed by, and subordinate to him alone (articles 115–17).

The very function of raising or lowering the status of a national unit is to a large extent a central function, by virtue of the constitutional requirement of Union approval of territorial-administrative changes, and, as recent experience has shown, elevation of the standing of a national unit on the territorial-administrative ladder has its counterpart in acts of degrading or downgrading in national-political status. Thus, in the course of the recent war, five autonomous republics and regions were liquidated, and their territories were either distributed among neighboring areas or changed into purely administrative regions. The first of these, the German Volga A.S.S.R., was abolished in the autumn of 1941, following disclosure of diversionist activities among its German population. Similarly, during 1943–5, the Kalmyk, Chechen-Ingush, and Crimean Autonomous Soviet Socialist Republics, and the Karachaev Autonomous Region were abolished on the ground that their populations did not offer opposition to treacherous collaborationist groups, which were formed among them during the German occupation and which fought alongside the Germans against the U.S.S.R.[103] In each case, changes in place names were made in order to remove the linguistic identity of the national group involved, and many of the inhabitants were resettled in other parts of the Union.

Lastly, there is the constant impact of the highly centralized Party structure on the entire territorial-administrative pyramid, and on the standing and operation of the national units at all of its levels.

This combination of centralized control with national political expres-

---

103. See Shabad, loc. cit.; *The New York Times,* 30 November 1945, 27 June 1946.

sion for the nationalities came — as did all other political power relationships in the Soviet state — under the designation of democratic centralism.

Economic Co-ordination

Centralism in General Direction and Unity of the Economic Plan. In
the field of economics, this same 'democratic centralism presupposes centralism in fundamental questions — in the general direction, in maximum
unification of all economic activity by one state-wide plan, in directing
industry with the aim of the rational and economical utilization of all
material resources of the country.' [104] Thus, plans for the economic development of the national territorial-administrative units are required to be an
integral part of and fully co-ordinated with the economic plan for the
entire U.S.S.R.

The Definitive Establishment of the Planning Principle. That socialist
economy would be planned and organized was one of the most prominent
ideas in the theoretical prognoses of Marx and Engels, and during the
early Soviet period the treaty relations between the republics sought
economic no less than military union.[105] From 1920 on, the question of
practical undertakings for all-round planning was raised periodically at
the Party and Soviet congresses, and as control of 'the commanding
heights' made for a progressive increase in the socialist sector of the
national economy, planning began to take on a political-compulsory nature, the warning being uttered at the Fifteenth Party Congress (1927)
that the plans are not attempts at forecasts or mere guesses 'but plans-
directives, which are *obligatory* upon the leading organs and which *determine* the direction of our *future* economic development on a scale
embracing the *entire* country.' The Five-Year Plans gave these views an
added impetus. On the assumption of unity of socialist economics as well
as a 'socialist division of labor between the parts of the state . . . based
on the fullest and many-sided development of the industrial and agricultural resources and possibilities of every part of the Union,' the Soviet
leaders did not hesitate to create economic regions that at times cut across
political-territorial lines. They took care, however, to increase the self-
sufficiency of the units without at the same time neglecting the more

---

104. *S.G.P.* pp. 220–21. As a Comintern thesis put it in 1920, 'socialism aims to tie up all
the regions, all the districts, all the nationalities by the unity of the economic plan,'
adding at the same time, 'But economic centralism, freed from exploitation of class by
class [and] nation by nation and therefore equally advantageous for all, is correlated —
without detriment — with genuine freedom of national development.' (*K.I. v Dok.*
p. 151. See also ibid. pp. 22–3 [1928].)
105. *S.G.P.* pp. 191–3.

concentrated utilization of their particular resources.[106] And co-ordinated economic activity was given supreme and definitive recognition by the inclusion of a special article on the planning principle in the new constitution (article 11).

Cultural Concordance

Uniformity of Content for the Diverse National Cultures. Lastly, cultural concordance — coherence with central pursuits and with one another — was to be secured for the various cultures of the nationalities through uniformity of content, whatever the differences in form of expression. Succinctly, the formula was given as follows:

Proletarian in content and national in form — such is the universal human culture toward which socialism is marching. Proletarian culture does not cancel national culture, but lends it content. National culture, on the other hand, does not cancel proletarian culture, but lends it form.[107]

Whatever the earlier attitude on national culture, the business of the proletariat, once established in power, was actively to support it. If the nationalities benefited from earnest, unstinting, and persevering efforts at the elevation of their cultural endowment, said the Bolshevik leaders, so did the Soviet polity, 'for it need hardly be shown that ignorance and unenlightenment are the most dangerous enemies of Soviet government.' Also, it was pointed out, national culture, no less than national statehood, was placed 'at the service of socialist construction.'[108]

The Propagation of a 'Proletarian Content' in the Cultures of the Nationalities. In order to implant a 'proletarian content' in the national cultures, a series of concrete measures was outlined in 1923: creation of special schools of political literacy and of a Marxist literature and periodical press in the native languages; extension of the activities of the University of the Peoples of the East and its branches in the localities, and formation of a Party discussion club — with the active participation of

---

106. Ibid. p. 256; Harper, *The Government of the Soviet Union,* pp. 9, 45. 'The Party rejected absolutely, as reactionary and nationalistic, projects for transforming individual republics into closed economic complexes on the one hand, and plans for planting monocultures in the individual republics, on the other.' (*S.G.P.* p. 256.)

107. *M.N.C.Q.* p. 210 (1925). See also *K.I. v Dok.* p. 22 (1928). 'What is national culture under the supremacy of the national bourgeoisie? A culture *bourgeois* in content and national in form, the aim of which is to infect the masses with the virus of nationalism and to consolidate the supremacy of the bourgeoisie. What is national culture under the dictatorship of the proletariat? A culture *socialist* in content and national in form, the aim of which is to educate the masses in the spirit of internationalism and to consolidate the dictatorship of the proletariat.' (*M.N.C.Q.* p. 260 [June 1930].)

108. Ibid. pp. 83, 259; *S.G.P.* p. 219.

Central Committee members — attached to it; and intensification of Party work in general, and among young people and women in particular, in the republics and regions.[109] Thus, the wide opportunities for national cultural assertion would not negate, but would contribute in the end toward the achievement of ultimate goals and aspirations. Said Stalin at the Sixteenth Party Congress (1930):

> It may seem strange that we, who are in favor of the *fusion* of national cultures in the future into one common culture (both in form and in content), with a single, common language, are at the same time in favor of the *blossoming* of national cultures at the present time, in the period of the Dictatorship of the Proletariat. But there is nothing strange in this. The national cultures must be permitted to develop and expand and to reveal all their potential qualities, in order to create the conditions necessary for their fusion into a single, common culture with a single, common language.[110]

Essentially, this position has been maintained to the present.

(3) THE CONSTITUTIONAL BALANCE BETWEEN CENTER AND CIRCUMFERENCE

The General Trend toward Centralization. On balance and in line with the theoretical views on the virtues of centralism, there has been a mounting tendency toward greater centralization and progressive augmentation of federal control, even while more and more nationalities not only were given economic and cultural opportunities, but were being endowed with territorial-administrative forms of political expression. In number and caliber, the governmental branches independently administered by the Union republics have diminished. Of the six original exclusively republic commissariats — Agriculture, Internal Affairs, Justice, Public Health, Education, and Social Security — only the last two remain as such. Agriculture was made a federated commissariat in December 1929; Internal Affairs was first eliminated (1930), then reintroduced as a joint commissariat (1936); while the departments of Justice and Public Health similarly became federated or Union-republic commissariats in July 1936.[111]

---

109. *M.N.C.Q.* pp. 146, 287; *VKP(b) v Rezol.* i, p. 541 (March–June 1923).

110. *M.N.C.Q.* p. 261 (1930). 'Such is the dialectical nature of the Leninist presentation of the question of national culture. It may be said that, presented in this way, the question is "self-contradictory." But is there not the same sort of "self-contradiction" in our treatment of the question of the state? . . . Whoever has failed to understand this peculiarity and this "self-contradictory" nature of our transitional times, whoever has failed to understand this dialectical character of historical processes, is lost to Marxism.' (Ibid. pp. 261–2.)

111. The commissariats of Internal Affairs of the republics were liquidated at the end of 1930, their functions being variously distributed; that of Communal Economy was reorganized into republic commissariats in the second half of 1931. On 10 July

At the same time the potency and quantity of the all-Union and joint commissariats have continuously climbed upwards. The five all-Union and five joint or Union-republic commissariats provided for in the constitution of 1924 had became eight and ten, respectively, by 1936.[112] A federal office of Procurator (state attorney) was created in 1933, and in the following year the Commissariat of Workmen-Peasants Inspection — a Union-republic or joint-jurisdiction commissariat — gave place to an all-Union Commission of Soviet Control, operating independently of any local authorities.[113]

The Increase in Federal Jurisdiction under the New Constitution. Further changes increasing the scope of federal jurisdiction were laid down

---

1934, an all-Union Commissariat of Internal Affairs was created, which by the new constitution became a federated commissariat. Education remained a republic commissariat, but from 1928 on its jurisdictional sphere was considerably circumscribed by the transfer of professional and technical training to economic departments and enterprises, and the formation of a Committee on Higher Technical Education at the C.E.C., U.S.S.R. (September 1932), later transformed into an all-Union Committee on Higher Education, at the Sovnarkom U.S.S.R. (May 1936). In 1934, republic commissariats of Local Industry were formed, there being, thus, four republic commissariats at the time of adoption of the new constitution: Local Industry, Education, Communal Economy, and Social Security. (See *S.G.P.* pp. 363–79, *passim*.)

112. To the original all-Union Commissariats of Foreign Affairs, Army and Navy, Foreign Trade, Ways of Communication (Railways), Posts and Telegraphs (renamed Communications in 1932) were added the Commissariats of Water Transport (1931), Heavy Industry (1932), and Defense Industry (December 1936). Moreover, all-Union committees and commissions with commissariat-like functions were formed from time to time. (See *infra*, pp. 281–2.) The five federated or joint commissariats of 1924 were: Finance, Supplies (succeeded by Internal Trade in 1924), Labor, Workers-Peasants Inspection, and Supreme Council of National Economy. In addition, there was the Unified State Political Administration, or O.G.P.U., of the U.S.S.R. which was to direct the work of the local authorities of state political administration or G.P.U., through its representatives at the sovnarkoms of the Union republics. In 1934, O.G.P.U. passed to the newly formed all-Union Commissariat of Internal Affairs, which became a joint or Union-republic commissariat in 1936. The Department of Labor was liquidated in June 1933 — its functions being transferred centrally and locally to the trade unions — and that of Workers-Peasants Inspection superseded in February 1934. A large increment to this group of commissariats — besides Agriculture, Internal Affairs, Justice, and Public Health indicated before — were the immediate and later offshoots of the Supreme Council of National Economy, which was broken up in 1932: Light Industry (1932, federated; 1934, all-Union), Timber Industry (1932, all-Union), Food Industry (1934, all-Union), all of which became federated or Union-republic by the Constitution of 1936, and State Grain and Livestock Farms (1936). (Cf. articles 37, 51–2, 61–3, 67–8, Constitution of 1924 in original and post-1930 editions, and articles 77, 78, 83, Constitution of 1936; and see *S.G.P.* pp. 265–8, 363, 379; and *infra*, pp. 456–7.

113. See *S.G.P.* pp. 258, 352, 375–8; and *infra*, pp. 307–8. For the function of the Commission of Soviet Control and its subsequent supercession, see *infra*, pp. 172–3.

by the new constitution. Whereas by the Constitution of 1924 the Union
had the right only to establish 'the bases' and general plan for the national
economy, 'the principles' of the judicial system, and 'fundamental legislation' concerning union citizenship, the Constitution of 1936 gives the
federal Union total powers of legislation in these matters. While under
the earlier constitution the federal authority was merely 'directing' foreign
trade, and the Union republics had the right — with its permission — to
contract foreign and domestic loans, control of these fields is now the
exclusive prerogative of the U.S.S.R. In lieu of the loose provision for
'adjusting questions concerning the alteration of boundaries between
Union republics,' which gave the republics, in fact, great leeway in reshuf-
fling territorial-administrative setups, the Union now exercises the veto
power on the formation of new territories, regions, autonomous republics,
and autonomous regions.[114] And more transformations along these lines
have been effected since the adoption of the new constitution.

To be sure, the constitutional reform of 1944, which granted the Union
republics the right of representation in foreign affairs and empowered
them to establish their own military formations and to enter into relations
with foreign states, is a move in the other direction, and would be of
considerable potential significance if it were permitted to develop fully.
Fundamentally, however, no radical change in prevailing relationships
has taken place.[115] The Union retains full powers to represent itself in
international relations, conclude and ratify treaties, organize the defense
of the Union, and direct 'all the armed forces of the U.S.S.R.' And, in
regard to the rights obtained by the republics in these fields, it specifically
reserves to itself the prerogative of establishing 'the general procedure in
the mutual relations between the Union republics and foreign states' and

---

114. *S.G.P.* pp. 268–9. The last-named provision of the new constitution, along with the
novel feature of detailed enumeration in the latter of the territorial-administrative units
of each Union republic, was introduced, as Stalin explained at the time, in order to put
a curb on the passion of some officials for endless rearrangements of territories and
regions: 'And that is very good, because what is needed here, as in many other things,
is an atmosphere of certainty; stability, clarity is needed.' (*O Konstitutsii,* p. 27.)

115. Outside of participation by the Ukrainian and Belorussian Republics at international
conferences, and a few agreements on repatriation concluded by them as well as by
the Lithuanian SSR with the Polish authorities in 1944, the constituent republics have
not, as yet, made much use of their new rights in the foreign field and apparently slow
going is expected for a time. 'During the initial period,' wrote Professor Trainin in
1945, 'the extension of the foreign-political connections of the Union republics, of
their mutual business relations with large and small states of the world, encounters the
tenacity of prejudices, [and] the habit of foreign states to have intercourse with the
all-Union government alone.' (*Sodruzhestvo,* p. 55.) Nor is there any present evidence
of any extensive creation of separate military formations in the Union republics.

the 'directing principles' of the organization of military formations of the republics (articles 14a and g, 18a, 60c and f, Constitution of 1936, as amended 1 February 1944). Under these reservations the federal government's powers of over-all direction and control remain strong.

View of Centralism in Relation to the National Entities. These manifestations of ascending power concentration are not regarded by Soviet theorists, however, as derogatory to and contradictory of the rights of the nationalities and the people at large, but as complementing and reinforcing them.[116] Increased unification, centralization, planning, and direction, it is said, were called forth by the dire needs of construction, the economic interdependence, and the cultural ties that have grown through time. What is more, the very fact of centralized direction has made it possible to render systematic assistance to the nationalities and 'not only does not infringe upon the special interests of the separate republics, but on the contrary, it contributes to their better satisfaction.'[117] If the Union is constitutionally bound to guard the sovereign rights of the Union republics, the independence of the latter, it is strongly emphasized, would lack all security were it not backed in fact by the concentrated resources and military might of the entire state, for 'the source of strength and sovereignty of the Union republics is in the U.S.S.R.'[118] The controlling principle of the prevailing relationships is visualized therefore as one of maximum correlation between the needs and ends of the parts and the whole, resting at base on Lenin's guiding principle that 'Unity in the fundamental, the cardinal, the essential is not violated, but is secured by

---

116. If, for instance, the statement is made that the economic plans composed by individual collectives, etc., issue from and 'in final analysis constitute the detailed and concretized, in time and space, state-wide economic plan' drawn up by the state organs (the Sovnarkom, Gosplan, etc.), it is also stated at the same time that 'the plans for the national economy — both at the stage of their preparation and at the stage of their execution — are a result of the political, economic, and organizing creativity of the wide masses of toilers, whose life interests form the essence of these plans. Around the fulfilment of these plans — as state-compulsory undertakings — the Party and government, as well as the mass, public organizations (trade unions, Komsomol, etc.), organize the productive initiative and self-activity of the masses. Soviet planning correlates state discipline with the self-activity of the masses.' (*S.G.P.* pp. 193–4.)

117. *S.G.P.* pp. 226–7, 256, 267–8. At the same time, such acts as the abolition of the Mid-Asian Bureau of the Central Committee and of the Mid-Asian Economic Council (1934), preparation of conditions for the formation of new republics from composite units (Transcaucasia, etc.), and the creation of republic Commissariats of Communal Economy and Local Industry were pointed to as items buttressing the 'independence' of the republics. (See ibid. pp. 257–8.)

118. Ibid. p. 273; article 15, Constitution of 1936; Trainin, in *Sov. Gos.* No. 2 (1938), pp. 95, 98, 100, 101.

variation in particulars, in local peculiarities, in modes of *approach* to the thing, in *methods* of effectuating control . . .'[119] The crowning conclusion is drawn that 'the wide sphere of competence of the federal government in the U.S.S.R. . . . is an index of the unity of the Soviet state and of the closest solidarity of the Soviet republics.' The changes introduced by the new constitution, in other words, are considered but natural extensions of earlier travel along a necessary road, perfecting the structure of the multi-national Soviet polity, adapting it to the conditions of a socialist order, and fortifying the might of the state in the face of recurring threats of external aggression.[120]

---

119. *S.G.P.* pp. 220–21, 266–7; Lenin, XXII, p. 166 (January 1918).
120. *S.G.P.* pp. 267, 268–9.

Chapter V · The Nationality Principle (II)

1. THE STRUGGLE OVER THE NATIONALITY POLICY

(I) EARLY OPPOSITION TO NATIONAL SELF-DETERMINATION

The Position of the Social-Democrats. The complex of views and practices comprising the concept of Soviet nationhood met with motley opposition at various stages of its evolution. Since their earliest days, the Bolsheviks faced on the one hand theories and arguments rejecting the slogan of self-determination of nations, and on the other projects offering cultural national autonomy as a solution of the nationality problem. Expounders of the first were the Polish and Dutch Social-Democrats[1] and of the second, primarily those of Austria-Hungary.[2] World War I increased the rifts and complications in the theoretical front of the social-democratic parties — the ideological-organizational predecessors of the communist sections. While some of the leaders of the Second International stepped forth with outright denials of the self-determination principle, others were equivocal in their statements on the question, and Lenin fought and condemned the position of both.[3]

---

1. Roza Luxemburg, Gorter, Pannekoek, etc. Their contention was that it was impossible to solve the national question under imperialism; that the development of great capitalist states rendered illusory the right of self-determination of small nations; and that socialist recognition of such right was equivalent to support for and playing into the hands of the bourgeois nationalism of the oppressed nations. The Bolshevik response was that in practice such views resulted in nihilism and were based on a complete lack of perception of the vital importance of a bond between proletariat and peasantry — including the peasantry of the oppressed nationalities. (Lenin, XVII, pp. 90, 120, 427–74; *K.I. v Dok.* p. 481; *S.G.P.* p. 205 [1913–14, 1925, 1938].)

2. Bauer, Springer, Renner, etc. In Russia these views were held chiefly by the Bund, a Jewish socialist organization. (See Lenin, XVII, pp. 117–18; XIX, p. 40; XXIX, pp. 230, 265; *M.N.C.Q.* pp. 75–6, 112, 114, and note 4; *S.G.P.* pp. 204–5; and *supra,* pp. 80–82.)

3. Kunow and Parvus, of Germany, and certain Fabian and trade-union leaders in England, etc., belonged to the first group, while considered prominent among those of the second were: Kautsky, Scheidemann, Hyndman, Vandervelde, Renaudel, etc., in western Europe, and Plekhanov, Martov, Trotsky, and Chkheidze in Russia. Lenin also

Early Opposition in the Communist Ranks. The fight involved even several close Russian collaborators at the time — Bukharin and Piatakov, who, following Karl Radek on the question of 'annexations,' i.e. self-determination of nations, gave vent to expressions contrary to the 1913 Party resolution on the matter.[4] This negation of the necessity for self-determination, with the correlative right of national secession, was carried by them to the very threshold of the Bolshevik Revolution, and reasserted again in March 1919 when the new Party program was being adopted.[5] Though the adoption of the program, completely embodying Lenin's outlook, laid down authoritative guidance in the matter for the future, from time to time there were occasional echoes of past conceptual differences on the national question.

(2) THE STRUGGLE AGAINST NATIONALIST REGIMES AND DEVIATIONS

The War on Nationalist Regimes in the Early Period. Another early battlefront of the Soviet nationality policy was the criss-cross struggle against the 'National Councils' or governments and nationalist parties that cropped up like mushrooms over wide areas in the west, south, and east of the Russian land during the Revolution and civil war. These included the Ukrainian Central Rada (April 1917–April 1918); the White-Russian Rada (July 1917–January 1919); the Sfatul Tarii or regional council of Bessarabia (November 1917–November 1918); the Kurultai in the Crimea (December 1917–January 1918); the Kurultai in Bashkiria (November 1917–19); the autonomous government in Turkestan (November 1917–February 1918); the national councils of Azerbaijan, Armenia, Georgia; and the Azerbaijan Mussavat, Armenian Dashnak, and Georgian Menshevik parties (replaced by Soviet regimes in April and De-

---

found it necessary to answer such lesser lights as Yurkevich, Libman, and Semkovsky in Russia, whose statements were reflections of Roza Luxemburg's views. (See Lenin, XVII, pp. 468–9, 472; XVIII, p. 323–8; XIX, pp. 44–8, 53, 263, 271–2.)

4. Lenin, XIX, pp. 195–235, 238, 262–72, 276–8; XXIX, pp. 230–32, 239, 263–5; XXX, pp. 250–56, 257–61; *S.G.P.* p. 206. Even Lunacharsky, later the first Commissar of Education, and Madam Kollontai had apparently leaned to such views at the time. (See Lenin, XXIX, pp. 237–8, 276–7.)

5. At the Seventh or 'April' Conference of the Party in 1917, Piatakov persisted in his views, maintaining that every national movement is a reactionary movement. His stand was supported at the time by F. Dzerzhinsky and F. Makharadze. (See Lenin, XX, pp. 276–8; *VKP(b) v Rezol.* I, pp. 230–31, 289; *M.N.C.Q.* pp. 66–7 and note 27. At the Party congress in 1919 Tomsky joined the Bukharin-Piatakov group with a speech hostile to national self-determination, which Lenin was not slow in answering. (See *Pravda,* 23 and 25 March 1919.)

cember 1920 and February 1921, respectively); and the regional governments of the Don, Kuban, Siberia, et cetera.[6]

The Fight on 'National Deviations' in the Party. Then, following the
disappearance of the nationalist regimes and polities in embryo, the
Bolshevik Party was periodically confronted with displays of nationalist
credos within segments of its own ranks — the so-called national deviations. Wrote Stalin in his theses for the Tenth Party Congress:

> On the one hand, the Great-Russian Communists working in these [border]
> regions, who have grown up under the conditions of a 'sovereign' nation, and who
> have never known national oppression, not infrequently minimize the importance
> of national peculiarities in Party work, or else ignore them altogether, and fail in
> their work to reckon with the peculiarities of class structure, culture, social life, and
> historical past of the given people, and so vulgarize and distort the policy of the
> Party on the national question. This circumstance leads to a deviation from com-
> munism towards the dominant-power spirit, the colonising spirit, the spirit of Great-
> Russian chauvinism. On the other hand, the native Communists, who have lived
> through the painful period of national oppression and have not entirely ceased to be
> haunted by the horrors of that period, not infrequently exaggerate the importance
> of national peculiarities in Party work, leave the class interests of the toilers in the
> background, or else simply identify the interests of the toilers of the given nation
> with the 'general national' interests of that nation, failing to pick out the former
> from the latter and to base their Party work on them. This circumstance in its turn
> leads to a deviation from communism towards bourgeois-democratic nationalism.[7]

Along with want of prudence in approach to the nationalities, the first
deviation was regarded as particularly deleterious to the Soviet cause.

Great-Russian Chauvinism. Initially based on the presence, in both the
central and local institutions of large numbers of old Party workers of
Russian descent — unfamiliar with the customs and mores of the diverse
nationalities — as well as on the fact that a substantial part of the proletariat of the national republics consisted of Russians, the deviation
towards Great-Russian chauvinism gained added momentum with the
introduction of the NEP in 1921. This deviation, according to the Party
leaders, took the shape of 'the rankest kind of nationalism, which strives
to obliterate all that is not Russian, to gather all the threads of administration into the hands of Russians.'[8] As the proceedings and resolutions

6. For brief accounts, see *M.N.C.Q.* notes 30–35, 44, 45, and pp. 71–4; *S.G.P.* pp. 240–45.
7. *M.N.C.Q.* pp. 96–7 (10 February 1921).
8. Ibid. pp. 145–6, 153–5, 282, 286 (March–April 1923). 'The national question·is also of
   importance to us,' said Stalin on 23 April 1923, 'not only because the formerly oppressed
   nationalities inhabit regions most essential from the point of view of economic development and most important from the point of view of military strategy, but first and

of successive Party congresses attest,[9] this nationalism, sometimes cloaked in verbal garments of internationalism, found expression in such views and tendencies as: the underrating of specific national and linguistic differences; oversimplification and mechanical transplantation of central models of economic development to the border regions; and efforts to pave the way for the liquidation of the national republics and regions, to undermine the principle of national equality, and to discredit the policy of naturalizing the administrative apparatus and cultural media. Great-Russian chauvinism likewise manifested itself in beliefs that considered the entrance of the Soviet state into the period of socialist construction as leaving only class, not nationality, questions before it and as calling for the elimination of national cultures.[10] Socially, the roots of this deviation were assessed as 'the striving of the moribund classes of the formerly dominant Great-Russian nation to win back their lost privileges' and it was considered itself to be a major contributing cause of the deviation toward local nationalism.[11]

Local Nationalism. Under this second deviation, influenced by a heritage of 'old national grudges' and 'a certain national aloofness and a lack of complete trust on the part of the formerly oppressed peoples in measures proceeding from the Russians,' came a number of acts and manifestations on the part of Communists in the national localities. These consisted of: overrating the specific national features; treating the nationality problem independently of the question of proletarian dictatorship; juxtaposing the culture and economy of a national republic — e.g. the Ukraine — to the Russian culture and Union economy; opposing the formation of federal administrations, such as an all-Union department of agriculture; substituting as a task the development of national consciousness in place of propagation of proletarian self-consciousness; spreading forcible

---

foremost because during the last two years we have introduced what is known as the New Economic Policy, as a result of which Russian nationalism has grown and become accentuated, the idea of Smenoveknism has been born.' He blamed this idea or current of ideas — developed in 1921 among Russian émigrés by V. N. Ustryalov and others and holding that the Communist Party would degenerate in time and with the aid of a strong man re-establish the old 'single and indivisible' Russia in the form of a bourgeois-democratic Russian republic — for intensified nationalistic moods among many of the Party's political workers. (See ibid. pp. 141, 149, 153–4, 282, and note 43.)

9. Ibid. pp. 104, 141–2, 213, 256–62, 278; *VKP(b) v Rezol.* i, pp. 396–7, 503–4; *XV S'ezd VKP(b)*, pp. 146–7; *XVI S'ezd VKP(b)*, pp. 105, 430–32; *XVII S'ezd VKP(b)*, pp. 70, 71–2, 141 (1921–34).

10. In the Ukraine, for example, some Communists proposed the introduction of Esperanto in place of the Ukrainian language in the schools. (See *XVI S'ezd VKP(b)*, p. 200.)

11. *M.N.C.Q.* pp. 157, 264, 287.

inculcation of a national language, such as compulsive Ukranization of schools; and concealing the activity of nationalists.[12] Its worst aspect was considered to be that in some of the republics inhabited by different peoples 'this defensive nationalism often turns into aggressive nationalism, into the outright chauvinism of the stronger nationality directed against the weaker nationalities of these republics.' The Party also considered this deviation harmful as hindering the cultivation of internationalism, retarding the amalgamation of the Soviet peoples into a single federal state, and playing into the hands of prospective interventionists; and analyzed its social source as 'the dissatisfaction of the moribund classes of the formerly oppressed nations with the regime of the proletarian dictatorship, their endeavor to separate themselves off into their national state and there to establish their own class supremacy.'[18] Accordingly, prominent Party members found to be manifesting this deviation were promptly removed from Party and government posts.[14]

Great-Russian chauvinism was for a time considered the greater threat of the two. At the Twelfth Party Congress (1923), Stalin strictly opposed, however, a proposal by Bukharin and Rakovsky to omit from the resolution any mention of the danger of local chauvinism, and ridiculed Bukharin's theory that only by artificially placing themselves 'in an inferior position' in relation to the other nationalities could the Russians, as a formerly dominant nation, win their full confidence. Answering the purport of the argument, Stalin said:

Yet it is clear that the political basis of the Dictatorship of the Proletariat consists mainly and primarily of the central, the industrial regions, and not the border regions, which are peasant countries. If we overemphasize the peasant border regions at the expense of the proletarian districts, a fissure in the system of the

---

12. Ibid. pp. 104, 142–3, 145, 169–70, 278, 283–4; *XV S'ezd VKP(b)*, p. 102; *XVI S'ezd VKP(b)*, pp. 105, 432, 436; *XVII S'ezd VKP(b)*, pp. 69–72 (1921–34). 'The essence of the deviation toward local nationalism consists in the attempt to isolate oneself and shut oneself up within one's own national shell, in the attempt to hush up class differences within one's own nation, in the attempt to resist Great Russian chauvinism by turning aside from the general current of Socialist construction, in the attempt to shut one's eyes to that which brings together and unites the toiling masses of the nationalities of the U.S.S.R. and to see only that which tends to estrange them.' (*M.N.C.Q.* pp. 262–3.) 'The result of this deviation is that they become divorced from socialism and degenerate into ordinary bourgeois-nationalists.' (Ibid. p. 214.)

13. Ibid. pp. 143, 145, 157–63, 263, 287; *XVI S'ezd VKP(b)*, pp. 432, 534.

14. Mdivani, Makharadze, Tsintadze in Georgia; Shumsky, Khvylevoy, Valuev, Skrypnik, etc., in the Ukraine; Maksum, Abdrakhmanov, Khodzhibaev in Central Asia, etc. (1923, 1926, 1933). (See *M.N.C.Q.* pp. 158–63, 229–31, 267–8, and note 47; *XV S'ezd VKP(b)*, pp. 626–6; *XVI S'ezd VKP(b)*, pp. 200, 436; *XVII S'ezd VKP(b)*, pp. 69–71, 105.)

Dictatorship of the Proletariat may result. This is dangerous, comrades. We must
not overshoot the mark in politics, just as we must not undershoot it.[15]

The Party strongly condemned both deviations, however; and the rule
was laid down in 1934 that 'the question of which is the major danger in
the sphere of the national question is determined not by futile and formal
controversies, but by a Marxist analysis of the situation at the given
moment, and by a study of the mistakes that have been committed in
this sphere.'[16] At the same time the view was expressed that 'the survivals of capitalism in the minds of men are much more tenacious in the
sphere of the national question than in any other sphere. They are more
tenacious because they are able to disguise themselves in a national cos-
tume.' And the point was stressed that the chauvinism of each nationality
should be combatted by Communists of the same nationality, since otherwise the fight would be interpreted as hostility toward the given nationality, and the achievement of internationalism in institutional development would become impossible.[17]

On several occasions the deviation toward local nationalism was found
to have slipped into counter-revolutionary activities.[18] The 1937–8 trials
presented a picture of the interlaced efforts of a conglomerate assemblage
of former internationalists, nationalists, deviators, and counter-revolu-
tionaries of most of the national republics and regions, directed toward
the dismemberment of the U.S.S.R. along national-territorial lines.[19]

---

15. *M.N.C.Q.* pp. 167–8, and note 48; *XII S'ezd RKP(b)* pp. 596–8.
16. *M.N.C.Q.* pp. 267–8.
17. Ibid. p. 170.
18. A notable earlier case was that of Sultan-Galiev, a Tatar member of the Commissariat
of Nationalities' collegium, who was discovered in 1923 to have formed a conspiratory
organization in Tataria and Bashkiria, with the aid of Mukhtarov, Mansurov, Sabirov,
Deren-Ayerly, Firdevs, Enbaev, etc. He was accused of transmitting secret information
to Pan-Islamist and Pan-Turkish circles in Persia and Turkey, and of seeking contact
with Validov — a former Communist, turned leader of the Basmachi revolt in Bokhara
and Turkestan — with the hope of creating a Pan-Turkish Eastern International juxtaposed to the Comintern. (Ibid. pp. 172–7 and note 51; *VKP(b) v Rezol.* I, pp. 537–8;
XVI S'ezd VKP(b), pp. 392–3, 479, 601.) In the Ukraine there was the S.V.U.
(1925–33), a nationalist military organization whose members penetrated into the
Commissariat of Education, the local representation of the Narkomindel, and other institutions. (*XVII S'ezd VKP(b)*, pp. 66, 69–71, 141, 199.) And in White Russia, too,
deviationist groups operating since 1924 were found in 1933 to have been connected
with the 'Polish Defensive' organization across the border, and later with the Fascists
of Germany. (Ibid. p. 72.)
19. See *Report of Court Proceedings in the Case of the Anti-Soviet 'Bloc of Rights and
Trotskyites,' Verbatim Report, passim; Bol'shevik,* No. 1 (1935), pp. 8–11, and No. 5,
pp. 66–74; *N.Y.T.,* 30 December 1937 and 4, 11 January 1938. That the Soviet gov-

(3) THE NEW SOVIET PATRIOTISM

The Vigorous Emphasis on Patriotism Since the Mid-'Thirties. Lastly,
it should be pointed out that since the mid-'thirties there has emerged in
the U.S.S.R. a vigorous patriotism, characterized by a mounting emphasis
on love of 'homeland,' 'motherland,' and 'fatherland.' This was an obvious departure from the early dictum of the Communist Manifesto that
'the workers have no fatherland,' on the ground that its application was
never intended within the territorial-political frame of a socialist society.
The components of faith and conviction of this new patriotism were the
endlessly repeated themes of the worth and success of the Soviet order,
with its socialist industry, collective agriculture, achievements in science
and culture, the new constitution, the unity of the social groups and of the
nationalities, the organization of the armed forces, and the leadership of
the Party.

In deed and pronouncement Soviet patriotism reached its highest pitch
during the recent war.[20] Along with appeals and exhortations to all the
peoples of the U.S.S.R. to rise in defense of the honor and independence
of 'the great Soviet motherland' came constant praise and glorification, in
the most exalting terms, of the skill, performance, and morale of the Red
Army and the homefront in the patriotic war. The entire Soviet people
was hailed as 'great,' 'victorious,' 'mighty,' as a people which through
miracles of heroism and selfless sacrifice saved the civilization of Europe
and 'rightfully won the fame of a heroic nation.' The cities of Leningrad,
Stalingrad, Sevastopol, and Odessa, which had withstood long sieges in
the war, were christened 'hero cities,' and the Party itself was acclaimed

---

ernment would not hesitate to transplant nationality segments of the population thought
to constitute potential fifth columns is evidenced by: the removal of the German colonies
around Odessa and the Dnieper to trans-Ural locations in 1936, the Soviet-German resettlement treaty of 10 January 1941, transferring 57,000 Germans from Lithuania,
Latvia, and Estonia to the Reich; and the Soviet decree of 28 August 1941, transplanting the entire German population of the Volga German Autonomous Soviet Socialist
Republic — 400,000 persons — to new habitats beyond the Urals. (See *B.S.U.,* 11 September 1941; *N.Y.T.,* 15 January 1941, p. 3.)

20. A great deal has been written on these themes. See e.g.: Kalinin, 'The Might of the
Soviet State,' pp. 20–37; editorial, 'The Great Strength of the Soviet Order,' pp. 1–7;
Gatovskii, 'The Industrial Foundation of the Military Might of the U.S.S.R.,' pp. 43–54;
Granovskii, 'The Strength and Viability of the Economic Base of the Soviet State,'
pp. 19–29; Kalinin, 'About the Moral Face of Our People,' pp. 11–30; editorial, 'The
Great Desert of the Soviet People before the History of Humanity,' pp. 1–8; Talenskii,
'The Great Victorious Army of the Soviet Union,' pp. 19–33; Laptev, 'The Strength
of the Kolkhoz Order.'

as 'the inspirer and organizer' of the Soviet victories.[21] Many of those themes have also been stressed since the end of hostilities.

Recognition of Russian Prominence. Along with the new patriotism came a considerable revival of the symbols of the Russian nation. Writers, actors, poets, Party notables, and statesmen have referred at length to 'the great Russian people,' its history and achievements in literature, art, science, et cetera, the 'wonderful richness' of the Russian language, and the exploits of old Russian heroes on the field of battle.[22] This development likewise reached its highest intensity after the outbreak of the war.[23] Four and a half months after the German attack on the Soviet Union, Stalin concluded a fervent appeal to the armed forces with the following words: 'Let the manly images of our great ancestors — Alexander Nevsky, Dmitri Donskoi, Kusma Minin, Dmitri Pozharsky, Alexander Suvorov, Mikhail Kutuzov — inspire you in this war!'[24] And similar statements and appeals were made by other leaders and writers throughout the War.

From the standpoint of the position of the Russians in the complex of nationalities, the significant thing is that they are publicly credited with having played a leading role in the November Revolution, the civil war, and the economic reconstruction and other programs and endeavors that followed. The latest authoritative expression of this sentiment was provided by Stalin himself, on 24 May 1945, at a Kremlin reception in honor of the Red Army officers. Stalin offered a toast to the Russian people as 'the most outstanding nation of all nations forming the Soviet Union' and as one 'which has won in this war universal recognition as the leading force in the Soviet Union among all the peoples' of the country. He ascribed to the Russian people 'a clear mind, staunch character, and

---

21. See also Stalin, *The Great Patriotic War of the Soviet Union, passim.*
22. See e.g. Volin, *Velikii Russkii Narod;* Kirpotin, 'Russian Culture,' pp. 47–63. As regards language, a pamphlet published under the auspices of the Komsomol contains the following statement: 'The Russian language, in which the great works of Lenin and Stalin are written, attracts not alone the peoples of the U.S.S.R., but all the toilers of the world. At one time the summit of European society made Latin the international language. Later, until very recently, French became the language of communion between peoples and governments. The Russian language is becoming the international language of socialist culture.' (Volin, op. cit. p. 18.)
23. See e.g. Korobkov, 'The Heroic Past of the Russian People,' pp. 59–64, and 'Russian Military-Naval Traditions,' pp. 50–64; Timiriazev, 'The Founders of Russian Physics,' pp. 32–42; Iovchuk, 'Leninizm and the Advanced Russian Culture of the XIX century,' pp. 35–50; K. Bazilevich, 'Documents concerning the Prowess and Heroism of Russian Soldiers and Officers,' pp. 59–64; B. Bazilevich, 'Peter I — Founder of the Russian Military Art'; Egolin, 'The Universal Significance of the Russian Literature.'
24. *The Great Patriotic War of the Soviet Union,* p. 38.

patience,' and thanked them for the confidence they had shown in the Soviet government during the trying years of 1941 and 1942.[25] This marks the highest official recognition of the prominent role played by the Russian nationality in the Soviet state.

Disclaimer of Differentiating Nationalism. There has been, at the same time, no attempt to depreciate in any way the culture, values, or historical past of the other nationalities. As one competent observer was able to note several years before the concrete proof supplied by the recent conflict, the new 'nationalism' was part of an effort to consolidate the country, in a world situation pregnant with war, in which the Russian people, constituting the numerical and geographical core of the land, would eventually bear the brunt of the fighting. [26] In fact, one of the strongest elements of the new patriotism, acclaimed as a major source of Soviet strength, is the friendship of the peoples of the U.S.S.R.[27] In a speech on 6 November 1944, Stalin declared:

The labor exploits of the Soviet people in the rear, like the immortal deeds of valor of our soldiers at the front, are rooted in their fervent and life-giving spirit of Soviet patriotism. The strength of Soviet patriotism lies in the fact that it is based not on racial or nationalistic prejudices, but on the people's profound devotion and loyalty to their Soviet homeland, on the fraternal partnership of the working people of all the nationalities in our land.

Soviet patriotism blends harmoniously the national traditions of the peoples and the common vital interests of all the working peoples of the Soviet Union. Far from dividing them, Soviet patriotism welds all the nations and peoples of our country into a single fraternal family.[28]

Nor has the new patriotism been accompanied by any disavowal of the ideal of internationalism; the development of the constituent and autonomous republics and the solidarity of the Soviet peoples has been hailed as proof of organized collaboration on principles of 'proletarian internationalism.' [29] Finally, it should be noted that, despite the acclamation

25. *Bol'shevik*, No. 10 (May 1945), pp. 1–2. See also editorial, 'The Russian People—Leading Force among the Peoples of Our Country,' pp. 3–12; and Lebedev, *Velikii Russkii Narod-Vydaiushchaiasia Natsia.*

26. See Harper, *The Government of the Soviet Union*, p. 186.

27. See Mitin, 'The Victory of the Ideology of Friendship among Peoples over the Ideology of the Beastly Nationalism of the Fascists,' pp. 22–32; editorial, 'The Friendship of the Peoples of the U.S.S.R. — Mighty Factor of the Victory over the Enemy,' pp. 1–9; Azizian, 'The Successes of the Lenin-Stalin Nationality Policy,' pp. 36–47; Matiushkin 'The Great Strength of the Soviet Multinational State,' pp. 18–29.

28. *The Great Patriotic War of the Soviet Union*, p. 135.

29. Trainin, *Sodruzhestvo*, p. 60.

of Russian patriotism of the past, a deliberate distinction is drawn between Soviet patriotism and Russian patriotism today.[30]

Complete disclaimers are entered, therefore, to any and all interpretations hinting at a return to the differentiating Russian nationalism of the pre-Soviet days or at a prospective evolution in that direction. On the contrary, Party theory is based on the premise that, since the peasantry's role as traditional carrier of national sentiments makes the national question 'virtually a peasant question,' the heart of its solution in Russia lies in a lasting understanding between the most potent part of the Soviet proletariat — the Russian working strata — and the widest mass of the peasantry — the peasantry of the nationalities.[31] Lastly, the Communist leaders maintain that, owing in fact to the set of views and practices described above, the Bolsheviks were initially helped to power by the diverse nationalities and, in the form of a historically novel type of flexible federation progressively knitting the separate national parts into a single whole, were subsequently able to solve — almost alone in the world — the vexing problem of inter-national relations in a multinational state.[32]

2. THE EVOLUTION OF THE FEDERAL UNION [33]

The development of the Soviet federal union falls into three main periods roughly corresponding to the major stages of the Soviet constitution. The first, or formative period, covering the years 1917–24, is characterized by a struggle for the retention and firmer attachment of doubtful

---

30. Soviet Ambassador Bogomolov is reported to have stated with great emphasis to a delegation of prominent Russian émigrés (headed by one-time Russian Ambassador V. A. Maklakov), who came to the Paris Embassy on 14 February 1945 to pay tribute to the Russian 'National Government' for its role in the war: 'There is a vast difference between the Russian patriotism of the émigrés and the Soviet patriotism of the peoples of the Union. The Union, as such, is higher than Russia, and Union patriotism is higher than Russian patriotism. The Union has united 120 nationalities. A new status, unheard of in history, has been created for the nationalities, and in this titanic struggle the peoples have demonstrated heroic devotion to the great, common Motherland — the Soviet Union . . . The confusion of the concepts of Russian and Soviet patriotism is a common thing now . . . But the emigration must find the strength of spirit and understanding to rise to the concept of Soviet patriotism.' (*Novoye Russkoye Slovo,* 7 March 1945, pp. 1–2.)

31. *M.N.C.Q.* pp. 149, 150, 201–2, 225, 227.

32. Ibid. pp. 91, 93, 102, 107, 124, 138–40, 155, 254–74; *VKP(b) v Rezol.,* I, pp. 503–6; *S.G.P.* 207–8, 214–20, 269; Stalin, *Constitution,* pp. 10–11, and Report at Eighteenth Party Congress, op. cit. p. 46; Molotov, *Constitution,* pp. 19–21.

33. Only the larger entities are treated here. For the development of the autonomous republics and regions, see *Lenin i Stalin O Sovetskoi Konstitutsii,* pp. 406–11, cited hereafter as *L. i S.; S.G.P.* pp. 245–7, 252–4, 282–7; Malitski, op. cit. pp. 347–9, 365–70; and Shabad, loc. cit.

peripheries, which at one time or other during the civil war and inter-vention were, in whole or in part, under foreign or anti-Soviet rule. The second, 1925–35, is largely one of development by internal transformation in the territorial-administrative structure; while the third, 1936–46, is a period of both redefinition of status within and territorial accretion from without.

(1) THE FORMATIVE PERIOD

The Slow Progress of Federalism at the Beginning of the Regime. Public pronouncements favoring federal arrangements for the state were made within a few weeks of the establishment of Soviet rule. Then, in the 'Declaration of Rights of Toiling and Exploited People,' the Third All-Russian Congress of Soviets (23–31 January 1918) proclaimed the Soviet Russian Republic a 'federation of Soviet national republics,' and declared that it limits itself to 'the establishment of the basic principles of feder-ation,' leaving it to the nations to decide at their own congresses 'whether they wish and on what bases to participate in the federal government and other federal institutions.' In another resolution, the congress specified that the method of participation of the Soviet republics and separate regions in the federal government as well as the delimitation of the relative spheres of activity 'would be determined, immediately upon the formation of re-gional Soviet republics, by the All-Russian Central Executive Committee and the central executive committees of these republics.'[34] The Declaration was embodied verbatim in the Constitution of the R.S.F.S.R. adopted on 10 July 1918.

If this juridical sanction of federation was in part an answer to the ex-treme tendencies toward decentralization current at the beginning of Soviet rule, federation remained, in the course of the next two years at least, within the realm of theoretical expression only. The civil war and intervention, which broke upon the new regime less than a year after its establishment, gave the question a different complection. The policy of War Communism, which gave its name to these years, meant not only central control in the R.S.F.S.R., whose domain was largely restricted at the time to the Great-Russian or central territory, but also efforts at close co-operation — primarily in the military field — with the provisional Soviet regimes that appeared and reappeared in the border regions.

Thus, due to the occupation of the Ukraine first by the German and then by the Denikin and Polish forces, successive Soviet regimes were

---

34. For the texts of these documents, see *L. i S.* pp. 278–81; and for the deliberations of the congress, 3.*V.S.S.* (verbatim report), pp. 72–94.

established and re-established there in December 1917, November 1918, and December 1919. Repeatedly these provisional governments declared themselves for a federation with the R.S.F.S.R. and called for a defensive alliance. Of particular importance in this connection were the proposals made by the Ukrainian C.E.C. in May 1919 that all the Soviet republics work out 'concrete forms of organization of a single front of revolutionary struggle,' and the response of the All-Russian C.E.C. of 1 June 1919 resolving upon the unification of the Soviet republics' administrations in the fields of military affairs, economy, railroads, finances, and labor. Though the provisions of this resolution were largely unrealized due to the actual military situation that developed soon after, the purport of the decisions was reaffirmed in December 1919 and May 1920 by the all-Russian and all-Ukrainian congresses of Soviets, respectively. Also, in accordance with the wish of the latter, expressed at that time, the All-Russian C.E.C. decided on 1 June 1919 to introduce into its own composition thirty members of the Ukrainian C.E.C., though it should be pointed out that the Soviet regime was not actually fully established in the Ukraine until the end of 1920.[35]

In White Russia a Soviet regime came into being on 1 January 1919, but was soon afterwards displaced by anti-Soviet forces. Following Red Army successes over most of its territory in the Russo-Polish war, a new White-Russian Soviet government proclaimed the independence of White Russia on 1 August 1920. At the same time it announced the placement of its army under a single command of all the armed forces of the Soviet republics, and its intention to co-ordinate its foreign policy with that of the R.S.F.S.R. and to partake in a unified economic plan for all the Soviet republics.[36]

The Treaty-Relations Period. These initial undertakings led to the inauguration of the so-called 'treaty-relations period,' 1920–22 — a direct steppingstone to the formation of the Union.[37] The pattern was laid by the treaty — and supplementary agreements — for a Military and Economic Alliance concluded on 30 September 1920 between the R.S.F.S.R. and the

---

35. See *L. i S.* pp. 315–18; *S.G.P.* pp. 238–42; and *7.V.S.S., Postanovlenia,* pp. 4–5. For English texts of several of these documents, see Batsell, op. cit. pp. 243–7.

36. *S.G.P.* pp. 240–43.

37. The R.S.F.S.R. itself first began to live up to its designation as a federation during this period, by the initiation of an intensive policy of territorial-administrative differentiation within it according to nationality. Most of its autonomous republics and regions were established in 1920–22 or in later years, only a few having originated in 1918–19. (See Ananov, *Ocherki Federal'nogo Upravlenia S.S.S.R.,* p. 9; and *L. i S.* pp. 406–11; and cf. *S.G.P.* p. 246.)

Azerbaijan S.S.R. (formed on 28 April 1920). It provided for a unification of the military organization and command, and of the administration and policies concerned with the economy, supplies and foreign trade, transport, communications, and finances. In substance, though not in all particulars and sometimes in several steps, this model was followed in a series of treaties entered into by the R.S.F.S.R. and the other outlying Soviet republics: the Ukrainian S.S.R. on 28 December 1920, the White-Russian S.S.R. on 16 January 1921, the Georgian S.S.R. (formed in February 1921) on 21 May 1921, and the Armenian S.S.R. (formed 29 November 1920) on 30 September 1921.[38]

Prominent features of these treaty relations were: the absence of an all-round multilateral treaty interconnecting all the independent Soviet republics, each of them being bound directly only to the R.S.F.S.R.; the fact that no new organs of legislation and administration were created, the organs and commissariats of the R.S.F.S.R. performing alliance or 'union' functions as well, and in some cases having representatives of the unified administrative branches in the sovnarkoms of these republics; and the fact that separate commissariats for foreign affairs were retained in the republics and a large measure of freedom of action in foreign trade in some of them as well. Inevitably, considerable confusion resulted from the exercise of two kinds of federalism by one and the same administrative setup — one *vis-à-vis* the autonomous units of the R.S.F.S.R. and another with regard to the treaty republics of the Ukraine, White Russia, and Transcaucasia outside of it. If a loose federation went against the grain of basic Soviet theory, the above-described arrangements accompanying it militated even more against the practical lessons in economic, political, and military necessity drawn by the Communist leaders from the preceding period of turmoil. Hence, almost as soon as they were inaugurated, the treaty relations were looked upon as inadequate, as a sort of trial marriage or preparatory stage. And an active campaign for the creation of a real union was begun in the second half of 1922.[39]

---

38. *L. i S.* pp. 318–20; *S.G.P.* pp. 243–4; *N.K.I.D., Sbornik Deistvuiushchikh Dogovorov,* I-IV (1921–3), cited hereafter as *Sbornik Dogorov.* The treaties were followed by other agreements in 1921–2 between the R.S.F.S.R. and these republics. Also the Treaty of Economic Union concluded by the R.S.F.S.R. with the Far-Eastern Republic on 17 February 1922 should be mentioned, though the latter voted itself out of existence on 13 November 1922 and its territory was incorporated into the R.S.F.S.R.

39. *S.G.P.* pp. 222, 248–50; Gurv!ch, op. cit. pp. 156–8, *M.N.C.Q.* pp. 92–3, 120, 140–41, 153. The question was first taken up at the leading Party organs and the projected theses on unification were approved by the Party Central Committee on 6 October 1922. Stalin is generally credited with being the moving spirit in the matter. Among the practical steps paving the way to complete unification was the protocol of 22 February

The Establishment of the Union. The formal initiative in the matter was taken by the Transcaucasian Socialist Federated Soviet Republic on 13 December 1922, the very day that it came into being juridically.[40] It was followed on the same day by a 'Declaration for the Formation of the Union' on the part of the Ukrainian S.S.R., and a similar decision three days later by the White-Russian S.S.R. On 26 December 1922, the All-Russian Congress of Soviets voted for union, and on 30 December the declaration and treaty for the creation of the U.S.S.R., providing for the formation of Union organs of power and the fusion of some and joint administration of other enumerated commissariats, et cetera, was adopted by the First Congress of Soviets of the U.S.S.R. Later, following their consideration by the central executive committees of the uniting republics, these acts were approved as the Union Constitution by the C.E.C. of the U.S.S.R. on 6 July 1923 and definitively adopted by the Second Congress of Soviets of the U.S.S.R. on 31 January 1924.[41] Thus, the first or formative period came to an end with the establishment of a single federal state comprising four constituent republics: the R.S.F.S.R., Ukrainian S.S.R., White-Russian S.S.R., and Transcaucasian S.F.S.R.

(2) THE MIDDLE PERIOD

The Creation of the Central Asiatic Republics. Toward the end of 1924, as a result of a territorial demarcation of Central Asia along national lines, the Uzbek and Turkmen peoples were grouped into two new Union republics, while the Tadzhik, Kazakh, and Kirghiz peoples were given the administrative-territorial status of autonomous republics. Formally, the Uzbek S.S.R. came into being on 17 February 1925 and the Turkmen S.S.R. three days later, both being admitted into the Union as the fifth and sixth constituent republics on 13 May 1925.[42] On 5 December 1929 the

---

1922, entered into by the R.S.F.S.R. on the one hand and the Soviet republics of Armenia, Azerbaijan, Georgia, Ukraine, White Russia, Khorezm, Bukhara, and Far-East on the other. This protocol empowered the R.S.F.S.R. to represent the latter at the Genoa conference.

40. The Transcaucasian Federation itself was achieved in several stages. During 1921 the railroads and foreign-trade administrations of Azerbaijan, Georgia, and Armenia were unified in practice, and Lenin urged the timeliness of federation of these republics. On 12 March 1922, the 'Federative Union of Transcaucasian Republics' — more a con-federation than a federation — was formed at a conference of delegates from the three republics, but on 13 December 1922 it was transformed into the Transcaucasian Socialist Federated Soviet Republic at the First Transcaucasian Congress of Soviets. (See *L. i S.* pp. 323–5; *S.G.P.* pp. 244–5; Gurvich, op. cit. p. 159; Ananov, op. cit. p. 19.)

41. *L. i S.* pp. 325–48; *S.G.P.* pp. 250–51; *M.N.C.Q.* pp. 120–36; Gurvich, op. cit. p. 159.

42. *L. i S.* pp. 348–53; *S.G.P.* pp. 252–4.

Tadzhik autonomous republic was transformed into a Union republic, becoming the seventh constituent republic of the U.S.S.R. and the change was confirmed by the Union Congress of Soviets on 17 March 1931.[43] While no more Union republics were created until the adoption of the new constitution, the territorial-administrative setup underwent unceasing rearrangements at the other levels of the national-territorial pyramid in the years 1925–35.

(3) THE LAST PERIOD

The Increase in the Number of Union Republics by the New Constitution. The new constitution opened the third period in the evolution of the federal union. In addition to other changes in the status of national units, it elevated the Kazakh and Kirghiz autonomous republics to Union republics and dissolved the Transcaucasian Federation, granting its members — Azerbaijan, Georgia, and Armenia — Union-republic status, thus raising the number of constituent republics to eleven in 1936. Though the more rigid rules on administrative-territorial change embodied in the new Fundamental Law were generally expected to result in considerably greater stability of the territorial setup, economic needs and administrative convenience were found to require further changes from time to time, particularly by the breaking up of the large territories and regions into smaller units.[44]

The 1939–40 Territorial Accretions and Addition of Constituent Republics. In 1939–40, with the dynamic alterations in the international balance of forces, came telling accretions to the territory and population of the U.S.S.R., with corresponding modifications in the political-juridical framework. Western Ukraine and Western White Russia were reincorporated into the domains of the Ukrainian S.S.R. and the White-Russian S.S.R. respectively, on 14 and 15 November 1939.[45] The end of the 1939–40 Soviet-Finnish War brought the reorganization of the Karelian autonomous republic, plus the acquired strips of Finnish territory, into the Karelo-Finnish S.S.R. and its admission, on 4 April 1940, as the twelfth constituent republic. Similarly, the Moldavian autonomous republic, with the addition to it of the greater part of re-acquired Bessarabia, was shaped into the Moldavian S.S.R. on 9 July 1940 — the rest of Bessarabia and

---

43. *S.Z.* 1929, No. 75, item 717; 1931, No. 17, item 162.

44. See Morrison, 'The Evolution of the Territorial-Administrative System of the U.S.S.R.,' pp. 25–46, and Shabad, loc. cit.

45. For a general Soviet account, see Trainin, *Natsional'noe i Sotsial'noe Osvobozhdenie Zapadnoi Ukrainy i Zapadnoi Belorussii*, pp. 71–9.

Northern Bukovina being added to the Ukrainian S.S.R. The Moldavian Union Republic was admitted as the thirteenth by vote of the Supreme Soviet of the U.S.S.R. on 2 August 1940. In like fashion were the newly absorbed states of Lithuania, Latvia, and Estonia admitted into the Union on 4–6 August 1940 as the fourteenth, fifteenth, and sixteenth constituent republics.[46]

The Recent Territorial Acquisitions of the Soviet Union. With the Nazi invasion of the U.S.S.R. on 22 June 1941, the western Soviet republics were progressively lost, and even parts of the R.S.F.S.R. itself. All of these territories were recovered in the course of 1944. Aside from changes effected in the form of administrative reorganizations and internal transfers of territory — on ethnic grounds — since 1941, the U.S.S.R. acquired a number of lands in Europe and Asia during 1944–5, and formally incorporated them into its territorial-administrative structure.[47] By the terms of the Finnish armistice of 19 September 1944, the U.S.S.R. obtained from Finland the Petsamo District, which was renamed the Pechenga Area. At the same time the Soviet Union leased from Finland the Porkkalla-Udd Peninsula for a naval base. In the early part of 1945, the Republic of Tannu Tuva was officially incorporated into the Soviet Union as the Tuvinian Autonomous Region. Later in the year, by a treaty signed in Moscow on 29 June between the U.S.S.R. and the Czechoslovak Republic (ratified by the Soviet Union on 27 November 1945) the Carpatho-Ukraine was ceded to the former and included as the Trans-Carpathian Region in the Ukrainian S.S.R. At the Potsdam Conference of the Big Three in August 1945, the U.S.S.R. had acquired, subject to definitive confirmation in the peace treaties, a part of East Prussia north of a line passing above Braunsberg and Goldap and embracing the city of Koenigsberg. This region was incorporated into the R.S.F.S.R. as the Koenigsberg Area, later renamed Kaliningrad Area. Lastly, by the beginning of September 1945, following the defeat of Japan, the Soviet Union had completed the occupation of

---

46. *N.Y.H.T.*, 5 April and 3, 7 August 1940; *N.Y.T.*, 10 July 1940.
47. For details, see Shabad, loc. cit. It should be pointed out, however, that in the Soviet-Polish Treaty of 16 August 1945, which was to set the boundary on the basis of the Curzon line, several deviations from the Soviet-German line of 28 September 1939 were executed in favor of Poland. The westernmost parts of the Ukrainian and Byelorussian Republics, including the cities of Przemysl, Suwalki, and Bialystok, were yielded to the Polish Republic. At that, the change in the Soviet-Polish border, as well as the subsequent acquisition of the Carpatho-Ukraine, brought all the territories inhabited by Ukrainians and Byelorussians within the respective Soviet republics and was officially acclaimed as fulfilling 'the ancient aspirations of the Ukrainian and Byelorussian people.' (See Molotov's statement in *Pravda*, 7 November 1945.)

Southern Sakhalin (Karafuto) and the Kurile Islands, which it subsequently incorporated into the R.S.F.S.R.[48]

This, in brief, is the evolution of the Soviet federal union to date. While the precise contours of future territorial-administrative arrangements cannot be foreseen yet, it may be recalled in conclusion that as a matter of general principle Communist political theory holds no bar to periodic redefinitions of the forms of Soviet federation.

3. NATIONALITY AND SOVEREIGNTY

(1) THE LOCUS OF SOVEREIGNTY IN THE MULTINATIONAL U.S.S.R.

National Equality from the Standpoint of Sovereignty. While its stand on some aspects of the sovereignty of the state has differed from time to time, Soviet jurisprudence has never asserted sole sovereignty for any nationality, even in the case of the Great-Russian people, whose role in the state has admittedly been outstanding. No hint has ever been put forth of greater sovereignty in one or several nationalities, the theme of equality being consistently maintained. But, though the claim of the international character of Soviet rule has never been abandoned, or the proclamations of the sovereignty of the Soviet nations rescinded, the tendency of late years has been to stress the sovereignty of 'the multinational Soviet people,' in the singular.[49] This is not in derogation of the recognized right of existence and development of the nationalities, but is an added assertion of the high degree of solidarity and cohesiveness attained in the Soviet state.

The Legal Nature of the U.S.S.R. As to the legal nature of the U.S.S.R., the majority of the earlier and the present-day Soviet jurists maintain that if any descriptive labels of non-Soviet jurisprudence are applicable at all to this novel polity,[50] the Soviet state is not a confederation or *Staatenbund*,

---

48. By the terms of the Yalta Agreement of 11 February 1945 (which was made public a year later) and by the provisions of the supplementary agreements to the Soviet-Chinese treaty of 14 August 1945, the U.S.S.R. also gained the right of joint control with China over Port Arthur as a naval base; recognition of the interests of the Soviet Union in Dairen (Dalny), which was to become a free port; and joint property and management rights over the Manchurian railways.

49. *S.G.P.* p. 262; Trainin, 'The Question of Sovereignty,' pp. 90–92; see also *supra*, pp. 48–9.

50. There is unanimous skepticism among Soviet jurists concerning such applicability, and at one time Professor Gurvich went so far as to suggest a break with the concepts of 'autonomy,' 'federation,' etc., as understood in the traditional legal science. (See his articles in *Sov. Pravo*, 1924, No. 3, and *Vlast' Sovetov*, 1924, No. 1. See also Trainin, 'The Question of Sovereignty,' p. 97.)

but a federation or *Bundestaat*.[51] To begin with, whatever may have been the juridical nature of the association of Soviet republics during the so-called treaty-relations period,[52] the relationship established since 1923–4 has most of the accepted earmarks of a federal union. Though it has arisen by virtue of a treaty between separate state entities, the U.S.S.R. has since been developing by its own law and custom and has its own constitution and supreme organs of power; and its acts are binding on the individual citizens and prevail throughout the territory. It has a wide sphere of direct rule and, above all, is possessed of *Kompetenz-Kompetenz*, i.e. of a capacity itself to alter and determine the extent of its control.[53] Where the Soviet Union departs from the general pattern of federation is in the right of withdrawal — usually a feature of confederation — constitutionally retained by its component republics. That, however, is one of the very distinctions that render it unique among federal states. Moreover, it is pointed out, the question whether the U.S.S.R. was to be a confedera-

---

51. Malitski, op. cit. p. 437; Gurvich, op. cit. pp. 154–8, *passim;* Ananov, op. cit. *passim; S.G.P.*, pp. 217, 248–51, 259, 274. Non-plussed by the simultaneous designation of the U.S.S.R. in the Treaty on the Formation of the Union as 'one federal state' and a 'Union of Soviet Socialist Republics,' and by such confederate features as the recognition of the sovereignty of the uniting republics and of their right of withdrawal, the jurists of the early period were having a hard time in rounding out their formulations. Professor Kotliarevsky would not 'without reservations' include the U.S.S.R. among federations. (Kotliarevsky, *S.S.S.R. i Soiuznye Respubliki,* pp. 12–17.) Reikhel would say that it is 'both a union of states and a union state, it is a synthesis of the one and the other — more precisely a permanently-voluntary union of states in the form of a federal state' or, in short, 'a *Soviet Federal state.*' (Reikhel', *S.S.S.R. Ocherki Konstitutsionnykh Vzaimo-otnoshenii Sovetskikh Respublik,* pp. 60–61.) Vaksberg, too, agreed that the U.S.S.R. is simply of a 'dual nature,' on the one hand a single state 'undoubtedly a federation with all its distinguishing juridical marks' and on the other a union possessed of a 'confederal base.' (Vaksberg, *Pravovoe Polozhenie Soiuznykh Respublic-Chlenov S.S.R.,* p. 20.) Professor Cheliapov would term it a federation, but, to distinguish it from others, he thought that 'it would be best to designate the U.S.S.R. as a *Soviet Federation.*' (*E.G. i P.*, III, p. 1416.) While Mikolenko, critical of the others, concluded that 'the question as to whether the Union S.S.R. constitutes a federal state or a union of states is a purely scholastic question. Being a single federal state it is, dialectically, at the same time "a union of equal state units."' (I. F. Mikolenko, 'Problems of Sovereignty in the Soviet System,' op. cit. p. 10.)

52. Professors Malitski and Reikhel consider the association of this period (1920–22) 'a Union of states, a confederation,' and Ananov also speaks of 'confederative interrelations,' while Professor Magerovsky held that after the admission of representatives of the other Soviet republics into the Congress of Soviets and C.E.C. of the R.S.F.S.R. early in 1922, it already was 'an effected federation, a realized Union of Soviet Socialist Republics,' even before the name was adopted. (See Malitski, op. cit. pp. 438–9; Reikhel', op. cit. p. 51; Ananov, op. cit. p. 20; Magerovsky, *Soiuz Sovetskikh Sotsialisticheskikh Respublik,* pp. 25–6.)

53. Reikhel', op. cit. pp. 52–61; Kotliarevsky, op. cit. p. 12; Malitski, op. cit. p. 440; Cheliapov, *E.G. i P.* III, 1415; Vaksberg, op. cit. p. 13.

tion or federation was in fact fought over and settled in favor of the latter during the period of political-juridical crystallization of the form of union, in 1922–4.[54]

The Sovereignty of the Union Republics. Soviet jurists balk, at the same time, at definitions of federation that insist that the federal state alone, not its component parts, is the one sovereignty, the true state. Starting from diverse angles and explanations, drawing no distinction between perfect and imperfect unions, and explicitly accepting neither the theory of a divided sovereignty nor the conception of sovereignty as the sole property of the parts that they have passed on to the federal power for a time, most of these jurists hold that the Union republics are sovereign states.[55] These republics, it is said, did not lose their sovereignty upon forming the Union, but only transferred to the latter a number of rights and functions in regard to vital matters of common concern (such as defense, foreign affairs, the economy, et cetera), voluntarily limiting their sovereignty in these spheres, but otherwise remaining sovereign.[56] Between

54. An echo of this debate was heard at the October 1924 session of the C.E.C. U.S.S.R., where Kursky, Krylenko, Skrypnik, and others opposed Kalinin, Antonov, Larin, et cetera, on decrees seeking greater unity in the system of justice, on the ground that they were encroaching on the sovereignty of the Union republics. The latter viewed these arguments as largely idle talk obstructing the necessary solidification of the Union. In an obvious dig at the strict interpreters of the nature of the Union, Foreign Commissar Chicherin bluntly emphasized at the same session that 'our federal Soviet state is not at all a union of states, but a single federal state.' (See Vaksberg, op. cit. pp. 3–5, 13.) Referring to the December 1922–January 1924 period, the authoritative public-law text states: 'Defending the creation of a single federal Soviet state, comrade Stalin stepped forth also against the Ukrainian project, which was defended by the nationalists and Trotskyites — a project that was aimed at interpreting the U.S.S.R. not as a single federal state, but as a union of separate republics, i.e. a confederation.' (*S.G.P.* p. 217.)

55. Malitski, op. cit. pp. 440–42; Reikhel', op. cit. p. 52; Mikolenko, op. cit. pp. 10–11; *S.G.P.* pp. 263–4; Trainin, 'The Question of Sovereignty,' p. 97. While the theories of Tocqueville, Waitz, Calhoun, Seydel, Laband, and Jellinek are discussed, no statements of choice in basing their own conclusions are given in most of these treatments. Vaksberg did think that 'The Constitution of the Union accepts the theory of a division of sovereignty.' (Vaksberg, op. cit. p. 20.) And a hint at distributive sovereignty is contained in Stalin's statement of 26 December 1922 (see *supra,* pp. 67–8.) Trainin, however, in one of the latest expositions on the subject, emphasizes that the Soviet conception of simultaneous sovereignty in the Union and the Union republics has nothing in common with the theories of Tocqueville, Waitz, etc., because the Soviet Union is a new type of state and 'the sovereignty of the Soviet federal state is not juxtaposed to the sovereignty of the union republics. The one complements the other.' ('The Question of Sovereignty,' pp. 97–8.)

56. Mikolenko, op. cit. p. 23; Gurvich, op. cit. pp. 339–40; Malitski, op. cit. pp. 437, 442–5; Stetsky, *Constitution,* p. 23; *S.G.P.* pp. 222–3, 271–4; Trainin, 'The Question of Sovereignty,' p. 100. For the new autonomous rights in regard to foreign affairs and defense, see *supra,* pp. 90–91.

the time of the adoption of the Treaty of Union and its incorporation in
the first Union constitution, special provisions were included and other
efforts made to proclaim the retention of independence and sovereignty
by the uniting republics. Taking up the question specifically at the Tenth
Party Congress, on 23 April 1923, Stalin added the following statement to
his other formulations:

> Some people ask a purely scholastic question, namely, whether after amalgamation
> the republics remain independent. This is a scholastic question. Their independence
> is restricted, for every amalgamation involves a certain restriction of the rights of
> the amalgamating parties. But the elements of independence of each of these re-
> publics undoubtedly remain, for each republic retains the right to leave the Union
> at its own discretion.[57]

The literature that has developed on the subject points to such items as:
the possession of their own constitutions by the Union republics; their
right of secession; the unalterability of their territory without their consent; the specific provisions in the federal constitution that declare that
their sovereignty is restricted only within the limits of the article on Union
competence, and that otherwise they exercise state power independently,
with the Union protecting their sovereign rights; the considerable competence, which they enjoy jointly with the Union, as well as the sphere of
activities left to them alone; and their participation on principles of parity
in the supreme organs of the federal government. All these are said to
constitute the positive features and guarantees of the sovereignty of the
Union republics.[58]

The Status of the Autonomous Republics. Finally, there are the autonomous republics. The older jurists, following the traditional criteria of
legal science, did not regard them as sovereign, and for the most part
even expressed doubts whether these republics were states at all, since
they were created by acts of the central government, and their constitutions are subject to confirmation by the Union republics, of which they
form a part.[59] Present-day Soviet jurists, however, leave no doubt that, in
line with the views expressed by Stalin at the Twelfth Party Congress, they
consider the autonomous republics states, even if possessed of less power

---

57. *M.N.C.Q.* p. 152.
58. *S.G.P.* pp. 263, 269–74; Trainin, 'The Question of Sovereignty,' pp. 98–101; N.
    Farberov, 'About the Sovereignty of the Union Republics,' *Izvestia,* 21 December 1945.
59. Cheliapov, *E.G. i P.* III, pp. 1081–2; Malitski, op. cit. p. 444; Reikhel', op. cit. pp. 54–6;
    Turubiner, *Ocherki Gosudarstvennogo Ustroistva S.S.S.R.,* p. 27. See also Magerovsky,
    op. cit. p. 35, and Gurvich, op. cit. pp. 151–4. Some of these jurists would regard the
    autonomous republics as 'federative parts,' or 'staatsfragmenten' in Jellinek's terminology.

than the Union republics.[60] And although they are not termed sovereign states, a considerable point is made of 'the sovereignty of nations in the autonomous republics.'

The 'National Sovereignty' of the Soviet Nationalities. In fact, recalling the entire gamut of pronouncement and policy in regard to the nationalities over the past decades as concrete proof of the 'national sovereignty' enjoyed by each Soviet nation, the conclusion is reached that '*all* the forms of Soviet national statehood constitute the political form of national sovereignty.'[61] This view was recently modified somewhat, to the effect that the nations of the autonomous units, i.e. autonomous republics, autonomous regions, and national areas 'do not possess their own state sovereignty' but realize 'national sovereignty, that is independence in utilizing all of their national capacities and abilities'; and that they participate in state sovereignty through the Union republic of which they are a part and through the U.S.S.R. — 'particularly through the Council of Nationalities, which guarantees the sovereign rights of the nations.'[62]

(2) THE UNITY OF SOVIET SOVEREIGNTY

The Question of International Status. There is, thus, an imposing variety of acclaimed sovereignties in the Soviet land. And yet, their presence is not held to have affected the growing unity of the state.[63] Facing outwardly, the U.S.S.R. has, until very recently, consistently been regarded by Soviet statesmen and jurists — whatever their differences on other points — as one sovereignty, a multinational yet single state, alone possessed of international status in the world system of states.[64] With the admission of the Ukraine and Byelorussia to the United Nations in 1945, at least two

---

60. See *supra*, pp. 72–3; *S.G.P.* pp. 282–7; Trainin, 'The Question of Sovereignty,' pp. 101–5. They dispute the earlier jurists' views on the question of a right of self-organization, etc., in these republics, pointing out that the autonomous republics have their own constitutions, territory, governmental organs, and, even by the preceding constitution, have had direct representation in the federal Council of Nationalities. (Ibid.)

61. *S.G.P.* p. 97 (1938); italics J.T.

62. Trainin, 'Questions of Sovereignty in the Soviet Federal State,' p. 23.

63. 'In what was formerly "single and indivisible" Russia,' said Molotov in 1936, 'there have arisen fifty republics, autonomous regions, and national areas . . . Far from shaking our state, the creation of numerous national republics and regions has served to reinforce it.' In short, the Soviet Union 'is becoming more and more welded into a single whole.' (Molotov, *Constitution,* pp. 19–20.)

64. Mikolenko, op. cit. p. 12; Vaksberg, op. cit. pp. 13, 20; Pashukanis, *Ocherki po Mezhdunarodnomu Pravu,* pp. 93–4; *S.G.P. passim;* Trainin, 'The Question of Sovereignty,' pp. 91, 92, 96, 97, 101.

of the Union republics acquired international status. This development, however, took place not only with the consent but at the instance of the Union, and the participation of the two republics at international conferences alongside the U.S.S.R. is hailed as emphasizing 'the unity of aims of the sovereignty of the Union and of the Union republics.'[65]

The Basic Unity of Sovereignty in the Soviet State. Internally, the fundamental features of the Soviet polity made for a singular oneness of power, notwithstanding the multiplicity of designates of sovereignty. 'Sovereignty in Soviet conditions,' writes a prominent Soviet academician, 'is indivisible in the sense that, despite all its forms, *its* essence is one: dictatorship of the working class.' Thus, the summary evaluation is arrived at that sovereignty in the U.S.S.R. means the sovereignty of the Soviet people, which is a voluntary union of nations; that this sovereignty is expressed through the Union state, which is itself a system of soviet republics; and that in these republics the toilers of numerous nations are equal masters of their destiny.[66]

As for the future of sovereignty in the Soviet state, it is deemed interrelated with and subject to the same process as all the other socio-political questions.[67] The community of the economic system and of political aims, the interchange of cultural experiences, the play of influences of nation upon nation under the guidance of the state are expected to lead to the gradual obliteration of dividing differences and to the final fusion of the nations of the U.S.S.R. But 'the road to this,' it is emphasized in conclusion, 'lies in the sovereignty of the Soviet nations, in the sovereignty of the Union republics, and the strengthening of the sovereignty of the single federal state.'[68]

Thus, the Soviet idea of sovereignty from the standpoint of nationality has followed the same pattern of development as the concept of Soviet nationhood. The wide imputation of sovereignty to national entities is part of and in line with the policy of progressively extended distribution of territorial-administrative power to the nationalities and of consciously curbing claims or manifestations of exclusive or preferred status for any national group in the state.

---

65. Trainin, 'Questions of Sovereignty in the Soviet Federal State,' p. 22.
66. Trainin, 'The Question of Sovereignty,' pp. 92, 96.
67. 'Sovereignty, in the conditions of the dictatorship of the working class, is not an independent and self-sufficient question. It is subordinate to the problems of struggle for Communism. It is most intimately tied up with the questions of the state, and as the latter, it is not an "eternal" question. It is subject to the same kind of dialectical process as the state and as the nation.' (Ibid. p. 106.)
68. Ibid. p. 108.

The Marxist program of a large, integrated state was substantially realized in the U.S.S.R. without sacrificing at the same time the sense of identity of the nationalities. Characterized by an evolution from an early condition of diffused authority to one of centralized direction of fundamental polity and policy; based on an anterior and continuing contiguity of peoples and national-territorial areas; and propelled by their joint perception of external insecurity, expectation of mutual advantage, and unifying ideology — this union is a new type of federal state in the world of nation-states. Much of its uniqueness stems from its twin origin, in the centrifugal breakup of Imperial Russia and the subsequent centripetal confluence of the severed parts into a new entity. Primarily, however, it is due to the erection of the federation as an intricate yet elastic conceptual-structural mechanism designed to reconcile the need for unity with the presence of diversity, national development with proletarian supremacy, and the urge for centralization with demands for autonomy. The association that has crystallized is, hence, the resultant of a complex interplay between the horizontal and vertical divisions of social cohesion, between the class and nationality principles in the Soviet constitutional order. Issuing, unlike the class principle, from an initial premise of deliberate non-discrimination, and, like the progressive evolution of that principle, based on a desire to enlarge the constitutional consensus behind the Communist government, the nationality principle found its realization in the particular development of the concept of Soviet nationhood. This concept of nationhood embraces the grants of cultural autonomy, economic equality, and administrative-territorial expression to the nationalities — and the related ideas concerning the nature and *loci* of national sovereignty in the Soviet state. Admittedly, it was always subordinate, however, to the paramount claims of the class principle. In part, this relationship was expressed in the tendency toward extension of the sphere of common concern administered by the central, federal government, and in the conception of the Soviet federation as a transitional form — a political-psychological safety system, affording an outlet for residues of national cravings, yet leaving the road clear for an ultimate all-round amalgamation of the Soviet nations. Eventually, it is believed, socialist substance will engender the subsidence of the national forms, with economic socialization and cultural-political communization acting as mixing-media, levelers, and cementers, molding the many-grained sands of nationality into one mortar — a solid socio-political whole. Yet, the undercurrents of national sentiment, and with them of national forms, are expected to continue for a long time to come in the Soviet state.

Part II

The Structure and Operation of
Government

Chapter VI · The Conception of the Party

1. THE PARTY AS A POLITICAL MONOPOLY

(I) RECOGNITION OF THE PARTY'S POSITION OF LEADERSHIP

The Party as 'Vanguard of the Proletariat' and 'Chief Leader' in the State. Although the Communist Party was accorded recognition for the first time in the Fundamental Law of the land by the new constitution's reference to it in 1936 as 'the vanguard of the toilers' that 'represents the directing kernel of all organizations of toilers both public and state' (article 126), its all-pervading function in the scheme of political power was never denied. 'Here in the Soviet Union, in the land of the dictatorship of the proletariat,' said Stalin, 'the fact that not a single important political or organizational question is decided by our Soviet and other mass organizations without directions from the Party must be regarded as the highest expression of the leading role of the Party.'[1] This role flows from the acknowledged position of the Party as supreme institutional embodiment of the class principle.[2] With the proletariat itself hav-

---

1. Stalin, *Problems of Leninism*, p. 34.
2. The Party branches in the national-territorial units are emphatically designated as expressions of the class rather than of the nationality principle. As early as the 'April Conference' of 1917, Stalin, following an even earlier postulate of Lenin (see Lenin, xvii, p. 67 [20 November 1913]), stated: 'We have still to settle the question of how to organize the proletariat of the various nations into a single, common party. One plan is that the workers should be organized according to nationality — so many nations, so many parties. This plan was rejected by the Social-Democratic Party. Experience has shown that the organization of the proletariat of a given state according to nationality only leads to the destruction of the idea of class solidarity. All the proletarian members of all the nations in a given state must be organized into a single, indivisible proletarian collective body.' (*M.N.C.Q.* p. 66; see also *VKP(b) v Rezol.* 1, p. 240.) And in March 1919, the Eighth Party Congress resolved that the existence of separate Soviet republics 'does not mean that the R.K.P. [Russian Communist Party] must in turn be organized on the basis of a federation of independent communist parties' and that 'it is necessary to have *one* centralized Communist party, with one central committee, directing the entire work of the party in all parts of the R.S.F.S.R. All decisions of the R.K.P. and its leading institutions are unconditionally binding upon all the parts of the party, regardless of their national composition.' (*VKP(b) v Rezol.*, 1, p. 313.)

ing been regarded all along as 'the vanguard of the toilers' and the Party
as 'the vanguard of the proletariat,' the Party stood out as vanguard of the
vanguard, or 'chief leader in the system of proletarian dictatorship.'[3] The
very endurance of the dictatorship was related to the existence of the
Party as the initial and continuing reservoir of leadership. The workers
themselves, said Lenin on 23 January 1921, do not know as yet how to
rule and would first have to go through years of schooling. Hence, 'in
order to rule, an army of revolutionaries — Communists hardened in battle is necessary. We have such; it is the Party . . . were the Party to be set
aside, there could in fact be no dictatorship of the proletariat in Russia.'[4]

(2) THE ESTABLISHMENT OF THE PARTY'S MONOPOLY OF POWER

View of the Party's Acquisition of Exclusive Status. The Communist
Party enjoys a status of monopolized legality in the state. Such position,
it is explained, is not a consequence of accident or artifice, but has accrued
to the Party historically, when the other socialist parties refused to go
along with the revolution:

We marched to October under the slogan of a dictatorship of the proletariat and
the poorest peasantry [said Stalin in 1927], and have formally realized such in
October [November 1917] in so far as we had a bloc with the Left S.R.'s [Social
Revolutionists] and shared the leadership with them,[5] though actually there was
already then a dictatorship of the proletariat, since we, Bolsheviks, constituted a
majority. The Dictatorship of the Proletariat *and* the poorest peasantry ceased, however, to exist formally after the Left S.R. *putch,* after the rupture of the bloc with
the left S.R.'s when leadership passed over *wholly* and completely into the hands of
one party, our party which does not share and cannot share the guidance of the state
with any other party. This is what we call in fact the dictatorship of the proletariat.[6]

*The Elimination of the Mensheviks and of Right and Center Social-
Revolutionists from Political Influence.* The Party monopoly was not
established all at once. When the Bolsheviks set up the new government
on 8 November 1917, by decree of the Second Congress of Soviets, most

---

3. See Stalin, *Problems of Leninism,* pp. 29–33; *Foundations of Leninism,* pp. 104–20; also
   rules of the Communist Party, adopted in December 1919 and re-adopted in amended
   form in 1922, 1925, 1934, and 1939, *VKP(b) v Rezol.,* I, pp. 326–31, 464–70; II,
   pp. 82–92, 596–604; and *A.Q.S.U.* April 1939, pp. 59–73, respectively, *passim,* all cited
   hereafter as Comparty Rules. See also *supra,* ch. III, pp. 31, 33–4.
4. Lenin, XXVI, pp. 103–4.
5. The first Soviet constitution read in fact: 'The principal object of the Constitution of
   the R.S.F.S.R., which is adapted to the present transition period, consists of the establishment of the *dictatorship of the* urban and rural *proletariat and the poorest
   peasantry,* in the form of the strong all-Russian Soviet power . . .' (Article 9, ch. V,
   second section; italics J.T.)
6. Stalin, *Voprosy Leninizma,* pp. 156–7, also pp. 182–3.

of the members of the moderate socialist parties that opposed them in the March-November period — Mensheviks, Social-Revolutionists of the Right and Center, et cetera — withdrew from that congress.[7] Efforts at an understanding between these parties and the Bolsheviks failed because each was proceeding from directly opposite assumptions: the first, unreconciled to the idea of Soviet rule and Bolshevik predominance, expected that these were but in temporary occupancy and that the scheduled Constituent Assembly would resolve the question of the content and form of governmental power; the second considered that this question had already been resolved and that only on the condition of recognition of the soviets and adoption of the Bolshevik platform as embodied in the basic decrees on land, peace, et cetera, would they find a provisional place for the Constituent Assembly in the scheme of government.[8] 'Constituent Assembly' became, in fact, a battle cry and rallying point not only for the socialist parties, but the Cadets (Constitutional Democrats) and other Rightists as well. And these latter, charged with leadership of the Kornilov-Kaledin uprising and with preparations for a new *coup d'état,* were outlawed on 11 December.[9]

Five weeks later, on 16 January 1918, the Constituent Assembly met. In the elections to the Constituent Assembly the Bolsheviks had received clear majorities in the capitals and larger cities, but, out of a total of about 36 million votes, they obtained over 9 million as against nearly 21 million for the S.R.'s and over 4½ million for the Rightist parties. Contending that the elections, based on pre-November lists, were not expressive at all of the actual state of public opinion, the Bolsheviks thought at first in terms of retrieving the vote by a decree on the right of recall and new elections as an alternative to the dissolution of the Constituent Assembly.

7. During the period of March–November 1917 the Mensheviks and Social-Revolutionists of the Right and Center supported and participated in the Provisional Government. Small Left-wing groups of 'Menshevik-Internationalists' and 'United Social-Democratic Internationalists,' etc., opposed the government but did not associate themselves with the Bolshevik program, while the so-called 'Mezhraiontsy,' or in-betweens, which included such future prominent names as Trotsky, Joffe, Karakhan, Lunacharsky, Pokrovsky, etc., opposed the government and actively supported the Bolsheviks, joining them formally in August. Also the Left S.R.'s opposed the Provisional Government, increasingly co-operating with the Bolsheviks and aligning with them in November. (See Bunyan and Fisher, op. cit. p. 3. For a description of the various parties in Russian politics, see Harper, op. cit. pp. 8–9, 20–23.)

8. See *Izvestia* for 15, 16, and 22 November 1917; *VTsIK, II Sozyva,* p. 176; Stalin, *Voprosy Leninizma,* pp. 96–97.

9. *Izvestia,* 12 December 1917. The Cadet leaders were ordered arrested (*S.U.* 1917, pp. 65–6) and similar action was taken against certain S.R.'s connected with their activities. (*Izvestia,* 4 January 1918.)

Later they became doubtful of the utility of such action. Accordingly they decided upon the contemporaneous convocation of the Third Congress of Soviets — to be augmented by deputies from a peasant congress — as the rightful popular assembly, and invited the Constituent Assembly, in the Declaration of Rights submitted for its acceptance, to recognize exclusive power in the soviets and confine its own task solely to the enunciation of the basic principles of a socialist society and of a federation of Soviet republics. But having rejected consideration of the Soviet decrees and of the 'Declaration of Rights of Toiling and Exploited People,' it was promptly dispersed by decision of the Central Executive Committee on the ground that it represented the old order and by its own acts had 'cut every tie which bound it to the Soviet Republic of Russia.'[10] The larger part of the Menshevik and Social-Revolutionist parties thus found itself outside the sphere of influence on government policy. The scope of this ban was further broadened six months later, when the Central Executive Committee, accusing these parties of widespread counter-revolutionary activity against Soviet authority, voted on 14 June 1918 'to exclude from its composition representatives of the parties of the Right and Center Social-Revolutionists and Mensheviks' and to propose to the local soviets to do likewise.[11]

The Exclusion of the Left Social-Revolutionists from the Soviets. Only the Left Social-Revolutionists enjoyed considerable participation in the government side by side with the Bolsheviks for a while. In the congresses of soviets and the Central Executive Committee they constituted the second largest group.[12] And although they declined to enter the Council of People's Commissars in mid-November 1917, an agreement with the Bolshevik leaders, arrived at soon afterwards, brought eight of their number into the government the following month.[13] But this party entente

10. See *S.U.* 1917–18, pp. 47–8, 216; Lenin, XXII, pp. 92–5, note 43, 184–90, note 87; *VTsIK, II Sozyva*, pp. 175–7; *Izvestia*, 15 December 1917 (editorial), 19 December 1917, p. 6 (Lenin), 17 and 20 January 1918; *Uchreditel'noe Sobranie* (verbatim report, Petrograd 1918), pp. 1–9, 87–8; Bunyan and Fisher, op. cit. p. 350.

11. *VTsIK, IV Sozyva*, pp. 36–7, 420–39; *S.U.* 1918, p. 538.

12. Together with the Bolsheviks the Left S.R.'s dominated the Third Congress of Soviets (23–31 January 1918), where there were only 54 opponents. (*T.V.S.S.* p. 87.) At the Fourth Congress (15–16 March 1918), the Bolsheviks had 795 and the Left S.R.'s 284 of the 1204 voting delegates (*Izvestia*, 17 March 1918. Cf. *Ch.Ch.S.S.* p. 83), while at the Fifth Congress (4–10 July 1918) the first had 773 and the second 353 of the 1164 voting delegates (*P.V.S.S.* p. 250.) The new C.E.C. of 198 elected at the Fourth Congress comprised 141 Bolsheviks and 48 Left S.R.'s, while the Presidium of 16, which it formed in turn, included 7 Left S.R.'s. (*VTsIK, IV Sozyva*, pp. 38–40, 50.)

13. *VTsIK, II Sozyva*, p. 21; *Izvestia*, 29 November 1917, p. 1; 10 December 1917, p. 8; 25 December 1917, p. 6.

was not destined to be long-lived. Brest-Litovsk proved the crucial stum-
bling block that led to a bitter parting of the ways. Following approval of
that Treaty of Peace by the Fourth, Extraordinary, Congress of Soviets
on 15–16 March 1918, the Left S.R. members of the Council of People's
Commissars resigned in protest. Through agitation in the army and other
acts, the leaders of the Left S.R. sought to force a change in policy toward
the German invaders; and their activities culminated in the assassination
of the German ambassador and the instigation of an armed revolt in the
capitals on 6 July 1918. The uprising was quickly suppressed, and the
Fifth Congress of Soviets, meeting at the time, passed a resolution that
read in part:

In regard to the Left S.R'.s, the All-Russian Congress of Soviets declares that in
so far as any sections of this party are in accord with the attempt to drag Russia
into war by the murder of Mirbach and the revolt against the Soviet government,
these organizations can have no place in the Soviets of Workers and Peasants
Deputies.[14]

This marked the end of the influence of the allied party on the political
fortunes of Russia and completed the circle of parties placed outside the
pale of power.

(3) RETENTION OF THE ONE-PARTY SYSTEM

Prohibition of Other Parties. Though insignificant groups of individual
members of other parties continued to appear for a time in Soviet assemblies, the parties as such ceased to function as effective political minorities.
Even the policy of a united front with socialist Internationals, pursued by
the Russian Communist Party from time to time abroad, was strictly interpreted as bearing no counterpart at home.[15] While, in exceptional cases
and upon meeting special, progressively more difficult conditions of admission, former members of other parties were subsequently permitted

---

14. *P.V.S.S.* pp. 208–9; see also pp. 20–36, 105–34.
15. 'The aim and meaning of the United Front consists in attracting more and more of the
     widest mass of workers to the struggle against capital, not stopping even before repeated
     offers proposing to the leaders of the II and II–½ Internationals to lead such struggle
     jointly. When [however] the majority of workers has already established its class, i.e.
     Soviet representation, and not an "all-national" one, i.e. a joint one with the bourgeoisie,
     when it has already overthrown the political domination of the bourgeoisie, then the
     tactics of the United Front cannot, of course, require any offer to such parties as the
     Mensheviks ("RSDLP") and S.R. ("party of socialist-revolutionaries") because they
     turned out to be opponents of Soviet rule.' (Resolution of the Eleventh Party Congress,
     29 March 1922, *VKP(b) v Rezol.* I, p. 426.)

to qualify for membership in the ruling Communist Party,[16] reinstatement of those parties themselves to any position of influence was completely and conclusively rejected.[17]

This exclusive position of the Communist Party has been reaffirmed numerous times. The continuance of the one-party monopoly at present is ascribed to the total absence of antagonistic classes in the state and hence of such a cleavage of interests as would seek expression in a multiparty system.[18]

2. THE PARTY AS A POLITICAL MONOLITH

(1) THE MONOLITHIC CONCEPT OF THE PARTY

The Principle of Party Unity. Closely connected with the conception of the Party as a monopoly is its conception as a monolith, resting on the premise that no monopoly of political power can be such in fact if torn within itself. The Party is conceived not as a 'conglomerate of different groups,' but as a single, granitelike, massive unity, 'a unified militant organization held together by conscious, iron, proletarian discipline.' Centralism and discipline — lack of these in the first and their presence in the second case — are deemed vital lessons learned from the defeat of the Paris Commune and the victory of the Bolsheviks in the civil war. Complete unity and solidarity in the Party ranks, from the lowest rung to top leadership, are considered a basic and absolute prerequisite for the success and survival of Soviet rule and the Party's directing role, whose very strength is ascribed to 'its coherence, unity of will, and unity of action.' [19]

16. Since 1922, the Party rules provide for admission of former members of other parties. While the 1922 rules called for a recommendation of 5 Party members of 5 years' Party standing and confirmation by a district Party committee, the rules since 1925 state that such admission is 'in exceptional cases' and only through an industrial Party cell, later a primary Party organization, requiring confirmation by the Central Committee and, since 1934, the recommendation of 3 Party members of 10 years' standing and 2 of pre-revolutionary Party status. (Cf. articles 2d and v, 3v, and 4d of the 1922, 1925, 1934, and 1939 Comparty Rules, respectively.)

17. See the resolution of the Twelfth Party Congress (4–7 August 1922), 'About Anti-Soviet Parties and Movements,' *VKP(b) v Rezol.* I, pp. 473–7.

18. Stalin, *Constitution,* pp. 22–3; Molotov, *Constitution,* p. 8; Strong, *Constitution,* pp. 85–6, 90.

19. Comparty Rules, 1934, 1939; Kalinin, *Stat'i i Rechi,* 1919–1935, pp. 256–8, 267; Lenin, xxv, p. 96 (April 1920); *XIV S'ezd VKP(b),* p. 520; *XV S'ezd VKP(b),* p. 133 (Kaganovich, in December 1927). See also *VKP(b) v Rezol.* I, pp. 313, 373–4. 'The Bolshevik Party can fulfil its historical assignment only through real ideational unity and monolithism.' (C.C. Resolution, 17 January 1925, *VKP(b) v Rezol.* I, p. 652.) 'If

(2) THE PROHIBITION OF FACTIONAL ACTIVITY

The Proscription of Factions and Groupings. Consequently, it is stressed, factions, groupings, independent platforms and clusters of opinion, and any manifestations of deliberate aloofness and separatist activity in the Party cannot and will not be tolerated.[20] In the resolution adopted on the question by the Tenth Party Congress (March 1921), continuously relied on since as supreme Party law in the matter, the Congress ordered 'the complete annihilation of any factionalism,' demanding of all Party organizations that they keep constant vigil against factional doings, and giving the Central Committee 'plenary powers, in case of a violation of discipline or the revival or allowance of factionalism, to apply all the measures of Party penalties, up to expulsion from the Party, and in regard to members of the Central Committee — their transfer to the status of candidates and even, as an extreme measure, their expulsion from the Party.'[21]

---

it [the Party] will be united and monolithic . . . we shall undoubtedly resolve the task of liberating humanity which fell to us.' (Voroshilov, 2 July 1930, *XVI S'ezd VKP(b)*, p. 516.)

20. 'As far as Trotskyism is concerned, the C.P.S.U.(B) should not be a unified, solidified, fighting party, but an assemblage of groups and factions having their own centers, their own press, etc. And what does that mean? It means proclaiming the freedom of political factions in the Party. It means that after freedom of political groupings in the Party must come freedom of political parties in the country . . . Could we, given such views concerning the Party, secure an iron discipline in the Party, secure an iron unity in the Party, which is necessary for a successful struggle with the class enemies? Clearly not.' (Stalin, in *XVI S'ezd VKP(b)*, p. 102 [June 1930].)

21. *VKP(b) v Rezol.* I, pp. 374–5 (article 7, first openly published in 1924). What constitutes a faction, factional action, etc.? The resolution above speaks of 'factionalism, i.e. the rise of groups with special platforms and with the aim to shut themselves off to a certain extent and create their own group discipline.' (Ibid. p. 373. For additional statements on 'freedom of groupings,' 'shades of opinion,' etc., see Lenin, xxvi, pp. 200–201 [1921]; *XIII S'ezd VKP(b)*, p. 243 [Stalin, 1924]; Kalinin, op. cit. p. 256 [1927]; *XVI S'ezd VKP(b)*, pp. 167–8 [Kaganovich, 1930].) In a speech at the Sixteenth Party Congress (1930), admitting that his relations with Bukharin and Rykov constituted 'embryos of factionalism,' Tomsky expostulated that 'group,' 'faction,' 'elements of factionalism' are not strictly defined concepts. When three Central Committee members meet for a political conversation they do not as yet constitute a 'group,' but if they prepare a joint document and iron out their differences, 'when, differences of opinion between Central Committee members on questions of policy should be overcome openly in the presence of the members of the Central Committee, then we have . . . elements of factionalism, from which factionalism may subsequently grow.' Only factional discipline, factional organs, and an apparatus are lacking then to make it a faction 'which in our conditions (as I said many times in many a speech) can lead nowhere else but to the creation of a second party, unless it is smashed in time by the Party.' (*XVI S'ezd VKP(b)*, pp. 263–4.)

The Meaning of Intra-Party Democracy. It would not do, it was stated repeatedly, for breakers of this law to shield themselves by appeals to 'intra-Party democracy.'[22] For, intra-Party democracy means, it is said, the carrying on of a constant struggle against bureaucracy, against the method of 'administering' in lieu of persuasion in the Party, and against decision-making 'in family fashion,' i.e. by failing altogether to criticize one's colleagues for fear of upsetting comradely relations; it means the electivity of the leading Party office-holders and collegia from the bottom up, 'widespread self-criticism and the colossal activity of the Party masses guided by the Party,' more participation of the rank and file in meetings that

---

22. 'We are not liberals. For us, Party interests are higher than formal democracy.' (Stalin, December 1925, *XIV S'ezd VKP(b)*, p. 503.) 'For us, however, intra-Party democracy and self-criticism are a means to guarantee the fighting capacity of the Party.' (Kaganovich, June 1930, *XVI S'ezd VKP(b)*, p. 157.) One of the most interesting phenomena in the development of the political process in the Soviet state is the fact that at one time or another every single member of the highest leadership, including the heads — whatever their subsequent utterances — of the successive oppositions, made resounding pronouncements in favor of monolithism. Thus, Trotsky, 26 May 1924: 'In it [the C.C. resolution of 5 December 1923] it is made clear that under no circumstances does intra-Party democracy presuppose freedom of factional groupings, which are very dangerous for the ruling party because they always threaten to split in two or rend asunder the government and state apparatus as a whole. This I deem undisputed and indisputable. And we have agreed unanimously to rely on the resolution of the Tenth Congress . . . I never recognized and do not recognize the freedom of Party groupings because in the present historical conditions a grouping is but another name for a faction.' (*XIII S'ezd RKP(b)*, pp. 159–60.) 'And if the Party makes a decision that any one of us considers unjust, he must say: just or unjust, but this is my party and I shall bear the consequences of its decisions to the end.' (Ibid. p. 168. Cf. his *The Third International after Lenin*, pp. 149–50.) Zinoviev threatened the Trotsky opposition with the severest measures in January 1924 (*Pravda*, 25 January 1924) and in May 1924 he emphasized: 'We need a monolithism that is a thousand times greater than the one up to now . . . we cannot allow ourselves to go so far as to permit the freedom of factions or even the freedom of groupings.' (*XIII S'ezd RKP(b)*, p. 112, also pp. 261–3, 269. Cf. his statement in December 1925, *XIV S'ezd VKP(b)*, pp. 465–7.) At the Fourteenth Party Congress (December 1925), Rykov and Tomsky took Zinoviev and Kamenev — then in opposition — to task with biting excerpts from their former statements, such as Zinoviev's 'with a party that rules the state, freedom of factions would mean freedom to form parallel governments in embryo.' They concluded: 'What can you propose by way of democracy? . . . Nothing but the old well-known slogans of freedom of opinion, freedom of discussion, freedom of shades of opinion. But we call that disorganizing Lenin's party.' (*XIV S'ezd VKP(b)*, pp. 284, 289, 419.) While at the Seventeenth Party Congress (1934) Radek, reversing his former position on factions, averred that 'even a mere shadow of opposing oneself to the Party signifies the political death of a fighter for socialism, his going over into the camp of the foreposts of counter-revolution.' (*XVII S'ezd VKP(b)*, p. 628; see also p. 118. For Bukharin's statements, see *XIV S'ezd VKP(b)*, p. 152; *XV S'ezd VKP(b)*, p. 730; *XVII S'ezd VKP(b)*, p. 125; and for Kamenev's utterances cf. *XIII S'ezd RKP(b)*, pp. 212–25 [1924] with *XIV S'ezd VKP(b)*, p. 522 [1925] and *XV S'ezd VKP(b)*, p. 246 [1927].)

elect Party organs, more speeches, reports, and proposals of candidates, et cetera; it signifies the enlistment of thousands of workers for 'mass control' over the Soviet apparatus, that is the combatting of red tape, slothfulness, and nepotism through factory patronage of Soviet offices and the recommendations of factories for removal of bureaucratic officials; and it also means the promotion of hosts of workers to positions in the state machine and to leading work in the Party.[23]

But it does not mean avalanches of discussion and campaigns of criticism. From the end of the civil war on, speaker after speaker rose at congress after congress to voice indignation at the endless repetition of opposition. The sharp debates and bitter wranglings, they pointed out, were fraught with harm and danger externally and internally. Abroad the struggles were re-echoed in the Comintern, affecting in it adversely the prestige of the Communist Party of the Soviet Union, while unfriendly governments were interpreting them as welcome, long-awaited signs of weakness in the Soviet regime. Within the country, too, they were weakening the standing and influence of the Party in the wide non-Party masses, and were wittingly and unwittingly serving as trumpets and vehicles for the interests and activities of enemies of the revolution. Opposition to the Party line and leadership was growing into opposition to the Party itself, and with its reverberations outside the Party walls it was becoming a struggle against the dictatorship, against Soviet rule. Lastly, and not least, it was insisted times without number, the dragged-out discussions periodically inflicted upon the Party were a terrific drain upon the Party's strength and time, an unpardonable luxury when tremendous tasks of construction were at stake, when the crying all-round need was work not words.[24]

(3) THE LIMITS OF CRITICISM AND DISCUSSION

Metes and Bounds of Criticism and Discussion in the Party. Hence, although the Party rules recognize the right of a Party member 'to criticize any Party worker at Party meetings,' and provide that 'the free and businesslike discussion of questions of Party policy in individual organiza-

23. *VKP(b) v Rezol.* I, pp. 368, 548; *XV S'ezd VKP(b)*, p. 69; *XVI S'ezd VKP(b)*, pp. 79, 102, 139–40, 146, 163, 165–7. (Stalin; Kaganovich.)

24. *VKP(b) v Rezol.* I, pp. 373–4, 548–9, 553–4, 651 (1921–25); Lenin, XXVI, pp. 200–201 (1921); *XIII S'ezd RKP(b)*, pp. 205–10, 230–34, 237 (1924); *XIV S'ezd VKP(b)*, pp. 296, 300, 367, 418–19, 508 (1925); Kalinin, op. cit. p. 258; *XV S'ezd VKP(b)*, pp. 258, 295, 338, 351, 365–6 (1927); *XVI S'ezd VKP(b)*, pp. 102, 221, 245, 250, 263–70, 274, 285, 289, 365, 452–3 (1930). Besides the congressional resolutions, these comprise statements by Lenin, Stalin, Andreev, Kalinin, Kirov, Kosior, Krupskaia, Ordzhonikidze, Rudzutak, Rykov, Tomsky, Ulianova, and Yaroslovsky.

tions or in the Party as a whole is the inalienable right of every Party member, derived from internal Party democracy,' certain limits have evolved.[25] A line is drawn between factual, constructive criticism and factional, destructive critique. The stipulation is that Party men participate in 'businesslike discussion of practical questions of Party policy,' and critics are expected to be mindful of the conditions surrounding the Party and through their own work in public institutions to seek to rectify the Party's mistakes.[26] Above all, unbridled, uncontrolled campaigns of criticism and discussion are ruled out, the provision of the Party rules being that:

. . . extensive discussion, especially discussion on an all-Union scale, of questions of Party policy, must be so organized that it cannot lead to attempts by an insignificant minority to impose its will upon the vast majority of the Party, or attempts to form factional groupings that break the unity of the Party, attempts at a split that may shake the strength and endurance of the dictatorship of the working class.[27]

These rules further provide:

Therefore a wide discussion on an all-Union scale can be regarded as necessary only if: (a) this necessity is recognized by at least several local Party organizations whose jurisdiction extends to a region or a republic; (b) if there is not a sufficiently solid majority in the Central Committee itself on very important questions of Party policy; (c) if, in spite of the existence of a solid majority in the Central Committee advocating a definite standpoint, the Central Committee still deems it necessary to test the correctness of its policy by means of a discussion in the Party.

The Tenor of Self-Criticism. Wide discussion, thus, means organized discussion. The pattern of inquiry and fault-assessment is one of 'self-criticism,' i.e. criticism aimed at discovering deficiencies in practical work, removing bureaucratic abscesses in the Party apparatus, and adapting its

---

25. See rules 3 and 25 of the 1939 and rule 57 of the 1934 Comparty Rules, respectively. The earlier rules carried a provision in the section on 'Discipline' that: 'at the same time, within the Party, the discussion of all debatable questions of Party life is entirely free until such time as a decision has been adopted.' While a resolution of January 1924 read in part: 'In order to forestall it [the transformation of episodic differences of opinion into factional groupings], it is necessary that the leading Party organs should pay attention to the voice of the wide Party masses, should not consider every criticism a manifestation of factionalism and thereby push conscientious and disciplined Party men into the road of seclusion and factionalism.' (*VKP(b) v Rezol.* I, p. 548.)

26. *VKP(b) v Rezol.* I, p. 374 (1921); rule 3a, 1939 Comparty Rules 'Keeping clear of Trotskyist "critique," which proceeds from the other side of the barricades and has as its aim the discrediting and weakening of Soviet rule, the Party declared as the task of self-criticism the merciless revelation of the shortcomings of our work in order *to improve* our structure, in order *to strengthen* the Soviet government.' (Stalin, in *XVI S'ezd VKP(b)*, p. 79 [1930].)

27. Rules 25 and 57 of the 1939 and 1934 Comparty Rules, respectively.

organs and institutions toward greater and better fulfilment of the tasks
resolved upon, thereby fortifying in fact the staying power and the ef-
fectiveness of the regime.[28] And the Party itself, through its leading
organ — the Central Committee — is the one that provides guidance with
regard to the timeliness, propriety, tenor, and extent of complaints and
accusations, and the concrete goals sought through self-criticism.[29]

As part of the system of rights and duties, these rules on the limits of
political assertion in the Party, it is claimed, are set as equally binding for
all the organizations, even the most important ones, and all the members,
no matter how highly placed, in the pursuit of comprehensive, all-embracing monolithism for the Party that directs the state.[30]

3. THE ROAD TO MONOLITHISM

(1) EARLY OPPOSITION GROUPS

Oppositions in the First Year of the Regime. The road to monolithism,
however, was a long and difficult one. Hardly a congress or conference,
hardly a year of the first two decades of Bolshevik rule, passed without
some focus of opposition within the Party. As early as May-November
1917, the majority of the Central Committee met with the opposition of
several prominent members (Kamenev, Zinoviev, Preobrazhensky, et
cetera) to its orientation for a socialist revolution and its later decision
to seize political power. Then, in the very first weeks of establishment of
power, came strong disagreement on the part of a minority in the Committee's midst on the question of continuance of negotiations with and
the extent of concessions to be granted to some of the other socialist parties
for the purpose of possible formation of a joint government. (This minority comprised Kamenev, Zinoviev, Rykov, Nogin, Milutin, Larin, and
Riazanov.) Again, the first months of 1918 witnessed violent opposition

---

28. *XVI S'ezd VKP(b)*, pp. 79, 139–40, 146, 165–9. 'We never were and never will be
    afraid openly to criticize ourselves and our mistakes before the entire Party. Truly speak-
    ing, the strength of Bolshevism consists in the fact that it is not afraid of criticism,
    and in the criticism of its faults it draws energy for further progress forward.' (Stalin,
    XV S'ezd VKP(b), p. 71 [1927].)
29. 'The joint plenum of the C.C. and C.C.C. resolves that . . . the Politbureau of the
    C.C. and the Presidium of the C.C.C. should see to it that a discussion should be con-
    ducted within such frame and in such a tone as are compatible with Party affiliation
    and comradely relations.' (23 October 1927, *VKP(b) v Rezol.* II, p. 224.) 'The Central
    Committee headed the uplifting of mass self-criticism, decisively unmasking and over-
    coming both the suppression of criticism and biting criticisms.' (*XVI S'ezd VKP(b)*,
    p. 166 [1930]; see also ibid. pp. 79, 165–9; *XV S'ezd VKP(b)*, p. 71.)
30. Comparty Rules, section on discipline; *XV S'ezd VKP(b)*, p. 79; Kalinin, op. cit. p. 258.

on the part of the so-called 'Left Communists,' headed by Bukharin, to the conclusion of the annexationist Brest-Litovsk Peace, advocated by Lenin as the only available means of attaining an indispensable breathing spell for the Soviet republic.[31]

The 'Democratic Centralism,' 'Labor Opposition,' and Other Groups. Though there was relatively much greater unity on policy during the period of civil war and intervention, the Eighth Party Congress (18–25 March 1919) had to fight off a military opposition, headed by Smirnov and directed against the utilization of military specialists and the creation of a regular, disciplined army. It also saw the appearance of the 'Democratic Centralism' group, led by Sapronov and Osinsky, which — until dispersed in 1921–2 — fought against the principle of single-manager responsibility in industry, et cetera, against the Party's direction of the Soviet state apparatus and, above all, against a centralized order and the principle of monolithism in the Party. On these issues, as well as on the question of the need of a bond between the working class and peasantry, it was joined by the 'Labor Opposition,' headed by Shliapnikov and Medvedev, and a host of other groups, particularly activized about the time of the inauguration of the NEP.[32]

(2) THE OPPOSITIONS OF THE MIDDLE PERIOD

The Trotsky Opposition. Then began the long and bitterly fought opposition of Trotsky, whose following was augmented by remnants of the above-mentioned opposition groups. His proposals to utilize 'toil armies' in industry for the reconstruction of Russia (1920), his views on the relation of the Party to the trade unions (1921), and his plan for industrial organization, submitted against the then-proposed monetary reform and price policy (early in 1923), were rejected in succession by the majority of the Politbureau. His differences with the others of the top leadership began in earnest in the autumn of 1923, with his 8 October pronouncement and subsequent letter and brochure on 'The New Course.' In these statements he accused the Party of degeneration, juxtaposed it to its leading apparatus, posited the thesis that the younger generation — the student youth — is the best barometer of sentiment within the Party, defended the freedom of factions, and prophesied the doom of the revolution with the continuation of the policies pursued. The controversy revolved around current questions as well as fundamental postulates: concessions to foreign

31. See *VKP(b) v Rezol.* I, pp. 230–31, 258, 279–87, 702–5.
32. See ibid. pp. 289, 304–11, 322, 336, 364–5, 373–7, 424, 459–61; *Protokoly Deviatogo S'ezda RKP(b)*, pp. 53–65, 97; *Pravda*, 11 March 1921.

capital; assessment of blame for Comintern failures in 1923, et cetera; the interrelation between proletariat and peasantry, industry and agriculture, and the Party and state and economic organs; and the nature of the Party — the conception of its total unity and the impermissibility of factions or of assertions positing a 'struggle of generations' within it. It also embraced the question of correct historical evaluation of the role of the Party and of its Central Committee, of Lenin, and other leaders in the October Revolution. Last and most important, it concerned the view of the primary nature and program of that revolution — the crucial question of the possibility and desirability of building 'socialism in one country,' the U.S.S.R., as against Trotsky's thesis of 'Permanent Revolution.' Over these multiple issues with their manifold angles, the debate with the Trotsky opposition grew progressively tenser and sharper.[33]

The New or 'Left' Opposition. It was mainly on the last-named item that Trotsky, who was divested of his post as War Commissar and Chairman of the Revolutionary Military Council in January 1925, was subsequently joined in opposition by Zinoviev and Kamenev. Questioning the possibility of erecting a socialist system of economy in such a technically backward country as Russia, without the aid of sustaining revolutions abroad — a view underlying their opposition as early as 1917–18 — Zinoviev and Kamenev broke with the others in the Politbureau in April 1925. By the time of the Fourteenth Party Congress in December of that year, they emerged as the 'New Opposition.' They criticized the policy of winning over the middle peasantry on the ground that it left intact the might of the kulaks, denied that the state industry was socialist in nature, and demanded freedom of groupings and discussions in the Party.[34] In April–July 1926 an association or 'bloc' between the Zinoviev and Trotsky groups was effected and there followed a number of secret and open meetings of these factions in factories, Party cells, et cetera, denouncing the leadership in control and eliciting mass discussions on policy. In consequence Zinoviev was first removed from the Politbureau (July 1926) and then relieved of his post in the E.C.C.I. (Executive Committee of the Communist International), while Trotsky and Kamenev were at the same time (23 October 1926) removed from the Politbureau — all three being warned against further factional work.[35] On 16 October 1926, the opposi-

---

33. *VKP(b) v Rezol.* I, pp. 336, 364, 480–81, 542–6, 551–6, 576, 649, 651–6; II, p. 3.
34. Ibid. II, pp. 46–7, 59–60. See also *XIV S'ezd VKP(b)*, pp. 135–6.
35. Ibid. pp. 106, 118–21, 128, 129, 154–61. Involved with them were a number of high office-holders and members of the highest Party organs: Lashevich, Piatakov, Evdokimov, Sokolnikov, Smilga, etc.

tion submitted a declaration of capitulation before the Party and cessation
of its struggle. This declaration notwithstanding, various oppositional activities — the printing and distribution of factional literature, denuncia-
tory speeches by Trotsky, Zinoviev, et cetera — continued well into the
summer of 1927. Severe criticism was leveled against the majority of the
Politbureau and Central Committee for its tactics and policies in regard
to the Chinese Revolution and Anglo-Russian trade-union relations. The
majority group was accused of 'Thermidorian degeneration,' of catering to
the kulaks, and of following a national-conservative line. Professing to
see greater danger in the existing Party regime than in an external threat
of war, despite the mounting tension in Anglo-Soviet relations at the time,
the opposition expressed doubt of the desirability of organizing the defense
of the country unless the personnel of its ruling organs was replaced.[36] In
reply, the Central Committee denounced the opposition's activity as a
road leading to a new party in the country and a split in the Comintern.
The Central Committee threatened to expel Trotsky and Zinoviev from
its midst unless they withdrew their damning accusations; this they did
to a considerable extent in a declaration of 8 August 1927, renouncing a
number of their views and expressions as erroneous. Two and a half
months later, however, on 23 October, the threat was carried out against
them on charges of duplicity — of having continued their factional struggle at home and abroad despite their earlier promises.[37] Then, what was
regarded as the last straw came on 7 November 1927, when the opposition
attempted to organize a street demonstration during the celebration of the
tenth anniversary of Soviet rule. Viewed with consternation as an appeal
— over the heads of the established leadership — not alone to the men of
the Party, but to the populace at large, and thus cutting across both the
monopoly and monolithism power principles, this act was immediately
and widely condemned as 'open counter-revolution.' On 11 November,
Trotsky and Zinoviev were excluded from the Party, Kamenev from the
Central Committee, et cetera, and a month later the Fifteenth Party Congress (2–19 December 1927) sought to make a clean sweep by expelling
from the Party seventy-five members of the opposition, including Kamenev, Piatakov, Radek, and Rakovsky.[38]

36. Ibid. pp. 176–85, 195–9, 672–3, 673–6.
37. Ibid. pp. 200, 224, 225.
38. Ibid. pp. 226–7, 264–6, 667–70. Though Zinoviev, Kamenev, and a number of others,
    severing relations with Trotsky, whose policy resulted in exile from the country, declared
    at the Fifteenth Party Congress the complete subordination of 'their will and their views
    to the will and views of the Party' and were later readmitted into the Party, they re-
    mained outside the sphere of active influence on policy and were again expelled from

The 'Right Opposition.' The echoes of the 'Left Opposition' struggle had barely died down when a new 'Right Opposition,' headed by Bukharin, Tomsky, and Rykov, began to emerge prior to the July (1928) plenum of the Central Committee, revealing its platform more fully in January–February 1929. Advancing contentions that, domestically, current policies resulted in 'tribute-bearing' by the peasantry and in the planting of bureaucracy and of a political commissar system in the Party, while abroad they were bringing about the splitting up of the Comintern sections, this opposition revived the old arguments regarding freedom of factions. It pressed for a slowing down of the tempo of industrialization, for a liberalization of the trade and especially the kulak-taxation policies — the consequences of which it feared most of all — and also for a modification of the policy of weeding out social-democratic and other non-Communist elements inaugurated within the Comintern. Rejecting these contentions as based on wrong evaluations of the total situation at home and as flowing from Bukharin's erroneous theory of 'the stabilization of capitalism' abroad, the majority of the Party's leadership condemned the opposition's pronouncements and actions. Bukharin's attempt in July 1928 to form an oppositional coalition with Kamenev and the dissident leaders' repeated tenders of resignation and refusals to execute directives, were denounced as intolerable violations of Party discipline. Bukharin was relieved of his posts as editor of *Pravda* and secretary of the Comintern, and Tomsky as head of the Central Council of Trade Unions, on 23 April 1929. In July, the E.C.C.I. followed suit by removing Bukharin from its presidium, and on 17 November of that year he was also divested of membership in the Politbureau, while Tomsky and Rykov were at the same time warned against any further struggle against the decisions of the Central Committee and E.C.C.I.[39] Later, they were also expelled from the Politbureau. Though all three declared at the Sixteenth Party Congress (June–July 1930) their complete capitulation to the Party, they never really regained their former positions of influence.

(3) THE ATTAINMENT OF MONOLITHISM .

Realization of Total Unity at the End of the 'Thirties. Thus, all major opposition seemed to have collapsed by 1930 and Stalin was able to state

it on 9 October 1932 for failing to communicate to the Party knowledge of the existence of the counter-revolutionary group of Riutin, etc.

39. Ibid. pp. 318–30, 331–2, 367, 396, 398–9, 679–81. Another prominent Right oppositionist, Uglanov, was removed from candidacy in the Politbureau in April 1929, and expelled from the Party in 1932. (Ibid. pp. 366, 670.) Also Syrtsov and Lominadze were excluded for such opposition in December 1930. (Ibid. pp. 668–9.)

at the time that 'the Sixteenth Congress is one of the few congresses in our Party at which there is no longer any crystallized and solid opposition capable of opposing its own line to that of the general line of the Party,' a claim repeated by the leadership also at the succeeding congress, in the beginning of 1934.[40] That all was not well, however, despite the new atmosphere of unanimity that reigned at the Party gatherings, was soon revealed by the assassination, on 1 December 1934, of Kirov, an outstanding leader of the Party, and the long and serious aftermath of the purges and trials of 1936–8 involving the total liquidation of the various oppositionists with their active adherents throughout the land. Only the last Party congress, which met in March 1939, reflected in fact a complete, all-round unity of purpose and policy at all the branches and levels of the Party domain. The perfect monolithism, striven for so long, was realized at last.

In conclusion, it should be noted that, though thoroughly deplored at the time of its occurrence, every round of opposition was evaluated at its termination as having served as a sort of purifying process, bearing in its incidence also the beneficial consequences of sifting the ranks and consolidating them ever more strongly around the leadership of the central, guiding Party organs.[41]

Resting on these political power principles, and counting with its auxiliaries — the Communist Youth League and the Pioneers — over one sixth of the approximately 193 million Soviet population in 1946, the Party was composed of a membership especially schooled, tried, and selected on the basis of training, merit, and probation. Closely knit by an iron discipline of devotion and obedience and backed by sanctions periodically purging those found faulty or faithless, the Communist Party of the Soviet state constitutes a ruling revolutionary order, singularly shaped for the perpetually mobilizing and directing function cast for it in the system of the dictatorship.

---

40. *XVI S'ezd VKP(b)*, p. 110, also pp. 415, 517. Recalling that even the leadership of Lenin himself 'did not succeed in achieving genuine, complete, and unconditional unity at the Party Congresses,' Voroshilov claimed that such had been attained at the Seventeenth Party Congress, which will go down as 'the first congress of Bolshevik unity.' (*XVII S'ezd VKP(b)*, p. 224.)

41. See e.g. *XIII S'ezd RKP(b)*, p. 210; *VKP(b) v Rezol.* II, p. 161; Kalinin, op. cit. p. 258; *XVI S'ezd VKP(b)*, p. 171.

Chapter VII · The Party Structure (I)

1. THE PYRAMIDAL ARRANGEMENT

(i) THE HIERARCHICAL ORGANIZATION OF THE PARTY

The Party Tiers. Structurally, the Party represents a power pyramid erected on a territorial-production basis, i.e. a Party organization serving a given area being regarded as superior to all Party organizations serving part of that area; and the same holds true of a Party organization serving a whole branch of work as against those serving only part of one.[1] The floor of this pyramidal structure consists of a mosaic of primary Party organizations, formerly known as 'nuclei' or 'cells,' varying in size but numbering not less than three Party members in the whole or a part of a given enterprise or unit in industry, agriculture, transport, distribution, educational institutions, offices, parts of the armed forces, et cetera. Over this floor rise the tiers of the Party organizations in the urban and rural districts, areas, regions, territories, and Union republics, culminating in the highest, i.e. the central, all-Union, Party organs.[2] The interrelation between the tiers is governed by the principle of Democratic Centralism, which is described as:

(a) The application of the elective principle to all leading bodies of the Party, from the lowest to the highest.

(b) The periodical accountability of the Party bodies to their respective Party organizations.

(c) Strict Party discipline and subordination of the minority to the majority.

(d) The absolutely binding character of the decisions of the higher bodies upon the lower bodies.[3]

---

1. Rule 19 of the 1939 and 1934 Comparty Rules. Cf. rule 11 of the 1919 and 1922, and rule 13 of the 1925 Comparty Rules.
2. Corresponding to the then existing territorial-administrative divisions there were listed in March 1939: 113,060 primary Party organizations, 212 city, 336 city district, and 3,479 rural district Party committees, 30 areal, 104 regional, 6 territorial, and 11 central Party committees, headed by the Central Committee of the all-Union Communist Party (b). (See Stalin, Report to the Eighteenth Party Congress, op. cit. pp. 56–7.)
3. Rule 18 of the 1939 and 1934 Comparty Rules. Cf. rule 10 in the 1919 and 1922 and rule 12 in the 1925 Comparty Rules.

(2) THE TRIPARTITE DIVISION OF AUTHORITY

The Representative Bodies. Within each of the Party units there is a tripartite division of authority and responsibility. First, there is the representative or so-called 'highest leading body,' a general meeting for the primary Party organizations; a Party conference for the urban and rural district (once a year), and for the areal, regional, and territorial Party organizations (once every year and a half); a Party congress in the case of the Union-republic parties (once every year and a half); and a Party conference (not less than once a year); and Party congress (not less than once in three years) for the all-Union Communist Party.[4] Of these, the primary organizations choose the delegates to the city and district conferences, the latter to the area, region, and territory conferences and the Union-republic congresses, and the last named to the all-Union Party congress. Since 1937 elections have been by secret ballot.

The 'Executive Bodies.' Second, there it an 'executive body' — from the city and district Party organizations and upward — a committee elected by and for each of the above-mentioned representative bodies and charged with guidance of the current work of its organization.[5] The conferences of the city and district, area, region, and territory Party organizations, and the congresses of the Union-republic Party organizations elect Party committees (rules 44, 49, and 52 of the 1939 Comparty Rules). A bureau is elected by a general meeting of a primary Party organization numbering not less then fifteen members; otherwise, a secretary is elected (rule 62). The plenums of the city and district committees must meet not less than once every month and a half, while the regional and territorial committees and the central committees of the Union-republic parties are required to convene at least once in three months (rules 47, 55). The importance of the Party organs of this category lies in their more frequent sessions, and in the work that they are required to perform: to organize and guide various Party institutions as well as enterprises of general importance within their respective geographical limits; to distribute therein the Party forces and resources; and, most important of all, to lead the Party groups in the non-

---

4. See parts II–IX of the 1939 Comparty Rules, *passim.* 'The highest leading body of each organization is the general meeting, conference, or congress.' (Rule 13, of the 1919 Comparty Rules. Same in subsequent rules.)

5. The 1919–34 Comparty Rules provided that: 'The general meeting, conference, or congress elects a committee that is its executive organ and guides all the current work of the respective organization.' This provision was amended in 1939 to read 'bureau or committee' (rule 22).

Party organizations — the soviets and other state, economic, or public institutions (rules 46, 51, 54, 60). The responsibility of these committees to
the representative Party bodies, by which they were chosen and which they
call into session, is shown by the usual provisions to the effect that the
latter hear and adopt the reports of the former, et cetera (rules 44,
49, 52).

The Lesser Bureaus and the Secretaries. Last, there are the further
carved-out, still smaller bodies, the bureaus and their secretaries, set up by
the Party committees.[6] These are in permanent or frequent session and
through constant attendance to Party tasks and interests at the functional-
territorial links of the pyramidal edifice exercise a tremendous influence
on the daily operation of the entire Party apparatus.

(3) THE PARTY AUXILIARIES [7]

The Komsomol. The closest auxiliary of the Party is the Komsomol or
Young Communist League. As early as 1903, the Bolsheviks accepted
Lenin's recommendation for a special Party organization among young
people, but only during March–November 1917, especially after the Sixth
Congress of the Party in August, which adopted a resolution on the subject, did they succeed in their efforts to gain large-scale adherence of
youth groups to their program. A year later, at a congress of youth or-

---

6. While a Party committee is itself an 'executive organ' of a congress, conference, etc., and
'guides all the current work' (rule 22), it is, at least in the case of the region, territory,
and republic Party organizations, also 'the highest body' in the interval between their
conferences and congresses (rule 43) and it 'appoints, for *current work,* corresponding
executive bodies to consist of not more than 11 persons and 4 or 5 secretaries, including
a First Secretary, a Second Secretary, a Secretary for Cadres, and a Secretary for Propaganda, to be confirmed by the Central Committee C.P.S.U.(B). The secretaries must
have Party standing of not less than 5 years.' (Rule 45; italics J.T.) An Area Committee
elects a bureau of not more than 9 persons and 4 secretaries of at least 3 years' Party
standing, while a City and District Committee elects a bureau of 7 to 9 and 3 secretaries
of like standing. (Rules 50, 53.) The higher Party status, which was always required of
secretaries in greater or lesser degree, as well as the provisions for their confirmation by
higher Party instances, are indicative of the importance attached to their role. (Rules 45,
50, 53, 61, 62. See also *VKP(b) v Rezol.* I, pp. 425, 445, 514, 590; II, 593.)
7. This section is based on the following sources: Lenin and Stalin, *O Molodezhi;* Gavrilin,
Leninskii Komsomol Rezerv I Pomoshchnik Kommunisticheskoi Partii; P.S. pp. 90–92,
393; Webb, op. cit. pp. 392ff.; editorial, 'The Fighting Reserve of the Bolshevik Party,'
pp. 5–15; Zhdanov, 'Speech at the Festive Plenum of the C.C. of the A.L.C.L.Y.,' pp. 38–
46; editorial 'Young Patriots of the Motherland,' pp. 11–18; Mikhailov, 'XXV Years of
the Leninist-Stalinist Komsomol,' pp. 45–55; editorial, 'Master Tirelessly Contemporary
Technology, Science, and Culture,' pp. 19–24; *Izvestia,* 15 June 1945; *Pravda,*
20 October 1942, 15 June and 1 and 2 December 1945, and 28 April 1946.

ganizations held from 29 October to 4 November 1918, the All-Russian Communist League of Youth was formed. In July 1924, following Lenin's death, its name was changed to All-Russian Leninist Communist League of Youth, and in March 1926 it adopted the designation All-Union Leninist Communist League of Youth. All along it has been popularly referred to by the abbreviated version of its Russian title — Komsomol.

Although the Komsomol is defined as a mass 'non-Party organization,' it is at the same time designated as 'the assistant of the C.P.S.U.(B) and its reserve.' [8] The accepted conception of the Komsomol embraces a double relationship: the role and standing of the Komsomol *vis-à-vis* the Party, and its duties toward Soviet youth. As regards the Party, which is called its 'mother' and which draws from its ranks a great proportion of members and leaders, the Komsomol is called upon to master the teachings of Marxism and to engage at all times in active aid to the Party in the execution of the program and directives of the latter. As for its role toward the youth of the country, the basic task of the Komsomol is stated to be 'assistance to the Communist Party [Bolsheviks] in the matter of educating the youth and children in the spirit of communism and of organizing the youth around the Soviet power.' [9] Here the Komsomol is viewed as 'a transmission belt that connects the Party with the masses and spreads the Party's influence to the masses of youth.' [10] By attracting great numbers of young people to its own ranks, and by serving as an example to Soviet youth in numerous spheres of activity, as well as by directing the work of children's organizations, the Komsomol serves as a mass training school, which provides young cadres not only for the Party but for all other organizations and institutions in the country.

Organizationally the Komsomol is patterned after the Party, with members in farms, factories, and every kind of institution throughout the country forming themselves into cells and electing committees that in turn select the secretaries of the respective units — the city or village, district, region, and republic committees. These committees and secretaries govern the day-to-day operation of their groups, while conferences and congresses meeting periodically resolve upon current tasks and a Central Committee appointed by the All-Union Congress of the Komsomol directs the work of the entire organization.

The controlling influence exercised by the Party in the affairs of the

---

8. *P.S.* pp. 90–91.

9. Ibid.; *Bol'shevik*, 18 September 1943, p. 11; Letter of the fourteenth Plenum of the C.C. A.L.C.L.Y. to Stalin, *Pravda*, 1 December 1945.

10. *Bol'shevik*, 15 October 1938, p. 7.

Komsomol is readily admitted and acclaimed. 'The C.C. [Central Committee] of the A.L.C.L.Y. [All-Union Leninist Communist League of Youth]' states a widely used text, 'being the leading organ of the Komsomol, is subordinate to the C.C. of the C.P.S.U.(B). The work of the local organizations of the A.L.C.L.Y. is directed and controlled by the corresponding republic, territorial, regional, city, and district Party organizations.'[11] This control and the co-ordination of the Komsomol's work with that of the Party are achieved through a number of organizational arrangements. The Party attaches great importance to the work of the Komsomol, and one of the highest Party leaders is usually assigned to look after this work. The Party has been instrumental in purging the Komsomol of oppositionist elements, and it not only guides the ideological orientation of the Komsomol, but exercises a controlling voice in the selection of candidates for the posts of secretaries of the higher Komsomol committees. From the district committees upwards, the secretaries of the Komsomol must at the same time be members of the Party, the required length of such membership rising with the grade of the secretaries. Stalin himself took an active part in the drawing up of the new program and rules of the Komsomol, adopted in April 1936. The ideological level, discipline, and nature of the Komsomol membership are watched with special concern by the Party leadership.[12]

The Komsomol comprises young people between the ages of 15 and 26. Before 1936 the age limits were 14 to 23. In practice, many young people stay on in the Komsomol beyond the age limit, in which case, however, they retain only a consulting voice in the organization. While admission to membership in the Komsomol was never as strict as in the case of the Party, there nevertheless existed for a long time a number of limitations with regard to admission of children of white-collar workers and intelligentsia.[13] These consisted of probation periods and of various requirements for recommendations by Party and Komsomol members. The rules of admission were gradually liberalized and during the war years the doors of the Komsomol were thrown wide open, resulting in a phenomenal growth in the organization's membership. The continuous growth of the Komsomol membership, especially since the 'thirties, is attested by the following figures:[14]

---

11. *P.S.* p. 91.
12. See *Bol'shevik,* 15 October 1938, pp. 12–14; October 1943, p. 51.
13. In April 1925, at a session of the Organizational Bureau, Stalin argued the need to secure 'the proletarian kernel' in the Komsomol. (*Bol'shevik,* 15 October 1938, p. 9.) In later years, however, progressively less attention was paid to this requirement.
14. See *P.S.* pp. 91–2; *Pravda,* 20 October 1942; *A.R.S.U.,* February 1946, p. 69.

DATE	APPROXIMATE KOMSOMOL MEMBERSHIP
October 1918	22,000
October 1919	96,000
October 1920	400,000
October 1921	415,000
July 1924	700,000
March 1926	1,750,000
May 1928	2,000,000
January 1931	3,000,000
April 1936	4,000,000
October 1939	9,000,000
October 1942	12,000,000
October 1945	15,000,000

Thus, the Komsomol has become in fact a mass organization, in its membership and activities, encompassing the greater part of Soviet youth.

Certain tasks have been required of the Komsomol over and over again and have become more or less permanent in nature: the communist education of Soviet youth; widespread activity in the village; the organization of multiple social and cultural undertakings for young people — clubs, theaters, excursions, and entertainments — and the promotion of physical-culture activities. On special occasions the Komsomol was called upon to assist the Party in particular, urgent undertakings, such as campaigns to liquidate illiteracy or to check up on bureaucratic practices and carry out purges in institutions, to help with the harvesting of seasonal crops, et cetera.

Of greater importance, however, than these permanent tasks were the primary ones on which the Komsomol was asked by the Party to concentrate at various periods. Thus, during the civil-war period, the Komsomol was urged to mobilize its members in defense of the new republic. It carried out several such mobilizations, sending thousands of young people to the front lines, and for its role in the victory of the regime it was awarded the Order of the Red Banner in 1928. In the years following the civil war, the Komsomol assisted in the reconstruction of the national economy. At the Party's bidding, it dispatched thousands of its members to the Ukraine, Urals, Siberia, the Donets basin, Karaganda, and other places, to help re-establish factories, shops, railroads, and mines. Then, in 1928, the Party called upon the Komsomol to assist with the execution of the industrialization and agricultural collectivization programs under the Five-Year Plan, and to promote the training of young specialists for the new economy.[15] In a long speech before the Eighth Congress of the Komsomol, in May 1928, Stalin declared: 'To master science, to forge new cadres of Bolsheviks — specialists in all branches of science, to study, study,

15. See Bol'shevik, 15 October 1938, p. 10.

study in the stubbornest fashion — that is the present task. A crusade of
revolutionary youth into science — that, comrades, is what we need now.'

The Komsomol produced from its ranks thousands of technical specialists for all branches of the economy and is generally credited with contributing greatly toward fulfilment of the Five-Year Plans. For its share
in the launching and prosecution of the first Five-Year Plan the Komsomol was awarded the Order of the Red Banner of Labor in 1939. The
contribution of the Komsomol was particularly strong in the collectivization of agriculture. Twice it sent mass expeditions of its members into the
village to assist in the collectivization program. Data for 1937 show that
103,640 Komsomolites, and young people below thirty associated with
them, were collective-farm chairmen; 210,790 were leaders of plant-grow-
ing brigades; 125,790 worked as statisticians and accountants; 61,931 were
commercial farm managers; and tens of thousands served as agronomists,
technicians, veterinaries, et cetera, in the village. During the years of the
first two Five-Year Plans alone, the Komsomol is said to have given the
country 118,000 engineers and technicians, 69,000 agricultural specialists,
19,000 teachers possessed of a higher education, 9,000 physicians, and tens
of thousands of highly qualified workers in other lines of specialization.[16]
It was also a prime mover in the Stakhanovite movement for labor efficiency in the middle 'thirties.

In 1935-7, the Komsomol was urged to concentrate on political study.
But several years later, along with such specific tasks as aid in the program of settling the Soviet Far East and of replenishing the ranks of
industrial workers through the migration of village youths into the city,
the emphasis turned largely to the promotion of measures to strengthen
the defensive capacity of the U.S.S.R.[17] The Eighteenth Party Congress,
in March 1939, formalized the position of the Komsomol as the Party's
assistant in all Party tasks, by a special resolution.

In this connection it should be stressed that from the early part of the
regime the ties between the Komsomol and the armed forces have been
particularly close. In October 1922 the Komsomol assumed the role of
patron of the Soviet Navy, and in January 1931 it did the same with
regard to the Soviet Air Force. In practice this meant that the Komsomol
took a special interest in these services, organized various welfare activities
for them, and sent great numbers of its members into their ranks. In
return the armed services provided the Komsomol with instructors for

16. Gavrilin, op. cit. pp. 27-8.
17. See Zhdanov's speech before the Komsomol Central Committee plenum, 29 October 1938,
    in Bol'shevik, 15 November 1938, pp. 45-6.

its numerous voluntary military study and physical-training groups. This relation has also aided in the recruitment of many servicemen — mostly peasant in origin — to the Komsomol. The Komsomol is also largely responsible for the organization and growth of Osoaviakhim — the voluntary Society for Assistance in Defense, and in Aviation and Chemical Development.

During the recent war years, the Komsomol was asked to concentrate all its efforts on victory over the enemy, and its members have been repeatedly acclaimed for feats of heroism and sacrifice at the front and in the rear. Official figures have pointed out that by December 1942, 242 out of 478 Heroes of the Soviet Union were members or former members of the Komsomol. Ten months later, the number of Heroes of the Soviet Union stemming from the Komsomol was given as 500, while 10 of these had held the title twice. During the first half of 1943, 100,000 Komsomol members at the front were awarded orders and medals, while in 1944 similar awards were made to nearly 600,000 Komsomolites, and at the end of the war, the Komsomol as an organization was given the highest Soviet award — the Order of Lenin — for patriotic services.[18]

In the more recent period, the Komsomol actively helped in the campaign for the 1946 elections to the Supreme Soviet. Currently, its two main tasks are declared to be assistance with the execution of the new Five-Year Plan, and concentrated attention on the pursuit of modern science and technology by the entire youth of the U.S.S.R. — helping to create new day and night schools and correspondence courses, and bringing the mass of young people into them.[19]

The Komsomol is, thus, a vital cog in the Party structure and has played a very important role in all spheres of activity in the U.S.S.R.

The Pioneers and Octobrists. Closely connected with the Komsomol (through which they are controlled by the Party), are the 'Children's Communist Organization of Young Pioneers of the Name of Comrade Lenin' — usually referred to as the Pioneers — which embraces children and adolescents from the ages of ten to sixteen, and the organization of 'Little Octobrists,' to which belong children aged eight to eleven. The Pioneers are directed by representatives of the Komsomol and along with the latter they in turn guide the Octobrists.

The organization of the Pioneers was founded at the Fifth Congress of

18. See *Bol'shevik*, September 1943, pp. 12–14, October 1943, p. 48; *Pravda*, 15 June and 2 December 1945.

19. See editorials in *Komsomolskii Rabotnik*, 21 November 1945, and *Pravda*, 2 December 1945, and 28 April 1946.

THE PYRAMIDAL ARRANGEMENT

Komsomol, in October 1922, after several earlier attempts to create a children's communist organization, and in May 1924 the name of Lenin was added to its title. The accepted conception of its role is that it helps the Soviet school to educate the children in the spirit of communism, and love for the country and the Party, and that it inculcates in them habits of cultural behavior, 'a strength of will, firmness of character, a yearning for knowledge.'[20]

Admission to the organizations of the Pioneers and Octobrists is not restricted. Regardless of social origin, children in the respective ages may enter these organizations and become members after a probational period of several months. Both organizations have increased tremendously in membership. The Octobrists embrace a good deal of the Soviet school population in the lower grades. As for the Pioneers, the extent of its growth is attested by the following figures:[21]

YEAR	APPROXIMATE MEMBERSHIP
1923	5,000
1925	1,000,000
1928	1,650,000
1930	3,300,000
1934	7,000,000
1939	11,000,000

The present membership of the Pioneers is probably higher by at least several millions.

The triple connection and graded control involved in the relation between the Party, the Komsomol, and the Pioneers and Octobrists is apparent from the set-up of the junior organizations.[22] The Pioneers are organized in 'links' and brigades; each ten members at a school, factory, farm, et cetera, form a link, and four links are joined in a brigade. Every brigade of Pioneers is attached to a Komsomol cell and led by a

---

20. *P.S.* p. 393.
21. For the 1923 and 1925 figures, see Webb, op. cit. p. 401; the other figures are based on statements at several Party congresses. See *XVI S'ezd VKP(b)*, p. 60, and Zakharov's speech in *Pravda*, 14 March 1939.
22. The intimacy of this relationship is impressed upon the members of the junior organizations through their pledges and slogans, the 'laws and customs' or rules that they are required to obey, and various symbols, such as the three-cornered kerchief worn by the Pioneers, which is supposed to signify 'the unity of three Bolshevik generations — the Communists, Komsomolites, and Pioneers.' (See *P.S.* p. 393 and Webb, op. cit. pp. 400–405.) The overlapping of the age categories in these groups is likewise designed to provide additional organizational-ideological bridges between them through simultaneous membership in two organizations by some of the members.

member of that cell. This brigade leader, together with the link leaders and another representative of the Komsomol cell, form a council of the brigade to consult in the running of its affairs. The work of the brigade leaders in a given area is directed and supervised by the section on Pioneers of the district committee of the Komsomol for that area, while the operation of all the sections on Pioneers of the Komsomol committees is in turn supervised by a commission on Pioneers of the central committee of the Komsomol. The organizational tie-up between the Komsomol and the Party we have noted earlier.

The Octobrists are organized in links and groups. Each five Octobrists constitute a link led by a Pioneer, while five links form a group that is integrated into a Pioneer brigade and led by a member of the Komsomol cell to which this brigade is attached. Thus, a thorough integration is achieved in the leadership and operation of the junior organizations.

The little Octobrists are engaged in supervised play and may assist the older Pioneers in such activity as clean-up campaigns, et cetera. The Pioneers make excursions of all kinds, engage in sport contests, train as sharpshooters, learn the rudiments of various mechanical skills, and frequently assist the Komsomol actively in its tasks. Throughout their existence, the emphasis in the work of the Pioneers and Octobrists has been on study, and more recently in the activity of all the junior organizations a good deal of stress has been placed on military subjects and physical culture, in connection with the introduction of the system of universal military education. Of considerable importance in the operation of the Pioneers organization are the periodic meetings of the links and brigades, at which discussions are conducted on political subjects, science, and sundry other topics, and at which an accounting is asked from the members on the progress of their studies and on compliance with the rules and purposes of the organization.

2. THE CONGRESS AND CONFERENCE OF THE PARTY

(I) THE PARTY CONGRESS

The Conception, Organization, and Procedure of the Congress. Of primary interest for our purpose is the apex of the pyramid, the central or higher bodies of the Party. First, there is the All-Union Party Congress, conceived as 'the supreme organ of the Party,' and regarded as the most authoritative interpreter of theory and the highest instance of Party appeal.[23] Elected on the basis of one voting delegate per one thousand members and one consulting delegate per two thousand candidates of the Party, the congress was composed of 104 delegates at its first meeting during the Soviet regime (March 1918). The number of delegates has risen steadily with the general growth of the Party, reaching 2,159 at the Sixteenth Party Congress in 1934, and then falling off, in connection with the purge, to 1,574 at the last congress, held in March 1939. At first convocable yearly and now every three years, the Party congress met annually till 1925. Thereafter, it convened at increasingly greater intervals, the Fifteenth in 1927, the Sixteenth in 1930, the Seventeenth in 1934, and the Eighteenth in 1939.[24] Extraordinary Party congresses, though stipulated in the rules, have never been held. Till 1925 it was provided that norms of representation to the congress were to be established by the Central Committee and the pre-congress Party conference. Since then the rules have called for apportionment of representation only by the Central Committee.

Sessions are called by the Party Central Committee, which is required to make known the scheduled agenda by publication a month and a half in advance. These sessions are held behind closed doors, attendance being restricted to delegates and invited guests — Communists and sympathizers as a rule. They last usually one to two weeks.[25] The established order of proceedings is to elect, immediately upon assembling, a presidium, a secretariat, and a mandate and an editorial commission for the conduct of the congress.[26] Then the reports of the Party Central Committee are presented: a political report on internal and external policy, an organiza-

---

23. Rule 20, Comparty Rules, 1919. Same in subsequent rules. 'The Party congress . . . the highest sovereign organ of our Party.' (Krestinsky in C.C. Report, March 1920, *Protokoly Deviatogo S'ezda RKP(b)*, p. 89.) 'The highest organ of the party . . . its congress.' (Litvinov, 14 December 1927, *XV S'ezd VKP(b)*, p. 916.) 'The congress . . . the most responsible assembly of the Party and the republic.' (Lenin, 9 March 1921, Lenin, xxvi, p. 232.) 'The congress is sovereign, it is not bound by any decision of any plenums, it is higher than any plenum [of the C.C.], it has full rights to overthrow any decision of a plenum.' (*Zinoviev*, 23 December 1925, *XIV S'ezd VKP(b)*, p. 436; see also ibid. pp. 237, 288-9.)

24. By the 1919, 1922, and 1925 Comparty Rules (rules 20, 20, 21, respectively) regular sessions were to be held yearly. Since 1934 the rules provide for the convocation of the congress 'not less than once in three years' (rule 27).

25. Of the twelve Party congresses held since 1918 the shortest lasted three days, the longest eighteen days. They sat a total of 137 days.

26. The tendency for increased membership in these bodies was reversed in the 'thirties, and the last Party congress (1939) elected a Presidium of thirty-five, a Secretariat of five, a Mandate Commission of twenty-nine, and an Editorial Commission of five. At several of the congresses an 'Honorary Presidium' of prominent guests from Comintern sections was elected.

tional report dealing with the Party and Soviet structures and their inter-relations, reports by control and auditing commissions, and specific reports on a wide variety of subjects. Numerous greeting statements from factories, collectives, army regiments, Comintern sections, et cetera, read or delivered through representatives and special delegations at the beginning of pro-ceedings, or interspersed throughout, act as supporting devices for policies pronounced by the Central Committee in the pre-congress theses and discussion. The delegates, familiar with the main contentions or proposals from these advance formulations, now developed or defined in the reports, proceed to debate. The rules of order allow forty-five minutes for a report — a provision never strictly insisted upon — and every group of forty voting delegates has a right to put forth its own co-reporter on a question of the agenda. However, in view of the striving after unanimity and the persistent efforts to iron out differences on policy before the convocation of the congress, an opposing co-report is in fact a rare occurrence. The delegates may speak twice on each agenda question, and can submit personal declarations, factual remarks, and inquiries on extra-agenda mat-ters in written notes to the Presidium.[27] The Presidium has a right to — and as a rule does — form sections and commissions on some of the sched-uled items before the congress on major individual questions of Party work, and these bodies deliberate and submit drafts of resolutions to the Presidium. Following the debate on a given report, the reporter makes a concluding statement, summarizing his proposals or offering additional explanations or some modifications in light of the debate and written in-quiries. Thereupon a resolution is offered, in the name of several Party delegations, embodying the basic conclusions arrived at on the part of the majority. A crystallized minority may present its own resolution. The vote is indicated by a show of hands — the raising of membership cards — though upon demand of fifteen voting delegates a roll call may be taken, and only a simple majority is required for decision. Thereafter, the rule obtains — and is asserted without any equivocation — that the majority rules, that the resolution adopted is Party law for all.[28]

---

27. See the Rules of Order of the Party Congress, *Protokoly Deviatago S'ezda RKP(b)*, p. 476. Fifteen minutes the first time and five the second are allowed to speakers in the debate. Inquiries and declarations are made public by the Presidium at its discretion, unless they are signed by 20 delegates. Points of order and proposals are also made in writing and one 'pro' and one 'con' speech, of 3 minutes duration each, are allowed on points of order, 5 minutes each on proposals, while 3 minutes are permitted to explain one's motives for voting in a certain manner. Reporters have 25 minutes for con-cluding statements.

28. At the Fourteenth Party Congress (December 1925), in connection with the debate on the opposition, Krupskaia attempted to argue against this rule, saying that 'the majority

The Jurisdiction of the Congress. As regards jurisdiction, the congress has the power of amending and revising the program and rules of the Party, it elects the Central Committee and other central Party organs, hears and confirms their reports, and 'determines the tactical line of the Party on the principal questions of current policy.'[29]

Operation in the Field of Domestic Affairs. Domestic policy predominated in the reports and debates. In the earlier part of the regime the questions that took up most of the deliberations dealt with the forms and forces of the new polity, items relative to: the structure, program, rules, resources, and internal arrangements of the Party; the 'conducting belts' of the dictatorship — the soviets, trade-unions, co-operatives, et cetera — and their interrelations with the Party; the application of the class and nationality principles to the constitutional order, et cetera. Gradually, from the end of the civil war on, economics — questions of finance, transport, trade, industry, and agriculture — came more and more to the fore and with the adoption of the Five-Year Plans they constitute the great bulk of the proceedings.

Role in Foreign-Policy Formulation. Foreign policy came before the congress primarily by two paths: the political report of the Central Committee, always considered the most important of all the reports and delivered by an outstanding member of the highest leadership,[30] and the report on behalf of the Party's delegation at the E.C.C.I. (Executive Committee of the Communist International), presented by a prominent Party

---

should not revel in the fact that it is the majority, but should impartially seek the right decision.' (*XIV S'ezd VKP(b),* pp. 165–6.) Her argument met, however, with a chorus of criticism claiming the principle as fully established since the earliest Bolshevik days: 'In a collective a question is decided by the majority and the minority must submit to the majority. This is a basic, Bolshevik rule of work.' (Andreev, ibid. p. 292.) 'The idea that the truth remains the truth is admissible in a philosophical club, but in the Party the decisions of the congress are obligatory also upon those who doubt the correctness of a decision . . . Our party is strong through the fact that the decisions of the majority are obligatory upon all not only in form, but in substance.' (Kalinin, ibid. p. 321.) 'And what does unity require? It requires that the minority should submit to the majority. Otherwise there is or can be no unity, no Party.' (Stalin, ibid. p. 508. See also ibid. pp. 167, 229, 287–8, 300, 417–19.)

29. Rules 31 and 29 of the 1939 and 1934 Comparty Rules. Earlier rules read 'determines the tactical lines of the Party on current questions.'

30. The first 5 reports, in 1918–22, were delivered by Lenin, the following 2, in 1923 and 1924, by Zinoviev, and the remaining 5 in 1925–39, by Stalin. The Foreign Commissar does not report to the Party congress on foreign policy, though on some rare occasion he may deliver an 'informational communication' — as Litvinov did at the Fifteenth Congress (1927) with regard to the work of the Soviet delegation at the preparatory disarmament commission in Geneva — which the congress 'takes note of.' (See *XV S'ezd VKP(b),* pp. 916–24.)

leader closely connected with Comintern work at the time.[31] The political report has evolved into an elaborate exposition, usually divided into three parts: the external situation of the U.S.S.R., its internal position, and the condition of the Party. The first part comprises the following elements:

(a) a statement on the international position of the Soviet state — an appraisal of the world situation and of the political and economic conditions and relationships of the major countries, and a diagnosis and prognosis with regard to the world tension level, i.e. the possibilities and probabilities of occurrence of wars and internal upheavals.

(b) a description, in broad and general terms, of the bright and dark sides of the Soviet position in this milieu, which usually involves brief references to the major treaties or other acts or actions of the Soviet state in the foreign area and a characterization of the sore spots, the outstanding threats in the policies or practices of other states affecting the U.S.S.R.

(c) an account of the fundamental pursuits of Soviet foreign policy, coupled with a warning to would-be aggressors against the Soviet Union, and expressed in language curt and simple enough to be converted into popular slogans.[32]

(d) an enumeration of the bases or pillars of Soviet foreign relations.

(e) a brief recapitulation of future tasks in foreign policy aimed at safeguarding the security and political-economic order of the U.S.S.R.

The rule became early established that, while a delegate to the Party congress has a right to acquaint himself directly or through a section or commission of the congress with the details of instructions given to Soviet diplomats by the Central Committee (i.e. its working collegia — the Political and Organizational Bureaus and Secretariat), it was not expedient or,

---

31. Four of these reports were made by Zinoviev, at the 8th, 10th, 11th, and 14th Congresses (1919, 1921, 1922, 1925); 1 by Radek, at the 9th Congress (1920); 3 by Bukharin, at the 12th, 13th, and 15th Congresses (1923, 1924, 1927); 1 by Molotov, at the 16th Congress (1930), and 2 by Manuilsky, at the 17th and 18th Congresses (1934, 1939).

32. 1930. 'We do not want a single foot of foreign land. But neither shall we surrender our land, even a single inch of our land to anyone.' (*XVI S'ezd VKP(b)*, p. 53.) 1934. Warning to would-be aggressors of 'a stunning rebuff to teach them not to poke their pig's snout into our Soviet garden again.' (Report to Seventeenth Party Congress, op. cit. p. 14.) 1939. 'We are not afraid of the threats of aggressors and are ready to deal two blows for every blow delivered by instigators of war who attempt to violate the Soviet borders.' (Report to Eighteenth Party Congress, op. cit. p. 23.) 'To be cautious and not allow our country to be drawn into conflict by warmongers who are accustomed to have others pull the chestnuts out of the fire for them.' (Ibid. p. 24.) These were warnings uttered by Stalin at the 16th, 17th, and 18th Party Congresses.

in practice, possible to present them at the congress.[33] And in point of fact there has, on the whole, been much less discussion and greater unanimity on questions of foreign policy than on any other items in these debates at the congress. With the sole exception of the debate at the Seventh Party Congress, assembled in March 1918 for the express purpose of passing upon the Brest-Litovsk Treaty, the overwhelming majority of the speakers at the succeeding congresses have dwelt on organizational relations, the nature and tasks of the economy, the various oppositions, and other domestic questions. References to foreign policy, when made in the debates on the political reports, have almost invariably been in praise of the line pursued by the Central Committee, only a bare few ever having spoken against it.[34] And of the resolutions of approval offered on these reports at the eleven congresses held since 1918, eight were adopted unanimously and the remaining three — the ninth (1920), tenth (1921), and fourteenth (1925) — by great majorities.[35]

As for the report of the Party's delegation at the E.C.C.I., it, too, was a long presentation as a rule, containing items on: changes in world economy and world politics and their effect on labor movements and the ebb and flow of revolutionary perspectives; the condition of the Comintern and its sections, its points of strength and weakness, deviations, causes of failure, and conditions for success; the growing threats of war without and menaces of internal reaction within states; and the requisite current tasks and tactics. Half of the time, from the Eighth to the Thirteenth Party Congresses (1919–24) and again at the last congress (1939) there were no debates at all on this report, and with only two exceptions — where the vote was by a great majority — the resolutions approving the line and activity of the Party's delegation at the E.C.C.I. were passed unanimously. When there were debates on this report, the number of participants was not large and consisted entirely of Comintern functionaries, guests from foreign sections, and a few veteran Party officials, all of whom, with but a rare exception, spoke in substantiation and support or expan-

---

33. Lenin, XXVII, pp. 226–7 (27 March 1922); *XIII S'ezd RKP(b)*, p. 57 (24 May 1924).

34. An example of one of the few times when issue was taken on foreign policy at the congress itself — whatever the differences in the pre-congress discussion — was Rakovsky's disagreement with Stalin's evaluation of the external situation at the Fourteenth and Fifteenth Congresses, in view of the Communist debacle in China and the rupture of Anglo-Soviet relations in 1927. (See *XV S'ezd VKP(b)*, pp. 182–3.)

35. Even in these 3 cases the indications were that it was the approval of the 'organizational' rather than the 'political' line of the Central Committee that the minority objected to, thus pointing to practically complete unanimity on foreign policy at the Party congress. (See *Protokoly Deviatogo S'ezda*, p. 97; *Protokoly X S'ezda*, pp. 138–43; *XIV S'ezd VKP(b)*, pp. 520–24.)

sion upon the subject matter of the report, rather than in opposition to it.[36]

To some extent, foreign policy items, especially threatening aspects of the external situation, were brought out in reports on military organization and speeches by the War Commissar and other military men at the congress. Their pronouncements on the condition of the armed forces and the state of preparedness served as warning signals to prospective violators of the Soviets' tranquility, giving notice of the mobilized might that would meet aggressors at the country's borders.[37]

Late Innovations in Congressional Procedure. Several innovations in procedure were introduced at the Seventeenth Party Congress (1934). Kirov's proposal to dispense with the usual framing of a resolution, and, in its place, 'adopt for execution, as Party law, all the postulates and conclusions of comrade Stalin's report,' was received with great acclaim, and the congress voted to approve the report and 'propose to all the Party organizations to guide themselves, in their work, by the theses and tasks advanced in this report of comrade Stalin.'[38] In view of the degree of unanimity displayed at the congress, the customary concluding remarks by the reporter, following debate, were also deemed unnecessary. And this practice was repeated at the last congress in 1939. 'Thus,' summarized *Pravda,* 'the Party, its supreme organ — the Eighteenth Congress — approved the political line and work of the Stalinist Central Committee and adopted for steady guidance, as immutable law, the directions of its leader and teacher.'[39]

The Basic Evolution and Position of the Party Congress. In general, the following features of development in the proceedings of the congress may be noted. The variety of agenda items has diminished. Since the First Congress the number of participants in debates has increased.[40] From the point of view of content, theory has receded before practice, and the high

---

36. See *XIII S'ezd RKP(b),* pp. 349–81 and *XIV, XV, XVI, XVII S'ezd VKP(b),* pp. 681–721, 605–734, 759–839, 323–50, respectively. The number of speakers in these debates was as follows: 2 at the 13th Congress, 5 at the 14th, 16 at the 15th, 13 at the 16th, and 9 at the 17th Congress.

37. Early Party congresses had special reports on military organization (1919, 1920, 1922). Later, some facts and figures of a general nature were occasionally given at the Party congress, mainly by the War Commissar. (See, e.g. *XVII S'ezd VKP(b),* pp. 224–35.) With the emergence of a definite threat of war a host of military speakers was arrayed at the last congress, the War Commissar frankly going into considerable detail, and all stressing the country's readiness to repel aggression. (See *Pravda,* 16–20 March 1939.)

38. *XVII S'ezd VKP(b),* pp. 252, 259–60.

39. See *Pravda,* 15 March 1939.

40. The number of speakers on the political report was as follows: Eighth Congress, 3; 9th — 16; 10th — 11; 11th — 16; 12th — 24; 13th — 16; 14th — 43; 15th — 43; 16th — 60; 17th — 57; 18th — 37.

theoretical formulations so prominent in the discussions of the earlier congresses have been crowded off by preoccupation with the consideration of
practical plans and programs. As for the tone of debate, while the stormy
thrust and parry of European parliamentary practice has never characterized the Soviet Party congress, considerable acrimony and argumentative-
ness were present in some of its proceedings during the first half of the
regime. Since then the discussions have run smoothly, uniformly, per-
meated with a spirit of complete unanimity. With the growth of its membership to unwieldy proportions, the element of deliberation at the congress has decreased while that of accounting by the participants has
increased, each speech, in most cases, being in fact a sort of miniature
report in itself on the fulfilment of the Party's directives — more particularly the economic quotas and objectives — in the speaker's own region —
a statement of achievements, defects, remedies, and promises of improvement.

Thus, the following conclusion seems warranted. Earlier in the regime,
the Party congress, meeting every year and in smaller numbers, was — in
a broad and general sense — an active participant in current policy determination, as a ratifying body of the ruling party. In the course of its
subsequent development, with its tremendous increase in membership,
rare convocations — only three meetings since 1927 — and altered manner
of deliberations, it became one of the policy-propagating organs. A high
consensus-building body or solemn *ad hoc* Party convention, as it were,
it was called from time to time to proclaim anew basic principles of polity
and lend the weight of its prestige to wide projects for the state's development and to the corresponding changes in socio-political arrangements.

(2) THE PARTY CONFERENCE

The Nature and Composition of the Party Conference. Partly to fill
the gap between the Party congresses, an All-Union Party Conference is
convoked by the Central Committee, by earlier provisions at least once a
year, later once in the interim between congresses, and by the last-adopted
rules (1939) again 'not less than once a year.' [41] From 1919 to 1926, except-

---

41. By a resolution of the Eighth Party Congress in March, and the Party rules adopted
in December 1919, the Party conference was to meet once in three months. (*VKP(b) v
Rezol.* I, pp. 312, 327–8.) This was changed to twice a year by a resolution of the
Tenth Party Congress in March 1921 (ibid. I, pp. 371–2) and to once a year in the
interim between congresses by the Party rules adopted in August 1922. (Ibid. I, p. 466,
rule 26.) As amended in December 1925, the rules read simply, 'once in the interim
between congresses.' (Ibid. II, p. 85, rule 27.) The new rules (1939) reintroduce the
provision for convocation of the conference not less than once a year in the interval
between congresses. (Rule 37.)

ing 1922, the conference met every year (twice in 1921), then at about two-and-a-half-year intervals (in 1929 and 1932), while in 1934 it was abolished altogether by the Seventeenth Party Congress. At the last congress (1939), it was again restored to a place in the Party structure. Composed of representatives of local Party organizations elected from among the regional and territorial Party committees and the Union-republic central committees of the Party, the conference constitutes a sort of conclave of the heads and highest functionaries of these bodies, and includes also leaders from the membership of the Party Central Committee.[42] Those members of the Central Committee who are not elected as delegates to the conference from local Party organizations can participate in it with the right of consultative voice. Numbering 118 delegates in 1919 at its first convocation following the establishment of Bolshevik rule, the composition of the conference increased at every gathering, attaining 911 representatives at the Seventeenth Party Conference, in 1932, while the last conference, held in February 1941, numbered 595 representatives, 457 of whom were voting delegates. The Party conference lasts three to four days on the average. Not differing markedly in procedure from the Party congress, it is a less solemn, less dignified, more simple body.

The Operation of the Conference. As regards function, it was originally provided that 'at these conferences the most important current questions before the Party are discussed.'[43] The new rules state that the objective of calling the conference is 'to discuss questions that arise concerning the policy of the Party' (rule 37). It should be noted here that they also give the Party conference the power to remove for cause individual members of the Central Committee, up to one fifth of its membership, replacing them with alternates and electing a corresponding number of the latter (rule 38).

As in the case of the congress, the practice of the conference shows that domestic questions took up most of its proceedings — items concerning the Party, the economy, and, to a lesser extent, the soviets, trade unions, and co-operatives. Yet, till 1926, reports and resolutions surveying the international situation and the condition of the Comintern figured prominently at the Party conferences.[44] The three conferences held since then

---

42. The 1939 Comparty Rules provide that the method of election and apportionment of representation to the conference are determined by the Central Committee (rule 37). This incorporates the actual practice, though no provisions on this point are given in the previous rules.

43. Resolution of the Eighth Party Congress, March 1919, *VKP(b) v Rezol.* I, p. 312.

44. Twelve reports bearing on foreign policy were made at the Party conferences in 1919–26: 2 political reports, 5 'on the international situation,' and 5 on the Comintern, there being

were preoccupied only with domestic matters, almost exclusively with questions of the national economy. There were fewer debates and even greater unanimity in the vote on resolutions than at the congresses.

The Place of the Conference in the Party Structure. Basically, the Party conference occupies a dependent position in the Party power scheme, the provision being that 'the decisions of the All-Union Conference must be ratified by the Central Committee,' as only decisions so ratified bind the Party organizations (rule 39, Comparty Rules 1939).[45] Its function, when it meets, is primarily that of an opinion-tapping and effort-mobilizing agency, helping the central leadership better to assess conditions, sentiments, and possibilities in the localities, to gauge the measure of the assembled officials' work, and to line them up in behalf of effective organization or execution of pending Party drives and undertakings.

3. THE CENTRAL COMMITTEE OF THE PARTY

(1) THE OPERATION OF THE CENTRAL COMMITTEE

The Organization and Composition of the Central Committee. The most important Party organs and indeed the most important bodies of the entire system of government are the Central Committee, and the Politbureau, Orgbureau, and Secretariat, constantly identified with the Central Committee in public reference and together with it comprising the summit of the Party pyramid.[46] Always elected by secret ballot at the Party congress, and standing in place of the congress in prestige and authority of decision during the interval between congresses, the Central Committee directs the entire work of the Party. The relevant provision of the Party rules read in full:

---

considerable interlapping of subject matter in them. Of these, 2 were delivered by Lenin, 5 by Zinoviev, 2 by Radek, and 1 each by Chicherin, Sokolnikov, and Bukharin.

45. As Lenin put it in February 1918 when he argued for the convocation of a congress rather than a conference to pass on the Brest-Litovsk Peace, on the ground that the decisions of a congress are, while those of a conference are not, binding on the Central Committee: 'the conference is only [a means of] catching the Party's opinion, which it is necessary to set [yet].' (See Lenin, xxii, pp. 245–6, and note 108.)

46. 'The Party,' said Lenin in 1920, 'is directed by a central committee of nineteen, while the current work in Moscow has to be done by still narrower collegia, namely the so-called "Orgbureau" (Organizational Bureau) and "Politbureau" (Political Bureau) composed of five C.C. members each, elected at the plenary sessions of the C.C. . . . not one important political or organizational question is decided by any one state institution in our republic without guiding instructions of the C.C. of the Party.' (Lenin, xxv, p. 192.)

The Central Committee during the interval between congresses, directs the entire work of the Party, represents the Party in its relations with other parties, organizations, and institutions, forms various Party institutions and guides their activities, appoints the editorial staffs of the central organs working under its control, and confirms the appointment of the editorial staffs of the Party organs of large local organizations, organizes and manages enterprises of public importance, distributes the forces and resources of the Party, and manages the central funds.

The Central Committee directs the work of the central Soviet and public organizations through the Party groups in them (rule 36, 1939 Comparty Rules).

Consisting of 15 members and 8 candidates in March 1918, the Central Committee has progressively grown in membership, becoming stabilized since 1927 at 71 members and, a little later, at 68 alternates or candidates, who replace dropping-out members and participate in plenary sessions with the right of a consultative voice.[47] At first the Central Committee was required to meet twice monthly, later once in two months, and now 'not less than once every four months.'[48] As far as published resolutions disclose, the Central Committee met on the average of three times a year, with sessions lasting about two to three days and the longest about a week. These are presided over by a presidium, which is supposed to represent the Central Committee when the latter does not sit.[49] The Committee itself sets the dates of the regular plenary sessions. According to a congressional resolution of 1923, a date thus set can be changed only in exceptional cases, by the joint decision of the Orgbureau and Politbureau, while extra plenums are convocable by decision of the Politbureau or upon demand by one fourth of its members.[50] On occasion, the roster of leading Party and state officials that comprise its membership was joined in session by invitees from among the ranks of important Party workers in the national republics, or joint plenums were held with the Party's Central Control

47. There were 50 candidates elected in 1927, 67 in 1930, and 68 in 1934 and again in 1939. The composition of the Central Committee is determined by the Party congress, and until recently replacements by alternates were supposed to be made 'in the order determined by the congress.' (Rule 30, 1934 Comparty Rules. Same in previous ones.) This proviso is dropped by the new rules, which institute a form of replacement by the Party conference. The right of participation with consultative voice was first introduced for candidates in 1921. (See *VKP(b) v Rezol.* I, p. 372.)

48. By resolution of the Eighth Party Congress and the 1919 Party rules, two sessions a month were required. (*VKP(b) v Rezol.* I, p. 312.) In 1921, the Tenth Party Congress modified the requirement to once in two months, stating that 'for the guidance of current organizational and political work the system of the Org- and Politbureau of the Central Committee is preserved.' (Ibid. I, p. 372.) And this frequency was called for by the Party rules until changed in 1934 to 'not less than one plenary session every four months' (rule 31), which is also the present provision (rule 33).

49. Harper, op. cit. p. 65; Webb, op. cit. I, p. 366.

50. See *VKP(b) v Rezol.* I, p. 512.

Commission. The agenda for the sessions is prepared by the Politbureau and pertinent materials are distributed beforehand to the members of the Central Committee.

The Scope of Central Committee Decisions. All the most important political and organizational questions not in need of immediate solution are supposed to be reserved for consideration by the Central Committee, and the Politbureau is enjoined, especially the last two to three weeks before the scheduled Central Committee sessions, to transfer such questions to the plenum of the latter.[51] The plenum of the Central Committee hears reports of the Politbureau, Orgbureau, and other organs on past activity or projected action, discusses their content, and votes upon the theses proposed. While details on procedure are not available, since verbatim records of proceedings at the Central Committee are not made public as a rule, some of the reports or speeches in the discussions may appear in the press, and the resolutions, unless of a secret nature, are published and often given wide publicity.

As these resolutions indicate, a limited number of questions is taken up at a time, and from the quantitative standpoint questions of the economy have occupied first place, followed in order by questions of the Party structure, Soviet structure, 'work in the village,' foreign policy, the Comintern and its auxiliaries, other 'political' questions, matters of the trade-union and co-operative movements, and miscellaneous items. Elections to the top working organs and other appointments are in a class by themselves and are frequently scheduled on separate agenda. Few of the resolutions on foreign policy are given *in extenso,* the volume of published resolutions indicating merely that the reports or informational communications on the foreign situation were approved or noted.[52] For the period

51. Ibid. 1, p. 511. As between the two, the vast majority of policy questions falls in fact within the orbit of decision of the Politbureau. Thus, to illustrate from the early period, when the practice — increased since — had taken root, during the year covering 25 April 1923 to 1 May 1924, the Politbureau held 5 times as many sessions as the Central Committee, 86 as against 17. Out of 1,914 points on the agendas of these sessions, 1,815 were before the first, 99 before the second body; while of a total number of 3,923 questions considered, 3,671 were passed upon by the Politbureau, and only 252 by the Central Committee. (See *XIII S'ezd RKP(b),* p. 77. Also *infra,* pp. 160–3.)

52. Typical summary statements are: 'The reports of c. Zinoviev about the situation in foreign comparties, of c. Litvinov about the international situation, and the communication of c. Tomsky about the congress of English trade unions were taken note of by the plenum.' (3–10 October 1925, *VKP(b) v Rezol.* II, p. 33.) 'Having heard the communication of the Politbureau about the decisions it has adopted in connection with the last international events (the strike of the English miners, the *coup d'état* in Poland, the events in China, etc.), the plenum approved the activity of the Politbureau and of the C.P.S.U.(B) delegation in the E.C.C.I. in the international question.' (14–23 July

since the middle of 1928, no references to foreign-policy decisions by the Central Committee are contained therein.

The Established Conception of the Central Committee. There was more strife in the Central Committee during the earlier part of the regime than in either the congress or conference of the Party, since it met more often and served as a sort of arbiter on policy differences in the interim between congresses. And the recurrent tug of war within it came to be regarded almost as a tradition, albeit an unpleasant one.[53] The fight for monolithism in the Party, however, led to the firmer establishment of the conception of the Central Committee as director of the Party rather than as mere registrar and mediator between divergent currents within it, and to its more frequent public designation as managerial staff of the Party and the revolution.[54]

(2) THE POSITION OF THE CENTRAL COMMITTEE IN THE PARTY STRUCTURE

The Extent of the Central Committee's Accountability. The Central Committee is accountable to the Party congress. In addition, the Central Committee has a recognized duty to inform the lower Party organizations of its work.[55] But the extent of such information is left to its own discre-

---

1926, ibid. p. 106.) However, on the occasion of what was regarded as a grave threat from the outside, in July–August 1927, an extensive resolution 'About the International Situation' was published. (See ibid. pp. 176–85.)

53. 'In the course of the work within the C.C. during the past six years there have arisen (and could not but arise) certain habits and certain traditions of intra-Central-Committee struggle, which at times create an atmosphere that is not so good . . . and here I noted that the intervention of people from the localities often decides everything. We need people who are independent of these traditions and of these personal influences, in order that, entering the C.C. and bringing there their experience of positive work and ties with the localities, they should serve as a cement capable of welding the C.C. together as a single and inseparable collective which directs our party.' (Stalin, 19 April 1923, *XII S'ezd RKP(b)*, pp. 182–3.)

54. *VKP(b) v Rezol.* 1, pp. 553–4; *XVI S'ezd VKP(b)*, pp. 203, 208, 377.

55. In 1919 it was provided that, while matters subject to wide publicity were to be published in the newspapers every two weeks if possible, the Central Committee should send the Party committees of the capitals and the provinces a written report of its activity not less than once a month. (*VKP(b) v Rezol.* 1, pp. 312, 328.) The presumed content of such appears from a resolution of the Tenth Party Congress (1921) to the effect that: 'the Central Committee shall inform all the provincial committees in special sealed letters concerning the internal and international political situation, the condition of the Party and the nearest tasks placed upon them by the Central Committee.' (Ibid. 1, p. 372.) By the 1922 Party rules the Central Committee was to send a written report to the provincial committees once in two months (ibid. 1, p. 466), while a 1924 decision provided that the regional and provincial committees were to receive the verbatim reports of the Central Committee's plenary sessions (ibid. 1, p. 571). All subsequently adopted party rules state simply that 'the Central Committee keeps the Party organizations

tion, just as, in the last analysis, the Central Committee itself decides what, if any, questions of high policy it would give for discussion to the lower levels of the Party pyramid. The *raison d'état* behind this position was early thrown into relief by Stalin's lengthy exception to Lutovinov's conception of democracy within the Party:

He [Lutovinov] wants real democracy, that all, at least the most important questions should be discussed in all the cells from bottom up, that the whole Party should get going on every question and should take part in the consideration of that question. But, comrades . . . with such an arrangement our party would be transformed into a discussion club of eternally jabbering and never-deciding [people], while our party must, above all, be an acting one, because we are in power. Besides . . . there is no reason to suppose that the enemies who surround us are not engaged in some preparatory work for blockade or intervention. That is the situation. Can we in such circumstances carry all questions of war and peace into the street? Yet, to discuss a question in 20,000 cells means to carry the question out into the street . . . It must be remembered, that in the conditions of being surrounded by enemies, a sudden stroke on our part, an unexpected maneuver, speed, decide everything. What would have become of us, if, instead of discussing our political campaign for the Lausanne Conference in an intimate circle of trusted persons of the Party, we had carried all that work out into the street, revealed our cards? Enemies would have discounted all the minuses and pluses, undermined our campaign, and we should have departed from Lausanne in shame. What would become of us if, questions of war and peace — the most important of all important questions, we should first bring out into the street . . . Why, we should be given a sound thrashing to the count of two. It is clear, comrades, that for organizational as well as political reasons Comrade Lutovinov's democracy is a utopia, a democracy of Manilovism.[56] It is unfit and unnecessary.[57]

The Basic Evolution and Position of the Central Committee. To conclude, the Central Committee, originally a small, compact organ, and *the* deciding body of the Party, has become more and more of a ratifier rather than an out-and-out decision-maker, operating to confirm, periodically, important decisions, especially when a vital project is at stake or when lack of complete unity of point of view in the Politbureau, et cetera, make its sanction desirable. Its developmental tendency was aptly noted and candidly characterized by Lenin as early as January 1923:

The plenum of the C.C. of our party has already disclosed its tendency to develop into a kind of higher Party conference. It meets on the average not oftener than once

---

regularly informed of its work.' (Rules 28, 35, 41 of the 1925, 1934, 1939 Comparty Rules, respectively.)

56. Perhaps best translatable as 'a dream world' or 'unfounded phantasy,' the term is derived from the personality pattern of a Gogol character, Manilov, of an indolent, sentimental, unrealistic make-up.

57. *XII S'ezd RKP(b)*, pp. 181–2 (April 1923).

in two months, and the current work is, as is known, carried on in the name of the C.C. by our Politbureau, our Orgbureau, our Secretariat, et cetera. I think that we should complete this path onto which we entered and definitely convert the C.C. plenums into higher Party conferences, gathering once in two months, with the participation of the C.C.C. [Central Control Commission] in it.[58]

Inasmuch as the frequency of Central Committee sessions has ultimately decreased further by one half, while the total number of its members and candidates has tripled since then, the characterization above holds even more true today. Thus, the Central Committee can be assessed as an opinion-tapping and policy-crystallizing organ. Helping to check up periodically — through the leaders from all parts of the Union who make up its membership — on the state of execution of policies previously adopted, it also serves to confirm policies currently enacted or approved by the Politbureau, Orgbureau, and the Secretariat.

---

58. Lenin, XXVII, p. 402.

Chapter VIII · The Party Structure (II)

1. THE POLITICAL BUREAU

(1) THE POSITION OF THE POLITBUREAU IN THE PARTY STRUCTURE

The Topmost Working Organs of the Central Committee. Vital stations of control and policy determination at the peak of the Party structure are the topmost working organs organized by the Central Committee: 'a Political Bureau for political work, an Organizational Bureau for the general guidance of the organizational work, a Secretariat for current work of an organizational-executive nature.'[1] The first two meet several times weekly, while the last named is in daily attendance.[2] Numbering five in each in 1919, the membership of the bureaus has remained fairly restricted. At present there are ten and eleven members, respectively, in the Politbureau and Orgbureau, with four candidates in each. Except for occasional fluctuations, the membership of the bureaus and Secretariat stood, according to available figures, as follows:[3]

---

1. Rule 34 of the 1939 Comparty Rules. Same since 1922 and a similar one in the 1919 rules. The bureaus are usually referred to by their abbreviated version — Politbureau, Orgbureau. A proposal by Preobrazhensky at the Eleventh Party Congress to form also an Economic Bureau, or Econombureau, was rejected by Lenin as impractical. (See *Protokoly Odinnadtsatago S'ezda RKP(b)*, pp. 87–91, and Lenin, xxvii, p. 264.)

2. Originally, in March 1919, it was provided that the Orgbureau should meet 'not less than three times a week.' (*VKP(b) v Rezol.* i, p. 313.) Otherwise, there is no mention anywhere of any required frequency of sessions on the part of the bureaus. During the year of March 1919–March 1920 the Politbureau had 72 sessions, i.e. an average of 6 a month. (*Protokoly Deviatogo S'ezda RKP(b)*, pp. 486–7.) Nineteen sessions were joint ones with the Orgbureau. In 1923–4 it held 86 sessions, or an average of over 7 a month. (*XIII S'ezd RKP(b)*, p. 77.) Since its published work-plans for 1926 and 1928 also indicate that at least 2 to 3 and sometimes 5 to 6 or even more major reports were to be presented to the Politbureau monthly, it is obvious that, with other current work added, the Politbureau meets not less than several times weekly, except during the summer vacations, short-notice sessions being called as occasion demands.

3. See *VKP(b) v Rezol.* i, pp. 312–13, 466, 511–12, 638; ii, pp. 93–4, 270, 444–5, 502, 607, 626; *Pravda*, 23 March 1939; *Bolshevik*, No. 6 (March 1946), p. 3.

YEAR	POLITBUREAU		ORGBUREAU		SECRETARIAT	
	M.	C.	M.	C.	M.	C.
1919	5		5		6	
1923	7	4	7	4	6	
1924	7	6	11	6	5	
1925	9	8	11	5	5	2
1927	9	8	13	7	5	3
1934	10	5	10	2	4	
1939	9	2	9		4	
1946	10	4	11	4	5	

In function, standing, and interrelationship the three organs have undergone a considerable evolution.

The Conception and Place of the Politbureau in the Party Hierarchy. The Politbureau early emerged as the most authoritative of the three organs. The gradation of authority between the three as intended in the earlier period is evidenced by a 1923 provision to the effect that decisions of the Secretariat can be appealed to the Orgbureau while those of the Orgbureau can be appealed to the Politbureau.[4] Originally formed on 23 October 1917, at the time when the seizure of power was decided upon by the Bolsheviks, the Politbureau, along with the Orgbureau, was established as a permanently functioning organ by a resolution of the Eighth Party Congress in March 1919. A year later, Lenin reported to the following congress that 'the Politbureau decided all questions of international and internal policy' during the period that had elapsed.[5] Thus, the Politbureau came to be designated as the 'directing collective' or 'kernel' of the Central Committee.[6] Despite the conception of the Party congress, which was pointed out earlier, the Politbureau is viewed, in fact, as the highest Party organ in the country.[7]

While primarily political matters dominated its sessions during the so-called War-Communism Period, economic questions came up for its atten-

---

4. *VKP(b) v Rezol.* I, p. 512.

5. Lenin, xxv, pp. 95, 597, note 63.

6. In speeches at the Party congress, etc., the Politbureau was referred to as 'the directing collective,' 'the Bolshevik kernel,' and 'the leading organ' — of the Central Committee — and also as 'leading center,' 'leading summit,' 'fundamental Leninist kernel,' 'directing kernel' or 'general staff' of Leninism; 'general staff,' 'directing staff' of the Party, etc. (See e.g., *XIV S'ezd VKP(b)*, pp. 114, 292, 298, 453, 459, 461, 485; *XVI S'ezd VKP(b)*, p. 230.)

7. 'Our Politbureau of the C.C. is the organ of operative direction of all branches of socialist construction.' (Kaganovich, February 1934, *XVII S'ezd VKP(b)*, p. 564.) 'The Politbureau is sovereign as it is, it is higher than all the organs of the C.C., except the plenum.' (Stalin, December 1925, *XIV S'ezd VKP(b)*, p. 508.) 'The Politbureau is the highest organ not of the state but of the Party and the Party is the highest directing force of the state.' (Stalin, ibid. p. 51.) 'The Politbureau is the highest Party organ in the country.' (Ordzhonikidze, ibid. p. 222. Cf. the conception of the Party congress, *supra*, p. 144.)

tion more and more following the introduction of the NEP. In April 1923, the Party congress ordered specifically that planned direction by the Politbureau of the state and especially of the economic organs should be expanded. Yet, because of the intra-Party situation at the time, this directive was not fully realized until 1925–6, when the fundamental attitude prevailing toward policy-determination by the Politbureau was that it inevitably embraced economic as well as political matters, and when the greater application of the planning principle in the operation of the Politbureau made possible better co-ordination of its work with that of the Council of People's Commissars and the Council of Labor and Defense.[8]

(2) THE SCOPE OF THE POLITBUREAU'S COMPETENCE

The Range of Decision-Making by the Politbureau. The extraordinary scope of the Politbureau's field of decision is illustrated by its published work-plans for 1926 and 1928. The list of organs scheduled to report before it included the State Planning Board, the Supreme Council of National Economy, the Finance, Trade, Justice, Labor, Agriculture, and Communications commissariats, the Central Council of Trade Unions, the State Political Administration, the Revolutionary War Council, several high Party committees, a number of governmental and Central Committee commissions, the Orgbureau, and a commission set up by the Politbureau itself.[9] The many subjects covered nearly ran the gamut of public policy with regard to the political, economic, and social order, taking up such spheres of action as the party and Soviet structures, the territorial-administrative set-up, industry, agriculture, transport, budget, credit and finance, trade, labor, co-operatives, education, national defense, et cetera. A number of the reports were checked by supplementary co-reports of the organs of verification — the Central Control Commission and the Workmen-Peasants Inspection Commissariat — while others were carried over to the plenum of the Central Committee. Interestingly enough, while reports were scheduled on such items as the export-import and foreign-cur-

---

8. *XV S'ezd VKP(b)*, pp. 105–6. Efforts at unified economic direction through more direct participation of the Politbureau in the solution of economic questions, to be implemented by delegating Stalin and Kuibyshev to the Council of Labor and Defense, were opposed by Kamenev, head of the Council at the time, and for a while there was created instead a special consultation on economic questions by the Politbureau. (See *XIV S'ezd VKP(b)*, pp. 337–40.)

9. *VKP(b) v Rezol.* II, pp. 103–5, 283. Lenin frowned upon the practice of profuse commission-forming by the Politbureau, and it has evidently diminished considerably in later years. (See Kuibyshev's statement at the Thirteenth Party Congress, *XIII S'ezd RKP(b)*, pp. 281–2.)

rency plans, the structure of the foreign-trade apparatus, the state of defense of the country, the condition of the war industry, and the condition and structure of the Red Army, no reports either by the Narkomindel (the Commissariat for Foreign Affairs) or any special commission on foreign policy as such were listed.[10] That, however, was not because of any lack of consideration of such questions by the Politbureau, but because, on the contrary, a particularly close, direct, and continual relationship existed between the Politbureau and the Narkomindel in the conduct and control of foreign affairs.

The Politbureau-Narkomindel Relationship in the Conduct of Foreign Affairs. The understanding has early developed that problems or conditions bearing even remotely on foreign policy — from the status of foreign correspondents within the country to questions of political and economic relations and military alliances with other states — are of particular concern to the Politbureau and require its decision or sanction before formal state action is taken. Consequently, affairs of the Narkomindel constituted, in fact, an important part of the Politbureau's agenda.[11] And Lenin considered this fusion of functions of a Party and a Soviet organ so singularly beneficial that he held it up as a model arrangement:

Did anyone fail to note [wrote Lenin in March 1923] that in a commissariat like the Narkomindel such amalgamation is extremely useful and is practiced from the very beginning? Are not petty as well as large-scale questions of 'moves' on our part in answer to 'moves' of foreign powers in order to forestall, let us say, shrewdness — to avoid a less decorous expression — on their part, discussed in the Politbureau from the Party standpoint? And is not this elastic fusion of Soviet and Party [elements] the source of the extraordinary force that our [foreign] policy possesses? I think that that which has justified itself, which has become consolidated in our foreign policy and turned into a custom that no longer calls forth any doubts in this sphere, would be just as appropriate (and I think even more appropriate) with regard to our entire state apparatus.[12]

Other Aspects of the Politbureau's Work. The Comintern angle of its international politics was implemented by the Politbureau through the

10. The 1928 work-plan lists a report on the program of the Comintern without indicating the organ reporting.
11. Even in 1923–4, i.e. before relations with other states had become as extensive as in later years, matters of the Narkomindel occupied second place among the questions that preoccupied the Politbureau. Quantitatively the percentages stood as follows: (1) economic questions — 26.8; (2) questions of the Narkomindel — 17.2; (3) questions of the Party structure — 14; (4) questions of the Soviet structure — 13.5; (5) personnel appointments — 9.7; (6) political questions — 7.3; (7) Comintern, Profintern — 4.2; (8) questions of the co-operative movement — 1.8; (9) questions of the trade-union movement — 1.1; (10) miscellaneous — 4.4. (See *XIII S'ezd RKP(b)*, p. 77.)
12. Lenin, XXVII, p. 413.

C.P.S.U.(B) representation at the E.C.C.I., the members of the delegation being appointed by it, working under its control, and referring all policy differences back to it. And as the directing organ of the leading party of the Comintern, the Politbureau exercised a dominant influence upon the tactics, policy, and personnel of the former.[13] Also, though evidently in a lesser degree and on a higher plane than in earlier years, the Politbureau plays the role of judge and adjuster of jurisdictional conflicts and differences of opinion on projects and procedures between top officials of the state.[14]

The minutes of the Politbureau are kept secret. Nevertheless, Central Committee members not entering the Politbureau, as well as members of the Presidium of the Central Control Commission, were accorded the right of being supplied with documents of the Politbureau.[15] In peacetime, members are, as a rule, within easy reach for instant convocation, and they not only vote upon but record their signatures to the resolutions adopted.[16] Members of the Central Committee who are not also Politbureau members are supposed to have access to the sessions of the latter, with the right of consultative voice. Occasionally, particularly when attempts to iron out grievous disagreements among the leaders were involved, joint sessions with the Presidium of the Central Control Commission were held by the Politbureau.

The Politbureau is considered accountable to the Central Committee. Originally, a biweekly report by the Politbureau to the Central Committee was required. With the practice of rarer sessions by the latter, it was provided in 1923 that the Politbureau should present a report at each Central Committee plenum concerning its activity during the interval.[17]

---

13. See e.g. *XIII S'ezd RKP(b)*, pp. 335, 337 (May 1924); *XIV S'ezd VKP(b)*, pp. 641, 661, 663–4, 689, 697, 698, 709 (December 1925); *XV S'ezd VKP(b)*, pp. 580–81 (December 1927). For the rare instance of a complaint of insufficient preoccupation by the Politbureau with Comintern questions, see *XIV S'ezd VKP(b)*, p. 685.

14. At the Eleventh Party Congress (March 1922) Lenin complained that 'while it is necessary to carry to the Politbureau all difficult state problems,' an end must be put to the practice where 'everything is being dragged from the Sovnarkom to the Politbureau.' He asked the congress to confirm directives to the effect that 'It is necessary to free the Politbureau and C.C. of petty matters and increase the work of responsible officials. It is necessary that the People's Commissars should answer for their work and not, as is the case, that they first go to the Sovnarkom and then [appeal] to the Politbureau. Formally we cannot abolish the right to complain to the C.C. [i.e. the Politbureau], because our party is the sole governmental party. What is necessary here is to cut short every appeal in minor matters, but it is also necessary to raise the prestige of the Sovnarkom in this respect . . .' (Lenin, xxvii, pp. 250, 257–8.)

15. See *VKP(b) v Rezol.* i, pp. 511–12.

16. Louis Fischer, *Men and Politics*, p. 233.

17. See *VKP(b) v Rezol.* i, pp. 312–13, 511.

2. THE ORGANIZATIONAL BUREAU AND SECRETARIAT

(I) THE ORGBUREAU

The Sphere of Decision of the Orgbureau. The guidance of the organizational work, which the Orgbureau was to exercise in accordance with the erstwhile division of functions, meant general direction of the various departments attached to the Central Committee 'for the practical work of carrying out Party decisions.' It entailed the effectuation of measures to maintain the Party's role and influence among the toiling strata, the nationalities, women, youth, et cetera, and especially the distribution of the Party's forces in industry, agriculture, Soviet institutions, the Red Army, et cetera.[18]

As regards the departments of the Central Committee, it should be pointed out that departments for special forms of Party work — among women, youth, nationalities, et cetera — have been organized in the Secretariat of the Central Committee all along. While at the time of the Sixteenth Party Congress (1930), the central apparatus was reorganized on the functional principle, it was decided at the following congress (1934), to set the departments up along production rather than functional lines, i.e. to concentrate within each department all of the Party work on organization, personnel, propaganda, and supervision of fulfilment of Party decisions for a given branch. As announced in 1939, the organization of departments, though combining both the functional and production principles, is more a return to the former. It consists of the following: the Administration of Cadres; the Administration of Propaganda and Agitation; the Organizational-Instructional Department; the Agricultural Department; the Department of Schools; and the Political Administrations of the Army, Navy, and Transport, considered in status as departments of the Central Committee. For most of these, corresponding departments exist in the Party organizations of the localities.[19]

The sphere of decision of the Orgbureau was never either completely

---

18. In general, for items relating to the work of the Orgbureau, see *VKP(b) v Rezol.* I, pp. 313, 327, 372, 407, 575–6, 638, 649; II, p. 194; *Protokoly IX S'ezda RKP(b)*, pp. 41–2; *XV S'ezd VKP(b)*, pp. 92–3.

19. See the following of the Comparty Rules per year adopted: 17 for 1919, 17 for 1922, 19 and 78 for 1925, 25 and 52 for 1934, and 27, 35, and 67 for 1939; also Stalin's reports at the Seventeenth and Eighteenth Party Congresses, op. cit. pp. 81–92 and 55–65, respectively; Vladimirsky, in *XVI S'ezd VKP(b)*, pp. 176–7; Kaganovich, in *XVII S'ezd VKP(b)*, pp. 561–2.

autonomous or clearly and absolutely defined. For, as Lenin pointed out only a year after their establishment, no strict delimitation of operation between the Politbureau and Orgbureau was possible, because of the impossibility of any mechanical separation of the political and organizational. Politics and organization are in fact inseparable in that no policy can be carried into execution without being expressed in the appointment and transfer of personnel. Consequently, any organizational question may take on political significance, and vice versa.[20] Hence it became the established practice to remove any problem that could be assessed as political from the Orgbureau to the Politbureau for decision.[21] From the standpoint of competence, the Orgbureau also lost some ground to the Secretariat, which was associated with it in the supervision of the Central Committee departments. In fact, the Secretariat largely superseded the Orgbureau as active daily overseer of the work of these departments. In general, the Secretariat rose tremendously in status and stature.

---

20. Lenin, xxv, pp. 94, 112; also xxvii, p. 264. The view that has evolved is that while organization is secondary to politics, success requires a skilful combination of both. In May 1924, Stalin maintained that, provided the Party's policy is right, it can never perish of organizational shortcomings: 'The basis of Party life and Party work does not consist in the organizational forms that it takes or may take at a given moment, but in the politics of the Party, in its domestic and foreign policy. If the Party's policy is correct, if it correctly posits the political and economic questions that are of decisive importance for the working class, then organizational defects cannot have any decisive significance, policy will come to the rescue.' (*XIII S'ezd RKP(b)*, pp. 245–6.) Later expressions, however, modify the emphasis. 'After the correct line has been given, after a correct solution of a problem has been found, success depends on the manner in which the work is organized, on the organization of the struggle for the application of the Party's line, on the proper selection of workers, on supervising the fulfilment of decisions of the leading organs. Without this the correct line of the Party and the correct solutions are in danger of being severely damaged. More than that, after the correct political line has been given, the organizational work decides everything, including the fate of the political line itself, i.e. its success or failure.' (Stalin, January 1934, *XVII S'ezd VKP(b)*, p. 33; see also his report at the Eighteenth Party Congress, op. cit. p. 58.) 'Lenin always stressed the subservient role of the organizational practice of the Party to its politics . . . Without an able combination of correct policies with correct organizational practice we would never have achieved the tremendous successes of which c. Stalin reported yesterday.' (Kaganovich, June 1930, *XVI S'ezd VKP(b)*, p. 112.) 'If organizational work built on a neglect of politics is bad, politics that does not find its embodiment in organizational work is also bad.' 'Only the subordination of organizational policy to the correct political line . . . only an elastic combination of politics and organizational tasks . . . would secure the success of the Party.' (Manuilsky, ibid. pp. 758–9, 762; see also p. 786.)

21. A declaration of even one Central Committee member, for whatever reasons, was sufficient, said Lenin, to have a question considered political and transferred to the Politbureau. (xxv, pp. 94, 112; xvii, p. 264.)

(2) THE SECRETARIAT

The Secretariat's Jurisdiction. In March 1919, the Secretariat consisted of one responsible secretary — a member of the Orgbureau — and five technical secretaries. A year later it was decided to strengthen the Secretariat by bringing into it three Central Committee members for permanent work and 'to transfer to the jurisdiction of the Secretariat as thus composed current questions of an organizational and executive nature, while preserving for the Orgbureau . . . the general direction of the organizational work of the Central Committee.' [22] The provision was embodied in the Party rules of 1922. It was at this point that the Secretariat entered upon a path of thorough transformation.

The Cardinal Transformation of the Secretariat. As Lenin explained in March 1920, in order to assure co-ordination and consistency between the decisions of the Politbureau and Orgbureau, it was found necessary that the responsible secretary, or Secretary-General as he came to be called, be a member of both bureaus. But the understanding had been that the Secretariat was a purely 'executive organ' of the Central Committee, that the Secretary-General was solely and exclusively an executor of the will of the Central Committee, only carrying out decisions of the latter and of its collegia — the Orgbureau and Politbureau.[23] The subsequent development of the Secretariat, however, transcended this early understanding. Stalin was appointed to the post of Secretary-General in May 1922. And here a phenomenon not unfamiliar in other polities — under conditions when a particularly strong personality becomes associated with a focally placed office — came into play. Structure plus personality yielded a new political equation. Daily attendance by the Secretariat upon current organizational-executive problems meant active charge of the work of the central Party apparatus, constant contact with the local Party organizations and officials, and vigilant check on the work and status of Party men everywhere. As it later developed, it also meant the integration by the Secretary-General of the operation of the various Central Committee de-

---

22. *VKP(b) v Rezol.* I, pp. 313, 352–3. The Secretariat consisted of 5 members in 1924–30, having several candidates at times. From the end of the latter date it was composed of 4 members. In March 1946 a Central Committee announcement again indicated a membership of 5 in the Secretariat. One of these secretaries, Stalin, has been the Secretary-General since 1922. (For items relating to the structure, composition, and function of the Secretariat, see ibid. I, pp. 313, 327, 352–3, 362, 363, 407, 466, 511–12, 638; II, pp. 93–4, 270, 607; *XV S'ezd VKP(b)*, pp. 108–9; *XVI S'ezd VKP(b)*, pp. 172, 175–7; *Pravda,* 12 March 1939.)

23. Lenin, xxv, p. 94; *Protokoly IX S'ezda RKP(b)*, p. 33.

partments, his overriding of departmentalism in attitude, and the effecting of an all-party approach in their joint or several treatment of parallel tasks.[24] Add the fact that in this plexus of Party-state activity the Secretary-General was required to be in continuing touch with both the Politbureau and Orgbureau for the very purpose of bridging their functions, and it is obvious that structurally the Secretariat was the embryonic hub of the Party with all the prerequisites for becoming a focal point of control.

Into this potential pivot Stalin stepped early in 1922, just at a time when the end of the period of civil war and intervention made possible fuller assertion of the Party's role in all spheres of the country's life. He brought with him to his new position not only an extremely vigorous, determined, and able personality, but a political experience born of many years of intensive Party work. He also had an unusually specialized knowledge of the nationality and peasantry problems, garnered from close study dating to pre-World War I days and from six years of administration of the Commissariat for Nationalities, and a trouble-shooter's understanding of the minutiae of the state machinery, acquired in his direction of the Workman-Peasant Inspection Commissariat.[25] It was this combination of office and man that changed the nature of the Secretariat, transforming it from an executant agency into a mighty policy-making organ.

The Struggle over the Secretariat's Role. Like many another political transformation in the Party, the change did not occur without a struggle. At a meeting of a number of Party leaders called together by Zinoviev in the summer of 1923, two alternate plans were broached: either to make the Secretariat a purely servicing organ, or, on the contrary, to 'politicize' it by bringing several Politbureau members into it so that it should become 'something in the nature of a small Politbureau.' The second plan was preferred and was forwarded to Stalin, but in subsequent conversations with him his counterproposal — to introduce three Politbureau mem-

---

24. As the Central Auditing Commission's report to the Sixteenth Party Congress showed, a certain parallel in the work of these departments is unavoidable. If the Organizational-Instructional Department supervises the work of the Party groups in non-Party organizations, so does the Department of Cadres by its allocation of the necessary officials. Likewise, the duties of the former department and those of the Department of Propaganda cross and coalesce in such tasks as mass campaigns, control of the shock-brigade, and socialist-competition movements, etc. But it is the presiding secretary who links up the work of the separate departments in an all-round approach to the tasks performed. (See *XVI S'ezd VKP(b)*, pp. 176–7.)

25. Stalin was Commissar for Nationalities from the moment that the Commissariat for Nationalities was formed up to the time of its liquidation in 1923. From March 1919 to May 1922 he was also Commissar for Workman-Peasant Inspection.

bers into the Orgbureau instead — was adopted.[26] Of the three named, Zinoviev, Trotsky, and Bukharin, only the first attended a few sessions of the Orgbureau, and nothing came of the attempt.

In December 1925 the issue was reopened at the Fourteenth Party Congress. Reviving the first of the plans, Zinoviev, Kamenev, et cetera, now in opposition, argued against the joining up of the political and organizational work in the Secretariat and called for a rearrangement to make the Politbureau 'really sovereign' and the Secretariat 'servicing and subordinate to the Politbureau' and merely executing technically the decisions of the latter. The theoretical potency of these arguments for structural change was largely vitiated, however, by the opposition's simultaneous attacks against the personality of the Secretary-General. Pointing up the personal angle behind the proposals, the majority of the congress completely rejected them. Some contended that the Secretariat is in fact subordinate to the Politbureau — appointments of officials of regional rank, for instance, require Politbureau confirmation, et cetera — while others insisted that the fusion of functions in the Secretariat was perfectly feasible, and that it was neither necessary nor desirable to reduce the Secretariat to the position of a technical executor of the will of the Politbureau. And Stalin himself also questioned the utility of 'technicizing' the Secretariat, expressing serious doubt whether a purely technical Secretariat would be capable of laying the groundwork for the solution of the many problems which it was required to get ready for the bureaus.[27]

(3) THE SECRETARY-GENERAL

The Interlocking Directorate under the Secretary-General. The subsequent evolution of the three organs marks their growing together into an interlocking, closely knit directorate, in which the Secretary-General exercises a dominant influence. While, from the standpoint of membership, the Secretariat and Orgbureau have often served as steppingstones to the Politbureau, the tendency has emerged to arrange double and even triple membership for the secretaries, i.e. to have them enter two or all three organs in order to facilitate the integration of their operation.[28] The

---

26. *XIV S'ezd VKP(b)*, pp. 455–7.

27. Ibid. pp. 274–5, 297–8, 335–6, 374–5, 396–8, 401, 468, 484–5, 506.

28. Of the four secretaries elected in 1934 — Stalin, Kaganovich, Kirov, and Zhdanov — the first 3 were also members of both bureaus, while the last-named was only in the Orgbureau. Of the 4 elected in 1939 — Stalin, Andreev, Zhdanov, and Malenkov — the first 3 entered the two bureaus also, while the last was a member of the Orgbureau, but not of the Politbureau. Currently, 3 of the 5 secretaries — Stalin, Malenkov, and Zhdanov

greater homogeneity of the leading personnel, along with the complete acceptance of Stalin as the outstanding leader, has rendered less important the earlier segregation of functions; consequently there is considerable interchange and joining of effort in various spheres by the three bodies.[29]

The Full Emergence of the Secretary-General's Role. The controlling influence exercised by the Secretary-General in the concentrated authority at the summit of the only ruling party — hence in the affairs of the Soviet state as a whole — was for a long time kept formally separate from official action toward foreign powers by virtue of the non-official standing of the Party. A gradual change in this practice began to take place in the early 'thirties, with the realization of full recognition abroad of Stalin's position. Though up to that time his few interviews with foreigners had been confined to writers and labor delegations, in November 1932 on the death of his wife he received condolences from members of the diplomatic corps and subsequently conferred, though still on rare occasions, with a number of ministers and ambassadors of foreign powers (Ambassador Bullitt, Laval, Eden, emissaries from China, Ambassador Davies, et cetera.) Finally, in mid-1939 he commenced to take an open and most active part in the eventful negotiations of the Soviet government with Germany, the Baltic states, Turkey, and Finland. It is thus that the actual status and role of the Secretary-General has fully emerged, becoming generally recognized and accepted even before Stalin's assumption of the governmental posts that he now holds.

3. THE ORGANS OF VERIFICATION

(1) THE AUDITING AND CONTROL COMMISSIONS

The Central Auditing Commission and the Commission of Party Control. In addition to the above-described organs, the central Party hierarchy includes the Central Auditing Commission, elected by the Party congress and numbering 22 at present, which checks the accounts of the central Party organs and their enterprises,[30] and the Commission of Party Control,

---

— are members of the Politbureau and Orgbureau, the other 2 — Kuznetsov and Popov — enter only the last-named organ.

29. See e.g. *XV S'ezd VKP(b)*, p. 111; *XVI S'ezd VKP(b)*, p. 153.

30. When formed in 1919, it consisted of 3 members and was termed the Auditing (or Revision) Commission, the membership increasing to 22 by 1934. Since 1922 it has borne the name Central Auditing Commission. (See rules 28, 22, 30, 37, and 42 of the 1919, 1922, 1925, 1934, and 1939 Comparty Rules, respectively; *XVII S'ezd VKP(b)*, p. 37.)

formerly elected by the Congress and now formed by the Central Committee. The prerogatives of the Commission of Party Control, according to
the new rules, are: 'verification of the fulfilment of the decisions of the
Party and of the Central Committee . . . by the Party organizations and
by the Soviet-economic organs,' checking up on the work of the local
Party organizations, and institution of proceedings against violators of the
Party program and rules of Party discipline (rules 34 and 35, 1939 Comparty Rules).

(2) THE PARTY'S SYSTEM OF CONTROL

The Role of the Party Groups in Public Organizations and Institutions.
One must distinguish here between the organs of political-directive control, with the technique of direction employed by them, and the organs of
administrative-operative control and the system of verification evolved in
the complex Party-Soviet structural set-up. It should be pointed out, however, that the two are often intertwined and overlapping and are continuously undergoing alterations in scope, emphasis, and methods of application.[31] As the Party rules have always decreed, 'the Central Committee
directs the work of the central Soviet and public organizations through
the Party groups in them.' The special departments and administrations
of the Central Committee from which the downward stream of directives
and instructions flows to the Party groups and units were discussed earlier.
These groups or 'fractions' are organized at all state and public congresses,
conferences, consultations, organs, and institutions where there are at
least three Party members. Their declared task is 'to consolidate the influence of the Party in every respect, carry through its policy in the non-
Party milieu, and secure Party control over the work of all the institutions
and organizations.'[32] And for the achievement of this purpose each Party
group or 'fraction' in a given institution is required to propose candidates
for all the leading positions therein, decide at a caucus of its own members
every problem before the institution, and then vote as a unit at the session
of the latter, always being guided in its action by the decision of the

31. No more than a bare outline of the major changes in the checking and verification sys-
    tem can be given here. To trace its development through successive Party resolutions,
    see *VKP(b) v Rezol.* I, pp. 314, 377–8, 450–51, 469, 482, 508–12, 549–50, 587, 590–94;
    II, pp. 53–7, 88–90, 193–5, 232, 346, 356, 407–14, 457–8, 572–3, 590, 595.
32. Rules 60, 60, 93, 55, 70 of the 1919, 1922, 1925, 1934, and 1939 Comparty Rules,
    respectively. Marking the more open assertion of a functional interrelationship between
    the Party and Soviet pyramids, the rules, since 1934, introduce into the article the items
    'to strengthen the iron Party and *Soviet* discipline, to struggle with bureaucracy, to
    verify the fulfilment of Party and *Soviet* directives.' (Italics J.T.)

higher Party bodies and the voice of its immediately superior Party committee.[33]

(3) THE EVOLUTION OF THE INSTRUMENTS OF VERIFICATION

The Central Control Commission and Rabkrin (1921–34). Paralleling this system of direction, though at times duplicating or reinforcing some of its functions, were a number of Party instruments of verification, mostly operating in close association with similar Soviet organs. In 1921, the Party established a Central Control Commission to look after the fidelity and fitness of the Party membership, while a year earlier a Commissariat of Workers-Peasants Inspection, termed Rabkrin, superseded a Commissariat of State Control, formed in 1918, in checking the accounting and practices of governmental organs and the loyalty and efficiency of state employees. Soon afterwards the possibility was visualized of turning the Rabkrin into an institution permanently attending to the improvement of the state machinery, in the triple capacity of detector of defects, fighter against bureaucracy, and promoter of efficiency. Since, however, these tasks were considered inseparable from the still more vital aims of perfecting cohesion in the Party ranks and vigilantly maintaining the Party's leadership in the state, the Twelfth Party Congress (1923), following Lenin's suggestion, resolved upon the closest co-operation between the Rabkrin and the Central Control Commission of the Party. The commission was raised in composition from 7 to 50, subsequently attaining a membership of nearly 200; and there were provisions for an interlocking personnel, a pooling of resources and information, and joint sessions with the Rabkrin at least once in two months.[34] Together, the Central Control Commission and the Rabkrin became the eyes and ears of the Party, inaugurating mass checking devices to battle bureaucracy, carrying out *chistkas* or purges of the state, public, and Party organs, and acting as co-reporters on subjects reported on by these bodies before the Politbureau and Central Committee, in order to point out discrepancies and deficiencies. They studied and suggested ways and means for the rationalization of operation and perfection of performance by sundry organs and organizations of the entire governing structure.[35] Additional duties, such as

---

33. Rules 62–6 of the 1919 Comparty Rules. Same in later adopted rules up to those of 1934. Cf. rules 60, 61 of the 1939 Rules.
34. See Lenin, xxvii, pp. 402–5, 406–18; *VKP(b) v Rezol.* I, p. 512.
35. See Harper, op. cit. pp. 103–6; Steklov, *Sovetskaia Demokratia, passim;* Ananov, op. cit. pp. 122–32, 200–208; Speransky, 'Ten Years of the Rabkrin,' pp. 21–40; Bertsinsky, 'The Lenin Road of Development of the R.K.I.,' pp. 40–53; also *XVI S'ezd VKP(b),*

actively aiding in the recruitment and promotion of personnel for the state and economic organs, were placed upon these twin trouble-shooters from time to time, but a resolution of the Fourteenth Party Congress emphasized that 'the most important tasks of the C.C.C. [Central Control Commission] and R.K.I. [Rabkrin] should, as before, be the checking of the execution of the decisions and directives of the Party and the state, and control over the activities of the key parts of the state apparatus.'[36] Reiterating the paramountcy of these tasks, Stalin declared in 1934, however, that the Central Control Commission and the Rabkrin were no longer adequate to perform them because of an accumulation of and diffusion over too many additional functions and because of their need to rely on local agencies in the pursuit of their work.

The Commission of Party Control and Commission of Soviet Control (1934-40). Accordingly, on his suggestion, the Seventeenth Party Congress (1934) decided to supplant them with two new organs, a Commission of Soviet Control and a Commission of Party Control. The Commission of Soviet Control was shaped out of a Commission of Fulfilment that was attached to the Council of People's Commissars up to that time, while the Rabkrin was abolished. The provision was that, in order that the Commission of Soviet Control 'may have sufficient authority and be able, in the event of necessity, to take proceedings against any responsible worker,' its membership should be nominated by the Party congress and confirmed by the Council of People's Commissars and Central Executive Committee. But in 1939 the requirement for the nomination of the commission by the Party congress was dropped.[37]

The Commission of Party Control was to be elected by the Party congress. The first commission was to concentrate on 'the work of control, the work of supervising the fulfilment of the decisions of the central bodies of the Soviet government'; and the second, on 'the work of supervising the carrying out of the decisions of the Party and its Central Committee.' Both commissions were to have their own representatives in the localities, who were to act entirely independently of the local authorities. And again, like their predecessors, the Commission of Party Control and Commission

---

pp. 79, 144–5, 346, 538, 563–8, 582–3, 616–17, 634, 635, 637, 643, 687, 713–4. For a concrete example of their work, see the joint report of the Central Control Commission and Rabkrin to the Fifteenth Party Congress on the Soviet state apparatus, its main faults, and methods for reshaping and improving it, in *XV S'ezd VKP(b)*, pp. 387–421, 550–56, 1284–8.

36. *VKP(b) v Rezol.* II, pp. 54, 55, 57.

37. See *XVII S'ezd VKP(b)*, pp. 35, 673–4; S.Z. 1934, items 58 and 75; *Pravda*, 20 March 1939, p. 4 (Zhdanov's report).

of Soviet Control, numbering 61 and 70 respectively, operated in close collaboration.[38]

Subsequent Changes in the Machinery of Verification. The last changes in the system of checks and controls were introduced in 1939–40 and have been carried further since 1944. To facilitate and make concrete the guidance of Soviet and public institutions by the Party bodies it was decided to break up the former into smaller entities. Accordingly, a subdivision of commissariats and territorial-administrative units was carried out at the end of the 'thirties and has been repeated several times since. While the primary Party organizations have the right of control over the activity of the administrations in economic enterprises, 'the Party organizations in the People's Commissariats, which, because of the special conditions of work in Soviet offices, cannot exercise functions of control, are obliged to give warning of the shortcomings of the offices, pointing out the deficiencies of the work of the People's Commissariat and of its individual workers, and to send these materials and considerations to the Central Committee C.P.S.U.(B) and to the leaders of the People's Commissariat' (rule 61, 1939 Comparty Rules).[39] The Commission of Soviet Control was abolished in September 1940, being replaced by a new Commissariat (now Ministry) of State Control, which is 'to establish strictest control over accounting and expenditure of state funds and material values, and over execution of governmental decisions.' The Commission of Party Control continues in its prerogatives of control over fulfilment of Party decisions by the Party, state, and public institutions.

The Position of the Verifying Organs. In conclusion, it should be underscored that the organs of verification are not evaluated as politically

---

38. See *VKP(b) v Rezol.* II, pp. 572–3; *XVII S'ezd VKP(b)*, pp. 562–647, 670–74; Antipov, 'The Work of the Commission of Soviet Control,' pp. 9–16.

39. To handle expeditiously the enormous number of complaints that pour into the Secretariat of the Central Committee from all groups of the population about carelessness, abuses, personal injustices, distortion of Party and government directives, red tape, etc., in the operation of public, Party, Soviet, and economic institutions, a Correspondence Bureau was established at the Secretariat of the Central Committee in November 1930. The complaints are examined and forwarded to the organs of verification (Central Control Commission, Rabkrin, etc.), the office of the Procurator General (State Attorney), and the relevant ministries or local Party and Soviet organizations in order to be investigated and remedied, execution of the decision taken in the matter usually being entrusted to responsible officials, such as directors of the Central Committee departments or of regional and district Party committees and directors of Soviet governmental institutions. Complete files are kept of each case and the complainant can learn of the disposition made. In the first three years of its existence alone the Correspondence Bureau attended to 12,500 complaints. (See the reports of the Central Auditing Commission, *XVII S'ezd VKP(b)*, pp. 39–41; *Pravda,* 12 March 1939.)

self-sufficient. Whatever may have been the original conception of the position of the Party Control Commission in the scheme of power,[40] the definite understanding has evolved that the Control Commission is not a separate and distinct seat of power, standing above or apart from, and exercising any function of control over, the political center, but that it is a part and instrument of the latter, maintained for the very purpose of guarding its unity and that of the Party as a whole on the basis of the political line arrived at by a majority of the leaders comprising this center.[41]

While the view of the Party as a political monopoly, assembling all the channels of effective influence under its roof, found full institutional realization early in the Soviet regime, the associated conception of the Party as a political monolith, embracing the complete coherence of the will and action of its members, took two of the three decades of Soviet existence to achieve. Given the crucial significance attached by the Communist Party to its exclusive control of power in the vast and conglomerate Soviet state, the severe and uncompromising struggle for total unity within its own ranks followed as a matter of course. Thus the doctrine of monolithism was born, with all the conceptual and organizational consequences that flow from it: the definition of the meaning and content of intra-Party democracy, the institution of bounds and limits of legitimate criticism and discussion, and the prohibition of factions or groupings and related practices deemed productive of dangerously dividing divergences. The monopoly and monolithism principles were also among the generating causes of the changes or re-emphases that took place in the theory and allocation of authority in the Party hierarchy. These changes involved: (a) the acceptance of the view of the Central Committee — hence also of its working organs, the Politbureau, Orgbureau, and Secretariat — as primarily the manager of a unified disciplined party, not the mediator

---

40. Judging by the view expressed in regard to creation of control commissions in individual Comintern sections, the Party Control Commission was at one time conceived as a parallel elected center in a duality of power with rather than in subordination to the political center. (See *The Communist International between the Fifth and Sixth World Congresses*, 1924–8, pp. 27–8.) And Lenin also regarded it as a sort of check on the Politbureau, stating that 'members of the Central Control Commission, who should be present in a certain number at every session of the Politbureau, must constitute a solid group which, "personalities notwithstanding," would have to see to it that no one's prestige should prevent them from making an inquiry, verify documents, and in general obtain absolute awareness and [secure] the strictest order of affairs.' (Lenin, XXVII, p. 405 [23 January 1923]. See also Ordzhonikidze, in *XVI S'ezd VKP(b)*, p. 538.)
41. See *XVI S'ezd VKP(b)*, pp. 35, 580, 581, 585, 588.

between opposing currents within it; (b) the assessment of the Party's Commission of Control as an aid of, rather than as a co-equal power center with or checking instrument over, the policy-making summit of the Party; and (c) the concentration of decisive authority in the above-mentioned working organs, which have evolved into an interlocking and intimate directorate presided over by the Secretary-General. Of these the last-named was by far the most remarkable development. Generally, historical justification for the mounting centralization was found in the lessons of survival gleaned from the Communist past. But paradoxically enough, such democratically earmarked manifestation as the extensive growth of the Party's membership, i.e. the increase in the relative proportion of the ruling pyramid to the country's populace, served as a contributory factor in the concentration of ultimate control in the continuously operating Party directorate — the Politbureau, Orgbureau, and Secretariat. For the rise in Party membership found reflection in progressively increased representation in the Congress and Central Committee of the Party, transforming these organs into unwieldy bodies capable of approval but hardly of formulation of basic policy in their customary relatively short meeting time. And this fact, coupled with the growing practice of rarer convocations of the congress and the restricted number of Central Committee plenums per year, left the actual determination of policy to the earlier-mentioned directorate, especially in conditions where instantaneous decision and rapid alteration of courses of action were required. As for the extraordinary position of influence attained by the Secretary-General in that directorate, it owes its establishment to the singular confluence of the particular personal qualities of the incumbent and the power potentialities inherent in his office in the early part of the 'twenties.

Chapter IX · The Conception of the Soviets

1. THE SOVIETS AS THE FORM OF THE DICTATORSHIP

(1) DESIGNATIONS OF THE SOVIETS

The Soviets as the 'Political Foundation of the U.S.S.R.' and 'the State Form of the Dictatorship.' The soviets are constitutionally designated as the political foundation of the U.S.S.R., having given their name to the regime from its inception. From the standpoint of fundamental theory the soviets are conceived as 'the state form of the dictatorship of the proletariat,' reckoned to remain such until the institution of the state itself passes from the social scene.[1]

(2) THE ADOPTION OF THE SOVIET FORM

The 1905 *Councils as Models for the Revolution.* How did this form come to be adopted? The model was supplied by the soviets or councils of 1905, primarily sporadic strike committees delegated by factories of the larger Russian cities in the revolution of that year. Even then the Bolsheviks regarded the soviets as incipient organs of power. Though they were suppressed at the time, Lenin evaluated them soon after the event as organs of rule — a government in embryo.[2] It was during this period that Lenin also developed his theory about the bourgeois-democratic revolution growing into a socialist one. And when a decade later, in 1915, he stated as the Bolshevik aim for the ensuing period the winning of 'a revolutionary-democratic dictatorship of the proletariat and peasantry,' he pointed to the soviets as the appropriate state form of this dictatorship.[3]

---

1. Stalin, *Voprosy Leninizma*, pp. 30–32; *S.G.P.* pp. 5, 137, 147–54; *VKP(b) v Rezol.* I, pp. 314–15; *K.I. v Dok.* pp. 107–8, 113. 'Dictatorship of the working class' is the current designation.
2. Lenin, VIII, p. 408 (December 1905); IX, pp. 116–18 (April 1906).
3. *S.G.P.* p. 139.

The Crystallization of the Bolshevik Attitude toward the Soviets in 1917. March 1917 brought to the fore two centers of power in Russia — the Provisional Government and the Soviets of Workers and Soldiers' Deputies — which the Bolsheviks regarded as an intertwining of a dictatorship of the bourgeoisie with a dictatorship of the working class and peasantry, at once advancing the slogan of 'All Power to the Soviets.' Paradoxically enough, as compared with subsequent theory, the Bolsheviks at this time looked forward to the dissolution of the diarchy by educational means of propaganda, persuasion, and criticism. They expected — in line with Lenin's formulation of 1905 — that the revolution would 'develop into' a socialist one, and they thought — as Lenin explained in August 1917 — that the slogan of a transfer of power to the then existing soviets 'guaranteed the peaceful further development of the entire revolution and, in particular, the possibility of peacefully overcoming the struggle of classes and parties *within* the soviets.' [4] But with the bloody fate accorded by the Provisional Government — participated in by the Mensheviks and S.R.'s, who dominated the soviets at the time — to the 4 July demonstration in favor of power to the soviets, the Bolsheviks decided upon a course for a new revolution.[5] The slogan of soviets as organs of power was abandoned, but only for a while. By the end of October the Bolsheviks were in the majority of the soviets of the cities and 7–8 November 1917 they took power and soviet rule was proclaimed. Thus, says Stalin, the soviets became 'the political form so long sought and finally found . . . The Paris Commune was the embryo of this form. Soviet rule is its development and consummation.' [6] And the credit for discovering the suitability of this form is given entirely to the views and formulations of Lenin.[7]

(3) THE BASIC CONCEPTION OF THE SOVIETS

The Soviets as 'Conductors of the Party Line.' But form alone, it is said, is not enough. The crux of the matter lies in the question of who supplies the content of the form — who directs the work of the soviets?

---

4. Lenin, xxi, p. 82 (1 September [19 August o.s.] 1917); also xx, pp. 78–9, 88, 90 (April 1917); *S.G.P.* pp. 144–5; Denisov, *Sovety-Politicheskaia Osnova SSR*, pp. 12–13.
5. See Lenin, xxi, p. 82; *K.I. v Dok.* pp. 112–13.
6. *Voprosy Leninizma*, p. 33; see also *K.I. v Dok.* pp. 18, 112, 477.
7. In this, it is said, Lenin picked up the threads of theory where Marx left off, Marx having at first thought that a 'Republic' in general was the appropriate form of political organization for the period of transition to communism, but later — after the Paris Commune — specified that it must be a republic of the Paris-Commune type. Lenin developed this view further by pointing to the soviets as the requisite type of state form. (See Denisov, op. cit. pp. 10–13.)

From this cardinal angle the primary assessment of the soviets stems —
their conception as 'conductors of the general line of the Party.'[8]

2. THE EVOLUTION OF THE PARTY–SOVIETS RELATIONSHIP

(1) THE RELATIONSHIP OF THE FIRST YEARS

The Original Ambiguity of the Relative Spheres of Activity. The development of the theory of the relationship between the Party and the
soviets, which gave substance to this conception, falls into several distinct
phases. By the Revolution of November 1917 the Bolshevik Party was
transformed from an underground or opposition party, pursuing primarily
propaganda and agitation, into a ruling party, gaining for the first time
the material and technical means to play such a role. The leaders of the
Party, from Lenin down, had all taken posts in the Soviet government.
But the intensity of the civil war kept the Party leaders from clearly defining the relation between the Party and the soviet structure, especially
since the latter structure was itself being hewed out at the time.[9]

(2) THE DEMARCATION OF PARTY–SOVIET FUNCTIONS

The Definition of the Party-Soviets Relationship. A definition of rela-
tionship providing for a demarcation of the respective functions of the
Party and the soviets was first offered by the Eighth Party Congress, in
March 1919:

> The Communist Party poses as its task the conquest of a most decisive influence
> and complete direction in all the organizations of toilers: trade unions, co-opera-
> tives, village communes, et cetera. The Communist Party seeks especially the realiza-
> tion of its program by and [the achievement of] its complete dominance in the
> contemporary state organizations — the soviets . . . By practical, daily, self-sacrific-
> ing work in the soviets, by putting forth its most stable and devoted members for all

---

8. See Stalin, 11 January 1933, *Voprosy Leninizma*, p. 519; *VKP(b) v Rezol.* II, p. 455
   (December 1930); Shchebletsov, 'The Soviets — Conductors of the General Line of the
   Party,' pp. 21–4.
9. At the center, the association — formal and actual — between the Party and the soviets
   was very close and the Party's control was strong. But in the localities the Party's influence was much weaker, since the local Party organizations received their finances from
   the local soviets — the executive committees — and such dependence was not conducive
   to the exercise of control by the first over the second. This situation was changed toward
   the beginning of 1920 when the Party Central Committee undertook to finance the local
   Party organizations from the center. (See C.C. Report at the Ninth Party Congress,
   Protokoly IX S'ezda RKP(b), pp. 31–3, 36.)

soviet posts, the R.C.P. must conquer for itself undivided political dominance in the soviets and actual control over all their work.

But the functions of the Party collectives must on no account be confused with the functions of the state organs — the soviets. Such confusion would produce fatal results, especially in military affairs. The Party must carry out its decisions through the soviet organs, *within the frame of the Soviet constitution.* The Party should endeavor to guide the activity of the soviets, not to supplant them.[10]

Similar statements were made at several subsequent Party congresses against action that would tend to erase the lines of demarcation between the Party and the soviet organs, i.e. to make the Party compete with the soviets rather than guide them.[11] Yet in these same years, the leadership in control fought determinedly against all attempts to juxtapose the soviets and the Party, repeatedly and unequivocally asserting the supremacy of the Party's directing role in the soviets, and incessantly calling for further expansion of that role.[12]

---

10. *VKP(b) v Rezol.* I, pp. 314–15; Lenin, XXIV, p. 721; see also *S.G.P.* p. 154.

11. *VKP(b) v Rezol.* I, pp. 352, 425, 444, 483, 512; II, pp. 7–8 (1920–25). 'Keeping for itself the general guidance and direction of the entire politics of the Soviet state, the Party must carry out a much more precise demarcation between its own current work and the work of the Soviet organs, between its own apparatus and that of the soviets. Such a systematically executed demarcation should secure more systematic consideration and decision of economic questions by the Soviet organs, at the same time raising the responsibility of every Soviet official for the work entrusted to him, and on the other hand, make it possible for the Party to concentrate properly on the basic Party work of general guidance of the work of all state organs . . .' (Resolution of the Eleventh Party Congress, March 1922, *VKP(b) v Rezol.* I, p. 425.)

12. *VKP(b) v Rezol.* I, pp. 322, 481, 483, 485, 512, 552–3; II, pp. 7–8, 47, 52, 158, 231 (1919–27). 'The Twelfth Congress confirms, for undeviating fulfilment, the resolutions of the preceding congresses about the need for a precise division of labor between the Party and the Soviet organizations . . . But the congress warns against too wide an interpretation of the above decisions, which might create political dangers for the Party. The Party can by no means content itself now with general propaganda and agitation only . . . the main responsibility for the work of the economic and state-wide organs rests upon the RCP, because it alone is historically called upon to be the real executor of the dictatorship of the working class.' 'Therefore the Twelfth Congress emphasizes especially the need also in the future to adhere to the tactics which . . . secure for the Party the actual direction of the entire Soviet, and particularly the economic, apparatus of the Soviet republic.' (Ibid. I, pp. 483, 485.) 'In order to endow the Party's leadership of the Soviet organs with greater elasticity and methodicity . . . to recognize the need of strengthening the personnel ties between the leading Party and Soviet organs, by having, for example, the secretary and several members of the bureau of a Gubkom [Party committee of a province] enter the membership of the presidium of the Gik [executive committee of a province], while the chairman of the Gik presidium enters the bureau of the Gubkom; the same in the districts, etc.' (Ibid. II, pp. 7–8 [April 1925].) 'What tasks then do we visualize in the matter of directing the state apparatus? It seems to me that the tasks are: first, to increase the influence and direction of the Party with regard to both the leading organs of the state apparatus and the entire body

The Distinction between the Respective Roles of the Party and the Soviets. Theoretically, therefore, the problem of this relationship resolved itself into a demand not to confuse the Party with the soviets — the 'core of the state power' with 'the state power' — and into a double injunction against either 'commanding' or 'tailism' (following, instead of showing initiative) in the Party's exercise of its prerogatives of leadership within the soviets. As regards the first, Stalin sought a conclusive clarification of the subject in a statement on 25 January 1926:

> The Party realizes the dictatorship of the proletariat. 'The Party is the direct governing vanguard of the proletariat; it is the leader.' (Lenin.) In this sense the Party *takes* power, the Party *governs* the country. But this does not yet mean that the Party realizes the dictatorship of the proletariat separately from and without the state power; that the Party governs the country apart from the soviets, and not through them. But this does not yet mean that the Party can be identified with the soviets, with the state power. The Party is the core of this power, but it is not and cannot be identified with the state power itself. 'As the ruling party,' writes Lenin, 'we could not but merge the "upper stratum" of the Party with the "upper stratum" of the soviets; we have merged them, and they will continue so.' . . . But he never stated that the Party is the state power, that the soviets and the Party are one and the same. The Party . . . leads the soviets, with their national and local ramifications . . . but it cannot and should not replace them by itself.[13]

As for the second, a series of warnings were issued by the higher Party organs to Party bodies and fractions at all the levels of the pyramid that they should endeavor to guide, lead, teach, and correct the errors and shortcomings of the soviets in which they operate, and not command and order them around. At the same time the Party bodies were warned that they must under no circumstances find themselves dragging behind, at the tail end of the procession, in the operation of the soviets, that they must never forget their primary objective of leading in the promotion, stimulation, and initiation of desirable action by the soviets.[14]

Such was the theoretical position concerning the Party-soviets relationship, at least up to the early 'thirties, with its chief reflection in practice in the official separation of Party directives from the laws and enactments of the soviet government organs, and in the formal distinction between the operation of the Party and soviet pyramids. It is important to point out

---

of the state apparatus as a whole.' (Molotov, in the C.C. organizational report at the Fourteenth Party Congress, 19 December 1925, *XIV S'ezd VKP(b)*, p. 72. For a similar statement at the Sixteenth Party Congress, in the organizational report of Kaganovich, see *XVI S'ezd VKP(b)*, p. 152 [June 1930].)

13. *Problems of Leninism*, pp. 38–9.

14. *VKP(b) v Rezol.* II, pp. 111, 112, 172, 355–6; *XV S'ezd VKP(b)*, p. 101.

here, however, that in his own time Lenin was not at all against a progressively greater fusion of Party and soviet functions, wherever it seemed necessary for the good of the cause; that the effort to keep the two separate was to a large extent a concession to various oppositions of the earlier period; that admitted exceptions to the theory of separation of the Party and government functions were known at least in several instances: the Politbureau-Sovnarkom, Politbureau-Narkomindel, and the Central Control Commission-Rabkrin working combinations;[15] and that, as in all other fields, the Party reserved for itself full freedom to alter the forms of its own organization, operation, and relationships.[16]

(3) THE OPERATIVE INTEGRATION OF THE PYRAMIDS

Mounting Functional Fusion of the Party and the Soviets. In 1929–30, about the time when the industrialization and collectivization programs went into full swing, a more open fusion of the Party and government began to emerge. First, there appeared the frequent public association of the Party and government in authoritative Party pronouncements.[17] Then, a number of resolutions directed specifically to higher government bodies, commissariats, and various government enterprises were issued by the Party Central Committee, calling upon them for certain action. These resolutions were followed as a rule by simultaneously promulgated official laws covering the same points, though at times they took full effect entirely by and of themselves.[18] Lastly and even more significantly, since

---

15. See *supra,* pp. 130, 162–3, 171–4.
16. '1. The party of revolutionary Marxism fundamentally denies any search for an absolutely proper form of party organization, as well as methods of work, fit for all stages of the revolutionary process. On the contrary, the form of organization and methods of work are entirely determined by the peculiarities of the given, concrete, historical conditions and the tasks that flow directly from these conditions. 2. From this standpoint it is clear that every organizational form and its corresponding methods of work can, through a change in the objective conditions of the development of the revolution, become transformed from a form of development of the party organization into fetters upon such development; and vice versa, an organizational form that has become unfit may again become a necessary and solely expedient one with the recurrence of corresponding objective conditions.' (Resolution of the Tenth Party Congress, March 1921, *VKP(b) v Rezol.* i, p. 365.)
17. See *VKP(b) v Rezol.* ii, pp. 347–8, 413 (April 1929, June 1930). This association in public pronouncement has become particularly strong since 1934, joint reference being constantly made to 'Party and Soviet' or 'Party and government' discipline and directives, 'decisions of the Party and Soviet centers,' etc. (See ibid. ii, pp. 571, 592, 596, 603; rules 72–4, 1939 Comparty Rules.)
18. See e.g. the Central Committee resolutions of 2 April and 30 July 1930 in *Izvestia* for 3 April and *Pravda* for 2 August 1930, respectively. For other instances, see *Pravda* for 5 January, 27 March, 3 April, 28 and 29 August 1932, and 13 February 1933.

January 1931, numerous formal laws and enactments have been published in the official Gazette and Collection of Laws in the joint name of the Council of People's Commissars and the Central Committee of the C.P.S.U.(B), signed by Molotov as Chairman of the Council and Stalin as Secretary of the Central Committee.[19] No precise criteria have been publicly suggested in regard to the nature or subject matter of the laws that were to be so promulgated, though practice indicates that this form was, in the majority of cases, used to underscore the primacy of certain legislation or the vital current urgency of the items embraced by these laws.[20]

The Amalgamation of the Summits. The cycle was completed in 1941, with Stalin's assumption of the chairmanship of the Council of People's

---

19. The first laws so promulgated, dated 15 January, 21 January, and 5 February 1931, deal with railroad transport, contraction of summer sowings, and river transport, and were published respectively on 29 January, 22 January, and 9 February 1931. (*S.Z.* 1931, I, items 80, 81, 82.) It may be interesting to note that though Stalin is generally referred to as 'Secretary-General,' he signs these laws simply as 'Secretary,' evidently in line with the customary listing of all members of the Secretariat as 'Secretaries' in the statements of election by the Central Committee.

20. The authoritative public-law text offers this concise explanation: 'when a law defined the general norms of political and economic life . . . [and] if such law was at the same time also an important Party directive, practice has established the signing of this law also by the secretary of the C.C. C.P.S.U.(B) along with the signature of the leader of the high Soviet organ.' (*S.G.P.* p. 302.) An investigation of the Collection of Laws for 1 January 1931 through the issue of 23 August 1941 (Part I only; Part II deals with official appointments and international agreements) reveals the following points. Out of 5,455 official enactments, 367 were promulgated in the joint name of the Sovnarkom (the Council of People's Commissars) and the C.C.: 11 in 1931 (missing issues Nos. 30, 36, were not consulted), 16 in 1932, 40 in 1933, 25 in 1934, 82 in 1935, 35 in 1936, 9 in 1937, 7 in 1938, 34 in 1939, 83 in 1940, and 25 in 1941. On a few single occasions a third Soviet body, such as the Supreme Council of National Economy, the Commissariat of Agriculture, or the Central Council of Trade Unions, was joined. (See *S.Z.* 1931, item 291; 1932, item 143; *S.P.R.* 1939, item 1.) The first of these laws were titled 'Obrashchenie' i.e. appeal or address, and couched primarily in language of recommendation; the later ones are decisions phrased as directions or commands. In nature they are both brief and extensive, general and specific, and cover a range of subjects almost as wide as that of the rest of the laws. The vast majority of them deal with agriculture: sowing, harvesting, animal raising, accumulation of reserves, and every phase of the regime of the state and collective farms. Quantitatively, next in line, were items on transport, education, the coal, food, etc., industries, power and irrigation, privileges for Siberian and Far-Eastern settlements, formation, structure or break-up of named commissariats and councils, and considerable miscellanea: on accounting, census, consumption goods, agricultural exhibitions, movie themes, cultural, housing and other projects, as well as jubilees for specified cities and republics, and such seemingly petty items as postal parcels, etc. It appears, thus, that the form of joint promulgation and the occasional variation in the title and signature were successive devices to stress the particular significance attached to the items so promulgated.

Commissars on 7 May. Enactments promulgated in the joint name of the government and the Party for a time bore the sole signature of Stalin as 'Chairman of the Council of People's Commissars and Secretary of the Central Committee of the C.P.S.U.(B).'[21] Stalin — like Lenin before him — is now both the acknowledged highest leader of the Party and the official head of the government. And even more than during Lenin's earliest tenure, the Party and government are publicly associated and closely amalgamated in personnel, operation, and performance of the all-embracing function of preparation and promulgation of general and fundamental, as well as current and specific, activity-guiding norms.

3. THE SOVIETS AS A SYSTEM OF BAROMETERS

(1) AVOWED CHARACTERISTICS OF THE SOVIETS

Popular Features considered Inherent in the Polity. In evaluating further the nature and role of the soviets, Soviet statesmen and jurists from time to time have advanced the following characteristics as being basic and inherent: (1) a pronounced mass character;[22] (2) an international quality; (3) a structure facilitating proletarian leadership of the masses; (4) the combination of legislative and executive functions in the same state organs; (5) the wide exercise of the right of recall with regard to delegates to the soviets; (6) an army converted from an instrument of oppression into one of liberation; (7) a singular capacity to attract mass organizations 'into constant and unconditional participation in the administration of the state.'[23]

---

21. See e.g. *S.P.R.* item 331 (9 August 1941). The practice of two signatures has now been resumed with Stalin signing as Chairman of the Council of Ministers and one of the members of the Secretariat signing for the Central Committee.

22. 'Wherein lies the strength of our state apparatus? In the fact that through the soviets it connects the government with the millions of masses of workers and peasants. In the fact that the soviets are a school of governing for tens and hundreds of thousands of workers and peasants. In that the state apparatus does not fence itself off from the millions of the popular masses, but is fused with them through a vast multitude of mass organizations, all kinds of commissions, sections, consultations, delegates' assemblies, etc., which encompass the soviets and prop up thereby the organs of government.' (Stalin, 3 December 1927, *XV S'ezd VKP(b)*, pp. 62–3.)

23. Stalin, *Foundations of Leninism*, p. 56. 'The soviets unite in their ranks tens of millions of toilers and should aim to unite in their ranks the entire working class and the entire poorest and middle peasantry.' (Eighth Party Congress, March 1919, *VKP(b) v Rezol.* i, p. 314. See also *K.I. v Dok.* p. 501, item 31.)

(2) REJECTION OF SEPARATION OF POWERS

Preference for Combining the Legislative and Executive Functions.
Because of the importance attached to it over a long period of time, point
4 of the foregoing enumeration deserves particular attention. This is one
of the most emphasized aspects, and has as its model the Paris Commune,
since it is held to be a type of government in which 'the parliamentarians
themselves must work, themselves execute their laws, themselves verify
what becomes of them in life.' Parliamentary institutions, said Lenin in
the summer of 1917, yes; he could not imagine a democracy, 'even a proletarian democracy,' without parliamentary institutions; but parliamentarism, no.

The way out of parliamentarism, he said, quoting Marx, is to be found, of course,
not in the abolition of representative institutions and elections, but in the transformation of the representative institutions from talking shops into 'working' institutions.
The Commune was to be not a parliamentary institution, but a working one,
legislating and executing the laws at the same time.[24]

And on the eve of the assumption of power he expressed the conviction
that the soviets are the kind of state apparatus that offers 'the possibility
of combining the benefits of parliamentarism with the benefits of direct
and plain democracy, i.e. of combining in the persons of the elected
representatives of the people both the legislative function and the execution of laws' — a theory emphatically repeated in his basic pronouncements
of the two following years, and subsequently expounded equally firmly
by Stalin.[25] This theoretical stand prevailed even at the time of the ex-
ploratory deliberations on the structure of power, before a formal instrument to define governmental arrangements was adopted. And to this
position the practical argument of the benefits of quick, centralized decision and action was added on the day when the first Fundamental Law
was proclaimed for the Soviet state.[26] Lastly, from the moment that the

---

24. Lenin, XXI, pp. 401–2 (August–September 1917).
25. Ibid. p. 258 (October 1917); XXII, pp. 239, 371; XXIV, pp. 14, 95. 'The Soviet government
    . . . abolishes the negative features of parliamentarism, especially the separation of
    legislative and executive powers.' (The Program of the Party, adopted in March 1919,
    VKP(b) v Rezol. I, p. 294, item 5.) 'Wherein lie the characteristic features of Soviet
    rule? . . . In that Soviet rule, combining the legislative and executive powers in a single
    state organization . . . connects the workers and the toiling masses in general directly
    with the apparatus of state administration and teaches them how to administer the
    country.' (Stalin, *Voprosy Leninizma*, pp. 32–3 [April 1924].)
26. 'While bourgeois constitutions, which are imbued with the doctrinairism of the pos-
    sessing classes and take into account the internal struggle of separate groups of bourgeois
    society, have set up an artificial separation between individual elements of power (legis-

governing structure was set up under that constitution, Soviet jurists have consistently maintained that it completely rejects as fictitious and unnecessary the principle of separation of powers.[27] Their view was that the Congress of Soviets is composed of deputies who are practicing executives and administrators from all over the land, rather than legislating parliamentarians; that the Central Executive Committee, its Presidium, and the Council of People's Commissars are both legislative and executive organs; and that what does exist in the Soviet polity is not a separation of powers but a technical distribution and gradation of functions and spheres of activity, a system of division of labor whereby the constitution communicates to different organs different scopes of competence, with varying degrees of legislative and executive power.[28]

Persistence of the Theory of Non-Separation of Powers. Under the new constitution, as we shall see later, the legislative function was to be the exclusive prerogative of the Supreme Soviet. Public statements have strongly stressed this change, pointing out likewise that the increase in branches of administration that resulted from the establishment of a socialist economy has necessitated a more precise definition of these distinct functions of each organ of government. Nevertheless, there has been no

---

lative, executive, judicial), we, in our constitution, aim to concentrate as far as possible all these elements in one central organ; and such [organ] is the all-Russian Congress of Soviets, the Central Executive Committee that it elects, and the Council of People's Commissars, which is accountable to both of them. This is necessary in order that, at a time that calls for the greatest effort and speed of action on the part of the government in solving the militant and military tasks before it, it should be able to display a maximum of energy, to utilize all forces and skills, quickly to adopt and carry out decisions in behalf of tasks placed by history upon it.' (*Piatyi Vserossiiskii S'ezd Sovetov*, p. 185.)

27. As a political principle of power balancing power, formulated in the writings of Locke, Montesquieu, Kant, etc., the Soviet jurists ascribe the origin of the separation-of-powers doctrine to the struggle for power between the bourgeoisie and the aristocracy in the period of the emergence of the former. Initially reflecting an effort to crystallize juridically a state of comparative equilibrium existing between the two social forces, a true separation of powers was actually achieved nowhere (these jurists maintain), for there followed demands for the supremacy of parliament over the executive — the king and his ministers — once the bourgeoisie was more firmly entrenched, and later, with its complete triumph, a reverse process actually set in — the growth and 'preponderance' of power in the executive branch of government, as the more elastic organ capable of quicker action in the interests of the dominant classes. (See Gurvich, *Osnovy* . . . pp. 72–6, 81–2; Malitski, op. cit. pp. 52–5; Cheliapov, in *E.G.i P.* iii, pp. 632–6; Engel', op. cit. pp. 164–72; *S.G.P.* pp. 159–60, 295–300. See also Strong, *Constitution*, pp. 72–3; Stetsky, *Constitution*, pp. 30–32.)

28. See Gurvich, *Osnovy* . . . pp. 82–5; Malitski, op. cit. pp. 33–4, 48, 55–6; Cheliapov, in *E.G.i P.* iii, pp. 637–8; and Vyshinsky, ibid. ii, p. 486; Engel', op. cit. pp. 172–4; *S.G.P.* pp. 160, 167–8, 300–303, 346.

retreat in Soviet theory from the position of total rejection of the principle of separation of powers.[29]

(3) THE SOVIETS AS STRUCTURAL BAROMETERS

Barometers of Popular Sentiment instead of Checks and Balances. To the political principle of separation of powers, wherein power balances power, the soviets oppose the principle of Democratic Centralism, wherein power is subordinate to power on a defined scale of territorial and administrative gradation. Rather than a system of checks and balances, the dominant concern of the framers of the Soviet polity was the forging of a system of structural barometers accurately and instantaneously, or periodically, to gauge all variations in the state of public sentiment and reactions to changing programs and events. As Stalin formulated this consideration on 23 April 1923:

In our Soviet country we must evolve a system of government that will permit us with certainty to anticipate all changes, to perceive everything that is going on among the peasants, the nationals, the non-Russian nations, and the Russians; the system of supreme organs must possess a number of barometers which will anticipate every change, register and forestall . . . all possible storms and ill-fortune. That is the Soviet system of government.[30]

In the years that followed, this remained a primary concern of the leadership, and, along with the other views comprising the conception of the soviets' nature and role, it influenced considerably the actual development of the Soviet structure.

---

29. See *S.G.P.* pp. 300, 302–3, 316, 346; Stetsky, *Constitution,* pp. 30–33; Vyshinsky, 'Stalin's Constitution,' pp. 9, 12.

30. *M.N.C.Q.* p. 165.

Chapter X · The Soviet Structure (I)

1. THE PYRAMIDAL ARRANGEMENT

(1) ELECTION OF THE SOVIET PYRAMID

The Hierarchical Organization of the Soviets. The soviets are built on the same hierarchical principle as the Party itself and as the other 'conducting belts' — they constitute a structural power pyramid.[1] At the base of this pyramid are the city and village soviets, over which rise successively the administrative-territorial tiers of the districts and areas, regions or territories and autonomous republics, constituent republics, and the central, all-Union organs.

Electoral Rights.[2] Under the new constitution all the soviets, from village and city upwards, are elected in accordance with the four-tailed formula of universal, equal, direct, and secret suffrage. Except for the insane and persons convicted by a court of law whose sentences include deprivation of their electoral rights, all citizens who have reached the age of 18, irrespective of race or nationality, sex, religion, educational and residential qualifications, social origin, property status, or past activities, have the right to vote in the election of deputies. And any citizen who has reached the age of 23 may be elected as a deputy.[3]

---

1. There are, thus, about half a dozen principal pyramidal structures intertwined in the system of rule — the Party, the Soviets, the trade unions, the agricultural collectives, the artisans' *artels,* the consumers' co-operatives — of which the first two are the most important. (See Webb, op. cit. pp. 4–7.)

2. The next three sections are based largely on a detailed examination of the editorial and other material on elections in *Pravda* and *Izvestia* for November and December 1945–January 1946 and the following sources: ch. xi, Constitution of 1936; *S.G.P.* ch. x; Bregman, *Vybory v Verkhovnyi Sovet SSSR i Profsoiuzy; The Election System of the Union of Soviet Socialist Republics;* U.S.S.R. Election Regulations, *E.B.* 24 November 1945, cited hereafter as Election Regulations; Gorkin, *Izbiratelnyi Zakon Sovetskogo Gosudarstva;* Vakhmistrov, *Agitatsionno-Massovaia Rabota na Izbiratelnom Uchastke.*

3. Until the 1946 elections to the Supreme Soviet of the U.S.S.R., a citizen of the U.S.S.R. — according to article 135 of the Constitution of 1936 — could both elect and be

There was no such universality of suffrage under the earlier two constitutions, which — while granting extensive electoral rights to 'toiling people' — deprived the urban bourgeoisie, the richer peasants, and several other population groups of the franchise. The theory was that this disfranchisement need not last indefinitely and could be dispensed with when the Soviet regime was consolidated. Beginning with the 'thirties there was a progressive liberalization of the rules governing the reinstatement of electoral rights of the disfranchised, and in 1936 the new constitution instituted universal suffrage.[4]

All Soviet constitutions gave women and members of the armed forces equal rights with all other citizens to elect or stand for election to the soviets.[5] But before the adoption of the new constitution, workers enjoyed a number of electoral privileges. First, the workers' vote was weighted as opposed to the peasantry: the soviets of cities and workers' settlements sent representatives to the federal Congress of Soviets on the basis of 1 deputy for 25,000 electors, while representatives from the provincial soviets were chosen on the basis of 1 deputy for 125,000 inhabitants. Similar differences favoring the urban as against the rural localities existed in regard to elections to the regional and territorial congresses of soviets. Secondly, while elections were conducted by production units (factories, shops, mines, et cetera) in the cities and workers' settlements,[6] and the latter were directly represented at the congresses of soviets of the higher tiers, rural settlements carried out their elections on a territorial basis and were only indirectly represented in the regional and higher con-

elected at the age of 18. Soviet jurists boasted of the absence of any distinction between the right to elect and be elected. (*S.G.P.* pp. 602, 611.) Experience, however, has apparently suggested the desirability of more mature deputies in the Soviet, for on the suggestion of the Legislative Commissions of the two chambers of the Supreme Soviet, the Presidium of the Supreme Soviet issued a decree on 10 October 1945 raising the age requirement for election to the Supreme Soviet U.S.S.R. to 23 and proposing a corresponding amendment of the constitution. (*V.V.S.* 12 October 1945; Gorkin, op. cit. pp. 6–7; *Izvestia,* 15 March 1946.)

4. *S.G.P.* pp. 602–7.

5. To implement these rights for members of the armed forces serving beyond the boundaries of the U.S.S.R. the Presidium of the Supreme Soviet decreed (on 14 October 1945) the formation of special electoral areas in the units and formations of the Soviet army and navy abroad on the basis of a quota of 100,000 voters per area. (Gorkin, op. cit. pp. 14–15.)

6. This electoral feature was considered highly important for bringing the state apparatus closer to the masses (see the Party Program, *VKP(b) v Rezol.* 1, p. 294, item 5; Strong, *Constitution,* p. 35; Williams, *The Soviets,* p. 42), but was never absolute in so far as even in the urban elections the 'unorganized population,' i.e. housewives, pensioned persons, etc., voted in district meetings, and elections to the higher-placed congresses of soviets were on a territorial basis.

gresses of soviets. This contrast, as a concrete application of the conception of the electoral law as the will of the dominant class, was regarded by the Bolshevik leadership as historically inevitable and justifiable in view of the social set-up of the Russian village at the beginning of Soviet rule.[7] There were, thus, elections at four stages: first, the electors choosing their village and city soviets; second, the plenums of the village and city soviets electing their own executive organs as well as delegates to the district congress; third, the district congress electing a district executive committee and delegates to the territorial or regional congress; fourth, territorial and regional congresses electing their executive committees and delegates to the congress of soviets of the constituent republic and to the All-Union Congress of Soviets. Under the new constitution all elections are direct and conducted on a territorial basis; no distinction is made between city and village soviets. Each citizen has only one vote and is entered on one electoral list, and each electoral area sends one deputy to the Supreme Soviet of the U.S.S.R.

Voting at the elections of deputies is secret. The earlier constitutions did not define the manner of voting, and the practice was to vote openly by a show of hands. This practice, it is said, was not altogether free from opportunities for abuse.[8] The new constitution has introduced the secret ballot, which, the Soviet leaders claim, has become possible owing to the liquidation of counter-revolutionary groups and the rise in the cultural level and political consciousness of the populace. Like the previous constitutions, it also provides for the right of recall: the deputy of a soviet is required to report to his electors, who can recall him by majority decision at any time (article 14a, Constitution of 1936). Generally, the new electoral rights are viewed as a natural and not unforeseen outgrowth of the high degree of integration attained by Soviet society.

Electoral Procedures. Elections to the Supreme Soviet of the U.S.S.R. are held on a non-working day (between 6 A.M. and 12 P.M.) set by the Presidium of the Supreme Soviet and announced by it not later than two months in advance of the appointed date.[9] The executive committees

---

7. *S.G.P.* pp. 595, 616–17, 628.

8. 'Soviet electoral laws strictly forbade the use of any pressure whatever on the voters . . . Nevertheless, in individual instances bureaucratic and opportunist elements in the soviet and trade-union apparatus have sought to utilize the open form of voting to push through candidates they desired.' (*S.G.P.* p. 624.)

9. During the recent war, elections to the Supreme Soviet were successively postponed each year by the Presidium of the Supreme Soviet. On 5 October 1945, the first elections in over 8 years were ordered by the Presidium to take place on 10 February 1946, and on that date the Supreme Soviet of the second convocation was elected.

of the city and village soviets compile the voters' lists, form election precincts, approve the precinct election commissions, and supply the printing presses, buildings, means of communication, and other material conditions for the conduct of the elections. Voters' lists are prepared on the basis of residence registers, collective-farm books, and house-to-house canvasses, and are posted in public thirty days before the elections. Any complaints concerning errors in these lists are entered with the executive committees of the soviets, whose decisions can be appealed to a People's Court. In case of a change of residence after the voters' list has been published, the elector can secure from the respective executive committee a 'Certificate of the Right to Vote' entitling him to vote at his new abode.

All candidates are nominated according to electoral areas. For elections to the Supreme Soviet of the U.S.S.R., electoral areas are set up by the Presidium of the Supreme Soviet and made public at least two months before the elections. In accordance with the constitution (articles 34, 35), electoral areas for elections to the Council of the Union are established on the basis of 300,000 people to each area, while electoral areas for elections to the Council of Nationalities are set up as follows: 25 areas in each Union republic, 11 areas in each autonomous republic, 5 areas in each autonomous region, and 1 electoral area in each national area.[10] In the first elections to the Supreme Soviet of the U.S.S.R., held in 1937, there were 1143 electoral areas: 569 for the Council of the Union, and 574 for the Council of Nationalities. For the second elections, held in February 1946, 1287 electoral areas were formed: 656 for the Council of Union and 631 for the Council of Nationalities, with 26 special areas, representing the armed forces abroad, added for the elections to each chamber.

The territory of the cities and districts that enter into electoral areas are divided into election precincts, common for elections to the Council of the Union and the Council of Nationalities, where the ballots are cast and the

10. The electoral areas for elections to the supreme soviets of the Union and autonomous republics are formed by their respective presidiums. The constitution of each Union republic sets the population quotas on the basis of which the electoral areas within it are formed, and these quotas have ranged from 5000 inhabitants in the Tadzhik or Kirghiz Republic to 100,000 in the Ukrainian Republic and 150,000 in the R.S.F.S.R. These differences, which obviously affect the total number of deputies elected to the Supreme Soviet of the U.S.S.R., are ascribed 'exclusively to the number of population in these republics.' The population quotas for the formation of electoral areas for elections to the supreme Soviets of the autonomous republics ranged from 2000 persons in the Nakhichevansk A.S.S.R. to 20,000 in the Bashkir A.S.S.R. Similar differences in the various regions existed with regard to the elections of the territorial or regional, area, district, and village soviets. (See S.G.P. pp. 628–31.)

votes counted. These precincts must be set up not later than forty-five days prior to the date of elections. In urban and rural settlements with a population of more than 2000, election precincts are formed on the basis of 1 precinct for every 1500 to 3000 inhabitants; a separate election precinct is organized in each rural settlement (village, stanitsa, kishlak, or aul) with between 500 and 2000 inhabitants. And provision is also made for separate election precincts with much smaller numbers of electors in sparse and remote settlements, hospitals, and sailing vessels, the declared purpose being to reach every eligible voter.[11] There were close to 136,000 election precincts in the 1937 elections and over 150,000 in the 1946 elections.

To supervise the conduct of the elections and keep the necessary records and registers, the following election commissions are formed: the Central Election Commission, for the entire U.S.S.R.; commissions for elections to the Council of Nationalities in the Union and autonomous republics, autonomous regions, and national areas; area commissions, separate for elections to the Council of the Union and for elections to the Council of Nationalities; and precinct elections commissions, for elections to both chambers of the Supreme Soviet. The election regulations provide for the recruitment of the membership of these commissions from trade unions, co-operatives, Party organizations, youth groups, cultural, technical, and scientific societies, and other public organizations, as well as meetings of workers, employees, servicemen, and peasants. Each election commission has a chairman, vice-chairman, and secretary, while the number of members ranges from 8 in the area commission to 12 in the Central Election Commission; precinct election commissions have 4 to 8 members. The following table, pertaining to the election commissions of the R.S.F.S.R. during the 1938 elections, illustrates the nature of the composition of the election commissions:[12]

---

11. See ibid. p. 631; Election Regulations, ch. iv. Separate election precincts are permitted: (a) in settlements or groups of settlements counting only between 300 and 500 inhabitants, where they are at a distance of over 10 kilometers from the central election precinct; (b) in settlements with not less than 100 inhabitants in remote northern and eastern districts; (c) in national areas in the north and also in mountain and nomad districts with a population of between 50 and 100 inhabitants; (d) in military units and formations, on the basis of 500–3000 electors; (e) on vessels in transit with not less than 25 electors; (f) in hospitals and invalid homes with not less than 50 electors; (g) on long-distance trains, for the purpose of receiving ballots from travelers holding a 'Certificate of the Right to Vote.' (Ibid.)

12. Election Regulations, ch. v; S.G.P. p. 635.

PRECINCT ELECTION COMMISSIONS

TOTAL NUMBER OF ELECTION COMMISSIONS	TOTAL NUMBER OF MEMBERS OF THE ELECTION COMMISSIONS	PARTY AFFILIATION			SOCIAL COMPOSITION				WOMEN PARTICIPATING
		C.P.S.U. (B) Members	Komsomol Members	Non-Party People	Workers	Peasants	Employees	Others	
91,880	609,993	135,597 22.2%	141,733 23.2%	332,663 54.6%	101,796 16.7%	284,138 46.6%	220,601 36.2%	3,458 0.5%	158,919 26.1%

AREA ELECTION COMMISSIONS

727	7,993	4,189 52.4%	1,391 17.4%	2,413 30.2%	2,383 29.8%	1,991 24.9%	3,411 42.7%	208 2.6%	2,458 30.8%

By the Constitution of 1936 (article 141), the right to nominate candidates is secured to public organizations and societies of the working people, Communist Party organizations, trade unions, co-operatives, youth organizations, and cultural societies. This right has been extended by the election regulations to include general meetings of workers, employees, servicemen, and collective farmers, as well as general meetings of all peasants in the villages and rural counties. Candidates must be registered by their nominating organizations with an area election commission not later than thirty days before the elections, and they are then entered on the ballot. Refusal on the part of an area commission to register a candidate may be appealed to a higher commission and the Central Election Commission. Nominating organizations as well as citizens are guaranteed by the election regulations the right to campaign for the candidate of their choice.

The date and place of polling are made known each day for twenty days before the elections. To assure the secrecy of marking the ballot, special rooms or partitions are provided in the election precincts. The voter is required to leave on each ballot the name of the candidate for whom he is voting and strike out the names of the other candidates.[13] Ballots with more than one name left on them, or otherwise violating the regulations, are declared invalid. The votes are counted and recorded separately for the elections to the Council of the Union and to the Council

---

13. Each voter marks two ballots, one for the elections to the Council of the Union, the other for those of the Council of Nationalities. Voters residing on the territory of autonomous republics, autonomous regions, and national areas mark three ballots, the third for elections to the Council of Nationalities from the respective autonomous republic, autonomous region, or national area, according to election areas formed for the elections from these units. Different colors were ordered for the ballots in the 1946 elections: white for the elections to the Council of the Union, pale blue for those to the Council of Nationalities from the Union republics, and rose for the elections to the Council of Nationalities from the lower national-administrative units. (See Gorkin, op. cit. pp. 14, 23.)

of Nationalities. Authorized representatives of public organizations have a right to be present during the counting of the votes. A candidate receiving more than half of all the votes cast in the area is certified as elected. Provisions are made for the holding of a balloting of the two highest candidates where none received an absolute majority of votes, and for new elections in an area where less than half of the eligible electors have voted. And the penalty of imprisonment is provided for interference with a citizen's exercise of his electoral rights.[14]

Election Practices. Basically, elections in the U.S.S.R. are conceived as not merely a method of recruiting the personnel of the soviets, but as a means of demonstrating to the population and the world at large the unity of Soviet society behind the Party and the government, and an occasion to rouse the people to further efforts. Election campaigns in the Soviet Union, it is stated, 'have always been a school of education for millions of Soviet people,' constituting a 'mighty instrument for the further political education and organization of the masses' and one more 'powerful means to rally further the Soviet people and strengthen the Soviet state.' [15] It is this conception of the nature and purposes of elections in the U.S.S.R. that gives content and direction to the election practices of the Soviet Union.

There is ample evidence to indicate that public organizations and societies throughout the U.S.S.R. display a large measure of initiative in proposing candidates for nomination in the elections to the soviets. Indeed, this initiative is encouraged by the Party, since it aids in spotting candidates who would be popular with their constituencies, and helps to increase the reserve of political cadres for possible future assignments to managerial positions. This, however, in no way diminishes the role of the Party in influencing the choice of candidates. The elections are conducted and candidates are proposed in the name of a 'bloc of Communists and non-Party people,' and it is repeatedly emphasized that only persons 'who are devoted to the cause of Lenin-Stalin' are worthy to stand for election.[16] A candidate need not necessarily be a member of the Party, but he must have demonstrated complete loyalty to the regime, as well as contributed to the welfare of the state through superior performance in his line of work. As a result, candidates elected, for example, to the Supreme Soviet of the U.S.S.R., represent the élite of various fields of endeavor — ranging

---

14. Election Regulations, chs. VI, VII, VIII.
15. See Gorkin, op. cit. pp. 17–18, 32; *S.G.P.* pp. 601, 646–7; Vakhmistrov, op. cit. pp. 5, 8–10; Bregman, op. cit. p. 5.
16. Vakhmistrov, op. cit. pp. 5, 10; Gorkin, op. cit. p. 32.

from cotton pickers and coal miners to industrial managers, scientists, marshals, and members of the highest governing bodies. The actual nominations, even at the lower levels, are made jointly by the respective Party organization and public organizations at area and inter-area pre-election consultations, where the various candidates proposed are discussed.[17] The Party exercises, thus, a decisive initial influence on the selection of candidates to the soviets, and there is little likelihood that a person hostile to the regime or the existing leadership would be nominated in the first place.[18]

Nonetheless, should such a nomination occur, the candidate would most likely be refused registration by the area election commission.[19] Moreover, as the first elections to the Supreme Soviet have shown, in certain circumstances — as when their loyalty has been called into question — candidates can be replaced by others even after their names have been put on the ballot.[20] The possibility of nominating a candidate who is *persona non grata* to the Party is made more remote by what has become a common practice in Soviet elections — to have but one nominee for an office. In these circumstances, failure of the respective Party organization to consent to a candidate proposed by a public organization would amount to a veto of that candidate. On the other hand, agreement among the Party and public organizations of an area to sponsor a certain candidate is tantamount to election, since as a rule, most of the public follows the lead of the articulate part of the community. A total scratching of the candidate's name by all the voters in the area would be necessary to defeat a nominee.

Once the candidates have been selected, the attention of the vast machinery of the Party, Komsomol, trade-union, and other public organizations is turned to a wide propaganda campaign to bring out the vote. Generally, the elections to the soviets are one of the chief large-scale means publicly

17. There is considerable emphasis on the joint nature of the nominations of candidates: 'The Party of Lenin-Stalin teaches: the main thing in the electoral campaign is not to separate from the non-Party people, together with them to nominate candidates, to arrive at an agreement with the non-Party people for a common candidate.' (Bregman, op. cit. p. 24. See also Vakhmistrov, op. cit. p. 10.)

18. In November 1936, in his speech on the new constitution, Stalin remarked, 'if people here and there do elect hostile persons, it will show that our propaganda work was organized very badly indeed and that we fully deserve such a disgrace.' (Stalin, *Constitution*, p. 29.) In the subsequent elections to the soviets, this dictum served as a point of departure for vigorous participation by the Party bodies in the nominating process.

19. The area election commissions consist of engineers, officials, teachers, army men, scientists, and other persons prominent in their respective fields, and — as we have seen earlier (*supra* p. 192 this chapter) — are overwhelmingly Communist in membership.

20. See *N. Y. T.* 13 December 1937.

to identify the Party with the masses, and to give the people a sense of active participation in the processes of government. If the trade unions, co-operatives, youth organizations, and cultural societies take part in the nomination of candidates, the mass of the citizenry gets a chance during the campaign to discuss the candidates and their field of work, and to ask questions about local as well as international problems — schools, municipal services, and rationing, as well as foreign affairs and conditions abroad.[21] In the process of preparing and executing this campaign the Party associates thousands of 'activists' from among the public organizations and even the unorganized population, many of whom are subsequently brought into the Party ranks or recruited for governmental and administrative positions. Thus, in the case of the trade unions, for example, tens of thousands of propagandists and agitators are searched out and trained for the election campaign by the factory-shop committees with the aid of the Party.[22]

The center of the propaganda work is the electoral precinct, and the primary Party organizations are attached to these precincts for the purposes of the campaign. The task of organizing the propaganda by places of residence falls upon 'trustees' elected by the area pre-election consultations, while the actual work of agitation is conducted by agitators selected by the Party organizations attached to the precincts. For the purpose of direct acquaintance with the voters and of conducting propaganda in line with their interests, each agitator is assigned to a specific group of electors — 1 agitator for every 20 to 30 voters in the urban settlements, and 1 for every 10 to 12 peasant households in the village.[23]

The trustees and agitators receive systematic instruction and guidance for their work at frequent consultations and seminar sessions with representatives of the Party committees. The agitators are urged to enlist the aid of 'activists' from among the voters themselves and even of Pioneers and school children in organizing discussions, distributing literature, writing slogans, et cetera. For the duration of the campaign, agitation points (*Agitpunkty*) are set up in the election precincts — in clubs, reading rooms, houses of culture, et cetera — where discussions and lectures are held, information is given out to the voters, and political literature is kept on hand. Both general meetings of voters, in every conceivable enterprise and institution, and meetings for special audiences — for women,

---

21. See Vakhmistrov, op. cit. pp. 19–23.
22. Bregman, op. cit. pp. 5–13, 29.
23. See Vakhmistrov, op. cit. pp. 11–24; *Izvestia*, 2, 8, and 25 December 1945; *Pravda* 19 December 1945.

young people, teachers, doctors, et cetera — are conducted in the course of the campaign. Use is made also of such varied and multiple channels and tools as libraries, study circles, excursions to museums, amateur performances, the press, wall newspapers, pamphlets and leaflets, lectures, talks, radio broadcasts, recordings of leaders' speeches, photographs, placards, and motion pictures.

In addition to the biographies of the candidates, questions of production, local conditions, and some subjects of current politics, the chief themes of the speeches, lectures, and discussions in the campaign cover such topics as: the Soviet electoral system; the Soviet constitution and the socialist order, the Bill of Rights, and national equality guaranteed by it; the might of the U.S.S.R. and its armed forces; the achievements of Soviet industry, agriculture, science, culture, and art; gains of the Soviet citizens, especially women and young people, under the Soviet regime; and the role of the Party and its leaders — of Stalin in particular — in engineering these attainments and securing the victory of the U.S.S.R. in the recent war. In all of these discussions comparisons are drawn with life under Tsarist and other political systems to show the advantages of the Soviet system and to identify the Party with the progress of the Soviet state.[24] Also, throughout the campaign, the speakers and the press exhort the electorate to new exploits in industry, agriculture, et cetera, and the populace responds with numerous public promises to engage in 'Socialist competition' — to double or triple the output of their factories, shops, farms, or institutions in honor of the elections.

A picture of the results of the election campaigns can be gained from the tables on the next two pages.[25] Lastly, it should be pointed out that since the elections are regarded essentially as a sort of plebiscite — constituting a periodic public endorsement of the leadership — voting on election day is carried out in a festive spirit. The outcome — which is a foregone conclusion — is widely celebrated by the citizenry.

---

24. Vakhmistrov, op. cit. pp. 6–10, 19–22; Samoilov, *Kak Proiskhodili Vybory Pri Tsarizme.* Agitators are warned to adjust their approach to the cultural level of their hearers, to use simple, brief, and precise language, to avoid boring their audiences with too many figures, not to use foreign phrases needlessly, and above all to make sure that they are well-versed in economic questions and will be able to tie up their talk with concrete problems of the work of the voters whom they address. (Vakhmistrov, op. cit. pp. 24–31.)

25. See the statement of the Central Election Commission in *Izvestia,* 14 February and 15 March 1946; *A.R.S.U.* August 1946, p. 28; Gorkin, op. cit. p. 13.

ELECTION OF THE SUPREME SOVIET OF THE U.S.S.R. IN 1937 AND 1946

	TOTAL		COUNCIL OF THE UNION		COUNCIL OF NATIONALITIES	
	1937	1946	1937	1946	1937	1946
Number of Election Areas	1,143	1,287 *	569	656	574	631
Number of Eligible Voters	94,138,159	101,717,686	94,138,159	101,717,686	94,138,159	101,717,686
Number and Percentage Who Voted	91,113,153 (96.8%)	101,450,936 (99.7%)	91,113,153 (96.8%)	101,450,936 (99.7%)	91,113,153 (96.8%)	101,450,936 (99.7%)
Number and Percentage Who Voted for the 'Bloc of Communists and Non-Party People			89,844,271 (98.6%)	100,621,225 (99.2%)	89,063,169 (97.8%)	100,603,567 (99.2%)
Number and Percentage Who Voted Against the Bloc			632,074 (1.4%)	819,699 (0.8%)	562,402 (2.2%)	818,955 (0.8%)
Invalidated Ballots			636,808	10,012	1,487,582	28,414
Number of Deputies	1,143	1,339	569	682	574	657
Of the Deputies: Number and Percentage of Men	954 (83.5%)	1,062 (79%)	492 (86.5%)	566 (83%)	462 (80.5%)	496 (75.5%)
Number and Percentage of Women	189 (16.5%)	277 (21%)	77 (13.5%)	116 (17%)	112 (19.5%)	161 (24.5%)
Number and Percentage of Party Members and Candidates	870 (76.1%)	1,085 (81%)	461 (81%)	576 (77.5%)	409 (71.3%)	509 (84.5%)
Number and Percentage of Non-Party People	273 (23.9%)	254 (19%)	108 (19%)	106 (22.5%)	165 (28.7%)	148 (15.5%)

* This figure does not include the 52 Special Election Areas for the armed forces, 26 for the elections to each chamber.

THE VOTE IN THE UNION REPUBLICS IN THE 1946 ELECTION OF THE SUPREME SOVIET U.S.S.R.

	NUMBER OF ELIGIBLE VOTERS	PARTICIPATED IN THE VOTING		VOTED FOR THE 'BLOC OF COMMUNISTS AND NON-PARTY PEOPLE'			
				IN THE COUNCIL OF THE UNION		IN THE COUNCIL OF NATIONALITIES	
		Number of Voters	% of Voters	Number of Voters	% of Voters	Number of Voters	% of Voters
R.S.F.S.R.	56,851,348	56,773,337	99.86	56,331,954	99.22	56,349,246	99.25
Ukrainian SSR	20,613,669	20,581,354	99.84	20,392,737	99.08	20,382,214	99.03
Byelorussian SSR	4,043,284	4,036,592	99.83	4,011,161	99.37	4,011,081	99.37
Azerbaijan SSR	1,420,360	1,419,535	99.94	1,415,493	99.72	1,411,414	99.43
Georgian SSR	1,941,151	1,939,789	99.93	1,937,780	99.90	1,936,261	99.82
Armenian SSR	643,733	643,113	99.90	641,254	99.71	641,051	99.68
Turkmen SSR	622,843	621,809	99.83	620,207	99.74	618,768	99.51
Uzbek SSR	3,106,589	3,103,498	99.90	3,096,932	99.79	3,096,058	99.76
Tadzhik SSR	725,536	725,310	99.97	723,889	99.80	722,545	99.62
Kazakh SSR	3,302,139	3,298,932	99.90	3,284,296	99.56	3,285,836	99.60
Kirghiz SSR	778,951	777,460	99.81	773,891	99.54	770,585	99.12
Karelo-Finnish SSR	210,011	209,858	99.93	208,654	99.43	207,398	98.83
Moldavian SSR	1,294,667	1,291,582	99.76	1,286,652	99.62	1,284,614	99.46
Lithuanian SSR	1,378,951	1,265,638	91.78	1,207,200	95.38	1,208,234	95.46
Latvian SSR	1,248,411	1,237,982	99.16	1,223,310	98.81	1,224,743	98.93
Estonian SSR	770,899	760,981	98.71	719,803	94.59	718,068	94.36

(2) THE BASE — THE LOCAL SOVIETS

The Local Soviets in the Early Period. In their general features, the governmental hierarchies of the constituent and autonomous republics follow the pattern of the central system. Before 1937 there was a Congress of Soviets, a Central Executive Committee and its Presidium, a Sovnarkom, i.e. Council of People's Commissars, and a number of commissariats in each of these republics. Since then the place of the Congress, Central Executive Committee, and its Presidium was taken by a Supreme Soviet and its Presidium, just as in the system of all-Union organs. In March 1946, the Sovnarkom was renamed Council of Ministers.

Here we shall consider briefly the main lines of development of the base of the Soviet pyramid — the local soviets, i.e. the tiers below the grade of constituent and autonomous republics.[26]

The first constitution (1918) provided for: city and village soviets (councils); congresses of soviets in the regions, provinces, districts, and counties; and in all these units were executive committees, which for purposes of administration had the right to form various departments. The city and village soviets were to be elected for a term of three months, with regular sessions called once a week in the city and twice a week in the village soviet, or upon decision of their executive committees or half of their membership. Congresses of soviets were to be called by the corresponding executive committees not less than twice a year in a region, once in three months in a province, and once a month in a county.[27] These local soviets and congresses of soviets, and, in the interim between their convocation, their executive committees as well, were termed by the constitution 'the highest power within the limits of the given territory' (articles 56, 60). Their responsibilities were described therein as follows:

(a) the execution of all the decisions of the respective higher organs of the Soviet government.

(b) the adoption of all measures looking toward the cultural and economic uplifting of the given territory.

---

26. For detailed treatments of the local soviets, see *S.G.P.* pp. 387–445; Trainin, *Mestnye Organy Gosudarstvennoi Vlasti V SSSR I 'Samoupravlenia' V Kapitalisticheskikh Stranakh.*

27. This frequency of convocation was curtailed by a statute adopted in December 1919 to 'not less than twice a year' for the regions, provinces, and districts, and 'not less than once in three months' for the counties. For the manner of composing these congresses, see *S'ezdy Sovetov RSFSR V Postanovleniakh i Rezoliutsiakh*, pp. 148–9, cited hereafter as *S'ezdy Sovetov RSFSR.*

(c) the solution of all problems of purely local significance (for the given territory).

(d) the unification of all Soviet activity within the bounds of the given territory ... (article 61).

Unlike the structural set-up at the higher tiers, no provision was made for Sovnarkoms (Councils of People's Commissars) in the local soviets. For, despite the high significance publicly attached to the local soviets at the time of the inception of the Soviet government, the Bolshevik leadership regarded the wholesale formation of Sovnarkoms in the regions, provinces, and districts as unwarranted excesses in the application of the 'All power to the Soviets' slogan, and accordingly ordered the liquidation of such Sovnarkoms in April 1918. A new organ, a presidium composed of several members to direct the current work of administration, emerged about the middle of 1918, and was sanctioned for the provinces and districts by a statute adopted in December 1919; later it appeared also in many city soviets. The same statute also defined the departments that were to be set up in the executive committees of the local soviets. It provided for 15 departments in a province (administration, military, justice, labor and social security, education, post and telegraph, finances, agriculture, food, state control, people's economy, health, statistics, extraordinary commission, and communal); 12 departments in a district (same as above except for justice, post and telegraph, and extraordinary commission); and such departments in a county executive committee or soviet of a factory settlement as the related higher-placed provincial executive committee would sanction.[28]

It should be pointed out that the civil-war conditions of the period (1918–20) put the intended operation of the local soviets considerably out of gear. The administrations of numerous city soviets were fused with those of the provinces and districts, while the regional organizations established by the Constitution of 1918 ceased to exist altogether. A major role at this time was played in fact by the so-called 'Revkoms' or Revolutionary Committees, brought into being to aid the defense of the regime and to maintain order in the immense territories enveloped in the struggle.

The Local Soviets in the Post-Civil-War Decade. The years following the end of the civil war brought a number of changes in the structure of the local soviets. Those city soviets that went out of existence earlier were restored, and in October 1925 it was also provided that such soviets should be organized in all workers' settlements, even in such where the population was less than 10,000. At the same time cities with over 50,000 inhabit-

28. See *S.G.P.* p. 403.

ants were empowered to form district soviets. The city soviets were to be elected once a year and hold plenary sessions not less than twice a month. The executive committees of the city soviets were allowed to form four departments (administration, education, communal economy, and health). They could also establish several so-called city sub-departments within the departments of a provincial or district executive committee standing immediately above it. Besides an executive committee a city soviet could elect as its working organ a presidium of as many as eleven members.

In the village, the structural changes followed a different, more restrictive tendency. By a statute adopted in February 1920, the departments of the village executive committees were abolished, the membership of these committees was reduced, and only rural settlements with a population of over 10,000 were permitted to elect executive committees. The provision was somewhat relaxed in 1924–5 to allow a soviet of a large village settlement with a smaller population to elect — with the permission of the superior provincial executive committee — an executive committee, and, where such a committee was composed of more than twenty persons, to form also a presidium.[29] In the vast majority of the larger rural settlements the role of executive was played by the Chairman of the Village Soviet, and this soviet was a body re-elected yearly, whose sessions were reduced at this time from twice a week to twice a month. In small rural settlements the place of a village soviet was to be taken by a *skhod* — a general meeting of electors — with the chairman of the meeting exercising the functions of village executive in the interim between these meetings.

Other enactments of the period called for: the convocation of all of the local congresses of soviets only once a year; more frequent sessions by the executive committees, which were being largely displaced in operation by the presidia; and for enlarged consultations by all these executive committees with representatives of the respective lower-placed executive committees and soviets. It should be pointed out here that whatever the changes in structure brought about during the post-civil-war decade and whatever the variations in grade of these local organs, the fundamental nature of their jurisdiction remained the same. It was strictly local, embracing such subjects as the local budget, communal facilities, civic improvements, and local cultural and economic undertakings. In these spheres the local soviets had the right to issue obligatory ordinances and impose administrative fines.[30]

29. See ibid. p. 410.

30. See *S'ezdy Sovetov RSFSR*, pp. 179, 219; also *S.G.P.* pp. 407, 410–11, 414.

Changes in the Local Soviets in the Early 'Thirties. In the early 'thirties, the liquidation of *okrugs* (areas) and the intensification of the industrialization and collectivization programs brought with them several rearrangements in the structure of the local soviets. Cities having a population of over 50,000 and constituting industrial, cultural, and political centers were singled out as 'independent' administrative-economic units, i.e. their soviets were to be subordinate directly to a territorial executive committee, to a presidium of an autonomous republic or to the Presidium of the Central Executive Committee of the U.S.S.R. Within a radius of one district, villages abutting a city of this type could join it; they retained their own village soviet while participating in the election of the city soviet. These city soviets, as compared with ordinary city soviets, which were subordinate to district executive committees, were entitled to set up eleven administrative departments. Ordinary city soviets could form only three departments and three inspectorates.

In general, by a statute on city soviets confirmed in 1933, the position of a city soviet was — within the limits of its territory — comparable in jurisdiction to that of a district (*rayon*) executive committee following the liquidation of areas.[31] Owing to the abolition of areas, as well as to a 1934 decision of the Party to form additional districts in the new economic centers that sprang up around the machine-tractor stations, the number of districts has greatly increased. The district with its organs became the basic link in the system of local soviets.[32]

As for the village soviets, though they appeared to be overshadowed by the rapid growth of large, collectivized, agricultural economies, and actually decreased in number, they were left intact.[33] At the time their main task was visualized as that of participation in the composition of the

---

31. For details, see *S.G.P.* pp. 417–26. When the areas (*okrugs*) were liquidated in 1930, 5 of them, formed on a nationality basis or sharply distinguishable by economic condition, or by distant or border location, remained in existence. By 1 October 1938 the number of such areas increased to 30, of which 11 — all in the R.S.F.S.R. — were national areas. As for cities, 157 out of 711 that existed in 1930 did not enter the districts upon liquidation of the areas but became instead distinct units of the type described above. To many of these cities adjoining villages were joined. By 15 September 1938, there were 807 cities, 709 workers' settlements, and 200 other urban-type settlements in the U.S.S.R.

32. The number of districts rose from 2,443 on 1 January 1934 to 3,463 on 15 September 1938 (ibid. pp. 424–6).

33. In 1928 there were 74,500 village soviets. This number fell to 68,209 in 1931 and to 62,824 by 1934. Several years later the number of village soviets had picked up somewhat, as there were 63,036 in September 1938. (Ibid.)

production plans of the collectives and looking after deliveries by the latter of their quotas of products to the state. They were also allowed to set up their own village budgets.

To summarize, before the new (1936) constitution came into effect, a congress of soviets was considered the highest organ of power in the structure of the local soviets. With its closing session, however, its powers formally passed to the executive committee that it elected. As in the case of the higher soviets, the understanding was that these executive committees were not mere 'executive' organs, but that they possessed all the powers of the congresses between convocations of the latter. Since, as a rule, a local congress of soviets was convoked for a few days only once in several years, even its function of adopting the yearly budget fell in practice to its executive committee, and the operation of the congress consisted merely in electing representatives to higher congresses as well as to its own executive committee, and occasionally hearing a report by the latter.[34] Finally, except for the passing of the budget, the executive committees of the local units were at times supplanted in actual operation by their presidia, which carried on the current work in the interim between executive committee sessions. As for the rural localities, the day-to-day bearer of village authority came to be the chairman of the village soviet or general meeting.

The Local Soviets under the New Constitution. Under the new constitution there are six basic links in the structure of the local soviet organs, namely, the soviets of: (1) the territories and regions, (2) autonomous regions, (3) areas, (4) districts, (5) cities, and (6) villages.[35] The system of local organs that prevails in most of the constituent republics consists in fact of only three links: (1) territorial or regional organs, (2) district soviets, (3) city and/or village soviets.

There are no more congresses of soviets. Their place was taken by the 'soviets of toilers' deputies,' which are elected for a term of two years in accordance with ratios of representation determined by the constitutions of the Union Republics (articles 95, 96, Constitution of 1936). Unlike the earlier constitutions and interpretations, a deliberate distinction is drawn between the soviets of deputies and the executive committees that they

---

34. *S.G.P.* p. 439.
35. Ibid. p. 427. The constitutions of the Union republics mention an additional link — the district soviets within large cities. The city soviets remained, as before, of two types: those subordinate to a district and those carved out of districts and subordinate to one of the higher links of local soviets — those of a territory or region — or to a supreme soviet of an autonomous or Union republic.

elect. The emphasized conception is that the soviets of deputies are 'organs of state power,' performing directive functions, while the executive committees are only 'the executive and administrative organs of the soviets of toilers' deputies.'[36] The frequency of convocation of these local soviets of deputies is determined by the constitutions of the Union republics. According to the provisions of most of these constitutions, territorial and regional soviets are convoked not less than four times a year, area and district soviets not less than six times a year, and city and village soviets not less than once a month. Sessions are conducted by a temporary chairman and secretary elected for that purpose. An exception is made in the case of village soviets, where a permanent chairman of the village soviet, who is also the chairman of the executive organ of the soviet, conducts its sessions. The soviets of deputies are convoked by their executive committees, and a village soviet by its chairman.

As for their functions, the federal constitution provides that the soviets of deputies 'adopt decisions and give orders within the limits of the rights granted to them by the laws of the U.S.S.R. and the Union republic' (article 98). More specifically, they 'direct the activity of the organs of administration subordinate to them, ensure the maintenance of state order, the observance of the laws, and the protection of the rights of citizens, direct the local economic and cultural construction, and establish the local budget' (article 97). Also, the soviets of deputies of the territories, regions, autonomous regions, and areas elect the corresponding courts for a term of five years (article 108).

The soviets of deputies choose executive committees, which — as was pointed out earlier — are deemed their 'executive and administrative organs' and consist of a chairman, vice-chairman, a secretary, and members (article 99). In small rural settlements a chairman, deputy, and secretary elected by the village soviet constitute its executive and administrative organs (article 100). These executive organs are directly accountable both to the soviet of deputies that elected them and to the executive organ of the superior soviet of deputies (article 101). Their function, too, is stated to be the exercise of 'direction of the cultural-political and economic construction' on the territory of the given unit, but 'only on the basis of decisions of the soviets of toilers' deputies that elected them and of the higher-placed state organs.'[37]

The constitutions of the Union and autonomous republics enumerate in detail the departments that are organized in the executive committees,

36. Articles 94, 99, 100, Constitution of 1936; S.G.P. pp. 430–31, 438–9.
37. S.G.P. p. 439.

though it should be pointed out that none is formed in the village soviets. These departments are of two kinds: obligatory, and those necessitated by the particular conditions of a given territorial unit. The following are the obligatory departments of the executive committees of all the links of the local soviet structure, i.e. of the territorial and regional, district, and city soviets: (1) finances, (2) trade, (3) popular education, (4) health, (5) social security, (6) general, (7) a planning commission, (8) a sector of cadres at the office of the chairman of the executive committee. In addition there are: departments of land, local industry, communal economy, roads, and arts in the territorial-regional executive committees; departments of land and roads in the district executive committees; a department of communal economy in the city executive committee; while some of these departments may be formed in the lower links by approval of the higher ones. In addition, various federal commissariats have their local representatives or administrations attached to these executive committees.[38]

Basically, it may be stated in conclusion, the competence of the local soviets under the new constitution remains, as before, strictly local in nature and extent, and, in fundamental aspects, much controlled by the norms of the higher or federal organs.

(3) THE LISTENING POSTS AND AUXILIARIES

Drives to Enliven the Soviets. It was this vast network of links and organs of the Soviet pyramid, spreading over the length and breadth of the U.S.S.R. and reaching every layer of its populace, that was regarded by the Soviet leaders as that ideal system of 'barometers that will anticipate every change . . . register and forestall all possible storms' — of which Stalin spoke as early as 1923.[39] Outside of the items discussed in earlier chapters, the story of the Soviet polity since the mid-'twenties — and especially since 1929 — is a story of an expanding program of arrangements for what may be called political listening posts and attraction devices. Among such arrangements in the Soviet pyramid are the drives for 'enlivenment' of the soviets, the campaigns to encourage the practice of recall in them, and particularly the 'deputy groups' and so-called *aktivs* in their sections and commissions.

As a result of special drives to 'enliven the soviets,' carried on since 1924, more than a twofold increase in the number of participants in elections to the soviets was achieved between that year and the time of the

---

38. Ibid. pp. 440–41.
39. See *supra,* p. 186.

adoption of the new constitution.[40] This was regarded as both a prerequisite for and proof of the attraction of wider strata of the population to the Soviet government and their consolidation around the programs and policies it pursued.[41] Between 1930–31 and 1934–5 the progressive restoration of electoral rights to various categories of formerly disfranchised citizens decreased the percentage of disfranchised from 3.7 per cent in the villages and 4.9 per cent in the cities to 2.6 per cent and 2.4 per cent, respectively, thereby also contributing to wider participation in the elections to the soviets.[42] In addition, the new constitution (article 135) removed all restrictions from such participation, establishing universal suffrage for the first time in the U.S.S.R.

Recall Campaigns. Another part of the program of revitalizing the soviets was a series of campaigns to encourage the utilization of the right of recall in order to unseat unfit or inactive deputies, especially in the primary units. Apparently, there was a double aim: to render the soviets — particularly the lowest ones, which are in continuous contact with the vast majority of the populace — into more sensitive opinion-gauging instruments by quick removal of all slothful elements; and to stimulate the election of new members so as to give more people the experience of activity in the soviets.[43] For a while, therefore, wide use was made of the right of recall, which resulted in a considerable turnover in the personnel of the city and village soviets.[44] This right, as we have seen, remains in full force,

---

40. The following percentages on participation in the elections of the cities and villages are indicated (*S.G.P.* p. 605):

YEAR	CITY		VILLAGE	
	All	*Women*	*All*	*Women*
1922	35.5		22.3	
1923	38.5		37.2	
1924	40.5	16.6	28.9	10.8
1925	48.7	25.8	36.9	19.9
1926	52.0	42.9	47.3	28.0
1927	58.4	49.8	48.4	31.1
1928–9	70.8	65.2	61.8	48.5
1930–31	79.6	75.3	70.4	63.4
1934–5	91.6	88.2	83.3	80.3

41. *S'ezdy Sovetov RSFSR*, pp. 126, 169; *VKP(b) v Rezol.* II, p. 356; Denisov, op. cit. p. 33; *S.G.P.* pp. 413–25, *passim*.

42. *S.G.P.* pp. 605–6.

43. See Harper, *Government of the Soviet Union*, p. 48; Strong, op. cit. pp. 37–8; Gurvich, op. cit. pp. 80–81; and Shostak, 'About the Recall of Deputies by the Electors,' pp. 96–110.

44. Thus, with the impetus given the practice of recall by a special decision of the Fifteenth Party Congress (December 1927), which called for a check-up on the exercise of the right of recall, about 23,000 deputies of the village soviets and 1000 of the city soviets in the R.S.F.S.R. (not counting the autonomous units) were recalled practically immediately after the 1930–31 elections. (Shostak, op. cit. p. 104.) For the years 1931–4

though its liberal use is no longer encouraged because of a current desire to rear more experienced government cadres.

Deputy Groups and 'Aktivs.' The most important of the special devices in the barometer system are the 'deputy groups' and the *aktivs,* or active elements in the sections and commissions of a soviet. Deputies of a soviet who work in the same enterprise or institution organize into a 'deputy group' to which other members of the institution are invited to bring complaints, suggestions, et cetera. Through such mutual consultation the group has an opportunity to estimate the current sentiment of the unit on various questions of public interest, and in the process of exchange to get non-deputies interested in the work of the soviet.[45]

The same objectives are pursued through the *aktivs.* Here, the sections and commissions of a soviet, that is the working committees that are set up to handle particular problems, seek to enlist volunteers or 'active elements' from among the citizenry to participate in their work. Again, through these groups of active outsiders, the deputies learn at first hand the needs and reactions of various strata in regard to various economic, administrative, and cultural matters. They use this information in their own work and pass it on to superior organs. At the same time this work is expected to engross the majority of the voluntary participants sufficiently to make them more permanently interested as well as proficient in the problems of the soviet, thus preparing them for possible formal membership later.

'Democratic Centralism' in the Soviets. In conclusion, it should be stated that, like the other pyramidal structures in the U.S.S.R., the Soviet hierarchy is governed by the principle of democratic centralism discussed earlier. In operation, this meant an upward stream of political intelligence, suggestion, and accounting from the lower organs and a downward stream of laws, decrees, and instructions from the apex, or central organs.[46]

---

an average of 10 deputies from the village soviets and 32 from the city soviets of the R.S.F.S.R. were recalled, which meant a turnover of 37 per cent of personnel in the case of the village soviets, 17.8 per cent in the city soviets. (Ibid. p. 105.) As for causes for removal, for every 100 deputies recalled in 1931–2, 37.3 were removed 'for inactivity,' 21.5 'for inefficiency,' 4.1 'for abuse of power,' 8.8 'for distortion of the class line,' and 28.3 for other reasons. (Ibid. p. 106.) These are held to be representative figures. Even after the 1934–5 elections to the soviets, which were deemed to have produced a better caliber of deputies, 30,165 deputies were recalled from 36,078 village soviets in the R.S.F.S.R. during the first half of 1935, i.e. an average of about 1 deputy per village soviet. (*S.G.P.* p. 645. For a detailed historical and statistical-interpretative treatment of the subject, see Shostak, op. cit. pp. 96–110.)

45. Harper, op. cit. p. 49; Denisov, op. cit. p. 32.

46. On this point cf. the view of the Webbs, op. cit. pp. 4–5, 7; and see also Gurvich, *Osnovy Sovetskoi Konstitutsii,* p. 87.

At the Sixteenth Party Conference (April 1929), where measures for ensuring popular support for the Five-Year Plan were considered, the question of the concrete meaning to be given to the democratic-centralism principle in the work of the soviets came to the fore. Along with decisions to continue the 'enlivement of the soviets' program and to increase the number of 'deputy groups' and *aktivs*, the conference adopted a resolution calling for the decentralization of operative functions with the simultaneous centralization of planning and direction, thus offering a formal and realistic assessment of democratic centralism in the operation of the soviet structure.[47]

As thus applied, the principle is regarded as leaving sufficient leeway for popular initiative, without hindering the central guidance which is held to be dictated by the needs of the new economic system.[48]

Within the hierarchy of the soviets this guidance was to be provided by the all-Union organs: the Congress of Soviets, Central Executive Committee, and its Presidium, which were replaced in 1938 by the Supreme Soviet and its Presidium, and the Council of People's Commissars, now called the Council of Ministers. A proper understanding of the evolution of the Soviet structure to the present, requires also consideration of the Congress of Soviets, the Central Executive Committee, and the Presidium of the Central Executive Committee of the U.S.S.R., which formed integral parts of the Soviet pyramid for two decades.

*

2. THE CONGRESS OF SOVIETS

(1) THE ORGANIZATION OF THE CONGRESS OF SOVIETS

The Life Span of the Congress. As an organ of Soviet rule, the Congress of Soviets began to function on 7 November 1917.[49] Four Congresses of

---

47. Denisov, op. cit. pp. 19, 29–30. 'The local Party and soviet organs must carry out unfailingly the Party and government directives and ordinances, at the same time posing before the central organs the question of all such changes the necessity for which becomes apparent in the local experience. Only such *mutual control* of the ordinances of the center by the practice of the localities and the practice of the localities by the direction of the center would not only make possible the undeviating fulfilment of the proposals and decisions of the central institutions, but would introduce into them necessary corrections in accordance with the lessons of the local experience.' (*VKP(b) v Rezol.* II, p. 348. [April 1929].)

48. Denisov, op. cit. pp. 29–30.

49. There was a Congress of Soviets before the establishment of soviet rule — the First Congress of Soviets, which held sessions during 3–24 June 1917. Of the 777 delegates from various socialist parties present at this congress, only 105, i.e. 13%, were Bol-

Soviets were held before the adoption of the first Soviet constitution — the Constitution of the Russian Socialist Federated Soviet Republic, or R.S.F.S.R. — on 10 July 1918. And five more Congresses were called between that date and 30 December 1922, when the Union of Soviet Socialist Republics was formed and the second or Union Constitution was introduced. As assemblies representing the entire state, these Congresses of Soviets, termed 'All-Russian,' were supplanted by 'All-Union' Congresses of Soviets after the Union was established. In all, eight 'All-Union' Congresses of Soviets were held, the last in December 1936. By the new constitution adopted at that time, the place of the Congress of Soviets, as well as that of the Central Executive Committee, was taken by the Supreme Soviet.

The Conception, Composition, and Procedure of the Congress. The Congress of Soviets was formally conceived as the 'supreme authority' (article 24, Constitution of 1918), 'supreme organ of power' (article 8, Constitution of 1924) of the state, and was regarded as constituting — by its very composition — the expression of the unity of the toiling strata of the entire populace.[50] Numerically, this composition has risen progressively to over three times its original size. The Congress of Soviets was elected on the basis of one representative of the city or township soviets per 25,000 electors, and one representative of the provincial congresses of soviets per 125,000 inhabitants (article 24, Constitution of 1918; article 9, Constitution of 1924). It grew in numbers from 649 delegates in November 1917 to 1,296 (963 voting and 333 consulting delegates) a year later, and 2,214 delegates (1,673 voting, 541 consulting) at the congress that decided on the formation of the U.S.S.R. in December 1922. The number of delegates continued to mount at the Union congresses of Soviets, reaching 2,562 (2,022 voting and 540 consulting delegates) at the last regular congress at the beginning of 1935. The Eighth Congress of Soviets of the U.S.S.R. (25 November–5 December 1936), the last actually held, was an extraordinary one called for the special purpose of adopting the new con-

---

sheviks, while the Socialist-Revolutionists had 285 and the Mensheviks 105 delegates. The latter two parties thus dominated the congress, which co-operated with the Provisional Government and opposed the idea of transferring 'all power to the Soviets' advocated by the Bolsheviks. It was the Second Congress of Soviets, where the Bolsheviks were in the majority — having 390 out of a total of 649 delegates — that proclaimed Soviet rule. (See *S'ezdy Sovetov RSFSR,* pp. 2–3, 12–13.)

50. *Tretii S'ezd Sovetov Soiuza SSSR, Stenograficheskii Otchet,* p. 148. These individual verbatim reports of the all-Union Congresses of Soviets will be cited hereafter as *S'ezd Sovetov SSSR,* with an arabic numeral in front of the title indicating the particular congress.

stitution. There were 2,016 voting delegates at the congress, but no consulting ones. These delegates to the Congress of Soviets were a motley group — representing all the areas and nationalities and a great number of occupations — and, in their vast majority, they were also members or voluntary participants in the administrations of their localities.

At the beginning, the Congress of Soviets was convocable first every three months and then every six. This was changed to once a year in 1921 and later, in 1927, to once in two years.[51] In practice the Congress of Soviets of the R.S.F.S.R. met five times in the first year of Soviet rule and once every year during the period of November 1918–December 1922. The Congress of Soviets of the U.S.S.R., which superseded it, at first met at intervals exceeding a year (the second in January–February 1924, the third in May 1925), and then once every two years until 1931. The last regular congress (the seventh, January–February 1935), however, was held nearly four years after the preceding one. On the average, sessions lasted about a week, the shortest lasting one day and the longest eleven days. Over the period of its existence (1917–36) the Congress of Soviets sat a total of 104 days.

The Congress of Soviets was called into session by the Central Executive Committee, and, unlike the practice that prevailed at the Party congress, foreign diplomats and journalists were allowed to witness the sessions. The regular procedure was to elect, immediately upon assembling, a Presidium of the congress to preside over its sessions, and a mandate commission to check the credentials and determine the exact composition of the delegate body. After that the congress would vote acceptance of the rules of order and agenda and proceed with the reports and debates, interspersed with numerous greetings from organizations, institutions, and

---

51. By the 'Resolution on Federal Institutions,' 28 January 1918, the Congress of Soviets was required to meet 'not less than every three months' (*L. i S.* p. 280). The first constitution (10 July 1918) provided for convocation 'not less than twice a year' (article 26). This provision was changed to 'once a year' by the Ninth All-Russian Congress of Soviets on 28 December 1921 (*S'ezdy Sovetov RSFSR*, p. 218), and was later embodied also in the Constitution of the U.S.S.R. (article 11). The change to 'once in two years' was made at the Fourth All-Union Congress of Soviets, on 26 April 1927, and was motivated by the explanation that a new tempo was abroad, that 'such quick turns in fundamental policy as would require the yearly conduct of large, mass [election] campaigns — all the way through to an all-Union Congress — will not be necessary. On the contrary, what is needed is profound work of construction, which requires a concentration of attention.' The lengthened term, it was said, would mean less detraction from their daily tasks of the great numbers of people ordinarily participating in such campaigns and would gain greater experience for the officials. (4 *S'ezd Sovetov SSSR*, pp. 586–7.)

groups from every part of the country, and sometimes from abroad.[52]

The rules of procedure of the Congress of Soviets were not markedly different from those of the Party congress.[53] A reporter on a given subject was allowed an hour for his report and thirty minutes for concluding remarks following debate, though in point of fact he was never held to these time limits. A group of delegates numbering 250 could furnish its own reporter. It should be noted that there were only a few co-reports in the practice of the Congress of Soviets and these signified no opposition but were arranged for convenience in handling the particular topic of the agenda. Delegates were allowed to speak twice on each agenda item in the order in which they signed up, though the assembly could vote to limit debate and has done so on many occasions. The rules in regard to time allotments for speeches in the debate, points of order, and proposals were exactly like those of the Party congress. The practice of oral interpellations, so customary in European parliaments, was unknown at the Congress of Soviets, but delegates could submit in writing extra-agenda inquiries, personal declarations, and factual remarks to the Presidium, which at the end of the session would decide at its own discretion whether or not to make them public. Inquiries and declarations signed by a hundred delegates or more, however, had to be announced by the Presidium immediately, though no debate in regard to them was permitted. The Presidium had a right to form sections on separate items of the agenda and such sections were frequently formed for the purpose of working out the final text of a decision or resolution to be voted on and published

---

52. The congress had a right to add to or remove items from the scheduled agenda. Thus, at the Sixth All-Union Congress of Soviets on 8 March 1931, the reports on heavy industry, Soviet structure, and the Red Army were cut from the agenda on the proposal of several delegations urging the shortening of proceedings in order to permit the delegates to return to practical tasks that could not be delayed, such as the spring-sowing campaign already begun in South Russia and the Ukraine, and the coal, metal, and transport work programs. (6 *S'ezd Sovetov SSSR,* Bulletin No. 1, pp. 4–6. See also 2 *S'ezd Sovetov SSSR,* p. 60.) This action, at a time when the Five-Year Plan was being pushed relentlessly, may explain the four-year interval between this and the succeeding congress and also throws light on the inception of the practice of legislation by joint decree of the Council of People's Commissars and the Party Central Committee, which began in 1931. (See *supra,* p. 182.)

53. There were several variations in the rules over the years, such as: changes in the schedule of sessions, which usually ran from 10 a.m. to 3 p.m. and from 6 to 10 p.m., and an increase — from 100 to 250 — in the number of delegates a group had to claim in order to put forth its own reporter, etc. (Cf. the rules given in 2 *S'ezd Sovetov SSSR,* p. 216, referred to in the text above, with those of the verbatim reports of the Fifth and Seventh All-Russian Congresses and Third and Fourth All-Union Congresses of Soviets, pp. 204–5, 6, 5, 598, respectively.)

by the congress. In this case the original draft submitted by the reporter was taken as a basis, and suggestions brought out in the debate, as well as in the written inquiries and remarks of the delegates, were taken into consideration at the deliberations of the particular commission. All decisions and resolutions of the Congress of Soviets required only a simple majority and were voted by a show of hands.[54]

The Jurisdiction of the Congress of Soviets. As regards jurisdiction, the Constitution of 1918 declared 'all questions of state-wide importance' to be within the competence of the Congress of Soviets and the Central Executive Committee. It specifically enumerated such powers as: confirmation and amendment of the constitution; 'the general direction of foreign policy' (declaration of war, conclusion of peace, trade and tariff treaties, financial agreements, and loans); the admission of new members into the federation, alteration of frontiers, determination of administrative divisions and of their competence, confirmation of regional unions and settlement of disputes between them; establishment of the principles and organization of the armed forces; establishment of the principles and of the general plan of the national economy and its separate branches; confirmation of the budget, national taxes and duties, and the system of weights, measures, and coinage; legislation concerning the judicial system and procedure, civil and criminal codes, et cetera; establishment of general rules on citizenship and rights of foreigners; the right of amnesty; and appointment and removal of the Council of People's Commissars and of its individual members, and confirmation of its Chairman (article 49).

In addition, these two organs were given the blanket power of passing upon 'all questions which they deem to be subject to their determination' (article 50). At the same time the constitution provided that the establishment, supplementation, and amendment of the 'basic principles' of the Soviet constitution, and the ratification of peace treaties were to be exclusive prerogatives of the Congress of Soviets. In such spheres, however, as the establishment and alteration of frontiers, alienation of territory or rights of the republic, and 'relations with foreign states, declaration of war and conclusion of peace,' the Central Executive Committee could act when it was impossible to convene the Congress of Soviets (articles 51, 52).

The Constitution of the U.S.S.R. adopted in 1923–4 enlarged upon this competence. To quote the relevant article (article 1) in full, to the jurisdiction of the U.S.S.R., 'in the person of its supreme organs' — which

---

54. According to the Rules of Order, a roll call would have to be taken when demanded by 200 voting delegates.

according to article 8 were again the Congress of Soviets and the Central Executive Committee — belonged:

(a) The representation of the Union in international relations, the conduct of all diplomatic intercourse, and the conclusion of political and other treaties with other foreign states;

(b) The modification of the external frontiers of the Union and the regulation of questions dealing with the alterations of boundaries between the constituent republics;

(c) The conclusion of treaties for the admission of new republics into the Union;

(d) The declaration of war and the conclusion of peace;

(e) The contracting of foreign and domestic loans by the U.S.S.R., and the sanctioning of foreign and domestic loans of the constituent republics;

(f) The ratification of international treaties;[55]

(g) Control of foreign trade, and establishment of a system of internal trade;

(h) Establishment of the basic principles and of a general plan for the whole national economic system of the Union; determination of the branches of industry and of separate industrial undertakings which are of federal scope; and the conclusion of concession agreements, both of federal scope and in behalf of the various Constituent Republics;

(i) The control of transport, posts, and telegraphs;

(j) The organization and control of the armed forces of the U.S.S.R.;

(k) The approval of a single State budget for the U.S.S.R. comprising the budgets of the Constituent Republics; determination of the taxes and revenues applying to

55. In regard to clauses (a) and (f), it should be noted that by several subsequent decrees a distinction was drawn between treaties that did and those that did not require ratification. In the first category were placed treaties of peace, treaties for the alteration of frontiers of the Union, and treaties where ratification was called for by the laws of the state with which they were concluded or by the mutual agreement of the parties; in the second category all other treaties. Treaties of the first category were to be concluded in the name of the Congress of Soviets, where the Congress voted to conclude them; in the name of the C.E.C. in other cases. Treaties of the second category were to be entered into in the name of the Sovnarkom. Negotiators of treaties requiring ratification were to be appointed and recalled by decrees of the C.E.C. or its Presidium, their full powers being signed by the Chairman and Secretary of the C.E.C. and countersigned by the Foreign Affairs Commissar. Negotiators of treaties not requiring ratification were to be appointed by the Sovnarkom, their full powers being signed by the Chairman of the Sovnarkom and countersigned by the Foreign Affairs Commissar. All treaties were to be submitted by the Narkomindel [Foreign Affairs Commissariat] to the Sovnarkom for preliminary approval. The treaties of the first category were to be ratified by the Congress of Soviets and the C.E.C., and in the interim between sessions of the latter, by the Presidium C.E.C., the Narkomindel being required to submit such concluded treaties for examination by the Sovnarkom, which would pass them on to one of the ratifying bodies. Treaties of the second category that were not enforced immediately upon signature were to be submitted by the Narkomindel to the Sovnarkom for examination and final approval. (See the decrees of 22 May 1923 and 21 May and 2 October 1925, *S.Z.* 1925, I, pp. 530, 572, 1009–10; 3 *TsIK I Sessia*, pp. 4–5, 8–10, 17–18; see also Diablo, op. cit. pp. 28–30, and Harper, editor, *The Soviet Union and World Problems*, pp. 230–31.)

the whole U.S.S.R., as also of deductions therefrom and additions thereto for the budgets of the Constituent Republics; authorization of additional taxes and dues for the budgets of the constituent republics;

(l) Establishment of a single currency and credit system;

(m) Establishment of general principles governing the distribution and use of land, and the exploitation of mineral wealth, forests and waterways throughout the whole territory of the U.S.S.R.;

(n) Union-wide legislation on migration from one republic to another, and establishment of a migration fund;

(o) Establishment of basic principles for the structure and procedure of the courts and the civil and criminal legislation of the Union;

(p) The establishment of fundamental labor laws;

(q) Establishment of the general principles of public education;

(r) Adoption of general measures for the protection of public health;

(s) Establishment of a system of weights and measures;

(t) The organization of Union-wide statistics;

(u) Fundamental legislation in the matter of Union citizenship in relation to the rights of foreigners;

(v) The right of amnesty extending over the whole territory of the Union;

(w) The repeal of decisions adopted by the Soviet congresses and central executive committees of the several constituent republics infringing upon the present constitution;

(x) Settlement of controversies arising between the constituent republics.

Also by this constitution, the confirmation and amendment of the 'fundamental principles' of the constitution were declared to be within the exclusive competence of the Congress of Soviets (article 2).

(2) THE POSITION AND ROLE OF THE CONGRESS

The Operation of the Congress in Practice. During practically the entire R.S.F.S.R. period of its existence (1917–22) the Congress of Soviets was preoccupied with problems of constituting and solidifying the new regime, and with external relations and military affairs, economic questions taking third place.[56] Prominent in the proceedings of the congress during this period were its appeals to Russian groups to align themselves with Soviet rule, its expressions of revolutionary solidarity with workers' organizations abroad, and its appeal to foreign governments and peoples to establish peace. In the succeeding, U.S.S.R., period (1922–36) domestic policy clearly predominated quantitatively at the Congress of Soviets with economic problems and questions concerning the constitution and

---

56. A rough statement of the topics and number of the resolutions of the Congress during this period would stand as follows: (1) establishment and solidification of the regime — 45; (2) foreign policy and military affairs — 34; (3) economic questions — 28; (4) education — 2; (5) miscellaneous — 3. (See *S'ezdy Sovetov RSFSR*, pp. 513–19.)

Soviet structure occupying the major part of its agenda.[57] But foreign policy was by no means neglected, and during the first half of the regime it often actually gave the tone to the entire proceedings of the Congress. Generally, it may be said that the Congress of Soviets exercised only a small part of its wide range of competence. It came closest to a full use of its prerogatives only in the field of constitutional change. The first and last Congresses of Soviets of the U.S.S.R. (1922, 1936) were entirely devoted to the adoption of the two Union constitutions, and, with the sole exception of the Fifth Congress of Soviets (May 1929), constitutional questions, dealing with the admission of new soviet republics as constituent members of the Union, administrative-territorial rearrangements, and changes in the structure and practice of the central and local soviet organs, et cetera, were before every Congress of Soviets of the U.S.S.R.

The Role of the Congress in the Field of Foreign Relations. To illustrate the operation of the Congress of Soviets more concretely, let us take one specific field — that of foreign relations. As far as types of activity are concerned, if the field be viewed under the headings of treaty making, war making and foreign-policy formulation, it becomes apparent that no international treaties were specifically voted by or concluded in the name of the Congress of Soviets. Only a few treaties — chiefly between the R.S.F.S.R. and the other Soviet republics — were ratified by it. Even the treaties of peace concluded in the early period were ratified mostly by the Central Executive Committee, despite the exclusive prerogatives in regard to the ratification of such treaties which the Congress possessed by virtue of the Constitution of 1918.[58] There is no case on record of any declaration of war by the Congress in the only instances of hostilities engaged in by the Soviets during the lifetime of the Congress: the 1918–20 wars with the border states and the display of force in Manchuria in 1929. But from its

---

57. A tabulation of the number of decisions of the Congress during this period by major fields — whether such decisions were embodied in separate resolutions or were covered in the resolutions on the government report — yields the following: (1) economic questions — 29; (2) questions of the constitution and of the Soviet structure — 24; (3) foreign policy and defense — 12. (See *S'ezdy Sovetov SSSR*, pp. 288–90.) There were only two appeals by the Congress to the outside world during this period: one by the Second Congress (26 January 1924) on the occasion of Lenin's death, and another by the Third Congress (16 May 1925) in regard to the white terror in Bulgaria. (Ibid. pp. 37–9, 81.)

58. See *S'ezdy Sovetov RSFSR*, pp. 69–70 (Ratification of Brest-Litovsk Treaty of Peace); 8 *Vserossiiskii S'ezd Sovetov*, pp. 231–4; *L. i S.* p. 319 (Ratification of Treaty between the RSFSR and the Ukrainian SSR, 29 December 1920); and 10 *Vserossiiskii S'ezd Sovetov*, pp. 184–9; *L. i S.* p. 328 (Ratification of the Treaty of Union, 30 December 1922). See also Taracouzio, *The Soviet Union and International Law*, pp. 238–45.

very inception, the Congress of Soviets did serve — on the occasions of its meetings — as an authoritative tribune from which many foreign policy pronouncements were made and given the sanction of approval of a publicly acclaimed representative body.[59]

Except in the first year of the regime, there were no separate reports on foreign policy at the Congress of Soviets. Foreign policy came before the Congress chiefly by way of the so-called 'accounting report of the government,' and in part also in the reports on the armed services.[60] The government report was considered the most important of all the reports presented at the Congress and was delivered by the Chairman of the Council of People's Commissars, or by his deputy.[61] Divided about equally

---

59. See the following decisions and resolutions of the Congress: Decree on Peace, 8 November 1917; On the Question of Peace, 27 January 1918; in re the Brest-Litovsk Peace Treaty, 15 March 1918; in re Wilson's Message, 14 March 1918; An Appeal to the Governments That Are Conducting War against Russia with a Proposal to Begin Negotiations for the Conclusion of Peace, 6 November 1918; About the International Situation, 8 November 1918; To All Workers, Peasants, Soldiers of All Nations Struggling for Peace and Socialism and to Their Leaders, 6 November 1918; A Proposal for Peace Negotiations, 5 December 1919; Declaration about the International Position of the R.S.F.S.R., 28 December 1921; An Appeal of the Tenth All-Russian Congress of Soviets to All the Peoples of the World, 27 December 1922 (*S'ezdy Sovetov RSFSR*, pp. 20–22, 43–4, 69–70, 70–71, 116, 117, 121–2, 136–7, 239–43, 273–4); About the *de jure* Recognition of the U.S.S.R. by Great Britain, 2 February 1924 (*S'ezdy Sovetov SSSR*, p. 63). See also the resolutions on the government report adopted at the 3rd, 4th, 5th, and 6th congresses of Soviets of the U.S.S.R. (16 May 1925, 20 April 1927, 22 May 1929, 12 March 1931, respectively), which with but slight variations in detail spoke of the threat of new world conflicts, of attempts on the part of some states to forge a hostile ring around the U.S.S.R. or to prepare armed aggression against it, and of directives by the Congress to the government to keep up the struggle for peace as a basic policy, develop economic relations with other states, and strengthen the Red Army as the surest guarantee against external attack. (Ibid. pp. 78–80, 123–6, 165–70, 198–201.)

60. From November 1917 to November 1918 there were several separate reports on foreign policy, all presented to the congresses by Lenin. At the Seventh All-Russian Congress of Soviets, December 1919, there was a report on the Comintern by Zinoviev, in addition to Lenin's report for the government. After that the conduct of foreign policy was presented to the congress in the government report. The Foreign Commissar did not report to the Congress of Soviets. The only exceptions are provided by the Second All-Union Congress, which heard a brief communication by Litvinov, on 2 February 1924, about *de jure* recognition by Great Britain and adopted a resolution that he suggested without debate, and by the Third All-Union Congress, where Chicherin was brought into the debate on 14 May 1925. (See 2 *S'ezd Sovetov SSSR*, pp. 197–9 and *infra*, p. 219.)

61. Lenin reported at the Second to Ninth All-Russian Congresses (1917–21), Kamenev at the Tenth All-Russian and Second All-Union Congresses (1922, 1924), Rykov at the Third, Fourth, and Fifth (1925, 1927, 1929), and Molotov at the Sixth and Seventh (1931, 1935) All-Union Congresses. Up to 1924, this report on the work of the gov-

between foreign and domestic policy, this report constituted as a rule a comprehensive statement obviously designed both for internal and external consumption. In its foreign-affairs part, it would review the Soviet position in world politics in the period which had elapsed since the preceding congress and indicate broadly the policies currently pursued. It almost always presented the following elements: (a) the basic motivating factors in the foreign relations of the non-Soviet powers, such as their domestic situation, political and economic rivalries, interests, et cetera; (b) specific acts aimed at the Soviet Union — press campaigns, formal notes, agreements and alliances, restrictions against Soviet trade, violations of the immunity of Soviet trade and diplomatic representatives, et cetera; (c) the Soviet view of outstanding international questions, such as Locarno, disarmament, the outlawry of war, the London Economic Conference, et cetera; (d) Soviet efforts and contributions toward peace in international relations, such as the Moscow disarmament conference, the Litvinov protocol, the Soviet neutrality and non-aggression treaties, the convention defining aggression, et cetera; (e) a review of the Soviet Union's political and economic relations with individual countries; (f) a statement, in conclusion, of continued Soviet desire for peace and trade with other nations, coupled with a warning of military preparedness in view of latent hostility toward the U.S.S.R.

The report on the government's activity was usually followed by debate.[62] The verbatim accounts of proceedings show that the great majority of the participants in this debate addressed themselves to problems of domestic rather than foreign policy. Those who did take up questions of the Soviets' foreign affairs spoke overwhelmingly in favor of the policies pursued by the government in regard to both relations with other nations and measures of defense. Efforts at radical alteration of the government's foreign policy through the power of the purse, through refusal to approve budgetary and financial plans, were unheard of in the Soviet scheme. Yet, the debates at the Congress reveal considerable pressure on governmental policy during the first half of the regime, particularly on the part of the delegates from the frontier Soviet republics. To illustrate, at the Third All-Union Congress of Soviets, on 14 May 1925, Staryi — a delegate from the Moldavian Autonomous Soviet Republic —

---

ernment was presented as 'the report of the Central Executive Committee and of the Council of People's Commissars,' but since then as the report 'of the Council of People's Commissars' or of its chairman.

62. Only at the Ninth and Tenth All-Russian Congresses (December 1921, December 1922) was there no debate on the government's report.

bitterly denounced certain foreign powers for recognizing Roumania's seizure of Bessarabia despite their recognition of the Soviet Union and their strict adherence to the property principle at home, and demanded that the government should declare at the Congress that it would some day present Roumania with a bill for the harm it was doing to Bessarabian citizens. He concluded with a plea to the Congress:

> to instruct our future Central Government to declare aloud . . . declare to all the bourgeois countries that any ratification of this grab [by them] would be like distributing land on the moon, that the . . . Moldavian people themselves will do the ratifying.[63]

He was followed by Zharyn, a peasant from White Russia, who spoke of the oppression of White Russians and the suppression of their culture in Poland, and demanded some action of Chicherin, 'who knows what is stated in which paragraph' of the treaty with Poland, concluding: 'We must say firmly to our Union government that it should show more toughness in its policy in this respect.'[64] Shumsky, a Ukrainian leader, pointed out the shortcomings in the Soviet foreign policy, speaking of the relations with England, Germany, France, and particularly Poland. Accusing the last-named of wholesale violation of the Treaty of Riga and reminding the Congress that Poland answered Chicherin's friendly overtures with the murder of Vechorkevich and Baginsky on the border and with acts of terror against the Ukrainian population of the Western Ukraine, Shumsky stressed the need for stronger Soviet assertion:

> All of these facts show that the course and tone of our foreign policy is too mild, that our Red diplomacy still clings to the tone that was appropriate when all [the powers] confronted us as an armed wall and we had to tear a breach in that wall by all means and conclude some kind of an agreement, be it even with third-rate states. But that time is past . . . It is necessary that our diplomacy should conduct its work in such manner that, while unswervingly pursuing a policy of peace, it should nonetheless not place us before all kinds of sudden surprises that stir public opinion . . . It is necessary that our diplomacy should maintain a firmer tone corresponding to the dignity of our Union.[65]

Khalikov, a delegate from Bashkiria, complained of the disappointing results of the *de jure* recognitions by England and France, and implied that the government had erred in promising MacDonald some payment on the Tsarist debts on condition of obtaining a 40-million pound loan, because that gave the Entente powers the idea that they would get more

63. 3 *S'ezd Sovetov SSSR*, pp. 66–70.
64. Ibid. pp. 71–2.
65. Ibid. pp. 72–8.

by waiting longer. Khalikov asked the Congress to direct the government to seek more practical results from recognition.[66] Lastly, delegate Kireev reminded the Congress of Poincaré's promise that the Russian fleet, which was carried away by Wrangel and placed in the harbor of Bizerte, would be returned to the lawful government of Russia, and of a similar promise by Herriot; and he demanded that now that the Soviets were recognized by France the logical conclusion should be drawn:

Maybe the French government is not responsible for the actions and words of Herriot and also for the actions and words of Poincaré, but we hold that it is necessary for our Commissariat of Foreign Affairs and our government to pose, most categorically, the question of the immediate return of these ships to our Soviet ports.[67]

The rising pitch of these demands for action caused the Council of People's Commissars to interpose at this point an unscheduled speech by Chicherin, which was not limited in time and was virtually a report in itself. Chicherin began by observing that 'the criticism that was heard here and the numerous written inquiries received from those present show with what lively interest the Congress, and consequently our Soviet public, regard questions of foreign policy.' Noting also that the chief criticisms were directed against Poland for its non-observance of the treaty guarantees of cultural development for national minorities, Chicherin gave a long and exhaustive statement on the foreign policy of the government, its milieu, bases, purposes, and expectations. The gist of his answer, struck at the very outset of his speech, was that the Soviet Union could not push things to a point where war might result, when its entire policy is built on peace:

Really, what do the comrades who come forth with this criticism want? Do they want that we should start a war? There are, perhaps, a couple of odd fellows who think in such terms, but not wide [sections of] Soviet public opinion, in any case.[68]

While the debate on foreign policy subsided after this speech and swung around largely to domestic affairs,[69] Rykov, in his concluding remarks on

---

66. Ibid. pp. 78–81.
67. Ibid. pp. 81–3.
68. See ibid. pp. 83–100.
69. There were several more demands later in the debate. A delegate from White Russia told the Congress of border attacks by armed bands from Poland, which alarmed the people of White Russia, and he demanded that the federal government should decisively remonstrate with Poland about such incidents. (Ibid. pp. 114–17; see also ibid. pp. 130–31.) Other delegates insisted that the government should not pay the Tsarist debt; a non-Party peasant named Spitzyn said that the peasants were amazed at the foreign bankers' nerve in expecting payment of this debt despite 'the blood and tears' shed by

the government report, also sought to meet the open and implied pressure for stronger action with its occasional world-revolutionary overtone:

The declarations that were made here in regard to the foreign policy of the U.S.S.R. are characteristic in that in all or in the majority of the speeches made from this platform there were expressions of solidarity with the oppressed peoples and oppressed classes of the entire world, and, if one may thus call it, a demand for an active foreign policy . . . By our positive work alone, within the Union, we simultaneously achieve the greatest liberating revolutionary results in regard to the entire world, in regard to all the toilers. In the measure that we come nearer to organizing socialism, that we destroy poverty, organize industry, raise wages, fight ignorance — in the measure of this struggle, the desire of all the oppressed peoples and of all the oppressed classes to do likewise at home, in their own country, must rise. But the liberating factor . . . is the struggle of the oppressed classes and oppressed nations themselves for their liberation on the basis of internal revolutionary forces in these countries.

Our policy must be and is a policy of non-intervention and peace . . . The particular interests of our Union coincide in this case with the interests of the toilers of the entire globe.[70]

This illustration of the proceedings at the Third All-Union Congress of Soviets is not an exception. Similar instances of pressure on the government's foreign policy have occurred at several of the other congresses.[71] This pressure did not go unnoticed. While at certain times it played,

---

the Soviet people in the blockade, etc., and concluded: 'The diplomatic corps is here. Let them know what a non-Party peasant says and tell it to the governments that sent them.' (Ibid. pp. 117–18, 145, 146–7.)

70. Ibid. pp. 148–9.

71. In addition to the critical speeches and declarations by the representatives of the other socialist parties — Dan, Martov, Volsky, etc. — still present at the early Congresses of Soviets (see 7 *Vserossiiskii S'ezd Sovetov*, pp. 56–66, 68–71; 8 *Vserossiiskii S'ezd Sovetov*, pp. 33–43, 45–57, 61) — see particularly the following speeches and answers at the All-Union congresses: Second Congress, 30–31 January 1924: Skrypnik, in re Poland; Kamenev in answer, in re Poland and Bessarabia (2 *S'ezd Sovetov SSSR*, pp. 105–8, 115); Fourth Congress, 19–20 April 1927: Malkovich, in re White Russia and Bessarabia; Morozov, in re British note; Staryi, in re Bessarabia; Rykov in answer to some of the above and in re liquidation of the Soviet-Swiss conflict. (4 *S'ezd Sovetov SSSR*, pp. 95–7, 103–6, 133–5, 204–17.) Fifth Congress, 21–22 May 1929; Butsenko, in re Polish oppression of minorities, murder of Voikov, and attempt on Lazarev; Kior, in re Bessarabia. (5 *S'ezd Sovetov SSSR*, Bull. 4, pp. 3–6, 28–31.) Sixth Congress, 9–12 March 1931: Trolov, in re need of firmer line in foreign policy; Goloded, in re Poland's bad-neighbor role; Dimitriu, in re Bessarabia; Molotov's concluding remarks (6 *S'ezd Sovetov SSSR*, Bull. 3, p. 23; Bull. 6, pp. 18–24; Bull. 8, p. 21; Bull. 10, pp. 7–12). Typical examples are the following: 'The workers and peasants often ask us also such questions as these: If the Union of Soviet Socialist Republics is strong and mighty, why does it not react to the oppression that exists in White Russia and Bessarabia, places dear to our heart, which only an accident separated from us? We in White Russia hear such questions very frequently from our peasants. These are not

in fact, into the government's hands, strengthening its position in dealings with other states, at other times, when it seemed out of tune with the official line, an effort was made to answer all objections that had appeared in the debate or in the written remarks to the Presidium, by re-introducing and re-emphasizing the government's considerations in the résumé following debate. And as the resolutions adopted on the government report show, the foreign policies presented by the Council of People's Commissars have practically always received unanimous approval at the Congress of Soviets.[72]

Foreign-policy problems were often brought out at the Congress in the reports and statement on the Red Army, the contents of which suggest that they were designed to mobilize and reassure public opinion at home, as well as to warn off hostile neighbors or other prospective foreign foes.[73] The pattern of presentation evolved in these reports shows

---

words of the Soviet Government or of officials of the apparatus; such declarations are constantly heard at the meetings of our workers and peasants. We heard these declarations at all the area congresses of soviets without exception. The answer of our leaders — that the peoples themselves have to free themselves from the oppression of the capitalists — does not satisfy the [Soviet] toilers.' (Malkovich, in 4 S'ezd Sovetov SSSR, pp. 95–7.) 'There isn't a village or district meeting, not a single congress of soviets of the Moldavian Republic, where the question of the Bessarabian situation is not being raised. To the toilers of the Moldavian Republic, who are freely developing in the Union of Soviet Republics, it means nevertheless that the Union Government has not given sufficient attention to the problem of Bessarabia. In his report comrade Rykov spoke of the ratification [of the Bessarabian protocol by Italy], yet he failed to say what, from the point of view of the Federal Government, are the nearest prospects in regard to the liberation of Bessarabia. It may be, comrades, that in the total sum of problems of an international nature the problem of Bessarabia is not a big one, but after all there is a three million population there — a population that has overthrown Tsarist autocracy in February [March 1917] and has established Soviet rule in October [November 1917] together with us — smarting under the yoke of the bourgeoisie.' (Staryi, ibid. pp. 133–5.)

72. It is not clear from the verbatim reports whether the vote at the Eighth All-Russian (December 1920) and Sixth All-Union (March 1931) Congresses was a majority or unanimous one, though it was probably the latter. At all other congresses since mid-1918 the vote on the government report was unanimous.

73. These reports were made ordinarily by the Commissar of War. Such reports were presented at the Fifth to Ninth All-Russian Congresses (1918–21) by Trotsky, and at the Third and Fourth All-Union Congresses (1925, 1927) by Frunze and Voroshilov, respectively. At the Sixth All-Union Congress (1931) S. S. Kamenev, deputy Commissar of War, spoke at length about a French plan for military intervention uncovered at the then current trial, while Budenny made a sharp warning that aggressors against the Soviet Union would be beaten into the dust. (6 S'ezd Sovetov SSSR, Bull. 4, pp. 1–6; Bull. 8, pp. 31–2.) Likewise, at the Seventh All-Union Congress (1935) deputy Commissar of Defense Tukhachevsky presented figures on the personnel, organization, and equipment of the Red Army, crediting Ordzhonikidze, Voroshilov, and 'especially Stalin who personally and daily directed this matter' for the technical acquisitions made, and

the following elements: (a) a statement of the condition, nature, composition, training, and equipment of the Red Army; (b) a review and comparison of some facts and figures concerning the armies and armaments of neighbors or other powers; (c) a warning in regard to some concrete foreign policy incidents; (d) a declaration of the Soviet desire for peace; (e) a re-assertion of the need for a strong and modern Red Army as the most trusted guarantee of peace; (f) a concluding warning to possible aggressors of the military readiness of the armed forces and the populace. Thus, to illustrate in part the use of these reports in the conduct of foreign relations, let us look at portions of War Commissar Frunze's report at the Third All-Union Congress of Soviets on 19 May 1925. Referring to news that Estonia was about to yield the island of Ezel and Dago to Great Britain, he warned:

Should this be confirmed, should the English flag really be planted on the islands of Ezel and Dago, it would mean that English dreadnaughts could stand at the walls of Kronstadt and Leningrad within twenty-four hours, while in one hour and a half their air fleet would hover over the shops and factories of our Leningrad. You understand that this is far from being a matter of indifference to us. Therefore, though we do not desire to intervene in the internal affairs of Estonia, we must nevertheless declare aloud that we shall consider a fact of this sort as a direct challenge to our workers-peasants state . . . I should like to state in friendly fashion to Estonia and the other little states bordering upon us, that not on this road, not on the road of armaments exhausting the last means of their peoples, not on the road of threats and challenges addressed to the Soviet Union, would they, in the last analysis, secure their economic and political well-being and independence. Without the Russian people and the other peoples of the Union, and against them [i.e. their interest], no one would solve these problems. No! In the last analysis the question of this well-being will depend upon whether or not they will be able to regulate their interrelations with their Eastern neighbor, the mighty multimillion Union of Soviet Socialist Republics. We on our part are ready to do everything possible to facilitate the creation of honest, sincere, good-neighborly relations. The turn is theirs, not ours.[74]

Turning to Poland and Roumania, Frunze showed that, although Soviet feeling about the mistreatment of Ukrainians in those countries ran high and that their liberation would make a popular slogan, the Soviets have shown forbearance and want peace not war:

If it only depended upon us, we should gladly leave the solution of all questions in dispute, including the dispute about the condition of the national minorities in

---

concluding with the warning that war is being rapidly prepared against the Soviet Union, but that 'as one man, the country and the people under Voroshilov, under the Communist Party headed by the great Stalin, will smash the interventionists.' (7 S'ezd Sovetov SSSR, Bull. 5, pp. 29–38.)

74. 3 S'ezd Sovetov SSSR, pp. 483–4.

Poland and Roumania, to the peaceful march of history. We are deeply convinced that in the struggle between the system of Soviet statehood and socialism on the one hand and the bourgeois-parliamentary one on the other, victory will be on our side. Therefore, we are perfectly ready to renounce argumentation through the force of arms and have proved it in fact by a series of political statements. These took place at The Hague, in Genoa, and finally in Moscow, where it was none else but Poland that tore down our proposals for disarmament . . . We regret very much that we are unable in any way to prove to our neighbors the sincerity of our peaceful sentiments. We are powerless [to do so], so long as every step of ours, every speech, is interpreted in a reverse, hostile sense.[75]

Finally, after going into great detail about the condition of the Red Army, Frunze concluded with the type of warning to foreign aggressors that has virtually become a traditional conclusion in all reports and statements on foreign policy and defense made on behalf of the government in the years that followed:

After hearing this report, in which I tried to throw light, openly and directly, on the bright and dark sides of our work, you may ask me: Well, then, should the Red Army have to step out now unto the field of battle, would it be able to defend the Soviet Union or not? I think that I shall not be in error by saying: If anyone should get a desire to feel out with bayonet the strength of the Soviet house, the Red Army will prove that now it would be infinitely easier to enlarge this house by way of new Soviet buildings, than to destroy it.[76]

There were few debates on the military reports at the Congress,[77] and the vote taken on them shows that their statements and recommendations were received with complete unanimity by the Congress of Soviets.

The Basic Evolution and Position of the Congress of Soviets. To summarize, the development of the Congress shows the following features. The composition of the delegate body has risen tremendously in numbers, while the frequency of its convocation has fallen. Viewed through time the number of participants in the congressional debates has increased.[78] Up to the end of 1919 there were members of other socialist parties present at the Congress, and the debates were often characterized by sharp

75. Ibid. p. 485.

76. Ibid. pp. 489–514.

77. Only at the Third and Fourth All-Union Congresses were there debates on the military reports, with 6 and 12 participants, respectively. The tenor of their speeches was high praise for the Red Army and demands for more and better means and working conditions for it.

78. Since the time of the adoption of the first constitution (July 1918), the number of participants in the debate on the government report, at those congresses where debates were held, was: All-Russian congresses, 6th — 4, 7th — 6, 8th — 4; All-Union congresses, 2nd — 9, 3rd — 30, 4th — 56, 5th — 59, 6th — 98, 7th — 43. Similar increases were to be noted in regard to the debates on other reports at the congress.

and bitter clashes.[79] Since then, though considerable moral pressure has been brought into the debates at times, their tone was largely even, conforming, and approving. In practice the Congress of Soviets has utilized only a part of its wide sphere of competence, with problems of solidification of the regime — including its international position — being dominant at the first few congresses and economic questions at the later ones. As its operation in the field of foreign relations shows, the Congress of Soviets was used primarily as a popular platform from which — on the occasions of its meetings — the Council of People's Commissars could make pronouncements on policy to the populace at home as well as to foreign powers, which have become in time fairly stereotyped in form. The Congress of Soviets may be evaluated, thus, as having served partly as a policy-ratifying but chiefly as a policy-propagating organ during the two decades of its existence.

3. THE CENTRAL EXECUTIVE COMMITTEE

(I) THE ORGANIZATION OF THE CENTRAL EXECUTIVE COMMITTEE

The Crystallization of the C.E.C.'s Place. Like the Congress of Soviets, by which it was formed, the Central Executive Committee, or CEC, began its official existence on 7 November 1917, when Soviet rule was proclaimed.[80] Also like the Congress of Soviets in whose place it stood in the interim between congresses, it was 'All-Russian' until 30 December 1922; and although an 'All-Russian' C.E.C. continued to function for the R.S.F.S.R., it was the 'All-Union' C.E.C., created by the Union Constitution, that represented the entire state, the U.S.S.R., from that date on.[81] In the early years of the regime, even after the adoption of the first constitution (July 1918), the precise place of the C.E.C. in the Soviet hierarchy was not crystallized, owing partly to the lack of a clear view

---

79. See e.g. 5 *Vserossiiskii S'ezd Sovetov, passim,* especially pp. 16–17, 31; 7 *Vserossiiskii S'ezd Sovetov,* pp. 60–66.

80. When the Second Congress of Soviets assumed power on that day, there was in existence a Central Executive Committee elected by the First Congress of Soviets in June 1917. The first act of the Second Congress was to issue a proclamation declaring that 'the powers of the reformist C.E.C. have ended.' (*L. i S.* p. 257.)

81. The 'all-Russian' and 'all-Union' central executive committees, termed 'VTsIK' and 'TsIK,' respectively, as abbreviations of their Russian titles, were usually referred to as of the First, Second, etc., 'Sozyv' (call or convocation) to denote the particular congress of soviets by which they were elected. These designations, with arabic numerals indicating the successive committees, will be used hereafter in citing the verbatim reports of their proceedings.

concerning its duties and its relation to the Council of People's Commissars, and partly to the conditions of the civil war. By 1919–21, though efforts were made to clarify its status, the position of the C.E.C. in the scheme of authority was considerably affected by the emergence of its own Presidium as a governmental organ with a number of powers and prerogatives.[82] Then the constitution of the U.S.S.R. created a somewhat different structural set-up for the All-Union C.E.C., by making it a bicameral body. As we shall see later, however, a definite pattern of C.E.C. activity

82. The 8 November 1917 decree forming the Council of People's Commissars, or Sovnarkom as it is called, declared that 'control over the acts of the People's Commissars and the right of recall' belongs to the C.E.C. (*S.U.* 1917, p. 1.) Four days later, the Sovnarkom itself stated in a decree that the C.E.C. 'has a right at any time to suspend, modify, or annul any decision of the government.' (Ibid. pp. 10–11.) At the time, however, the C.E.C. appears to have been more interested in setting up shop for itself on lines similar in some respects to the Sovnarkom. For, on 15 November 1917, the C.E.C. adopted a project that provided for: (1) large and small sessions of the C.E.C., the latter to be held when one-quarter of the members were present, though the former alone was to be considered a controlling and directing organ; (2) a Presidium, which was to be a 'representative as well as executive organ'; and (3) 11 commissions or 'working organs of the C.E.C.,' with fields of activity not dissimilar to some of the commissariats, which would account weekly to the Presidium and be subject to the veto of the latter. (2 *VTsIK*, pp. 19–20.) And on 17 November 1917, answering an inquiry by the Left S.R.'s as to 'why drafts of decrees and other acts are not submitted for consideration by the C.E.C.,' the C.E.C. stated that 'the Soviet parliament [i.e. the C.E.C.] cannot deny the Council of People's Commissars the right to issue decrees of immediate necessity in the spirit of the general program of the All-Russian Congress of Soviets without first submitting them to the C.E.C.' (Ibid. p. 31.) Yet, a fortnight later, on 30 November 1917, the C.E.C. passed a resolution calling for weekly accounts by each of the people's commissars to the C.E.C. and for an immediate reply to C.E.C. interpellations, and providing that, though the Sovnarkom, 'with the reservation of its responsibility to the C.E.C.,' could adopt directly measures against counter-revolution, 'all legislative acts and ordinances of major political importance' would have to be submitted to the C.E.C. for examination and confirmation. (Ibid. p. 71; see also 4 *VTsIK*, p. 42.) These conflicting aims and attempts reflected a struggle within the C.E.C. itself on the question of establishing the principles of separation of powers and of executive responsibility in the evolving structure. Though little came of the accounting and control provisions, the result was considerable duplication of efforts and a recurrent tug of war between the C.E.C. and the Sovnarkom, which the Bolshevik leaders — while dismissing any conception of the C.E.C. as the legislative and Sovnarkom as the executive branch of the government — hoped to overcome by adoption of a constitution. (See Sverdlov's remarks, on 1 April 1918, in 4 *VTsIK*, pp. 66–9.) The Constitution of 1918 sought to delimit the relative spheres of action of the two organs, and some of the C.E.C. commissions (the Military, Peasantry, etc., Commissions) were subsequently fused with the relevant commissariats. (See 5 *VTsIK*, pp. 53–4.) But the constitution did not specify the manner and frequency of C.E.C. convocations — a condition not remedied until December 1919 — and they became rare during the civil war. Though some of the Bolsheviks questioned its utility, the C.E.C. was left in the Soviet pyramid, but, as we shall see later, in practice many of its powers fell away to its Presidium.

evolved during these and subsequent years. The C.E.C. went out of existence in 1937.

The Conception of the C.E.C. The formal conception of the C.E.C. inscribed in the first two constitutions (articles 12, 30, Constitution of 1918; article 8, Constitution of 1924) and averred in numerous public pronouncements, was that of a 'supreme organ of power' in the periods between the meetings of the Congress of Soviets. Associated with this conception was the view that the C.E.C. was functionally both a legislative and executive organ, the Constitution of 1918 specifically defining the C.E.C. as 'the highest legislative, administrative, and controlling organ' of the republic (article 31).[83] Lastly, by virtue of its usual composition, the C.E.C. was regarded as an organ singularly expressive of the interests of the localities,[84] and, since the introduction of bicameralism, as the embodiment of the class and nationality principles in its two chambers, the Union Council and Council of Nationalities, respectively.[85]

The Composition and Procedure of the C.E.C. The first constitution (July 1918) provided for a C.E.C. of not more than 200 persons, but this provision was altered to allow for an increase to 300 and later to 386 members by the eighth (December 1920) and ninth (December 1921) Congresses of Soviets. The constitution of the U.S.S.R. (1923–4) which set up the two-chamber system provided that the Congress of Soviets should

---

83. At the Eleventh Party Congress (March–April 1922) Lenin took sharp exception to Osinsky's proposal to change to 'a cabinet system,' to concentrate the legislative function exclusively in the C.E.C., while the Sovnarkom would act solely as its executive organ. (See Lenin, XXVII, p. 265 and note 116.)

84. In March 1919 the Eighth Party Congress declared in a resolution that 'the congress holds that the composition of the VTsIK should be altered in the sense that the members of the VTsIK should be recruited chiefly from among the public men of the localities who are carrying on constant work among the masses of peasants and workers.' (Lenin, XXIV, p. 720.) And in December of that year Kamenev expressed the official view that the C.E.C. was not an assembly of people empowered to sit in the capital and do nothing else but legislate: 'On the contrary, by the substance and spirit of our revolutionary practice, into the composition of the C.E.C. are placed comrades who, while legislating, are at the same time executing legislative proposals, thereby tying up living practice with the decisions of the central government . . . The Central Committee of the Russian Communist Party adopted a decision, and, in accord with it, you have now confirmed the composition of the C.E.C., which, in its vast majority, consists of officials of the local soviets. And were you to be told: yield us your local men, let them all sit in Moscow, let them detach themselves from local life and legislate here, you would, no doubt, refuse to leave these people here and say that such action would violate the interests of both the given locality and Socialist construction as a whole.' (7 *Vserossiiskii S'ezd Sovetov*, pp. 261–2.)

85. See *S'ezdy Sovetov SSSR*, p. 200; *S.G.P.* p. 225; and *supra*, ch. IV, pp. 71–4.

elect the Union Council from among the representatives of the Union Republics, in proportion to the population of each, 'to consist of 414 members in all.' The last clause was amended in May 1925 to read 'the number to be determined by the Congress of Soviets of the U.S.S.R.' (article 14). As for the second chamber, the Council of Nationalities, it was to be formed of the representatives of the Union and autonomous republics on the basis of five representatives from each, and of the autonomous regions on the basis of one representative from each; the membership of the Council of Nationalities as a whole was to be confirmed by the Congress of Soviets (article 15).[86] As was the case with most of the other central organs of authority, the actual composition of the C.E.C. continuously increased. From 246 (207 members, 39 candidates) in November 1918 it rose progressively to 513 (386 members, 127 candidates) in December 1921 during the R.S.F.S.R. period, and then again from 509 (371 members, 138 candidates) at the first convocation for the U.S.S.R., in December 1922, to 889 (587 members, 302 candidates) at the fifth convocation, in May 1929, decreasing relatively slightly to 757 when it was last formed in February 1935. Most of the C.E.C.'s membership consisted of people from the localities. But it always contained a considerable part from the center, which included many of the top men in the Party and the government — members of the Politbureau, the Sovnarkom, the high command of the Red Army, leading officials of the Foreign Affairs and other commissariats, a number of diplomats, and a few Comintern functionaries.

---

86. The actual selection of the members of the Union Council from among the delegate body of the Congress of Soviets, and apparently also the approval of the members of the Council of Nationalities designated at the congresses of the republics and regions, went through several stages of discussion at the Congress. It was considered by 'the Council of Elders' — something in the nature of an initial steering committee consisting of representatives of the various delegations — by the Communist fraction of the Congress and the 'Consultation of Non-Party Delegates,' and by a special commission that worked on the apportionment of the membership between the different republics and various groups. The lists thus drawn up were voted on by the Congress of Soviets *in toto* at its last session. That this system did not stand in the way of changes in the personnel of the C.E.C. in accordance with the Party's considerations and particular tasks is attested to by Enukidze, who claimed at successive congresses: that the percentage of non-Party men in the composition of the C.E.C. was increasing; that the representation of all parts of the U.S.S.R. was secured; that there were more women, more plain workers and peasants and fewer clerks and officials in it; and that of the Party men in the C.E.C. the number of officials from the localities and national units — many of them lower rung — was progressively increasing at the expense of the number of officials from the center. (See 3 *S'ezd Sovetov SSSR*, pp. 541–2; 4 *S'ezd Sovetov SSSR*, pp. 593–4; 5 *S'ezd Sovetov SSSR*, Bull. 20, pp. 6–7; 6 *S'ezd Sovetov SSSR*, Bull. 21, p. 17; 7 *S'ezd Sovetov SSSR*, Bull. 17, pp. 46–8.)

Members of the C.E.C. enjoyed certain privileges and immunities.[87] They had the right of inquiry and legislative initiative at the separate and joint sessions of the chambers. They could attend all sessions of the Presidium of the C.E.C., participate with consultative voice in the proceedings of the central and local institutions throughout the U.S.S.R., and receive all necessary information, except that attendance at secret sessions of these institutions and secret information was open to them only on special permission of the Presidium C.E.C. While they could be asked by the judicial or administrative organs to appear as witnesses, and were obliged to explain to the Presidium any refusal to do so, they could not be compelled to testify. Nor could they be arrested, detained, searched, or examined by these authorities without a special decision of the Presidium to that effect, except that in extraordinary cases such action could be taken upon the consent of the Chairman of the C.E.C., on condition that he report it to the nearest session of the C.E.C. Likewise, sentence could be passed against them by court decree or administrative order only on decision of the C.E.C. or its Presidium. In such cases, all investigatory material had to be submitted first to the Presidium C.E.C., which could render its own decision only after requesting an oral or written statement from the defendant. C.E.C. members were allowed free transportation.[88]

Candidates had the same right and privileges as members of the C.E.C., ordinarily participating in the sessions with a consulting voice, but having the right to vote, in the order of their seniority, when part of the C.E.C. membership was not present. According to the Statute on the C.E.C. (1923), members could be expelled from the C.E.C. during the interim

87. See Diablo, 'Immunitet,' pp. 140–41; rules 23–35 of the Statute on the C.E.C. R.S.F.S.R., adopted 17 December 1919, and articles 65–77 of the Statute on the C.E.C. U.S.S.R., adopted 12 November 1923, rendered in English in Batsell, op. cit. pp. 522–4, 533–6.

88. Until 1927, all members of the C.E.C., regardless of the place and kind of work in which they were engaged, received their remuneration from the C.E.C. in accordance with appropriations especially provided for C.E.C. members. (Article 76, Statute on the C.E.C. U.S.S.R. of 12 November 1923.) In that year, however, the C.E.C. amended its statute to provide that C.E.C. members occupying responsible posts in government institutions should get no additional pay for their C.E.C. membership, while members of the localities earning less than 100 rubles a month would get 60 additional rubles for expenses connected with their duties as C.E.C. members. In case of illness, members and candidates would receive a monthly sum equal to their last regular salary, while during C.E.C. sessions or when on missions of the C.E.C. or its Presidium taking them away from their regular jobs, members of the C.E.C. would receive a daily allowance of one thirtieth of the salary established for responsible officials of the center. All members and candidates retained the right to free railroad and river transportation. (4 TsIK 1 Sessia, pp. 17–19.)

between regular Congresses of Soviets only upon decision of extraordinary congresses, and in particularly urgent cases upon decision of the C.E.C. itself, provided a report on the action taken was submitted to the next Congress of Soviets. In practice, action in such cases was taken by the Presidium of the C.E.C. with subsequent submission to the plenary session of the C.E.C. for confirmation.[89]

The C.E.C. was not in continuous session, and this fact was considered a virtue rather than a vice. At first it was required to meet not less than once every two months. This was reduced to 'not less than three times a year' by provision of the Ninth All-Russian Congress of Soviets (December 1921), and this requirement was embodied in the Constitution of 1924 (article 21). In March 1931 the three-times-a-year convocation requirement was changed to 'not less than three times in the period of time between regular congresses of Soviets.'[90] In practice the meetings of the C.E.C. became progressively rarer. Following the civil-war period, the All-Russian C.E.C. met in regular session four times yearly during 1920–22. Sessions lasted from one to eight days; the longest was fifteen days. The yearly totals were: 1920, 20 days; 1921, 8 days; 1922, 25 days. The All-Union C.E.C. met on the average twice yearly during 1923–33 and once

---

89. A notorious example of such action was provided in the case of Zinoviev, Kamenev, Trotsky, Rakovsky, and four others who were excluded from C.E.C. membership by the Presidium C.E.C. on 30 December 1927, following their street demonstration on 7 November, at the time of the tenth anniversary celebration. Reporting this expulsion to the session of the C.E.C. on 19 April 1928, and basing it on article 29 of the constitution, which terms the Presidium 'the highest legislative, executive, and administrative organ of power' in the interim between C.E.C. sessions, Enukidze stated: 'You know the existing system of election to our C.E.C. The Congress of Soviets elects the members of the C.E.C., but the Congress of Soviets gives its sanction, its confidence, and vote to those comrades-Communists who are put forth by the Communist fraction of the Congress of Soviets . . . Continued presence within the ranks of the C.E.C. is unthinkable for a Communist who has lost the confidence of his party . . . And when the Party, in the person of its fraction in the Presidium of the C.E.C. U.S.S.R., informed us that they [the 8 members] were excluded from the Party, that the Party deprives them of its confidence for a definite period of time, the Presidium decided that the presence of these persons in the ranks of the C.E.C. would be unthinkable until such time as they regain the faith of the Party that has advanced them, morally supported them, shown them confidence at the time of the Congress of Soviets of the U.S.S.R.' (4 *TsIK* 3 *Sessia*, pp. 705–6. For other examples of removal from membership of the C.E.C., Presidium C.E.C., or both, see ibid. pp. 706–7; 8 *VTsIK*, p. 218; 6 *TsIK* 4 *Sessia*, Bull. 27, pp. 26–37.)

90. *S'ezdy Sovetov SSSR*, pp. 21, 48–9, 218. It may be interesting to note that the treaty forming the U.S.S.R. (30 December 1922) provided for the rotation of the sessions of the C.E.C., as well as of the Congress of Soviets, between the capitals of the Union republics (article 8). Only one such session, a meeting of the C.E.C. in Tiflis, appears to have been held outside of Moscow.

a year during 1934–7. It convened once in 1926, three times each in 1927 and 1931, and did not meet at all in 1930 and 1932. The yearly totals of these meetings ranged from 6 to 24 days, making an average of 11–12 days per year on the basis of a calculation for the years actually in session. The intervals between plenary sessions ranged from 2 to 13 months, averaging 6 to 8 months. In the 15 years of its existence (1923–37) the All-Union C.E.C. sat a total of 139 days.

The C.E.C. sessions were convoked by the Presidium of the C.E.C. They were open, as a rule, but occasionally discussion of a particular item was transferred to a closed meeting of the Party fraction of the C.E.C., at which, however, the non-Party members of the C.E.C. were allowed to be present.[91] At the first session of each convocation the C.E.C. would elect its Chairmen, Secretary, and Presidium. In accordance with the constitutional requirement, the chairmen of the C.E.C. were elected from among the members of the Presidium and corresponded in number to the existing constituent republics. Thus, following the addition of the Uzbek, Turkmen, and Tadzhik republics to the original four that formed the Union, by 1931 there were seven C.E.C. chairmen. These chairmen presided at joint sessions of the C.E.C., as well as in the Presidium, and performed a number of other duties on behalf of the C.E.C. and its Presidium by rotation, the order and term of which was fixed by the latter. The Secretary, besides acting as such at the sessions of the C.E.C. and of its Presidium, supervised the secretariat and technical apparatus of the C.E.C. Proceedings were based on complete equality of the chambers. Each chamber assembled only during the sessions of the C.E.C. Each would elect a presidium of nine of its members to arrange its sessions and conduct the work of the latter. Members of one chamber could not be members of the other. No bill pending before the C.E.C. could become law unless it was passed by both chambers. All communications with other Soviet organs and institutions were conducted through the C.E.C. The agenda of the C.E.C. sessions were set by the Presidium and were supposed to be published by the latter in *Izvestia* not later than a month

---

91. See e.g. 8 *VTsIK*, pp. 76, 183–4, 338, 364–5. The statement on procedure and organization which follows is based on: the Rules of Procedure adopted on 15 April 1918 (4 *VTsIK*, pp. 8–9, 124–5; see also ibid. pp. 20, 262); the Resolution of the Fourth Consultation of the Central Committee with Responsible Officials of the National Republics and Regions, 9–12 June 1923 (*VKP(b) v Rezol.* I, p. 539); the statutes on the C.E.C. R.S.F.S.R. and C.E.C. U.S.S.R. (see *supra*, note 87, this chapter); chapter IV, Constitution of 1924; the Rules of Procedure followed by the C.E.C. U.S.S.R. (see e.g. 3 *TsIK 2 Sessia*, p. 1102; 5 *TsIK 2 Sessia*, Bull. 18, p. 19, and the verbatim reports of proceedings of the C.E.C., *passim*.)

before the scheduled session was opened.[92] These agenda were voted confirmation at the opening of the plenary sessions and could be altered then or later in the proceedings. Both joint and separate sessions were held by the chambers. Since presentation of the same reports twice, before each of the chambers, was found cumbersome, it became the practice to hear the reports at joint sessions, and then debate and vote on them at separate sessions, though often the debates too were carried on at joint sessions. In the latter case, however, the vote was still taken separately.[93] The presence of one-third of its members was required in order to have a quorum within a chamber, and the combined quorums of both chambers constituted a quorum of the joint session. In case of disagreement between the chambers, the question under consideration was to be submitted to a Conciliation Commission set up by them on principles of parity. If no agreement was reached in the Conciliation Commission the question was to be referred back for a vote by a joint session of the chambers, and if no understanding was obtained at that time, either chamber could demand its submission to a regular or extraordinary Congress of Soviets for decision. Actually, no such case of disagreement has ever arisen. In the course of the proceedings, the plenary session as a whole or the separate chambers had a right to, and as a rule did, form temporary commissions for the examination of individual problems under discussion.[94] Generally,

---

92. The Statute on the C.E.C. R.S.F.S.R., which was adopted in December 1919, provided also that the materials, resolutions, decrees, etc., submitted for the consideration of the C.E.C. were to be supplied to all the members for their information 'as far as possible not later than two weeks before the opening of the session' (article 38), but this was found difficult of application and the provision was not repeated in the Statute on the C.E.C. U.S.S.R., adopted in November 1923.

93. During the first half of 1923, when the precise set-up of the central organs of the newly formed U.S.S.R. was being discussed by the various constituent republics, representatives of several of the latter — declaring that on questions of war and peace and other questions of foreign policy the constituent republics are not likely to have any special interests distinct from or opposed to those of the Union — proposed that, in deciding upon such questions. joint sessions should be held at which the vote would also be a joint one, a mere majority of the total of assembled delegates of both chambers sufficing for decision. In November of that year, however, when the plenary session of the C.E.C. considered the Statute for its own structure, the proposal was rejected on the ground that a separate vote was necessary in order to preserve the equality of the chambers in view of the numerical preponderance of the Union Council over the Council of Nationalities. (See Vaksberg, op. cit. p. 19.)

94. These commissions are not to be confused with the permanent and provisional commissions that the C.E.C. and its Presidium had a right to form (Decision of the Ninth All-Russian Congress of Soviets, 28 December 1921, *S'ezdy Sovetov RSFSR*, p. 219; articles 78 and 79 of the Statute on the C.E.C. U.S.S.R.), and with the various committees attached to it from time to time. In the R.S.F.S.R. period, the C.E.C. was fre-

the rules in regard to reports, proposals, debate, vote, et cetera, were not markedly different from those prevailing at the Congress of Soviets. The Presidium of the C.E.C. acted as a permanent steering committee; it received all drafts of decrees, reports, proposals, and inquiries from the chambers and their presidia, from the Sovnarkom, individual commissariats, the central executive committees of the constituent republics, and from the members of the C.E.C. U.S.S.R. themselves, and it arranged the consideration and disposal of these matters.

The C.E.C.'s Jurisdiction. The general scope of federal competence that the C.E.C. was empowered to exercise along with the Congress of Soviets was discussed earlier.[95] In addition, the constitutional provisions specifically enumerated a number of prerogatives granted to the C.E.C.: procedural, legislative, controlling-directive, and judicial. Thus, the C.E.C. was to convoke regular and extraordinary Congresses of Soviets and had the right to postpone such convocation under extraordinary circumstances (articles 26, 27, 34, Constitution of 1918; articles 11, 12, Constitution of 1924). It issued instructions and was the final instance of appeal in regard to elections to the soviets (articles 70, 77, Constitution of 1918). Its legislative powers included the examination of all decrees and decisions submitted by other organs and the issuance of codes, decrees, decisions, and ordinances of binding force throughout the U.S.S.R.[96] One pivotal article of the Constitution provided that:

quently called upon, in the resolutions of the Congress of Soviets, to form special commissions, and there existed at various times commissions on the federal structure, administrative problems, agriculture, the struggle against the famine, communal economy, transport, the budget, etc. (See *S'ezdy Sovetov RSFSR,* pp. 176, 179, 180, 212, 229–30, 232, 233, 265, 274; 8 *VTsIK,* pp. 4–5.) The Budget Commission was particularly important and was regularly elected at the plenary sessions of the C.E.C. The following commissions and committees, some of which were later set up under the Sovnarkom, were attached to the C.E.C. in the early 'thirties, in practice functioning under the supervision of its Presidium: the Budget Commission, Central Election Commission, Commission on the Care of the Central Archives, Commission on General Questions of Administrative Organization, Committee on Scientific Research and Progress, Committee on Higher Colleges, Supreme Council of Physical Culture, and All-Union Council of Communal Economy. (See 6 *TsIK* 2 *Sessia,* Bull. 19, p. 37; 6 *TsIK* 4 *Sessia,* Bull. 28, p. 36; and Webb, op. cit. pp. 90–91.) A somewhat analogous status in relation to the C.E.C. was occupied by the Supreme Court and the Procurator. (See *infra,* pp. 302–3, 306–7.)

95. See *supra,* pp. 212–13.

96. Article 33, Constitution of 1918; articles 16, 17, and 19, Constitution of 1924. From time to time the C.E.C. was specifically charged by the Congress of Soviets to issue or confirm various decrees and decisions. (See *S'ezdy Sovetov RSFSR,* pp. 117, 121, 152–3, 169–72, 180–82, 205–6, 208–13, 221, 223, 229–30, 232–3, 242–3, 262–4, 268–9, 270–71, 274; *S'ezd Sovetov SSSR,* pp. 25, 39–40, 53, 55, 61–2, 105.) It should also be pointed out that the C.E.C. enjoyed wide prerogatives of determination and approval of the

All decrees and 'decisions that determine the general norms of the political and economic life of the U.S.S.R., and also those which introduce fundamental changes in the existing practice of the state organs of the U.S.S.R., must be submitted for the examination and confirmation of the C.E.C. of the U.S.S.R. (article 18, Constitution of 1924).[97]

As for controlling-directive prerogatives, another article stated that the C.E.C. 'unifies the work of legislation and administration of the U.S.S.R., and determines the scope of activities of the Presidium of the C.E.C. and of the Council of People's Commissars of the U.S.S.R.' (article 17).[98] The C.E.C. could suspend or annul the decisions and enactments of the Presidium C.E.C., Council of People's Commissars, and the Commissariats of the U.S.S.R. (all of which were responsible to the C.E.C.), and of the Congresses of Soviets and central executive committees of the constituent republics, as well as other organs of power on the territory of the U.S.S.R.[99] The C.E.C. also occupied a unique position in regard to the judiciary. The Supreme Court of the U.S.S.R. was 'attached to the C.E.C.' (article 43, Constitution of 1924). Decisions, resolutions, and verdicts of the Supreme Courts of the Union Republics contravening federal legislation were to be appealed by the Supreme Court U.S.S.R., on motion of the Attorney General, to the C.E.C. The C.E.C. could request of the Supreme Court opinions in regard to the constitutionality of decisions of the Union republics. It was one of the organs that had a right to initiate action by the Supreme Court along the lines of the latter's jurisdiction (article 47, Constitution of 1924). And its approval, or that of its Presidium, was

budget and taxation in regard to both the federation and lower territorial units even by the Constitution of 1918. (See articles 81, 85, 86, and 88. For its budgetary powers under the Constitution of 1924, see article 1, clause k.)

97. An earlier decision, adopted by the Eighth All-Russian Congress of Soviets on 29 December 1920, contained an identical provision, adding that such 'decrees and decisions on questions of general political and economic significance, including all the important measures on military and foreign affairs, should be made public by the Presidium of the VTsIK [C.E.C.] not later than two weeks before the session, so that local soviets should have the time and possibility of discussing them before a final decision is adopted.' (S'ezdy Sovetov RSFSR, p. 175.)

98. A similar article in the Constitution of 1918 read: 'gives general direction to the activity of the Workers-Peasants' Government and of all the organs of Soviet rule in the country, unifies and co-ordinates legislative and administrative work, and supervises the observance of the Soviet constitution, the decisions of the all-Russian Congresses of Soviets and the central organs of the Soviet government.' (Article 32.)

99. Articles 40, 46, and 47, Constitution of 1918; articles 20, 36, 40, 41, and 60, Constitution of 1924. The Constitution of 1918, moreover, required the Sovnarkom to inform the C.E.C. immediately of all its decisions and to submit all decrees and decisions of major political significance, except measures of extreme urgency, for examination and confirmation by the C.E.C. (articles 39 and 41).

necessary before the Supreme Court could accept cases of exceptional importance affecting two or more republics, as well as cases involving members of the C.E.C. or of the Sovnarkom (article 48, Constitution of 1924). In the field of foreign policy, as we have seen earlier,[100] the C.E.C. also enjoyed a number of important prerogatives.

(2) THE POSITION AND ROLE OF THE CENTRAL EXECUTIVE COMMITTEE

The Operation of the C.E.C. in Practice. This array of power was only partly realized, however, in the actual operation of the C.E.C. In the nature of things, the procedural, controlling-directive, and judicial prerogatives did not lend themselves easily to execution by such a large body as the C.E.C., so that in practice they were exercised by the Presidium of the C.E.C. But to a large extent the same was also true in regard to legislation and matters of foreign policy, especially in view of the relatively infrequent convocation of the plenary sessions of the C.E.C. As the verbatim reports of the proceedings show, the C.E.C. busied itself in the early period with a lot of miscellanea; statements concerning the Soviet international position and military situation were prominent till 1920, while domestic matters — agriculture, other economic questions, the work of certain commissariats, law codes, reports from the provinces, et cetera — comprised the subjects of the sessions afterwards. With the establishment of the All-Union C.E.C., there soon emerged a fairly typical agenda, consisting of five subjects that were repeatedly presented, with a few occasional additions of one or several reports or an omission of a customary one. The five were: (1) the report of the government, which was later merged with the report on control figures of the national economy; (2) the report on the state budget; (3) a report on agriculture or some phase or measures concerning it; (4) a report by one of the constituent republics; (5) the report of the Presidium of the C.E.C. concerning fundamental decrees that were adopted in the interim between C.E.C. sessions. Of these, the first two reports were deemed the most important and drew the most extensive debates. The report of the government was delivered by the chairman of the Sovnarkom and, following its substitution by the report on the national economic plan (1929), was accompanied by a co-report made by the chairman of the State Planning Commission (Gosplan).[101]

100. See *supra*, pp. 212–13 and note 55, ch. x.
101. Rykov delivered 4 of these reports (31 March 1925, 12 April 1926, 15 October 1927, and 29 November 1929), Molotov, 5 (4 January and 22 December 1931, 24 January and 28 December 1933, and 10 January 1936); the last of Rykov's and all of Molotov's reports were accompanied by co-reports of the Chairman of the Gosplan.

The report on the state budget of the U.S.S.R. was presented by the Commissar of Finance on behalf of the Sovnarkom and was always accompanied by a co-report of the Budget Commission of the C.E.C.[102] The customary procedure was to vote acceptance of the Sovnarkom's project — together with the Budget Commission's proposed amendments — as a basis, and then to charge the Presidium of the C.E.C. with examining the 'directive decisions' concerning the budget. The next step was to have the Budget Commission prepare the final draft of the budget, with due consideration to the corrections suggested in the debate, and then vote this final draft at one of the last plenary meetings.

The C.E.C. and the Legislative Function. The decisions adopted by the plenary sessions of the C.E.C. on the reports presented were laws of the realm and to that extent the C.E.C. was a legislative organ. It should be pointed out, however, that the great majority of decisions, ordinances, and decrees operating as laws over the entire domain of the U.S.S.R. were passed or promulgated by organs other than the C.E.C.: by the Sovnarkom, the Presidium of the C.E.C., the Sovnarkom and Presidium together, the Council of Labor and Defense, the Central Committee of the Party together with the Sovnarkom, and occasionally some other organ.[103] To be sure, as we have seen earlier, by article 18 of the Constitution all decrees defining 'the general norms of the political and economic life' of the country or introducing 'fundamental changes' in the practice of state organs were required to be submitted for examination and confirmation by the C.E.C. Accordingly, a list of such decrees adopted by the Presidium of the C.E.C. and the Sovnarkom in the interim between C.E.C. sessions

---

102. On a few occasions there were as many as 4 reports on the budget and the debates on the economic plan and the budget were combined. (Sessions of 1928–31.) The Budget Commission was formed by the Presidium of the C.E.C., the list of its members being subsequently confirmed by the C.E.C., while the chairman of the commission was elected by the C.E.C. (See *S.Z.* 1931, 11, No. 5, item 60; 1935, 11, No. 3, item 18.)

103. An examination of the Collection of Laws of the U.S.S.R., Part 1, for the years indicated below, which were picked at random, yields the following in regard to the number of laws passed by each organ:

YEAR	TOTAL NO. OF LAWS	C.E.C.	SOVNAR- KOM	PRESID. C.E.C.	PRESID. AND SOVNARKOM	C.L.D.	C.C. AND SOV.	OTHER ORGANS
1925	643	64	220		228	109		22
1929	745	48	241		352	101		3
1933	456	10	211	24	94	40	40	37
1935	526	80	266		84	9	82	5
1937	379	41	247	5	77		9	

In the 'other organs' column the figure for 1925 represents 14 treaties and conventions (at this time still printed in Part 1) and 8 decisions of the Congress of Soviets; the figures for 1929 and 1935 are for decisions of the Congress of Soviets, and the figure for 1933 for decrees of the Commission on Fulfilment attached to the Sovnarkom.

would be distributed to the members of the C.E.C. during a given plenary session, and a report concerning them made by the Secretary of the C.E.C. on behalf of the Presidium. Admittedly, however, not all the important laws passed in the interim were covered in this list and report.[104] A great number of laws, which had a fundamental bearing on the political and economic life of the land and which certainly altered the 'existing practice' of the governmental bodies, were adopted by the above-mentioned organs, particularly by the Presidium and Sovnarkom.[105] It should be noted also that the decrees enumerated in the list submitted under article 18 attained the full force of law before their submission for approval by the C.E.C. Such approval became largely a *pro forma* matter, since there was no discussion of the interim decrees, the entire list being voted confirmation

104. See 5 *TsIK* 2 *Sessia*, Bull. 18, p. 7; 6 *TsIK* 2 *Sessia*, Bull. 18, pp. 24–5; 6 *TsIK* 4 *Sessia*, Bull. 27, p. 4. This can also be seen from the comparatively small number of interim laws contained in these lists: thus, for April–December 1928, 49 laws; December 1929–January 1931, 97 laws; March–December 1931, 39 laws; 1933, 34 laws; 1935, 66 laws. (4 *TsIK* 4 *Sessia*, Bull. 33, p. 12; 5 *TsIK* 3 *Sessia*, Bull. 20, pp. 34–9; 6 *TsIK* 2 *Sessia*, Bull. 19, pp. 37–40; 6 *TsIK* 4 *Sessia*, Bull. 28, pp. 35–7; 7 *TsIK* 2 *Sessia*, Bull. 27, pp. 29–34.)

105. 'I did not touch upon the vast majority of the decisions and laws that were adopted during the year. The figures alone will help you understand how many laws were adopted during this time by the Sovnarkom and Presidium of the C.E.C. U.S.S.R.: Legislative Acts — 425, various important secret decisions — 88, and general decisions not of major state significance — 538.' (19 April 1928.) 'These decisions of the Presidium C.E.C. U.S.S.R. are only separate links of the general system of measures of the Party and government for the year 1933 . . . In 1933 a series of the most important acts of the Central Committee C.P.S.U.(B) and Sovnarkom U.S.S.R. . . . was issued. Besides that, direct operative direction of the economic life of the country was being carried out by the Sovnarkom U.S.S.R. and Council of Labor and Defense. And it would be incorrect to look upon the decisions that are being brought [here] for your confirmation otherwise than as in a close and inseverable tie with the above-mentioned decisions of the C.C. C.P.S.U.(B), Sovnarkom U.S.S.R., and C.L.D. for the year 1933. All of them comprise a single system of strictly thought-out measures . . .' (4 January 1934, Enukidze, in reporting the interim decisions to the C.E.C. 4 *TsIK* 3 *Sessia*, p. 709 and 6 *TsIK* 4 *Sessia*, Bull. 27, p. 4, respectively.)

The issuance of joint Central Committee-Sovnarkom decrees was discussed elsewhere (see *supra*, pp. 181–2). As for the joint Presidium C.E.C.-Sovnarkom decrees, there was some confusion in their designation: the official Collection of Laws at times referring to them as 'decisions of the Presidium C.E.C.' and of 'the C.E.C. and Sovnarkom' even in the same volume, while in the reports made on interim decisions before the C.E.C. they were usually referred to as 'decisions of the Presidium and Sovnarkom.' The accepted public-law text offers this explanation: 'Practice has established also that when a law defined the general norms of political and economic life, such a law was promulgated by the joint signatures of the C.E.C. and SNK [Sovnarkom]' (*S.G.P.* p. 302). Since the verbatim reports of the C.E.C. sessions disclose no evidence of their individual adoption, it is obvious that if there was any consultation with the Sovnarkom at the time of promulgation, such was carried on by the Presidium.

as a whole without debate in practice.[106] The perfunctory nature of this procedure was not denied. But in explanation a series of statements was offered to the effect: that in any case the interim decisions followed the basic lines of policy charted by the Congress of Soviets, the plenary sessions of the C.E.C., the Party Congress, and Central Committee; that the important thing was to implement the plans for the national economy; that a vast amount of legislation covering all fields of endeavor, including the state structure itself, was necessary for that purpose; and that this paramount task was performed in fact by the timely enactments of the various organs that adopted them in the periods between the plenary sessions of the C.E.C.[107]

The Role of the C.E.C. in the Conduct of Foreign Affairs. As pointed out earlier, topics of the Soviets' foreign situation, tied up with accounts of the shifting fortunes of war in the struggle against intervention, were prominent in the agenda of the C.E.C. during the early period of Soviet rule. From the peace *pour-parlers* at Brest-Litovsk (1917–18) to the Genoa Conference (1922), representatives of the Soviet delegations reported before the C.E.C. Whenever the C.E.C. met during this period some report, 'informational communication,' or speech concerning the external position of the Soviet state or the general international situation was made on behalf of the Sovnarkom. At times, these were followed by brief debates — with a few participants — and most of the resolutions offered were

---

106. See 3 *TsIK 2 Sessia*, pp. 1036–7; 5 *TsIK 2 Sessia*, Bull. 18, p. 1. On 19 April 1928, delegate Poraiko complained that the result of this procedure was 'that the session of the C.E.C. — the supreme legislative organ — does not in essence discuss the laws, but adopts them wholesale, all the laws together.' He proposed that all important interim decrees should be put up individually for discussion by the C.E.C. session, while the petty laws should be grouped in one report delivered early in the session and be examined by a special commission. The session adopted the first part of his proposal, voting that in so far as possible the Presidium should present the most important of the decisions for individual discussion by the C.E.C. at the beginning of sessions. (4 *TsIK 3 Sessia*, pp. 712–14). At the following session, on 15 December 1928, Poraiko continued to press for some scheme that would enable the members to become acquainted with the interim laws beforehand and make sure that 'the entire C.E.C. session should be able to take an active part in the examination of our legislative acts.' (4 *TsIK 4 Sessia*, Bull. 33, pp. 17–19.) Subsequent practice shows that while a few extra reports were added to some of the agendas, there was no change from the earlier procedure.

107. See 4 *TsIK 3 Sessia*, pp. 709–10; 5 *TsIK 2 Sessia*, Bull. 18, pp. 1–2, 5, 8; 5 *TsIK 3 Sessia*, Bull. 18, p. 25; 6 *TsIK 2 Sessia*, Bull. 18, pp. 24, 34; 6 *TsIK 4 Sessia*, Bull. 27, p. 4. It should perhaps be added that one class of enactments, the joint Central Committee-Sovnarkom decrees, were not included at all in the list submitted for C.E.C. confirmation under article 18; the reporters on the interim decisions stated simply that it was not part of their task to report them. (See 7 *TsIK 2 Sessia*, Bull. 26, p. 2; 7 *TsIK 3 Sessia*, Bull. 8, p. 10.)

adopted unanimously. On a number of occasions direct appeals and declarations to foreign governments and peoples were made by the C.E.C. on
the suggestion of the Sovnarkom and Narkomindel.[108]

In the U.S.S.R. period of the C.E.C.'s operation (1923–37) the record
was somewhat different. No direct appeals or declarations by the C.E.C.
are to be noted. Reports on foreign policy do not appear to have been
among the 'must' reports on the agenda. Yet from 1924 to 1929 there was
at least one such report delivered each year by the Foreign Affairs Commissar at the plenary sessions of the C.E.C.[109] These reports seem to have
been made when the leadership thought the time appropriate for a public
statement of the Soviet stand on various international questions, though
on several occasions they were placed on the agenda in direct response to
requests by delegate groups.[110] Less comprehensive in scope than the
reports at the Party and Soviet congress, they were nonetheless substantial
surveys of the Soviet position in international relations at the given time.
Only a few debates are recorded during this period and all the reports
were voted unanimous approval.[111]

After 1929 there were no specific reports on foreign policy by the
Foreign Affairs Commissar at the C.E.C.[112] Brief references to such policy

108. See 5 *VTsIK*, pp. 21–3, 47–8, 218–20, 251–3, 273–4, 311–12; *Krasnaia Kniga*,
Gosizdat, Moskva, 1920, pp. 105ff.

109. Three of these reports were made by Chicherin in 1924 and 1925, and five by Litvinov
during 1926–9. (See 2 *TsIK 2 Sessia*, pp. 64–76, 565–9; 2 *TsIK 3 Sessia*, pp. 30–60;
3 *TsIK 2 Sessia*, pp. 1051–67; 3 *TsIK 3 Sessia*, 659–62; 4 *TsIK 3 Sessia*, 772–94;
4 *TsIK 4 Sessia*, Bull. 19; 5 *TsIK 2 Sessia*, Bull. 14.)

110. Of the latter category were Litvinov's reports of 24 April 1926, 21 February 1927, and
6 December 1928. (3 *TsIK 2 Sessia*, pp. 1051–67, 3 *TsIK 3 Sessia*, pp. 659–62; 4 *TsIK
4 Sessia*, Bull. 19.) In the case of the 21 February 1927 report, 28 C.E.C. members
addressed an inquiry to the Presidium of the C.E.C. two days earlier regarding the dis-
turbed state of Anglo-Soviet relations. (3 *TsIK 3 Sessia*, pp. 565–6.) The Presidium
gave the first three signers of this inquiry an opportunity to voice their apprehensions
on 21 February 1927 (Ibid. pp. 641–59), following which Litvinov's report of the
situation was given in answer. The session voted to take note of the inquiry and answer.
(Ibid. p. 662.)

111. It is interesting to notice the motivation offered at one of the sessions for passing up
the debate. On 4 December 1929, following Litvinov's report, Chubar took the floor
to suggest that the session could limit itself to a brief resolution of approval, since
Litvinov's theses are entirely clear, and that 'by adopting such a concise resolution without opening any debates, the session will have expressed full support to the Workers-
Peasants Government in its foreign policy, which [support] it needs and which will
help our Government also in the future to carry out the precise, clear policy of the
proletarian state in its struggle with the capitalist encirclement.' The proposal and
resolution were voted unanimously. (5 *TsIK 2 Sessia*, Bull. 14, pp. 20–21.)

112. Perhaps the one exception was Litvinov's 'supplementary communication' of 29 December 1933 in the debate on Molotov's report of the preceding day. (6 *TsIK 4 Sessia*,
Bull. 3.)

were made instead in the reports of the Chairman of the Sovnarkom on the national economic plans. In line with the general spirit of all public proceedings in the U.S.S.R. since the early 'thirties, these were given complete and enthusiastic approval in the debates and resolutions on these reports.[113]

There is no record of any war declaration by the C.E.C. The following may be said concerning its part in treaty making. Many treaties were concluded in the name of the C.E.C. According to the preambles of these treaties, the delegates to the negotiations were appointed by the C.E.C. Early practice offers a concrete example of such appointment in the extraordinary session of the C.E.C. called on 27 January 1922 for the purpose of electing a delegation to the Genoa Conference. At that session Chicherin reviewed the preceding negotiations and requested, on behalf of the Narkomindel, that 'a delegation with the widest powers' be sent to the conference, and also that the representatives of the allied Soviet republics in the delegation should act as one there. After five other speeches and a brief résumé by Chicherin, the chairman stated that the Presidium of the C.E.C. had already come to a preliminary understanding in this matter with the allied Soviet republics and was now proposing a definite list of delegates, which he read. The plenary session then took a vote approving the suggested composition of the delegation.[114] The verbatim reports of the subsequent years, however, do not disclose any similar vote of appointment by the plenary sessions of the C.E.C., and the conclusion seems warranted that such appointments were carried out by the Presidium of the C.E.C. The same may be said concerning the ratification of treaties. In the early period the Foreign Commissar brought before the C.E.C. treaties that required ratification. Thus, in the case of the treaties between Russia and Turkey (16 March 1921), Russia and Persia (26 February 1921), and Russia and Bokhara (4 March 1921), Chicherin presented these treaties in the plenary session of the C.E.C. on 20 March 1921, made a few remarks in which he reminded the representatives that 'materials in regard to these treaties were distributed to the members of the All-Russian C.E.C.,' and asked for their ratification. The session then voted the ratification of each of these treaties separately.[115] At the same time, Chicherin asked that the C.E.C. authorize the Presidium C.E.C. to examine and approve the treaty with Poland (18 March 1921) if no addi-

---

113. 5 *TsIK* 3 *Sessia*, Bull. 1, pp. 6–15; 6 *TsIK* 2 *Sessia*, Bull. 1, pp. 3–9; *Izvestia*, 24–27 January 1933; 6 *TsIK* 4 *Sessia*, Bull. 1, pp. 3–12; 7 *TsIK* 2 *Sessia*, Bull. 1, *pp*. 3–13.
114. 9 *VTsIK*, pp. 7–26.
115. 8 *VTsIK*, pp. 109–10.

tional C.E.C. session was scheduled within thirty days, since the treaty was subject to ratification in that period of time: 'If the All-Russian C.E.C. will empower the Presidium to examine and ratify this treaty, it will in that case have the same juridical force as if it were ratified entirely by the All-Russian C.E.C.' The C.E.C. voted the requested authorization.[116] Again, in view of the fact that later verbatim reports show no such action by the sessions of the C.E.C. in regard to the numerous treaties listed as ratified by the C.E.C., it seems proper to conclude that their ratification was carried out in practice by the Presidium of the C.E.C., which was in constant session and was legally empowered to do so in the interim between C.E.C. sessions.[117]

The Basic Evolution and Position of the C.E.C. Thus, in brief summary, the following evolution may be noted. The membership of the C.E.C. has greatly increased, while the length and frequency of its meetings has decreased. The number of agenda items has also decreased, becoming stabilized since the mid-'twenties at about five habitual and a few additional reports, almost exclusively devoted to domestic policy, though until 1929 reports and communications dealing with foreign policy were also made at the C.E.C. sessions. On the whole, the number of participants in the debates has risen.[118] Except for the early years of the regime, a high degree of agreement was exhibited at the sessions of the C.E.C., and since 1931 complete unanimity in its proceedings has practically become the rule. Like the Congress of Soviets, the C.E.C. has actually used only a fraction of its powers, as its procedural, controlling-directive, and judicial prerogatives, and, to a large extent also, its competence in regard to legislation and conduct of foreign affairs were exercised in practice by the Presidium of the C.E.C. The C.E.C. may also be evaluated, therefore, as having served in part as a legislative and policy-ratifying organ of the Soviet hierarchy, but mainly as a high policy-propagating body, whose formal powers passed largely to its Presidium. This brings us to a consideration of the development of the last-named organ.

---

116. Ibid.; see also 5 *VTsIK*, pp. 88–107.

117. See *supra*, p. 213 note 55. This conclusion seems to be warranted also by the fact that all acts of the C.E.C. and of the Presidium C.E.C. were alike signed by the Chairman and Secretary of the C.E.C., and that generally there was a tendency to identify the two in public reference. (Cf., however, Taracouzio, op. cit. p. 244, on this point.)

118. Thus, the number of participants in the debates on the Government report — later the report on the National Economic Plan — was as follows ('joint,' 'UC,' and 'CN,' standing for Joint Session, Union Council, and Council of Nationalities, respectively): 1925, joint — 12; 1926, UC — 46, CN — 36; 1927, joint — 23; 1929, joint — 12, UC — 43, CN — 36; January 1931, joint — 6, UC — 61, CN — 39; January 1933, UC — 36, CN — 27; December 1933, UC — 35, CN — 28; January 1936, UC — 46, CN — 36. The same tendency of an increase in participation up to 1931 and some drop afterwards is to be noticed in regard to other reports at the C.E.C.

Chapter XI · The Soviet Structure (II)

1. THE PRESIDIUM OF THE CENTRAL EXECUTIVE COMMITTEE

(I) THE EMERGENCE OF THE PRESIDIUM IN THE SOVIET STRUCTURE

The Growth of the Presidium's Jurisdiction in the R.S.F.S.R. Period.
There was no Presidium of the C.E.C. in the system of organs established on 7 November 1917. An unofficial body, a presidium of seven or eight persons, was soon set up by the C.E.C., however, for the purpose of preparing the materials for the sessions and of providing continuous supervision over the then existing departments of the latter.[1] In the course of the C.E.C.'s activity in the succeeding months, it became the practice of the C.E.C. to entrust certain work to this Presidium. Thus, the Presidium C.E.C. was frequently assigned the final editing of decrees adopted by the C.E.C., it determined the composition of the first constitutional commission, set the agenda and drafted the Standing Rules of the C.E.C., and took all preliminary decisions in regard to procedural matters. It was even empowered to remove for its own decision cases on appeal at the Cassation Division of the Revolutionary Tribunal, if it did not agree with the verdicts of the latter.[2] Paradoxically, however, the first Soviet constitution, which was adopted on 10 July 1918, did not include the Presidium among the organs of power, nowhere offering a description of its structure, functions, and prerogatives.[3]

---

1. For the changes in the numerical composition of the Presidium, which increased to 15 members and 12 candidates by 29 December 1921, see 4 *VTsIK*, pp. 38, 441–2; 5 *VTsIK*, pp. 440–42; 8 *VTsIK*, pp. 3–4; 9 *VTsIK*, pp. 3–4.
2. For the organization of the Tribunal and the Cassation Division, see 4 *VTsIK*, pp. 23, 28, 35, 314, 345–53, 412–18; also 5 *VTsIK*, p. 294.
3. Indeed, the only mention of the Presidium in the constitution indicating cognizance of such an organ is contained in article 45, which provided that members of a collegium of a commissariat could lodge complaints against the decisions of their commissar either with the Sovnarkom or the Presidium C.E.C. Before the constitution was adopted, a project was brought before the constitutional commission published in *Izvestia*, 22 June 1918, which would have given the Presidium: (a) the power to suspend the

Official recognition of the existing gap in the formal charter of power was taken for the first time a year and a half later, when the Seventh All-Russian Congress of Soviets adopted the following specific decision concerning the Presidium of the C.E.C., on 9 December 1919:

(1) The Presidium of the All-Russian C.E.C. conducts the sessions of the All-Russian C.E.C.
(2) Prepares the materials for the sessions of the All-Russian C.E.C.
(3) Introduces drafts of decrees for examination by the plenum of the All-Russian C.E.C.
(4) Supervises the observance of decisions of the All-Russian C.E.C.
(5) Conducts relations in the name of the All-Russian C.E.C.
(6) Is the leading center for instructing the entire work in the center as well as in the localities.
(7) Considers petitions for pardon, confirms awards of the Order of the Red Banner, and resolves other problems in the order of administration.
(8) Has the right, between sessions of the All-Russian C.E.C., to confirm decisions of the Council of People's Commissars, as well as to suspend decisions of the latter, transferring them to the nearest plenum of the All-Russian C.E.C. for decision. At the instance of the Council of People's Commissars, it appoints individual people's commissars.[4]

This decision was taken in pursuance of a resolution of the Eighth Party Congress (March 1919) that the functions of the Presidium should be formulated on the basis of experience and delimited from those of the Sovnarkom at the nearest Congress of Soviets.

The Eighth All-Russian Congress of Soviets followed suit on 29 December 1920. It gave the Presidium of the C.E.C. the right to annul decisions of the Sovnarkom.[5] And it also empowered the Presidium to issue all

promulgation of Sovnarkom enactments and transfer them to the C.E.C. for examination, or ask for their re-examination by the Sovnarkom; (b) the right to select and delegate C.E.C. members to participate and vote at Sovnarkom sessions at which enactments deemed of particular importance by the Presidium were being considered. Nothing came of this project at the time, however. (See Turubiner, 'The Organization of the Presidium of the Union C.E.C.,' p. 128.)

4. S'ezdy Sovetov RSFSR, p. 148; see Lenin, XXIV, p. 720; 7 Vserossiiskii S'ezd Sovetov, pp. 261–2; 8 VTsIK, pp. 11–12.

5. S'ezdy Sovetov RSFSR, p. 176. It was made amply clear that this right over such a powerful organ — staffed with high Party men — as the Sovnarkom was more formal than real, and that at any rate it was not intended as an independent power to be used outside the frame of Party considerations. When the Central Committee of the Party thwarted efforts of the Presidium C.E.C. to set up the Workmen-Peasants Inspection as a department of the C.E.C. rather than as a commissariat of the Sovnarkom, and stopped attempts to create commissions on C.E.C. agenda problems without the inclusion of the relevant commissars in them, several members of the Presidium C.E.C. complained loudly that this was intervention and constituted a curtailment of the scope of work of the Presidium, contrary to the decision of the Seventh Congress. In

necessary decrees in the name of the C.E.C., with the obligation to report to the regular sessions of the latter concerning its work; to decide problems of the administrative-territorial division of the republic; and to pass upon questions and conflicts arising in the interrelations between the central and local organs, giving the Presidium the right to annul decisions of the central commissariats, as well as of the local congresses of soviets, executive committees, and their presidia. While provincial executive committees could — 'only in exceptional cases' — suspend the execution of an ordinance of a central commissariat, the Presidium was empowered to subject to judicial action the party that was in the wrong in regard to the ordinance in dispute. Moreover, by its own decree of 14 September 1921, the Presidium could consider complaints of the central commissariats not only regarding decisions of the provincial executive committees, but also in regard to decisions of the central Sovnarkom concerning decrees that the commissariats wished to introduce for consideration by the C.E.C.[6]

A resolution, passed by the C.E.C. on 31 May 1921, sought to strengthen and increase the role of the Presidium as an organ for constant contact with, and guidance of, the local executive committees. This resolution emphasized that the Presidium was to utilize members of the C.E.C., as well as of the collegia of the central commissariats, for the purpose of instructing the local executive committees, and was to keep abreast of

---

a report at the Ninth Party Congress, on 29 March 1920, the Central Committee answered that the Presidium C.E.C. digressed from the letter and spirit of that decision: 'The comrades will perhaps point out that by the resolution of the Seventh Congress of Soviets the Presidium VTsIK was given the right to confirm certain decisions of the Sovnarkom and suspend the execution of others in the name of the VTsIK. Quite right. [But] exceptional cases were envisioned here, [cases] where the C.C. of our party, which controls and directs the work of the [Soviet] organs, comes to the conclusion that on account of its importance this or that decree should have been passed by the VTsIK, the plenum of which could not be convoked in time for technical reasons . . . When a given decision of the Sovnarkom must be annulled or suspended, the C.C. does it through the Presidium of the VTsIK. Therein lies the fundamental aim of the above right of confirmation and suspension, and not in any independent [power of] decreeing concerning decisions of the Sovnarkom given the Presidium VTsIK by the Seventh Congress.' (*Protokoly IX S'ezda RKP(b)*, pp. 45–7.) In view of his and his followers' subsequent views on the Party-soviets relationship, Trotsky's intervention in the debate on this point may be noted: 'Kiselev asked for additional time in order to tell how the C.C. sacrilegiously raised a hand against such an institution as the Presidium VTsIK, i.e. the summit of the Soviet parliament . . . under the guise of introducing more workers, it is desired to free some high Soviet institutions, like the Presidium of the VTsIK, from the control of the C.C. And I say to you: You can disperse the present C.C., but say to the new C.C. "Look with both eyes after all labor groups and after the highest institutions, including the VTsIK." ' (Ibid. p. 82.)

6. *S'ezdy Sovetov RSFSR*, pp. 176–7; *S.U.R.* 1921, No. 64, item 476.

developing relations between the center and the localities through periodic reports on local activity made to it both by the central commissariats and the provinical and district executive committees.[7]

Finally, the Ninth All-Russian Congress of Soviets, meeting in December 1921, especially provided that the permanent commissions of the C.E.C. should be headed by members of the Presidium, and the statute on the C.E.C., as well as several law codes adopted in 1922–3, gave the Presidium a number of important judicial prerogatives. The appointment of the members and chairman of the Supreme Court required the confirmation of the Presidium C.E.C., which alone had the right to remove them. By its own decision, the Presidium could stop a criminal prosecution at any stage in the process; it could propose to the Supreme Court to annul or alter the verdicts of any court in the republic, including those of the Judicial and Cassation collegia of the Supreme Court; and, as a corollary to its pardoning power, the 'highest measure of punishment,' i.e. the death sentence, could be carried out only if after a certain period of time no reprieve was received from the Presidium.[8]

The Activity of the Presidium during the R.S.F.S.R. Period. The practice of these years indicates that the Presidium was carrying out most of these functions. It continued to perform its customary procedural tasks in regard to the C.E.C.; it organized and supervised the work of various commissions; it ratified the treaty of peace with Poland and the treaty with the Far-Eastern Republic; it dealt with a number of federal questions and supervised the preparation of the statutes on the new, Union, organs — the C.E.C., Sovnarkom, Council of Labor and Defense, and commissariats of the U.S.S.R. (1923). But above all, the Presidium was in continuous association with local soviet organs, receiving solicitors and emissaries from all parts of Russia, bringing sundry complaints and inquiries; sending responsible agents there to investigate conditions and relations at the source; resolving conflicts between the central institutions and the localities and between the localities themselves; and sometimes annulling decisions of the local courts.[9] It was as a result of the last-named group of activities — which grew out of a simple early practice of local petitions to the Presidium — that the Presidium came to be looked upon as one of the best sources of information on local sentiment and as best suited for the role of judge and adjuster between the local and central Soviet organs. And this conception resulted in the vesting of the con-

---

7. 8 *VTsIK*, pp. 182–3.
8. *S'ezdy Sovetov RSFSR*, p. 219; Turubiner, op. cit. pp. 129–30.
9. See 8 *VTsIK*, pp. 4–5, 11–17, 92, 115–21, 143, 181, 189–90, 314–15, 381; *M.N.C.Q.* pp. 120, 126, 127; 1 *TsIK* 1 *Sessia*, p. 4.

trolling-directive, judicial, and pardoning powers in the Presidium. Thus, by the time the Union was being formed, an additional organ, the Presidium of the C.E.C., had become fully established in the Soviet hierarchy. The Union constitution included it in the system of Union organs with substantially the same functions and powers that it progressively acquired through legislative enactment and practice.[10]

The Organization and Jurisdiction of the Presidium C.E.C. under the Union Constitution. More specifically, the Union constitution for the first time defined the Presidium of the C.E.C., designating it as 'the highest legislative, executive, and administrative organ of power of the U.S.S.R.' during the intervals between the sessions of the C.E.C. to which it was accountable (articles 26, 29, Constitution of 1924). Interestingly enough, as already pointed out, article 8 listed only the Congress of Soviets and the C.E.C. as the supreme organs of power. The Presidium was to consist of 21 members, including the entire presidia of the two chambers of the C.E.C., and was to be formed at a joint session of the latter by a separate vote of each chamber (article 26, Constitution of 1924).[11] In

10. In view of the powerful role of the Sovnarkom in both legislation and administration, the older jurists appear to have been at a loss for a time to assess the exact nature and standing of the Presidium. Professor V. N. Durdenevsky declared that the Presidium was now the 'Government,' while the Sovnarkom had become a 'managing department' (cited in Turubiner, op. cit. p. 126.) Professor Stuchka thought that 'something in the nature of a diarchy or of a bicameral system' composed of the Presidium and Sovnarkom had come about, and he was not sure what the functional relationship between the two organs would be in the future. (Ibid. p. 127.) Professor M. A. Reisner likened the Presidium to 'a Senate, a State Council, and similar institutions,' the purpose of which is 'supreme activity in regard to guarding legality in the republic.' (Ibid.) Professor Engel' stated that there was a gradation in the respective legislative functions of the Congress of Soviets, C.E.C., Presidium C.E.C., and Sovnarkom, with the Presidium possessing a higher legislative competence than the Sovnarkom but a lower one than the C.E.C. (Engel', op. cit. p. 173.) Professor Gurvich held that both the Presidium and Sovnarkom were dependent and auxiliary organs of the C.E.C., but that while the Sovnarkom was 'specializing in the field of administrative functions,' the Presidium was concentrating on 'work in the field of legislation and control.' (Gurvich, *Osnovy* . . . pp. 83–4.)

11. It was specifically emphasized that the Presidium of the C.E.C. was a unit and exercised its competence as one. In June 1923, when the new Union structure was being considered at a consultation of the Central Committee of the Party with officials of the republics and regions, the Ukrainians demanded that two presidiums be created, to accord with the number of chambers, but they were overruled with the claim that: 'The Presidium is the supreme power of the Union, which acts constantly, uninterruptedly from session to session [of the C.E.C.]. The formation of two presidiums with legislative functions would inevitably create great complications at work. The chambers should have their presidiums, which are not to possess, however, any legislative functions.' (*VKP(b) v Rezol.* i, p. 539. See also *S.G.P.* p. 217.) Also, contrary to the claim of the Ukrainian representative, Skrypnik, the accepted understanding was that after

May 1925, the membership was raised to 27 and this number remained, in fact, stationary throughout. Members of the Presidium enjoyed all the privileges and immunities of C.E.C. members, and by the statute on the C.E.C. R.S.F.S.R. they were, moreover, entitled to immediate admission to all Soviet institutions on presentation of their credentials. The number of candidates for membership in the Presidium was less than that of the members and also remained fairly restricted. From 19 candidates in February 1924 the number rose to no more than 24 at the last election of the Presidium C.E.C., in February 1935.

The sessions of the Presidium were presided over alternately by each of the chairmen of the C.E.C., and the Secretary of the latter likewise served in that capacity for the Presidium. These sessions were not open to the public, nor were the protocols of the Presidium's proceedings published. Representatives of the constituent republics, however, had the right to take part in the sessions with an advisory vote, and the same was true of representatives of individual autonomous republics and regions when questions concerning them were under consideration. Also, by special decision, the Presidium could extend the right of participation in its proceedings to other persons (article 58, Statute on the C.E.C. U.S.S.R.). The exact frequency of the sessions of the Presidium is nowhere indicated, though apparently it averaged three to four sessions per week.[12] When the Presidium was not in session, the particular chairman then serving his turn as President of the C.E.C. was empowered to act in the name of the Presidium, later reporting on his action at the next session of the Presidium (article 63, Statute on C.E.C. U.S.S.R.). In practice, Kalinin as chairman, and with him the Secretary of the C.E.C., played the greatest role in the operation of the Presidium, since they were always on the spot while the other C.E.C. chairmen, who were simultaneously serving as chairmen of the central executive committees or sovnarkoms of the constituent republics, and many of the members of the Presidium, who also held high posts in the governments of those republics, of necessity had to be away from the federal capital a good deal of the time.

---

each chamber elected its own presidium of 7 — later 9 — the joint session not only elected the additional 7 to make up the Presidium of the C.E.C., but confirmed the composition of the Presidium as a whole. (3 *TsIK 1 Sessia*, pp. 12–15.)

12. In a report on the activity of the Presidium C.E.C. between 19 March and 30 May 1921, Kalinin stated that during that period there were 19 meetings of the Presidium: 10 of the 'Large Presidium' and 9 of the 'Small Presidium,' the reference apparently being respectively to meetings at which there was a full quorum and to those where only part of the membership was present. (8 *VTsIK*, p. 115.) This would make an average of over 3 meetings a week.

As regards jurisdiction, the Union constitution and the statutes on the Union organs adopted in November 1923 have embodied in the Presidium of the C.E.C. U.S.S.R. all the powers and prerogatives earlier possessed by the Presidium of the C.E.C. R.S.F.S.R., and have even extended them along several lines.[13] Thus, in the field of legislation, the Presidium was given the power to pass decrees and ordinances on its own initiative, and to examine and confirm drafts of enactments submitted to it by the federal Sovnarkom or individual commissariats, by the central executive committees of the constituent republics and their presidia, or by other departments of the government (article 33, Constitution of 1924). In exceptional cases, it was also allowed to adopt decisions embodying fundamental political and economic norms or effecting basic changes in governmental practice, provided it subsequently submitted such decisions for consideration and confirmation by the C.E.C. (article 52, Statute on C.E.C. U.S.S.R.).

In the judicial sphere, the Presidium was endowed with particularly important prerogatives, which are rather unique for an organ of this type. As was well pointed out of the Supreme Court of the U.S.S.R.: 'It exists at the C.E.C. of the Union, i.e. factually, of course, not at the short sessions of the C.E.C., which assemble three times a year, but at the uninterrupted working practical organ — the Presidium.'[14] The Presidium appointed the Chairman and Vice-Chairman of the Supreme Court. Of the plenary session of the Supreme Court, consisting of these two officials, a representative of the OGPU, the chairmen of the supreme courts of the constituent republics, and seven additional members, the last-named were also appointed by the Presidium (article 45, Constitution of 1924). The Presidium was one of the organs possessing the right to initiate action by the Supreme Court of the U.S.S.R., and the latter could perform a number of purely judicial functions only on the special

---

13. See articles 21, 26, 27, 29–36, 40–42, 45–8, 60, Constitution of 1924; the Statute on the C.E.C. U.S.S.R., *passim,* and the Statute on the Sovnarkom U.S.S.R., articles 3, 7, 8, in 1 *Sistematicheskoe Sobranie Deistvuiushchikh Zakonov SSSR,* pp. 16–25, 31–3, respectively. The only items that may be considered a slight diminution of the Presidium's earlier powers are the provisions that the Presidium may merely suspend the decisions of the congresses of soviets of the constituent republics, submitting them later for consideration by the C.E.C. (article 32, Constitution of 1924), and that only the appointment of deputy commissars would require the confirmation of the Presidium. (Item m, article 3, Statute on the Sovnarkom U.S.S.R.) On the other hand, by the same statute the Sovnarkom was required to report all of its decisions to the Presidium C.E.C. within 3 days after they have been taken. (Article 7, Statute on the Sovnarkom U.S.S.R.)

14. Turubiner, op. cit. p. 137.

decision of the C.E.C. or the Presidium C.E.C. in each case (articles 47, 48, Constitution of 1924; article 2, Statute on the Supreme Court of the U.S.S.R.).[15] It could request of the Supreme Court advisory opinions concerning the constitutionality of decisions of the federal Sovnarkom and of the central executive committees and sovnarkoms of the constituent republics. And it was empowered to entertain requests of the Supreme Court of the U.S.S.R. and of the central organs of the constituent republics to suspend or annul decisions, orders, and enactments of the central organs of the U.S.S.R. (except decisions of the Presidium itself and of the C.E.C.) and of individual commissariats, including the O.G.P.U. on grounds of unconstitutionality.[16] The Presidium had a right to consider protests of the Supreme Court of the U.S.S.R., initiated by the Attorney General,[17] against decisions and verdicts of the supreme courts of the constituent

15. Such special decisions of the C.E.C. or its Presidium were required for the examination of: cases involving the personal liability of members of the C.E.C. and Sovnarkom; cases pertaining to the accusation of the highest officials of the Union in service crimes; civil and criminal cases of exclusive importance affecting two or more constituent republics; and judicial disputes between the constituent republics.

16. See *supra*, pp. 23–4, and Turubiner, op. cit. pp. 137–8. As for requests to annul decisions of the central, federal organs on grounds other than constitutionality, the central executive committees of the constituent republics and their presidia had a right to appeal to the federal Presidium against decrees of the federal Sovnarkom, without suspending their execution (article 42, Constitution of 1924), while decisions of the Presidium itself could be protested by these committees to the sessions of the C.E.C. (article 53, Statute on the C.E.C. U.S.S.R.). For a time the constituent republics, especially the Ukraine, made very extensive use of these appeal rights, seeking their implementation through the medium of the federal Presidium. At the session of the C.E.C. on 19 April 1928, Enukidze called attention to the disharmony and delays in the execution of federal decisions caused by this practice. Speaking of petitions by the Union republics and the federal commissariats asking for revision of decisions of the C.E.C. U.S.S.R. and its Presidium as of 'a right which they have by the constitution,' Enukidze asked, in the name of the Presidium, that this right be altered so as to allow such petitions only 6 months after the decisions in question were taken, with the Chairman of the C.E.C. having the power to advance their consideration: 'We have become convinced that a law or a decision of the U.S.S.R. is best verified by experience, in the process of being carried out. It would be an inexpedient hindrance to the execution of laws, therefore, to suspend these laws only on account of theoretical or some kind of juridical considerations. Hence, because of all this, and keeping in mind that this measure will to a large extent curtail correspondence and red tape in the execution of the most important decisions, we have brought forth this amendment. Experience will show us whether it is useful, whether it will be necessary to shorten this term for complaints or to leave it at 6 months.' (4 *TsIK* 3 *Sessia*, pp. 689–90.) The proposal was accepted by the session.

17. By article 46 of the Constitution of 1924, the Procurator of the Supreme Court (Attorney General) and his deputy were to be appointed by the Presidium C.E.C. On 5 February 1935, this article was amended so as to make the Attorney General appointable by the C.E.C. itself. (See *S'ezdy Sovetov SSSR*, p. 248.)

republics alleged to be contrary to federal legislation or to impinge upon the interests of other republics (article 2, Statute on the Supreme Court U.S.S.R.). Finally, it could consider appeals from decisions of the Supreme Court itself, presented by the Procurator (Attorney General) or Sovnarkom of the U.S.S.R. and by the central executive committees of the constituent republics (articles 4, 22, Statute on the Supreme Court U.S.S.R.).

Earlier we noted the functions which the Presidium of the C.E.C. U.S.S.R. was authorized to perform in the field of foreign affairs.[18] Generally, the Presidium also derived various powers from the fact that it was formally charged with the conduct of all relations of the C.E.C. with the other state institutions and departments of government (article 59, Statute on the C.E.C. U.S.S.R.).

(2) THE POSITION AND ROLE OF THE PRESIDIUM

The Operation of the Presidium C.E.C. in Practice. Many of the above-described powers and functions were being carried out by the Presidium of the C.E.C. in its actual operation. The Presidium has given much time to such matters as the preparation and conduct of the C.E.C. sessions, the representation of the C.E.C. in the interim between sessions and the management of its commissions and committees, the exercise of the pardoning and amnesty powers, and the award of orders, medals, and other state insignia of recognition.[19] It has served as intermediary and arbiter between the central and local Soviet organs. In addition to the role it played in the system of legislation and in the conduct of foreign affairs,[20] the Presidium came to be regarded as a sort of ceremonial head in the

---

18. *Supra*, pp. 213–14, 234, 239–40 and note 55 ch. x.

19. From the time of the first award of the first military order introduced by the Soviets in September 1918 (5 *VTsIK*, p. 224), the Presidium of the C.E.C. was the organ exercising that power. It was not obliged to report its awards to the C.E.C., and if on some rare occasion it did so, as in the case of the award of the Order of the Red Banner to Kalinin, Rykov, and Petrovsky (reported on 19 April 1928), it was based on the motivation that approval by the C.E.C. 'will add the greatest prestige to this award.' (See 4 *TsIK* 3 *Sessia*, p. 708.)

20. See *supra*, pp. 234–7, 239–40. Except for the stock argument that the Presidium could not be considered to be unlimited in its legislative prerogative because the C.E.C. had the ultimate power of veto, Soviet jurists did not indicate clearly the concrete limits to the exercise of this prerogative by the Presidium, as distinguished from the other central organs. An interesting suggestion of criteria was offered by Professor Turubiner. According to him, there were 'almost no formulations concerning the difference of competence' between these organs. Whether a given problem was to be solved by the Congress of Soviets, C.E.C., Presidium C.E.C., or Sovnarkom, depended on the importance and urgency of the problem. From the point of view of importance the line followed from the Congress of Soviets down, while from the standpoint of urgency the order was reversed. (Turubiner, op. cit. p. 135.)

relations of the U.S.S.R. with foreign nations. While Kalinin headed most of the diplomatic receptions, the other C.E.C. chairmen, who also presided at the Presidium, often took turns in receiving newly arrived envoys, and as a rule several members of the Presidium participated in these formal receptions.

The Basic Evolution and Position of the Presidium C.E.C. Thus, the Presidium of the C.E.C. may be said to have evolved into a highly serviceable organ of the Soviet hierarchy, having performed such varied functions in the policy-shaping process as opinion tapping and fact finding and participation in the promulgation of legislative norms, as well as observance and adjustment of divergences arising between the central and local Soviet bodies in the execution of governmental policy.[21]

2. THE SUPREME SOVIET AND ITS PRESIDIUM

(1) THE SUPREME SOVIET OF THE U.S.S.R.

The Conception of the Supreme Soviet. The Supreme Soviet was elected on 12 December 1937 and was convoked for the first time on 12 January 1938.

From the point of view of its social significance, the Supreme Soviet — like the C.E.C. before it — is regarded as a representation and expression of both the common interests of the entire Soviet people and the specific national interests of the nationalities composing it.[22] From the standpoint

21. Nevertheless, statements that the Presidium was 'about the most influential organ of the constitution' (Webb, op. cit. p. 89), and 'the real source of power,' 'the real source of constitutional authority,' dominating the Sovnarkom in the official Soviet hierarchy (Batsell, op. cit. pp. 291, 506–7, 519–20) are gross exaggerations. Batsell argues that the Presidium included the political leaders and was centralized, but the same was even more true of the Sovnarkom. His statement that the Congress of Soviets and C.E.C. acted in matters already decided by the Presidium C.E.C. should be balanced with the statement that to a large extent these matters, the budget for example, were also passed upon by the Sovnarkom, which actually enacted a vast amount of legislation, and together with its commissariats, etc., served as the initial source of most of the legislation adopted by other organs.

22. *S.G.P.* pp. 292–3, 306–9; Stetsky, *Constitution,* pp. 27–9. The following features show the extent to which the Supreme Soviet reflects the interests of all the nationalities of the U.S.S.R.: the complete equality of representation within each national-territorial category in the Council of Nationalities so that, for instance, little White Russia and the huge R.S.F.S.R. have the same number of deputies — 25 each; the fact that 299 out of the 574 deputies in the Council of Nationalities (in the Supreme Soviet of the first convocation) represent the autonomous republics and regions and the national areas, while the remainder fall to the share of the constituent republics; and the fact that even the smallest national groups, such as the Koriaks and Evenks, counting no more than 13,000 and 6000 people, respectively, are represented by at least one deputy each, through their national areas.

of its status and function in the Soviet pyramid, the Supreme Soviet is conceived as the 'highest organ of state power of the U.S.S.R.,' to which all the organs of state power are subordinate (articles 30, 31, Constitution of 1936). For the first time, something akin to the 'supremacy of parliament' theory is asserted for a Soviet organ, the Supreme Soviet, since it is regarded as the embodiment of all authority — legislative, executive, and judicial — and is at the same time declared to be the sole and exclusive legislative organ, the laws of which constitute the source of authority and direction for the activity of the other Soviet organs (article 32, Constitution of 1936). Rejecting a proposed amendment that would have invested the Presidium of the Supreme Soviet with the right to issue provisional legislative acts, Stalin stated in December 1936:

We must at last put an end to the situation in which not one body but a number of bodies legislate. Such a situation contradicts the principle of stability of laws now more than ever. The legislative power of the U.S.S.R. must be exercised by one single body, the Supreme Council [Soviet] of the U.S.S.R.[23]

Election and Dissolution of the Supreme Soviet. The Supreme Soviet is elected by direct suffrage for a term of four years — the Council of the Union on the basis of 1 deputy for every 300,000 people and the Council of Nationalities on the basis of 25 deputies for a Union republic, 11 for an autonomous republic, 5 for an autonomous region, and 1 for a national area (article 33–6, Constitution of 1936).[24] In December 1937, in the first elections to the Supreme Soviet, 1,143 deputies were elected; in February 1946, the second election, 1,339 deputies. Theoretically, numerical equality between the two chambers is held desirable; though no article in the new constitution specifically provides for such, Stalin agreed at the time of its adoption that numerical equality 'offers obvious political advantages, for it emphasizes the equality of the chambers.'[25] Such equality was nearly achieved in the first of the elections above, with 569 deputies elected to the Council of Union, and 574 to the Council of Nationalities. In the second elections the number of deputies elected to these chambers were 682 and 657 respectively, and it is obvious that in practice it may prove difficult to maintain numerical equality between the chambers. On expiration of the four-year term, or in case the Supreme Soviet is dissolved by its Presidium in accordance with the constitutional provision in regard

---

23. Stalin, *Constitution,* p. 27. See also Stetsky, *Constitution,* pp. 32–3.
24. The original draft of the new constitution provided for direct elections of the Council of Union only, but was later amended to introduce the same form of elections for the Council of Nationalities on the ground that it would 'raise the prestige' of the latter. (See Stalin, *Constitution,* p. 26.)
25. See Stalin, *Constitution,* p. 26; also Molotov, *Constitution,* p. 20.

to disagreement between the two chambers, the election of a new Supreme Soviet is required to be scheduled by the Presidium for a date not later than two months after such dissolution. The newly elected Supreme Soviet is to be convened not later than three months after its election. (Articles 54, 55, 47, Constitution of 1936.)

The Standing and Duties of the Supreme Soviet Deputies. As for the deputies of the Supreme Soviet, the emphasized conception is that a deputy is 'a servant of the people, its messenger in the Supreme Soviet,' who must report back to his electors concerning his own and the soviet's work and who can be recalled by them at any time.[26] The deputy enjoys certain privileges, but must perform a number of duties. In addition to participation in the proceedings of the Supreme Soviet and in the work of its commissions, he may address inquiries to the government or to a particular minister, which must be answered orally or in writing within a period of three days (article 71, Constitution of 1936). He enjoys immunity from arrest and prosecution and cannot be held to legal responsibility without consent of the Supreme Soviet or — during the interim between the sessions of the latter — of the Presidium of the Supreme Soviet (article 52). He has the privilege of free transportation over rail and water routes throughout the U.S.S.R., and, in addition to a daily allowance during sessions of the Supreme Soviet, he receives a larger sum each month as 'reimbursement of expenses connected with the carrying out of a deputy's duties.'[27] Chief among these duties are considered to be the deputy's maintenance of contact with the electors of his district through correspondence and visits to farms and factories, as well as the reception of petitioners at home and the initiation of action by him in the local or central institutions directed toward the solution of problems brought to his attention by members of his electorate.[28]

26. Stalin, cited in *Vlast' Sovetov,* 1938, No. 1, p. 1; article 142, Constitution of 1936.
27. See *Pervaia Sessia Verkhovnogo Soveta, Stenograficheskii Otchet,* pp. 122–4, 205. These verbatim reports of proceedings of the successive Supreme Soviet sessions will be referred to hereafter as *Sessia V.S.,* with arabic numerals indicating the given session.
28. Ibid. The practice of the first years following establishment of the Supreme Soviet showed that the deputies experienced a number of complications — not completely overcome in subsequent years — in the execution of these tasks. First, there was the difficulty of finding time to receive callers and answer correspondence while holding down a regular job in industry, agriculture, etc. Second, since most of the requests and petitions dealt with complaints against some official action or lack of such, there was the delicate job of prodding the relevant governmental agencies along without appearing to be stepping into their shoes. Finally, since the nature of the problems that a citizen could take up with his deputy was not clearly defined, many deputies found themselves overloaded with petitions of a purely personal nature, requests for jobs, etc. (See e.g. Simonzhenkova, 'About the Work of a Deputy of the Supreme Soviet of the Union S.S.R.,' pp. 27–31.)

As in the case of the Congress of Soviets and the C.E.C. earlier, the delegate body of the Supreme Soviet is drawn from all walks of life, in accordance with Lenin's dictum about legislators who also execute the laws.[29] But to a much larger extent than before, this body represents the new élite, the people who have advanced most under the Soviet regime, ranging all the way from a champion miner or machinist to Marshal of the Red Army, and counting among its members Party and soviet officials, directors, managers and chairmen of large economic enterprises and collective farms, *stakhanovites,* men of the arts and sciences, and persons who won state awards in their particular line of endeavor.[30]

The Organization and Procedure of the Supreme Soviet. By the provisions of the constitution, regular sessions of the Supreme Soviet are convoked by the Presidium of the Supreme Soviet twice a year, while extraordinary ones are called by the latter on its own initiative or upon demand of one of the Union republics (article 46). These provisions were realized in practice up to the middle of 1941. The Supreme Soviet met twice in 1938, three times (for one regular and two extraordinary sessions) in 1939, twice in 1940, and once early in 1941. On the average sessions lasted about a week; the shortest lasted three days, and the longest twelve. Following the German invasion of the Soviet Union, regular meetings were suspended and the election of a new Supreme Soviet, scheduled for December 1941, was postponed. Four brief sessions were held during the war years: one in 1942, one in 1944, and two in 1945. The Supreme Soviet of the second convocation, elected in February 1946, met in regular session twice during the year.

Both chambers of the Supreme Soviet are required to begin and end their sessions simultaneously (article 41). As a rule, notice of convocation of the regular sessions is published several weeks in advance, and, as in the case of the Congress of Soviets and the C.E.C., foreign journalists and diplomats are permitted to observe the proceedings of the sessions from special loges in the hall of the Kremlin. Also present and frequently mingling with the deputies are delegates from various organizations and

---

29. See *supra,* pp. 184–5. The accepted Soviet view is embodied in the following description: 'The deputy of the Supreme Soviet is not a professional politician, not a professional "legislator," but a man connected with Socialist production, with science, etc. The Soviet deputy is a trustee of the bloc of Communists and non-Party people, a man of live experience and deed, a fighter for socialism. He does not "fence" with brilliant speeches, but as a deputy he aims to incorporate all of his creative experience into the matter of making laws that would secure the further development and strengthening of Socialism.' (*S.G.P.* p. 330.)

30. For details, see the reports of the Credentials Commissions of the Supreme Soviet (1938 and 1946), in *Sots. Zak,* 1938, No. 2, pp. 12–15, and *Izvestia,* 15 March 1946.

institutions bringing greetings to the Supreme Soviet.[31] The chambers in session are presided over by their respective chairmen — each assisted by two vice-chairmen — who are generally in charge of internal procedure (articles 42–4).[32] Joint sessions of both chambers are presided over alternately by the chairmen of the Council of the Union and the Council of Nationalities (article 45). Except for the constitutional provisions concerning the formation of the Presidium of the Supreme Soviet and of the Sovnarkom (now the Council of Ministers) at joint sessions of both chambers (articles 48, 56), there is no set rule on when sessions are to be conducted jointly and when separately. In practice, most of the reports were delivered at joint sessions, while most of the debates were conducted separately; and there were more separate than joint sessions.[33] Even at the joint sessions, the vote was taken separately as a rule, despite the fact that the argument of numerical inequality of the chambers no longer existed, at least during the first few convocations of the Supreme Soviet.[34] Exceptions to the rule were the votes confirming the composition of the Presidium of the Supreme Soviet, the Council of Ministers, and the Supreme Court, and appointing the Attorney General, as well as the vote adopting rules of procedure for the joint sessions.[35] The practice of a separate vote at joint sessions was in accordance with the constitutional provisions granting the same measure of legislative initiative to both chambers and requiring the approval of each for a law to be valid, as well as the constantly stressed conception of the complete equality of the chambers (articles 37–9).[36] In implementation of this equality, the new

31. The accepted Soviet public-law text offers this explanation: 'The democratic nature of the socialist parliament is also underscored by access to its sessions of toilers' delegations, who receive the right to speak from the rostrum of the Supreme Soviet in order to express their attitude towards its policy and work.' (*S.G.P.* pp. 325–6.)

32. The chairmen and vice-chairmen of the chambers are supposed to represent the latter and to keep up systematic contact with the deputies in the interim between sessions, and for that purpose 300,000 rubles a year per chamber are placed at their disposal. (See I *Sessia V.S.*, pp. 123–4, 205; *S.G.P.* p. 330.)

33. There was no logical reason for delivering the same reports at each chamber separately (see *supra*, p. 231) and this was rarely done, except for the reports on decrees adopted in the interim between the Supreme Soviet sessions by its Presidium. At first the latter reports were also made at joint sessions, but beginning with the sixth session (March–April 1940) of the Supreme Soviet of the first convocation they were delivered — in identical language and form — before separate sessions of the chambers, apparently to emphasize the indispensable legislative role of each.

34. See *supra*, p. 251.

35. See I *Sessia V.S.*, pp. 77–9, 125–47, 160–67; 2 *Sessia V.S.*, pp. 679–92; *Izvestia*, 13–20 March 1946.

36. 'Both of the chambers of the Supreme Soviet of the U.S.S.R. are equal in rights. This equality is genuine — there are no "upper" and "lower" chambers in the Soviet system.

constitution goes so far as to provide for the dissolution of the Supreme Soviet and the election of a new one whenever disagreement between the chambers over a question under consideration is not settled to the satisfaction of either of them by a joint conciliation commission (article 47). However, as in the case of the C.E.C., in practice no occasion for recourse to these provisions has arisen.

Generally, the rules of procedure and the actual proceedings of the Supreme Soviet thus far differ but slightly from those that prevailed at the earlier representative assemblies.[37] As before, practically all the reports and most of the proposals were made by the Sovnarkom. There were few co-reports. The only marked innovation was the creation of permanent commissions. In addition to Credentials Commissions, to pass upon the credentials of the deputies in each of the chambers, the Constitution of 1936 empowered the Supreme Soviet to appoint any investigating and revisional commissions it sees fit (articles 50, 51). At the first session of the Supreme Soviet (January 1938), each of the chambers elected three permanent commissions for the purpose of working through drafts of laws introduced for consideration by the chambers: a legislative commission, consisting of ten members in each chamber; a budgetary commission, of thirteen members in each; and a commission on foreign affairs, numbering eleven in the Council of the Union and ten in the Council of Nationalities. The commissions newly elected by the chambers on 18 March 1946 have a higher membership: nineteen in the legislative com-

---

A situation where the second chamber would hold back, hinder [the passage of] law projects of the first chamber, can have no place in the Soviet system. This is to be explained by the fact that the class nature and essence of both chambers of the Supreme Soviet is one — both the first and second chambers are elected by all the toilers of the U.S.S.R. Both the first and second chambers have one aim — the strengthening of Socialism.' (*S.G.P.* p. 306.)

37. The rules of procedure, adopted on 12 January 1938, and again on 12 March 1946 carry the following provisions: The Council of the Union meets from 11 A.M. to 3 P.M., the Council of Nationalities from 6 to 10 P.M. Reporters are confirmed for each chamber by the chairman of the latter, while persons scheduled to report at joint sessions are confirmed by the chairmen of both chambers. Each group of 50 deputies has a right to put forth a co-reporter in its own chamber or at the joint sessions. Reporters are allowed one hour for their reports, 30 minutes for conclusions following debate; co-reporters are given 30 minutes and 15 minutes respectively. Participants in the debate are permitted to speak 20 minutes the first time, 5 minutes the second. Personal declarations and factual remarks are made in writing and are announced by the presiding officer, immediately or at the end of the session, depending upon their content. Extraordinary inquiries are also made in writing and are immediately announced. Five and 3 minutes, respectively, are allowed for remarks in regard to a point of order and in motivation of voting. (1 *Sessia V.S.*, pp. 13, 77–9; *Sots. Zak.* 1938, No. 2, pp. 26–7, 30; *S.G.P.* p. 325; *Izvestia*, 13 March 1946.)

mission, twenty-seven in the budget commission, and eleven in the commission on foreign affairs.[38] Note should also be taken of the 'Council of Elders' or senior deputies of the Supreme Soviet, which consists of representatives of the deputy groups from the various republics and regions. While the function of steering legislation through the chambers belongs to the chairmen of the latter, the Council of Elders assists in working out the agenda of the sessions, and most of the proposals in regard to the election or alteration of the personnel of the Presidium of the Supreme Soviet, the Attorney Generalship, et cetera, were made at the sessions in the name of this council.[39] Lastly, it should be stated, decisions of the Supreme Soviet — unless they involve changes in the constitution, where a two-thirds vote is necessary — require but a simple majority vote in each of the chambers (articles 39, 146).

The Scope of the Supreme Soviet's Competence. The scope of the Supreme Soviet's jurisdiction is given as the exercise of 'all the rights granted to the Union of Soviet Socialist Republics according to article 14 of the Constitution' in so far as they do not come, by virtue of the latter, under the jurisdiction of the federal organs that are accountable to the Supreme Soviet: the Presidium of the Supreme Soviet, the Council of Ministers and the ministries (article 31). These rights are listed as follows (article 14):[40]

(a) Representation of the U.S.S.R. in international relations, conclusion, ratification and denunciation of treaties of the U.S.S.R., *establishment of a uniform system in the relations between the Union republics and foreign states;*
(b) Questions of war and peace;
(c) Admission of new republics into the U.S.S.R.;
(d) Control over the observance of the Constitution of the U.S.S.R. and ensuring conformity of the constitutions of the Union republics with the Constitution of the U.S.S.R.;
(e) Confirmation of alterations of boundaries between Union republics;
(f) Confirmation of the formation of new territories and regions and also of new autonomous republics and autonomous regions within Union republics;
(g) Organization of the defense of the U.S.S.R. and direction of all the armed forces

38. *Sots. Zak,* 1938, No. 2, pp. 26–9; *Izvestia,* 19 March 1946. These commissions in turn form preparatory and sub-commissions to analyze, rearrange, and reword the drafts of the laws submitted to them, and may invite relevant administrators and representatives of particular republics or governmental agencies, as well as outsiders, such as scientists, etc., to obtain expert opinion and factual information. For the work of these commissions, see *Vestnik Verkhovnogo Soveta,* cited hereafter as *V.V.S.,* No. 10, 1938, p. 4; Vasiliev, 'The Permanent Commissions of the Supreme Soviet of the U.S.S.R.,' pp. 137–53.

39. See *S.G.P.* p. 326; 1 *Sessia V.S.,* p. 124; 3 *Sessia V.S.,* p. 458; 6 *Sessia V.S.,* pp. 5–11, 15–20; 7 *Sessia V.S.,* pp. 157–8. Cf. *Izvestia,* 20 March 1946.

40. As given here the article embodies amendments through February 1947. Italics (J.T.) represent the 1 February 1944 amendments.

of the U.S.S.R., *establishment of the guiding principles of organization of the troop formations of the Union republics;*

(h) Foreign trade on the basis of state monopoly;

(i) Safeguarding the security of the state;

(j) Establishment of the national economic plans of the U.S.S.R.;

(k) Approval of the single state budget of the U.S.S.R. and the report of its execution; the establishment of the taxes and revenues that serve to form the budgets of the Union, the republics, and the localities;

(l) Administration of the banks, industrial and agricultural establishments and enterprises, and trading enterprises of all-Union importance;

(m) Administration of transport and communications;

(n) Direction of the monetary and credit system;

(o) Organization of state insurance;

(p) Contracting and granting loans;

(q) Establishment of the basic principles for the use of land as well as for the use of natural deposits, forests, and waters;

(r) Establishment of the basic principles in the spheres of education and public health;

(s) Organization of a single system of national economic accounting;

(t) Establishment of the principles of labor legislation;

(u) Legislation on the judicial system and judicial procedure; criminal and civil codes;

(v) Laws on Union citizenship; laws on the rights of foreigners;

(w) Establishment of the basic principles of legislation on marriage and the family;

(x) Issuing of all-Union acts of amnesty.[41]

As was pointed out earlier, the constitution specifically provides that 'the legislative power of the U.S.S.R. is exercised exclusively by the Supreme Soviet of the U.S.S.R.' (article 32). Other powers placed within the domain of the Supreme Soviet are: the amendment of the constitution; the election of the Presidium of the Supreme Soviet; the formation of the Council of Ministers; the election of the Supreme Court and of special courts of the U.S.S.R. for a term of five years; and the appointment of the Procurator General (Attorney General) of the U.S.S.R. for a term of seven years (articles 146, 48, 56, 105, 114, respectively).[42]

The Operation of the Supreme Soviet in Practice. The pattern of

---

41. For the competence assigned to the Presidium of the Supreme Soviet, the Council of Ministers, and the Ministries, see *infra*, pp. 266–8, 275–6, 280. That the qualifying clause of article 31 is intended as a general guide for practice rather than as an absolute limitation on the 'highest organ,' the Supreme Soviet, is indicated by the ratifications of the Soviet-German Non-Aggression Treaty of 23 August 1939 and of the Anglo-Soviet Treaty of 26 May 1942 by the Supreme Soviet. (See *infra*, pp. 262–3.)

42. There does not appear to be any actual difference between 'election,' 'formation,' and 'appointment' — the differential terms used — in practice, except that in the case of appointment or removal of ministers, which the Presidium of the Supreme Soviet is empowered to carry out in the interim between sessions of the Supreme Soviet, with

Supreme Soviet action in pursuance of its competence is illustrated by the proceedings of the sessions held thus far. From the point of view of content, the decisions adopted at these sessions, outside of those involving the exercise of the appointing power fall into fairly distinct categories: (1) the amendment of the constitution; (2) the admission of new territories and formation of new republics of the U.S.S.R.; (3) the passing of the budget; (4) the confirmation of decrees adopted by the Presidium of the Supreme Soviet in the interim between sessions of the Supreme Soviet; (5) the adoption of less than a score other laws on the judicial structure, citizenship, the ratification and renunciation of treaties, military duty, troop demobilization, the formation of several commissariats, changes in the titles of the Sovnarkom and the Attorney General and in the number of Presidium Supreme Soviet members, a number of various taxes, the new Five-Year Plan; and (6) the approval of reports on the foreign policy of the U.S.S.R.

Amendments to the constitution were adopted at six out of the twelve sessions of the Supreme Soviet of the First Convocation (the first, second, third, sixth, seventh, and eighth), and laws necessitating amendments and addenda in the text of the constitution were passed at the tenth session of the First Convocation and the first session of the Second Convocation. At the first session of the First Convocation a separate report concerning necessary constitutional amendments was made by the Secretary of the Presidium of the Supreme Soviet and six deputies spoke in approval of it. Subsequently, constitutional amendments were reported on together with the interim decrees adopted by the Presidium of the Supreme Soviet, and they were not debated.[43]

Between November 1939 and August 1940 the Supreme Soviet voted the admission of Western Ukraine and Western White Russia (1 and 2 November 1939), the transformation of the Karelian Autonomous S.S.R. into the constituent Karelo-Finnish S.S.R. (31 March 1940) and of the Moldavian Autonomous S.S.R. into the constituent Moldavian S.S.R. (2 August 1940), and the admission of Lithuania, Latvia, and Estonia

---

subsequent submission for confirmation by the latter (article 49 g), the proposal for confirmation is made in the name of the Presidium (see 2 *Sessia V.S.*, pp. 774–5; 3 *Sessia V.S.*, pp. 455–7; 6 *Sessia V.S.*, p. 298; 7 *Sessia V.S.*, pp. 159–60; 8 *Sessia V.S.*, pp. 306–10), while in the case of appointments to or removal from the post of Attorney General or membership in the Presidium, the proposals are made in the name of or with a statement of approval of the Council of Elders (see 3 *Sessia V.S.*, pp. 457–8; 7 *Sessia V.S.*, pp. 157–8, 160–61). The original source of selection in either case, of course, is the control center of the Party.

43. 1 *Sessia V.S.*, pp. 79–121, and reports on interim decrees, cited *infra* at pp. 260–61, *passim; Izvestia*, 2 February 1944; 15 March and 19 October 1946.

as constituent Soviet republics (3, 5, and 6 August 1940).[44] In each case the procedure consisted of a declaration by a representative of the respective territory asking admission, about a half dozen speeches by members of the delegations of these territories and by deputies from neighboring territorial units in approval of the request, and a proposal by one of the deputy chairmen of the Sovnarkom, speaking in the name of the latter, to admit or transform the petitioning territory as requested.

The procedure for adoption of the budget was not markedly different from that at the C.E.C. A report on the pending budget and on the execution of the one enacted two years earlier was made every year by the Commissar of Finance. It was always accompanied by separate co-reports delivered in each of the chambers by the chairmen of the respective budgetary commissions, and as a rule it drew a more extensive debate than any of the other reports. Suggested revisions were ironed out with the Finance Commissar (now the Finance Minister), representing the Sovnarkom, and embodied in a revised budget bill presented by the commissar for adoption, item by item, in each of the chambers, following his concluding remarks before the latter at the end of the debate.[45]

The various other laws were usually brought before the sessions and reported on by the relevant commissars (ministers): tax laws, by the Finance Commissar; the law on judicial structure, by the Commissar of Justice; the law on military duty, by the Commissar of Defense et cetera. An occasional bill was introduced by one of the permanent commissions.[46]

---

44. *V.V.S.* No. 36, p. 1; 6 *Sessia V.S.*, pp. 46–60; 7 *Sessia V.S.*, pp. 38–152.

45. See 2 *Sessia V.S.*, pp. 8–165, 322–38, 430–68, 617–49; 3 *Sessia V.S.*, pp. 8–25, 143–76, 182–96, 319–53, 357–90; 6 *Sessia V.S.* pp. 61–90, 93–108, 222–63, 417–56; 8 *Sessia V.S.*, pp. 25–63, 67–294, 315–28, 488–532; *Izvestia*, 29–31 January 1944, 24–25 April 1945, 16–20 October 1946.

46. Thus, the Legislative Commission of the Council of the Union introduced the bill on 'The State Tax on Horses of Individual Peasants' (2 *Sessia V.S.*, pp. 707–15, 281–316, 580–614) and the Legislative Commissions of both chambers presented co-reports in regard to the 'Law on the Judicial Structure' (ibid. pp. 166–81, 226–7, 469–83, 533–40), while the Foreign Affairs Commission of the Council of Nationalities introduced the bill on 'The Procedure for Ratification and Denunciation of International Treaties of the U.S.S.R.,' which was voted without debate. (Ibid. pp. 701–6.) Generally, while the Budget Commissions take an active part in the drafting and passage of the budget, drafts of general legislative bills do not necessarily have to go through the permanent commissions either during the stage of preparation or for the purpose of introduction of alterations suggested in the debate. For the latter purpose provisional commissions were set up by the chambers on several occasions. (See 4 *Sessia V.S.*, pp. 35–6, 50–83, 130–63.) As for the Commission on Foreign Affairs, while the purpose of its formation is stated to be the preliminary examination of all questions related to foreign affairs that come up for consideration 'by the Supreme Soviet, as well as its Presidium' (*S.G.P.* p. 326), the precise role to be played by it in practice remains to be clarified.

It is difficult to see, however, wherein the Supreme Soviet served as the 'exclusive' legislative body, in view of the relatively small number of laws actually passed by it as compared with the great number of activity-guiding norms — having all the earmarks of laws — adopted by the Presidium of the Supreme Soviet in the form of 'decrees,'[47] and by the Sovnarkom in the form of 'decisions and ordinances.'[48] To be sure, in normal times, a report concerning decrees adopted by the Presidium of the Supreme Soviet in the interim between Supreme Soviet sessions is regularly made by the Secretary of the Presidium when those sessions convene, with a request for confirmation by the latter.[49] These reports list decrees dealing with: (a) territorial changes — such as the delimitation of frontiers between the Soviet republics, the formation of new territories and regions through the break-up of large regions, et cetera; (b) changes in the system of commissariats — abolition of some and formation of new ones; (c) appointments to and removals from the Presidium of the Supreme Soviet and the Sovnarkom; (d) miscellaneous enactments

47. Both the laws of the Supreme Soviet and the decrees of the Presidium of the Supreme Soviet are published over the signatures of the chairman and secretary of the latter body and printed in the *Vedomosti Verkhovnogo Soveta.*, the 'News of the Supreme Soviet.'

48. An examination of the official Collection of Decisions and Ordinances — which contains enactments of organs other than the Supreme Soviet and its Presidium — for the period since the establishment of the Supreme Soviet and up to the year of the German invasion shows the following:

YEAR	TOTAL NO. ENACTMENTS	BY THE C.C. AND SOVNARKOM	BY THE ECO-NOMIC COUNCIL	BY THE SOVNARKOM
1938	329	7	32	290
1939	645	35	55	555
1940	818	80	56	680

OF THE SOVNARKOM ENACTMENTS

YEAR	Appointments and Removals	Diplomatic Agreements	Enactments of a Legislative Nature
1938	131	4	155
1939	302	6	247
1940	310	2	370

Besides decisions in regard to the structure of the commissariats and of the commissions, committees and administrations of the Sovnarkom, as well as their personnel below the rank of commissar, the enactments of the Sovnarkom cover such wide and varied fields as agriculture, industry, communications, commerce, taxes, duties, rates and standards, banks, state loans, labor, education, the arts, celebrations and commemorations, pensions, fellowships, ranks and titles for members of the Red Army command, and numerous lesser subjects.

49. See 2 *Sessia V.S.*, pp. 769–76; 3 *Sessia V.S.*, pp. 449–67; 6 *Sessia V.S.*, pp. 292–301, 486–95; 7 *Sessia V.S.*, pp. 155–65, 169–79; 8 *Sessia V.S.*, pp. 300–12, 539–52. No report was made during the war, but on 14 March 1946 the Secretary of the Presidium reported to the new Supreme Soviet on all decrees concerning the formation of commissariats adopted since the eighth session (1941). (See *Izvestia*, 15 March 1946.)

on a variety of subjects.[50] Most of these interim decrees become effective months before their confirmation by the Supreme Soviet.[51] And as was earlier the case in the matter of approval of interim decrees by the C.E.C., the practice is not to debate or discuss these decrees but to vote their approval as soon as they have been reported on. It should be pointed out, however, that the theory of exclusive legislative power in the Supreme Soviet is persistently maintained; and Soviet jurists invariably insist that the enactments of the Presidium of the Supreme Soviet and of the Sovnarkom, though absolutely obligatory throughout the U.S.S.R., are norms inferior to the 'laws' of the Supreme Soviet, and that they are issued on the basis and in pursuance of laws, but are not 'laws' themselves.

Lastly, the following may be noted concerning the role of the Supreme Soviet in the conduct of foreign affairs. Beginning with the third session (25-31 May 1939) reports on foreign policy (or bearing on the conduct of foreign policy, such as the report introducing the 1 February 1944 reform) were delivered by Foreign Commissar Molotov at every session of the Supreme Soviet of the First Convocation except the eighth (25 February to 1 March 1941), eleventh (24 April 1945), and twelfth (22-3 June 1945).[52] While the report at the third session is indicated to have been in response to a request of a group of seven deputies, including Marshal Timoshenko, at all the other sessions the reports were made on the Sovnarkom's own initiative; the fourth (28 August to 1 September 1939) and fifth (31 October to 2 November 1939) sessions, which assem-

---

50. As samples of the last-named category may be mentioned the 1940 decrees: in re establishing military titles for the commanding staff of the Red Army; in re transition to an 8-hour work day, 7-day work week, and prohibition of the quitting of enterprises and institutions by workers and employees; in re criminal responsibility for petty larceny in production; in re establishing labor reserves of the U.S.S.R.; in re instituting compulsory transfer of engineers, technicians, master-craftsmen, employees and qualified workers from their enterprises and institutions to other enterprises and institutions. (See 7 *Sessia V.S.*, p. 161; 8 *Sessia V.S.*, pp. 302–5.)

51. To illustrate, the decree concerning the transition to an 8-hour work day, etc. (see preceding note) became effective, by its own terms, on 27 June 1940 (*V.V.S.*, 1940, No. 20, p. 1), yet its confirmation by the Supreme Soviet took place on 7 August 1940. Such important decrees as those creating labor reserves, and instituting compulsory transfer of engineers, technicians, etc., from one industrial enterprise to another, were issued by the Presidium of the Supreme Soviet in October 1940 (*V.V.S.*, 1940, No. 31, p. 1; No. 42, p. 1), but were confirmed by the Supreme Soviet on 1 March 1941. (See preceding notes.) The same was true of most of the other interim decrees.

52. 3 *Sessia V.S.*, pp. 447–8, 467–76 (31 May 1939); 4 *Sessia V.S.* pp. 196–210 (31 August 1939); *V.V.S.*, 1939, No. 36, p. 1; Molotov, *O Vneshnei Politike Sovetskogo Soiuza;* 6 *Sessia V.S.*, pp. 26–45 (29 March 1940); 7 *Sessia V.S.*, pp. 22–37 (1 August 1940); *Stenograficheskii Otchet Zasedania Verkhovnogo Soveta SSSR 18 Iunia 1942 goda* (18 June 1942).

bled in extraordinary fashion, having been called largely for the very purpose of making statements of the government's foreign policy. No report on foreign policy as such was made at the first session of the Supreme Soviet of the Second Convocation (12–19 March 1946) — probably because several pronouncements on the subject were made by the Soviet leaders a month earlier, in the election campaign — nor at the second session (15 October 1946), which was devoted to the 1946 budget and confirmation of interim Presidium decrees. With the exception of the debate at the meeting of 18 June 1942, in which ten deputies voiced their approval of the Anglo-Soviet Treaty of 26 May 1942, and of the speeches in approval of the February 1944 reform, none of the foreign-policy reports were debated at the Supreme Soviet sessions. Customarily, following the delivery of the report, a prominent deputy would rise and propose to dispense with debate 'in view of the exhaustive clarity and consistency of the foreign policy of the government' and to adopt a brief resolution of complete approval of the government's foreign policy. Whereupon the chambers would vote unanimous approval, as was the case with every law and decision adopted by the Supreme Soviet.

Though, by article 49 of the constitution, international treaties are supposed to be ratified by the Presidium of the Supreme Soviet, the Supreme Soviet itself ratified the Soviet-German Treaty of Non-Aggression on 23 August 1939. It likewise ratified the Treaty of Alliance between the U.S.S.R. and the Kingdom of Great Britain in War against Hitlerite Germany and Her Associates in Europe and of Collaboration and Mutual Assistance Thereafter, concluded on 26 May 1942. This was done, however, because of the exceptional importance attached to these treaties at the time of their conclusion.[53]

The Position and Role of the Supreme Soviet in the Soviet Structure. To summarize, the Supreme Soviet constitutes a structural cross between the former Congress of Soviets and C.E.C. By combining in it the functions formerly performed by these two organs — amendment of the constitution, adoption of the budget, approval of foreign-policy reports,

---

53. See 4 *Sessia V.S.*, p. 206, and the last reference of the preceding note, p. 6. This may be inferred also from a recent Soviet statement on 'Organizational Forms of Modern Diplomacy,' which recognizes that, even without any specific legislation on the subject, treaties are often submitted by governments to their parliaments for ratification 'when a government deems it necessary to weaken its responsibility for the conclusion of a serious international agreement, or wishes to endow the latter with particular weight, or, lastly, when it wishes to induce the other contracting party to use a similar parliamentary procedure, in order to communicate to the treaty greater stability.' (*Istoria Diplomatii*, III, p. 768.)

confimation of interim decrees of other organs, and occasional passage of some specific laws — one rung was eliminated from the formal ladder of authority. Though theoretically the sole legislating organ in the Soviet pyramid, the Supreme Soviet, like its predecessors — large in composition and meeting for a brief period in the course of the year — has so far operated primarily as a ratifying and propagating body. Its chief purpose appears to be, periodically or as occasion demands, to lend the voice of approval of a representative assembly to governmental policy.

(2) THE PRESIDIUM OF THE SUPREME SOVIET

The Conception of the Presidium of the Supreme Soviet. The Presidium of the Supreme Soviet came into existence on 17 January 1938. It is listed in the constitution among 'the highest organs of state power' of the U.S.S.R.[54] While the functions allotted to it are chiefly those performed elsewhere by the head of the state, such as a president, the accepted Soviet conception — in accordance with Stalin's definition of the Presidium at the time of the adoption of the new constitution — is that the Presidium of the Supreme Soviet is a 'collective president.' In rejecting a proposed amendment of the draft of the constitution which would have the chairman of the Presidium elected by the people rather than by the Supreme Soviet, Stalin stated:

I think this amendment is wrong because it is not in conformity with the spirit of our constitution. According to the system of our constitution, the U.S.S.R. should not have an individual president elected by the entire population on an equal basis with the Supreme Soviet, who might essay to stand out against the Supreme Soviet. In the U.S.S.R. the president is a collective one — the Presidium of the Supreme Soviet, which also includes the chairman of the Presidium of the Supreme Soviet, elected not by the entire population but by the Supreme Soviet and accountable to the Supreme Soviet. The experience of history shows that such a structure of the supreme organs is the most democratic and insures the country against undesirable contingencies.[55]

As far as its position in the hierarchy of Soviet organs is concerned, this Soviet president, it is pointed out, unlike other heads of state, not only possesses no veto power over or any right to dissolve the 'Soviet parliament' — the Supreme Soviet — but is entirely subordinate and ac-

---

54. In this respect it is in company with the Supreme Soviet, as contrasted with the Council of Ministers. (See chs. III, v, Constitution of 1936, and Shlifer, 'The Presidium of the Supreme Soviet U.S.S.R.,' pp. 36–40.)

55. Stalin, *O Proekte Konstitutsii Soiuza SSR*, p. 41. Soviet jurists illustrate what was meant by 'undesirable contingencies' by references to Napoleon III, Hindenburg, and others. (See *S.G.P.* p. 313, and Shnaidman, 'The Presidium of the Supreme Soviet of the Union S.S.R. — a collective president,' pp. 38–46.)

countable to the latter, which can replace it at any time with a presidium of a new composition.[56] Like the Supreme Soviet and some of the earlier organs, the Presidium of the Supreme Soviet is regarded as a concrete application of the Soviet class and nationality principles at the present stage, i.e. as an organ whose essence and structure reflect the interests of the entire people as well as of the separate nationalities.

The Organization and Composition of the Presidium and the Role of Its Chairman. By article 48 of the Constitution of 1936, the Presidium of the Supreme Soviet was to consist of: a chairman, eleven vice-chairmen — to accord with the number of constituent republics existing at that time — a secretary, and twenty-four members, i.e. a membership of thirty-seven in all.[57] At the first session (January 1938) of the Supreme Soviet of the First Convocation, the Presidium was elected from among the members of the former in line with the above-stated provisions. On 7 August 1940, article 48 was amended to provide for sixteen vice-chairmen, in order to allow for the increase in the number of constituent republics. At the first session of the Supreme Soviet of the Second Convocation, on 19 March 1946, a law was adopted to reconstitute the Presidium of the Supreme Soviet as follows: a chairman, sixteen vice-chairmen, a secretary, and fifteen members, which would have reduced the total membership to thirty-three. Since, however, as a matter of established custom, the posts of vice-chairmen in the federal Presidium are filled by all the chairmen of the presidia of the supreme soviets of the Union republics, the actual present membership of the Presidium of the U.S.S.R. is thirty-two, because the chairman of the latter, Shvernik, is also the chairman of the Presidium of the Supreme Soviet of the R.S.F.S.R.[58] Normally, under the provisions of the Constitution, the tenure of office of the Presidium would last a little over four years, that is, until a newly elected Supreme Soviet convenes and elects a new presidium (article 53). However, due

56. *S.G.P.* pp. 310–13; articles 31, 48, Constitution of 1936.

57. The original draft of article 48 provided for 4 vice-chairmen in the Presidium of the Supreme Soviet. During the discussion of the constitution, an amendment was suggested to increase the number of vice-chairmen to 11 so that there may be one vice-chairman from each Union republic. Speaking on behalf of the Constitutional Commission, Stalin declared the amendment acceptable on the ground that 'it is an improvement and can only enhance the prestige of the Presidium of the Supreme Soviet.' (Stalin, *Constitution*, pp. 27–8.) As was earlier the case with the chairmen of the C.E.C., each vice-chairman of the Presidium of the Supreme Soviet is, as a rule, also the chairman of the Presidium of the Supreme Soviet of the constituent republic that he represents, and when he is transferred to a post outside of his republic he is dropped from membership in the Presidium. (See e.g. 3 *Sessia V.S.*, p. 458.)

58. See 7 *Sessia V.S.*, pp. 157–8, 171; 8 *Sessia V.S.*, pp. 310–12, 549–52; *Izvestia*, 20 March 1946.

to the suspension of elections following the German invasion, the Presidium of the Supreme Soviet elected in 1938 remained in office until 19 March 1946, when it was replaced by the present Presidium.

In consonance with the conception of the Presidium as a 'collective president,' the Chairman of the Presidium is deemed to have no distinct powers of his own, accruing to him by virtue of his position. Although laws of the Supreme Soviet are promulgated under his signature, and he signs the decrees of the Presidium, receives foreign envoys, et cetera, he acts, it is stated, always in the name of the Presidium, the decisions of which are collective decisions.[59] Nevertheless, the Chairman of the Presidium of the Supreme Soviet has stood out in practice as titular head of the Soviet state in its relations with other states.[60] For that reason he has generally been referred to outside of the U.S.S.R. as the Soviet President.

The Secretary of the Presidium countersigns the laws adopted by the Supreme Soviet and the decrees of the Presidium, and is in general charge of the latter's secretariat, which handles all the technical details of the Presidium's work and through which matters are cleared before they are passed upon by the Presidium.

The membership of the Presidium of the Supreme Soviet includes several members of the Politbureau and until recently included also several from the highest command of the Red Army. However, unlike the situation that existed earlier, when a number of commissars were at the same time also members of the Presidium of the C.E.C., it was specifically declared at the time of the first election of the Presidium of the Supreme Soviet in 1938 that no members of the Sovnarkom, no Commissars would belong to the Presidium of the Supreme Soviet.[61] The explanation was offered that under the old constitution there was no strict delimitation between the legislative functions of the supreme organs of power and executive and administrative functions, a condition that was reflected in the composition of the Presidium of the C.E.C., whereas the new constitution introduces a rigid demarcation of functions. It was explained also that, since the Sovnarkom and the individual commissars are accountable to the Presidium of the Supreme Soviet, it is not proper that the commissars should be members of the Presidium. Accordingly, on several occasions, when members of the Presidium of the Supreme

---

59. *S.G.P.* p. 311; Schnaidman, op. cit. p. 41.

60. See e.g. Kalinin's exchange of messages with President Roosevelt in regard to the latter's appeal to Hitler and Mussolini (*Pravda*, 17 and 22 March 1939), his congratulations to the President on the occasion of the third-term inauguration, and his Independence Day greeting to the U.S.A. in 1941. (*N.Y.T.* 7 February and 2 July 1941.)

61. 1 *Sessia V.S.*, pp. 124–5.

Soviet were appointed to commissar posts, they were relieved of membership in the Presidium.[62] Likewise, contrary to previous practice at the C.E.C. and its Presidium, the chairmen and vice-chairmen of the two chambers of the Supreme Soviet were not included in the membership of the Presidium. Here the argument was made that since these officers are in charge of the sessions of the Supreme Soviet, to which the Presidium is accountable, they should not become members of the latter body.[63]

The proceedings of the Presidium of the Supreme Soviet are not made public. While the frequency of its sessions is nowhere indicated, the Presidium is referred to as a 'daily working' organ.[64] The chairman, secretary, and a number of its members are always at the center, assuring a minimum operating quorum. Before the war emergency, full sessions were probably held by the Presidium several times a month.

The Prerogatives of the Presidium of the Supreme Soviet. By article 14 of the constitution the Presidium of the Supreme Soviet is one of the organs of state power that represent the U.S.S.R. in international relations, and a recent Soviet text refers to this role as 'the highest international representation.'[65] Generally, according to article 49 of the present constitution, specifically enumerating the competence with which the Presidium is endowed, the Presidium of the Supreme Soviet of the U.S.S.R.:

(a) Convenes the sessions of the Supreme Soviet of the U.S.S.R.;
(b) Issues decrees;
(c) Interprets laws of the U.S.S.R. in force;
(d) Dissolves the Supreme Soviet of the U.S.S.R. on the basis of article 47 of the Constitution of the U.S.S.R. and designates new elections;
(e) Conducts a general interrogation of the people (referendum) on its own initiative or on the demand of one of the Union republics;
(f) Annuls decisions and ordinances of the Council of Ministers of the U.S.S.R. and of the councils of ministers of the Union republics in case they do not conform to law;
(g) In the period between sessions of the Supreme Soviet of the U.S.S.R., relieves of their posts and appoints Ministers of the U.S.S.R. at the instance of the Chairman of the Council of Ministers of the U.S.S.R., with the subsequent submission for confirmation by the Supreme Soviet of the U.S.S.R.;

---

62. L. P. Beria, on 31 May 1939, because of his apointment as Commissar of Internal Affairs (3 *Sessia V.S.,* p. 458), Marshal Timoshenko, on 7 August 1940, in connection with his appointment as Commissar of Defense (7 *Sessia V.S.,* pp. 160–61), etc.

63. 1 *Sessia V.S.,* p. 125.

64. *S.G.P.* p. 314.

65. 'In the modern state, the highest international representation, in accordance with the generally recognized doctrine of international law, belongs to the head of the state, be that a physical person (a monarch, a president of a republic) or a collective (the Presidium of the Supreme Soviet of the U.S.S.R., the Swiss Federal Council).' (*Istoria Diplomatii,* III, p. 765.)

(h) Institutes decorations (orders) and medals of the U.S.S.R. and establishes titles of honor of the U.S.S.R.;

(i) Awards decorations and medals of the U.S.S.R. and confers titles of honor of the U.S.S.R.;

(j) Exercises the right of pardon;

(k) Establishes military titles, diplomatic ranks, and other special titles;

(l) Appoints and removes the higher commands of the armed forces of the U.S.S.R.;

(m) In the period between sessions of the Supreme Soviet of the U.S.S.R., proclaims a state of war in the event of armed attack on the U.S.S.R., or whenever necessary to fulfil international treaty obligations concerning mutual defense against aggression; [66]

(n) Proclaims general or partial mobilization;

(o) Ratifies and denounces international treaties; [67]

(p) Appoints and recalls plenipotentiary representatives of the U.S.S.R. in foreign states;

(q) Receives the credentials and letters of recall of diplomatic representatives of foreign states accredited to it;

(r) Proclaims martial law in separate localities or throughout the U.S.S.R. in the interests of the defense of the U.S.S.R. or for the purpose of ensuring public order and state security.

To underscore the primacy of the Supreme Soviet, as 'the sole bearer of the sovereignty of the Soviet people,' over the Presidium, descriptions of the competence of the latter emphasize that 'only the laws of the

---

66. The phrasing of this clause was obviously inspired by the Soviets' adherence to the Kellogg Pact. As one Soviet writer commented on it in 1938: 'Let us underscore once more that what is meant is not a declaration of war but a declaration of a *state of war*, that is, a declaration that a war was *thrust* upon us directly by a hostile state or issues from our treaty obligations toward other states for mutual defense against aggression.' (Shlifer, op. cit. p. 40.)

67. By the 'Law on the Procedure for Ratification and Denunciation of International Treaties,' adopted by the Supreme Soviet on 19 August 1938, it was provided that 'the denunciation of ratified international treaties of the U.S.S.R. is made on the basis of decrees of the Presidium of the Supreme Soviet.' (2 *Sessia V.S.*, pp. 705–7; *V.V.S.*, 1938, No. 11, p. 3.) This law, which supersedes earlier decrees on the subject (see *supra* note 55, ch. x) lists as subject to ratification: treaties of peace, treaties for mutual defense against aggression, and non-aggression treaties, as well as treaties at the conclusion of which the parties mutually agreed on subsequent ratification. The introduction of the last-named class of treaties, in place of treaties ratifiable by the laws of the state with which they were concluded — made subject to ratification by the earlier Soviet decrees — is hailed by Soviet jurists as corresponding more to the prestige of the Soviet state. (See *V.V.S.*, 1938, No. 17, p. 4, and Plotkin, 'International Law Questions at the Second Session of the Supreme Soviet U.S.S.R., pp. 83–4.) While the new law does not indicate what treaties are to be confirmed by the Council of Ministers, it is understood that treaties not subject to ratification by the Presidium of the Supreme Soviet may be confirmed as usual by the Council of Ministers. (Plotkin, op. cit. p. 54; see also *infra* p. 279.)

Supreme Soviet constitute the guiding line of the Presidium of the Supreme Soviet,' which does not issue any laws, but only interprets laws and issues decrees.[68] And it is also stressed that not the Presidium of the Supreme Soviet, but the Supreme Soviet itself appoints the judges of the Supreme Court and of special courts of the U.S.S.R., and that while the Presidium wields control over the activity of the government, its appointment and removal of ministers in the period between the sessions of the Supreme Soviet requires the subsequent confirmation of the latter.

As compared with the former Presidium of the C.E.C., the Presidium of the Supreme Soviet has no powers to annul or suspend decisions of the supreme soviets of the constituent republics and their presidiums, and although it convokes it does not conduct the sessions of the Supreme Soviet of the U.S.S.R. On the other hand, whereas by the Constitution of 1924 the right to interpret laws belonged not only to the Presidium of the C.E.C. but also to the Supreme Court of the U.S.S.R., by the new constitution this right belongs to the Presidium of the Supreme Soviet alone, which, though restricted in regard to the framework of substance, is free to choose the methods of interpretation.[69] The consent of the Presidium is required for judicial action against Supreme Soviet deputies in the interim between the sessions of the latter. And the Law on Citizenship of the U.S.S.R., adopted on 19 August 1938, places within the jurisdiction of the Presidium of the Supreme Soviet the right to admit foreigners to citizenship and to allow withdrawal from Soviet citizenship by special decrees of the Presidium in each case.[70]

---

68. 'Legislation cannot foresee the details of development of public relations. Legislation cannot render norms in such a general form as would fit all concrete situations. It can give general principles. The principles of the law are detailed in the form of decrees.' (*S.G.P.* p. 320.) 'Not only that which is directly stated in the law has universal obligatory force, but also that which explains existing law . . . In the U.S.S.R., the right to interpret laws is given to an organ that is accountable to the Supreme Soviet, to the collective president — the Presidium of the Supreme Soviet. Thereby is secured the greatest identity of the interpretation of the laws with the laws themselves . . . Thereby is also predetermined the nature of the interpretation of law in the U.S.S.R., its subordination to law.' (Ibid. pp. 318–19. See also Shnaidman, op. cit. pp. 42–3.)

69. *S.G.P.* pp. 319–20. See, however, *infra*, pp. 307–9 concerning the functions of the Procurator General.

70. *V.V.S.*, 1938, No. 11, p. 3. The right to admit to Soviet citizenship foreigners living on their respective territories is possessed also by the presidia of the supreme soviets of the constituent republics, but only the Presidium of the Supreme Soviet U.S.S.R. can grant permission to renounce Soviet citizenship by special decree in each case. Deprivation of citizenship takes place either by a decision of the Presidium, or, in certain cases, by the verdict of a court. (See Plotkin, op. cit. pp. 81–3.)

The Operation of the Presidium in Practice. The operation of the Presidium during the past nine years shows that it has been exercising fully most of its prerogatives. It has convoked the regular and extraordinary sessions of the Supreme Soviet, set election days and formed electoral areas, and decreed the postponement of elections and prolongation of the term of the Supreme Soviet during the war years. As far as its functioning under clause *b* of article 49 is concerned, the scope and nature of the decrees issued by the Presidium in the interim between sessions of the Supreme Soviet show that, despite the assertion of exclusive legislative power in the Supreme Soviet, wide latitude is allowed for the exercise of the decree power of the Presidium. This power is being used not only in situations where it is impossible or difficult to convene the Supreme Soviet, but also where the occasion seems to call for an edict by a high Soviet organ, yet does not seem to warrant the convocation of the Supreme Soviet.

The decrees passed by the Presidium fall into several groups. First, there are the decrees issued by the Presidium in pursuance of its own specific functions under article 49 of the constitution. Second, there are decrees in interpretation and implementation of laws.[71] The third group comprises decrees on matters of federal jurisdiction not specifically assigned to the Presidium, as well as decrees on matters explicitly or implicitly within the competence of the Supreme Soviet.[72] While decrees of

---

71. By way of illustration may be cited the decree nationalizing banks, industries, transport, and communications in the newly acquired territories of Bessarabia and North Bukovina (*V.V.S.*, 1940, No. 29, pp. 1–2), and the decree on the manner of acquiring U.S.S.R. citizenship by citizens of Lithuania, Latvia, and Estonia. (Ibid. No. 31, p. 1.)

72. This group contains decrees dealing with: (a) the approval of changes of boundaries between Union republics (e.g. the 1940 decrees establishing precise borders between the R.S.F.S.R. and Karelo-Finnish S.S.R., the Ukrainian S.S.R. and Moldavian S.S.R., the White Russian S.S.R. and Lithuanian S.S.R., 8 *Sessia V.S.*, pp. 305–6); (b) the approval of the formation of new territories and regions and of new autonomous republics within Union republics (e.g. the formation of the Murmansk region and the division of the Donets region into the Stalinsk and Voroshilovgrad regions, *V.V.S.*, 1938, No. 7, p. 1); (c) acts of amnesty (e.g. the 12 August 1941 decree granting amnesty to Polish citizens confined on the territory of the U.S.S.R. in accordance with the protocol to the Soviet-Polish agreement of 30 July 1941, *V.V.S.*, 1941, No. 37, p. 2) — which decrees by clauses e, f, and w, respectively, of article 14 of the constitution are within the jurisdiction of the U.S.S.R. 'as represented by its highest organs of power and organs of state administration'; (d) the formation of investigatory commissions (e.g. the 2 November 1942 decree forming an Extraordinary State Commission to investigate the crimes and damages committed by the German invaders in the U.S.S.R., *V.V.S.*, 1942, No. 40, p. 2); (e) changes in the system of commissariats (e.g. decrees of January, February, and April 1939 creating 20 commissariats out of 6 existing ones, 3 *Sessia V.S.*, pp. 450–51) — which by virtue of articles 48, 51, 70, 77, and 78 should be carried out by the Supreme Soviet; and (f) occasional other decrees on subjects presumably within

this group are held to require confirmation by the Supreme Soviet, they take effect immediately, as their subsequent approval is largely a matter of form. Finally, there are the decrees of the same category as the preceding one, but which have been enacted since the eighth session (25 February to 1 March 1941) of the Supreme Soviet of the First Convocation and, where still in effect, have only been confirmed by the Supreme Soviet of the Second Convocation, on 14 March 1946.[73]

The Presidium has never had to dissolve the Supreme Soviet on account of disagreement between the chambers. Nor has it initiated or been asked by a constituent republic to carry out a referendum of the people. But it has had occasion to utilize the rest of its prerogatives. It has annulled a number of existing decrees and ordinances in connection with the passage of new laws; made appointments and removals of Ministers, at the request of the Chairman of the Council of Ministers; has established and awarded numerous decorations, insignia, ranks, and titles of honor;[74] inaugurated celebrations and holidays; and exercised the right of pardon. As a rule, shifts in the high command, promotions to the rank of marshal, and similar changes in the status of political commissars in the Red Army were formally instituted through Presidium decrees.[75]

the competence of the Supreme Soviet (such as the 8 July 1944 decree on marriage, divorce, the family, and motherhood, *N.Y.H.T.* 10 July 1944).

73. As examples of these may be cited the following decrees: in re a regime of working time for workers and employees in time of war; in re establishing a temporary addition to the agricultural tax and income tax from the population for the war period; in re a tax on single men and single and childless citizens of the U.S.S.R.; in re the responsibility of workers and employees of war industries for leaving the enterprises on their own volition; in re a war tax; in re the mobilization of the able city population for work in industry and construction during the period of the war; in re local taxes and collections; in re abolishing inheritance and gift taxes for heirs of persons who have perished in defense of the fatherland; in re compulsory transfer of medical personnel from one medical institution to another during war time. (*V.V.S.*, 1941, No. 30, p. 1; No. 31, p. 2; No. 42, p. 3; 1942, No. 2, p. 4; No. 6, p. 4, No. 13, p. 4; 1943, No. 3, p. 4; No. 5, p. 4.)

74. This is by far the widest exercised of all the prerogatives of the Presidium. As a rule 9/10 and often the entire space of the 4-page *Vedomosti Verkhovnogo Soveta* is taken up with lists of awards of orders, medals, pins, certificates, dress insignia, and special designations and titles of honor, to excellent performers in every conceivable type of work, to institutions, cities, enterprises, to units, men and officers of the armed forces, and even to guerrilla fighters. New signs and symbols of distinction, most of which carry also material rewards, are added constantly, and a special Department of Registry at the Secretariat of the Presidium keeps track of them. (See *V.V.S.*, 1941, No. 5, p. 4.) Occasionally, the Presidium issues decrees depriving individuals of their awards. (See e.g. *V.V.S.*, 1939, No. 26, p. 4.)

75. See e.g. the decrees successively abolishing (12 August 1940), reinstituting (16 July 1941), and again abolishing (9 October 1942) political commissars in the armed forces. (*V.V.S.*, 1940, No. 28, p. 2; 1941, No. 33, p. 1; 1942, No. 38, p. 1.)

The Presidium has declared martial law and subsequently decreed its end, proclaimed the mobilization of the armed forces, and ordered partial demobilization on several occasions. Lastly, the Presidium has made full use of its prerogatives in foreign affairs: it has ratified international treaties;[76] it has appointed and recalled diplomatic representatives of the U.S.S.R.;[77] and it has received letters of credence and recall from diplomatic representatives of foreign states.

Although a State Defense Committee, in which 'the full plenitude of power in the state' was to be concentrated, was set up on 30 June 1941 in

76. The treaties and agreements published since the middle of 1938 show that: (1) the text of ratification is signed by the Chairman of the Presidium of the Supreme Soviet and countersigned by the Foreign Affairs Minister (see e.g. *V.V.S.*, 1939, No. 35, p. 3); (2) denunciation of a treaty is made by the Foreign Ministry in reliance on decrees of the Presidium (see e.g. ibid. No. 12, p. 1); (3) plenary powers to conclude treaties that are subject to ratification are issued under the signature of the Chairman of the Presidium of the Supreme Soviet, and plenary powers for all other international agreements, under the signature of the Chairman of the Council of Ministers (both bear also the signature of the Minister of Foreign Affairs); (4) most of the treaties were concluded in the name of the Presidium of the U.S.S.R., particularly when they were of a kind subject to ratification, such as the Soviet mutual-assistance treaties with Lithuania, Estonia, and Latvia (ibid. No. 37, p. 3), the Soviet-Finnish Peace Treaty of 12 March 1940 (*V.V.S.*, 1940, No. 14, p. 3), and the Soviet-Japanese Neutrality Pact, of 13 April 1941 (*V.V.S.*, No. 24, p. 4); (5) yet some treaties, although of a kind subject to ratification and subsequently actually ratified by the Presidium, were concluded in the name of 'the Government of the U.S.S.R.,' as, for example, the Soviet-German treaties of 23 August, 28 September, and 4 October 1939, and 31 August 1940, concerning 'non-aggression,' 'Friendship and the Border,' and 'Legal Relations on the Border' (*V.V.S.*, 1939, No. 37, p. 3; 1940, No. 10, p. 2; 1941, No. 14, pp. 2–4); (6) while the Law on Ratification, etc., makes treaties of mutual assistance against aggression subject to ratification, when quick understandings were desirable, the Soviet government entered into 'agreements' for mutual aid, etc., which specifically declared that they took effect immediately and were not subject to ratification, such as the Soviet-British, Soviet-Czech, and Soviet-Polish agreements of 12, 18, and 30 July 1941, respectively. (*V.V.S.*, 1941, No. 32, p. 1; No. 33, p. 1, No. 35, p. 1. See also *Istoria Diplomatii*, III, pp. 806–7, 809–10.)

77. On 9 May 1941 the Presidium of the Supreme Soviet decreed the establishment of the ranks of ambassador extraordinary and plenipotentiary, minister extraordinary and plenipotentiary, and chargé d'affaires in the Soviet diplomatic service, in order to bring the service in accord with general international practice. (*V.V.S.*, 1941, No. 21, p. 1.) On 14 June 1943, the Presidium issued a new decree setting up the following ranks: (1) ambassador extraordinary and plenipotentiary, (2) minister extraordinary and plenipotentiary of the first class, (3) minister extraordinary and plenipotentiary of the second class, (4) counselor of the first class, (5) counselor of the second class, (6) first secretary of the first class, (7) first secretary of the second class, (8) second secretary of the first class, (9) second secretary of the second class, (10) third secretary, (11) attaché. The Presidium bestows the first three ranks and accredits their holders. The other ranks are bestowed by order of the Foreign Minister, who likewise accredits the diplomats holding them. (See *Istoria Diplomatii*, III, pp. 774, 779.)

order to be able to act swiftly in the war emergency, the Presidium of the Supreme Soviet did not cease to function and has, in fact, been used to enact considerable legislation of vital, and sometimes extraordinary, import.[78]

The Position and Role of the Presidium in the Soviet Structure. To summarize, the Presidium of the Supreme Soviet, constitutionally classified as one of the highest organs of the state power, has — like its predecessor, the Presidium of the C.E.C. — fulfilled the need of a continuously operating body, representing the summit of the formal Soviet pyramid and performing a wide variety of functions. Though the competence assigned to it differs in several aspects from that of the Presidium of the C.E.C., particularly in the publicly emphasized lack of legislative power in the Presidium of the Supreme Soviet, the latter has not only acted as 'collective president' of the Soviet state, but has in fact served to a large extent as a legislative organ in the Soviet structure.

3. THE COUNCIL OF MINISTERS AND ITS ORGANS

(I) THE COUNCIL OF MINISTERS — FORMERLY THE SOVNARKOM

The Formation of the Council. The Council of Ministers of the U.S.S.R. was called Council of People's Commissars or Sovnarkom (abbreviated from the full Russian title *Sovet Narodnykh Komissarov*) until 19 March 1946, when its name was changed by the Supreme Soviet.

The Sovnarkom or Council of People's Commissars came into existence on 8 November 1917. On that date, in one of the first acts inaugurating the new regime, the Second Congress of Soviets issued a decree:

To form a Provisional Workers' and Peasants' Government, which would be called the Council of People's Commissars, in order to govern the country until the convocation of the Constituent Assembly. The management of individual branches of state life is entrusted to commissions [commissariats] . . . Governmental power belongs to a collegium of the chairmen of these commissions, i.e. to the Council of People's Commissars.[79]

---

78. See e.g. the decree of 28 August 1941, transplanting the Volga Germans to resettlement lands in Novo-Sibirsk, Omsk, etc., in the interests of national security. (*V.V.S.*, 1941, No. 38, p. 4.)

79. *L. i S.* p. 258. For the origin of the designation 'Council of People's Commissars,' see *E.G.i P.*, II, p. 1095. In view of the widespread employment of the name 'Commissar' at the time, an instruction was introduced in the early part of 1918 to restrict its use, and only members of the Sovnarkom could bear the title 'People's Commissars' (see 4 *VTsIK*, pp. 334–5), a provision embodied in the constitution adopted in July 1918 (article 48).

On 31 January 1918 the term 'provisional' was dropped from the designation of the Sovnarkom. With the formation of the U.S.S.R. a Union Sovnarkom was established in July 1923, and in January 1938 it was formally reconstituted as the government of the U.S.S.R. by the Supreme Soviet of the First Convocation.[80] In accordance with article 56 of the constitution, this government laid down its powers and was immediately reappointed (15–19 March 1946) by the Supreme Soviet of the Second Convocation. Along with the change in its name to Council of Ministers, adopted at that time, the Chairman of the Sovnarkom was renamed 'Chairman of the Council of Ministers of the U.S.S.R.;' his deputies, 'deputy-chairmen of the Council of Ministers;' the people's commissars, 'ministers;' and the commissariats headed by them 'ministries.' Similar changes in designation were made with regard to the governments of the Union and autonomous republics.[81]

The Conception of the Council of Ministers. According to the first Soviet constitution (1918) the Sovnarkom was formed 'for the general administration of the affairs' of the state, and to carry out this purpose it had a right to issue 'decrees, ordinances, instructions' and take all other necessary measures (articles 35, 37, 38). It was responsible and accountable to the Congress of Soviets, and also to the C.E.C., which could annul or suspend its decisions (articles 40, 46). The Treaty of Union of December 1923 termed the Sovnarkom 'the executive organ of the C.E.C.,' while the Constitution of 1924 designated it as 'the executive and administrative organ of the C.E.C. of the U.S.S.R.' (articles 11 and 37, respectively). By the Constitution of 1924 the Sovnarkom was declared

---

80. *Sovetskoe Administrativnoe Pravo*, p. 38 (this official Soviet text on administrative law will be referred to hereafter as *S.A.P.*); 1 *Sessia V.S.*, pp. 134–44, 151–67.

81. *Izvestia*, 16 and 20 March 1946. The motivation for the change is suggested by the organ of the Central Committee of the Party as follows: 'The law transforming the Council of People's Commissars of the U.S.S.R. into Council of Ministers of the U.S.S.R. and the councils of people's commissars of the Union and autonomous republics into councils of ministers of these republics reflects the increased role of the Soviet state, the increased range of competence and responsibility that the Constitution of the U.S.S.R. places upon the central organs and upon the persons who head the individual branches of state administration.' After pointing out that the old names were given during the formative period of Soviet rule, the statement continues: 'The transformation of the people's commissariats into ministries corresponds to the increased role of the state and the state apparatus, which calls for an ever more durable state discipline, order, performance on the part of every official in the post he occupies, and for securing the systematic growth of the cadres of the state apparatus.' (Editorial, *Bol'shevik*, No. 6, March 1946, pp. 4–5.) Professor Denisov offers the additional explanation that the change in titles was made by the Supreme Soviet's 'considering the generally accepted terminology.' (*A.R.S.U.* May 1946, p. 59.)

responsible before the C.E.C. and its Presidium, which could suspend and annul its decisions (articles 40, 41). At the time that the Sovnarkom was designated as an executive-administrative organ it was empowered to issue 'decrees and decisions that must be carried out on the entire territory of the U.S.S.R.' (article 38, Constitution of 1924), and it was freely regarded as a legislative no less than an executive-administrative agency of government. The new constitution and the Soviet legal literature interpreting it introduce a different conception of the Council of Ministers. In connection with the present constitution's provisions placing legislative power exclusively in the Supreme Soviets of the U.S.S.R. and the republics, extraordinary emphasis is placed upon the idea that all 'organs of state administration' are solely executive-administrative in nature, functioning strictly in reliance on constitutions and laws within their respective jurisdictions.[82] The Council of Ministers of the U.S.S.R., it is now emphasized, is not a legislative but an executive-administrative organ, and hence strictly subordinate to the legislative power, to the Supreme Soviet of the U.S.S.R. as the highest embodiment of the popular will. The Council of Ministers is designated by the present constitution as 'the highest executive and administrative organ of the state power of the Union of Soviet Socialist Republics.' In the performance of its duties — which encompass all branches of state administration within the competence of the Union — it has a right to publish 'decisions and ordinances' of binding force throughout the entire domain as well as to verify their execution (articles

---

82. *S.G.P.* p. 346; *S.A.P.* pp. 3–5, 56. The following definitions and criteria are offered. 'State,' i.e. public administration, is defined as 'the constant, current activity of the executive-administrative organs of power, carried on in the interests of the dominant class and directed toward the preservation and strengthening of the existing social and political order.' (*S.G.P.* p. 337.) In the activity of the Soviet organs of public administration, the guiding principle is provided by Lenin's dicta: 'not to tear administration away from politics,' 'to attain the complete subordination of the apparatus to policy,' 'the apparatus *for* politics . . . and not politics for the apparatus!!' (Cited ibid. p. 340.) Specifically, acts of Soviet public administration are described as acts issued on the basis of Soviet laws and Party directives by the sovnarkoms of the Union and the republics, the commissariats, the councils, committees, commissions, and administrations attached to them, and the executive committees or directors of departments and administrations of the local soviets of deputies. (*S.A.P.* p. 101.) These acts are deemed: (1) juridical, i.e. creating, altering, or terminating rights or duties of public bodies, organizations, and enterprises, as well as of citizens; (2) authoritative; (3) operative, i.e. aimed at live, concrete, and differentiated direction; and (4) 'sub-legal,' by which is meant that 'an act of administration can be issued only on the basis and in execution of a Soviet law.' (Ibid.) Lastly, it is claimed that 'Soviet administrative law, as distinguished from bourgeois, does not recognize any freedom of discretion for the organs of administration, i.e. any sphere of discretionary activity unbound by law.' (Ibid. pp. 102–3.)

64, 66, 67, and 14, Constitution of 1936). At the same time it is emphasized over and over again that such enactments are published only 'on the basis of, and in execution of, the existing laws' and that 'the Council of People's Commissars of the U.S.S.R. exercises exclusively executive-administrative functions.'[83] The Council of Ministers is responsible and accountable to the Supreme Soviet, and in the period between the sessions of the latter it is accountable to the Presidium of the Supreme Soviet, which can annul its decisions for non-conformance to law (articles 65, 49 f).

The Competence of the Council. The present constitution (article 68) gives the functions of the Council of Ministers as follows:

The Council of Ministers:
  (a) Co-ordinates and directs the work of the all-Union and Union-republic ministries of the U.S.S.R. and of other institutions under its administration;
  (b) Adopts measures to carry out the plan of the national economy, the state budget, and the strengthening of the credit-monetary system;
  (c) Adopts measures to secure public order, defend the interests of the state, and guard the rights of citizens;
  (d) Exercises general supervision in the sphere of relations with foreign states;
  (e) Determines the yearly quotas of citizens subject to call for active military service, directs the general organization and development of the armed forces of the country;
  (f) Forms, in case of necessity, special committees and chief administrations attached to the Council of Ministers on matters of economic, cultural, and defense organizations.[84]

---

83. *S.A.P.* pp. 38–9, 107; *S.G.P.* p. 346.
84. The Constitution of 1924 did not enumerate the specific functions of the federal Sovnarkom, but the statute concerning it — dated 12 November 1923 — detailed them as (a) direction of the activity of all all-Union and unified people's commissariats; (b) examination and ratification of the decrees and decisions of all-Union importance within the competence provided by the Constitution of the U.S.S.R., the act organizing the TsIK of the U.S.S.R., and other decisions of the TsIK of the U.S.S.R. or its Presidium, as well as the examination and execution of all measures necessary for the general administration of the U.S.S.R.; (c) preliminary examination of the drafts of all decrees and decisions submitted, in accordance with the Constitution of the U.S.S.R., for ratification by the TsIK of the U.S.S.R. or its Presidium; (d) examination of all matters that the TsIK of the U.S.S.R. or its Presidium shall find necessary to submit to the Sovnarkom of the U.S.S.R.; (e) examination of treaties and agreements with the governments of foreign states, as well as confirmation of those treaties that do not require special ratification; (f) examination and approval of concessionary agreements; (g) examination and submission of the all-Union budget for ratification by the TsIK of the U.S.S.R.; (h) examination and submission, for approval by the TsIK of the U.S.S.R. or its Presidium, of all drafts of decisions concerning the introduction of new or the increase of existing taxes; (i) examination of records of the activity of all-Union and unified people's commissariats of the U.S.S.R.; (j) settlement of differences that

Moreover, in branches of administration and the economy placed within the competence of the U.S.S.R., the Council of Ministers has the right to suspend decisions and ordinances of the councils of ministers of the Union republics and to annul orders and instructions of the ministers of the U.S.S.R. (article 69, Constitution of 1936).

The Operation of the Council of Ministers in Practice. All available evidence indicates that the Council of Ministers has more than performed the functions and powers with which it was formally endowed in that it has been the most continuously operating and the most potent organ of the Soviet hierarchy in both the administrative and legislative fields. If at its inception the Sovnarkom spoke the language of power in the form of decrees designed as much for propaganda as for administration, the purport and tenor of these decrees was changed to that of absolute, military-order-like commands in the conditions of the subsequent civil-war period. After that period the Sovnarkom engaged in wide legislative activity not only jointly with the C.E.C. or its Presidium but also entirely independently of them. Theoretically, a stop was put to this activity by the new constitution and the governmental reorganization that it inaugurated. Admittedly, the Council of Ministers still plays an active role in the preparation of legislation, which is subsequently introduced by the relevant ministers at the sessions of the Supreme Soviet. Actually, however, it does more than that. For, whatever the present theoretical distinctions between laws passed by the Supreme Soviet, decrees issued by the Presidium of the Supreme Soviet, and the 'decisions and ordinances' of the Council of Ministers,[85] the scope and volume of its enactments make it

---

may arise between the sovnarkoms of the Union republics in matters falling within the competence of the Sovnarkom of the U.S.S.R., as well as of differences between the People's Commissariats of the U.S.S.R., or between the latter and the sovnarkoms of the Union republics; (k) examination of protests and appeals against the decisions of the S.T.O. [Council of Labor and Defense], or commissions formed in the Sovnarkom and the S.T.O. and having administrative-executive powers, as well as against the actions of the People's Commissariats of the U.S.S.R.; (l) ratification of the personnel lists of the People's Commissariats and other institutions of the U.S.S.R.; (m) submission to the Presidium of the TsIK of the U.S.S.R. of recommendations concerning the appointment of deputy people's commissars, and approval of the appointment of members of the collegia of the People's Commissariats of the U.S.S.R., members of the S.T.O., presidents and members of the Gosplan [State Planning Commission], general concessions committee, legislation-drafting committee, administration-finance commission, collegium of the OGPU, director of the central statistical department, president of the state bank, as well as of other officials, provided that the Union legislation is consulted. (*Sist. Sobr. Deistv. Zak. SSSR,* I, pp. 31–3; *S.Z.* 1924, No. 19, p. 184.)

85. See *S.G.P.* pp. 316–21, 344, 350, 352. 'Decisions' are defined as acts establishing general rules, calculated to operate continuously until they are either annulled or have lost

abundantly clear that the Council of Ministers is the greatest producer of obligatory, state-enforced, activity-guiding norms in the Soviet system.[86] It is the Council of Ministers that enacts the numerous statutes, rules, and regulations in regard to industry, agriculture, transportation, education, et cetera. It approves the various operative plans for production, agricultural work and crops, the volume and movement of freight, construction, obligatory purveyance of agricultural products to the state, and the contracts between the collective farms and the state to supply the latter with particular yields at stipulated prices and premiums. In the preparation of the enormous state budget of the U.S.S.R. the Council of Ministers subjects individual budget plans and reports, as well as the draft of the budget as a whole, to detailed preliminary scrutiny and revision before submitting the completed budgetary bill for approval by the Supreme Soviet. The Council of Ministers proclaims public celebrations and commemorative undertakings, establishes many forms of reward and recognition, confirms the social insurance scales, and sets rates of taxes, utility rates, wage rates, et cetera, though a considerable number of enactments in regard to the economy are decided now by the Economic Council and were formerly handled by the Council of Labor and Defense. Since the end of the recent war a good many of the enactments of the Council of Ministers have revolved around rehabilitation of the national economy, repatriation, and veterans' aid. In decisions and ordinances of great importance, especially those that are directed toward the improvement of particular branches of the national economy, the Central Committee of the Party is associated in their enactment, and where crucial labor questions are involved or where the utmost co-operation of labor is sought, the All-Union Central Council of Trade-Unions may also be associated in the promulgation of given enactments of the Council of Ministers.[87]

A considerable part of the Council of Ministers' decisions have to do

force through attainment of their intended result, while 'ordinances' are defined as acts operating but one time and regulating individual, concrete cases. (Ibid. pp. 348–9.) Until 1938, the enactments of the Sovnarkom were published in the 'Collection of Laws of the U.S.S.R.' Since that year, because of the distinction drawn between the acts of the Supreme Soviet and its Presidium and the enactments of the Sovnarkom, the latter are published in the new 'Collection of Decisions and Ordinances of the Government of the U.S.S.R.,' which has taken the place of the former 'Collection of Laws,' while the laws of the Supreme Soviet and the decrees of the Presidium of the Supreme Soviet are published in the 'News of the Supreme Soviet.'

86. See *supra*, note 48, this chapter.
87. See *supra*, notes 103, 105, 107, ch. x; note 48, this chapter; *S.A.P.* p. 107; *N.Y.T.* 20 August 1945; *Izvestia*, 6 April and 20 September 1946.

with the organization and activity of the administrative organs subordinate to it. These concern the formation and liquidation of committees, commissions, and chief administrations attached to the Council of Ministers; statutes and regulations concerning the structure and functions of these organs, as well as of the ministries, bureaus, industrial administrations and trusts, et cetera; the appointment of deputy ministers, heads of the committees and chief administrations of the Council of Ministers and their deputies; the confirmation of the collegia of the ministries; and various decisions of the Council of Ministers about reports of individual ministries, containing evaluations of their work. Since the mid-'thirties the Council of Ministers has increased its control over the publication of departmental acts. All the ministries are required to present to the Council of Ministers copies of all acts issued by them in execution of the corresponding decisions of the Council, as well as other important orders and instructions.[88] In a number of instances commissariats have submitted their most important orders and instructions to the Sovnarkom for confirmation.[89] And on occasion the Sovnarkom has annuled acts of individual commissariats as improper.[90] The Council of Ministers has also had the final say over the calling of all-Union congresses, conferences, and consultations of officials and others working in particular branches of administration; such gatherings to consider measures for the improvement of given branches of administration are allowed only with the permission of the federal Council of Ministers.

In the military field the Council of Ministers co-ordinates the work of the ministries of the Armed Forces (formerly the Defense and Navy Commissariats), Armaments, Munitions, Aviation Industry, Shipbuilding Industry, and other departments related to national defense; supervises the general organization of the armed services; makes appointments to such posts as Deputy Minister of Defense; awards promotions to the

---

88. *S.G.P.* p. 383. 'Orders' are described as primarily operative acts, 'instructions' as norms of a general nature. (Ibid. p. 382.) Orders and instructions are issued by the ministers, the heads of the chief administrations, and the chairmen of the committees attached to the Council of Ministers and are published in the collection of orders and instructions and in the bulletins of individual ministries. (*S.A.P.* p. 18.)

89. *S.G.P.* p. 383. In these instances they were published in the 'Collection of Decisions and Ordinances of the Government' and are held to have the force of decisions of the Sovnarkom.

90. See e.g. *S.P.R.* 1939, No. 26, item 164. By the Constitution of 1924 both the Presidium of the C.E.C. and the Sovnarkom could suspend or annul acts of the commissariats (article 58). The present constitution's provisions giving the right to annual orders and instructions of the ministries to the Council of Ministers alone is deemed to be in line with the present differentiation between legislative and executive-administrative organs. (*S.G.P.* p. 383.)

ranks of 'General,' 'Admiral,' or their equivalents; [91] and confirms military delegations for negotiations of the U.S.S.R. with other countries.[92]

Finally, the Council of Ministers has had both a formal and active share in the conduct of Soviet foreign policy: [93] officially exercising general supervision over the current work of the foreign-affairs and foreign-trade organs and enacting specific measures in the field; [94] granting or withdrawing recognition, severing relations, and ordering acts of reprisal in regard to other states; appointing negotiators to treaties not requiring ratification, and appointing or replacing trade representatives of the U.S.S.R. on the recommendations of the Foreign Affairs and Foreign Trade Ministers; confirming treaties and agreements not requiring ratification; subjecting all treaties to its preliminary examination and approval; declaring Soviet adherence to international conventions; and entering into numerous agreements in its own name with the governments of other states.

The Composition of the Council. The Council of Ministers is formed by the Supreme Soviet. By earlier constitutions the Sovnarkom was formed by the C.E.C. by a rather cursory procedure involving little more than a vote of approval of the list presented. In January 1938 at the first election of the Sovnarkom by the Supreme Soviet, however, some criticisms of individual commissariats were offered, and the commissars of three of the commissariats involved were omitted from the list subsequently submitted for the confirmation of the Supreme Soviet.[95]

The Council of Ministers consists of the following officials: the Chairman of the Council of Ministers, the deputy chairmen, the Chairman of the State Planning Commission, the Chairman of the Committee on Arts, and finally the ministers — i.e. the heads of the ministries of the U.S.S.R. (article 70, Constitution of 1936). Its formal term of office is a little longer than that of the forming body, because it continues until a newly elected Supreme Soviet confirms its composition. In the interim

91. See e.g. *S.P.R.* 1939, No. 12, item 75, in re Timoshenko, Mekhlis, Apanasenko, Meretskov, Stern, and others.

92. E.g. the delegation composed of Voroshilov, Shaposhnikov, Kuznetsov, Loktionov, and Smorodinov, confirmed on 3 August 1939 for the talks with the military representatives of England and France. (Ibid. 1939, No. 47, item 363.)

93. See *supra*, pp. 216–23, 237–40, 261–2; note 55, ch. x; notes 67, 76, ch. xi; *S.G.P.* pp. 349–50; *S.A.P.* pp. 169–70, 176; *Istoria Diplomatii*, iii, pp. 767–8, 779–80, 806–7.

94. The constitution's vesting of powers of general supervision in the field of relations with foreign states in the Council of Ministers is explained by the official text on administrative law as owing to 'the inseverable connection between the external and internal policy of the Soviet state.' (*S.A.P.* pp. 169–70.)

95. See 1 *Sessia V.S.*, pp. 134–44, 151–67.

between sessions of the Supreme Soviet, individual ministers are appointed
and replaced, at the instance of the Chairman of the Council of Ministers,
by the Presidium of the Supreme Soviet, with the subsequent submission
of such appointments for confirmation by the Supreme Soviet (article
49g). The membership of the Council was fairly restricted until the mid-
'thirties, but has grown considerably since then. If it counted 13 members
at the time of the inception of the Sovnarkom, on 8 November 1917, there
were — besides the Chairman and his deputies — 15 voting members in
the Sovnarkom in 1921 (there were 17 commissariats at the time, but
Stalin and Dzerzhinsky held two posts each), 10 in 1925; 12 in 1931; 15 in
1935; 26 in 1938; while by the middle of 1946 the number of voting members in the Council of Ministers had reached 64.[96] This increase in
membership is due to the changes in the system of administrative organs
subordinate to the Council of Ministers, and is considered to be a reflection of the tremendous growth of the economy and the rise in military
needs, which have necessitated greater differentiation in administration.[97]

(2) THE SYSTEM OF ORGANS OF THE COUNCIL OF MINISTERS

The Ministries — formerly the Commissariats. By the summer of 1946
this central system of organs of the Council of Ministers consisted of
55 ministries, less than a dozen committees and councils, and about
half a dozen chief administrations, as well as a number of other organs
attached to it.[98] The ministries of the U.S.S.R. are two kinds: all-Union
and Union republic. The all-Union ministries direct the branches of state
administration entrusted to them throughout the territory of the U.S.S.R.
either directly or through organs appointed by them, while the Union-
republic ministries of the U.S.S.R. do so, as a rule, through corresponding
ministries of the Union-republics, administering directly only a limited
number of enterprises in accordance with a list confirmed by the Presidium
of the Supreme Soviet of the U.S.S.R. (articles 75, 76, Constitution of

---

96. See *S.U.* 1917, No. 1, item 1; 9 *VTsIK*, pp. 3–4; *S.Z.* 1931, II, No. 5, item 59; 1935,
    II, No. 3, item 14; 1 *Sessia V.S.* pp. 160–61, 203–4; *Izvestia,* 21 March 1946; *A.R.S.U.*
    August 1946, pp. 24–7. By the Constitution of 1918, there were to be 18 members in
    the Sovnarkom (articles 42, 43); by the Treaty of Union and the Constitution of 1924,
    10 members (articles 11, 37, respectively); by the new (1936) constitution, at the time
    of its adoption, 23 members (articles 70, 77, 78).
97. See Molotov's speech of 15 January 1938 in 1 *Sessia V.S.*, p. 109.
98. A complete description of this system, with the numerous structural and functional
    transformations within its individual units, would require a volume in itself and is
    beyond the scope of this study.

1936). The following are all-Union ministries at present:[99] Foreign Trade, Railways, Communications (Post, Telegraph, and Telephones), Maritime Transport, River Transport, Coal Industry of the Western Areas, Coal Industry of the Eastern Areas, Oil Industry of the Western and Southern Areas, Oil Industry of the Eastern Areas, Power Stations, Electrical Industry, Ferrous Metallurgy, Non-Ferrous Metallurgy, Chemical Industry, Aviation Industry, Shipbuilding Industry, Agricultural Machine-Building Industry, Armaments, Heavy Machine-Building Industry, Automobile Industry, Machine and Instrument Building, Agricultural Stocks, Construction of Heavy Industry Enterprises, Construction of Military and Naval Enterprises, Cellulose and Paper Industry, Machine-Tool Industry, Rubber Industry, Construction of Fuel Enterprises, Road and Construction Machine Building, Transport Machine Building, Geology, Medical Industry, Communications Industry, Material Reserves, Food Reserves, and Labor Reserves.

The Union-republic ministries are: Armed Forces, Foreign Affairs, Food Industry, Fish Industry — Eastern Areas, Fish Industry — Western Areas, Meat and Dairy Industry, Light Industry, Textile Industry, Timber Industry, Agriculture, Finance, Trade, Internal Affairs, State Security, Justice, Public Health, Building Materials Industry, State Control, Higher Education, Cinematography, Gustatory Industry, and State Farms. As the process of breaking up ministries into several new units and transforming committees, councils, and chief administrations into ministries continues, these lists of ministries can be expected to undergo further changes.

The Committees, Councils, and Chief Administrations. The Council of Ministers now has committees on: Arts, Radio, Physical Culture and Sports, Measures and Measuring Instruments, Geological Matters, Standards, Defense, and Architecture. It has councils on Collective Farm Affairs, Affairs of the Russian Orthodox Church, and Affairs of Religious Denominations. And it also has chief administrations of: Civil Aviation, Forest Guarding and Forest Planting, Geodetics and Cartography, the Hydro-Meteorological Service, the Northern Sea Route, Producers and Consumers Co-operatives, Military Construction, and the Sulphate-Alcoholic and Hydrolytic Industry.[100] Also there are other bodies attached to the Council of Ministers: State Arbitration Commission, the Migration Administration, the Main Committee on the All-Union Agricultural

---

99. Articles 77, 78, Constitution of 1936, as affected by changes up to March 1947; see Gorkin's report in *Izvestia*, 15 March 1946; *Izvestia*, 21, 22, and 27 March, 11 April 1946, and 26 February 1947; *Pravda*, 30 January 1946; *A.R.S.U.* August 1946, pp. 24–7.

100. See also *S.G.P.* pp. 350–57, *passim; S.A.P.* pp. 44, 46; *Izvestia*, 9 October 1946; *N. Y. T.* 12 November 1946.

Exhibition, the Academy of Sciences of the U.S.S.R., and the Telegraph Agency of the Soviet Union (TASS). The machinery of the committees and chief administrations follows mostly the all-Union ministry type of structure, there being only a few instances (the Committee on Physical Culture and Sports, for example), where such machinery is set up on the model of a Union-republic ministry of the U.S.S.R., i.e. with like-named administrations attached to the councils of ministers of the Union and autonomous republics.

Supervisory-Auxiliary Organs. In addition to all these bodies, the Council of Ministers has a number of organs of a supervisory-auxiliary or of a preparatory nature: the Economic Council, the State Planning Commission, the Administration of Affairs, and the Secretariat.

The Economic Council, successor to the Council of Labor and Defense (S.T.O.) since 23 November 1937,[101] has the status of a permanent commission of the Council of Ministers and is considered an authoritative 'organ of state administration.' It is presided over by the Chairman of the Council of Ministers and its members are deputy chairmen of the Council of Ministers, each of whom heads one of the six operative economic councils created 17 April 1940 for the purpose of better supervision over the economic commissariats and chief administrations in six specified fields. These six councils embrace Metallurgy and Chemicals, Machine Building, Defense, Industry, Fuel and Electricity, Consumption Goods, Agricultural Economy, and Reserves. The Economic Council functions primarily as an agency that reviews economic plans before they are submitted for confirmation, looks after the condition of individual branches

101. The Council of Labor and Defense (S.T.O.) was itself an outgrowth of the Council of Workers and Peasants Defense, formed on 30 November 1918 for the mobilization of the means and forces of defense and whose place S.T.O. took in April 1920. By a statute confirmed on 29 December 1920, S.T.O. was given the status of a commission of the Sovnarkom and charged with the co-ordination of departmental activities relating to defense and economic construction as well as with the setting up of a unified economic plan and direction of the economic commissariats. By decree of 21 August 1923, S.T.O. was established with similar functions in the then-forming system of Union organs. S.T.O. was composed of the commissars heading the defense and economic commissariats, the Gosplan, and Gosbank, and included Stalin in its membership. It was presided over by the chairman of the Sovnarkom. While its functions in regard to planning decreased in the 'thirties, its competence remained quite wide to the end. Decisions of S.T.O. could be appealed to the Sovnarkom, which had the right to suspend or annul them; but they became operative without prior approval by the latter and were, admittedly, 'legislative in nature' — binding on all central and local institutions. (See *S'ezdy Sovetov RSFSR*, pp. 108, 181; *S.G.P.* p. 351; *S.A.P.* pp. 41, 108; Batsell, op. cit. pp. 620–22; Webb, op. cit. pp. 101, 104–6. See also Voroshilov's speech in *XV S'ezd VKP(b)*, pp. 846–7.)

of the economy and adopts measures for their improvement, and passes on prices, labor, wages, the formation or liquidation of economic organs, and a number of other economic problems of an operative nature.[102] Unless annulled by the Council of Ministers the decisions and orders of the Economic Council are obligatory for all the ministries of the U.S.S.R., the councils of ministers of the Union republics, and the local soviets.[103]

The State Planning Commission or Gosplan is a preparatory organ engaged in continuous study of the conditions and perspectives of the national economy and in working out the yearly and quarterly economic plans for the Council of Ministers. Originally formed by decree of 21 February 1921 in the R.S.F.S.R. and later established by the statute of 21 August 1923 as a commission of S.T.O. in the system of the U.S.S.R., Gosplan became a permanent commission of the Sovnarkom by decision of the latter on 2 February 1938. With the growth of the Soviet economy and the definite establishment of the planning principle in it, Gosplan grew in importance and is considered one of the most important and distinct institutions of the Soviet system that differentiate the latter from other political systems. It is composed of leading economists and planning officials whose appointment is individually confirmed by the Council of Ministers, and it is now directly represented in the latter through its chairman. The Gosplan has a right to request materials and explanations from the central ministries and other departments in matters concerning fulfilment of the national economic plans, and its representatives in the localities have similar rights in regard to corresponding organs and economic enterprises. But generally, the projects of plans worked out by the planning organs of the Union republics and autonomous republics are confirmed by their own respective governments. Only in regard to the methodology of planning and in questions of verification of the execution of the economic plans does Gosplan of the U.S.S.R. possess the right to issue acts that are obligatory upon all central and local organs subordinate to the Council of Ministers.[104]

Preparatory Organs. To prepare the conduct of business at the sessions of the Council of Ministers, to take preliminary decisions in regard to matters of lesser importance, and to see to it that decisions of the Council of Ministers are started on the course of operation promptly and accurately, there are a Bureau of Administrative Affairs and a Secretariat at the

---

102. *S.A.P.* pp. 41–2; *Izvestia,* 18 April 1940.

103. They can be appealed by the federal ministers within a three-day period and by the governments of the Union republics in the course of a month.

104. See *S.G.P.* pp. 352–3, 357; *S.A.P.* pp. 43, 108, 117–18; Batsell, op. cit. pp. 618–20; Webb, op. cit. pp. 98, 105, 112.

Council of Ministers.[105] The Bureau of Administrative Affairs, or the Administration of Affairs of the Council of Ministers as it is usually referred to, is headed by the Administrator of Affairs of the Council of Ministers, who countersigns the decisions and ordinances of the Council. The Administrator is assisted by several deputies assigned to separate fields (economic questions, cadres, et cetera) and one of these deputies is the Manager of the Secretariat of the Council, who is in turn assisted by several deputy managers of the Secretariat.[106]

Attendance at the Council's Sessions. Not all the heads of the organs of the Council of Ministers treated in the preceding pages have a right to be present at the Council's sessions, or when present to take part in the vote. Only those who are considered its full-fledged members, i.e. the Chairman and deputy chairmen of the Council, the ministers, and the chairmen of Gosplan, and the committee on arts, have the right of deciding vote (article 70, Constitution of 1936). The heads of the other committees, councils, and chief administrations attached to the Council of Ministers enjoy merely a consulting voice. In addition, the Council can permit any person to attend its sessions. By earlier decrees, members of the C.E.C. U.S.S.R., the Chairman of the G.P.U., the Administrator of Affairs of the Sovnarkom and the chairmen of a number of Sovnarkom commissions, the chairmen of the central executive committees and sovnarkoms of the Union republics, representatives of these republics, and also (in cases where the matters discussed were submitted by them) commissars of the Union republics had the right to attend the sessions of the federal Sovnarkom with consulting voice.[107] There is no reason to doubt that the highest Party leaders were accorded the privilege of attending Sovnarkom sessions whenever they wished to do so, and some of them used it frequently.[108]

Sessions of the Council of Ministers are held when at least half of the voting members are present, probably several times a week, though

105. See decrees of 12 November 1923 and 17 February 1924 in Batsell, op. cit. pp. 598–9, 605; Webb, op. cit. p. 98. Earlier there existed the so-called Small Council of People's Commissars — a commission of the Sovnarkom — and a Preparatory Commission, which occupied themselves with expediting the business of the Sovnarkom. (See Lenin, XXVII, notes 58, 135; *S.G.P.* p. 351.)

106. See *S.P.R.* 1938, No. 32, item 199; 1941, No. 12, item 190. The Council of Ministers also confirms from time to time state counselors, who act apparently as technical advisers to it. (See ibid. 1941, No. 12, item 191; No. 13, item 222.)

107. See decrees of 7 August 1923 and 12 November 1923 in Batsell, op. cit. pp. 595–8, 598–9. For the rights of deputy ministers and members of the collegia of the ministries to attend the Council of Ministers sessions, see *infra,* note 122, this chapter.

108. See Webb, op. cit. p. 101.

the exact frequency is nowhere indicated. The general proceedings of the Council are secret and no minutes are published. A major part of its decisions, however, become known through formal publication in the 'Collection of Decisions and Ordinances' of the government.

The Relative Standing of the Members of the Council of Ministers. The Chairman or Premier. Since the Council of Ministers is designated as the 'government' of the Soviet Union, some consideration of the relative standing of its members seems necessary.

The most important position on the Council and one of the most crucial in the Soviet polity as a whole is that of the Chairman of the Council of Ministers — earlier the Sovnarkom — often referred to outside of the U.S.S.R. as 'the Soviet Premier.' The four incumbents of this office since the inception of the Soviet regime have all been top Party men. Lenin, the recognized leader of the party, held this position from 8 November 1917 until his death in January 1924, though owing to his illness he was inactive after the latter part of 1922. Rykov, who followed Lenin and held the post until December 1930, was a member of the Politbureau and a deputy chairman of the Sovnarkom when he assumed office. Molotov, who succeeded Rykov and held the office until 6 May 1941 — when Stalin was appointed to it — had been secretary of the Central Committee of the Party for ten years (1921–30) and a member of the Politbureau since January 1926, having previously been an alternate in the Politbureau (1921–6). Stalin has been the acknowledged highest leader of the Party at least since 1927. The Chairman of the Council of Ministers — who also holds the chairmanship of the Economic Council, and earlier held the chairmanship of the Council of Labor and Defense — presides at the Council's sessions, signs its decisions, ordinances, and other formal acts, exercises the right of suspension over orders of the ministers, and generally guides the work of the Council of Ministers. While the precise relationship between the Council and its Chairman has varied through time, the post has always been of the highest potency, and most particularly so during its occupancy by Lenin and Stalin, i.e. when the recognized highest Party leader held this office.[109]

The Deputy Chairmen of the Council. Next in importance are the deputy chairmen of the Council of Ministers. Originally, two deputy chairmen were appointed to the Sovnarkom in 1921, when it became evident that Lenin's illness might keep him away from his post for longer periods. On Lenin's suggestion, one of these was a member of the

109. See Vyshinsky, 'The Chief of the Soviet Government,' pp. 3–23; Tikhomirnov, *Viacheslav Mikhailovich Molotov, Kratkaia Biografia;* Batsell, op. cit. p. 601.

Politbureau and of the Presidium C.E.C., for liaison purposes, 'because these institutions must have contact, because without such a connection the basic wheels sometimes move out of tune.'[110] The other became the Chairman of Gosplan. In following years the number of deputy chairmen increased to three and at times to five, and, with the general increase in the number of commissariats and other Sovnarkom organs in the late 'thirties and early 'forties, it mounted further until it reached about a dozen deputy chairmen of the Sovnarkom by 1942. A number of these combined in their persons the chairmanship of vital organs in the Sovnarkom system — the Gosplan, the Commission of Soviet Control, the Gosbank, the Defense Committee — while others simultaneously held important commissar posts (State Control, Internal Affairs, Heavy Industry, Chemical Industry, et cetera).[111] This increase in the number of deputy chairmen in turn necessitated some differentiation in their status, and on 10 March 1941 the planning expert Nikolai Voznesensky — then an alternate member of the Politbureau — was appointed First Deputy Chairman of the Sovnarkom in regard to economic questions. Further gradation took place a year and a half later, when Molotov was appointed, on 16 August 1942, to the newly created position of 'First Deputy Chairman of the Sovnarkom of the U.S.S.R. on all questions of work of the Sovnarkom U.S.S.R.'[112] On 19 March 1946 the number of deputy chairmen of the Council of Ministers was reduced to eight, two of whom, Mikoyan and Kaganovich, hold down ministries, while the third, Voznesensky, is Chairman of Gosplan.

The People's Commissars — Now Ministers. The standing of the ministers is a product of considerable evolution. The present official conception of a minister is that he is a servant of the Soviet people, a pupil of Lenin, and an assistant of Stalin, and the 'personal director' of the branch of state administration that he heads.[113] In this position, according to the

---

110. Lenin, XXVII, pp. 257–8, 283–9, note 136.

111. See 2 *Sessia V.S.*, pp. 774–5; 3 *Sessia V.S.*, pp. 457–8; 7 *Sessia V.S.*, pp. 159–60; 8 *Sessia V.S.*, pp. 306–7; *V.V.S.* 11 June 1940, No. 15, p. 1; 28 March 1941, No. 13, p. 1; 1 April 1942, No. 10, p. 4. In January 1938, at the first session of the Supreme Soviet of the first convocation, Molotov requested that deputy chairmen of the Sovnarkom be relieved of positions of commissars in charge of specific commissariats. In practice, however, it was found impossible to follow this rule, and already at the second session, in August 1938, Kaganovich was appointed a deputy chairman of the Sovnarkom while heading at the same time the Commissariats of Railroad Transport and Heavy Industry. Similar instances followed. (Ibid.)

112. *V.V.S.* 28 March 1941, No. 13, p. 1; 25 August 1942, No. 34, p. 1. Italics J.T.

113. *S.G.P.* p. 358. Referring to Stalin's injunction that Supreme Soviet deputies must be copies of the model, Lenin, Molotov told the commissars on 19 January 1938 that this applies even more to them and to the Sovnarkom as a whole: 'We must remember that

new constitution (articles 72, 73), he issues, within the limits of the jurisdiction of his department, 'orders and instructions on the basis and in pursuance of the laws in operation, and also of the decisions and ordinances of the Council of Ministers of the U.S.S.R.,' and supervises their execution.[114] For his activity he bears a formal responsibility not only before the Supreme Soviet, but before the Council of Ministers as well.

While the ministers, even while they were called commissars, were generally considered the Soviet counterparts of ministers in Western parliamentary states, they differ sharply from the latter in many respects. The Soviet ministers, it was pointed out, are not provisional appointees from among the membership of parliament, whose tenure in office is limited to the duration of a particular political combination in that body, and who are often unacquainted with the techniques, procedures, and working details of the ministries they head — hence dependent upon and affected by the professional staff on which they have to rely.[115] By experience or long tenure they are experts themselves, fully acquainted with the affairs they administer. On the other hand, they have little opportunity to carry out their own policies with obstructionist and dilatory methods, for by unwritten law and open injunction they are required to be extremely alert to the contours and oscillations of the Party line. Formally elected in a body by the Supreme Soviet and individually appointed and replaced by the Presidium of the Supreme Soviet, yet actually selected and removed on decision of the Party center, the members of the Council of Ministers are in fact supersensitive to all angles and changes in high policy.[116] Here a distinction may be drawn between those ministers who

from the very beginning of its formation the Council of People's Commissars was headed by Lenin and must aim at being worthy pupils of the great Lenin, who laid the foundations for our entire cause. We wish to be assistants of our teacher, the leader of the peoples of the Soviet Union — the great Stalin. In all important questions, we, the Council of People's Commissars, will turn for advice and for directions to the Central Committee of the Bolshevik Party and, first of all, to comrade Stalin.' The commissars, he went on to say, must 'be worthy of our Socialist, people's parliament — the Supreme Soviet,' they must 'be worthy of the people.' (1 *Sessia V.S.*, pp. 157–60; *S.G.P.* p. 348.)

114. Orders are described as 'primarily operative acts,' and instructions as 'norms of a general nature.' These acts of the minister are norms that secure the conditions and define the order of executing the laws, but can 'neither develop law, nor interpret it.' They are published in collections of orders and instructions and in special bulletins issued by the individual ministries. (*S.G.P.* pp. 380–82; *S.A.P.* p. 18.)

115. See Malitski, op. cit. pp. 53–5 and *passim.*

116. When Kamenev was transferred from the post of Deputy Chairman of the Sovnarkom and Chairman of S.T.O. to that of Commissar of Foreign and Domestic Trade, the change was explained to the C.E.C. on 24 April 1926 as solely in the interest of maximum all-round efficiency. A complete record of the experience of groups and individual officials is kept and transfers are made in accordance with the urgency of

are members of the Party center — the Politbureau in particular — and those who are not. Ministers of the second category, though they enjoy a measure of discretion in their field of operation, are not policy-makers in the ultimate sense of the word, but high technical advisers and administrators — executants of the will of the Party summit. They render expert advice, draw up initial plans, and suggest policies that may be adopted, and they administer the execution of policies decided upon. To that extent they are participants in the process of policy-formulation. But the actual determination, the definitive word, on all fundamental courses of action lies with the Politbureau, which may busy itself with the details of a decision, or as is apparently often the case, adopt the substance of it, leaving its detailed consideration to the plenary session of the Sovnarkom.

The Position of the Ministers vis-à-vis the Collegia in their Departments. For a rounded-out view of the standing of the ministers, account must also be taken of their position in regard to the collegia in their ministries, which have undergone substantial changes. In the early months of the regime the commissariats were considered 'collegial' rather than 'single person' directed organs.[117] Attached to the commissar and presided over by him, there was within each commissariat a collegium, whose members were appointed by the Sovnarkom. Decision-taking and responsibilities were based on the 'collegiality' rule (*Kollegial'nost'*) rather than on the 'one-man management' principle (*edinonachalie*), i.e. they were the collective affair of the commissar and the collegium, not of the commissar alone. The principle of 'collegiality' in administration, Lenin stated later, was absolutely necessary at this first stage. The revolution had unleashed

---

particular jobs and the best utilization of available skills, stated Enukidze in the Presidium C.E.C. report, boasting that 'this side of the work of our state is, in its entirety, by far the most perfect one.' (3 *TsIK 2 Sessia,* pp. 1049–50.) Several years later, when Rykov was replaced by Molotov in the chairmanship of the Sovnarkom and other personnel changes were carried out in the Sovnarkom, Gosplan, and a number of commissariats, the replacements were frankly explained in the Presidium report to the C.E.C. (10 January 1931) in terms of 'the basic task of securing the decisive state posts for the best, most experienced Leninists . . .' (5 *TsIK 3 Sessia,* p. 24.)

117. According to the method of decision taking in them, the organs of state administration are either 'collegial' or 'single person' guided ones. Those of the first category, exemplified by the Sovnarkom, the Economic Council, or Gosplan, are headed by a collegium of officials and decisions are taken by majority vote, with the Chairman's vote deciding in case of a draw. The responsibility for decisions are borne by each collegium member personally and the collegium as a whole. In those of the second category, exemplified at present by the ministries, the chief administrations, and committees of the Council of Ministers, the collegia are considered consulting bodies to the head or minister, who takes personal responsibility for decisions and administers affairs on the basis of the 'single manager' principle. (See *S.A.P.* pp. 52–3.)

among the masses a widespread desire for political assertion, while the new rulers themselves were without administrative experience. Consequently, 'consideration, discussion, interpretation,' were the order of the day and, to give the people and their representatives a sense of power and first lessons in government, rallies and assemblies — or what Lenin termed 'meeting-ing' — were both unavoidable and desirable, said he, in this period of fashioning the new rule.[118] Moreover, the collegia of the commissariats, staffed with selected Party people, were considered useful checks on the commissars.[119]

After March 1918, however, Lenin began to demand the establishment of the 'single-manager principle' in administration, arguing the need for such in view of the transition to practical work. Lenin's basic view on the subject, sustained by him in subsequent years despite considerable opposition both within and outside the Party,[120] was that 'collegiality' was desirable in the process of discussion, but that the principle of 'one-man management' must operate in the commissariats in the adoption of decisions and in the process of execution.[121] The Constitution of 1918 — and

---

118. Lenin, xxv, p. 17; xxii, pp. 418, 463–4; see also Gribanov, 'Regarding the History of the Development of the Single-Manager and Collegiality Principles in the People's Commissariats,' pp. 61–9.

119. While occasionally complaints were heard at the Party congresses that the 'weak' composition of some of the collegia rendered the Party center's control over the commissariats involved 'quite weak' (see e.g., S. I. Polidarov's remarks at the Ninth Party Congress, March 1920, *Protokoly IX-go S'ezda RKP(b)*, pp. 78–79), the membership of the collegia was for the most part deemed satisfactory from the Party standpoint. As Molotov pointed out at the Fourteenth Party Congress, in December 1925, there were always 'almost exclusively Communists' in the collegia, and though a few non-Party individuals appeared in them that year, 'this was and can be — in the composition of the collegia of the people's commissariats — only by way of exception.' (*XIV S'ezd VKP(b)*, p. 72.)

120. Strong opposition to the introduction of the 'one-man management' or 'single-manager' (*edinonachalie*) principle in administration was exhibited by the 'Left Communists,' Socialist-Revolutionists, and Mensheviks in 1918 and by the 'Democratic Centralism' group, headed by Sapronov, Smirnov, and Osinsky and said to have been supported by Tomsky and Rykov, in 1920. (See Lenin, xxii, pp. 496–7, 501; xxv, p. 17; xxiii, pp. 447–8; *VKP(b) v Rezol.* i, p. 336; Gribanov, op. cit. pp. 64–5.)

121. A few citations from his statements illustrate his thought in the matter: There is nothing more erroneous, he said on 28 March 1918, than 'opinion that personal, dictatorial rule is incompatible with democracy or the Soviet type of state or collegiality of administration.' (xxii, p. 419.) 'Collegiality of consideration must be reduced to the necessary minimum and never allowed to hinder the speed and firmness of decision.' (xxiv, p. 534, November 1919.) 'Whether these be members of a collegium, assistant directors, or commissars — we need personal responsibility. Just as collegiality is necessary for the consideration of basic questions, so are both personal responsibility and personal direction necessary, so that there be no red tape, so that it should be impossible to evade responsibility.' (xxiv, p. 623, December 1919.) Technically, economically, and his-

following it the Constitution of 1924 — embodied a combination of the two principles. The commissar had the right to make decisions singly on all questions within the competence of his commissariat, and informed the collegium of these decisions. In case of disagreement with his decision, the collegium or any of its members, without suspending its execution, had the right to appeal the decision to the Sovnarkom.[122] The need for 'one-man management' in administration was emphasized from time to time.[123] But the difficulties encountered suggested the desirability of a prolonged period for its introduction, particularly in the commissariats that administered branches of the national economy. Therefore a series of transitional stages allowing for various combinations in the administration of industry were mapped out by the Party congress.

The transition to a policy of industrialization and collectivization led the Party Central Committee in 1929 to recommend measures for strengthening the 'single-manager principle' in the administration of industry, and at the Seventeenth Party Congress, on 26 January 1934, Stalin demanded the liquidation of the collegia altogether. The 'single-manager principle,' it was stated, was poorly rooted and frequently violated in practice. Under the cover of 'collegiality of direction' the diffusion or evasion of responsi-

---

torically, said Lenin, large-scale, machine industry requires 'the unconditional and strictest unity of will' directing tens of thousands of people. 'But how can the strictest unity of will be secured? By the subordination of the will of thousands to the will of one.' Given ideal consciousness and discipline on the part of the participants in the common work, this direction may remind one more of the soft guidance of a symphony leader. Or it 'may take the sharp forms of a dictatorship — if there is no ideal discipline and consciousness. But in either case *the absolute subordination* to a single will, for the success of the processes of work . . . is unquestionably necessary.' (XXII, p. 462.)

122. Articles 44, 45, Constitution of 1918; articles 56, 57, Constitution of 1924. The only differences in these articles were that by the Constitution of 1924 collegium members were appointed by the Sovnarkom and could appeal to it the commissar's decisions, while by the Constitution of 1918 they were confirmed by the Sovnarkom and could appeal to it or to the Presidium of the C.E.C. Besides the commissar, a collegium included the deputy commissars — the immediate assistants of the commissar — and several other officials of the given commissariat, the exact number of collegium members being determined by the Sovnarkom. Deputy commissars had a right to be present at Sovnarkom sessions with an advisory vote — a deciding vote when the commissars were absent. In the absence of both the commissar and his deputy one member of the collegium of a commissariat could participate in the Sovnarkom sessions with an advisory vote. (See Batsell, op. cit. pp. 598–9, 604.)

123. Lenin in particular appeared genuinely anxious that the commissars assume a greater role and urged them to learn to make decisions and take responsibility themselves rather than abide by scattered responsibilities in their commissariats and run with petty details first to the Sovnarkom and then to the Politbureau. He also urged them always to participate themselves rather than through their deputies in the Sovnarkom sessions. (See *supra,* note 14 p. 162 and Lenin, XXVII, p. 208.)

bility was widespread in the commissariats. A collegium would issue in its own name decisions that were obligatory on all institutions subordinate to the commissar. This lowered the personal responsibility of the commissar and created depersonalization in administration. Accordingly the collegia were abolished in March 1934.[124]

In place of the collegia councils were created in the commissariats. They were convokable twice a month and each consisted of from 40 to 70 persons of whom no less than half were representatives of local organizations and enterprises. These councils were to serve primarily as media for the establishment of closer ties and to insure an exchange of experience between the commissariats and the localities. The decisions of a commissariat's council were to be given effect in the form of orders of the commissar, if he agreed with them. No more than two deputy commissars were to exist in each commissariat. The commissar, in short, was installed as full boss in his commissariat — all authority was concentrated in his hands.

Four years later, in March 1936, the collegia were restored in all the commissariats. Their earlier liquidation, it was explained, did not result in the desired strengthening of the unity of administration of the various branches of work in the commissariats, or in improving the supervision of execution. A council of a commissariat could neither serve as an organ of systematic supervision over the carrying out of Party and government directives by the units and officials of the commissariat, nor meet often enough to discuss complex problems of direction. Only a collegium, composed of the leading officials in charge of the basic divisions of its work, could properly fulfil these functions in a given commissariat.[125] Hence, although the councils were left intact in the commissariats, the collegia were re-established. Also, in the years that followed, the number of deputy commissars was constantly increased in each commissariat.[126] In more recent months, however, there has been a tendency to reduce the number of deputy ministers, and they now average as a rule between 4 and 7, one of whom serves as Deputy Minister for General Affairs in the ministry.

---

124. *VKP(b) v Rezol.* II, pp. 348, 571, 592–5; *L. i S.* pp. 243–4; *S.G.P.* pp. 359–60; Gribanov, op. cit.
125. *S.G.P.* p. 359; Gribanov, op. cit. p. 67.
126. Thus, there were 10 deputy commissars in the Commissariat of Agriculture at the beginning of 1940, and by July 1941 the number of deputy commissars in the Defense Commissariat reached a total of 11. The increase of the number of deputy commissars, each of whom was assigned a definite branch of work, resulted in the institution of a first deputy for over-all assistance in many commissariats.

Under the present set-up, a collegium of a ministry — whose members are as before appointed by the Council of Ministers — consists of the minister, his deputies, and several important officials. The number of members in a collegium average now between 5 and 9. Its competence is described as: consideration of questions of practical management and of basic orders concerning the ministry, supervision of execution, the selection of cadres, hearing reports of the representatives of the ministry's local organs, and sending representatives into the localities to supervise the execution of the ministry's orders and instructions. But the collegium has no right to issue any acts whatever in its own name, and its decisions take force only on condition that the minister agrees with them and they are enacted in the form of his order. In case of disagreement between the minister and the collegium, the minister carries out his own decision. He is required, however, to report the differences to the Council of Ministers, and the members of the collegium have the right of appeal to the Council of Ministers and to the Central Committee of the Party.[127]

The restoration of the collegia is not viewed as a contradiction of the 'single-manager principle,'[128] because of the form that their decisions take and because the basic part of their work is considered to be not the performance of executive-administrative direction, but systematic supervision of the execution of governmental decisions and checking up on the cadres in their practical work. And the claim is made, in fact, that the re-establishment of the collegia has increased the unity of direction in the work of the ministries and has made it easier for the ministers, without violating the 'single-manager principle,' to meet the complex problems of administration.[129] It may be noted here that at the Eighteenth Party Congress

---

127. Gribanov, op. cit. p. 68; S.G.P. p. 360.
128. 'Thus . . . the new collegia do not contradict the "single-manager principle." But as distinguished from the former collegia, they are built so as to exclude depersonalization in administration and guarantee the people's commissar the conditions for the realization of unified direction and supervision of execution.' (S.G.P. p. 360.) Here, exception is taken to the views of several older writers on 'collegiality' and the 'single-manager principle': Professor Stuchka, who considered the collegia the most bureaucratic form of administration; P. Sirotinin, who viewed 'one-man management' as a capitalistic form of administration; E. F. Rozmirovich, who reduced the problem of 'one-man management' to a theory of administration on the model of a factory-conveyor system; and a writer in the Soviet Encyclopedia of State and Law, who held that 'collegiality' excluded administration on the 'single-manager principle.' (See Gribanov, op. cit. p. 61, note 2.)
129. Gribanov, op. cit. pp. 67–8. Other virtues now seen in the collegia are that they serve as schools of state administration, as it were; the participation of the collegia in the consideration of fundamental administrative questions and in the supervision of execution of governmental and Party decisions sharpens political alertness, generates self-criticism,

(1939), Zhdanov warned the Party cells in the commissariats not to attempt to create 'a commissariat within a commissariat,' not to seek to control the activity of the leaders of the commissariats, i.e. the ministers. Such control, said he, was the business of higher Soviet and Party organs, not of the cells, whose job it was only to note such irregularities as inattention to workers' complaints, poor personnel discipline, et cetera, and to apprise the Central Committee of the Party and the leaders of the commissariat about them.[130] Lastly, decisions taken in recent years in the fields of industrial direction and defense are pointed to as evidence that the 'single-manager principle' of administration is taking firm root.

The chairman of the Committee on Arts has the same standing as the ministers, while the Committee itself enjoys the rights of a ministry collegium.

(3) THE WARTIME CABINET — THE STATE DEFENSE COMMITTEE

The Composition and Functions of the State Defense Committee (1941–5). The State Defense Committee was created as a sort of War Cabinet by a joint decree of the Presidium of the Supreme Soviet, the Central Committee of the Party, and the Sovnarkom on 30 June 1941. Explaining the establishment of the Committee by the need for 'quick mobilization of the forces of the peoples of the U.S.S.R.' in the emergency created by the German invasion, the decree provided for concentration of 'the full plenitude of power in the state' in its hands, obliging 'all citizens and all Party, soviet, Komsomol, and military organs unfailingly to execute the decisions and orders of the State Defense Committee.'[131] At the time of its formation the Committee consisted of five members: Stalin, Foreign Affairs Commissar Viacheslav Molotov, Chairman of the Sovnarkom's Committee on Defense Kliment Voroshilov, Secretary of the Central Committee of the Party Georgii Malenkov, and Commissar of Internal Affairs Lavrentii Beria. Later, Commissar of Railways Kaganovich, Chairman of the Economic Council Nikolai Voznesensky, and Foreign Trade Commissar Anastase Mikoyan were added to the commit-

---

and lessens the chances of bureaucratization and petrification of the administrative apparatus, thereby helping to raise organizational leadership to the level of political leadership. 'Systematic supervision by the collegium of the work of the people's commissariat teaches people to execute the business entrusted to them quickly and precisely, cultivates in them qualities necessary for every Soviet patriot — persistence, firmness, decisiveness in bringing a matter begun to its conclusion. Reversely, the absence of control leads to complacency, political carelessness, bureaucracy, laxness, and irresponsibility.' (Ibid.)

130. *S.A.P.* pp. 74–6; *supra*, pp. 173–4.
131. *V.V.S.* 1941, No. 31, p. 1.

tee, and Marshal Voroshilov was replaced by General Nikolai Bulganin.[132] Exercising the highest directing power in wartime, with Stalin as its chairman and Molotov as vice-chairman, the State Defense Committee naturally occupied a position distinct and superior to the larger Sovnarkom.[133] By a decree of the Presidium of the Supreme Soviet, published 5 September 1945, which declared the need for the committee to have ended with the termination of the war, the State Defense Committee was abolished and its functions were transferred to the Sovnarkom.

The Role of the Chairman of the Committee and of the Council of Ministers. Stalin's leadership of the State Defense Committee from the time of its inception was followed by a series of steps designed officially to concentrate the supreme conduct of the war in his person. A deputy of the Supreme Soviet, a member of its Presidium since 1938, and Chairman of the Sovnarkom of the U.S.S.R. since 6 May 1941, Stalin was appointed to the post of Commissar of War on 19 July 1941. In the autumn of that year he became Supreme Commander-in-Chief of the Soviet armies, and on 6 March 1943 he was given the title of 'Marshal of the Soviet Union.'[134] Since his assumption of the chairmanship of the Sovnarkom, the official conduct of diplomacy at the highest level was also centered in his person and he participated in the wartime conferences of the Allies as one of the leaders of the Big Three. On 26 June 1945, the Presidium of the Supreme Soviet created the rank of Generalissimo of the Soviet Union as the highest military title in the land, and the following day this title was bestowed on Stalin for his leadership in the War. Simultaneously he was given four new awards: the Order of Victory, the title Hero of the Soviet Union, the Order of Lenin, and the Gold Star Medal.[135] On 25 February 1946, with the replacement of the Commissariats

---

132. Bulganin was formerly the Chairman of the Moscow Soviet and a week before his appointment to the State Defense Committee, on 15 November 1944, he was given the rank of Army General. On 21 November he was appointed Deputy Commissar of Defense (*N.Y.T.* 23 November 1944). Later he was made Deputy Minister for General Affairs in the Ministry of Armed Forces, serving directly under Stalin, and now he is Minister of the Armed Forces.

133. While the committee has published only a few orders — on general compulsory training of civilians for air raid and gas defense etc. (see *N.Y.H.T.* 3 July, *Izvestia,* 18 September and 21 October 1941), its co-ordinating activity unquestionably far exceeded them. In structure, personnel, and standing in the government system the State Defense Committee was a vastly more powerful body than the Revolutionary Military Council formed on 30 September 1918 for the defense of the Soviet state at the time. (For the prerogatives of the latter, see 5 *VTsIK,* pp. 23–4, 226–7.)

134. *V.V.S.* 1941, No. 20, p. 1, No. 33, p. 1; 1943, No. 11, p. 1.

135. *Izvestia,* 27, 28, and 29 June 1945. These were not the first awards conferred upon him. He already held from before three Orders of the Red Banner, the title Hero of Socialist

of Defense and Navy by a Commissariat of the Armed Forces, uniting all the land, air, and naval forces, Stalin was again named the People's Commissar for the Armed Forces and Supreme Commander-in-Chief of the Armed Forces of the U.S.S.R. While he has since relinquished the last-named post, he retains the chairmanship of the Council of Ministers. His progressive assumption of official posts has merely formalized his dominant role, as the highest leader of the Party, in the Soviet councils of state.

Labor and the Order of Lenin — awarded him on his sixtieth birthday — the Order of Suvorov First Class (November 1943), the Moscow Defense Medal (June 1944), and the Order of Victory (July 1944). (See *E.B.* 20 December 1945.)

Chapter XII · The Judicial System

1. THE SYSTEM OF COURTS

(1) MAIN FEATURES OF THE JUDICIAL SYSTEM

Election of the Courts. Justice in the U.S.S.R., according to the new constitution, is represented by the supreme courts of the U.S.S.R. and the Union republics, the territorial and regional courts, the courts of the autonomous republics and autonomous regions, the area courts, the special courts of the U.S.S.R. established by decision of the Supreme Soviet, and the People's Courts (article 102).[1] The Supreme Court and the special courts of the U.S.S.R., and the supreme courts of the Union and autonomous republics are elected by their respective supreme soviets for a term of five years, while the courts of the territories, regions, autonomous regions, and areas are elected for an equal term by the soviets of deputies of these units. People's Courts are elected by the citizens of the district for a term of three years (articles 105-9).

Participation by People's Assessors. Judicial proceedings are conducted in the language of the Union republic, autonomous republic, or autonomous region; and persons not knowing this language are guaranteed the right to acquaint themselves with the relevant materials through an interpreter and to use their own language in court (article 110). Unless otherwise provided for by law, cases must be heard in public and the accused guaranteed the right to be defended by counsel (article 103). In all of the courts, people's assessors participate along with the judges, except in cases specially provided for by law. By the Law on the Judiciary adopted in 1938, this means chiefly that two people's assessors sit with the chairman of the court, or a member appointed by him, in cases tried for the first time, while cases on appeal are reviewed by three members of

---

1. For details on the earlier development of the Soviet judiciary, see *S.G.P.* ch. VIII, *passim;* Batsell, op. cit. pp. 584–8; Webb, op. cit. 131–4, as well as the sources indicated in the footnotes below.

the court.[2] The regular member of the court acts as the presiding judge in the case, but the people's assessors enjoy equal rights with him, and all questions, including the verdict, are decided by majority vote. All citizens who possess electoral rights are entitled to be elected as judges or people's assessors (article 11, Law on Judiciary). Judges and people's assessors are removed by recall on the part of their electorate or on the basis of a court verdict in a criminal proceeding against them (article 17, Law on Judiciary). In practice, candidates for regular judgeships are usually people who have had professional training, who have served as judges, procurators, court clerks, investigators for ministries concerned with problems of security or supervision of execution of governmental directives, or who have at least been members of an *aktiv* interested in some phase of the judicial process.

The Form of Judicial Review. The decisions and verdicts of all the courts, except the Supreme Courts of the U.S.S.R. and the Union republics, can be appealed by the accused or their representatives, or by the procurator (article 15, Law on Judiciary).[3] There are no courts in the Soviet judicial system given over exclusively to appellate functions. The case goes up for review only to the next higher court, which is required to determine — on the basis of the record and materials presented by the contestants — whether the decision rendered by the lower court is supported by the facts in the case and accords with the law. If the decision of the lower court is found faulty on these counts, it may be changed or the case remanded for retrial. Where a People's Court has served as the court of original jurisdiction, the regional, territorial, or area court above is the court of appeal. Cases tried first in a regional, territorial, or area court are reviewed by the supreme court of the Union republic. In the autonomous republics the supreme court of the republic performs the cassational function with regard to cases decided by the People's Court, while in cases where the Supreme Court of the autonomous republic was itself the court of original jurisdiction the Supreme Court of the Union republic serves as the court of appeal. In cases where the Supreme Court of a Union republic acted as a court of original jurisdiction, the decisions and verdicts of the court are final and cannot be appealed. Thus, cases as a rule pass through only two judicial stages. Only in rare instances,

2. Articles 14, 34–6, 42–3, 49, 50, 55–6, 68, 70, 72–3, Law on the Judiciary. For the text of this law, see *Novyi Zakon O Sudoustroistve*, pp. 131–42.

3. The appeal must be made before the sentence or decision of the court has entered into force, otherwise it can be protested only by the procurator of the Union republic or the U.S.S.R. and the chairman of the supreme court of the Union republic or the U.S.S.R. (Article 16, Law on Judiciary.)

when it is established that in the normal course of consideration by two courts (trial and review) a patently wrong decision was rendered, the case may be reviewed on the basis of a protest made by either the Procurator of the Union republic, the Procurator General of the U.S.S.R., the chairman of the supreme court of the Union republic, or the Chairman of the Supreme Court of the U.S.S.R.[4]

(2) THE COURT STRUCTURE

The People's Courts. The People's Courts form the broad base of the system of courts. They are exclusively courts of original jurisdiction and the bulk of the criminal and civil cases pass through them. In the criminal field the jurisdiction of the People's Court embraces crimes against life, health, the liberty and dignity of citizens, property crimes, service crimes (abuse or non-use of authority by officials, embezzlement, et cetera), and crimes against the system of administration, such as violation of the electoral law, deliberate non-payment of taxes and duties, refusal to carry out the required deliveries of agricultural products to the state, evasion of military duty, and violation of the ordinances of organs of government. In the civil field, the court's jurisdiction embraces suits with regard to property, labor laws, alimony and inheritance (article 21, Law on Judiciary).

The number of People's Courts in each district is determined by the Council of Ministers of the Union or autonomous republic in which it is located at the instance of the respective Minister of Justice (article 26). The people's judges are elected for a term of three years, while the people's assessors are called upon to serve in the courts by turn, for not more than ten days a year (articles 12, 22).[5] Both the people's judges and people's assessors are elected by procedures similar to those that prevail at the elections to the soviets, on the basis of electoral areas that include the entire population of the territory on which the given People's Court operates (articles 22–5). The people's judges are required to report periodically to their electors on their work and the work of the People's Court (article 29).

The Courts of the Areas, Regions, and Autonomous Regions, and Republics. The regional or territorial and area courts, the courts of the autonomous regions, and the supreme courts of the autonomous republics have original jurisdiction in criminal cases relating to counter-revolu-

4. *S.G.P.* pp. 468–9.

5. According to the public-law text people's assessors for the area and higher courts are elected for a term of 5 years. (See *S.G.P.* p. 470.)

tionary crimes, cases of particular danger to the U.S.S.R., crimes against the state administration, the theft of socialist property, and cases of particularly important administrative and economic crimes. In the civil sphere their jurisdiction extends over cases of litigation between state and public institutions, enterprises, and organizations. They serve as courts of review for the People's Courts of their respective territories (articles 32, 40).[6] Each of these courts, as well as of the supreme courts of the Union republics, consists of a chairman, deputy chairman, members, and people's assessors — picked for service from panels of assessors specially elected by the respective soviets of toilers or supreme soviets. Each operates in the form of two collegia or benches — a collegium on criminal cases and a collegium on civil cases (articles 31, 33, 39, 41, 47, 48).

The Supreme Courts of the Union Republics. The highest judicial organ in a Union republic is its supreme court. It exercises supervision over the judicial activities of all the judicial organs of the Union republic, and of the autonomous republics, territories, regions and areas within the territory of the Union republic. This supervision is realized in the form of reviewing the protests of the Procurator General or Chairman of the Supreme Court of the U.S.S.R., or of the Procurator or Supreme Court Chairman of the Union republic, against verdicts, decisions, or other judicial dispositions that have gone into effect; and also by examining appeals and protests in regard to cases decided by the area and regional courts, the supreme courts of the autonomous republics, and — in Union republics that are not divided into regions — also of the People's Courts. The supreme court of the Union republic can set aside the verdict of any court within the republic. It has original jurisdiction in civil and criminal cases of exceptional importance, such as crimes in office by members of the highest governing bodies of the republic, as well as in cases brought before it by the Presidium of the Supreme Soviet — earlier by the Presidium of the Central Executive Committee — the Procurator, or the Ministry of Internal Affairs of the republic, or placed on its calendar by its own plenum.[7]

The Special Federal Courts. In addition to these courts, there are a number of special courts of the U.S.S.R. that operate in all parts of the Union. These are the military tribunals, railroad-transport courts, and water-transport courts, over which similarly named collegia of the Supreme Court of the U.S.S.R. act as courts of review (article 53, Law on

6. See also *S.G.P.* p. 470–71.
7. Articles 45, 51, Law on Judiciary; *S.G.P.* pp. 470–72; article 449, Code of Criminal Procedure, R.S.F.S.R.

Judiciary). Except where special laws provide for consideration by a collegium of three regular judges of the court, two people's assessors participate with the regular judge in all of these courts (articles 55, 56).

Military tribunals are formed: at military areas, fronts, and fleets; at armies, corps, other military formations, and militarized institutions, with the tribunals of the first category reviewing petitions and protests against decisions of the tribunals of the second category (articles 57–9). The jurisdiction of the military tribunals embraces military crimes, cases of counter-revolutionary activity, or particularly dangerous crimes against the system of government committed by military personnel or persons of a similar status. Furthermore, the jurisdiction of these tribunals extends to civilians as well as military personnel in all cases of treason, espionage, terror, arson, et cetera.[8]

Railroad and water-transport courts are formed along communication lines of the railroad and water-transport systems, and have jurisdiction over crimes aimed at undermining labor discipline or otherwise hindering the normal work of transport (articles 60, 61).

2. THE SUPREME COURT OF THE U.S.S.R.

(1) THE ORGANIZATION AND JURISDICTION OF THE SUPREME COURT

Supervisory and Original Jurisdiction. The Supreme Court of the U.S.S.R. is 'the highest judicial organ' of the land, elected for a term of five years (articles 104, 105, Constitution of 1936).[9] It supervises the judicial activity of the entire court system by examining the verdicts and findings of the lower courts on protest of its own Chairman or the Procurator General of the U.S.S.R., as well as by reviewing the decisions of the special courts of the U.S.S.R. (articles 63, 64, Law on Judiciary). The Supreme Court of the U.S.S.R. acts as a court of original jurisdiction in criminal and civil cases of great importance and of all-Union scope.

The Organization of the Supreme Court. The Supreme Court is composed of a Chairman, deputy chairman, and members — at present

---

8. See *S.G.P.* p. 471–2.

9. Supreme Court judges as well as judges of the special courts are removable before the expiration of their term only in case of a criminal prosecution instituted against them by decision of the Procurator General with the sanction of the Presidium of the Supreme Soviet of the U.S.S.R.; the judges of all the other courts by similar action of the Procurator of the Union republic with the sanction of the presidium of the supreme soviet of the latter (article 18, Law on Judiciary).

68 judges in all, as well as 25 people's assessors.[10] It operates in five divisions designated as the criminal, civil, military, railroad transport, and water transport collegia (article 65, Law on Judiciary). When a collegium sits as a court of original jurisdiction, it consists of two people's assessors and a member of the court; when it acts as a court of review it is composed of three members of the court (articles 68–73). The Chairman of the Supreme Court of the U.S.S.R. can act as the presiding justice in any case under consideration by a collegium of the Supreme Court, and he has a right to remove a case from the calendar of any court of the U.S.S.R. or the Union republics and protest its findings before the full plenum of the Supreme Court (article 74). Such a plenum, consisting of the entire membership of the court — with the presence of the Procurator General obligatory and that of the Minister of Justice optional — is called not less than once in two months, in order to consider verdicts, decisions, and rulings of the court's collegia, brought up for reconsideration by the Chairman of the court or the Procurator General, or to issue guiding instructions for general court practice on the basis of the Supreme Court's decisions (article 75).

(2) THE POSITION AND ROLE OF THE SUPREME COURT

The Basic Conception of the Supreme Court and of the Soviet Judiciary. Fundamentally speaking the Supreme Court has been considered always as an auxiliary and not a superior or independent branch of the government. It has long been an axiom of Soviet political theory that 'every court is an organ of power of the class that is dominant in the given state; it defends and guards its interests.'[11] The Soviet court, say the Soviet jurists, is no exception; in aims, interest, and composition it is a class court, dedicated at its inception to the twin purpose of suppressing the formerly dominant classes and inculcating Socialist principles and labor discipline

---

10. This is the composition of the Supreme Court elected by the Supreme Soviet of the second convocation on 19 March 1946 (see *Izvestia*, 20 and 21 March 1946). The court elected by the Supreme Soviet of the first convocation, 17 August 1938, counted 45 judges and 20 people's assessors. (See *Vlast' Sovetov*, 1938, No. 16, pp. 28–30.) For the evolution of the Supreme Court's composition before the adoption of the new Constitution, see *S'ezdy Sovetov SSSR*, pp. 88, 150, 219, 247.

11. *S.G.P.* p. 448; Krylenko, *Osnovy Sudoustroistva S.S.S.R. I Soiuznykh Respublik*, pp. 5, 7. 'The judiciary in every state plays a tremendous role as a fighting organ for the guarding of the class dominant in the given state. The judiciary is a mighty means for the strengthening of the social and political relations dominant in this or that country . . . which reflect the interests of the class dominant in the given society.' (Vyshinsky, in the discussion of the Law on the Judiciary at the second session of the Supreme Soviet of the first convocation, 15 August 1938, *Novyi Zakon O Sudoustroistve*, p. 49.)

among the workers themselves.[12] Said Commissar of Justice, N. M. Rychkov, in 1938:

The Soviet judiciary is an important and sharp weapon of the dictatorship of the working class in the cause of strengthening socialist construction and defending the conquests of the October Socialist Revolution. That is why it is the duty of all judicial officials, all local Party and Soviet organs, properly to organize the organs of the judiciary, to improve their work, to select and advance for the judicial organs new, honest, and devoted to the cause of socialism, Party, and non-Party Bolsheviks.[13]

The Status and Competence of the Supreme Court before 1938. The political nature of the Supreme Court, hence the subordination of its operation to over-all Party guidance of the system of government, was not denied.[14] But also in the official hierarchy of Soviet organs, its status was for a long time essentially dependent. As we have noted earlier, under the preceding constitution and statutes, the Supreme Court of the U.S.S.R. was attached to the Central Executive Committee (C.E.C.) — which in practice meant to the Presidium of the C.E.C. — and its functions were largely advisory. At the request of the Presidium C.E.C. of the U.S.S.R., the Supreme Court would render advisory opinions concerning the constitutionality of decisions of the central executive committees and sovnarkoms of the Union republics. On the motion of the Procurator (Attorney General), the Court would examine and appeal to the Presidium C.E.C. decisions and verdicts of the supreme courts of the Union republics that contravened federal legislation or were impinging on the interests of other

---

12. Vyshinsky, ibid. pp. 57, 60–61.
13. Rychkov, 'The Soviet Court — Fighting Organ of the Dictatorship of the Working Class,' p. 33. In Tsarist Russia, stated Rychkov, 70% of the members in the chambers of justice came from officers' families, and 12% from the merchant estate. By contrast, the judges of the People's Courts in Soviet Russia were by origin 43% workers, 34% clerks, and 23% peasants in the year 1937. Of these 84.8% were Party members, and 10% were members of the Communist Youth League — the Komsomol. Women judges, he said, constituted 18% in these courts. (Ibid. pp. 23, 25.)
14. 'The Supreme Court,' declared Kalinin at the tenth-anniversary celebration of the court, 'is under the eyes of the C.C. [Central Committee] of the Party and the C.E.C. [Central Executive Committee] of the U.S.S.R., and its decisions correspond fully to the Party line.' Speaking further about the people's judge, the district procurator, and the people's investigator as 'the most important links in the Party's struggle to overcome the survivals of capitalism in economics and in the conscience of people,' Kalinin stated: 'If a judge is a good Marxist, a dialectician, an experienced practical worker, a cultured, literate person, then it can be firmly said that 99 per cent of his verdicts and decisions would have positive political significance, would constitute one of the best forms of propaganda of Soviet laws, propaganda of the Party's directives. If the judge is a poor Marxist, who does not know the Party decisions, is unable to fight strongly enough for the Party decisions, and lets himself be led by local organizations, he is no good.' (10 *Let Verkhovnogo Suda Soiuza SSR,* 1924–34, p. 5. See also Malitski, op. cit. pp. 83–4.)

Union republics.[15] In the latter case, an increase in the jurisdiction of the Supreme Court took place in February 1935, when it was accorded the right itself, and on its own initiative, to annul decisions and verdicts of the supreme courts of the Union republics on the grounds stated above.[16] As regards the Sovnarkom of the U.S.S.R., the Supreme Court would, at the request of the Presidium C.E.C., submit to the latter advisory opinions concerning the constitutionality of Sovnarkom enactments; it could entertain cases involving members of the Sovnarkom only with the preliminary approval of the C.E.C. or its Presidium; and it could make representations to the Presidium C.E.C. suggesting the suspension or annulment of decisions and ordinances of the Sovnarkom or individual commissariats on grounds of unconstitutionality. But it had no right to annul such acts itself. On the other hand, the Sovnarkom on its part had the right to appeal decisions of the Supreme Court to the Presidium of the C.E.C.

The Present Position of the Court in the Soviet Structure. The new constitution has introduced several innovations. The Supreme Court stands out now as a separate body, charged as we have seen, with 'the supervision of the judicial activities of all the judicial organs of the U.S.S.R. and of the Union republics' (article 104). Its judges — like all judges in the Soviet Union — are declared to be 'independent and subject only to the law' (article 112). The last provision is strongly emphasized in recent Soviet theory, which fosters a higher conception of the judiciary.[17] There is no suggestion, however, of freedom from considerations of governmental policy. What the constitution has in mind, states the authoritative public-law text, is that it is the right and duty of the judges to

15. 'The decisions of the Supreme Court of the U.S.S.R. have no independent significance, since they are subject to confirmation by the Presidium C.E.C. U.S.S.R.' (Diablo, op. cit. p. 28, note 1 [1928].) 'This function of guarding the Constitution by way of verification of the constitutionality of laws, which in the United States is given to the Supreme Court, we — in connection with the idea of concentration of power — give to the Central Executive Committee and its Presidium; the Supreme Court of the Union only renders opinions.' (Turubiner, op. cit. pp. 137–8 [1924].)

16. Constitutional amendment passed by the Seventh Congress of Soviets of the U.S.S.R., *S'ezdy Sovetov SSSR*, p. 247.

17. By contrast, earlier Soviet jurists did not hesitate to call the judges 'dependent.' 'The third principle,' wrote former Commissar of Justice N. V. Krylenko in 1927, 'is the dependence and removability of our court. Whereas the basic principle of the bourgeois court is its independence, the irremovability of the judge . . . we say plainly that our judge is both removable and dependent; inasmuch as he is an organ of state power, an organ of the proletarian dictatorship, he is, therefore, both removable and dependent upon the proletariat, the state, the toiling class, whom he is called upon to serve.' (Krylenko, op. cit. p. 21.)

render decisions in accordance with their own inner convictions based on socialist conscience, the circumstances of the case under consideration, and the dictates of the law.[18] But, as one jurist put it, 'the independence of judges in examining concrete cases does not at all exclude the duty to follow the general policy of the government. The judiciary is an organ of state power and therefore cannot be outside of politics. The demand that the judiciary remain outside of politics is nowhere and under no circumstances realized.'[19] Consequently, as before, only men who have proved their devotion to the cause of socialism and are capable of keeping abreast of the unfolding policies and principles of the Party and the government are deemed worthy of election as judges.[20]

The Soviet Supreme Court has never possessed the power of judicial review of legislation. It never had the right to annul enactments of the federal Congress of Soviets, C.E.C., or its Presidium, and it possesses no such right in regard to the Supreme Soviet of the U.S.S.R. now. As far as its power with regard to the Council of Ministers is concerned, it will be noted that the Supreme Court is given no express right by the new Constitution to annul the Council's decisions. The Council of Ministers has played an important role from the very beginning in evolving a higher tribunal; it has introduced structural changes in the judiciary including the last-adopted Law on the Judiciary; and one of its members, the Minister of Justice, has not only been charged with supervision of the administrative side of the operation of the law courts, but participates regularly in the plenary sessions of the Supreme Court.[21] In the light of

---

18. *S.G.P.* p. 461.

19. Poliansky, 'The Stalin Constitution on the Judiciary and the Procurator's Office,' p. 83. 'It is self-evident that the independence of the judges does not release them from the duty to obey political directives, which of course also cannot go against the Soviet law that expresses the will of the people, the law-giver, directed by the dictatorship of the proletariat.' (Ibid. p. 82.)

20. See the speech of A. E. Badaev in introducing the list of Supreme Court judges at the second session of the Supreme Soviet of the first convocation, 17 August 1938, *II Sessia V.S.*, pp. 677–9; Rychkov, op. cit. p. 31. 'The election of courts would immeasurably strengthen our judicial organs, would make the Soviet judiciary an even mightier instrument in the hands of the working class. The daily aid and attention paid to the Soviet judiciary by our government and by the nearest colleague of the great Stalin — by Vyacheslav Mikhailovich Molotov personally — is a guarantee for that. The fact that we are led by the great Communist Party, its Central Committee, and our wise, great, dear, and beloved comrade Stalin is a guarantee for that.' (Concluding part of Commissar Rychkov's speech introducing the Law on the Judiciary at the same session, 15 August 1938, *Novyi Zakon O Sudoustroistve*, p. 23.)

21. Rychkov, op. cit. p. 26; *Novyi Zakon O Sudoustroistve*, pp. 8, 20; *S.G.P.* p. 472; *S.A.P.* p. 11; Golunsky, 'The Supreme Soviet U.S.S.R. and the Organs of Justice,' p. 90. The Ministry of Justice is charged with the tasks of training qualified judicial personnel,

the conception of the role of the judiciary in the state, it is highly improbable that the Supreme Court would essay to void Party-sanctioned decisions of the Council of Ministers.

3. THE OFFICE OF THE PROCURATOR GENERAL

(1) EMERGENCE OF THE OFFICE OF PROCURATOR

The Status of the Procurator before 1933. Between the judiciary and the Office of the Procurator (*Prokuror*) or Attorney General — renamed Procurator General on 19 March 1946 — organic functional ties are deemed to exist, and the latter no less than the former is depicted as an integral lever of the proletarian dictatorship directed by the Party.[22] The evolution of the Soviet Procuratorial Office represents a steady climb toward the goal of complete centralization. An Office of Procurator was first set up by the all-Russian C.E.C. in May 1922. The fundamental principles that were to govern its organization were suggested in a communication 'about "dual" subordination and legality' sent by Lenin to Stalin for the Politbureau. 'Legality,' Lenin wrote, 'cannot be one in Kaluga and another in Kazan, but it must be one, all-Russian, and even one for the entire federation of Soviet Republics,' and to attain such uniformity regardless of local differences and despite local influences the Procuratorial Office must be centralized and made entirely independent of local organs of power.[23] The idea was that the Procuratorial Office

creating the material conditions for the proper functioning of the judicial organs, and preparing the elections for the People's Courts.

22. *S.G.P.* pp. 446–7, 452; *Izvestia,* 20 March 1946. 'In instituting or investigating criminal cases, in acting as prosecutor in court, in examining complaints, in making protests against unlawful decisions of any organ of power, the Soviet procurator is a guardian of socialist legality, a carrier of the policy of the Communist Party and Soviet authority, a fighter for the cause of Socialism.' (*S.G.P.* p. 484.) 'The Central Committee of our Party and our government devote much attention to the Procuratorial Office, look after the replenishment of its cadres with worthy people, after strengthening its material base. The duty of every worker of the Procuratorial Office consists in justifying this high confidence, in answering this care with genuine Bolshevik work, with a genuinely Bolshevik struggle for the great cause of the party of Lenin-Stalin, for Communism!' (Editorial in the organ of the Attorney General's Office, *Sotsialisticheskaia Zakonnost'*, cited here as *Sots. Zak.* 1938, No. 7, p. 4.)

23. Lenin, XXVII, pp. 298, 301; *L. i S.* pp. 83–5. Lenin was moved to write this letter, suggesting that the matter was important enough to be transferred to the Politbureau for decision, by the fact that a majority of the members of a C.E.C. commission considering the question were in favor of 'dual' subordination of local procurators to both the central and local authorities and were against giving the procurators the right to protest decisions of the local authorities. These commission members defended their position as a legitimate struggle against bureaucratic centralism and 'the arrogant attitude of the center to

should not act as an administrative organ, making decisions itself, but that it should see that decisions of the local organs of power do not contravene the law, making such surveillance effective by protesting unlawful enactments successively up to the highest organs of state power, which would pass upon them definitively. Likewise, besides instituting criminal proceedings for law violations of a criminal nature and prosecuting such cases in court, the Procuratorial Office would protest court verdicts it considered groundless or violative of the law, carrying such protests all the way up to the highest instances.[24] Local and Union-republic procuratorial offices were formed, but apparently due to strong local pressures, the principle of complete subordination to one center was not fully realized at the time.

Soon ofter the Union was established an office of Procurator was indeed set up, but it was attached to the Supreme Court of the U.S.S.R. — it was not an independent, federal organ designed to unify and direct the activity of procurators throughout the U.S.S.R. The local procurators were subordinate to the Procurators of the Union republics (i.e. State Attorneys) who were members of the Commissariats of Justice of these republics.[25] As for the Procurator of the Supreme Court of the U.S.S.R., who, together with his deputy, was appointed by the Presidium C.E.C., his

the members of the provincial executive committees.' Deploring these views as destructive of efforts to disseminate legality and culture, Lenin claimed that the localities were amply protected, since the procurators do not decide cases themselves and the courts of first instance are the local courts. And pointing out that it would be impossible at that time to find hundreds of trusted communists with legal training who would be invulnerable to local influences, he presented the following argument: 'In the center, however, we should find about ten men who would exercise the central procuratorial power in the person of the Procurator General, the Supreme Tribunal, and the collegium of the People's Commissariat of Justice . . . These ten men, located in the center, would work under the closest supervision and in most direct contact with three Party institutions, which constitute a maximal guarantee against local and personal influences, namely: the Orgbureau of the C.C. [Central Committee], the Politbureau of the C.C., and the C.C.C. [Central Control Commission]; while this last institution, i.e. the C.C.C., responsible before the congress of the Party alone, would be built in such a manner that no holding of two or more offices by the members of the C.C.C., whether it be in any people's commissariat, any individual department, any organ of the Soviet government, would be possible in the slightest. Clearly, under such conditions we would have a greater guarantee than any heretofore devised that the Party would create a small central collegium, capable of withstanding in fact local influences, local and any other bureaucracy, and of establishing a really uniform application of legality in the entire republic and the entire federation. Possible errors of this central juridical collegium, therefore, would be corrected here on the spot immediately by those Party organs that establish in general all the basic concepts and all the basic rules for our entire Party and Soviet work in the republic.' (Lenin, XXVII, pp. 298–301.)

24. *S.G.P.* pp. 473–4.
25. Editorial in *Sots. Zak.* 1938, No. 7, pp. 1–2.

duties were: (1) to render opinions on questions that were subject to the decision of the Supreme Court, (2) to act as prosecutor at Supreme Court sessions, and (3) to supervise the legality of O.G.P.U. actions on the basis of a special decree of the C.E.C. U.S.S.R. Also, as we pointed out earlier, he could ask the Supreme Court to examine and protest before the C.E.C. decisions and verdicts of the supreme courts of the Union republics, he had a right to protest to the Presidium of the C.E.C. U.S.S.R. decisions of the plenary sessions of the Supreme Court U.S.S.R. with which he disagreed, and his office was one of the organs on whose initiative questions within the Supreme Court's competence could be referred to the latter for examination.[26]

Establishment of the Office of Procurator of the U.S.S.R. A big step toward centralization was taken in June 1933 when an Office of Procurator of the U.S.S.R., i.e. an Office of Attorney General independent of the Supreme Court U.S.S.R., was established, though for a time a measure of dual subordination by local organs of this Office to the Procurator of the U.S.S.R. and the commissars of justice of the Union republics was preserved.[27] The duties of the office, as indicated by the amended text of the federal constitution were: (a) to see that decisions and enactments of the administrative departments of the U.S.S.R. and the Union republics and of the local organs of power were in accord with the constitution of the U.S.S.R. as well as the decisions of the federal government; (b) to look after the correct and uniform application of the laws by the judicial institutions; (c) to institute criminal cases and prosecute them in all judicial instances on the territory of the U.S.S.R.; (d) to supervise the legality and propriety of the activities of the Commissariat of Internal Affairs and its organs; (e) general guidance of the activity of the procurators of the Union republics; (f) protestation of Supreme Court decisions before the Presidium C.E.C.[28] The centralization of the Procuratorial Office on an all-Union scale was completed by the law of 20 July 1936 and later by the constitution, which entirely separated the offices of procurators from the Commissariats of Justice of the Union republics and made them fully subordinate to the Procurator of the U.S.S.R.[29] As for the standing of the Procurator in the pre-1937 period in relation to the federal Sovnarkom, in whose sessions he had a right to participate

---

26. Articles 43b, 46, 47, and 63, Constitution of 1924. The other organs were the C.E.C. U.S.S.R., its Presidium, the O.G.P.U., and the procurators of the Union republics.
27. *Sots. Zak.* 1938, No. 7, p. 2; *S.G.P.* p. 474; 6 *TsIK 4 Sessia*, Bull. 28, pp. 35–7.
28. Article 46, Constitution of 1924 as amended by the Seventh Congress of Soviets of the U.S.S.R., 5 February 1935; *S.Z.* 1935, No. 8, item 68.
29. *S.Z.* 1936, No. 40, item 338; *S.G.P.* p. 474; *Sots. Zak.* 1938, No. 7, p. 2.

with consulting voice only, it may be noted that before the new constitution was enacted the Procurator was constitutionally responsible not only
to the C.E.C. of the U.S.S.R. and its Presidium, but also to the Sovnarkom
of the U.S.S.R.[30]

(2) THE PRESENT POSITION AND ROLE OF THE PROCURATOR GENERAL

The Powers of the Procurator General under the New Constitution.
Since the adoption of the new Constitution, the Procurator's — now Procurator General's — Office has been acclaimed by Soviet jurists as one of
the highest in the state, with wider powers than those enjoyed by procurators in other countries.[31] Article 113 of the Constitution of 1936
vests in the Procurator General of the U.S.S.R. 'the highest supervision
over accurate execution of the laws by all ministries and institutions subordinate to them, as well as by individual officials and citizens of the
U.S.S.R.' This, it is pointed out, gives the Procurator General a broader
supervisory competence than that of the Supreme Court of the U.S.S.R.,
whose supervision extends only over the activity of the judicial organs.[32]
The Procurator General's presence at the plenary sessions of the Supreme
Court is required, and like the Chairman of the Supreme Court he has
a right to remove cases from any court of the U.S.S.R. or the constituent
republics to the plenum of the Supreme Court (articles 74–7, Law on
Judiciary).

The office of the Procurator General of the U.S.S.R. is highly centralized
and it operates on the principle of one-man management. It is the
Procurator General who appoints, for five-year terms, the procurators
(state attorneys) of the constituent republics, territories, regions, autonomous republics, and autonomous regions; and procurators of the districts,
areas, and cities are appointed for similar terms by the procurators of the
Union republics subject to his approval (articles 115, 116, Constitution of
1936). The theory is that the Procurator General alone bears the procuratorial power, all the other procurators possessing such power only in
so far as it is delegated to them by him.[33] The constitution, moreover,
specifically provides that 'the organs of the Procurator General carry

---

30. Article 46, Constitution of the U.S.S.R.; *S.Z.* 1935, No. 8, item 68; *S'ezdy Sovetov SSSR,*
    p. 248.
31. See *Sots. Zak.* 1938, No. 7, p. 3.
32. Poliansky, op. cit. pp. 83–4.
33. Golunsky, 'The Supreme Soviet of the U.S.S.R. and the Organs of Justice,' p. 92;
    S.G.P. pp. 474–5. Hence the constitution of each Union republic provides that the highest
    supervision over the execution of the laws on its territory is exercised by the Procurator
    General of the U.S.S.R. directly as well as through the procuratorial office of the par-
    ticular republic. (See *S.G.P.* p. 474.)

out their functions independently of any local organs whatsoever, being subordinate only to the Procurator General of the U.S.S.R.' (article 117). This provision is given strong public emphasis.[34]

The Position of the Procurator General in the Soviet Structure. The Procurator General's singular present status is also accentuated by the position currently ascribed to him in regard to the executive power. By the terms of the constitution the Procurator General is not a member of the Council of Ministers. While in other countries, it is stated, the Procuratorial Office is a departmental organ headed by a member of the government — the Minister of Justice — it is not so in the U.S.S.R. where the Procuratorial Office is established as an extradepartmental organ directly subordinate to the Supreme Soviet. Consequently, 'no departmental hierarchical considerations can influence the Soviet Procuratorial Office in the execution of the tasks placed upon it.'[35] The Procurator General is not appointed by the Council of Ministers and he enjoys a higher term of appointment — seven years — as compared with the usual four-year term of the ministers (article 114, Constitution of 1936).[36] He is not an agent of the executive power, but occupies a position side by side with it, with the special assignment of 'guardian of legality.'[37] In short, the Procurator General exercises supervision over the carrying out of the laws by the organs of the executive power, but is himself 'independent' of this power.[38]

---

34. At the same time, the strict centralization of the Office of Procurator, it is claimed, does not diminish its democratic nature, manifested in the ties that it maintains with the people. In substantiation of this claim it is pointed out that the Komsomol, the trade unions, the factory and village correspondents, generally assist the Procurator General's office in the pursuit of its functions, while more specific, active assistance is rendered to it by its own social 'aktiv,' i.e. voluntary 'groups of assistance to the Procurator's Office' and 'sections of revolutionary legality' whose members act as public prosecutors, etc., and constitute a citizen reservoir from which the cadres of procurators are replenished. (*S.G.P.* pp. 475–6.)

35. Golunsky, op. cit. p. 91.

36. 'Such a long term, exceeding all other terms set by the Constitution for the occupancy of any of the offices, is explained by the fact that for an organ that supervises legality, stability of leadership is of particular importance . . . The requirement of stability of the laws concerns not only the issuance of laws, but also their application. And supervision over the application of the laws constitutes the fundamental duty of the Procuratorial Office.' (*S.G.P.* p. 475.)

37. 'At one time, the English philosopher and political scientist Locke, denying that the judicial power was an independent power, viewed the judicial function as auxiliary with regard to the legislative function. This view, erroneous with regard to the judicial function, would not be without foundation were it to be applied to that function of supreme supervision over the execution of laws that is entrusted to the Procurator General of the Union.' (Poliansky, op. cit. pp. 83–4.)

38. Ibid; *S.G.P.* p. 477. It may be pointed out here that, despite this allegation of 'independence' from the government, it is often stated that the Procurator General performs tasks

Thus, though the primary conception of the soviets has been that of 'conductors of the general line of the Party,' their development over more than a quarter of a century has resulted in their becoming a closer partner of the Party in the governance of the state, with the unique consequence of a practical merger of the two pyramids at the highest level. The unwritten understanding concerning the maintenance of structural barometers in the system of rule, and the rejection of the principle of separation of powers in favor of the principle of Democratic Centralism have led in practice to the concentration of most of the formal executive, as well as legislative, powers in the Council of Ministers, while legislative functions are to a lesser degree lodged in the Presidium of the Supreme Soviet. The more popular and rarer assemblies — the Supreme Soviet, earlier the Congress of Soviets, and the Central Executive Committee — serve primarily as sentiment gauging and mobilizing organs behind the policies decided upon by the highest Party instances and implemented by the ministers with the aid of lower Party and Soviet bodies. At the same time, the evolution of fundamental theory from the conception of exclusive pre-eminence in the working class to the view of the essential oneness of the entire Soviet people has brought about a renewed emphasis on popular sovereignty, with a concomitant assertion of sole legislative power in the Supreme Soviet and of complete responsibility of the executive — the Council of Ministers — before it. Basically, however, centralized direction from the top — in the Soviet instance the Council of Ministers — always working in closest relation with the Party summit and frequently associated with it in official enactments, has never ceased to be a prime desideratum and fact. And the search after insurance of accord between action in the numerous localities over the vast domain of the land and the will of the ruling summits of both pyramids, expressed in Party directives and Soviet norms, is chiefly responsible for the peculiar position occupied by the judiciary and the Procurator General in the Soviet hierarchy. While in wartime the supreme expression of the functional principle of concentrated control has been the State Defense Committee, the personnel of the latter, headed by Stalin as Chairman, constitutes in fact the controlling kernel of the highest authority operating regularly in the Soviet state and bears testimony alike to the degree of fusion attained between the Party and Soviet pyramids and to Stalin's singular role in them.

---

placed upon it by the Party and 'the government,' the latter — by the terms of the Constitution — being the Council of Ministers of the U.S.S.R. (See *Sots. Zak.* 1938, No. 7, pp. 3–4.)

Part III
The Dynamics of Political Power

Chapter XIII · The Socio-Political Balance

1. SOCIAL FORCES

(1) THE SOCIAL GROUPS

As we have seen, Soviet political theory began with the thesis of an intense and continuing conflict of classes in Russia. It proceeded with formulations concerning the elimination of the upper classes and processes of differentiation within the peasantry and the intelligentsia, and it has evolved to the concept of class peace between the two remaining classes — the workers and peasants — as well as between them and the intelligentsia, with all class differences being rapidly obliterated and the entire populace developing into one, closely knit, harmonious society.

In practice, the differentials in remuneration and the introduction of marked distinctions in ranks and emoluments before the war have created a strong impression of a new, incipient process of social stratification. It is too early, however, to conclude with any degree of certainty that a new dominant class is emerging, both because of the principles of social cohesion arrived at and emphasized by the Soviet leaders on and since the eve of World War II, and because of the relatively high degree of fluidity that still characterizes all social groups in the Soviet Union.[1] The social

---

1. The question of the rise of new dominant classes in the Soviet Union has been the subject of considerable debate recently. Solomon M. Schwarz essayed the thesis that there was an increasing trend before the war to block workers and their children from advancement to administrative positions and from access to higher education, while the industrial managers had become the nucleus of a new ruling class tending to make its privileged standing hereditary. (See Bienstock, Schwarz, and Yugow, *Management in Russian Industry and Agriculture*, pp. 28–30, 111–12, 121–4, cited hereafter as *Management;* also Schwarz's articles in *Social Research*, September 1942 and *Sotsialisticheskii Vestnik*, 5 January 1943.) Schwarz's deductions were not shared by his co-authors Bienstock and Yugow, the last-named advancing challenging data and arguments concerning the existence of factors counteracting any tendency toward the formation of a dominant class. (See his articles in *Novyi Put'*, December 1942, February 1943.) Professor Jacob Marschak, in an extensive introduction to the *Management* book, likewise did not find Schwarz's hypothesis sufficiently supported by facts. David J. Dallin

groups are at present politically balanced to an extent that would prevent exclusive assertion or usurpation of power by any one of them. There has been a shift in the social ladder. The intelligentsia — numerically the weakest class — now enjoys the highest social prestige and is playing a greater political role than before; the working class — numerically larger — is next in line politically and socially, and is followed by the peasantry — numerically the largest social stratum. But a deliberate effort is made to offer psychological and material satisfactions to all social groups and to hold them all to a strict sense of unity and discipline.

The Workers. Originally the avowed sole ruling class, and still giving name to the dictatorship, the working class has for a long time had a higher share in government than the other social strata and has benefited in social prestige from the official theories of proletarian dictatorship.[2] With the admission in the 'thirties of the peasantry and intelligentsia to a footing of equality with it, political participation by the working class has quantitatively diminished somewhat; and its prestige as a social group has likewise been deflated to some extent by the newer theories and practices, as well as by the heavy current emphasis on the importance of study and scientific attainment — hence on the role of the intelligentsia — for the present and the future of the Soviet state. At present this decrease is only relative, and the position of the working class — social as well as political — is still strong in Soviet society.

The working class has greatly increased in numbers. Official figures give the number of 'workers and employees' as follows: 1913 — 11.4 million; 1936 — 25.8 million; 1937 — 27 million; 1940 — 30.4 million; while in 1941 there were to be 31.6 million workers and employees according to the estimates of the third Five-Year Plan. In percentages the growth of this category in the population is represented as: 1913 — 16.7 per cent; 1928 — 17.3 per cent; 1937 — 34.7 per cent; while the 1939 census gives the per-

---

holds that there were four principal classes in the Soviet Union at the beginning of the war: the state employees, the workers, the peasants, and forced labor; and that the process of formation of new classes through social differentiation has not ended. (Dallin, *The Real Soviet Russia,* pp. 96, 134, 139, 145, and *passim.*) According to Professor Timasheff, the Soviet social structure consists of four classes: the 'upper class,' comprising the ruling élite; the 'non-Party Bolsheviks,' high-income executants, not policy-makers; the 'toilers,' consisting of workers, employees, peasants, and artisans; and the 'disfranchised,' who are destined to disappear. The two upper groups, not sharply demarcated, display a tendency to become hereditary, and though further social changes are probable, vertical social mobility has so sharply declined, Professor Tima-sheff concludes, that future historians will probably assess 1940 as the year ending the Russian Revolution. (*The American Journal of Sociology,* July 1944, pp. 9–21. See also the *American Sociological Review,* June 1944, pp. 236–41, 267–78.)

2. See *supra,* ch. III, *passim.*

centage of workers and employees together with their families as 49.73 per cent or a total of over 84,310,000 people.[3] 'Employees,' however, means white-collar workers or the intelligentsia.[4] Workers alone constituted with their families 32.19 per cent of the population in 1939 or 54,560,000, i.e. almost double the number of 'employees,' which was 29,758,000 or 17.54 per cent of the population.[5]

The pace of industrial expansion, however, has called continuously for additional workers. In 1940 special trade and factory schools were set up to train labor reserves. From these schools, numbering 1,550 before the war and 2,700 now, about two million young men and women were graduated by 1944, with 350,000 more trainees enrolled in the autumn of that year. The Ministry of Labor Reserves has recently stated that it plans to increase the number of schools to 6000 and expects no less than 1,500,000 skilled young workers to graduate from them in 1950.[6] Thus, the working class is largely a new class and its numbers will undoubtedly grow in the coming years.

Indices concerning the representation of the workers' stratum in the local soviets, at the Congress of Soviets, the Central Executive Committee, the Supreme Soviet, as well as in the Party and at the Party congress, suggest a rising scale throughout the 'twenties, with a diminished degree of participation setting in at the beginning of the 'thirties:[7]

PERCENTAGE OF WORKERS AMONG THE MEMBERS OR DEPUTIES

CONGRESS
OF SOVIETS

U.S.S.R.	1922	1924	1925	1927	1929	1931	1935	1936
	44.4	49.0	40.3	49.2	56.4	54.4	46.5	42.0

C.E.C.

U.S.S.R.			1922	1927	1931	1935		
			47.7	43.1	47.6	39.0		

SUPREME SOVIET

U.S.S.R.					1937	1946		
					42.0	39.0		

3. 20 *Let Sovetskoi Vlasti*, pp. 7, 11; *Bol'shevik*, Nos. 15–16 (1939), p. 113; No. 10 (1940), p. 17; also *A.Q.S.U.* November 1940, pp. 92, 100; Voznesensky's report at the Eighteenth Party Conference, *Pravda*, 19 February 1941.

4. Thus, when workers and employees were listed separately in statistics on the social composition of a Congress of Soviets, the term actually used was 'employees (intellectuals).' (*S'ezdy Sovetov RSFSR*, p. 203.)

5. Professor Timasheff believes that of the 49.73% of 'workers and employees,' the working class alone must approximate 44%. (Timasheff, op. cit. p. 20.) That would be about 75 million people. Yugow gives the percentage of workers in the population as of the 1939 census as 29.9%. (*Novyi Put'*, 14 February 1943, p. 376), while Dallin's estimate is 20 to 22% or 18 to 20 million of the 'active population.' (Dallin, op. cit. pp. 96–8.)

6. *E.B.* 6 October and 18 November 1944; *ARSU*, August 1946, p. 78.

7. The figures for this and other parts of the Social Forces section were drawn from or calculated on the basis of data given in the following sources: *S'ezdy Sovetov RSFSR*,

It will be seen that the lowest percentage above is still higher than the percentage of workers in the population. Figures for the local soviets are very scanty. Those that are available show — as could be expected — a relatively low percentage of workers in the rural soviets, though it is apparently higher than the percentage of workers in the rural electorate.[8] In the regional soviets, last elected in 1939, workers constitute 26.8 per cent of the deputies. The workers' element was always strong in the city soviets, though as the following figures show the percentage dropped in the 1939 elections as compared with previous years: 1925 — 38.8 per cent; 1927 — 47.9 per cent; 1929 — 54.0 per cent; 1931 — 56.5 per cent; 1939 — 38.9 per cent. It should also be pointed out that about 85 per cent of all the workers belong to trade unions, which now total more than 27 million. These trade unions serve to a large extent as centers for the social and political activity of Soviet labor.[9]

In the Party, though the injunction of the Thirteenth Party Congress (1924) that 'the vast majority of Party members should in the near future consist of workers directly employed in production,' i.e. 'workers-at-the-bench,' was never realized, several mass membership drives (1924,

---

pp. 16, 40, 67–8, 82–3, 115, 131–2, 165, 202–3, 254; *S'ezdy Sovetov SSSR*, pp. 16, 35–6, 75–7, 122, 163–4, 196–7, 235–6, 265; *I S'ezd Sovetov SSSR*, p.19 and appendix I, pp. 9–12; *II S'ezd Sovetov SSSR*, pp. 191–2; *III S'ezd Sovetov SSSR*, p. 531; *IV S'ezd Sovetov SSSR*, pp. 587–90; *V S'ezd Sovetov SSSR*, Bull. 20, pp. 1–2; *VI S'ezd Sovetov SSSR*, Bull. 21, pp. 1–3; *VII S'ezd Sovetov SSSR*, Bull. 11, pp. 52–5; *Sots. Zak.* No. 2 (February 1938), pp. 12–16; *XI S'ezd RKP(b)*, pp. 40–53, 386–8; *XIII S'ezd RKP(b)*, pp. 122–4, 533, 558–60; *XV S'ezd VKP(b)*, pp. 404–5, 1104–8; *XVI S'ezd VKP(b)*, pp. 83, 598–600; *XVII S'ezd VKP(b)*, pp. 303–4, 556–7; Malenkov's reports in *Pravda*, 15 March 1939, pp. 5–6, 16 February 1941, p. 2; *A.Q.S.U.* November 1940, pp. 92, 97, 100; Kareva, 'The Composition of the Congresses of Soviets, Executive Committees, and Soviets,' pp. 29–37; Vasil'ev, 'About the Composition of Deputies [the Membership] of the Local Soviets of Toilers,' p. 4.

8. Thus, while the percentage of workers in the electorate of the village was 4.2 in 1931, the percentage of workers in the village soviets was 5 in 1927, 7.4 in 1931; among the chairmen of the village soviets this percentage was 3.1 in 1927, 8.3 in 1929, 15 in 1931, while in the county executive committees it stood as 10.2 in 1927 and rose to 30.5 in 1931. (See Kareva, op. cit. p. 32.)

9. Although strikes are illegal in the U.S.S.R., and the fundamental conception of the trade union is that of an auxiliary arm, actively engaging in raising labor productivity and the general standard of living, rather than in a test of strength with management and government, the trade unions are the main organizations for the protection of the workers' rights and interests. They are required by law to attend to social insurance, the adjustment of wages and work norms, examination of the labor provisions in the economic plans, safety measures in the factory, and various welfare functions concerned with factory restaurants, housing, educational and recreational activities for the workers, etc. (See Rabinowitch, 'Soviet Trade Union Functions and Activities,' pp. 3–16.)

1927, and 1930) did secure a steady rise in workers' membership and participation in the Party until the early 'thirties, when it began to fall off.

PERCENTAGE OF WORKERS AMONG MEMBERS AND DELEGATES

	1921	1922	1923	1924	1925	1927	1930	1934
IN THE PARTY								
% of Workers	41.0	42.0	44.9	46.0	58.1	56.3	68.2	
% of 'Workers-at-the-bench'			17.0	35.3	40.8	37.5	48.6	
AT THE PARTY CONGRESS (among voting delegates)								
% of Workers		47.7	53.0	63.2	62.0	71.0	71.2	60.0
% of 'Workers-at-the-bench'				11.4		18.4	17.7	9.3

No figures on the social composition of the Party after 1930 and of the last Party congress (1939) are available, but in all probability the percentage of workers decreased further.

There is no definitive evidence, however, of a deliberate policy of discrimination against workers' participation in politics or advancement to higher positions.[10] The explanation, it is suggested, lies not only in the new position of equality accorded the peasantry and the intelligentsia, but in the transition of many workers — including Party members — to

10. Contrary interpretations base their deductions chiefly on three items: a Central Committee decision of 20 October 1930 forbidding 'the promotion of workers-at-the-bench into the administrative apparatus' for two years; the decree of 2 October 1940 introducing tuition fees in higher educational institutions and the last three grades of secondary schools; and a decrease in the percentage of manual workers and their children in higher educational institutions and technicums (vocational high schools) after 1933, as evidenced by the following tables:

	1928	1931	1933	1935	1938
ALL SCHOOLS					
Higher Institutions	25.4	46.6	50.3	45.0	33.9
Technicums	25.8	42.6	41.5	31.7	27.1
INDUSTRY AND TRANSPORTATION SCHOOLS					
Higher Institutions	38.3	61.9	64.6	59.8	43.5 (Industry) / 48.8 (Transport)
Technicums	38.5	60.1	62.2	51.7	40.0 (Industry) / 42.8 (Transport)

(See Schwarz, works cited in note 1, p. 313, and Timasheff, op. cit. pp. 18–19.) The 1930 decision, however, taken to preserve a nucleus of skilled workers at a critical period, was of limited duration. The tuition decree is to a large degree counterbalanced by a wide distribution of scholarships to deserving students, over 90% of the students of higher institutions having received scholarships in 1939. The drop in the percentage of workers among students of the higher educational institutions in the mid 'thirties was not unnatural in view of the abolition of special workers' privileges and the opening of access to higher education to children of the intelligentsia at that time. As the tables show, moreover, the percentage of workers in higher educational institutions in 1938 was still higher than the percentage of workers in the population.

the ranks of the intelligentsia.[11] In 1930, Kaganovich gave the percentage of the workers' stratum in the administration of industry as 56.0 per cent of the chairmen of trusts; 61.4 per cent in the general administration of plants; 71.0 per cent of the factory directors; and 69.4 per cent of their deputies and assistants.[12] In the 'thirties many 'stakhanovites,' that is, top-efficiency workers, moved up to administrative positions, and by the middle of that decade, it is pointed out, the intelligentsia itself was to a large extent labor-descended. In 1929, 38.7 per cent of the engineers and technicians in the industry of the U.S.S.R. were workers and children of workers, 10.8 per cent were peasants and children of peasants. In 1936, 80 to 90 per cent of the Soviet intelligentsia was, according to official figures, derived from 'the working class, the peasantry, and other toiling strata.'[13] Opportunities are still open to workers and children of workers to become members of the intelligentsia, to study, perfect their skills, and win recognition, which in the Soviet case means government recognition, accompanied by material benefits and social prestige — medals, titles, and orders — as well as by membership in some public body. Lastly, it should be pointed out, that as far as official attitudes are concerned, the workers as a class are highly praised for their patriotic performance during and after the recent war.[14]

Thus, though the conception of the workers' status and their relation to other strata has changed, the working class still occupies a recognized place in Soviet society, and does not loom as a focus of political opposition to the regime.

The Peasantry. Socially and economically the peasantry has undergone a more radical transformation than all the other classes. Politically, as we pointed out earlier, the designation 'Workers and Peasants' Government' was for nearly two decades interpreted as signifying not an equal sharing of state power by the two classes but a policy of forging an alliance between them under the guidance and leadership of the workers as the 'ruling class' in the dictatorship. In accord with this conception, the weight of the peasantry's participation in political life was relatively limited, especially in the councils of the Party. The removal of the suffrage and other inequalities between the workers and the peasants in the mid-

---

11. *XV S'ezd VKP(b)*, p. 101; *XVI S'ezd VKP(b)*, pp. 79–80; *XVII S'ezd VKP(b)*, p. 528.
12. *XVI S'ezd VKP(b)*, p. 79.
13. See *supra*, p. 44; Seleznev, 'About the New Socialist Intelligentsia,' pp. 39–40.
14. See I Kuz'minov, 'The Working Class of the U.S.S.R. in the Great Patriotic War'; editorial, 'The Glorious Working Class of the U.S.S.R.'

'thirties, following the fundamental execution of the collectivization program in the village, was officially explained at the time as a perfection of the alliance between the two classes — an 'expansion of the base' but not a dissolution of the dictatorship 'belonging to the working class as the advanced class of society.' This theory still stands, but the emphasis has been on the equality of the classes and on approaching 'classlessness.' In 1939 admission to the Party was equalized for the peasants, workers, and the intelligentsia.[15]

On the whole, political participation by the peasantry is still relatively low, though it will probably increase by slow degrees. Socially, the prestige of the peasantry as a group was low for a long time, because of the struggles continuously waged against various peasant groups in the effort to collectivize the countryside. The social standing of the peasantry can be expected to rise in the future in proportion to the further mechanization, urbanization, and culturalization of the village.

Before the revolution the peasantry was the largest class in Russia. Outside of the large-estate owners, who were eliminated during the civil-war period, in 1913 the kulaks or rich peasants accounted for 12.3 per cent and the rest of the peasantry (with a small group of artisans) for 65.1 per cent of the population. The total percentage of 77.4 per cent thus represented more than three fourths of the population. Though its numbers have diminished, the peasantry is still the largest class, but its face and body have changed.[16] In 1928, following the decision taken by the Fifteenth Party Congress in December of the previous year to collectivize agriculture, collective peasants and co-operative artisans constituted 2.9 per cent of the population, while individual peasants and non-co-operative artisans accounted for 72.9 per cent. In 1937 the relative percentages were 55.5 and 5.6 and in 1939 46.9 and 2.6, respectively. Collective peasants alone constituted with their families in 1939 44.6 per cent of the population or 75,600,000 persons, while individual peasants numbered only three million or 1.8 per cent. The kulaks were liquidated during 1929–34. By 1937 there were 243,700 collective farms (*kolkhoz*) embracing 18,500,000 peasant households; that is, 93 per cent of all the peasant households, covering 99 per cent of the peasant sowing area, were collectivized.[17] Three

---

15. See *supra*, pp. 38–46.

16. The figures quoted here are based on the following sources: 20 *Let Sovetskoi Vlasti*, p. 43; *Bol'shevik*, Nos. 15–16 (1939), p. 113, No. 10 (1940), p. 17; *A.Q.S.U.* November 1940, pp. 92, 100; Mikhailov, *Land of the Soviets*, p. 51.

17. Of the agricultural land, measured in millions of hectares, 152.5 million belonged to the large-estate owners, the Tsar's family, and the monasteries; 214.7 million to peasant

years later the percentage of collectivized households had reached 96.9 per cent. Thus, the peasantry is practically entirely collectivized.

The peasantry's role in political activity was fairly restricted for over two decades. As was to be expected, its participation in the Soviet organs was greater than in Party ones, since the soviets were regarded as a school of political training for the 'non-proletarian' strata.

PERCENTAGE OF PEASANTS AMONG THE MEMBERS OR DEPUTIES [18]

CONGRESS OF SOVIETS U.S.S.R.	1921	1922	1924	1925	1927	1929	1931	1935
	20.0	26.8	26.0	29.2	31.4	24.8	25.6	23.4
C.E.C. U.S.S.R.		11.4	15.5	23.4	23.7	20.9	16.3	14.9
SUPREME SOVIET U.S.S.R.					1937	1946		
					29.5	26.0		

As far as the local soviets are concerned, the peasant element was strong in the rural soviets, but weak in the city soviets. It should be noted, however, that at the last election to the local soviets, held in 1939, the percentage of peasants in the village soviets dropped by 15 per cent as compared with the elections of the decade before.[19] This is an indication that the new, predominantly young, village intelligentsia is beginning to take its place in the membership of the rural soviets, and this trend is apparently encouraged as part of a policy to assure the program of further modernization of the village.

At the Party congress the percentage of peasants among the voting delegates remained consistently low:

	1922	1923	1924	1927	1930	1934
	7.7	1.9	5.4	5.7	6.7	8.0

---

households in Tsarist Russia — a total of 367.2 millions of hectares. In 1937, Soviet state farms (*sovkhoz*) comprised 51.1 million and the peasant households — collective and individual — 370.8 million hectares. (20 *Let Sovetskoi Vlasti*, p. 44.)

18. Figures in this table are based on sources of note 7, p. 315. Collective peasants constituted 62.2% of the peasant delegates at the Congress of Soviets in 1931, 71% in 1935. At the extraordinary congress, convoked to adopt the new constitution in 1936, all the peasant delegates were collective farmers, and comprised 40% of the delegate body.

19. In 1927 the percentage of peasants in the village soviets was 81.1, in 1937 65.9. Data for 1927 shows the percentage of peasants to have been 90.2 among the chairmen of the village soviets, 55.2 in the county executive committees. In the local soviets elected in 1939 the peasant percentage was: 5.5 in the city soviets, 65.9 in the village soviets, 35.8 in the district soviets, and 28.3 in the region soviets.

'The Party is primarily a city party, not a village one,' declared Molotov in 1922, pointing out that there were three-and-a-half times as many Party members in city cells as in village cells of the Party.[20] The truth of this statement was borne out in subsequent years by the percentage of peasants in the entire Party membership:

1923	1924	1925	1927	1930	1934
25.7	24.6	24.0	22.0	20.4	28.5

Although an intensive recruiting drive in the village brought this percentage up to 28.5 per cent by 1934, Kaganovich complained to the Seventeenth Party Congress that year that 50 per cent of the collective farms still had no Party organizations.[21] In 1939, at the Eighteenth Party Congress, Andreev voiced a similar complaint: that only 12,000 collectives out of more than 243,000 had primary Party organizations, that some collectives had only Komsomol (Communist Youth League) groups, and that over 100,000 collectives had neither Party nor Komsomol organizations.[22] In 1941 the percentage of peasants in the Party membership still stood at the low figure of 19.0 per cent.

To the Soviet leaders these figures spelled general and political backwardness in the village. Regarding this backwardness as the greatest danger to the regime, they sought to remove it primarily in three ways: urbanization, tutelage by the city, and education and mechanization of the village.

Urbanization was constantly altering the balance between town and country in favor of the former. Migration from village to city meant an increase in the number of workers — viewed for so long as the mainstay of the regime — and continued replenishment of the industrial labor force from the seemingly inexhaustible peasant reservoir. Changes in the correlation of the urban and rural populations are expressed in the following table:[23]

YEARS	PERCENTAGE OF CITY POPULATION	PERCENTAGE OF VILLAGE POPULATION
1914	15.0	85.0
1920	15.6	84.4
1923	15.5	84.5
1926	17.9	82.1
1939	32.8	67.2

20. XI S'ezd RKP(b), p. 52.
21. XVII S'ezd VKP(b), pp. 556–7.
22. Pravda, 14 March 1939, p. 3.
23. Sul'kevich, Naselenie SSSR, p. 13.

Between 1926 and 1939 the urban population had increased from 26.3 million to 55.9 million. The manner of this increase is shown by the following table:[24]

	POPULATION IN MILLIONS OF PERSONS		
	RURAL	URBAN	TOTAL
Population by 1926 census	120.7	26.3	147.0
Migration from village to city in the course of twelve years	−18.5	+18.5	——
Natural increase	+18.2	+ 5.3	+23.5
Persons in points transformed from villages into cities	− 5.8	+ 5.8	——
Population by 1939 census	114.6	55.9	170.5
Difference between 1926 and 1939	− 6.1	+29.6	+23.5

Migration from the village to the city, thus constituted the largest factor in urbanization, taking up the natural increase of population in the village. It is likewise expected to absorb the surplus of manpower resulting in the village from the mechanization of agriculture.

While urbanization is a continuous process, tutelage by the city of the village was considered a passing phase. Tutelage took the form of assistance to the countryside during seasonal campaigns, the sending of permanent organizers there, and the establishment in the village of political departments staffed with people recruited from the city. Over a quarter of a million people were sent by the Party from the cities to the villages during 1928–30 to aid in the various campaigns during the initial period of collectivization. Kaganovich called it 'the quantitative expression of the organizing role of the proletariat with regard to the village, of the help of the city to the village.'[25] Twenty-five thousand specially selected city-dwellers went to the country for permanent work, and although many of the 'twenty-five-thousanders,' as they were called, knew nothing about agriculture, they were good organizers and were expected to learn quickly and show the peasants the road to collectivization. Another form of tutelage was the so-called *shefstvo* or patronage by industrial regions over agricultural regions producing raw materials used by the factories of the former. Thus, the Moscow, Leningrad, and Ivanovo-Voznesensk regions constituted *shefstvo* over the mid-Volga and central black-soil regions, Tadzhikistan, and part of Uzbekistan, in order to increase the growing of flax for the textile factories of the former through organizational assistance and production compacts. Later, the 'twenty-five-thousanders' were deemed insufficient and, on Stalin's initiative, political departments

24. Ibid. p. 15.
25. *XVI S'ezd VKP(b)*, pp. 67–9.

(*politotdely*) were created in the village for which 'tested, strong people who would be able to solve the tasks standing before the Party' were recruited from the city.[26] Not less than half of the chiefs of these political departments, said Kaganovich, were 'people from Leningrad and Moscow.' This move set an example for every region to send tried organizers from the cities into the collective farms.

From the outset, however, a more permanent solution for the new kind of agriculture was seen in the raising of loyal, qualified cadres from the village itself. 'If we speak of the commanding staff,' declared Kaganovich in 1930 at the Sixteenth Party Congress, 'the future of the village belongs to that commanding staff which is being raised from among the peasants themselves.'[27] At the following congress, in 1934, he adduced figures to show that the number of higher agricultural educational institutions rose from 30 in 1928 to 116 in 1933 and the number of students in them from 29,000 to 99,000. For the same years the number of agricultural technicums rose from 204 to 928, and the students in them from 30,000 to 121,000. In consequence, while there were 18,000 agricultural specialists at the beginning of the first Five-Year Plan, the number of specialists with a higher and medium agricultural education rose to 126,000 by the end of 1933.[28] This figure grew larger in subsequent years, and by 1938 the percentage of peasants among students in universities and colleges, which reached up to 20 per cent before the Revolution, was once more 21.6 per cent.[29] Thousands of skilled agricultural workers and higher agricultural personnel, as well as chairmen and administrators of the collectives and members of the local soviets, have risen from the ranks of the peasantry itself; on the eve of the recent war, one and a half million collective peasants — men and women — held leading positions in agriculture as chairmen of administrations, brigade leaders, and farm managers.[30] Thus, though peasants probably have less opportunities than workers to become members of the Soviet intelligentsia, because of the vastly greater number of peasants, such opportunities are not closed to them as a class.

The Soviet leaders had hoped that the agricultural revolution had solved the peasant problem.[31] The behavior of the Red Army, which is

26. Kaganovich's report at the Seventeenth Party Congress, 6 February 1934, *XVII S'ezd VKP(b)*, p. 530.
27. Report of 28 June 1930, *XVI S'ezd VKP(b)*, p. 69.
28. *XVII S'ezd VKP(b)*, p. 529.
29. See Schwarz, *Management*, p. 112.
30. *Izvestia*, 27 December 1945.
31. See *supra*, pp. 41–2.

to a large extent peasant in origin, and of the peasantry itself during the recent war, leaves no doubt that fundamentally the peasantry is loyal to the regime; and Stalin has hailed the patriotic contribution of the peasantry in the War as a demonstration by it of 'a high consciousness of the interests of the entire nation unheard of before in the history of the village.'[32] Many peasants have become genuinely reconciled to collectivized agriculture and the Soviet system. The wide distribution of emoluments to peasant boys in the army, and perhaps also the fact that some of the outstanding Soviet generals and marshals derive from the peasantry have been a source of psychological satisfaction. Still, peasant individualism dies hard, and some residues of dissatisfaction with the new order linger on in the village. Even the grant giving the peasants the right to own small individual plots of land did not entirely do away with dissatisfaction. The Party retains fundamental control over the village through the M.T.S. (machine and tractor stations) with their political departments, propaganda instruments, and actual possession of the agricultural machinery, without which the wheels of collectivized agriculture would stop.[33] Ultimately, it is believed, a peasant generation will be reared that will have never known any other form of agriculture but the collectivized form. And even transition to the *sovkhoz* or state-farm system sometime in the future is not altogether excluded.

As at present constituted, the peasantry has neither the will nor the capacity for effective political opposition to the regime. Its loyalty to the latter would probably become unshakeable were the supply of consumers' goods and other amenities of life to become ample in the countryside.

The Intelligentsia. From a legally unequal and politically suspect social stratum the intelligentsia has become an equal and acclaimed member of Soviet society. It has greatly grown in numbers and altered considerably in composition. With these changes, its participation in the political process has likewise increased. The intelligentsia is bound to grow further both in numbers and in influence. Evidence, however, points toward measures to prevent the development of a sense of separate identity in the intelligentsia, and to instill generally the concept of the 'Soviet people' — embracing the members of all social groups as 'toilers' of a unified society.

As of January 1937, the intelligentsia — according to figures given by Molotov — numbered 9,591,000 and, together with the members of their

---

32. See editorial, 'The Patriotism of the Soviet Peasantry,' *Izvestia,* 27 December 1945.
33. The M.T.S., focal points around which the collectives are grouped, numbered 158 in 1930, 2,916 in 1933, and 5,617 in 1937. In 1937 they controlled the use of 356,800 tractors and 96,300 combines in the collectives. (20 *Let Sovetskoi Vlasti,* p. 48.)

families, constituted 14 per cent of the population.[34] The 1939 census
gives the figure for 'employees' with their families, i.e. for the intelligentsia
(including minor officials), as 29,758,000 or 17.54 per cent of the population. This represents an approximate growth of six to seven times by
comparison with the pre-revolutionary intelligentsia.

The ranks of the old intelligentsia were considerably decimated during
the years of the civil war and Revolution. Soviet policy toward it wavered
between cautious acceptance and repression, conditioned on the one hand
by the indispensability of its services, and on the other, by distrust of its attitude toward the Soviet program, as well as fear of its influence on the
state apparatus.[35] The first steps in the gigantic industrialization and
collectivization programs disclosed to the Soviet leaders a general shortage
of intellectual and technological forces and an even greater shortage of
Party members with the requisite education and training. At the Sixteenth
Party Congress (June 1930) Kaganovich complained that a survey on
1 September 1929 had shown that while among non-Party men holding
positions as administrators of economic trusts and directors of enterprises
the percentage of persons with a higher education was 88 and 62, respectively, the percentage of Communists in the same positions possessing
a higher education was only 12 and 2.6 respectively.[36] These disclosures
led to a definite turn in policy toward the remnants of the old intelligentsia (inaugurated with Stalin's statement of 23 June 1931) and to
intensive efforts to create a new intelligentsia. At the following Party
congress (February 1934) Kaganovich reported that the number of higher
educational institutions had increased from 129 in 1928 to 600 by 1933,
and the number of students attending them from 160,000 to 491,000. The
percentage of Party members among these students rose from 15 to 22,
and of Komsomol members from 19 to 30. For the same years the number
of technicums had increased from 1,033 to 3,522, and the number of
students in the technicums from 188,000 to 672,000, with the percentage of
Komsomol members among them rising from 36 to 42. As a result of
these changes, Kaganovich concluded, the number of specialists with a
higher education had increased from 179,000 in 1928 to 303,000 by 1933,
and those with a medium technical education from 313,000 to 669,000.[37]

Before the revolution there were 90 colleges and universities with

34. Yaroslavsky, op. cit. p. 28.
35. See *supra*, pp. 37–8, 43–4.
36. *XVI S'ezd VKP(b)*, p. 79.
37. *XVII S'ezd VKP(b)*, p. 528. Cf. *20 Let Sovetskoi Vlasti*, pp. 81, 82; *E.B.* 2 Novem-
    ber 1944.

111,000 students in attendance; by 1938 the number of higher educational institutions reached 700, with 550,000 students in attendance. In the same year the number of students in technicums was about 700,000. Sergei Kaftanov, Minister of Higher Education, estimated that well over a million specialists graduated from these schools between 1928 and 1944: 198,000 during 1928–32; 323,000 during 1933–37; 477,000 during 1938–42; and over 200,000 during the war years of 1941–44.[38] By the spring of 1946 these schools were said to have been completely restored. They are expected to enroll 962,000 students in the period of the current Five-Year Plan (1946–50) and to graduate about 600,000 additional young specialists during these years.[39]

What these figures have meant by way of growth of the ranks of the intelligentsia is illustrated by the following comparative table:[40]

COMPOSITION OF THE SOVIET INTELLIGENTSIA
(in thousands of persons)

	1926	1937 (1 *January*)	INCREASE
(1) Heads of enterprises, institutions, workshops, state farms, collective farms, et cetera	384.6	1,751.0	4.6 times
(2) Engineers and architects (excluding heads of enterprises and workshops)	31.5	250.0	7.9 "
(3) Intermediate technical personnel (technicians, engineer assistants, foresters, station masters, et cetera)	175.3	810.0	4.6 "
(4) Agronomists	18.0	80.0	4.4 "
(5) Other agricultural personnel (surveyors, land specialists, agricultural technicians, animal husbandmen)	13.3	96.0	7.2 "
(6) Scientific workers (professors, college instructors, et cetera)	13.5	80.0	5.9 "
(7) Teachers	347.6	969.0	2.8 "
(8) Cultural-educational workers (journalists, librarians, club directors, et cetera)	58.5	297.0	5.1 "
(9) Workers of the arts	53.8	159.0	3.0 "
(10) Physicians	70.0	132.0	1.9 "
(11) Intermediate medical personnel (medical attendants, midwives, nurses)	129.8	382.0	2.9 "
(12) Economists, statisticians	250.0	822.0	3.3 "
(13) Bookkeepers, accountants	375.4	1,617.0	4.3 "
(14) Judicial-procuratorial workers (judges, procurators, investigators, et cetera)	27.1	46.0	1.7 "
(15) Students of the higher educational institutions	168.0	550.0	3.3 "
TOTAL	2,116.4	8,041.0	3.8 "
(16) Other groups of the intelligentsia (including the military intelligentsia)	No data	1,550.0	
GRAND TOTAL		9,591.0	

38. *E.B.* 13 October and 2 November 1944. Nearly 50 million people, wrote Kaftanov, were studying in one form or another on the eve of the war. (See *Bol'shevik*, No. 5 (1944), p. 18.)

39. Editorial, *Izvestia*, 12 April 1946.

40. Seleznev, op. cit. p. 40; Yaroslavsky, op. cit. p. 37.

'Salt of the Soviet earth,' Party historian Yaroslavsky called this new intelligentsia in 1939, and more recently it has even been publicly referred to as 'the most advanced and most cultural part of Soviet society.' [41]

Politically, these changes found expression in increased participation in government by the intelligentsia, beginning with the 'thirties.[42]

PERCENTAGE OF INTELLIGENTSIA AMONG THE MEMBERS OR DEPUTIES

CONGRESS OF SOVIETS								
U.S.S.R.	1921	1922	1924	1925	1927	1929	1931	1935
	41.0	28.8	25.0	30.5	19.4	18.8	20.0	30.1
C.E.C. U.S.S.R.		40.4	40.3	34.7	33.2	32.6	36.1	46.1
SUPREME SOVIET U.S.S.R.[43]				1937	1946			
				28.5	35.0			

In the local soviets elected in 1939,[44] the percentage of the intelligentsia was 34.78; it was 55.6 in the city soviets, 44.9 in the region soviets.[45]

Available statistics on the composition of the Party indicate a gradual decline in membership and participation by the intelligentsia until the 'thirties, when the percentage of the intelligentsia in the Party councils began to rise sharply.

PERCENTAGE OF INTELLIGENTSIA AMONG MEMBERS AND DELEGATES

	1923	1924	1925	1927	1930	1934
IN THE PARTY	25.7	24.6	24.0	22.0		
AT THE PARTY CONGRESS (among voting delegates)	34.4	31.4	30.9	23.0	22.1	32.0

---

41. Yaroslavsky, op. cit. p. 35; *Izvestia,* 29 December 1945, 12 April 1946. At the same time members of the intelligentsia are called 'workers of intellectual toil.' (*Izvestia,* 12 April 1946.)

42. For the sources of these figures on the role of the intelligentsia, see note 7, p. 315.

43. The strength of the Soviet intelligentsia in the Supreme Soviet is also indicated by the following facts: 33% of the deputies elected in 1946 have a higher education, 5% an incomplete higher education. Among the 1,339 deputies are academicians, writers, artists, engineers, doctors, teachers, agricultural brigade and link leaders and chairmen of collective farms, and master craftsmen of industry, transport, and the mines. 68% of the deputies in the Council of Nationalities and 78% in the Council of the Union are holders of government awards; and among these there are 102 Heroes of the Soviet Union, 52 Heroes of Socialist Labor, and 35 Stalin Laureates. (See *Izvestia,* 15 March 1946.)

44. In the local soviets elected the decade before, the percentage of the intelligentsia was 5.6 in the village soviets, 2.9 among the chairmen of the village soviets, 27.5 in the county executive committees.

45. Deputies with a higher or secondary education constituted 45.4% of the membership in the city soviets, 29.5 in the district soviets and 47.6 in the region soviets. For data on the intelligentsia of the local soviets by specialties, see *V.V.S.* 25 June 1941, p. 4.

While no exact figures are available, the percentage of members of the intelligentsia had unquestionably risen further by the last Party congress in 1939.

Another indication of an increase in the strength of the intelligentsia in the Party is the rise in the educational level of the Party membership. As a result of the cultural strides of the first two Five-Year Plans, Party Secretary Malenkov stated in March 1939 that the number of Communists with a higher education had increased from 9,000 to 127,000, and those with a secondary education from 110,000 to 335,000.[46] The change was reflected in the Party congress: in 1924 6.5 per cent of the voting delegates had a higher education, in 1930 7.2 per cent (4.4 per cent complete, 2.8 per cent incomplete), in 1934 about 10 per cent, in 1939 — at the Eighteenth Party Congress — 31.5 per cent (26.5 per cent a complete higher education, 5 per cent an incomplete one); while at the Eighteenth Party Conference in 1941, the percentage of delegates with a complete higher education was 41.8.[47]

Despite the present importance of the intelligentsia in Soviet life, a number of deliberate practices contradict the idea that it is being groomed or permitted to assume the role of a dominant class, standing apart and above the other social groups. The heavy toll among the ranks of the intelligentsia during the 1936–8 purge, the decree of 19 October 1940 on compulsory transfer of engineers, economists, planning experts, et cetera — along with skilled workers — 'regardless of territorial location,' and the more recent purges of industrial and agricultural officials and of professionals in other fields show that despite its economic advantages and social gains the intelligentsia is not a privileged class. The entire official emphasis, endlessly repeated in public pronouncements and the press, is that it is a 'people's intelligentsia' derived from and fused with the people, that it is 'yesterday's workers and peasants advanced to commanding posts.'[48] As a social category, 'Soviet intelligentsia' is defined very broadly, and, as a previous table shows,[49] it already comprises some groups with no

46. *Pravda*, 15 March 1939, pp. 5–6.
47. The percentage of delegates with a secondary education changed as follows: 17.9 in 1924, 15.7 in 1930, about 31 in 1934, 22.5 at the Eighteenth Party Congress in 1939, the statistics for which also give the figure of 46% for delegates with an incomplete secondary and a primary education. At the Eighteenth Party Conference in 1941, the percentage of delegates with an incomplete higher education and a secondary education was 29.1.
48. See *supra*, p. 44; Yaroslavsky, op. cit. pp. 4–5, 33, 36; A. Rakhlin, 'The Soviet Intelligentsia,' *Sots. Zak.* No. 12 (1938), pp. 28–9; Editorials, *Izvestia*, 29 December 1945, 12 April 1946.
49. See *supra*, p. 326.

more than vocational training. There is a growing tendency to interpret it even more broadly by making efficiency the criterion and presenting record-breaking workers — the 'stakhanovites' — as foremost examples of the intelligentsia, who point the road toward 'abolition of the contradiction between physical and mental toil' through high productivity.[50] This foreshadows wider inclusion of skilled workers within the concept of 'intelligentsia,' and indeed Party propaganda goes so far as to hold out the prospect that 'the entire Soviet people will become a people of intelligentsia.'[51]

These conceptions have contributed toward continued growth of an élite of efficiency: rewards for performance have made the people of the U.S.S.R. the greatest title-bearing and medal-wearing nation in the world.[52] But they have hardly been conducive to the crystallization of an overriding sense of group solidarity among the various elements of the intelligentsia.[53] The Soviet élite has not reached the point of saturation where restrictive arrangements to protect and perpetuate a privileged position for it might be inaugurated. The vastness of the Soviet Union and its resources, plus the scope of modern invention, may provide for decades to come opportunities for the children of all social groups to rise to a higher station. Since no sons of leaders as such have been pushed into special prominence, no privilege from birth is as yet indicated.[54] At the same time, through constant ideological indoctrination, the Party has been consistently guarding against the development of a separate 'class consciousness' or political opposition in the intelligentsia.[55]

50. See Rakhlin, op. cit. p. 29; Yaroslavsky, op. cit. pp. 30, 39–40; Kaftanov, 'The Soviet Intelligentsia in the Great Patriotic War,' p. 25.

51. Ibid.

52. See supra, note 74, p. 270; note 43, p. 327, and infra, pp. 357, 584, 587. As of 1 October 1944, 2,868,962 persons have been decorated with government orders and medals during the recent war alone. (E.B. 23 December 1944.) For descriptions of the orders and medals, see E.B. 20 July, 16 November 1944.

53. Cf. Dallin, op. cit. pp. 142–4, and Timasheff, op. cit. p. 18.

54. A seeming exception is provided by the establishment of the Suvorov Military Schools in August 1943, where sons of soldiers have the privilege of admission to train for army careers. (Izvestia, 22 August 1943.) But this exclusiveness is of limited scope, since there are many other military schools where sons of civilians can train, subsequently rising to high military status on merit. The high earnings of some citizens and recent laws on property inheritance have, of course, created the possibility of a future 'leisure class.' None has as yet emerged, however, and counter-measures are likely to prevent its rise. In this connection, see the provision of the new constitution (article 12) that 'toil in the U.S.S.R. is an obligation' for every citizen fit to work.

55. See supra, pp. 3–4; Yaroslavsky, op. cit. pp. 38–40. The patriotic performance of the intelligentsia during the war is considered 'a direct result of the gigantic work of the Party . . . for the ideological-political education of the Soviet intelligentsia.' (See

To summarize, because of the extraordinary current demand for a continuing increase in scientific and skilled personnel, the ranks of the intelligentsia are bound to increase in all spheres of activity, including the political. Individuals and small groups of this stratum have the capacity for political leadership. Whether, in the foreseeable future, the Soviet intelligentsia would produce from its midst leadership for effective opposition to the regime is to be seriously doubted. For one thing the Party and government have appropriated the intelligentsia, which is in fact the greatest present beneficiary of the existing order. At the same time, like any other social stratum, the intelligentsia is watched and curbed in the interest of the larger unity. It has as yet no real sense of a separate class identity; it is too large by definition and is still growing by design. And in the complex of attitudes assiduously bred at present in the U.S.S.R., the concepts of 'the people' and 'the toilers' are still given first place.

Women. Woman occupies a high social status in the U.S.S.R. The predominance of women in the Soviet population, and the complete equality of rights accorded them by law have resulted in a high degree of participation by them in the economy, education, the health services, and in a number of trades and professions. These factors have found lesser reflection in the field of politics, though since the beginning of Soviet rule women's participation has been on the increase.

Before World War I the number of men and women was nearly the same in Russia. In 1926 there were five million more women than men, in 1939 over seven million more. For every 100 men there were 107 women in 1926, 109 women in 1939. In the critical age group of 20 to 45 years, the ratio was 90 males per 100 females according to one estimate, and as a result of the war losses it was expected to fall to 82 in 1945.[56]

Together with equalized opportunities, this preponderance of women found expression in a progressive increase of their numbers in the entire national economy. In 1936 women constituted 34 per cent of the 'workers and employees,' in 1938, 35 per cent, in 1940, 37 per cent, and by March 1942, 45 per cent.[57] In industry the percentage of women workers was

Kaftanov, op. cit. p. 20.) Following a special decision on propaganda, taken by the Party Central Committee on 14 November 1938, the Party committees of the big cities organized so-called 'universities of Marxism-Leninism,' which were attended chiefly by members of the intelligentsia: scientists, engineers, artists, etc. In the school organized by the Moscow Party committee, for example, the 2500 who audited the courses during 1939–40 included 73 Doctors of Science, 349 candidates for science degrees, 65 professors, 276 associate professors, 790 instructors and science assistants, etc. About 300 of these were persons over fifty years of age. (Ibid. p. 21.)

56. See Lorimer, 'Recent Population Trends in the Soviet Union,' p. 221.
57. 20 *Let Sovetskoi Vlasti*, pp. 91, 92; Mikhailov, op. cit. p. 33; *B.S.U.* 14 May 1942.

over 28 in 1928, 39 in 1936, and over 70 during the war years of 1941-4. By 1938, women constituted 30 per cent of all scientific personnel and 41 per cent of the students in higher educational institutions. Two years later the percentage of women in higher educational institutions was 43 and women constituted over 50 per cent of all physicians, as compared with 15 per cent and 9.7 per cent, respectively, which they held in these categories in 1914.[58]

In the field of political activity, woman's participation was less spectacular, especially until the late 'thirties.[59]

PERCENTAGE OF WOMEN AMONG THE MEMBERS OR DEPUTIES

	1922	1924	1925	1927	1929	1931	1935	1936
CONGRESS OF SOVIETS U.S.S.R.	3.5	3.0	7.1	7.7	14.2	20.4	18.7	21.0
C.E.C. U.S.S.R.	2.4		5.5		15.0	20.4	13.3	

	1937	1946
SUPREME SOVIET U.S.S.R.[60]	16.5	21.0

In the local soviets women were about one fifth of the deputies and now constitute approximately one third of the membership:

PERCENTAGE OF WOMEN DEPUTIES

	1920	1922	1923	1924	1925	1927	1929	1931	1939
VILLAGE SOVIETS		1.0	2.2	9.0	10.1	11.8	19.0	20.9	32.4
CITY SOVIETS	5.7			18.6				25.9	37.4

In the local soviets elected in 1939, the percentage of women deputies is 32.9: 24.35 in the territories, 28.65 in the regions, 28.18 in the areas, 32.39 in the districts, and 39.27 in the districts-in-cities.[61]

---

58. Ibid; *Bol'shevik,* No. 16 (1938), p. 49; No. 5 (1944), p. 18. On 8 March 1946, *Pravda* listed the following figures on the place of women in Soviet society: 119,789 recipients of government medals and awards; 62 holders of the title Hero of the Soviet Union and 3 holders of the title Hero of Socialist Labor; over 250,000 engineers and technicians; 33,000 in scientific research, 1,498 recipients of science stipends and awards, 118 doctors of science, and 76 professors; 116 laureates of the Stalin prize; 254,000 leaders of tractor brigades and 350,000 leaders of brigades on livestock farms; 15,000 chairmen and vice-chairmen of collective farms; 1,030,000 in education work, 750,000 of whom are teachers; over 1,049,000 in public health services, of whom nearly 100,000 are doctors.

59. The figures cited below are based on the sources of note 7, p. 315.

60. There were 189 women deputies in the Supreme Soviet elected in 1937 (77 in the Council of Union, 112 in the Council of Nationalities), and there are 277 women deputies in the Supreme Soviet elected in 1946 (116 in the Council of the Union, 161 in the Council of Nationalities). There are 848 women deputies in the Supreme Soviets of the Union republics, 588 in the supreme soviets of the autonomous republics.

61. Women deputies constitute 422,279 out of the 1,081,008 deputies elected to the local soviets in 1939. (See *E.B.* 8 March 1945.)

In the Party, women have for a long time constituted less than one fifth of the membership, and were represented even to a lesser extent among the voting delegates of the Party congress.

PERCENTAGE OF WOMEN AT THE PARTY CONGRESS
(Voting Delegates)

1922	1923	1924	1925	1927	1930	1934	1939
1.7	1.0	2.7	2.4	4.6	7.7	7.2	9.1

The last Party congress (1939) was told by Stalin that of 500,000 young persons promoted to 'leading state and Party posts' during 1934–9, 20 per cent were women.[62] This appears to be now the approximate average at which the percentage of women participating in Soviet politics tends to stabilize.

Recent legislation on marriage and the family, as well as decrees establishing separate schools for boys and girls,[63] may tend to work in the direction of drawing many women back to the home and diminishing their numbers in economic and political life. Several factors, on the other hand, would probably counterbalance such a tendency: the numerical predominance of women over men (by about twelve million or more), along with the general shortage of industrial manpower; the injunction that some form of social activity is a must, even for housewives, or women not otherwise gainfully employed;[64] and the fact that a certain minimum of participation by women in government is watched by the Party as a tangible demonstration on its part of woman's equality in the Soviet state.[65]

There has been far less disaffection among women than among men in Soviet politics, and there is, generally, nothing to indicate that women's influence has been in any way detrimental to the regime.

Youth. Young people have been playing an increasingly greater role in all spheres of activity in the Soviet Union, including the political. Two factors are responsible for this phenomenon: the predominance of young people in the population, and a long-standing policy of promoting younger persons to positions of responsibility.

---

62. Report to the Eighteenth Congress of the C.P.S.U.(B), p. 60.
63. See *infra*, p. 364.
64. See Svetlov, 'Marriage and the Family under Capitalism and Socialism,' pp. 44–58.
65. At practically every Party congress, the number of women delegates present was deemed to be too small and officially deplored. A recent official article, asserting that the number of women promoted to government posts was constantly growing, has acclaimed this tendency as 'one of surest proofs of the triumphs of true popular democracy.' (See *E.B.* 8 March 1945.)

Over 63 per cent of the entire Soviet population was under 30 years of age in 1939, according to the census taken that year, while only 13 per cent were 50 and over. From the standpoint of political and military activity, it is interesting to note that over 71 million people, or about 42 per cent of the population, were between the ages of 20 and 50; about 56 million persons, or almost 33 per cent of the population, were 20 to 40 years old.[66] The Soviet Union has sustained tremendous losses in the younger age groups during the recent war. Nevertheless, according to an authoritative statement made in January 1946, 100 million of the present population of 193 million in the U.S.S.R. are persons born after the revolution of 1917.[67] This means that nearly 52 per cent, or more than half of the present Soviet population, is under 30.

These figures constitute one of the major causes of the relative youthfulness of Soviet managerial personnel. In 1934, the Party congress was told by Kaganovich that young persons constituted more than half of all the industrial specialists: 58 per cent in the coal industry, 66 per cent in machine building, 68 per cent in the oil industry, 70 per cent in the aviation industry, et cetera. Over 60 per cent of the heads of shops and production shifts, he said, were young specialists.[68] On the eve of the War, about one tenth of the top industrial executives in the country were under 30 years of age.[69] During the War, millions of youths poured into industry, filling 60 to 70 per cent of the jobs in many enterprises, and altering radically the age structure of Soviet labor. Since the Soviet leaders feel that these newcomers have brought with them daring, enthusiasm, and an urge to perfect the norms and processes of production,[70] every effort is being made to train and recruit more young people for the ranks of skilled labor and management.

In the political field, too, Soviet youth has attained a prominent position, largely owing to the Party's policy since the mid-'twenties. At the Thirteenth Party Congress, in May 1924, Stalin rejected Trotsky's thesis that the student youth was the best barometer of Party opinion and that the problem of intra-Party democracy has become a question of the relations of 'generations' within the Party. At the same time he welcomed the accession of younger members to the Party cadres, criticizing what he

---

66. See *A.Q.S.U.* November 1940, p. 97.
67. Statement of G. F. Aleksandrov, Chief of the Propaganda Department of the Party Central Committee, on 22 January 1946, reported in *N.Y.H.T.* 23 January 1946.
68. *XVII S'ezd VKP(b)*, p. 529.
69. *B.S.U.* 30 April 1942.
70. See editorial, *Izvestia*, 26 December 1945.

called a conception of the cadres that would make of them 'a closed
entity, a privileged caste admitting no new members into its midst.'
Pointing out that less than 1 per cent of the Communists in the armed
forces had entered the Party before 1917, and only 3 per cent during
March–November 1917, he concluded that the army was served 'almost
exclusively by Party youth.'[71] Kaganovich noted a decrease in the percentage of Party-congress delegates with a Party status dating to the period
before the Revolution, and likewise explained its political significance as
'a tendency to promote the youth.'[72] Similar statements were made at the
subsequent congresses, though at the same time attention was called to
the fact that the percentage of delegates with pre-revolutionary and civil-
war Party status was larger than the percentage of such members in the
Party itself, and this was explained as due to an effort to utilize the old
cadres along with the new ones.[73] As the table below shows, however, the
younger element was in great preponderance.[74]

AGE CATEGORIES OF THE PARTY–CONGRESS DELEGATES
(in percentages)[75]

AGE OF DELEGATES	1924 13TH PARTY CONGRESS	1927 15TH PARTY CONGRESS	1930 16TH PARTY CONGRESS	1939 18TH PARTY CONGRESS	1941 18TH PARTY CONFERENCE
20–29	27.4 } 82.6	13.8 } 75.8	10.0 } 70.0	81.5	78.4
30–39	55.2	62.0	60.0		
40–49	15.4	20.0	25.0	15.5	19.8
50 and over	2.0	4.2	5.0	3.0	1.8
	100.0	100.0	100.0	100.0	100.0

Thus, at every Party congress the percentage of delegates who were 40
years of age or younger was not less than 70 while more than 95 per cent
of the delegate body was 50 or under.

Another index of the influence of the younger element in the Party is
seen by a comparison of the percentage of so-called 'undergroundists'
(Party members whose status dates back to the period before the Bolshevik
Revolution) and, on the one hand, of members who entered the Party
during the civil-war period and, on the other, members who joined the

71. XIII S'ezd VKP(b), pp. 122–4, 242–3.
72. Ibid. pp. 559–60.
73. Moskvin's report, 16 December 1927, XV S'ezd VKP(b), pp. 1105–6; Ezhov's report,
    1 February 1934, XVII S'ezd VKP(b), p. 303; Malenkov's report, 14 March 1939;
    Pravda, 15 March 1939.
74. This table is based on sources indicated in note 7, p. 315.
75. In the columns for 1939 and 1941 the first figure represents the age group of 20
    through 40, the second 41 through 50, the third 51 and over.

Party after the civil war, and especially after the critical year of 1929.[76] In 1922 there were 10,431 Party members with 'undergroundist' status, constituting 2.7 per cent of the total membership. By 1927 there were 1.2 per cent of 'undergroundists' and by 1939 this figure was no more than 0.3 per cent. 'Undergroundists' and civil-war entrants together constituted 10 per cent of the Party membership in 1934, 8.3 per cent in 1939. In the latter year 70 per cent of the entire membership were persons who entered the Party since 1929.

The comparative evolution of these status categories in the Party was illustrated even more sharply at the Party congress:

STATUS CATEGORIES OF THE PARTY–CONGRESS DELEGATES
(in percentages)

PARTY STATUS CATEGORIES	1923 12TH PARTY CONGRESS	1924 13TH PARTY CONGRESS	1927 15TH PARTY CONGRESS	1930 16TH PARTY CONGRESS	1934 17TH PARTY CONGRESS	1939 18TH PARTY CONGRESS	1941 18TH PARTY CONFERENCE
'Undergroundists' (1903–17)	59.2	48.7	38.5	26.9	22.6	2.4	5.0
Civil-War Entrants (1917–20)		14.0	33.0	55.5	57.4	17.0	15.0
Post-Civil-War Entrants (1920–29)		37.3	28.5		17.4	37.6	45.0
Entrants since 1929					2.6	43.0	35.0

The renovationist process at the Party congress thus spelled an accretion of newer and younger members. First, the civil-war period entrants were increasing at the expense of the 'undergroundists' or 'Old Bolsheviks'; then both categories dropped sharply during the purge period of the late 'thirties, while the number of members who entered the Party in the post-civil-war period, and especially since 1929 — predominantly young — climbed to preponderant proportions.

As we indicated earlier,[77] there are approximately 15 million Komsomol members and 13 million Pioneers, the membership of these two junior auxiliaries of the Party constituting 14.5 per cent of the population.

The younger element is also predominant in the soviets, although since the adoption of the decree raising the lower age limit of Supreme-Soviet candidates from 18 to 23 (October 1945), there is a tendency to elect somewhat older deputies.[78]

---

76. The figures and table given below are based on sources given in note 7, p. 315. See also *The Communist International between the Fifth and Sixth World Congresses*, pp. 505–6.

77. See *supra*, pp. 140, 143.

78. Figures based on sources of note 7, p. 315.

AGE CATEGORIES OF THE DEPUTIES IN THE SOVIETS
(in percentages)

LOCAL SOVIETS ELECTED IN 1939		SUPREME SOVIET U.S.S.R.		
			ELECTED IN 1937	ELECTED IN 1946
Age of Deputies		*Age of Deputies*		
Up to 24		Up to 25 inclusive	8.5	3.5
inclusive	15.2	26–40	64.2	42.4
25–39	59.8	41–50	} 27.3	41.3 } 54.1
40–49	19.8	50 and older		12.8
50 and older	5.2			

Thus, in the local soviets three fourths of the deputies are under 40 years of age. While the percentage of the older categories of deputies has increased in the newly elected Supreme Soviet, the significant fact is that the overwhelming majority of the deputies — over three fourths of them — are under 50. Younger persons are also coming to the fore in agriculture and scientific pursuits, while a high proportion of the generals and marshals who won fame during the recent war were in their thirties and forties at the time.

The percentage of young adults in the population structure is expected to stay high for many years,[79] and the tendency to entrust young persons with positions of responsibility and leadership in all fields, including the military and political spheres, will in all likelihood continue.

(2) THE NATIONAL GROUPS

The Russians hold the balance of political power in Soviet society. Proportionately, the share of controlling and responsible positions that they occupy is larger than the percentage of Russians in the population. From the standpoint of prerequisites for the peaceful operation of the political process, however, it is also significant that the other nationalities play a far greater role in Soviet politics than they ever played in Tsarist Russia. On the whole, the Soviet nationality policy seems to make for harmonious relations in the political process of the U.S.S.R. and would probably operate against cataclysmic disintegration in crisis.

The Soviet leaders have visualized the nationality question in the Soviet Union as primarily a problem of the relations between the central, industrial, and ethnically largely Great-Russian regions on the one hand, and the outlying, non-industrial, and ethnically to a large extent non-Russian regions. As part of the solution of that problem, they have charted a program whereby the central regions, and the Russians as the leading nationality, would assist the other regions and nationalities to economic

79. See Lorimer, op. cit. p. 221; Notestein, *The Future Population of Europe and the Soviet Union, passim.*

and cultural progress. In part as a result of this still continuing program, and partly as a consequence of the shifting of industrial enterprises to the East during the War, the balance between the central and peripheral regions in economic and cultural sinews of power is gradually evening out. The main instrument employed by the Party in evolving these relationships has been the federal Union itself, as a flexible solvent and supreme unifying symbol, holding in the perspective of the more distant future the possibility of amalgamation of the cultures and peoples of the U.S.S.R.

The Russians. The leading position among the constituent republics is held by the Russian Soviet Federated Socialist Republic, or R.S.F.S.R., which embraces the entire northern and central belt of the Soviet Union. As the accompanying tables show, the R.S.F.S.R. is first among the Union republics both in territory, which was 78 per cent of the territorial domain, and in population, which was over 64 per cent of the total population in 1939.[80] Before the War it likewise occupied first place economically, producing 70 per cent of the industrial output of the whole U.S.S.R., and it may be recalled that at least in the early 'twenties the Soviet leaders held that the political basis of the dictatorship consists mainly of 'the central, the industrial regions and not the border regions, which are peasant countries.'[81]

Russians make up three fourths of the population of the R.S.F.S.R. and live in considerable numbers in most of the other republics. They constituted nearly three fifths of the entire population of the U.S.S.R. in 1939. Moreover, they are culturally and economically the most advanced of the Soviet nationalities and have the longest experience in administration.

These factors are reflected in the extent of the Russians' participation in Soviet political life.[82] At the Party congress, the Russians constituted 65.2 per cent of the voting delegates in 1924, 62 per cent in 1927, and 57.8 per cent in 1930. By comparison, the Ukrainians, for example, constituted 4.4 per cent, 9.8 per cent, and 9.6 per cent respectively, during the same years, while the percentage of the Byelorussians at the congress did not

80. These tables are based on the following sources: the 1926 and 1939 census data; Sul'kevich, op. cit. *passim;* Mikhailov, *Land of the Soviets,* p. 77. The figures on the national origins of the main population groups are taken from the appendix in Corliss Lamont, *The Peoples of the Soviet Union.* For similar data on national origins of the population groups in the autonomous republics, autonomous regions, and national districts, consult that appendix.
81. See *supra,* p. 97.
82. For the sources of the figures given below, see note 7, p. 315.

THE UNION REPUBLICS

REPUBLIC	AREA, IN SQUARE MILES 1939	POPULATION 1926	POPULATION 1939	NATIONAL ORIGINS OF MAIN POPULATION GROUPS (IN PERCENTAGE OF TOTAL AS OF 1926 CENSUS)
(1) Russian S.F.S.R.	6,375,000	93,457,996	109,278,614	Russian, 73.4; Ukrainian, 7.8; Kazakh, 3.8; Tatar, 2.8
(2) Ukrainian S.S.R.	171,950	29,042,934	30,960,221	Ukrainian, 80; Russian, 9.2; Jew, 5.4
(3) Byelorussian S.S.R.	48,960	4,983,240	5,567,976	Byelorussian, 80.6; Jew, 8.2; Russian, 7.2
(4) Georgian S.S.R.	28,875	2,677,233	3,542,289	Georgian, 67.7; Armenian, 11.6; Turkic, 5.2
(5) Azerbaijan S.S.R.	33,200	2,313,744	3,209,727	Turkic, 63.3; Armenian, 12.4; Russian, 9.7
(6) Armenian S.S.R.	11,580	881,290	1,281,599	Armenian, 84.7; Turkic, 8.2
(7) Kazakh S.S.R.	1,059,700	6,073,979	6,145,937	Kazakh, 57.1; Russian, 19.7; Ukrainian, 13.2
(8) Turkmen S.S.R.	171,250	998,154	1,253,985	Turkmen, 72; Uzbek, 10.5; Russian, 7.5
(9) Uzbek SSR	146,000	4,565,432	6,282,446	Uzbek, 76; Russian, 5.6
(10) Tadzhik S.S.R.	55,545	1,032,216	1,485,091	Tadzhik, 78.4; Uzbek, 17.9
(11) Kirghiz S.S.R.	75,950	1,001,697	1,459,301	Kirghiz, 66.6; Russian, 11.7; Uzbek, 11

1940 Additions

				(Estimate 1941)
(12) Karelo-Finnish S.S.R.	76,656		469,145	Karelian and Finn, 43; Russian, 57
(13) Estonian S.S.R.	18,353		1,126,413	Estonian, 87.7; Russian, 8.2
(14) Latvian S.S.R.	25,400		1,950,502	Latvian, 75.6; Russian, 11.3
(15) Lithuanian S.S.R.	22,959		2,879,070	Lithuanian, 85; Russian, 2.5
(16) Moldavian S.S.R.	13,124		3,500,000	Moldavian, 70

exceed 3.1 per cent. No data regarding the nationality factor are available for the subsequent congresses, but there is no doubt that the Russians continued to constitute more than 50 per cent of the delegates.

As for the soviets, the percentage of Russians was always low in the Council of Nationalities of the Central Executive Committee of the U.S.S.R., since that body was specifically constructed to allow representation to every nationality in the Union, including the very smallest. Thus, the percentage of Russians in this council stood as 17.9 in 1925; 13.1 in 1929; and 11.6 in 1931. For the same reason, Russians constituted only 25.4 per cent of the Council of Nationalities deputies in the Supreme Soviet of the first convocation (1937–45) and now comprise about one third of the membership of that chamber. But in the Union Council of the Central Executive Committee, Russians consistently formed more than half of the membership: 58.9 per cent in 1922, 56.2 per cent in 1924,

THE NATIONALITIES OF THE U.S.S.R.
(according to the 1939 census) *

NATIONALITY	NUMBER OF PERSONS INCLUDING FAMILIES	PER CENT OF TOTAL
Russians	99,019,929	58.41
Ukrainians	28,070,404	16.56
Byelorussians	5,267,431	3.11
Uzbeks	4,844,021	2.86
Tatars	4,300,336	2.54
Kazakhs	3,098,764	1.83
Jews	3,020,141	1.78
Azerbaijanians	2,274,805	1.34
Georgians	2,248,566	1.33
Armenians	2,151,884	1.27
Mordvinians	1,451,429	0.86
Germans	1,423,534	0.84
Chuvashs	1,367,930	0.81
Tadzhiks	1,228,964	0.72
Kirgizians	884,306	0.52
Dagestan peoples	857,371	0.50
Bashkirs	842,925	0.50
Turkmenians	811,769	0.48
Poles	626,905	0.37
Udmurts	605,673	0.36
Mariis	481,262	0.28
Komis	408,724	0.24
Chechens	407,690	0.24
Osetins	354,547	0.21
Greeks	285,896	0.17
Moldavians	260,023	0.15
Karelians	252,559	0.15
Karakalpaks	185,775	0.11
Koreans	180,412	0.11
Kabardinians	164,106	0.10
Finns	143,074	0.08
Estonians	142,465	0.08
Kalmyks	134,327	0.08
Letts and Letgauls	126,900	0.07
Bulgarians	113,479	0.07
Ingush	92,074	0.05
Adigeians	87,973	0.05
Karachaevs	75,737	0.04
Abkhazians	58,969	0.03
Khakasians	52,602	0.03
Oirots	47,717	0.03
Kurds	45,866	0.03
Balkarians	42,666	0.03
Iranians	39,037	0.02
Lithuanians	32,342	0.02
Chinese	29,620	0.02
Czechs and Slovaks	26,919	0.02
Arabs	21,793	0.01
Assyrians	20,207	0.01
Others	807,279	0.48
TOTAL	169,519,127	100.00

* The Western Ukraine and Western Byelorussia are not included.

56.4 per cent in 1925, 54.5 per cent in 1929, and 51.7 per cent in 1931. Again it may be pointed out by way of illustration that the percentage of Ukrainians in the Central Executive Committee was 6.5 in 1922; 10.3 in 1924; 12.5 in 1925; 12.6 in 1929; while that of the Byelorussians did not go above 2.3 per cent.

At the Congress of Soviets, the percentage of Russians was:

1922	1924	1927	1929	1931
62.5	61.0	56.9	58.1	59.7

No figures are indicated for 1935 and 1936, but delegates from the R.S.F.S.R. constituted 54.5 per cent and 64.9 per cent respectively during these two years. The highest percentage of Ukrainian representatives at the congress was 15.7 per cent, of Byelorussians 3.5 per cent.

Most of the time there were less Russians than non-Russians in the Presidium of the Central Executive Committee, but this situation was reversed in the Council of People's Commissars, especially in the years following 1938. Very rough estimates of the strength of the Russians in the higher federal organs of the Soviets in 1946 would be: in the Council of Ministers, 70 per cent; in the Presidium of the Supreme Soviet, 25 per cent; in the Council of Union of the Supreme Soviet, about 60 per cent; in the Supreme Court of the U.S.S.R., about 60 per cent.[83] In the military arm of the state, among the members of the general staff, marshals, generals, and commanders of other ranks, the Russians are overwhelmingly predominant. But the other nationalities, most of whom were not permitted even to serve in the army in Tsarist times, have produced an amazing number of officers during the recent war.[84] The Foreign Office and Foreign Service, where a good many of the higher posts were once held by non-Russians, have been completely dominated by Russians since the late 'thirties.

The outstanding role of the Russians in the state was never accompanied by any doctrine of a master race. No privileges are claimed for the Russians, no exclusive sovereignty has ever been asserted for the Russian people. The Russian language and Russian culture are highly praised, in great part probably with an eye to their serving as integrating and

83. Since there were no other criteria available for determining nationality but the sound and spelling of names and the electoral district in which the candidates stood for election, these percentages are merely approximations.

84. Among the military men represented at the Supreme Soviet elected in 1946, there are — besides Stalin, Beria, Khrushchev, and Mekhlis, who are also political leaders — such non-Russians as Marshals Timoshenko and Fedorenko, army Generals Bagramian and Eremenko, Admiral Tributs, Major-General Kokkinaki, and several dozen other non-Russian colonel-generals, major-generals, lieutenant-generals, colonels, and majors.

assimilating media, but no agitation for a single state language or any talk of the superiority of the Russian culture over the cultures of the other nationalities is tolerated. Earlier we have noted also Stalin's stricture against 'Great-Russian chauvinism' as, in its extreme form, striving 'to gather all the threads of administration into the hands of Russians.'[85] The conception that has evolved and is carefully fostered, now even more than before, is that the Russian people, with their culture and language, are simply *primus inter pares* in regard to the other peoples of the U.S.S.R., that it is the 'older brother' in the Soviet family of equal nations and is recognized by the latter as the leading nation because it is aiding them in their own progress and has borne the brunt of the recent struggle for the survival of the Union.[86]

The Other Nationalities. If the Russians predominate in public administration, the role of the other nationalities is nevertheless considerable, especially if one remembers that under Tsarist rule most of them had no share in the political life of the country.

As we have noted in previous chapters, a considerable framework of administrative arrangements operates to assure to the non-Russian nationalities a substantial measure of political expression. The Council of Nationalities, the vice-chairmen of the Presidium of the Supreme Soviet, the separate constitutions, councils of ministers, supreme courts, and other organs in the national republics, and the more recent reform on separate foreign ministries and national military formations are all designed to offer channels for political expression and to foster a sense of political participation by the nationalities. It should be pointed out, of course, that the representation of the separate national units in the Council of

---

85. See *supra*, pp. 82–3, 95–6.
86. Expressions such as the following abound now in the Soviet press and public pronouncements: 'The great Russian people — the older brother in the equal family of peoples of the U.S.S.R., occupies a special place in the Soviet companionship of peoples. The first among all the peoples of our country and of the entire world to have begun the great socialist revolution, it has not only renounced its former privileged position among the peoples of Tsarist Russia, but is tirelessly rendering every aid to the formerly oppressed and backward peoples in the matter of quick economic, political, and cultural development . . . Every people in the Soviet Union understands perfectly well that the main, decisive role in the achievement of victory over the enemy in the Great Patriotic War — in which the fate of the freedom and independence of all the peoples of the U.S.S.R. was being decided — was played by the great Russian people. That is why the prestige of the Russian people is so immeasurably high among the other peoples; that is why the peoples of the U.S.S.R. bear toward it boundless confidence and a feeling of tremendous love and gratitude.' (Statement of P. A. Sharia, Chairman of the Credentials Commission of the Council of Nationalities, at the Supreme Soviet sessions of 14 March 1946, *Izvestia*, 15 March 1946.)

Nationalities of the Supreme Soviet, and even the separate governments of the national units are not composed exclusively of the nationals for whom they are named. This is due primarily to the fact that the various nationalities, and the Russians in particular, overflow their national territorial-administrative units, although mixed representation is probably also encouraged in order to prevent the development of a sense of national exclusiveness and to cultivate the habit of joint political work by different nationals. But within each national republic, the 'root' or basic nationality whose name it bears is mostly predominant in the Soviet organs, especially in the local soviets.

Thus, for example, in the central executive committees of several of the Union republics in 1931, in four cases out of five the basic nationality was in the majority.[87]

THE NATIONAL COMPOSITION OF THE C.E.C.'S OF THE UNION REPUBLICS
(in percentages)

	RUSSIANS	THE BASIC NATIONALITY	OTHER NATIONALITIES
The C.E.C. of the R.S.F.S.R.	70.0		30.0
The C.E.C. of the Belorussian S.S.R.	9.2	56.8	34.0
The C.E.C. of the Transcaucasian S.F.S.R.	10.4	79.2	10.4
The C.E.C. of the Tadzhik S.S.R.	13.4	36.4	50.2
The C.E.C. of the Uzbek S.S.R.	22.3	67.6	10.1

In the village soviets elected during that year, the basic nationality constituted over 81 per cent of the members in each of the Union republics, except the R.S.F.S.R., where the Russians constituted 71.7 per cent; Azerbaijan, where the Turkic representatives were 79.2 per cent; and Tadzhikistan, where the Tadzhiks comprised 64.2 per cent of the delegates, with the Uzbeks next in line with 28.7 per cent. Again, in each of the Union republics, the overwhelming majority of the deputies elected to the local soviets in 1939, is of the basic nationality of the republic:

Ukrainian S.S.R.	— 84.22%	Ukrainians
Byelorussians S.S.R.	— 79.35%	Byelorussians
Azerbaijan S.S.R.	— 68.63%	Azerbaijanians
Georgian S.S.R.	— 72.32%	Georgians
Armenian S.S.R.	— 80.04%	Armenians
Uzbek S.S.R.	— 70.88%	Uzbeks
Kirghiz S.S.R. etc.[88]	— 63.44%	Kirghizians

The dissolution of a number of autonomous republics for collaborationist activity or passivism during the War[89] is proof that disaffection still

87. See Kareva, op. cit. p. 34.
88. Ibid.; *V.V.S.* 25 June 1941.
89. See *supra*, p. 85.

exists among some of the nationalities. The national units that were liquidated embraced over two million people, and some separatist sentiments
exists also in the Ukraine and the Baltic republics. But the same war experience has also shown that the great majority of the Soviet nationalities
fully identify themselves with the U.S.S.R. Despite general awareness of
the degree of control emanating from the federal center and of the illusory
nature of the Union republics' secession right, the promotion of cultural
and economic growth in the national units and particularly the absence of
ethnic discrimination in regard to the elevation of members of the various
nationalities to high positions of power have taken the sting out of the
old political grievances of the nationalities. Russians are bound to play a
leading role in the Soviet state for a long time, but individuals of other
nationalities are also gaining in education and status, and can be expected
in increasing numbers to fill managerial positions in all fields, the political
not excluded.

The Union. Conceivably, some groups among the predominant Russians
might be tempted in time of overwhelming crisis to restore a national
Russia, with a preferred status for the Russians. Or, conversely, some of
the dissatisfied border nationalities might attempt to utilize favorable
circumstances to separate from the U.S.S.R., particularly under stimulus
and support from the outside. Actually, neither seems very likely in the
foreseeable future.

Meanwhile — in the structural form of the federal Union — the political
formula of equality of opportunity for all the nationalities, with the Russians playing a leading role among equals, seems to assuage all the national
sensibilities concerned and is growing into a constitutional custom which,
in time, no one may wish to upset.[90] Such assimilating factors as the increasing diffusion of the Russian language and literature, free intermin-
gling and widespread intermarriage between individuals of the different
national groups, and common political, economic, and cultural patterns
help the centralized agencies of the Party and the government to control
the balance of national influence and are bound to lead also to increasing
substantive integration of the nationalities.

---

90. It is a silent tribute to the successful combination of inclusiveness and flexibility in
the Soviet national solution that at one and the same time former Russian Whites in
China and France are becoming Soviet citizens in the obvious conviction that the
U.S.S.R. is keeping together the Russian national domain and protecting traditional
Russian interests, while Armenians are returning to the Soviet Union from the Near
East in the firm belief that only in the Armenian Soviet Republic, under the aegis of
the U.S.S.R., can they lead a true national life.

2. POLITICAL FORCES

(1) THE PARTY

It is clear that the Party itself is the supreme political force, regulating the balance of all the other forces — political, social, and ideological. The Party has attained a status of monopolized legality in the country and a state of monolithic unity within its own ranks; and it has increased tremendously in numbers. The main questions are, therefore: under these conditions, how does the Party guard itself against ossification and stultification, and what kind of balance is maintained between its own forces.

The Growth in Party Membership. From a group of Bolshevik Social-Democrats numbering 8,400 in 1905, and only 23,600 in 1917, the Bolshevik Party — which was renamed Russian Communist Party (Bolsheviks) in 1918, then All-Union Communist Party (Bolsheviks) in 1925 — came to number 6 million members and candidates by 1946. As the following table shows, the Party has displayed a tendency toward progressive numerical growth, and the rate of increase became particularly accelerated at the beginning of the 'forties.[91]

DATE	PARTY MEMBERSHIP
1905	8,400
1917	23,600
1921	800,000
1922	532,000
1923	485,000
1924	735,000
1927	1,236,000
1930	1,972,000
1934	2,807,000
1939	2,477,000
1940	3,400,000
1941	3,876,000
1942	4,610,000
1944	5,000,000
1946	6,000,000

Together with its auxiliaries the Party numbers some 32 millions, or over one sixth of the population.[92] In its present dimensions, it represents a reversal of the conception prevalent in the early years of the regime, when the Soviet leaders considered a relatively small membership an indispen-

---

91. The figures on membership are based on the sources of note 7, p. 315; *The Communist International between the Fifth and Sixth World Congresses*, p. 495; *The U.S.S.R. at War* (New York, 1942), p. 44; *A.R.S.U.*, April 1941, p. 66, February 1946, pp. 69–70; *Bol'shevik*, No. 6 (1944), p. 2; *Pravda*, 19 February 1941, 16 May 1945.
92. See *supra*, pp. 140, 143.

sable condition for the Party's success.[93] It now comes closer than ever before to being a mass party, though even its present numbers do not alter essentially its nature as a revolutionary order comprising the select in the state.

This tremendous quantitative growth reflects in part the growth of the Soviet population, but is due primarily to the Party's desire to widen its base in the populace and keep up its role as 'leading kernel' in the expanding activities of the U.S.S.R. at home and abroad. If, on the one hand, increased admissions into the Party serve to reward Soviet citizens for patriotism and skill, it is obvious that on the other hand such admissions are employed by the Party to assimilate within its own ranks the best emerging talent in the country.

The Dynamism of the Party's Composition. Earlier we have detailed the establishment of a monopoly of power and of monolithism in its own ranks by the Party.[94] Even the introduction of the category of 'non-Party Bolsheviks' in the mid-'thirties, and the conduct of elections to the Soviets in the name of a 'bloc of Communists and non-Party men' cannot be properly interpreted as steps in diminution of the Party's monopoly on political leadership, but rather as an effort to broaden its popular appeal and widen its recruiting area. A ruling party, having no opposition parties with which to contend and having removed all organizational possibilities for conflicting factions to form in its midst, obviously stands in danger of ossification — of acquiring a sense of complacency in its power and of having its capacities for leadership dull or atrophy. The Soviet leaders seek to meet this danger through conscious pursuit of a quality of dynamism in the Party's composition.

The method is twofold: to attract and maintain a high proportion of younger persons, and to renovate periodically the membership of the Party and of its popular bodies. During the 'twenties and the 'thirties hundreds of thousands of members and candidates were expelled in Party

93. See Lenin, xxiii, p. 326; *VKP(b) v Rezol.* i, p. 582. 'The most general intra-Party task is not the quantitative enlargement of the Party ranks, but their qualitative improvement.' (*VKP(b) v Rezol.* i, p. 368 [1921].) 'We fear an excessive enlargement of the Party, because to a governmental party there invariably seek to attach themselves careerists and adventurers.' (Adoratsky in *E.G. i P.* i, p. 934.)

94. See *supra,* pp. 120–34. Even as individuals, former members of other political parties who were admitted to the Communist Party on fulfilment of special conditions progressively diminished in proportion. At the Eleventh Party Congress they still constituted 16.7% of the voting delegates. At subsequent congresses the percentage stood at 14.7 in 1923, 11.6 in 1924, 9 in 1927 and 1930, 8.6 in 1934, undoubtedly decreasing further in subsequent years. (See sources of note 7, p. 315.)

purges on grounds of insufficient alertness or devotion to Party tasks. At the same time, in addition to regular recruitment, special membership drives were carried out in 1924–5, 1926–7, 1930, and during the years of the recent war.[95] The process of membership renewal at Party conclaves is illustrated by the percentage of delegates attending the Party congress for the first time.[96]

PERCENTAGE OF DELEGATES ELECTED TO THE PARTY
CONGRESS FOR THE FIRST TIME

	ELECTED THE FIRST TIME	ELECTED A SECOND TIME	ELECTED A THIRD TIME
15th Party Congress (1927)	50.0		
16th Party Congress (1930)	58.0	15.3	8.6
17th Party Congress (1934)	48.5		

The percentage of first-time delegates was no doubt higher at the last Party congress, in 1939.

Earlier we noted the strength of youth in the Party cadres and the continuous decrease in members with underground status — the Bolshevik Old Guard — and members who entered the Party during the civil war. By 1945 two thirds of all the members and candidates of the Party were of recent Party status; a majority were complete newcomers, who were outside its ranks before the war.[97] There can be no doubt that, in greater or lesser measure, these renovationist practices will continue in the future.

The Circulation of the Political Élite. This dynamism of the Party's composition means that the balance between the diverse forces of the Party is held and controlled by the fairly stationary peak of the Party summit — the directorate comprising the Politbureau, Orgbureau, and Secretariat. It also means that except for this directorate, in which relatively few personnel changes have taken place since the end of the 'twenties, there is considerable circulation of the political élite in the Soviet Union. For the levels of the Party pyramid below the peak embrace members who hold leading positions in the soviets, the armed forces, and the economic and cultural enterprises, and the repeated turnover in the Party membership involves changes in the entire political-administrative personnel of the state — appointments to office, removals, transfers, promotions, and exclusions, which are designed to keep the managerial groups keyed to specified levels of performance.[98]

The criteria for staying and advancing in the ranks of the political élite

95. See *supra*, pp. 31, 33, 129–34.
96. See sources of note 7, p. 315.
97. See *Bol'shevik*, No. 6 (1944), p. 3, and *N.Y.T.* 5 June 1945.
98. See also *infra*, pp. 347–8.

are no longer years of Party membership, or even — in and by themselves — education and technical knowledge, on which so much store has been placed since 1929. A citizen's role in the recent conflict weighs heavily in the Party's scale of values, but is hardly the determining factor in assessment. The sole lasting criteria for political advancement, one may deduce from the practices that have prevailed in the last decade and a half, are and will continue to be skill and perfection in the execution of designated tasks in the service of the state, coupled with supreme devotion to the highest leadership of the Party and the government.

Fundamentally, the Party's position does not appear to have been weakened by the experience of the War. On the contrary, while it suffered great casualties among its members, it has come out of the conflict with an increased membership and heightened popular prestige. In the balance of forces at play in the Soviet state, the Party continues as before in the role of integrator, director, and adjuster, and there is nothing to indicate any change in its position in the immediate future.

(2) THE SOVIETS

Through several stages of development in the relationship between the soviets and the Party, the conception has become firmly established that the soviets serve the dual role of a primary transmission belt for the Party — linking the latter with the people — and a school of governance for the masses, drawing in and training wide sections of the citizenry in public administration. One of the major consequences of this functional conception has been the high rate of turnover in the membership of the soviets; another, the continued presence of a large percentage of non-Party people in the local soviets, as well as deliberate indulgence of a considerable proportion of non-Party members in the popular bodies of the central Soviet hierarchy, but not in the Council of Ministers or the collegia of the ministries. The soviets are not an independent political force, but a subordinate, auxiliary arm of the Party, helping it to rule the country and to identify its leadership with the interests of the people.

Renovation in the Membership of the Soviets. The rate of renewability in the membership of the soviets has always been high. In 1927, a fairly typical year for the 'twenties, deputies elected for the first time to the local soviets constituted 57.2 per cent of the membership of the village soviets, 37 per cent of the chairmen of village soviets, and 49.3 per cent of the membership of the county executive committees.[99] In 1931, the rate of

---

99. *XV S'ezd VKP(b)*, pp. 404–5.

renewability of the lower and middle links of the soviets was said to have stabilized at 50 per cent or more of the membership of these soviets.[100] In the Central Executive Committee of the R.S.F.S.R. the percentage of entirely new members coming in with each election has increased from 26.3 to 68.8 between 1922 and 1931, while in the Central Executive Committee of the U.S.S.R. it was stated to be 'over fifty per cent at all the convocations.'[101] Similarly, at the Congress of Soviets of the U.S.S.R., the percentage of deputies elected for the first time was given as 71.8 in 1931; 66.8 in 1929; 66.2 in 1927; and never less than 54.8 at the preceding congresses. All of the above figures were acclaimed as proof that 'great masses of the population go through a practical course in government.'[102] There can be little doubt that the turnover in membership has continued high in the soviets, although there is a recent tendency toward greater stability in their composition.

The Party's Numerical Strength in the Higher Executive Organs of the Soviets. The struggle over definition of the Party-soviets relationship and the emergence of the soviets as a subordinate yet close partner of the Party in the governance of the state[103] meant in practice increasing staffing of the highest, continuously operating, soviet organs with Party members, and a consequent merger of the summits of the two pyramids. Thus, since the early part of 1918 — when the Left Socialist-Revolutionists had left the Soviet government — the Sovnarkom, comprising the people's commissars as the heads of the various commissariats, has been continuously staffed with Party men. This also became the rule in the sovnarkoms of the Union republics. As for the other responsible officials of the commissariats — members of the collegia, directors of departments, and their assistants — Stalin indicated as early as 1924 that the percentage of communists among them had reached 86,[104] and this percentage has most likely long since reached the 100 mark.[105]

---

100. Kareva, op. cit. p. 37.
101. Ibid.
102. Ibid.
103. See *supra*, pp. 178–83.
104. *XIII S'ezd VKP(b)*, p. 120.
105. While continuous efforts were also made to augment the number of Party members among the general personnel of the commissariats or ministries, the pressure was less insistent. In 1927 the average percentage of Communists in the central commissariats was roughly 20%, representing an increase of only 7% in three years. (See the tables presented by Ordzhonikidze to the Party congress on 7 December 1927, *XV S'ezd VKP(b)*, pp. 402–3.) This percentage has probably doubled or tripled by now, but a considerable percentage of non-Communists remain among the lower personnel of the ministries.

The Predominance of Non-Party Members in the Local Soviets. A different situation has obtained in the local soviets and in the more popular bodies of the central soviets — the Congress of Soviets, the Central Executive Committee, and the Supreme Soviet. Because of the official conception of the soviets as 'a school of political education' and a medium to draw the Soviet people 'into administration of their socialist state,'[106] a high proportion of non-Party men was not only permitted but encouraged in the local soviets, although the top officers in the higher links of the local soviets are largely Communists. In 1927, the Party Central Committee demanded that the representation of non-Party workers and peasants at the congresses of Soviets should be increased, that 'new forces from the non-Party mass' should be promoted to more responsible work in the soviets, and that non-Party members must in the future constitute not less than one third of the membership in the county, provincial, and higher executive committees.[107] In consequence the percentage of non-Party people in the local soviets has remained large:[108]

PERCENTAGE OF NON–PARTY PEOPLE IN THE LOCAL SOVIETS

	1927	1931	1939
Village Soviets	87.4	85.4	
Chairmen of Village Soviets	65.9	41.0	Percentage
Presidia of Village Soviets		64.1	in
County Congresses of Soviets		56.3	local
County Executive Committees	40.5	34.7	Soviets
Chairmen of County Executive Committees		0.5	as a
Presidia of County Executive Committees		24.6	whole,
City Soviets		50.5	69.9
Chairmen of City Soviets		4.5	
Presidia of City Soviets		31.7	

It can also be seen from these figures that the lower the tier in the Soviet pyramid or the responsibility of the position in it, the higher the percentage of non-Party men.

The Progressive Increase in Non-Party Men in the Popular Federal Assemblies. Viewed over the entire period of the regime, a striking rise in the proportion of non-Party members has taken place in the popular federal assemblies of the Soviets, the memberships of which have comprised large representations from the localities.[109] Before the formation of the Union organs, the percentage of non-Party members at the Congress of Soviets rose from 1.4 in March 1918 to 3.5 in December 1919 and to 6.7

106. *P.S.* p. 519; *V.V.S.* 13 November 1939, p. 1.
107. *VKP(b) v Rezol.* II, pp. 173–4.
108. The figures in the following table are based on data in *XV S'ezd VKP(b)*, pp. 404–5; Kareva, op. cit. p. 31; Vasil'ev, loc. cit.
109. The figures and table given below are based on the first two sources of note 7, p. 315; *Sots. Zak.* No. 2, February 1938, pp. 12–15; *Izvestia,* 15 March 1946.

in December 1921. In subsequent years the percentage of non-Party members at the popular federal assemblies increased further three- and four-fold.

PERCENTAGE OF NON–PARTY PEOPLE IN THE POPULAR
FEDERAL ASSEMBLIES

	1922	1924	1925	1927	1929	1931	1935	1936
CONGRESS OF SOVIETS U.S.S.R.	5.9	10.0	21.9	27.3	27.4	24.7	21.0	28.0
CENTRAL EXECUTIVE COMMITTEE U.S.S.R.	2.6	9.0	15.9	30.3	28.2		28.3	

	1937			1946		
	TOTAL	COUNCIL OF THE UNION	COUNCIL OF NATIONALITIES	TOTAL	COUNCIL OF THE UNION	COUNCIL OF NATIONALITIES
SUPREME SOVIET U.S.S.R.	23.9	19.0	28.7	19.0	22.5	15.5

It will be noted that this percentage tends toward stabilization or some decrease, and that may well be the tendency in the future, reflecting the probable increase of the intelligentsia in the village and the assumption of more positions in the countryside by younger Party members.

No other basic changes loom in the position of the soviets in the political balance. The soviets will most likely continue in the role of a primary link between the Party and the populace, with perhaps a greater merger of forces and functions taking place at other levels, besides the summits, of the two pyramids. Occasional relaxation of some of the centralized features of the Soviet structure may occur, though the Party itself would in any case assure central guidance of the Soviet polity through its own established position.

(3) THE ARMY

The Army is not an independent political force. It was always regarded as an instrument of the dictatorship, with emphasis on national or international aims shifting in accordance with Party policy. For two decades there was a deliberate effort to favor workers in recruitment for certain services and the training of commanding personnel, but in the late 'thirties opportunities were equalized for all social groups. Separate nationality military formations have existed on a small scale from time to time, and some are planned for the future, to be closely integrated, however, within the Union military structure. The conception of an army divorced from the political process has never prevailed in the U.S.S.R., and there are many military men in the Party and soviet bodies. But the monopoly and monolithism principles of the Party have been enforced in the Army just as strictly as in all public organizations, and the Army is watched for possible Bonapartist tendencies and is not expected to 'play politics' as a separate and distinct entity. Through a constant increase of the Party element in the military services, perfection of the special political apparatus in the armed forces, and a number of material-psychological measures, the Party continues to maintain strong control over the military arm of the state. The prestige of the armed services has progressively mounted. While serious disaffection occurred among a considerable part of the commanding personnel in the 'thirties, the Army as a whole has been loyal to the regime and its present leadership, and is not likely to become a spearhead of political opposition to the latter.

The Accepted Conception of the Army. On the occasion of the tenth anniversary of the Red Army, in February 1928, Stalin spoke of 'three specific features of the Red Army.' The first and basic one, said he, was that 'it is the army of the emancipated workers and peasants, it is the army of the October Revolution, the army of the dictatorship of the proletariat'; secondly that it is 'the army of fraternity of the peoples' of the U.S.S.R., its whole being and structure resting on the idea of 'protecting the freedom and independence of the Socialist Republics that constitute the Soviet Union'; the third consists of 'the spirit of internationalism, the feelings of internationalism' in which the Red Army was trained from the moment it was born, 'in the spirit of respect for other nations, in the spirit of love and respect toward the workers of all countries, in the spirit of maintaining and confirming peace between countries.'[110] The first feature, Stalin went on to say, means that the Red Army would have back of it a strong home front; the second, that in a critical moment, it would be supported by all the Soviet nationalities; while the third feature makes it the army of the workers of all countries, and in case of attack on the Soviet Union, it would have friends and allies in all parts of the world.[111]

There are, thus, two aspects, a national and international one, in the accepted conception of the Red Army. The international aspect was predominant during the first half of the regime; the national has been almost exclusively emphasized ever since, especially during the recent war. In line with this emphasis, the name of the Red Army was changed to 'Soviet Army' in the summer of 1946.[112] But both aspects are components of the conception of the armed forces.[113]

---

110. *Bol'shevik,* No. 4 (1938), pp. 9–11.

111. Ibid.

112. *N.Y.T.* 21 September 1946.

113. At the Eighteenth Party Congress, in 1939, War Commissar Voroshilov cited Stalin's characterization of the Red Army, stating that the political work of the Army is based

The Social Composition of the Armed Forces. Soviet political theory and fear of serious repercussions in a largely peasant army, once collectivization of agriculture got under way, dictated a policy of 'proletarianizing' the armed forces. Consequently, for nearly two decades every effort was made by the Party to increase the number of workers in the rank and file and commanding personnel of the Army, and to allocate large proportions of worker-recruits to the more crucial arms.[114] But no substantial increase in the workers' percentage in the army was possible until the industrialization program of the first Five-Year Plan, initiated in 1927-8, began to take effect.

THE SOCIAL COMPOSITION OF THE ARMY
(in percentages) [115]

Year	SOCIAL ORIGINS OF THE RANK AND FILE			SOCIAL ORIGINS OF THE COMMANDING PERSONNEL		
	Workers	Peasants	Employees and Others	Workers	Peasants	Employees and Others
1918	14.1					
1921	14.8			12.0		
1923	15.7			13.6	52.7	33.7
1925	17.7					
1926	18.1	71.3	10.6	16.0	57.2	26.8
1927	19.8	63.4	16.8	22.4	56.0	21.6
1929	24.3	60.0	15.7	28.5		
1930	31.2	57.9	10.9	31.2		
1932	38.7			40.0		
1933	45.8	42.5	11.7	42.3		
1937	43.0					

Despite the increase of the 'proletarian kernel' in the army since the late 'twenties, it is obvious that the peasant-derived servicemen remained equally strong in numbers. At least until the 'thirties, they constituted a surprisingly strong element even in such specially watched parts of the service as the Navy, the military schools, and the Party organizations of the armed forces.[116] But as a result of collectivization, the nature of the peasant component of the Army changed radically in the 'thirties. Official

upon it. (*Pravda*, 15 March 1939. See also E. Aleksandrov, 'The Army of the Soviet People and the Capitalistic Encirclement,' pp. 58-9.)

114. An instruction enacted in 1925 called for a compulsory minimum of 50% 'proletarians' for the personnel of the armored and railroad troops, 40% in the air force, 30% in the signal corps, but only 12% for the cavalry and 8% for the infantry. (See Fedotoff White, *The Growth of the Red Army*, p. 260.)

115. See Fedotoff White, op. cit. pp. 205, 262, 296, 331, 368, 414; statements by Ordzhonikidze, Kaganovich, and Voroshilov, in *XV S'ezd VKP(b)*, pp. 398-9, *XVI S'ezd VKP(b)*, pp. 115, 512, *XVII S'ezd VKP(b)*, pp. 232-3.

116. Servicemen and students of peasant origin constituted 60.5% in the navy and 51% in the normal military schools in 1927, 32% in the Party organizations of the armed forces in 1928, as against 29.4%, 38% and 41%, respectively, of workers in the same categories. And the following table for 1926 reveals the great strength of the peasant

figures indicate that whereas in January 1930 only 5.3 per cent of the peasant-soldiers came from the collectivized peasantry, this percentage reached 76.7 in January 1934, and by 1937 non-collectivized peasants constituted no more than 2.3 per cent in the Army.[117]

The principle of social selectivity in the composition of the armed forces affected, however, the size of the Army's potential reserve. With the changes in the social structure detailed earlier, and the emergence of the Nazi threat, this principle was abandoned and the concept of 'class' gave place to the concept of 'the people' in the recruitment of the armed forces. The Constitution of 1936 (articles 132, 133) made universal military service the law of the land, and declared defense to be 'the sacred duty of every citizen of the U.S.S.R.' These principles were embodied in the universal military service law adopted 1 September 1939, and the military schools were thrown wide open to the citizenry without regard to social origin.

In a sense the change was presaged by the vast network of voluntary military organizations and a number of other practices introduced years before. Osoaviakhim — a voluntary, mass organization formed in 1927 on the basis of a merger of several organizations of civilians interested in military science, chemical defense, and aviation — has trained millions of citizens in air-raid protection, parachute jumping, marksmanship, skiing, and rudimentary military techniques, and offered its younger members regular pre-draft training. Since in 1930 only 35 per cent of its members were workers, despite the fact that it operated mainly in the cities, it is clear that not only peasants but members of the intelligentsia were among the chief beneficiaries of this training. From a membership of 2,950,000 in 1927, it grew to 5,100,000 by 1930, and, while its membership apparently stood still in the mid-'thirties, extraordinary interest in its work was subsequently taken by the Party and government. The membership increased to 13 million by 1945, with local branches in all factories, offices, farms, and institutions.[118] The work of Osoaviakhim,

---

element in the middle command as well as the high percentage of former Tsarist noncoms and officers, in the categories of 'Peasants' and 'Others':

	Workers	Peasants	Others
Highest Commanders	7.3	31.2	61.5
Senior Commanders	9.3	46.0	44.7
Middle Commanders	18.0	61.4	20.6

(Fedotoff White, op. cit. pp. 206, 216, 248, 324.)

117. XVII S'ezd VKP(b), pp. 232–3; Fedotoff White, op. cit. p. 414.
118. See XVI S'ezd VKP(b), p. 115; Gorshenin, 'Strengthen the Defense Organization Osoaviakhim,' pp. 31–9; A.R.S.U., August 1941, pp. 1–10; Kournakoff, Russia's Fighting Forces, pp. 58–9; E.B. 28 July 1945.

together with the relationships engendered between popular organizations and military units under the patronage system, and the regular pre-draft training reaching down to fifth-grade pupils under the 1939 law, raised military training of the populace in the U.S.S.R. to a point where it came close to approximating the concept of 'an armed people.'

It was this preparedness that enabled the U.S.S.R. to increase its armed forces considerably with the mounting threat of war and to mobilize millions of partly trained citizens when hostilities began. Counting less than 100,000 volunteers when it was officially formed, on 23 February 1918, the Red Army grew to a force of 4,100,000 in the course of the civil war. Following the demobilization at the end of 1921 from 1924 to 1934 it was left with a standing force of 562,000. On the Nazi rise to power in Germany, Stalin uttered the dictum (before the Seventeenth Party Congress in 1934) that 'in our times, it is not the custom to give any consideration to the weak — consideration is only given to the strong,'[119] and from then on the Red Army grew steadily in technical equipment and numbers. That year it was raised to 940,000 men, in 1935 to 1,300,000, by 1938 to about 2 million, and by 1939 to an estimated 5 million or more.[120] During the recent war it became the largest mass organization of the U.S.S.R., numbering perhaps upwards of 15 million at its greatest strength. While many millions are being demobilized, the Soviet leaders have indicated in their statements that the armed forces of the U.S.S.R. will remain strong.[121]

Currently, the Soviet Army consists primarily of young people, drawn from all social strata, and far better educated than their predecessors in the Tsarist Army or the Red Army of civil-war days. Former Tsarist officers, numerically strong in the Red Army during the civil war, and still constituting 10.6 per cent of the Soviet commanders in 1930,[122] are now reduced to a fraction of the officers corps. Likewise, Soviet commanders who won their spurs in the civil war, and formed the overwhelming majority of the highest and middle commanding personnel in 1934, have been greatly reduced in proportion by the purges of 1937-8,[123] and by the influx of younger officers who have matured in the recent con-

---

119. XVII S'ezd VKP(b), p. 13.
120. See VKP(b) v Rezol. I, pp. 438-9, 482-5; Voroshilov, in XVII S'ezd VKP(b), pp. 229-30, Pravda, 15 March 1939; Fedotoff White, op. cit. pp. 358-9; Kournakoff, op. cit. pp. 54, 84.
121. See N.Y.T. 23 June 1945.
122. XVII S'ezd VKP(b), p. 513; Fedotoff White, op. cit. pp. 206, 367.
123. Ibid. pp. 367, 390.

flict. The average age of the present marshals and generals at the beginning of the War was about 42.[124] As regards social origin, the honors
seem to be about equally divided between workers and peasants in the
ranks of the two dozen or more marshals.[125] Among the hundreds of
generals, there are probably more who derive from the peasantry than
from the working class, and a smaller proportion from the intelligentsia;
while in the ranks below the proportions may be more equalized, but
there are no specific data on these points.

The National Complexion of the Army. No figures on the national
composition of the Soviet Army in recent years are available,[126] and the
data on national military formations are somewhat scanty. Briefly, the
following can be said. A number of small national units, Moslem, Lettish,
Estonian, and other detachments, participated with the Red Army in the
civil war.[127] In 1923, the Party decided to create military schools in the
national republics and regions to train native military cadres for national
military formations, and to organize such separate formations at once
within nationalities that were permitted to serve in Tsarist times and,
consequently, had some military cadres.[128] The contribution of this step
toward internal peace, as well as defense, was duly taken into consideration; nor was sight lost of its possible effect on the national aspirations
of colonial peoples.[129] National military divisions were immediately organized or consolidated in Transcaucasia, the Ukraine, and Byelorussia, and
national regiments were created in the Tatar and Bashkir republics. In
the following six years national regiments were also established in the
Tadzhik, Uzbek, Turkmen, and Kazakh republics and smaller national
localities.[130] The number of national military units increased considerably
in the early 'thirties.[131] But they were entirely abolished about 1937–8, and
their personnel was merged with the rest of the Red Army. Explaining
this change, Voroshilov told the Party congress in March 1939 that the
existence of such military formations, permanently attached to their

124. Kournakoff, op. cit. p. 106.
125. See pamphlet by Burroughs, *Who's Who in the Red Army.*
126. In 1925, the national percentages in the Army were indicated as follows: Russians — 64, Ukrainians — 22, Byelorussians — 4, others — 10. (Fedotoff White, op. cit.
p. 273.)
127. See *supra,* note 77, p. 75.
128. *VKP(b) v Rezol.* I, pp. 540–41.
129. Ibid; Fedotoff White, op. cit. p. 272.
130. *VKP(b) v Rezol.* I, p. 540; Fedotoff White, op. cit. pp. 202, 273; Kournakoff,
op. cit. p. 56.
131. There were 10 Ukrainian, 3 Byelorussian, 4 Transcaucasian, and lesser numbers of
other national formations. (Fedotoff White, op. cit. p. 285.)

respective territories, contradicted the basic principles of the new Constitution and the principle of extraterritoriality in the recruitment of the armed forces.[132] It is obvious, however, that the revelations of the 1937–8 trials concerning separatist plots in some of the national republics had a lot to do with the liquidation of the national military formations.

Only a few small national contingents, operating as parts of armies, existed during the recent war. They are not to be confused with the 'Ukrainian,' 'Byelorussian,' and other armies in the war, which were Union armies bearing the names of particular fronts. The creation of separate military formations in the Union republics is called for by the 1944 constitutional reform. But, although national military cadres are available and these formations are expected to add to the armed might and international prestige of the U.S.S.R.,[133] their actual establishment is apparently proceeding very cautiously. When such formations were first decided on in 1923, it was specifically provided that 'the Party and social composition of the national detachments, and especially of the commanding staff, should be sufficiently safeguarded.'[134] Delicate questions of national sensibilities, the balance of national influences, external relations, and the effect on the Army as an intergrating and assimilating medium, are all involved in this measure. When established in the Union republics, these military formations will probably contain national contingents of the more compact minorities within these republics. This policy would implement further minority rights, serve as an additional means to keep up some sense of internationalism, and indirectly contribute toward the role of the Union as ultimate arbiter on nationality problems. Generally, their organization will no doubt reflect a careful consideration of the interrelationships between the national, social, and Party forces existing in the various localities.

While the Russians play a predominant role, there is no national discrimination with regard to admission and promotion in the Army. There are generals, colonels, or lower-ranking officers in the Soviet armed forces representing practically every nationality in the Union. A partial statement of awards granted to members of the various nationalities in the Red Army, from the beginning of the War till the last part of 1944, gives the following figures: [135]

---

132. *Pravda*, 15 March 1939.
133. See *Bol'shevik*, Nos. 3–4 (1944), pp. 12, 19–20.
134. *VKP(b) v Rezol.* p. 540.
135. Editorial, *Bol'shevik*, No. 23–4 (1944), p. 6.

AWARDS TO REPRESENTATIVES OF SOVIET NATIONALITIES

	RECIPIENTS OF THE TITLE HERO OF THE SOVIET UNION (22 JUNE 1941–1 OCTOBER 1944)	RECIPIENTS OF ORDERS AND MEDALS (22 JUNE 1941–1 DECEMBER 1944)
Total Number of Recipients	5,901	over 3,000,000
Russians	3,798	2,183,326
Ukrainians	961	441,806
Byelorussians	105	111,253
Tatars	93	59,500
Kazakhs	57	34,342
Jews	52	59,003
Uzbeks	39	24,185
Georgians	39	19,337
Armenians	33	24,856
Mordvinians	32	
Bashkirs	27	10,570
Chuvashs	22	18,323
Azerbaijanians	18	12,460 [136]
Osetins	16	
Turkmenians	9	
Maris	9	
Tadzhiks	7	
Estonians	6	
Karelians	6	
Komis	6	
Letts	4	

Altogether, representatives of 172 nationalities are stated to have received military orders and medals.

The Strength of the Party Element in the Armed Forces. Even more compelling than the former policy of 'proletarianization,' in the eyes of the Party leaders, was the need to increase the strength of the Party element in the armed forces. Not until the early 'thirties, however, did the Party succeed in outbalancing the non-Party element among the rank and file of the Army.[137]

PERCENTAGE OF PARTY–AFFILIATED PERSONS IN THE RANK AND FILE OF THE RED ARMY

YEAR	KOMSOMOL	PARTY	TOTAL PARTY AFFILIATED	NON-PARTY
1921		10.0		
1924			16.0	84.0
1925	10.7	12.1	22.8	77.2
1926	16.3	13.6	29.9	70.1
1927			36.0	64.0
1928			37.0	63.0
1930	18.4	15.9	34.3	65.7
1933	24.0	35.0	59.0	41.0
1934	23.9	25.6	49.5	50.5
1939			over 50.0	below 50.0

136. This is only a partial list. For figures on awards to 56 more nationalities, referring, however, to an earlier date, see Minz, *The Red Army*, p. 142.

137. See *XVII S'ezd VKP(b)*, p. 232; *Pravda*, 15 March 1939; Fedotoff White, op. cit. pp. 250, 322–3.

Among the commanding personnel, the percentage of those with Party affiliations increased more rapidly, and even by 1927 Party members constituted a majority of the commanders in the Red Army. In December 1927, Ordzhonikidze presented to the Party congress the following picture of growing Party strength in 'the brain of the army': [138]

PERCENTAGE OF PARTY MEMBERS IN THE COMMANDING
PERSONNEL OF THE RED ARMY

1920	10.5
1921	20.0
1922	22.5
1923	29.6
1924	31.8
1925	43.3
1926	47.0
1927	54.0

At the beginning of 1930 the percentage was 52.5, and in July 1934 it reached 67.8; these figures together with 4 per cent Komsomol members among the commanders make the percentages of Party-affiliated in the command 56.6 and 71.8, respectively, in the two years. The percentages were even greater in the technical arms, having increased from 70.1 to 84.3 in the tank divisions, and from 55.9 to 84.6 in the air force, between 1930 and 1934.[139] In some specialized branches of the Army the percentage of Communists among the commanding personnel reached over 90, and even most of the former Tsarist officers, said Voroshilov in 1934, had become Party members.[140] Commanders comprised the greater part of the Party members in the Army, while the non-commissioned officers and rank and file constituted a majority of the Komsomol members in the Army.[141] Despite the extensive purges of the preceding years, Voroshilov told the Party congress in 1939 that more than half of the Army consisted of Party and Komsomol members, and the rest of the servicemen, he added, were also 'genuine non-Party Bolsheviks whose lives belong entirely to the Red Army and their socialist Fatherland.'[142] The top level of the command was almost certainly 100 per cent Communist at the outbreak of the War.

In the course of the War, the Party sustained tremendous membership losses, owing to the high casualty rate among its members in uniform. It lowered its admission requirements and carried out several intensive

138. *XV S'ezd VKP(b)*, p. 398.
139. *XVII S'ezd VKP(b)*, p. 232.
140. *XVI S'ezd VKP(b)*, p. 513.
141. Fedotoff White, op. cit. p. 323.
142. *Pravda*, 15 March 1939.

membership drives, concentrating on the armed forces.[143] Long regarded by the Party leaders as a school of political indoctrination, for the peasant boys in particular,[144] the Army now became the largest recruiting ground for Party membership as well. The pressure was particularly great to enroll decorated men and officers winning rapid promotions.[145] Thus, by the end of the War, a majority of the Party's own membership consisted of members recruited during the War from the ranks of the armed forces.

The Nature of the Army's Participation in Politics. The conception that an army's business is to fight and that it need have no share in politics has never taken root in the Soviet Union. The constitution (article 138) specifically provides that citizens serving in the armed forces have the right to elect and be elected on equal terms with all other citizens. Many Red Army men have in fact been elected to soviets, and citizens holding public office have been frequently enabled to continue to discharge their public duties, as far as possible, even after they have been called to the colors.[146]

Generally, the Army is less represented in the Party than in the soviets, and military men have been less in evidence in the high Party councils since the second decade of the regime, especially since the late 'thirties. Outside of General Bulganin, who is a political appointee of recent years, Marshal Voroshilov is the only real military man in the Politbureau. A relatively small number of marshals and generals are members or candidates of the Party Central Committee. A much larger number of military men are elected to the Party congress. On the other hand, there is a conscious attempt to honor deserving higher officers with election to the Supreme Soviet, and at the same time publicly associate them with the decisions enacted. There are 155 Army officers in the Supreme Soviet elected in 1946, comprising 11.5 per cent of the deputies. The military in the Supreme Soviet include almost all the marshals — 20 in number — 11 army generals, 5 admirals, and dozens of generals of lower ranks, colonels, and majors. The Presidium of the Supreme Soviet contains one Army man at present, Marshal Budenny, and there are less than a dozen military men among the ministers, half of them former civilians put in uniform during the War.

High-ranking generals have participated at diplomatic receptions. They have been called in to take part in international military consultations, and

143. See *Pravda*, 26 January 1942, 22 May and 13 February 1943; *N.Y.T.* 4 June 1945.
144. See *XVI S'ezd VKP(b)*, p. 115.
145. See *N.Y.T.* 4 June 1945.
146. Minz, op. cit. p. 108.

several have acted as chairmen of Allied Control Commissions. But generally they are expected to concentrate their attention on their own tasks, and participate in political administration and consultation only within bounds requested and delimited by the Party. The rules on factionalism, discussions, and other forms of political activeness apply to the military perhaps even more strictly than to other groups. Army men are taught to understand that the Army is the offspring of the Party, living and operating by the rules and laws laid down for it by the Party and the government. And the Army is carefully watched not only against mass disaffection, but against any taint of Bonapartism in its officer cadres and any suggestion of an attempt to raise it into an autonomous entity, free from Party control.

The Maintenance of Party Control Over the Armed Forces. Party control over the Army is maintained by an elaborate system of material and psychological arrangements, designed to keep the entire personnel loyal and satisfied, to prevent any political opposition or moods of exclusiveness from developing in the Army, and to check such tendencies if they do develop.

For the rank and file, food, quarters, clothing, pay, cultural outlets, and training for useful trades while in service have constantly improved in the past twenty-five years.[147] With the progressive professionalization of the service, the material rewards and status of the commanding personnel have also been made more and more attractive. In the ten-year period between 22 September 1935 (when military ranks up to grade of general were established) and the end of 1945, personal ranks — including the ranks of marshal, general, and admiral — special decorations and uniforms, obligatory saluting, epaulettes, orderlies, and other forms of distinction between officers and men were progressively introduced, with the avowed purpose of strengthening discipline in the Army and adding to the military dignity and authority of the commanding personnel.[148]

These material conditions of army life are co-ordinated with a most extensive system of political indoctrination, permeating all levels of the services. In charge of this work is the Political Administration of the Army, a branch of the Ministry of the Armed Forces, which has for a long time held simultaneously the status of a department of the Central Committee of the Party. The Political Administration operates through political officers — formerly known as political commissars and military

---

147. See *Pravda,* 15 March 1939; Fedotoff White, op. cit. pp. 201, 344, 402.
148. Ibid.; Kournakoff, op. cit. p. 106; *Izvestia,* 17, 28 January 1943; *N.Y.T.* 3 September 1945.

commissars — who have the status of deputy commanders in every unit, from front or army group down to regiment and battalion; it carries on its work through the commanders themselves in company units.

The system of political commissars has had quite a checkered career.[149] Originally the institution of political commissar, then known as military commissar (*Voenkom*), was established early in 1918 to watch over, and also to protect, Tsarist officers serving the Red Army, or as the official order put it 'to see to it that the Army does not become a thing apart from the entire Soviet system and that the various military establishments do not become foci of conspiracies or instruments against workers and peasants.'[150] The commissar was the official *alter ego* of the commander in each unit, and his signature and assent were required for the validity of military orders. This system lasted until 1924, when the urge of the commanders to take full control of their units was recognized by a declaration of the Central Committee, admitting the 'one-man management' principle (*edinonachalie*)[151] for the structure of the Red Army. In practice a majority of the commanders became single managers of their units during the period of 1924–37, with a subordinate assistant on political matters conducting the actual political work of the unit. The rest of the commanders had commissars functioning side by side with them in their units.[152] In connection with the purges of 1937–8, military commissars were reinstituted (in 1937) in all the units as 'the eyes and ears of the Party and the government in the Army,' operating on a complete footing of equality with the commanders.[153] This new duality of control has apparently led to extensive friction between commanders and commissars, and the commissars were abolished on 12 August 1940, only to be reintroduced again on 16 July 1941, when tens of thousands of new, non-Party officers were enrolled in the Army on the outbreak of war. Finally, on 9 Octboer 1942, the military commissars were again abolished and the principle of unity of command was re-established. The explanation offered is that the new commanders have proved 'quite mature both politically and militarily' and that it was best 'to place full responsibility for all the activities of his unit upon the commander.'[154]

---

149. The evolution of this system has been traced in the excellent work of Fedotoff White, *The Red Army, passim;* see also, R.S.M., 'Red Army "Morale Builders," ' *A.R.S.U.* October–November 1941, pp. 11–24.
150. Cited in Fedotoff White, op. cit. p. 74.
151. See *supra,* pp. 288–93.
152. R.S.M. op. cit. pp. 13–14.
153. *Pravda,* 8 September 1938.
154. Minz, op. cit. p. 110.

The vast political apparatus in the Army was not disbanded with the new reform. Former military commissars and other political workers in the Army, many of whom have acquired regular military skills following repeated urgings by the Party since 1934,[155] were given military ranks and status, and, as deputies to the commanders, they carry on as before the work of building the morale and guarding the loyalty of the armed forces. This apparatus is carefully chosen for proved devotion to the Party leadership. In case of a serious threat to the regime developing in the midst of the Army, it would have the backing of the troops of the Ministry of Internal Affairs, which — though now intergrated in standing, uniform, and ranks with the regular Army machine — are composed 100 per cent of Party members, specially recruited on the basis of absolute loyalty to the existing leadership. In the past, this leadership has proved capable of executing transfers, removals, and other redispositions in the Army, including changes in the highest command, and there is no reason to doubt that it would be able to do so in the future. Relinquishment of Party control over the Army is most unlikely. But the forms of the exercise of this control, a repeated source of friction in the past, will probably undergo further changes to meet the inherently difficult problem of maintaining Party control and at the same time preventing it from acting as a fetters on the initiative and skill of the military commanders.

Lastly, we may note a number of measures adopted during and since the War, which tend to assert further the Party's supremacy and counteract any excessive sense of exclusiveness on the part of the professional élite of the Army. In the autumn of 1943, several civilian services were given the prestige of rank and uniform: the employees of the railroad network, the procurators, members of the Foreign Affairs Ministry and the foreign service.[156] In addition to Stalin, a number of top Party officials were endowed with high military ranks. Zhdanov, Kaganovich, Khrushchev, Shcherbakov, and later Bulganin of the Politbureau and many close associates of Stalin in the Central Committee were made generals. In July 1945, Beria, a member of the Politbureau and then head of the Ministry of Internal Affairs, was made a marshal, while other ranks, orders, and medals were conferred on his aides in the ministry.[157] The most significant item in this group of measures is the singular emphasis given in the press and public statements since the latter part of 1943 to the role of the Party in the War and of Stalin as embodiment of the supreme *military* leader-

---

155. See *XVII S'ezd VKP(b)*, p. 233.
156. See *Izvestia*, 5 and 25 September, 9 October 1943.
157. *Pravda*, 19 June 1944, 14 October 1945, 6 July 1946; *A.R.S.U.* February 1946, p. 60.

ship. While the military leaders who emerged during the War are praised as a group — very rarely as individuals — it is Stalin's role in bringing them out and co-ordinating their strategy and operations that is given the highest emphasis.[158]

Basically, the Army as a group has remained loyal to the regime in crises. Few troops joined the enemy camp in the War, and the misbehavior of some units in occupied countries was more a front-line phenomenon than an expression of political disaffection. Discipline, moreover, has been tightened more and more in the ranks of the Army, as in all organized groups. In the light of all that has been detailed above, it does not seem likely that the Army would become a focus of serious political opposition in the near future, unless unity were broken within the ranks of the highest Party leadership itself.

3. IDEOLOGICAL FORCES

(1) TRADITION

In the course of the recent war, and in some fields a number of years before, a return to traditional patterns has taken place in the U.S.S.R. Its effect has been felt particularly with regard to Russian lore, the family, the church, and the question of Slavic solidarity. It is, however, only a partial and controlled return, which would not permit tradition to take the place of the dominant ideology, but only to blend with and become a part of the latter. Since the middle of 1943, and especially since the end of the war, the emphasis has shifted back from tradition to ideology.

Russian Lore. Guard units, cadet schools, ranks and orders in the Army; the re-establishment of a school system, which has abandoned coeducation, curtailed political education in the lower grades, and restored discipline, uniforms, and a large part of the pre-revolutionary curriculum;[159] the rehabilitation in the teaching of history of Russia's past rulers who consolidated the country into a centralized state; and the glorification of Russia's cultural and scientific achievements — all have marked a consider-

---

158. 'All the successes of our army in the patriotic war are inseparably connected with the name of the Supreme Commander-in-Chief, Marshal of the Soviet Union comrade Stalin . . . The unsurpassed strategy of the patriotic war, the brilliant operations of our troops — are the genius creations of the great Stalin. He was raising and educating the Red Army in the years of peaceful construction. He is raising and perfecting it in the days of the war . . . The Supreme Commander-in-Chief, Marshal of the Soviet Union comrade Stalin, is in full measure the father and leader of the Red Army, the creator of all of its great victories.' (*Bol'shevik*, No. 3–4 (1944), pp. 23–4.)

159. See Timasheff, 'The Soviet School Experiment,' pp. 72–87.

able return to the traditional national values of pre-Soviet Russia. Their intensive propagation by the Soviet press during the critical years of 1941–2, helped to rally the populace and stem the tide of invasion. But even in those years, there was some differentiation in approach, with the publications catering to factory workers and to Party and Komsomol members and concentrating chiefly on orthodox ideology.[160] More general emphasis on the latter began with the turn in the fortunes of war, and currently there is a definite attempt to combat the nationalist moods that took hold during the War.

The Family. Since the mid-'thirties there is a new emphasis in the Soviet Union on the family as a social unit, on parental authority, and on the worth of motherhood. Monogamy is declared a *must* under socialism; and complete equality and mutual respect between spouses, and love and culture in the family circle have become the signs of the model Soviet family.[161] Under the system of separate schools for boys and girls, inaugurated in 1942–3 on the ground that the different rates of physical and mental development of boys and girls make such separation necessary, the curriculum for boys is to be concentrated on technical subjects. Girls are to be trained in pedagogy, handicrafts, domestic science, personal hygiene, and the care of children; essentially they are being prepared for the role of mother and for a career in the home, if they should choose such.[162] Large families are encouraged through the taxes on childless persons or families with no more than two children, and substantial state subsidies as well as special government orders and medals for mothers of many children.[163] At the same time mothers are protected by special legislation concerning working hours, leave and compensation prior to and after childbirth, as well as free clinics, nurseries, and kindergartens. Divorce is permitted, but with the strict injunction that it is not to be taken lightly. There is a rising scale of fees in multiple divorces, and, above all, in place of the former practice of mere registration with an administrative bureau on the whim of one of the parties, the granting of a divorce is now a matter for decision by a court on the merits of the case; and any license is strongly condemned.[164]

---

160. See Werth, 'The Outlook in the U.S.S.R.,' pp. 29–30.

161. Svetlov, op. cit. pp. 44–58.

162. Timasheff, 'The Soviet School Experiment,' p. 82; Medynsky, 'Schools and Education in the U.S.S.R.,' pp. 290–91.

163. See Decree of 8 July 1944, *Izvestia,* 9 July 1944; *E.B.* 25 July 1944.

164. Ibid.; Svetlov, op. cit. pp. 55–8. No stigma of illegitimacy, however, is attached to children born out of wedlock. They take the mother's family name and enjoy equal rights and privileges with all other children.

All this is a far cry from the instability of family relations that was so frequent in earlier years.

The Church.[165] The recent war gave a strong impetus to the *rapprochement* between Church and State in the U.S.S.R. which was begun in 1936. The constitution adopted that year, it may be recalled, reiterated the principle of separation of Church and State, first proclaimed in 1917 and embodied in previous constitutions. 'In order to ensure to citizens freedom of conscience,' it declared, 'the Church in the U.S.S.R. is separated from the State, and the School from the Church. Freedom of religious worship and freedom of anti-religious propaganda, is recognized for all citizens' (article 124). But at the same time, the constitution restored legal rights to the clergy along with other formerly disfranchised citizens (article 135). There were other signs of a new tolerance, interrupted, however, by the purges of 1937–8.[166] Anti-religious propaganda continued, though beginning with 1939 it was considerably restrained.

The trend toward reconciliation was accentuated by the outbreak of the War. At the very outset of hostilities all the religious denominations of the Soviet Union, and the Russian Orthodox Church in particular, pledged support to the government in the war effort. The Acting Patriarch Sergius, and the other prelates of the Russian Orthodox Church, repeatedly appealed to their followers to rise in defense of the country, condemned collaboration with the enemy, called on the Balkan Slavs and Greeks to rally against the common invader, collected huge funds and gifts in kind for the Red Army, and actively participated in the civilian defense program.[167] Moreover, in several special messages to Stalin, they called him 'the wise God-willed leader of the peoples of our great Union' and expressed their complete and abiding loyalty to the government.[168]

The government responded by suspending the anti-religious publications in the autumn of 1941, appointing a year later Metropolitan Nicholas of Kiev to an official commission for the investigation of crimes committed by the German invaders, and awarding defense medals to members of the clergy, including the highest prelates, for their share in civilian defense

---

165. For the status of the Church before the recent war, see Curtiss, *Church and State in Russia, 1900–1917;* Hecker, *Religion under the Soviets;* Timasheff, *Religion in Soviet Russia.*

166. Melish, 'Religious Developments in the Soviet Union,' pp. 282–3.

167. Ibid.; *Pravda o Religii v Rossii, passim;* E.B. 12 January and 27 June 1942, 3 February 1943; *Izvestia,* 12 September 1943, 24 October 1944.

168. *Izvestia,* 10 November and 29 December 1942, 21 May 1944; E.B. 23 May and 6 June 1944.

measures.[169] On 4 September 1943, Stalin and Molotov received in audience Acting Patriarch Sergius, together with Metropolitans Alexei of Leningrad and Nicholas of Kiev; and in response to the prelates' statement of intention to convene a council of bishops in order to elect a Patriarch and form a Holy Synod, Stalin expressed the government's sympathy with these objectives. Four days later, Sergius was elected Patriarch of Moscow and All Russia by a council of nineteen bishops, and on 12 September he was officially enthroned in the presence of the Archbishop of York, who came on a special visit to the Russian Orthodox Church.[170] At the same time a Holy Synod was established, to function under the Patriarch and publication was begun of the *Journal of the Moscow Patriarchate*.[171]

On 7 October 1943, the government set up at the Sovnarkom a Council for Affairs of the Russian Orthodox Church, to maintain contact with the Patriarchate in regard to all matters requiring government decision and to supervise the implementation of legislation concerning the Russian Orthodox Church.[172] And on 30 June 1944 a similar Council for Affairs of the Religious Denominations was established to act as a liaison body between the government and the Roman Catholic, Protestant, Jewish, Mohammedan, and other religious groups not affiliated with the Orthodox Church.[173]

Following the death of Patriarch Sergius on 15 May 1944, an Assembly (*Sobor*) or General Council of the Russian Orthodox Church was convened during 31 January–4 February 1945 to elect a successor. Present at this Assembly, in addition to 3 Metropolitans, 41 archbishops and bishops, and 126 representatives of the clergy and laity of the U.S.S.R., as well as the Catholicos-Patriarch of Georgia, were the Patriarchs of Alexandria and Antioch, representatives of the Patriarchs of Constantinople and Jerusalem, and representatives of the Serbian and Rumanian Orthodox Churches.[174] The government sent G. G. Karpov, chairman of the Council for Affairs of the Russian Orthodox Church, to address the Assembly, and he expressed the conviction that the decisions of the Assembly would 'contribute to the strengthening of the Church and will serve as an important point of departure for the further development of the activities

169. *N.Y.T.* 6, 7 October 1941, 5 November 1942; *E.B.* 23 May and 20 October 1944.
170. *Izvestia*, 5, 12 September 1943; *Pravda*, 9 September 1943; *N.Y.T.* 13, 15, 18, 19, 23 and 24 September and 11 October 1943.
171. See *Moscow Daily News*, 8 September 1943.
172. See *Pravda*, 8 October 1943; *N.Y.T.* 8 October 1943, 12 August 1944; *The Call of the Russian Church*, p. 13.
173. *Pravda*, 1 July 1944.
174. *The Call of the Russian Church*, pp. 3–6.

of the Church aimed at assisting the Soviet people in the achievement of the major historical tasks which confront it.' Karpov concluded by promising that his council would 'take every measure in the future to eliminate all obstacles in the way of the exercise by Soviet citizens of the freedom of conscience proclaimed by the constitution.'[175] On 2 February the Assembly unanimously elected the *locum tenens,* Metropolitan Alexei, as Patriarch of Moscow and All Russia, and he was enthroned two days later.[176] Before dispersing, the Assembly sent a message of thanks to the Soviet government and issued separate appeals to the Russian Orthodox Church, to Christians the world over, and to the nations of the whole world, calling on everyone to rally for the destruction of Fascism and pray for final victory over the enemy.[177] The following spring representatives of the Moscow Patriarchate paid return visits to the Orthodox Churches of Bulgaria and Yugoslavia, and to the Church of England, while the Patriarch himself visited the Eastern Patriarchs of Antioch, Jerusalem, and Alexandria.[178]

Thus, without any change in the constitution or existing legislation, a place was found for the Church in the Soviet scheme of things. Both Church and State have gained from the new relationship. The Church has emerged from its semi-surreptitious existence and has won official recognition to a much larger extent than before. It obtained the right to establish theological schools, print religious publications, and open more churches, where it could prove the need for such.[179] Also conceded was the right of parents to teach religion to their children in the privacy of their homes or have them instructed in groups by priests in private fashion in the homes of the latter.[180] In consequence of its improved status, the Russian Orthodox Church won unity in its own ranks and communion with other Orthodox groups in the U.S.S.R. The splinter group of the Renovated or Living Church dissolved itself, its clergy and parishes submitting to the Patriarchate. The Greek Orthodox Church of Carpatho-

175. Ibid. pp. 10–13.
176. Ibid.
177. Ibid. pp. 18–31. The Appeal to the Nations of the Whole World began with the words: 'Representatives of the Orthodox Autocephalous Churches gathered at the General Council of the Russian Orthodox Church held in Moscow . . . having considered the international situation, raise their voices against those — especially the Vatican — who are attempting to shield Hitler Germany from the responsibility for the crimes she has committed.' (Ibid. p. 31; see also p. 3, and *Russky Golos,* 8 April 1944.)
178. *Izvestia,* 10, 13 April and 9, 13, 20 June 1945.
179. See *E.B.* 20 April 1944; *N.Y.T.* 12 August 1944; *Russky Golos,* 18 December 1944, 27 January 1945.
180. See *N.Y.T.* 15 September 1944; *Christian Science Monitor,* 30 September 1944.

Russia; the Uniate Churches of the Western Ukraine, which have submitted to the authority of Rome since 1596 and embrace some six million
adherents; [181] and many smaller Orthodox churches scattered in Russian
émigré communities in Western Europe, the Near East, the Americas,
and the Far East, likewise rejoined the jurisdiction of the Moscow Patriarchate, while the autonomous Orthodox Churches of Georgia and Armenia renewed their communion with the Russian Orthodox Church.[182]
Lastly, the Russian Orthodox Church has taken the path of a *rapprochement* with the Anglican Church,[183] and has again acquired first place
among the eight Eastern Orthodox Churches, emerging as the leading
force in World Orthodoxy.

On its part, the government gained, during a critical period in the
state's struggle for survival, the valuable support of the considerable body
of believers still existing in the U.S.S.R.[184] The regularized relationship
gives the government better means of surveillance and control over the
scope of the Church's activities. And through the Church's newly won
prestige and relations abroad, the Soviet government obtained a sought-
after counterweight to the Vatican in the religious sphere, and has won
considerable influence in the Orthodox communities of the Balkans and
the Near East. In the Moslem world, apparently a much lesser degree
of influence has accrued to the Soviet government from its friendlier
attitude toward Moslem religious centers in the U.S.S.R., probably because

181. For the Vatican-Soviet dispute concerning the Uniates, see *N.Y.T.* 7, 13 and 19 March
     1946; *Izvestia,* 27 January 1946; *E.B.* 16 April 1946. The text of the letter of the
     Uniate *Sobor* in Lvov to Stalin, dated 8 March 1946, and informing him of the de-
     cision to break with Rome and rejoin the Russian Orthodox Church, is given in *Russky
     Golos,* 19 March 1946.
182. See *N.Y.T.* 9 May and 17 December 1944; *Izvestia,* 14 December 1944; *Zhurnal
     Moskovskoi Patriarkhii,* Nos. 2, 3, 10 (1944); *Russky Golos,* 10 March 1945. See also
     Anderson, *People, Church and State in Modern Russia,* pp. 166–83.
183. See Anderson, op. cit. pp. 186–7, 206–7.
184. In 1932 Yaroslavsky estimated the number of believers in the Soviet Union at 100
     million, or more than 50% of the population. This percentage was probably smaller,
     but still very high at the time of the outbreak of the war. In 1941 there were reported
     to be 30,000 religious associations, 8,338 places of worship, and 52,442 ministers, of
     all denominations. There were 4,225 Orthodox churches and 5,665 priests, as compared
     with 46,457 and 50,960, respectively, at the time of the revolution; 28 Orthodox
     bishops and 38 Orthodox monasteries in 1941, as compared with 130 bishops and
     1,026 monasteries in 1917. (See Anderson, op. cit. pp. 17, 115–16, 159.) Another
     estimate indicates that the figures above on places of worship and ministers comprised:
     1,744 Roman Catholic churches with 2,309 priests; 1,000 Evangelical societies; 1,011
     synagogues and 2,559 rabbis; and 1,312 mosques with 8,052 mullahs. (See Melish,
     op. cit. p. 283.) This would reduce the figure for Orthodox churches by about one
     thousand.

the social and economic changes brought about by the Soviet regime cut deeper into traditional Moslem modes of living than was the case with other religious groups.

Does the *modus vivendi* arrived at point toward a policy of augmenting the force of religion in Soviet society in the future? Will the State permit loyalty to the Church to grow stronger than loyalty to itself? The answer seems to lie in the negative. While the leaders of the Party have come to recognize the persistence of religious faith among sections of the populace, and have accorded the Church a place in the State, they remain fundamentally opposed to religion and other teachings that they believe to be anti-scientific or supernatural in content.[185] The most responsible positions in the state are occupied by Party members, who are required to be non-religious. While freedom of worship is permitted, it is not the same as freedom of political organization, and the Church as an organized group can only play a political role if, when, and as the state wills it. The chief strength of the Church is in peasant communities, largely among older people and women, and it is there that the Party expects its modernizing efforts and the passage of time to have the greatest effect. The Church has gained greater access to the young than it had before, and it possesses the appeals of its traditional pageantry and symbolism. But as against the private instruction that is now permitted, there is the vast force of the school system, the Komsomol and Pioneer organizations, the radio, press, and official pronouncements — all propagating the materialist outlook of the accepted ideology; and there is the powerfully organized pageantry and symbolism of the Party, soviet, and related bodies. It is doubtful, therefore, whether the Church will be able to do more than hold its own in the future.

Slavic Solidarity. The recent war years have also witnessed the birth of a positive attitude toward Slavic solidarity on the part of the Soviet leaders. The Nazis' openly proclaimed design to reduce the Slavs to a status of serfdom has induced a feeling of unity among Slavic peoples who had hitherto stood widely apart. Organizationally, it took the form of an All-Slav Committee — established in Moscow on 10–11 August 1941 at a meeting initiated by refugee representatives of various Slav countries — which

---

185. In May 1943, answering queries of propagandists serving with the Red Army, Kalinin stated: 'One must remember that we do not persecute anyone for religion. We believe that religion is an error and are combating it by enlightenment. Since religion still grips considerable strata of the population, and some people are deeply religious, we cannot combat it by ridicule. Of course, if some young people find it amusing, it is not so terrible. It is very important, however, that this laughter should not develop into mockery.' (*Sputnik Agitatora*, No. 10 (May 1943), p. 8. See also *N.Y.T.* 17 June 1943.)

has actively sought to promote united efforts by the Slavic peoples of Europe, and by Slavic groups and organizations everywhere, for the defeat of the Nazi invaders.[186] Politically, the strongest expression of this solidarity are the treaties of friendship, mutual assistance, and post-war collaboration between the U.S.S.R. and Czechoslovakia, Yugoslavia, and Poland.[187]

As far as its external aspect is concerned, the main themes and postulates of the new conception of Slavic solidarity, as evidenced by statements of Soviet writers and of its exponents in the Slavic groups represented in the All-Slav Committee, are as follows:[188]

(a) Not merely ties of a common ancient origin, a similarity of languages, and the nature of their cultures, but an affinity of fate — the need to defend their independence against common enemies — binds the Slavic peoples. The persistent German *Drang nach Osten,* seeking the enslavement or destruction of the Slavs, has ever constituted a deadly threat to Slavdom. Under the Nazis it became a reality of gruesome proportions.

(b) The defeats of the Slavic countries in the past were due to their feudal order, their military and economic weakness, their internal divisions, and, above all, to the absence of a common front among them. There were the quarrels between Poles and Russians, Ukrainians, and Byelorussians; the friction between Serbs and Croats, Czechs and Slovaks; the enmity between the Bulgars and the Serbs; and the oppressive policies of Russification practiced by Tsarist Russia toward Ukrainians, Byelorussians, and Poles.

(c) One of the chief lessons of the past is that the Russian people are the decisive force in the struggle of the Slavs against German aggressors, the rampart of Slavdom. If Tsarist opportunism was digging a precipice between the Russians and the other Slavs, the popular emancipation movements in Russia, on the other hand, called forth the sympathy of the

---

186. See the issues of *Slaviane,* the monthly journal of the All-Slav Committee.

187. For the texts of the treaties, see *Slaviane,* No. 1 (1944), pp. 26–8, and *A.R.S.U.* August 1945, pp. 105–8. Czechoslovak President Benes told the All-Slav Committee on 21 October 1943: 'My journey to Moscow seems to me to be symbolic. Such journeys will in the future be made also by all the Slav peoples. My trip here is a manifestation of Slavic solidarity, which has a cultural and political significance for all the Slavs . . . I want to state that for future policy, for the future of Czechoslovakia, this road, the symbolic road of Slavdom, which is secured by our treaty [of mutual assistance with the U.S.S.R.] is the only right road. Our aim is decisively to cut off the German offensive to the East. This is a matter of common Slav policy, this must be, and this will be.' (*Slaviane,* No. 1 (1944), pp. 33–4.)

188. See Kuznetsov, 'The Victory of the Slavic Peoples in the External Struggle against German Aggressors,' pp. 25–37; Clementis, *'Panslavism' Past and Present;* and the issues of *Slaviane, passim.*

Slavic peoples and stirred similar movements among them, thereby paving the way for genuine and enduring Slav friendship. And the recent role of the Red Army in the liberation of the Slavic countries has proved that the U.S.S.R. was their 'natural ally.'

(d) Another lesson to be learned from the past is the lesson of Slavic unity — the realization that only complete Slavic solidarity can create a reliable barrier against German expansion in Eastern Europe.

(e) This unity must be built on foundations other than the old Pan-Slavism, which as far as its exponents in Tsarist Russia were concerned was based on ideas of subordinating the Slavs to Russia, fusing their national cultures, and uniting them with the Russians on the basis of Orthodoxy. The new solidarity must be based entirely on Slav reciprocity and equality. The manifesto issued by the first All-Slav meeting in Moscow, 11 August 1941, declared:

> We are uniting as equals with equals. We have one task and one aim: the defeat of Hitler's armies and the destruction of Hitlerism. We have one warm, all-embracing wish: that the Slav nations, just as all other nations, may be able to develop in peace and freedom within the framework of their own statehood. We resolutely and firmly reject the very idea of Pan-Slavism, as an altogether reactionary movement, profoundly hostile to the high goals of equality of peoples and of the national development of all states, a movement that was exploited by Russian Tsarism in the pursuit of its imperialist aims.[189]

(f) Slavic solidarity does not mean Slavic self-seclusion or exclusiveness, fostered for purposes of aggression or directed against world peace.[190]

---

189. *Vseslavianskii Miting V Moskve*, p. 6. This part of the manifesto was based on the speech made at the meeting by the Russian writer Alexei Tolstoy, who also declared: 'No small contribution was made by Slavdom to the world's treasury of culture and civilization. The Fascists try to deny it. We thank the German people for excellent music, for philosophy, for good old poetry, but we warn that it will have to cleanse itself of the dirt of Hitlerite Fascism, in order to save its existence.' (Ibid. pp. 11–12.)

190. Apparently to emphasize this point, every speaker at the all-Slav meeting in Moscow in 1941 referred to the non-Slav countries fighting Hitlerism, Great Britain in particular, as worthy allies in the common cause, and the meeting was concluded with addresses by two exiled German writers, who associated the silent German masses with the Slavs' struggle for their independence. (Ibid. *passim*, and pp. 52–5.) At the beginning of 1946, Dr. Benes, after stating that World War II brought the Slav problem 'directly and unexpectedly close to a definite solution,' and that if the Slav peoples will radically reform their political, social, and economic life, they will approach each other so closely that disputes among them will be easily solved, concluded: 'By this I do not wish to formulate a new ideology of pan-Slavism, nor do I wish to herald the creation of a new political bloc in Europe that would exclusively comprise Slav peoples and would represent a new constellation of Powers from which other peoples would be excluded or by which they would be threatened.' (Yugoslav radio broadcast, 1 January 1946.)

The borders of Poland 'and of the whole Slav world' have been shifted to the West, and an end was made of the disunity of the Slavic peoples, which was used in the past to conquer them one at a time.[191] The mutual-assistance treaties between the Soviet Union and Czechoslovakia, Yugoslavia, and Poland 'are directed against any new German aggression' and constitute a guaranty of the security of all the Slavic peoples in the future. As such they 'contribute to universal peace, and are, therefore, in the interest of all the United Nations.'[192]

This exegesis of the new movement for Slavic solidarity lacks a good deal of the Slavophile mysticism and romanticism of the older Pan-Slavism, especially as it was preached by its early West Slav founders, and some of the later Russian and Czech groups.[193] Yet the movement probably has greater chances of success than its predecessors, since it is being backed by regimes of greater affinity, and is taking the form of binding political-military arrangements, accompanied not only by measures for cultural co-operation, but — for the first time — by definite efforts at economic collaboration between the Slavic countries.

As for the internal aspect of the concept of Slavic solidarity in the U.S.S.R., it should be noted that the Soviet leaders have generally refrained from claiming any particular unity between the Soviet Slavic peoples — the Russians, Ukrainians, and Byelorussians — comprising together over 150 million persons or more than 75 per cent of the population of the U.S.S.R. In 1944, Kalinin declared specifically in the organ of the All-Slav Committee: 'In our country, with its fraternal collaboration of peoples, there exists no Slavic problem, as an aim to unify specially and distinguish the Slavs or, even more so, to juxtapose in some fashion the Slavic peoples to the other peoples, inhabiting the Soviet Union.'[194] There is no evidence that Slavic unity, as an ideal, has excited the popular fancy, or will be permitted to become the subject of a wide popular movement in the U.S.S.R., superseding or seriously competing with the established conception of complete equality and solidarity of all the Soviet peoples — Slav and non-Slav alike.

The revival of interest in some of the Russian national values has created a bridge to the past, psychologically stabilizing for the younger generation and gratifying to the older groups, whose allegiance is likewise strengthened by the new church policy. This policy has also won friends

191. Kuznetsov, op. cit. pp. 36–7.
192. Ibid.
193. See Clementis, op. cit. *passim*, and Kohn, 'Pan-Movements,' pp. 545–7.
194. *Slaviane*, No. 1 (1944), p. 6.

for the Soviet Government in Orthodox circles abroad. The newer attitudes in the fields of family relations and education are strengthening the basic unit of social cohesion, leading to further increases in population, and helping to inculcate discipline and respect for authority, which will inevitably find reflection in the political sphere. And the change in the Soviet attitude on Slavic solidarity was the point of departure for intimate collaboration between the U.S.S.R. and the Slavic countries on its periphery. All of these elements benefit the regime in greater or lesser degree, adding to its strength and political influence internally and externally.

(2) IDEOLOGY

At the very beginning of this study we pointed out the extraordinary importance attached to ideology in the Soviet Union.[195] During the recent war, ideology took a back seat. While the basic tenets of Marxism remained, and were at times reiterated in Party statements, the overwhelming emphasis was on national values, on the need to meet the invasion of hearth and home, and on all-out effort in the struggle for survival.

In the summer of 1943, following the victory at Stalingrad early in the year, a re-emphasis on ideology began to emerge, gaining progressively in intensity. Pointing to the growing success in the War as a vindication of the Party's policies and of the teachings by which they are guided, the Party leaders once more called for extensive study of Marxist theory by the large numbers of new, ill-prepared recruits to the Party, by members of the intelligentsia and other social groups, and by the officials of soviet, economic, and Party institutions themselves; and organized for this purpose numerous additional courses and schools throughout the U.S.S.R.[196]

Recently, special campaigns have been carried out in the cultural field, to make sure that the theater, motion pictures, newspapers, magazines, and other publications will in the future conduct their activities in com-

---

195. See *supra*, 3-4.
196. See *Pod Znamenem Marksizma*, No. 7-8 (1943), p. 56; *Partiinoe Stroitel'stvo*, No. 17-18 (1943), pp. 16-18; editorials: 'The Education of the Young Communists — One of the Fundamental Tasks of the Party Organizations,' *Bol'shevik*, No. 6 (1944), pp. 1-6; 'About the Marxist-Leninist Education of the Personnel of the Soviet Intelligentsia,' ibid. No. 9 (1944), pp. 1-8; 'Intensify the Ideological-Political Work of the Party Organizations,' ibid. No. 17-18 (1944), pp. 1-8; 'Tirelessly Raise the Ideological-Theoretical Level of the Party — Soviet Cadres,' ibid. No. 22 (1944), pp. 1-7; Kuzmin, 'The Marxist-Leninist Dialectics — Mighty Ideological Weapon of Our Party,' pp. 12-23; G. Aleksandrov, 'Some Tasks of the Social Sciences in the Contemporary Conditions,' pp. 12-29; Voznesensky, 'Temper Our Students Ideologically.'

plete concord with the ideological and political postulates of the state.[197] And much of the content of current theoretical statements and cultural practices is directed toward keeping the revival of tradition and interest in the past within bounds, and balancing them with strong emphases on the achievements and tasks of the present.[198] Thus, as far as can be presently foreseen, ideology will most likely continue to be the dominant spiritual influence on the Soviet scene, deeply affecting political habits and sentiments in Soviet society.

To conclude, three concepts are the keys to the present socio-political balance in the U.S.S.R.: unity, discipline, and performance. The Party controls them all, watching the interplay of forces and making adjustments in the balance, in line with current estimates of the correlation between them, the outer world, and the goals of the Soviet state.

---

197. On 26 August 1946, the Central Committee of the Party adopted a decision concerning the repertoire of the drama theaters. Complaining that present-day themes were practically eschewed by the dramatists and theaters, that the small number of plays that dealt with such themes caricatured Soviet life, and that cheap foreign plays were brought to the Soviet stage, the Central Committee took to task the dramatists, theater critics, and Union of Soviet Writers for forgetting 'that the Soviet theater can fulfil its important role in the matter of educating the toilers only if it will actively propagate the politics of the Soviet state, which is the vital foundation of the Soviet order.' It also complained that *Pravda, Izvestia,* and other papers were devoting too little attention to questions of art. The Central Committee directed that the chairman of the Committee on Art, dramatists, theaters, and newspapers should remedy these shortcomings, so that dramatic presentations reflect the progress of Soviet life and help to develop character, and that they should fight 'against apoliticism and ideal-less critique.' (*Bol'shevik,* No. 16 (1946), pp. 50–53.) Similar statements were made with regard to the cinema and literature. (Ibid. pp. 45–9; *Pravda,* 8 September 1946.)

198. The Central Committee of the Party severely criticized, for instance, the glorification of a Golden Horde leader as a national hero in the Volga Tatar Republic. (See *Bol'shevik,* No. 19–20 (1944), p. 57.) And pointing out both the extremely limited nature of the theater repertoire in the Union and autonomous republics, and 'the passion of the local dramatists for themes of the distant past,' it directed that translations be made of the best works of Soviet dramatics into the languages of the various nationalities and included in the repertoires of the localities. (Ibid. No. 16 (1946), pp. 48–9.)

Chapter XIV · The Nature of the Polity: Conclusions

1. THE DYNAMISM OF THE CONSTITUTIONAL ORDER

(1) THE FLUX OF FORMS

In the preceding pages we sought to portray the moving panorama of political power in the U.S.S.R. Here we shall attempt to draw conclusions concerning the nature of the Soviet polity and bring out the main features that distinguish it from other polities in the modern state system.

One of the chief points of difference is revealed in the constant stream of change in the implements and mechanisms of the Soviet state. In less than two decades, three constitutions (1918, 1924, and 1936) have followed each other. No constitution in the world has been amended as frequently as the Fundamental Law of the Soviet land. Hardly a year has gone by without alterations in the political-territorial framework, in the structure of Soviet organs, and in the system of administrative departments. By the new constitution the Congress of Soviets, Central Executive Committee, and Presidium of the Central Executive Committee were replaced by the Supreme Soviet and its Presidium, and a new definition of legislative and executive functions was introduced. The commissariats, committees, councils, and chief administrations have been undergoing an unending process of subdivision and separation, fusion and reintegration, addition of new units, and changes in nomenclature. In 1934 the collegia of the commissariats were abolished, only to be re-established again in 1937. In the latter year preferential, indirect, unequal, and open elections to the Soviets were replaced by universal, direct, equal, and secret suffrage. The secret vote was likewise introduced in Party elections. At the beginning of the regime the term Minister was discarded as too reminiscent of the old order, and the name People's Commissar was adopted in its place. Before the regime ended its third decade it reverted to the term Minister, in line with the practice prevailing in other states.

In the Army, the institution of political commissars was established three times and abolished three times. Ranks, titles, and other forms of distinction, done away with on the outbreak of the revolution, were reinstituted during the decade of 1935–45, and a similar restoration took place with regard to ranks in the Foreign Service. Since 1919 the Party Rules have been amended five times, the last time in 1939, when admission into the Party ranks was liberalized. In the same year the Party Conference — dating in origin to the early beginnings of Bolshevik organization, but eliminated in 1934 — was restored to its former position. Considerable fluctuations have attended the organs that supervise and verify the execution of Party and Soviet directives, as well as the instrumentalities of economic management. And even the frequency of convocation of Party and Soviet bodies has been subjected to numerous changes.

Most notable of all has been the elasticity in forms and degrees of autonomy and federalism in the U.S.S.R. Nothing, perhaps, illustrates better the practice of organizational change than the revision of the Soviet position on separate representation in foreign affairs for the constituent republics. From the abolition of the Commissariats of War and Foreign Affairs in the Union republics in 1923, to repeated removals of officials seeking the restoration of these commissariats and separate diplomatic representation abroad for the Union republics, to the constitutional reform of 1944 granting the Union republics the right to re-establish such commissariats and enter into agreements with foreign powers, to the winning of separate representation for the Ukrainian and Byelorussian republics in the United Nations in May 1945 — such has been the cycle of evolution of arrangements for a share in the conduct of Soviet foreign relations by the constituent republics.

Parallel developments are evident in every phase of activity in the U.S.S.R.

(2) THE SHIFTING OF FORCES

In politics, form and substance are not altogether separable. The extraordinary flux of forms indicated above was conditioned by and in turn induced changes in the nature and balance of political forces. The transformations in town and countryside, industry and agriculture, mores and culture, the alterations in the standing of the workers, peasants, intelligentsia, and other groups in Soviet society, the periodic renewals of the membership of the Party, soviet, and other bodies, all have reflected and affected the social composition of authority. The growth in territorial-administrative units and the changes in the federal structure have mirrored and helped to bring about alterations in the national distribution of power. The introduction of a national anthem in addition to the 'Internationale,' the altered attitude toward pre-Soviet traditions of Russia, and the fundamental revisions of theory concerning the nature and future of state, law, constitution, and Party in the U.S.S.R. reflect a basic change in estimates of the international balance of power.

(3) THE PRINCIPLE OF ELASTICITY

Three factors can be said to be primarily responsible for the extreme fluidity of Soviet socio-political arrangements. To begin with, the Soviet Union has never had a prolonged period of normality, with tranquil conditions making for massive stability in governmental forms and slow changes in the equilibrium of socio-political forces. The setting up of the regime in 1917 was followed by the civil war and intervention (1918–20). The next period (1921–7) was characterized by an initial struggle over the establishment of a close federal Union, uncertainties in the balance between the New Economic Policy and the efforts at socialization of the economy, and bitter intra-Party strife. The first Five-Year Plan (1928–32) brought with it the rigors of industrialization and collectivization. The period of the second Five-Year Plan (1933–8) coincided with the emergence of a definite external threat to the U.S.S.R. and, toward the end, with the violent purges of 1937–8. And the last years before the War (1939–41) were occupied with intense preparations for the expected conflict.

The second reason is the fact that the Soviet leaders have been learning through trial and error as they went along. For, despite their belief in Marxism as a science of society, they were early confronted with the difference between theoretical dogma and the complexities of reality, and came to regard adaptability as an indispensable condition for survival and success.

The third and most important factor is the magnitude of the revolution itself, comprising in fact five revolutions in one — political, social, industrial, agricultural, and cultural — each dependent on the other and all in a race against time.

For these reasons, any claim that because of the decline in vertical social mobility 1940 might be regarded as the year ending the Russian Revolution,[1] or estimate of a similar nature, is premature. The rate of change, particularly in some fields, will no doubt decrease, but substantial political architecture and social engineering are by no means over. As we have seen,

---

1. See Timasheff, reference *supra*, note 1, p. 313.

the Party is committed to resilience in theory and practice; [2] and change itself will remain a constant factor for a long time to come in the U.S.S.R. Elasticity is a primary principle of the Soviet polity, and dynamism is the first feature of its constitutional order distinguishing it from other polities.

2. THE QUINTESSENCE OF POLITICAL CONTROL

(1) THE BOUNDS OF LIBERTY AND AUTHORITY

Characteristics of Soviet Constitutionalism. Soviet constitutionalism is *sui generis.* Deriving in part from ideas of the constitutional charters of the West, which came into being for the very purpose of limiting governmental power in the interest of individual liberty; and simultaneously drawing its inspiration from Soviet Marxist theory, which prescribes an amplitude of power for a long transition period leading to individual liberty in a society devoid of coercive authority, it frequently reflects in practice the dualism of its origin, though the Marxist teachings as a rule carry by far the greater weight. On the one hand, the Soviet constitution is a charter of power, defining the attributes of government and standing as the supreme law of the land. On the other hand, constitutionalism is not regarded as a sacrosanct imperative, and the flexibility of Soviet constitutional practice negates the idea that governmental power is definitively barred from any sphere in the U.S.S.R. The postulates of Soviet political theory and practice envision as safeguards against abuse of governmental authority not so much the specific enumeration of the powers of government in the constitution, as the consciousness of ideologically schooled administrators, alertness on the part of the populace, and a growing habit of observance by all — governors and governed alike — of the rules of the community, ultimately doing away with the need for state power altogether. This is, in fact, a peculiarly Marxist conception of 'government of laws and not of men,' with the weight of emphasis on 'men' in the present and 'laws' in the future. As Soviet society progresses toward more stabilized relationships, the emphasis, it is claimed, will be directly reversed. In this divergence in the current weight of emphases lies another difference between the Soviet and the Western constitutional systems.

The set-up of the Soviet governmental structure is similarly in a class by itself. The central organs of the Soviets resemble in their organization more the British parliamentary scheme than the American executive system

---

2. See *supra,* pp. 4, 21–3, 25–6, 45–6, 62–4, 87–8, 109.

of government. Neither in theory or form, nor in practice, as we pointed out earlier, is the American doctrine of separation of powers accepted by Soviet constitutionalism.[3] The organs designated by the new constitution as legislative, executive-administrative, and judicial are not co-ordinate and equal branches of government, acting as checks and balances upon each other. Nor does the American doctrine and practice of judicial review of legislation have any counterpart in the Soviet scheme of government. On the other hand, while — as we have seen — in practice other central organs besides the Supreme Soviet issue legislative norms, recent theory emphasizes the Supreme Soviet as the source of all legislative power.[4] This, together with the Supreme Soviet's power to appoint the Council of Ministers, Presidium of the Supreme Soviet, and Supreme Court, brings the central soviets, as far as constitutional theory is concerned, close to the British constitutional system of parliamentary supremacy. And although the Soviet constitution does not require the Council of Ministers to resign and invoke new elections on a vote of non-confidence by the deputies of the Supreme Soviet, there is a similarity to the British principle of ministerial responsibility in the articles of the Constitution of 1936 declaring the Council of Ministers and Presidium of the Supreme Soviet responsible and accountable to the Supreme Soviet.[5]

In actual performance, however, the Soviet structure differs radically from the parliamentary governments of Great Britain and the Continent. The Supreme Soviet, like the popular assemblies of the Soviets which preceded it, is much less an organ relied on for continuous legislation than a high-level barometer of public opinion, periodically helping to gauge popular sentiment and secure popular approval for governmental policy. The Council of Ministers, on the other hand, is a much more powerful body than appears from the constitution; it functions as a direct assistant or executive extension of the Party summit — the real seat of governmental power.

In its federal features the U.S.S.R. resembles more the United States than the British commonwealth, but by written constitution or unwritten attitude it has also some confederative and strongly unitary characteristics. The nationality aspects of Soviet federal arrangements, which distinguish the U.S.S.R. from all other federal states, constitute a unique contribution to political theory and practice.

Another basic peculiarity of Soviet constitutionalism is the emphasis

3. See *supra,* pp. 184–6, and chs. x–xii, *passim.*
4. See *supra,* ch. xi, *passim.*
5. See *supra,* pp. 263–4, 273–4.

placed by it on economic arrangements, duties, and rights. Lastly, its chief distinction lies in the fact that it operates — and this is openly proclaimed — within the context of Party guidance and ideology.

These, in brief, are the general lines of distinction between Soviet and Western constitutionalism. More specifically, they are expressed in the range of government and the content of individual and local liberties in the Soviet polity.

The Scope of Government Functions. In no country in the world is the province of government so great, the concern of authority so total in scope, as in the U.S.S.R. Government in the Soviet Union embraces in full measure the social, economic, political, and spiritual experiences of its citizenry. While the forms, degrees, and methods of legislation, regulation, guidance, and direction differ and change at various times and places, political control by the Party remains.

Through its 'conducting belts' or transmitters — the soviets, the trade unions, the co-operatives, the Komsomol, the Army, and voluntary associations — the Party controls the instruments of compulsion, persuasion and education, directing, regulating or guiding administration, industry, and agriculture, culture, and art. Through the medium of the economic plan, government in the U.S.S.R. plots the course of the future and controls the progress of the present in almost all phases of group activity and all geographical areas, from the smallest hamlet to the constituent republics and the Union itself. In one form or another, its supervision, instruction, counsel, or observation reaches farm and factory, production and distribution, science and education, literature, music and dramatics, medicine and jurisprudence, journalism and publishing, cinema, radio, and sport.

The chief secret of this scope of power lies in the magnitude of its undertaking. The leaders who seized power in Russia on 7 November 1917 undertook nothing less than to recreate Man and Society on new foundations. From the outset, they assumed the need of ample governmental power to meet the inertia of old ways in a vast and backward country and to reckon with the possible challenge of a hostile world. Deducing a lesson of centralism from the experiences of the Paris Commune, and preparing to act in times of crisis, they had no compunction about large and concentrated authority.

Still the conception of the range and probable life-span of government in the Soviet Union was milder in the earlier years, and much talk was tolerated about the 'softening' of the dictatorship and the 'withering away of the state.'[6] As, however, the enormity of the transformation sought

6. See *supra*, notes 30, 32, 39, 42, ch. I.

revealed itself in the process of prosecution, and crises multiplied within and without, the Soviet leaders' conception of the scope and duration of governmental power also grew.[7] And the Soviet government has actually operated as a crisis government over the greater part of its existence, making extensive use of the immense authority of the dictatorship to mobilize men and materials for titanic tasks of construction, war, and reconstruction.

Objective factors, such as the size, backwardness, and diversity of country and people, and the tensions of international relations have thus contributed to the extension of the area of government in the Soviet Union. But the main conditioning element in this development has been the subjective factor of the conviction of the Soviet leaders that massive power must remain in the state until a socialist society, as well as a unified outlook of its citizenry is established in the U.S.S.R. beyond the possibility of internal or external challenge.[8]

The Essence of Individual Liberty. If the range of government is so extensive in the U.S.S.R., what, if any, are the spheres of freedom left to the individual and the locality?

The immensity of governmental authority has not nullified all liberty in the Soviet Union. Some freedoms have been completely abolished, others curtailed, and still others permitted a considerable area of assertion. The chief difference between the U.S.S.R. and the Western democracies in the province of liberty is not that the former has quashed the freedoms altogether, but that it has endowed many of them with different meanings or emphases, on the assumption that the government itself must remain for many years the ultimate arbiter of all liberties: individual, local, and national.

Many of the basic ideas of the British Magna Carta (1215), the American Declaration of Independence (1776) and Bill of Rights (1789), and the French Declaration of Rights of Man and Citizen (1789, 1791) are to be found in the Bill of Rights of the Soviet Constitution. The value and dignity of the human personality, the idea of fundamental human rights

---

7. See *supra*, pp. 12–17, 27, 36–7.

8. 'The process of overcoming the residues of capitalism in the consciousness of people in our country has not ended . . . But the creation of new forms of social life, new arrangements of human cohabitation, is a very lengthy process. New arrangements and rules of community life could not appear all at once, because this new society has still not freed itself from the survivals of the old order from which it just emerged . . . Ahead of us is still prolonged and systematic . . . work, to liquidate definitively the heavy legacy left us by the old society, to educate all the citizens in a spirit where they will respect and fulfil all the rules of the socialist community.' (*S.G.P.* pp. 575–82.)

and freedoms, gaining increasing public recognition everywhere,[9] have been given much attention in Soviet political theory, despite the fact that the latter asserts that the socialist order, rather than the concepts of 'natural rights' and 'inalienable rights,' is the source of individual rights in Soviet society.[10] But the Soviet Bill of Rights and Soviet political writings introduce a number of radical innovations in the pattern of rights customarily inscribed in constitutional charters.

From the standpoint of implementation, the freedoms can be classed as negative and positive, depending upon whether the state merely has to refrain from action or whether it must undertake regulatory arrangements in order to give them effect.[11] In the Bill of Rights of the new constitution, the Soviet Union has followed the Western democracies with regard to the negative freedoms, while it has pioneered in the introduction of a number of positive freedoms. Thus, this constitution contains articles providing for such customary civil rights as freedom of conscience and religious worship (124), and freedom of speech and the press (125). Although it does not provide for a writ of habeas corpus, the equivalent of 'due process of law' in the constitutional bills of rights of the Western states is to be found in its articles on 'inviolability of the person' (127), 'inviolability of the homes of citizens and privacy of correspondence' (128), trial of cases in all courts 'with the participation of public assessors' (103), and the guarantee to accused of 'the right to be defended by counsel' (111). Likewise, the equivalent of 'equal protection of the laws' is contained in the articles of the Soviet constitution that provide for complete equality of all citizens regardless of race, nationality, or creed (110, 123, 135), and for equal rights for women (122, 137).

Again, the political rights inscribed in the Soviet constitution cover such habitual rights of the democratic polities as 'freedom of assembly,' including mass meetings, street processions, and demonstrations (125), the right 'to unite in public organizations' (126), universal suffrage (134-40), and the right to be elected to public office (135).

9. See Wright, 'Human Rights and the World Order,' pp. 238–62; Shotwell, 'The Idea of Human Rights,' pp. 551–61; and the text of the 'Bill of Human Rights,' drafted by the Executive Committee of the Committee on Human Rights, *International Conciliation*, No. 389, pp. 562–4.

10. See e.g. Kirpotin, 'Socialism and Personality,' pp. 54–66; F. Konstantinov, 'Concerning the Marxist Understanding of the Role of Personality in History,' pp. 47–61, and *Znachenie Lichnykh Sposobnostei I Truda Pri Sotsializme* (The Significance of Personal Abilities and Work under Socialism), Partizdat, 1938; Gak, 'Concerning the Role of the Personality and the Popular Masses in History,' pp. 45–56, and 'Socialist Society and Personality,' pp. 51–66.

11. Wright, 'Human Rights and the World Order,' pp. 245, 255–7.

The most radical differences appear in the sphere of economic rights. The right to private ownership of the means of production, land, and natural resources has been abolished. In its place the constitution of the U.S.S.R. provides for 'socialist ownership' in the form of state property or co-operative and collective farm property (4–8). But a small plot of land, a dwelling house, livestock, poultry, and minor agricultural implements are allowed to each household of a collective farm as personal property (7), and a small private economy of peasants and handicraftsmen 'based on personal labor and precluding the exploitation of the labor of others' is permitted by law (9), with the owners free to dispose of the products of these properties. Outside of these allowances, however, the Soviet Bill of Rights does not recognize any freedom of private trade or enterprise. All citizens have a right to personal ownership of their incomes from work, their savings, their dwelling houses and subsidiary household economy, and their furniture, utensils, and articles of personal use, as well as the right to inherit personal property (10). A novel economic right, which the Soviet constitution is the first of contemporary constitutions to introduce, is 'the right to work' — a guaranteed right to employment and payment in accordance with the quantity and quality of performance (118).

Similar innovations are made by the inclusion of a series of social rights in the Soviet constitutional charter: 'the right to rest and leisure' (119), the right to 'maintenance in old age' and in case of sickness or loss of capacity to work (120), and 'the right to education' (121). Each of the articles describing them contains also a statement of conditions to ensure their realization.

Finally, the Soviet Bill of Rights exhibits the unique feature of listing in detail the duties of citizens along with their rights: work as 'a duty and a matter of honor for every able-bodied citizen in accordance with the principle: "He who does not work, neither shall he eat"' (12); the duty to abide by the constitution, observe the laws, maintain labor discipline, honestly to perform public duties, and 'to respect the rules of socialist intercourse' (130); the duty 'to safeguard and strengthen public, socialist property as the sacred and inviolable foundation of the Soviet system' (131); and military service as an honorable and 'sacred duty' of every citizen of the U.S.S.R. (132, 133).

The Soviet Bill of Rights contains, thus, an impressive number of provisions to protect human freedoms and welfare. In practice, however, some of its rights, particularly in the field of civil liberties, have been honored more in the breach than in the observance, or have been hamstrung with restrictive interpretations. The ease with which life and liberty have been extinguished on a number of occasions in the U.S.S.R. has served in the past to negate the viability of the personal inviolabilities. The correctional labor camps, even if — in the absence of authentic figures — the number of their inmates has been exaggerated abroad, are a blot on the record of constitutionalism in the U.S.S.R. In other cases, the potency of some of the freedoms is reduced by the narrowed definitions given them in practice.

Thus limits are set by the Party for freedom of speech and the press.[12] In regard to such practical matters as the businesslike operation of economic enterprises, municipal services, et cetera, criticism and discussion are not only tolerated but solicited; in regard to important political questions touching on the internal balance or problems of foreign policy, the expression of public opinion is guided and organized; while no free criticism whatever (except to some extent during periods set aside by the Party for discussions by its members) is tolerated with regard to Soviet fundamentals: the principles of the economic system, the bases of the social order, the status of the Party, and the role of the highest leadership. Soviet law specifically forbids 'the issuance, publication, and dissemination of works containing agitation and propaganda against the Soviet government and dictatorship of the proletariat,' and recognized Soviet publicists openly declare that in the U.S.S.R. 'there, naturally, is or can be no place for freedom of speech, press, et cetera, for the enemies of socialism' and that any attempt by the latter to utilize these freedoms 'must be classified as a counter-revolutionary crime.'[13]

A more liberal interpretation than in preceding years has been given during the past decade to freedom of religious worship.[14] Freedom of movement, on the other hand, does not mean in practice any right to travel abroad at will, and the right of citizens to unite in public organizations does not extend to formation of another political party or to organization of any opposition against the government.[15]

Since crucial importance is attached to these understandings as prerequisites for the survival of the Soviet system, institutionalized violence, i.e. force as a tool of government, has been much more in evidence in the Soviet Union than in any of the Western democratic states. The G.P.U. (later N.K.V.D. and now M.V.D.), said Stalin in 1922, was 'the indefatigable guardian of the Revolution, the unsheathed sword of the proletariat,'

12. See *supra,* pp. 125–9.
13. *S.G.P.* pp. 554–5.
14. See *supra,* pp. 365–9.
15. See *supra,* ch. VI, *passim.*

which it would be unsafe for the Soviet state to relinquish.[16] While in the early 'thirties a beginning was made in whittling down its prerogatives, the effort was arrested by the aftermath to the Kirov murder in 1934, and this political police force still retains extensive powers of exile, imprisonment, and surveillance, which inevitably impinge upon the area of individual freedom in the U.S.S.R.

Besides the political considerations responsible for limitations on the concept of freedom, the desire of the Soviet leaders to provide the highest protection to their new economic order accounts for many of the restrictions on individual liberty and much of the severity of police measures. Both the new constitution and the still valid law of 7 August 1932 declare public, socialist property to be 'sacred and inviolable' and place offenses against it on a par with political crimes and treason, calling their perpetrators 'enemies of the people.'[17] Since so much of property and activity is public, chances for violations are extensive, and because it is the state that is involved, what are merely torts elsewhere become crimes in the U.S.S.R. This factor likewise bears heavily on the scope of individual liberty.

In considering the theory and practice of individual rights in the U.S.S.R., several basic points of difference between the Soviet Union and the Western states become apparent. The pattern of a social-economic 'free-for-all' as the best vehicle for maximum individual self-realization is completely rejected in the U.S.S.R. and governmental guidance is substituted in its place. Society and the individual are not considered inherently antithetic. But where the two come into conflict, society invariably takes priority over the individual. Furthermore, in the current Soviet scale of values, social and economic rights are strongly emphasized over political and civil rights. The Bill of Rights puts the social and economic provisions (right to work, leisure, security in old age, et cetera) in the first place; and Soviet political theory proceeds from a fundamental assumption that economic equality — not in the absolute sense of equality in the quantity and type of possessions, or of an egalitarian leveling of needs and tastes, but in the relative sense of economic opportunity — must precede the flowering of individual liberty.[18] And finally, in the implementation of these priorities, even constitutional guarantees take a back seat at any

---

16. Stalin, *Voprosy Leninizma* (9th ed., 1933), p. 312.

17. *S.G.P.* pp. 584–5.

18. 'We did not build this society in order to restrict human liberty, but in order that the human personality may feel really free. We built it for the sake of genuine personal liberty, liberty without quotation marks . . . Real liberty exists only where exploitation

indication of a threat or impediment to the new fundamentals of the Soviet state.

Liberty has never been an absolute or a constant. It is always related to time and place, to environment and historical period. As far as goals are concerned, 'life, liberty, and the pursuit of happiness' are as much aims of the Soviet Union as they are of the Western democracies, but these concepts are given a narrower interpretation by the former. As far as practice is concerned, Soviet citizens do not enjoy many of the highly prized liberties of the West, the first of which is the power to change periodically the highest rulers of the state. Yet it is probably true that the majority of the Soviet citizens are not laboring under any undue sense of deprivation of freedom. While most of them, it can be reasonably assumed, would greatly welcome curtailment of the ubiquitous surveillance of the M.V.D., there is nothing to suggest that they are at present conscious of lacking the freedoms prevailing in the West.

There are several reasons for this. In the first place, they have no tradition of the Western type of liberty, as they enjoyed no such freedoms under previous regimes. The long emphasis on economic rights, associating welfare arrangements with liberty, has created a new popular conception of freedom, and the Soviet citizens are more eager for realization of these rights than for freedom to criticize or change the Politbureau. For diverse groups of citizens, moreover, the present regime represents personal freedom, as compared with their previous condition. For many members of backward nationalities, who have received access to education and forms of national-political expression for the first time, these acquisitions spell freedom. The same is true of Soviet women, who were given equality with men by the present regime; and even more so of young people, who have never known any other regime and in great numbers are placed in

---

has been abolished, where there is no oppression of some people by others, where there is no unemployment and poverty, where man is not haunted by fear that tomorrow he may lose his job, home, or bread. Only in such a society is real — and not paper — personal and every other kind of liberty possible.' (Stalin in his interview with Roy Howard, *Beseda s Roi Govardom,* Partizdat, 1937, pp. 12–13.) 'It is natural, hence, that despite all the guarantees of the [citizens] rights by the first Soviet Constitution, it was impossible to realize at once the full assimilation of these rights by the widest masses of toilers. In order that all the toilers should be able to assimilate in full measure these rights, granted them by the Constitution, should learn to use them, it was necessary to liquidate unemployment, to raise the cultural level of the masses, to liquidate illiteracy; it was necessary to emancipate woman in actuality, to do a tremendous job in order to associate the toilers of the formerly oppressed nationalities in conscious political life; it was necessary to raise the general material standard of living of the toilers of city and village.' (*S.G.P.* p. 505.)

positions of trust. Intellectuals, apparently, feel the strictures of conformism in their creative efforts in much greater measure, but this applies more to social scientists and literary writers than to the bulk of physical scientists and men of technical skills. The fact that scientists and technicians have made great progress in the U.S.S.R., often displaying great boldness of spirit and a novelty of approach, that soldiers of all ranks have demonstrated a capacity for improvisation and flexibility in military operations during the recent war, and that similar abilities for innovaton were exhibited in other groups, suggests that the scope of governmental controls has not quashed all sense of individuality and initiative in the Soviet citizenry. Maximum attainment, however, in Soviet society — as in any other society — hinges on higher creativity of its individual citizens, which in the last analysis would flourish best only under much greater freedom from external constraints than exists at present.

The status of individual liberty in the U.S.S.R. is directly related to the state of Soviet society at present. By the yardstick of history, this society is not as old as we may think. It is just emerging from the backwardness of yesterday. The need and demand for higher personal freedoms come with the rise of culture and education. Liberty waxes on enlightenment. It seems obvious that the U.S.S.R. has unlocked tremendous talent in its vast masses through education and access to cultural opportunities. For the moment, in fact, the essence of individual liberty in the U.S.S.R. consists chiefly in the citizen's chance to grow — in his freedom and opportunity to develop himself and to gain social recognition in the process. In time, the growth of culture may lead to wider demands for greater personal liberty. Among the brighter sides of the total picture is the fact that the constitutional framework for the human freedoms exists, and that there is nothing in Soviet theory to prevent it from materializing at some point in the future.

The Spheres of the Localities and the Center. One of the most crucial problems of the century is to reconcile local liberties with central authority in such a manner as to secure adequate integration of administrative functions without sacrificing the sense of participation in government of the various segments of the community. In the politics of a world shrunk by modern invention into a community of neighbor-states, differing little in geographic proximity from the municipalities of yesterday, this problem is particularly difficult, since the obvious need for greater unity of regions and areas continues to meet with the persistent urge for separate political identity and self-expression by the various nationalities and ethnic groups. Essentially, it is the old question of distribution of public power and responsibility between the center and the circumference in sundry forms of autonomy and federalism, rendered more difficult by the peculiarities of the times. As a multinational state of great ethnic diversity the U.S.S.R. appears to have come close to a solution of this problem. But in doing so it has arrived at federative arrangements that set the Soviet Union off to a large degree from other federal states.

From the standpoint of constitutional theory, the Soviet Federation resembles partly the United States, partly Great Britain and the British Commonwealth of Nations. Although federal features prevail in its structure, it has some confederative characteristics, while in practice it is in many respects unitary in nature.

As in the United States, the constitution allocates governmental powers between the Union and the states — the constituent or Union republics — with the latter possessing all residual powers not specifically assigned to the Union. Both possess state sovereignty emanating from the people, and there are two spheres of authority: separate organs of government and fields of law, and a dual citizenship — federal and Union republican. In case of conflict with the constitutions and laws of the Union republics, the federal constitution and laws prevail. But the distribution of powers itself cannot be altered without a constitutional amendment requiring a two-thirds vote of each of the chambers of the federal Supreme Soviet, i.e. without participation by the Council of Nationalities in which the constituent republics are equally represented.

Unlike the United States, the Soviet Federation possesses the confederative feature of a constitutional right of secession vested in each of the Union republics. Nor does the American doctrine of judicial supremacy have any counterpart in the Soviet federal structure, since not only the Supreme Court of the U.S.S.R., but the federal Presidium can annul decisions and ordinances of the republican councils of ministers, while the federal Council of Ministers has the power to suspend such decisions and ordinances, and the Procurator General of the U.S.S.R. has strong supervisory powers over strict execution of laws by all local units. These prerogatives are more like the practices of Great Britain and the states of the Continent, where the central legislative and executive organs have large powers of nullification over the enactments of local entities. Furthermore, the autonomy reform of 1944, empowering the constituent Soviet republics to maintain separate military formations and to conduct their own foreign affairs, and the international status won for the Ukrainian and Byelorussian Republics through their admission to the United Nations, have brought the U.S.S.R. closer to the British Commonwealth of Nations.

In practice the Soviet Union is anything but a loose federation. The unitary tendencies found in all federal states in the twentieth century are even more pronounced in the U.S.S.R. Even formally, as we pointed out before, the Union retains strong powers of central control. In actual operation, all important branches of state administration, such as military affairs, foreign relations, finances, et cetera, are highly centralized, and the economy of the entire Union is directed on the basis of a unified economic plan. The frequency of territorial-administrative changes, without any rigid adherence in the past to the constitutionally prescribed distribution of authority, and other practices of constitutional flexibility have often partaken of unitary rule. And, above all, the highly centralized function of Party policy and ideology have given a singular unitary tenor to political direction in the Soviet Union.

This applies to a large extent also to local entities below the constituent republics: the autonomous republics, autonomous regions, national areas, and city and village soviets. At the same time, the vast network of administrative organs and institutions created in the various localities of the U.S.S.R. is wholly unprecedented and shows consideration of local peculiarities and sensibilities. The welfare and economic progress of the localities are taken into account and opportunities are provided for local languages and cultures. For the very reason that the scope of government is so extensive there are also more administrative functions to assign to local entities. Moreover, whatever the actual range of local authority, local liberties have appeared large because of the many forms of national self-expression provided. Consequently, there is a substantial sense of participation in government in the localities.

The wide diffusion of administrative functions, however, has not resulted in any relinquishment of effective central control. Outside of centralization of the chief branches of state administration, and the unity of economic direction, higher administrative bodies are empowered to supply guiding principles for the work of the lower bodies. This is the opposite side of the endowment of local entities with administrative functions.

The sphere of authority in the localities is twofold: responsibility for carrying out directives of the higher authorities — from the bodies immediately above to the central federal government — and considerable autonomous jurisdiction in local affairs. Little activity of a local nature is *ultra vires* in the U.S.S.R. — all local Soviets are free to deal with local needs, provided their actions do not conflict with the operation of higher organs. Local initiative is encouraged both in the execution of central plans and policies and in attention to local interests. Local soviets are urged to make maximum use of local forces and resources, to generalize from local experience and forward suggestions up the scale of the Soviet pyramid. While the constitution uses the term 'local organs of state power,' and the concept of 'local self-government' is not employed in the Soviet political vocabulary, self-activity in the localities is widely practiced and is a frequent theme in official pronouncements.

At the same time — and therein lies one more difference of government in the Soviet Union — there is no absolute autonomy in the U.S.S.R. Each Soviet body can be interfered with and overruled by the bodies standing above it, and the center retains the power of veto over any and all activities of the localities. The function of supreme supervision and verification is centralized; the Ministry of State Control (formerly the Commission of Soviet Control), the Party Control Commission, and the organs of the Procurator General, all operate in the localities free of any local checks for the very purpose of preventing any particularistic tendencies from impeding central objectives. In short, in terms of priorities, local autonomy and initiative are subject to central control; local liberties are not fixed and unalterable, but must always yield to the Union.

On the whole, this zoning of governmental authority appears to have achieved a workable balance between the geographic-political core and the periphery — between the center and the localities in the U.S.S.R. In general it may be said that to the extent that much of this zoning concerns different nationalities, it serves to sustain the thesis that a good deal of political and economic centralization may be feasible in a multinational state, provided adequate consideration is given to economic development and autonomous cultural expression in the national localities.

(2) THE PATTERN OF ADMINISTRATIVE LEADERSHIP

The Concept of Leadership. The Soviet concept of leadership can be best understood when it is compared with other recent theories based on the leadership principle.

Reduced to its essentials, the 'leadership principle' evolved in the recent Italian and German dictatorships comprised the following elements: (a) government by the few, headed by a dictator in whose person all authority was concentrated, i.e. one-man rule, with power organized from the top down; (b) irresponsibility of the governors to the governed, i.e., on the assumption of a self-decreed trusteeship of the nation, the dictatorship rejected the principle of consent of the governed on the ground that the masses are inherently incapable of knowing their interests, choosing their representatives, and reviewing or controlling the acts of their leaders; (c) political inequality as a basis of the governing system; (d) assertion of the permanence of the supreme leadership and of the utmost concentration of government as the definitive goal, according to the basic theory of the dictatorship.[19]

The Soviet concept of leadership differs in many respects on all of these counts. Power is indeed organized from the top down in the U.S.S.R. And the functional conception of leadership by an élite has been, and to some extent still is, a tenet of Soviet theory. Lenin's conception of a small party of professional revolutionaries, bound by ideology and discipline and flexible in method and tactics, had carried over to the period following the seizure of power, on the ground that such a party was necessary to maintain the gains of the Revolution and act as a mobilizing and coordinating force for the variegated framework of formal authority. But since this party has progressively grown with its auxiliaries to a membership of over thirty million, and the 'non-Party Bolsheviks' comprise many millions more, it would probably be more accurate to speak of government by a minority of the people than of 'government by the few' in the U.S.S.R. For in its broad sense 'government' in the Soviet Union embraces many millions of persons, while in the narrower sense of supreme leadership and ultimate control it is unquestionably limited to the small circle of the Party summit.

Neither in theory nor in practice is the idea of a single dictator, who irrevocably concentrates all authority exclusively in his own person, accepted in the Soviet dictatorship, despite the extraordinary role of Stalin — and of Lenin before him — in the governance of the U.S.S.R. As far as theory is concerned, Stalin rejected (in 1923) the principle of one-man rule over the country, on the ground that, though it may have the advantage of simplicity, it was fraught with the danger of conflict and consequently would be costly in the end.[20] In Lenin's time, his decisive influence notwithstanding, the accepted view was that the leadership of the Party — hence of the state — was collective. This view prevailed when, upon Lenin's death, his duties devolved upon a sort of steering committee of three (Stalin, Zinoviev, and Kamenev), and was reasserted on all sides during the intra-Party struggle in the mid-'twenties. For a number of years afterwards all public references were to 'leaders' of the Party. Only in the 'thirties do public references to Stalin as 'leader' begin to appear first with the adjectives of 'great,' 'beloved,' 'iron,' et cetera, and then in the

19. Merriam, *Systematic Politics*, pp. 120, 184–6.
20. *M.N.C.Q.* pp. 164–5.

form of the designation 'the leader' of the Party, people, or peoples of the U.S.S.R. Thereafter, Stalin's role in the state has been repeatedly emphasized and given singular connotation in public pronouncements, though he himself normally never speaks in terms of supremacy concerning his leadership.

Several reasons appear to be behind this stress on the singularity of Stalin's role. Initially, it may have been a form of belated or compensatory recognition, following the victory over his rivals, for the earlier underestimation and underplay of Stalin's contribution to the fashioning of Soviet rule and the winning of the civil war. And it was accompanied by a deliberate suppression of the records of some of the other early leaders, Trotsky in particular, on the ground that they were exaggerations or misstatements. The mounting and continuing emphasis on Stalin's leadership in later years is related in a large measure to his role in the promotion of the Five-Year Plans and the conduct of the War, and even more so to the apparent determination of the Soviet leaders to set him up as a symbol of the state, both for internal and external purposes. To no small degree, it may be due also to a desire to bring even the highest governing group into line with the trend toward managerial responsibility.[21]

Thus, the highest leadership assumes a double aspect. The theory of *collective* leadership remains. Like the Central Committee, the Politbureau is considered a collective organ. In practice also its decisions are collective. Though Stalin's influence is great, all of the members of the Politbureau take part in the consideration of questions before it, and their votes are of equal value. Differences of opinion can and do develop, and Stalin has been outvoted on occasion. But once a decision has been reached by majority vote, the Politbureau acts as a team under Stalin as manager in carrying out the decision. This is a different conception from the *Führerprinzip*.

Another difference concerns the theory of responsibility to the governed. Nowhere in Soviet theory is the principle of 'consent of the governed' rejected, or the irresponsibility of the governors asserted. Soviet theory, in fact, abounds in formulations concerning the value of mass judgment and the need for mutually controlling relations between the leaders and the people. Soviet writers echo times without number such dicta of Stalin as the statement that 'the fates of people and states are decided nowadays not only by the leaders, but first of all and chiefly by the millions of masses of toilers,' and the remark that 'Leaders come and

21. See *supra*, pp. 288–93.

go, but the people remain. Only the people are immortal. Everything else is transient.'[22] And the general thesis is maintained that the Soviet leaders themselves possess 'endless faith in the masses, in their strength, wisdom, creative ability,' that they believe in the need 'not only to teach the masses, but to learn from the masses,' and that they find in this conception the source of their own and the Party's strength.[23]

In practice the theory of leader responsibility finds differential application at the lower and higher administrative levels. The responsibility of officials below the top level can be enforced by removal from above and, in elective bodies, also by recall from below.[24] At the highest level, however, responsibility depends largely upon the conscience of the leaders themselves, and upon the checks that they can exercise upon one another. Removal at this level can only proceed upon decision of the governing collective itself — the Party summit — and the measure of responsibility of this collective before the governed is, in the last analysis, likewise set by the summit. Past experience shows that the highest leaders reserve the right to overrule popular sentiment when, in their opinion, occasion demands it. At the same time the Kremlin keeps a constant ear to the ground through various conferences, councils, meetings, organizations, Party secretaries, newspaper correspondents, et cetera. And it endeavors to demonstrate to the populace the responsiveness of the governors to the will of the governed not only by keeping up the elaborate structure of the soviets, but through such instrumentalities as the Correspondence Bureau of the Party's Central Committee, and the Reception Office of the Presidium of the Supreme Soviet, where the complaints of the citizens against bureaucratic abuses, as well as their many requests, are considered.[25] Here the concept of 'responsibility' is given more the aspect of a concept of 'responsiveness.'

This again is, in its totality, a different conception from the irresponsibility of the governors, which was openly proclaimed in the theories of the Italian and German dictatorships, on the premise of inherent human inequalities. Also, Soviet theory is increasingly narrowing the concept of political inequality as a basis of the governing system in the U.S.S.R., and this theory differs fundamentally from those of the Italian and German

22. See Konstantinov, in *Bol'shevik*, No. 10–11 (1938), pp. 48, 60.

23. Ibid. p. 60.

24. See *supra*, p. 206.

25. See *supra*, note 39, p. 173, and *Izvestia*, 17 April 1945. See also *Izvestia*, 22 and 23 October 1946, for a Presidium Supreme Soviet decision calling for establishment of a universal system of hearing complaints by citizens against the executive departments of territorial, regional, and lower executive committees of the Soviets.

concepts on the questions of permanence of the highest leadership and concentration of power as the ultimate goal. The theory of the dictatorship in the U.S.S.R. has always posited the duration of the dictatorship on a number of limiting factors grouped under the concept of 'the transition period,' and has always spoken of the ultimate goal as the 'withering away' of the state, to be arrived at through the gradual growth of institutions and habits of responsibility.[26] While the merging of the time element of the dictatorship with the concept of 'capitalist encirclement' has meant postponement to the distant future of this final goal, the very idea of a time limitation distinguishes the Soviet concept of leadership and might, under normal international conditions, bear to some extent upon the internal political development in the U.S.S.R.

Lenin and Stalin as Prototypes. The Soviet concept of leadership includes also a number of personal qualities encouraged in Soviet administrators, before whom Lenin and Stalin are held up as models.

Discussions of leadership in the U.S.S.R. invariably bring in the name of Marx, as founder and teacher of a new science of society that has guided the establishment of the Soviet state. Marx is held to have discovered the laws of history, explained social phenomena on a scientific basis, and created a new world view which places on the agenda of history the need to change the world.[27] In these discussions, Lenin is described not only as the founder of the Bolshevik Party and the father of the Soviet state, but, following the death of Marx's collaborator, Engels, as the 'teacher' of the Marxist science. Lenin is pictured as Marx's 'great pupil,' who has continued and developed the teachings of Marx, has generalized from the experience of his own epoch, has discovered new laws of social development, and has foreseen and predicted the march of events.[28] In short, Lenin's chief contribution is stated to consist of: discovery of 'the law of unequal development of capitalism' in different countries, which led to his theory that socialism can be victorious even in a single country; prediction of the advent of the socialist revolution in Russia; discovery of the soviets as a governmental form; laying the foundation of the economic policy of the Soviet state; advancing ideas for the industrialization and agricultural collectivization of the U.S.S.R.; formulation of the organizational principles of the Party; and teaching the need of a mighty military organization.[29]

26. See *supra*, pp. 11–17.

27. See *supra*, pp. 3–4; editorial, 'Leninism — the Most Advanced World View,' *Bol'shevik*, No. 1 (1944), pp. 3–4.

28. Editorial, *Bol'shevik*, No. 1 (1944), pp. 3–5.

29. Ibid. pp. 4–8.

In turn, Stalin is depicted as the 'great pupil' of Lenin, the 'continuator and developer' of Lenin's teachings, and the greatest theorist and teacher of Marxism since the death of Lenin. Like Lenin, Stalin is presented as a prophet and seer of things to come, and as the leader who has defined and realized in practice Lenin's ideas, and — generalizing from the experiences of his own times — has made special contributions to the theory of the state, nationality relations, the organizational principles of the Party, and the formulation or solution of many other questions.[30] Even more than Lenin, Stalin is pictured as a great strategist, who has made an immense contribution to military science and organization in the U.S.S.R. Generally, the names of Lenin and Stalin are repeatedly linked as close collaborators and Stalin is called 'today's Lenin.'[31]

Soviet writings offer no reliable clue to who might be Stalin's successor. But that the same kind of relations and attributes may be expected of such a successor is indicated by Vyshinsky's characterizations of Molotov in 1940, when Molotov was Chairman of the Council of People's Commissars. Not only was he described as a true pupil of Stalin — a designation now customary for all the members of the Politbureau — but as 'the first assistant' of Stalin in all undertakings of foreign and domestic policy, 'the outstanding theoretician' of the Party, 'the outstanding member of the Politbureau,' as well as the outstanding man of public affairs 'of the genuinely Leninist type.'[32]

Since, however, essentially the inheritance of power would be in the Party summit, and the conception of the Politbureau as a collective leader would permit a relatively prolonged period of operation without any single successor as the highest leader, it is pertinent to know the qualities generally sought in the Soviet leaders, the features emphasized as most desirable in Soviet administrators. Using Lenin as a model, Stalin stated in 1937 that Soviet political leaders must be: clear and determined in their actions; fearless in battle and merciless to enemies of the people; free of all forms of panic when things become complicated and danger appears on the horizon; wise and unhurried in deciding intricate questions, where all-round orientation and all-sided consideration of pros and cons are called for; just and honest; and loving their people, as Lenin did.[33] Stalin himself is also constantly presented as a model to follow. The characteristics others ascribe to him and that are commonly reiterated in Soviet

---

30. Ibid. pp. 5–8, 10.
31. Ibid. p. 6; *E.B.* 20 December 1945.
32. Vyshinsky, 'The Chief of the Soviet Government,' pp. 3–22.
33. *Bol'shevik*, No. 3 (1938), pp. 63–4; No. 10–11 (1938), p. 61; *E.B.* 30 January 1945.

statements are: wisdom and common sense, breadth of knowledge, courage, cool-headedness and complete inner coherence, a passion for clarity, undeviating consistency, firmness and strength in decision-making, and constant care in recruiting personnel.[34]

Finally there is the emphasis placed on the requirement that leaders should be able to combine theory and practice, politics and organization, broad imagination and a practical common sense.[35] Two features, said Stalin in 1924, make for a proper style in Party and state work: 'the wide outlook of the Russian revolutionist' and 'American practicality.' Russian revolutionary scope, said he, is an antidote against routine, mental stagnation, and a slavish following of ancestral traditions. It awakens thought, pushes forward, breaks with the past. But the chances are that in practice it will degenerate into 'empty "revolutionary" phrase-mongering,' unless it is combined with American practicality in work. American practicality is an antidote to such phrase-mongering and 'flights of "revolutionary" fancy.' It is 'that indomitable force, which knows and recognizes no obstacle, which by its businesslike perseverance washes away all and every impediment, which simply must go through with a job begun even if it is of minor importance, and without which any serious constructive work is impossible.' But American practicality, Stalin maintained, runs the risk of degenerating into narrow and unprincipled commercialism, unless it is fused with the wide outlook of the Russian revolutionist. Only a combination of both, he concluded, produces 'a finished type of Leninist worker, the Leninist style of work.'[36]

This conception has endured till the present. But, roughly speaking, earlier in the regime the public emphasis was on practicality, on businesslike methods, on learning the know-how of running economic and other establishments, since the Party then had plenty of members with a knowledge of Soviet theory, but lacked men with managerial experience and technical skills. Before the recent war, the emphasis had changed to some extent, because, although the managerial and technical personnel had greatly increased, it was found lacking in knowledge of the theoretical principles and teachings of the Party.

The Mold of the Managerial Personnel. These views on leadership, and the changing needs of the times have had a profound influence on the recruitment of managerial personnel in the U.S.S.R. In the days of the

---

34. *Bolshevik*, No. 22 (1943), p. 5; *XVII S'ezd VKP(b)*, p. 115.
35. See *supra*, pp. 3–4, 373–4, note 20, p. 165. For a discussion of qualities generally expected of successful political leaders, see Merriam, op. cit. pp. 108–12.
36. Stalin, *Voprosy Leninizma*, pp. 72–4; *Foundations of Leninism*, pp. 121–3.

Party's underground existence, and during the period of the seizure of power and the civil war, agitators, propagandists, theorizers, and verbalizers inevitably emerged in strength in positions of leadership. For the skills possessed by such persons, especially their ability to induce new psychological-political identifications through verbal appeal, find ample play in situations of this sort. When the sharpest phase of socio-political upheaval is over, however, and a new regime settles down to the practical task of making a going concern of the system it introduced, the propagandist, agitator, and theorizer almost invariably yield to the executive, administrator, and political organizer — to the men whose chief assets are works rather than words.

Thus it was that in the intra-Party struggles of the 'twenties, most of those who lost out, from Politbureau members down, were — with few exceptions — skilled in verbalization and symbolization rather than in organization. In the 'thirties, the slogan was advanced that 'cadres decide everything,' that the U.S.S.R. would be thoroughly vulnerable unless it acquired good and numerous cadres in industry, agriculture, transport, and the army.[37] With this slogan came a thorough revamping of the entire administrative personnel. The managers who have come to the fore in the vast network of administrative units and economic enterprises embody to a remarkable degree the features so assiduously fostered in the Soviet concept of leadership. Soviet managerial personnel consists overwhelmingly of energetic administrators, mostly young, sparing of words, supreme realists, persevering and hard workers, extremely devoted to their jobs, and faithful to the Party and its highest leadership.

(3) THE FUNDAMENTAL PRINCIPLE OF CONTROL

Popular Participation in Government. The bounds of liberty and authority in the U.S.S.R. are weighted heavily in favor of authority. Yet the Soviet theory of leadership bases the exercise of that authority on the principle of 'the consent of the governed.' What the nature of such consent or assent is, or, to put it differently, what the form, extent and purpose of popular participation in government in the Soviet Union are, we shall review in the present section.

Popular participation in government in the U.S.S.R. takes the forms of: (a) conciliar organs — councils, conferences, meetings, soviets; (b) occasional use of quasi-plebiscite methods; and (c) citizen participation in elections, policy-execution, and law enforcement. The most extensive net-

---

37. See *supra,* pp. 43–5, 314, 317–8, 323–30.

work of conciliar organs is provided by the soviets. At the lower levels, the soviets are decision-makers. Within their respective spheres of authority the local soviets function as direct organs of authority, with the power to command and enforce obedience. Since the local soviets embrace hundreds of thousands of members, and non-Party people, moreover, predominate in them,[38] they are one of the most tangible expressions of popular participation in government. At the higher levels the soviets are primarily ratifying and popularizing bodies. For instance, the federal Congress of Soviets, Central Executive Committee, and now the Supreme Soviet have not in practice possessed any large powers of decision, and it is highly doubtful whether these representative organs were ever intended to act as a check upon the arbitrary powers of government. Nevertheless, at least four important categories of decisions have been brought periodically before these bodies for official enactment or *ex post facto* approval: the budget and national economic plan, interim decrees, important international agreements, and constitutional amendments. This obviously demonstrates a desire to attach to these decisions the sanction of approval of a popular, representative assembly in order to mobilize or strengthen community consensus through the formalities of common deliberation.

Other examples of conciliar organs are the numerous congresses, conferences, and meetings of trade unions, co-operatives, cultural and scientific societies, and professional groups, for consultation and discussion of work in their fields. The deliberations and decisions of these groups, often arranged for the very purpose of exposing shortcomings in existing practices, have a distinct bearing on governmental policy.

Occasional employment of quasi-plebiscite methods is exemplified by the popular discussion of the draft of the new constitution. Elections to the soviets, where the voice of citizen organizations carries a good deal of weight in the nomination of candidates, and recall campaigns are other forms of popular participation.[39] Lastly, perhaps the most concrete form of direct citizen participation are the *aktivs* or active groups of citizens, who participate in commissions of the soviets, assist in the work of the procurators, and perform other public duties in their spare time, on a voluntary basis. Reflecting an exaggerated notion on the part of the Soviet leaders earlier in the regime that mass participation in administration is a cure-all for maladministration, such groups were once given all kinds of spectacular assignments, including participation in inspection tours and purges to combat bureaucracy in all state institutions. In more recent years,

---

38. See *supra*, pp. 203–5, 349.
39. See *supra*, pp. 26–7, 193–4, 206.

these groups, numbering in the thousands in every locality, have proved most effective in public activities of the most immediate interest to the citizens — civic improvement, sanitation, transportation, local industries, et cetera.

In these forms, comprising in their totality the 'system of barometers,'[40] popular participation in government is extensive and is considered part of the learning process, which is expected — at least in theory — ultimately to lead to popular self-administration without 'government' in the accepted sense.

The essential purpose of such participation is twofold: to provide the Soviet leaders with indispensable political intelligence concerning the state of the public mind; and to aid in promoting popular approval of governmental policy and in inducing initiative, enthusiasm, and active support in policy execution. From these aims flows the fundamental nature of popular participation in government in the Soviet polity. In such problems as civic improvement or local activity, the widest expression and citizen intervention are encouraged. In other spheres, popular participation consists not in questioning fundamentals, or bringing up for unauthorized discussion basic political decisions,[41] but in helping the carrying out of policy through discussions, 'self-criticism,' public promises of assistance in its implementation, and actual activity.

The Crux of the Principle of Control. These methods of popular participation in government have distinct implications for political control, which can be summarized as follows:

(1) The Party summit keeps all ultimate controls in its own hands.

(2) It can and does receive a good deal of political intelligence through the conciliar organs and other 'barometers' on what the traffic will bear — how far the populace accepts its policies and how much active assistance can be elicited in their execution.

(3) More often than not it acts on the basis of this intelligence, and to that extent the will of the masses — though it can be and frequently is overruled — finds reflection in governmental decisions.

(4) The Party summit associates considerable sections of the people in the process of implementation and execution of governmental policies.

(5) As compared with Tsarist Russia, there has been an increase in popular participation in government in the U.S.S.R., especially on the part of workers, peasants, young people, women, and the nationality groups.

40. See *supra*, p. 186.
41. See *supra*, pp. 127–9, 207–8.

(6) Some tendencies of the last decade, such as adoption of the Constitution of 1936, the liberalization of Party rules, the growth of the Party's
membership, the predominance of non-Party people in the local soviets,
the increase in non-Party members in the representative federal assemblies,
point toward potentialities for participation in government by wider
sections of the populace.

The Soviet system of popular participation in government is far removed, however, from the system prevailing in the Western democracies,
where legislative bodies not only approve but make decisions, and where
the electorate can periodically check and altogether repudiate the political
leadership. Yet, under its own system of popular participation in government, the populace of the U.S.S.R. — which, in its overwhelming mass,
is only a decade or two removed from the backwardness of Tsarist Russia
— is learning something of the purposes and processes of government,
and — other things being equal — such participation could ultimately lead
to the growth of democratic practices in the U.S.S.R.

In sum, the basic principle of political control in the U.S.S.R. can be
stated in the following terms: fundamental policy formulation is a Party
prerogative, exercised by the Party summit, without the possibility of any
effective check by the people at present; but the people are actively associated in the propagation and execution of policy, and are instilled with a
growing sense of participation in government.

3. THE CRUCIBLES OF THE GOVERNMENTAL SYSTEM

(1) THE COMPASS OF THE COMMON WEAL

In a broad and general sense, the ends of government everywhere consist of assuring for the citizens, organized in the commonwealth, five
basic satisfactions: external security, internal order, justice, welfare, and
freedom.[42] While the forms, degrees, and justifications of these ends may
vary in time and place, the measure of their substantial attainment
constitutes the gauge of the common weal. And upon such attainment,
or a demonstrated striving after fulfilment, hangs, to a large extent,
the kind of popular support that makes for the essential stability of a
regime.

The Question of Stability of the Regime. As far as internal factors are
concerned, there can be little doubt of the present stability of the Soviet
regime. The strongest proofs of such stability are supplied by the extraor-

42. Merriam, op. cit. pp. vii, 31, 117.

dinarily long tenure of the leadership in office and the absence of any large-scale revolts. If the purges of the 'thirties bore witness to strong dissatisfaction among some of the social and national groups, the civil war, the period of the Five-Year Plans, and the recent war have *volens nolens* constituted plebiscites that indicated widespread support for the regime among the populace as a whole.

Essentially, this stability is compounded of the following physical-material and political-psychological elements:

(1) Ability of the regime to command an abundance of natural resources and manpower, considerable technical skills, and strong military forces, in behalf of its goals.

(2) The existence of numerous political barometers to detect trends and moods in the community before they reach an explosive state.

(3) A readiness on the part of the leaders to take such trends into consideration wherever possible, and to use considerable flexibility in deciding upon and implementing governmental policies.

(4) Employment of a combination of 'persuasion and coercion' — propaganda and violence — in pushing through policies, which the leaders deem necessary, even when they are ahead of the public.

(5) A considerable habit of discipline in the people, which has been inculcated from the earliest days of the regime.

Theoretical indoctrination has been a standard commodity in the political stock-in-trade of the Soviet regime for such a long time that it has unquestionably built up a high degree of popular consensus behind the existing constitutional order, with the people at large accepting the theses that the Party's judgment has been vindicated by events, that the Party has periodically posed the correct alternatives and defended the national interest throughout, that the state is moving in planned and organized fashion toward purposeful objectives promising a brighter future, and that the sacrifices exacted from the people were the indispensable price of survival.

As against these elements that tend to uphold the regime, there are a number of factors that work in the other direction. Chief among these are: (1) the fact that theoretical postulates have often proved wrong or irrelevant in practice; (2) dissatisfaction with economic shortages and material inequalities, which emerges from time to time among various social groups; and (3) manifestations of national discontent that crop up among the nationalities of the peripheral regions. Contributory factors are the state of devastation and dislocation caused by the War, and to a lesser extent also popular fear of external attack, although in the past such fear has been successfully utilized for mobilization of the people behind governmental policy.

On the whole, it would seem that at present the bonds of internal cohesion outweigh the elements of disunity and disaffection, and that no serious fissures in the regime are apparent.

The Problem of Efficiency in Government. Reviewing the record of three decades, it cannot be said that the Soviet government has failed to pursue external security, to establish internal order, and to institute a workable system of justice in the U.S.S.R. To be sure, for about half of that period the system of justice was consciously and deliberately built on class foundations, to the distinct disadvantage of certain categories of citizens. Subsequently, however, the class principle was eliminated from the operation of the judicial system, which became uniform for all groups of citizens.

In the total field of government, nonetheless, the record of performance is far from being generally positive. The worst features of government in the U.S.S.R. are not personal corruption or selfish rule on the part of the leaders (though like most rulers everywhere, or perhaps even more so, these leaders undoubtedly cherish the power that their positions give them), but they are widespread bureaucracy and inefficiency, with red tape and delay hampering the execution of administrative and managerial tasks.

Government in the U.S.S.R. has attained its greatest efficiency in fields and tasks where the system of highly centralized control offers the advantages of extensive economic planning and rapid as well as thorough mobilization of men and materials. Thus, organizationally, some of the best results have been obtained by the Soviet government in the military field, as well as in specific task campaigns — industrial, agricultural, cultural, civilian defense, et cetera — where the application of concentrated pressure and mass mobilization of forces and resources for a definite purpose and over a definite period have brought about the desired results. Generally, governmental performance in the domestic field has varied with different incumbents and different branches of administration. And the volume of 'self-criticism' at official and semi-official gatherings leaves no doubt of considerable bureaucratic confusion, evasion of responsibility, and procrastination, born of conflicting activity by too many officials and of fear on the part of some of them to take responsibility for decisions.[43]

In the foreign field, the tight control wielded by the Party directorate

---

43. See references of note 45 below.

gives it certain advantages of surprise maneuver, rapid alteration of a course of action, and singular concentration on particular objectives.[44] But the very fact that some of the highest Soviet diplomats are unable to move without frequent instructions from the center, is disadvantageous in the long run. For, whatever gains are achieved through the extraordinary tenacity of point of view, tactical skill, and purposefulness of the Soviet diplomats, the delays and inflexibility arising from the need to await orders antagonize the other parties to the negotiations and consequently diminish rather than increase the chances for maximum success.

Bureaucratic deficiencies in the U.S.S.R. are due chiefly to the following factors: the extraordinary size of the governmental apparatus; the fact that a much smaller margin of error is allowed to Soviet administrators and managers than to their counterparts in other countries; knowledge on the part of officials that their performance will be carefully scrutinized, and, hence, fear on the part of some of them to take responsibility for decisions; and the novelty and complexity of administrative problems in a vast and still backward country so recently embarked upon large-scale transformation.

Few problems have received so much attention in the U.S.S.R. as the problem of efficiency in government. Hardly a single Party or Soviet congress has passed without discussions and decisions to fight bureaucracy and improve the carrying out of Party and Soviet decisions.[45] As far back as 1922, Lenin urged a relentless struggle against *Oblomovshchina* (fanciful talk without capacity to accomplish things) on the part of Soviet officials, by examining periodically the fitness of individual office holders and by checking up on their actual performance.[46] Persistently the Party sought to fight bureaucracy through such diversified material and psychological devices as rationalization of administrative operations and routines, introduction of labor-saving instruments, 'socialist competition,' increases in remuneration and honors, propaganda and purges, organized visits by *aktivs* of citizens to government offices to check up on complaints of bureaucratic practices, introduction of the principle of 'one-man management' (*edinonachalie*) in most of the branches of administration, and numerous changes in the organs that verify and control the execution of governmental policy.[47]

---

44. See *supra*, pp. 157, 162.
45. See especially *XIII S'ezd RKP(b)*, *passim*; *XIV S'ezd VKP(b)*, *passim*; *XV S'ezd VKP(b)*, pp. 62–4, 383; *XVI S'ezd VKP(b)*, pp. 73, 79, 86–7, 617–19, 664–5, 674, 689–90; *XVII S'ezd VKP(b)*, pp. 33–4. See also *supra*, pp. 127–9, notes 9, 14, ch. VIII.
46. Lenin, XXVII, pp. 177–9.
47. Ibid.; see *supra*, pp. 140, 171–4, 206–7, 288–93.

As a result of these efforts and of growing experience, the quality of administration has greatly improved in the Soviet Union. Still the problem of efficiency in government remains and is likely to persist for a long time. The large area of governmental control, the rapid pace of construction and change in the country, and the backwardness of many parts of the population leave a wide range for the manifestation of bureaucratic perversion and maladministration. The need for technically trained, more cultured, and more efficient personnel is still felt widely in all fields of endeavor, including the field of government.

Concern for the Common Welfare. The word 'welfare' is writ large in Soviet-Marxian theory. According to this theory definitive socialism without abundance is unthinkable, and progress toward socialism was to be marked with mounting material well-being for all and the ultimate realization of the principle: 'from each according to his ability, to each according to his needs.'[48] Yet now, three decades after the inception of the Soviet regime, the realities of accomplishment are lagging far behind this vision of plenty and popular expectations.

The U.S.S.R. has enacted a large amount of welfare legislation covering social insurance against sickness, old age and loss of capacity to work, accident and crime prevention, free medical services, hours and conditions of work, leave and vacations, protection of mother and child, and protection of the property rights of citizens. It has secured notable results in eradicating illiteracy, liquidating unemployment, diffusing knowledge of technical skills, health preservation, and promotion of education and culture.

At the same time it remains true that few peoples in the world have suffered as many bitter privations and sacrifices, and for so long a period, as have the Soviet people. Except, perhaps, for a brief interlude of relative prosperity in the mid-'thirties, the mass of the people of the U.S.S.R. have always known the meaning of shortages in housing, clothing, and even in food, as well as the burdens of hard labor and continuously pressing social duties.

This chasm between aspirations and achievements is due in large measure to the low productivity of individuals and the general difficulties of erecting a highly modernized as well as novel economy in a backward country. Its chief cause, however, probably lies in a deliberate choice of priorities among state ends on the part of the Soviet leaders, who have interpreted the common good in terms of the precedence of external

---

48. See *supra,* pp. 11–12, 14–15.

security over internal welfare. In this choice, large-scale industrialization, the mechanization of agriculture, and military preparedness were pushed far ahead of production of consumers' goods, partly on the basis of estimates of the international position and tasks of the U.S.S.R., and in part in the belief that capital investment in big industry would ultimately increase the capacity of the economy to provide the populace with the amenities of life. This basic choice still prevails and seems destined to continue, at least during the period of restoration of the war-ravaged industries, though considerable attention is promised for the problem of more adequate production of consumers' goods.[49] Whether this problem can be satisfactorily solved while the above-mentioned priority among state ends continues remains to be seen.

Implicitly, if not explicitly, the problem of citizen welfare is increasingly coming to include considerations of psychological or spiritual satisfactions for the masses of the people. The *miranda* and *credenda* of power, sustained by embellishment of the symbols of authority, myths of special virtue or superiority, and assertions of identity between citizenry and state, are playing an increasingly effective role in every state.[50] In the U.S.S.R., propaganda has from the very beginning been considered an indispensable tool of government, and it has attained a respectable position by the side of the instruments of administrative compulsion and institutions of popular consent in the scheme of political power. Perhaps for the very reason that material satisfactions are often so meager in the U.S.S.R., there is a prodigious effort to provide psychological satisfactions in abundance. Such human cravings, anxieties, or compulsions as the desire for honor and response, the dread of public ridicule, the admiration of courage and strength, the yearning after recognition and success, and the urge for new experience [51] are made use of and provided for through public meetings, official statements and the press, the system of honors and awards, the new attitude toward the family, school, and home, the stress on science, the extraordinary emphasis on patriotism, and the attempt to accord a modicum of deference to every social group.

Thus, the intellectuals are told that they are 'the salt of the Soviet earth' and 'the most advanced and most cultured part of the Soviet society.' But to keep them psychologically in line, from the standpoint of the sensibilities of other social strata, they are also called 'workers of intellectual

49. Editorial, 'Create an Abundance of Basic Consumers' Goods,' *Izvestia,* 14 April 1946.
50. See Merriam, op. cit. pp. 81–93, and *Political Power* (New York and London, McGraw-Hill, 1934), ch. IV.
51. See Wright, 'Human Rights and World Order,' p. 252.

toil.' On the other hand, Stakhanovites or record-breaking field and factory workers are praised as foremost representatives of the intelligentsia. Aside from progress through study, a worker need only learn to increase his labor skill, to raise his productivity, in order to feel among the select.[52] Scientists are overwhelmingly praised, but at the same time the idea is fostered that practical workers who note scientific, technological, or efficiency facts in their own experience and contribute their observations, are comrades-in-arms of the scientists. In short, besides the political élite, the U.S.S.R. has created and nurtured the conception of numerous élites, with a wide variety of psychological gratifications.

The public emphasis on the thesis that work in the U.S.S.R. has become 'a matter of *honor*, a matter of *glory*, a matter of *valor* and *heroism*,' as well as a key to individual success,[53] has been conducive to labor discipline. Even more important are the official emphases on class and national solidarity. For the assertion of conflict breeds conflict, while the assertion of unity tends to promote unity. Whatever the actual substance of the concepts of popular sovereignty and friendship among nationalities, the psychological gains of their constant iteration are immense.

While the dire material needs of a people cannot be perpetually assuaged by psychological props or substitutes, it seems reasonably clear that the propagation of unifying concepts and ingenuity in devising psychological satisfactions in the U.S.S.R. have, on the whole, contributed substantially toward peaceful operation of its internal political process.

(2) CAPACITY FOR POLITICAL ACCOMMODATION

Politics is the art of the possible only. Political action that seeks the impossible ends in frustration and futility. Hence, to augment and insure its chances of survival and success, a government must of necessity find ways of political accommodation, both external and internal — modes of co-operation with other states in the community of nation-states and means of domestic change to adjust the needs and interests of groups and individuals in its own community. The alternatives to accommodation are friction and war without, revolution and subversion within.

Capacity for International Co-operation. Roughly speaking, there are two main criteria to gauge the capacity of the U.S.S.R. for international co-operation: the presence or absence of constitutional mechanisms for participation in international relations, and the record of the past.

As far as the first criterion is concerned, there can hardly be any doubt

---

52. See *supra*, pp. 318, 326, 328–9.
53. Stalin, *Voprosy Leninizma*, p. 393; *S.G.P.* pp. 510–11.

that the Soviet Union possesses the constitutional capacity for international co-operation. It has long established the necessary organs and instruments to formulate foreign policy, conduct diplomatic negotiations, conclude treaties and agreements, make war, and participate in international organizations. In more recent years, changes in diplomatic ranks, in other practices, and even in the nomenclature of the government were specifically motivated for greater accord with generally accepted custom and terminology in the international community.[54]

A proper review and evaluation of the record of the past, with the patterns of foreign policy that have emerged, would require a volume in itself and is beyond the scope of this study. We can merely touch upon this question here. The foreign-political record of the U.S.S.R. comprises an initial period of non-co-operation and open conflict with the international community, subsequent periods of varying degrees of co-operation, and again — since the end of the recent war — a period of mounting friction between the Soviet Union and the Western Powers. During the periods of co-operation the U.S.S.R. is estimated to have lived up in considerable measure to most of its international obligations.[55] Essentially, such co-operation was motivated by self-interest, first of all by the all-pervading goal of survival. Similar considerations could operate in the future to induce greater international co-operation on the part of the U.S.S.R. In the more immediate future perhaps the most that could be hoped for would be a *modus vivendi* based on some sort of understanding between East and West concerning legitimate bounds of security and influence. From the longer-range point of view, however, enduring co-operation — rather than provisional accommodation — can develop only on the basis of a vastly increased and wholehearted participation by the Soviet Union in international measures for cultural exchange, economic reconstruction, and collective security in the community of nations.

Capacity for Internal Change. The problem of maintaining a balance between the needs of stability and the necessities for change is felt again and again in every polity.[56] For upon a government's ability to conserve what is useful and viable in the state, and to adjust or replace what has become superannuated or defective, depend in no small degree its chances to secure a peaceful political development and to diminish opportunities for internal violence. This problem, however, assumes a special nature in

54. See the references of notes 65, 67, 76, 81, ch. xi.
55. See Florinsky, 'The Soviet Union and International Agreements,' pp. 61–89; Dean, 'Russia's Foreign Economic Policy,' p. 269.
56. See Merriam, *Systematic Politics,* ch. vii.

a state, like the U.S.S.R., that has undergone a fundamental revolution. For here rapid and repeated change is likely to be the norm for a prolonged period, resulting in a sort of habit of dynamism in political arrangements, and necessitating in the end special efforts to instill a wider disposition toward greater political stability.

In the Soviet Union, the power-holders themselves have long accepted the view that technological change and scientific discovery make periodic change inevitable, including change in the field of government. Their Marxist belief in the determinism of the historical process and the primacy of economic factors as sources of change has not deterred them from an equal belief that man can and must assume control over the course of social and political change. The pace of political change has been so rapid, however, that in the mid-'thirties the Soviet leaders called a halt, asserting the need for greater stability in legislation, territorial-administrative arrangements, and other political practices.[57]

This declaration of intentions notwithstanding, the subsequent pace of internal mutation has been considerable not only in times of intense crisis, but in periods of relative calm. Though greater progress toward equilibrium between stability and change appears to be in prospect, it will hardly bar further changes in governmental forms, forces, and functions. Structural change, most frequent in the past, will probably be slowed up to some extent, but will certainly not be entirely halted in the future. The political climate is less favorable for changes challenging fundamental institutions and principles. Here the element of ideological faith often displays a tenacity bordering on the fanatical. Still, the Soviet leaders are anything but slaves to tradition, custom, or dogma, and have in the past demonstrated a marked capacity for flexibility, even in regard to basic principles, to meet what they held to be the needs of particular periods. In its own time, the N.E.P. was a radical innovation. Subsequent fundamental modifications have included such changes as the new attitude toward family and school, the allotment of individual plots to collective farmers, the differentiation in the Army, the revised policies on social groups, and the altered concepts with regard to the state.

More in the category of sacrosanct values, where conservation rather than mutation is likely in the foreseeable future, are the socialized state of the economy, collectivized agriculture, and the Party's monopoly of power. Yet even in regard to these institutions some modifications in practice are not altogether excluded. Additional changes can be expected

---

57. See *supra*, pp. 107, 251.

in the administrative-territorial framework, the constitution, various aspects of the political system, the managerial personnel, and the status of social groups. A new tendency to seek security against unwise change is to be noted in the increasing practice of calling in technical specialists for advice in connection with proposed measures of legislation, planning, or management. This tendency, however, will not prevent political change, induced not only by conscious considerations, but by new technological inventions and the alterations in power relations flowing from them.

As we have seen in preceding chapters, the adaptability of theory, the flexibility of the constitution, the variability of state forms, the membership changes in the Party and the soviets, and other shifts in the balance of socio-political forces, all go into the making of a principle of elasticity freely acclaimed in the Soviet polity. Though deviations from fundamental patterns are likely to be slow and few, the polity appears to have the capacity for internal change.

(3) PROSPECT AND RETROSPECT

The U.S.S.R. is a strict dictatorship with a number of democratically earmarked features, operating on a principle designated as 'democratic centralism.' The main dictatorial features of the Soviet polity are the paucity of circulation of the highest élite — the virtual absence of change in the personnel of the top echelon of the Party which holds the monopoly of leadership; the degree of restriction and suppression of free exchange of ideas on socio-political fundamentals; and the extent of violence permitted in the system of rule. Its chief ameliorative features are the practices of equality for the nationalities, the multiplicity of conciliar organs, and the encouragement of popular participation in the implementation of policy.

As far as bases of internal stability are concerned, probably the main elements of the regime's strength lie in the government's claim to credit for widespread elimination of illiteracy and ignorance, in its promise of welfare and extensive opportunity for personal growth to the masses of the citizenry, and in its skill in devising psycho-political satisfactions. From 'Russia One and Indivisible' to a federation of nationalities, to a 'monolithic' U.S.S.R.; from dominion in 'one class' to a partnership of classes, to a singular unity of the populace; from a limited sphere of public prestige — practically restricted to Tsar, nobility, and clergy — to political exclusiveness for proletariat, Party, and Party leadership, to wide diffusion of public emoluments among all social groups — such has been the path of official attitudes, apparently leading to extensive acceptance of the conception of an identity of interests between state and society, Union and nationalities, leaders and masses, community and individuals. The chief elements of weakness in the regime are the abyss between the low standards of living and the millennial vision of plenty held forth by the official ideology, and the equation of ends and means in Soviet political philosophy — the failure to see that violence and conformism have a way of feeding on themselves and growing into a habit, which may destroy the very basis for an improved society in the U.S.S.R.

The highest point of development of individual liberties was the period of the mid-'thirties, when the new constitution was being drafted and some of the most restrictive practices of the regime were being liberalized. This was also a period of relative prosperity in the U.S.S.R. The peaks of emphasis of dictatorial features were the periods of War Communism, mass collectivization of agriculture, and the purges of 1937–8. Again, with the progressive deterioration of the international situation since the end of the recent hostilities, the pressure for conformism and other restrictive practices have increased in the Soviet Union. In retrospect and prospect, the generalization seems justified that more liberal practices might grow during periods of substantial external security and internal prosperity, while the dictatorial and centralist aspects would become accentuated in periods of actual or fancied threats from outside and material straits within.

We find here a distinct connection between internal factors conditioning the system of power in the Soviet Union and external expectations and relations. The political problem that stands out in boldest relief in the complex of unresolved problems of the U.S.S.R. is precisely the issue that most divides the Soviet Union from the democracies of the West, and, indeed, is the issue of our time: whether political liberty can be reconciled with economic democracy, and whether both can be nurtured and strengthened side by side in all polities. In the current era, two worlds are facing each other across the shrunken space of the earth, the Soviet and non-Soviet worlds. Whether they will progress in peace depends — perhaps more than on anything else — on whether their conceptions of political power and economic welfare can be adjusted in time, ultimately leading to international stability and world order. No one can predict with any degree of certainty that such a development will prove possible. Much will depend on the readiness of the Soviet leaders explicitly or implicitly to revise some of their most important ideological conceptions. Soviet political theory suggests the following chain of internal links to liberty in the U.S.S.R.: discipline — skill — productivity — abundance — equality — liberty. From the standpoint of predominantly external factors the road to personal freedom is visualized in the following sequence of concepts: 'Socialism in one country' or internal impregnability of the U.S.S.R. — dilution of the 'capitalist encirclement' or attainment of a high degree of external safety — victory of world socialism or absolute security — the 'withering away of the state' everywhere or supreme individual liberty. It will be seen that the two key concepts of the respective sequences are 'productivity' and 'capitalist encirclement.' Persistence of the concept of communist expansion in Soviet ideological statements has generated apprehensions and at various times counteractions on the part of other states, with inevitable consequences not only for the external position of the U.S.S.R., but for its internal political development as well.

The Soviet leaders have maintained all along that, given the opportunity of lasting peace, they would create a productive community in which liberty would be realized to the fullest extent. But in the age of the atom, more than ever before, lasting peace depends upon the stabilization of international relations, which in turn hinges in large measure upon the propagation of ideas of peaceful processes among nations rather than of concepts of struggle. In this sphere, therefore, the Soviet leaders themselves could make a vital contribution to peace through substantial modification of the concepts for the external security of the U.S.S.R. that they have posited. Such a modification would entail in the first place a re-evaluation of the strength, efficacy, and capacity for social justice of the capitalist democracies. And sooner or later — whether in years or in decades — if enduring peace is to be achieved, there would have to be progress, however slow and painful, toward a universal consensus on basic human values. It will undoubtedly be difficult to move toward a consensus on race and nationality relations, on the nature of economic welfare, on the role of the state and the standing of the individual, on freedom of migration, contact, and communication for citizens of all states, and similarly vital issues. Yet, a high degree of agreement on these problems will probably have to be attained as a foundation for genuine understanding between the 'two worlds' gradually leading toward 'one world.'

Whether any such appraisal will take root in the U.S.S.R., fundamentally conditioning the future development of political power in that state, time alone can tell.

Charts

Chart 1 THE PARTY PYRAMID

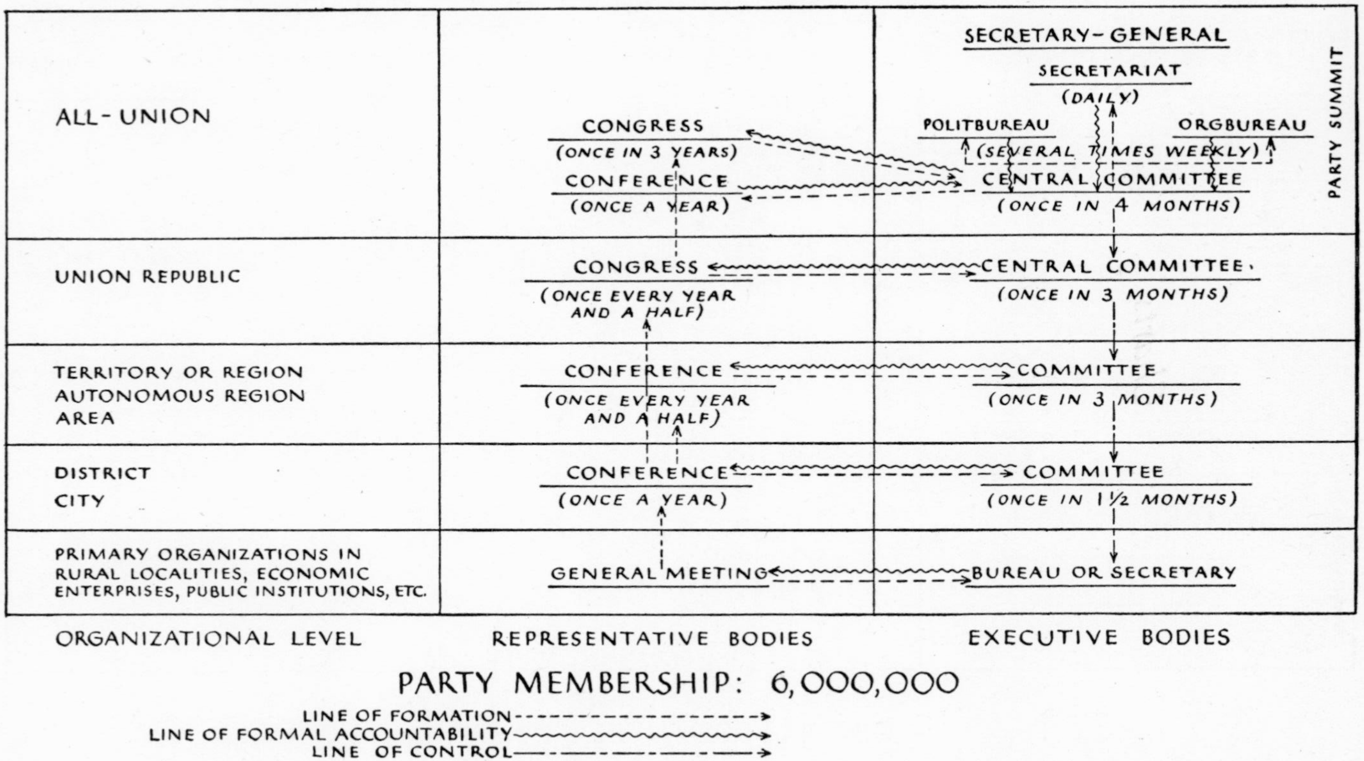

PARTY SUMMIT

SECRETARY-GENERAL
SECRETARIAT
(DAILY)
POLITBUREAU
(SEVERAL TIMES WEEKLY)
ORGBUREAU
CENTRAL COMMITTEE
(ONCE IN 4 MONTHS)

CONGRESS
(ONCE IN 3 YEARS)
CONFERENCE
(ONCE A YEAR)

CENTRAL COMMITTEE
(ONCE IN 3 MONTHS)

CONGRESS
(ONCE EVERY YEAR AND A HALF)

COMMITTEE
(ONCE IN 3 MONTHS)

CONFERENCE
(ONCE EVERY YEAR AND A HALF)

COMMITTEE
(ONCE IN 1½ MONTHS)

CONFERENCE
(ONCE A YEAR)

BUREAU OR SECRETARY

GENERAL MEETING

ALL-UNION

UNION REPUBLIC

TERRITORY OR REGION
AUTONOMOUS REGION
AREA

DISTRICT
CITY

PRIMARY ORGANIZATIONS IN
RURAL LOCALITIES, ECONOMIC
ENTERPRISES, PUBLIC INSTITUTIONS, ETC.

ORGANIZATIONAL LEVEL

REPRESENTATIVE BODIES

EXECUTIVE BODIES

PARTY MEMBERSHIP: 6,000,000

LINE OF FORMATION
LINE OF FORMAL ACCOUNTABILITY
LINE OF CONTROL

414

Chart 2   THE SOVIET PYRAMID

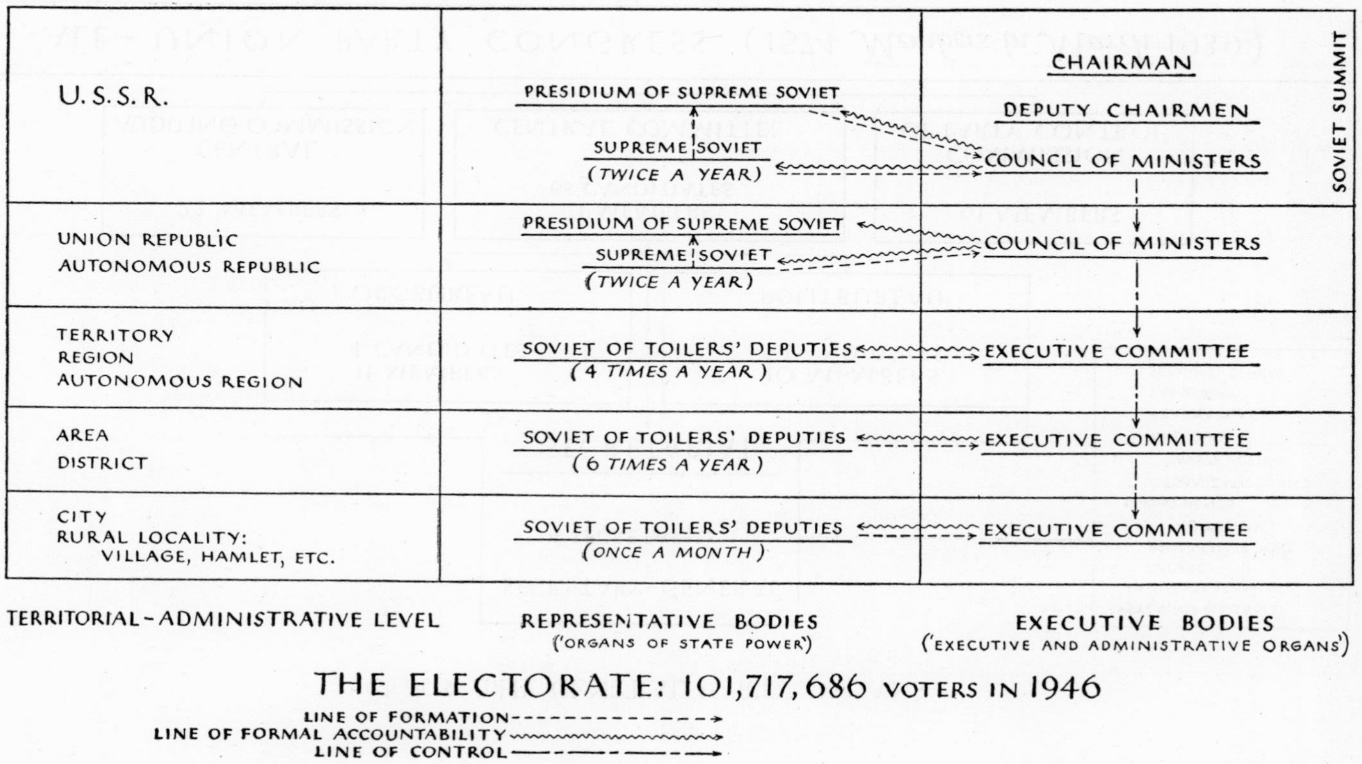

SOVIET SUMMIT

CHAIRMAN
DEPUTY CHAIRMEN

TERRITORIAL–ADMINISTRATIVE LEVEL	REPRESENTATIVE BODIES (ORGANS OF STATE POWER)	EXECUTIVE BODIES (EXECUTIVE AND ADMINISTRATIVE ORGANS)
U.S.S.R.	PRESIDIUM OF SUPREME SOVIET — SUPREME SOVIET (TWICE A YEAR)	COUNCIL OF MINISTERS
UNION REPUBLIC AUTONOMOUS REPUBLIC	PRESIDIUM OF SUPREME SOVIET — SUPREME SOVIET (TWICE A YEAR)	COUNCIL OF MINISTERS
TERRITORY REGION AUTONOMOUS REGION	SOVIET OF TOILERS' DEPUTIES (4 TIMES A YEAR)	EXECUTIVE COMMITTEE
AREA DISTRICT	SOVIET OF TOILERS' DEPUTIES (6 TIMES A YEAR)	EXECUTIVE COMMITTEE
CITY RURAL LOCALITY: VILLAGE, HAMLET, ETC.	SOVIET OF TOILERS' DEPUTIES (ONCE A MONTH)	EXECUTIVE COMMITTEE

THE ELECTORATE: 101,717,686 VOTERS IN 1946

LINE OF FORMATION -------
LINE OF FORMAL ACCOUNTABILITY ~~~~~~~
LINE OF CONTROL ------->

415

Chart 3 THE CENTRAL PARTY ORGANS

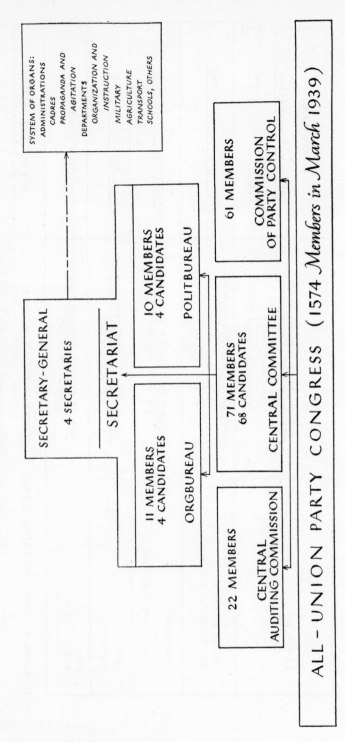

SYSTEM OF ORGANS:

ADMINISTRATIONS
CADRES
PROPAGANDA AND
    AGITATION
DEPARTMENTS
ORGANIZATION AND
    INSTRUCTION
MILITARY
AGRICULTURE
TRANSPORT
SCHOOLS, OTHERS

SECRETARY-GENERAL
4 SECRETARIES

SECRETARIAT

10 MEMBERS
4 CANDIDATES
POLITBUREAU

11 MEMBERS
4 CANDIDATES
ORGBUREAU

71 MEMBERS
68 CANDIDATES
CENTRAL COMMITTEE

61 MEMBERS
COMMISSION
OF PARTY CONTROL

22 MEMBERS
CENTRAL
AUDITING COMMISSION

ALL-UNION PARTY CONGRESS (1574 *Members in March* 1939)

416

Chart 4 THE CENTRAL SOVIET ORGANS

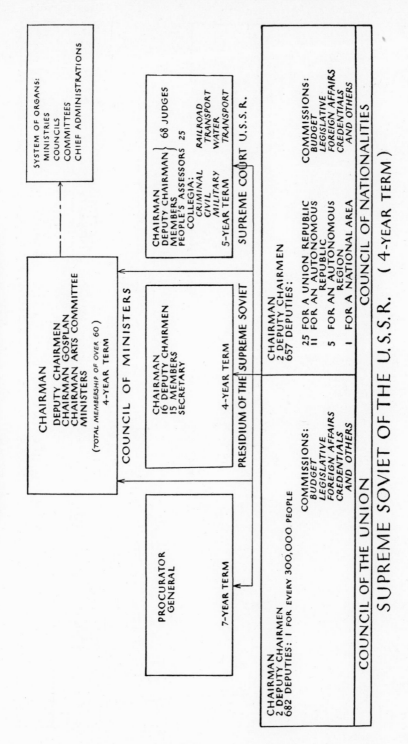

Bibliography

1. BOOKS, TREATISES AND PAMPHLETS

Ananov, I. N. *Ocherki Federal'nogo Upravlenia S.S.S.R.* [Outlines of the Federal Administration of the U.S.S.R.]. Leningrad-Moskva, 1925.

Anderson, Paul B. *People, Church and State in Modern Russia.* New York, 1944.

Batsell, Walter Russell. *Soviet Rule in Russia.* New York, 1929.

Bienstock, Gregory; Schwarz, Solomon M.; and Yugow, Aaron. *Management in Russian Industry and Agriculture.* New York, 1944.

Bloom, Solomon F. *The World of Nations.* New York, 1941.

Bregman, S. *Vybory v Verkhovnyi Sovet S.S.S.R. i Profsoiuzy* [The Elections to the Supreme Soviet of the U.S.S.R. and the Trade Unions]. Moskva, 1937.

Bunyan, James, and Fisher, H. H. *The Bolshevik Revolution, 1917–1918.* Stanford University, 1934.

Burns, Emile. *A Handbook of Marxism.* New York, 1935.

Burroughs, E. G. *Who's Who in the Red Army.* London, 1944.

The Call of the Russian Church. London, 1945.

Clementis, Vladimir. *'Panslavism' Past and Present.* London, 1943.

The Communist International between the Fifth and Sixth World Congresses, 1924–8. London, 1928.

Curtiss, J. S. *Church and State in Russia, 1900–1917.* New York, 1939.

Dallin, David J. *The Real Soviet Russia.* New Haven, 1944.

Denisov, A. *Sovety — Politicheskaia Osnova S.S.S.R.* [The Soviets — the Political Basis of the U.S.S.R.]. Moskva, 1940.

Diablo, V. K. *Sudebnaia Okhrana Konstitutsii* [Judicial Guarding of the Constitution]. Moskva, 1928.

The Dictatorship of the Proletariat. New York, 1936.

Duguit, L. *Manuel du droit constitutionnel.* 2nd ed., Paris, 1911.

The Election System of the Union of Soviet Socialist Republics. London, 1945.

Engel', E. A. *Osnovy Sovetskoi Konstitutsii* [Principles of the Soviet Constitution]. Gos. Izd., 1923.

Engels, Frederick. *Herr Eugen Dühring's Revolution in Science.* Trans. by Emile Burns. New York, 1939.

——. *The Housing Question.* London, 1942.

——. *The Origin of the Family, Private Property and the State.* New York, 1942.

Fischer, Louis. *Men and Politics.* New York, 1941.

Gavrilin, I. *Leninskii Komsomol Rezerv i Pomoshchnik Kommunisticheskoi Partii* [The Leninist Komsomol, Reserve, and Assistant of the Communist Party]. 'Molodaia Gvardia,' 1939.

Gierke, Otto von. *Das deutche Genossenschaftsrecht.* 4 vols. Berlin, 1868–1913.

———. *Die Genossenschaftstheorie und das deutche Rechtssprechung.* Berlin, 1887.

Gumplowicz, L. *Rasse und Staat.* Wien, 1875.

———. *Rechtstaat und Sozialismus.* Innsbruck, 1881.

———. *Der Rassenkampf.* 2nd ed., Innsbruck, 1909.

Gurvich, G. S. *Istoria Sovetskoi Konstitutsii* [History of the Soviet Constitution]. Moskva, 1923.

———. *Osnovy Sovetskoi Konstitutsii* [The Principles of the Soviet Constitution]. 5-e izd. Moskva, 1926.

Harper, S. N. (ed.). *The Soviet Union and World Problems.* Chicago, 1935.

———. *The Government of the Soviet Union.* New York, 1938.

Hecker, Julius F. *Religion Under the Soviets.* New York, 1927.

Jellinek, Georg. *Allgemeine Staatslehre.* Berlin, 1900.

———. *Verfassungsänderung und Verfassungswandlung.* Berlin, 1906.

Kelsen, Hans. *Sozialismus und Staat.* Leipzig, 1923.

———. *Allgemeine Staatslehre.* Berlin, 1925.

Konstantinov, F. *Znachenie Lichnykh Sposobnostei i Truda pri Sotsializme* [The Significance of Personal Abilities and Work Under Socialism]. [Moskva], 1938.

Korovin, E. A. *Mezhdunarodnoe Pravo Perekhodnogo Vremeni* [International Law of the Transition Period]. Moskva-Petrograd, 1923.

Kotliarevsky, S. A. *S.S.S.R. i Soiuznye Respubliki* [The U.S.S.R. and the Union Republics]. Moskva, 1924.

Kournakoff, Sergei N. *Russia's Fighting Forces.* New York, 1942.

Krabbe, H. *The Modern Idea of the State.* The Hague, 1922.

Krylenko, N. V. *Osnovy Sudoustroistva S.S.S.R. i Soiuznykh Respublik* [The Principles of the Judicial Structure of the U.S.S.R. and Union Republics]. Moskva, 1927.

Lamont, Corliss. *The Peoples of the Soviet Union.* New York, 1946.

Lasswell, Harold D. *World Politics and Personal Insecurity.* New York, 1935.

Lebedev, V. *Velikii Russkii Narod — Vydaiushchaiasia Natsia* [The Great Russian People — the Outstanding Nation]. Moskva, 1945.

Lenin, V. I. *State and Revolution.* New York, 1935.

———. *Sochinenia* [Works]. 30 vols., 3rd ed., Leningrad, 1935–7.

Lenin i Stalin. *O Molodezhi* [About the Youth]. 'Molodaia Gvardia,' 1938.

Lowie, Robert H. *The Origin of the State.* New York, 1927.

MacIver, R. M. *The Modern State.* Oxford, 1926.

McLeod, W. C. *The Origin and History of Politics.* New York, 1931.

Magerovsky, D. A. *Soiuz Sovetskikh Sotsialisticheskikh Respublik* [The Union of the Soviet Socialist Republics]. Moskva, 1923.

Malitski, A. *Sovetskaia Konstitutsia* [The Soviet Constitution]. 4-e izd. Kharkov, 1928.

Marx, Karl. *The Civil War in France.* London, 1941.

———. *Critique of the Gotha Programme.* London, 1943.

Marx and Engels. *The Communist Manifesto.* New York, 1932.

———. *Selected Correspondence, 1846–1895.* London, 1943.

Merriam, Charles E. *Systematic Politics.* Chicago, 1946.

Mikhailov, Nicholas. *Land of the Soviets.* New York, 1939.

Minz, I. *The Red Army.* New York, 1943.

More, Sir Thomas. *Utopia*. Robinson's trans., 1556. Birmingham, 1869.

Notestein, Frank W. *The Future Population of Europe and the Soviet Union*. League of Nations Series. Geneva, 1944.

Oppenheimer, Franz. *The State*. Trans. by J. M. Gitterman, Indianapolis, 1914.

Pashkukanis, E. *Obshchaia Teoria Prava i Marksizm* [The General Theory of Law and Marxism]. Moskva, 1927.

——. *Ocherki po Mezhdunarodnomu Pravu* [Outlines on International Law]. Gos. Izdat. Sov. Zak., 1935.

Politicheskii Slovar' [Political Dictionary]. [Moskva], 1940.

Pravda o Religii v Rossii [The Truth About Religion in Russia]. Moskva, 1942.

Reikhel', M. O. *S.S.S.R. Ocherki Konstitutsionnykh Vzaimootnoshenii Sovetskikh Respublik* [The U.S.S.R. An Outline of the Constitutional Interrelations of the Soviet Republics]. Kharkov, 1925.

Sabine, George H. *A History of Political Theory*. New York, 1937.

Samoilov, F. N. *Kak Proishkodili Vybory pri Tsarizme* [How Elections Took Place Under Tsarism]. [Moskva], 1945.

Sovetskoe Administrativnoe Pravo [Soviet Administrative Law]. Moskva, 1940.

Stalin, I. [sic]. *Voprosy Leninizma* [Problems of Leninism]. 10-e izdanie. [Moskva], 1934.

Stalin, Joseph. *Foundations of Leninism*. New York, 1932.

——. *Problems of Leninism*. New York, 1934.

——. *Marxism and the National and Colonial Question*. New York: International Publishers.

——. *Marksizm i Natsional'no-Kolonial'nyi Vopros* [Marxism and the National and Colonial Question]. Moskva, 1937.

Steklov, Iu. M. (ed.). *Sovetskaia Demokratia* [Soviet Democracy]. Moskva, 1929.

Stetsky, A. *Pobeda Sotsializma v S.S.S.R. i Novaia Sovetskaia Konstitutsia* [The Victory of Socialism in the U.S.S.R. and the New Soviet Constitution]. [Moskva], 1936.

——. *The Constitution of the Socialist State*. Moscow, 1936.

Strachey, John. *The Theory and Practice of Socialism*. London, 1936.

Strong, A. L. *The New Soviet Constitution*. New York, 1937.

Stuchka, P. *S.S.S.R. i R.S.F.S.R., Sovetskaia Konstitutsia v Voprosakh i Otvetakh* [The U.S.S.R. and the R.S.F.S.R., the Soviet Constitution in Questions and Answers]. [Moskva], 1924.

Sul'kevich, S. *Naselenie SSSR* [The Population of the USSR]. [Moskva], 1939.

Taracouzio, T. A. *The Soviet Union and International Law*. New York, 1935.

Tikhomirnov, G. A. *Viacheslav Mikhailovich Molotov, Kratkaia Biografia* [Vyacheslav Mikhailovich Molotov, A Short Biography]. [Moskva], 1940.

Timasheff, N. S. *Religion in Soviet Russia*. New York, 1942.

Trainin, I. *Natsional'noe i Sotsial'noe Osvobozhdenie Zapadnoi Ukrainy i Zapadnoi Belorussii* [The National and Social Liberation of Western Ukraine and Western Byelorussia]. Moskva, 1939.

——. *Mestnye Organy Gosudarstvennoi Vlasti v SSSR i 'Samoupravlenia' v Kapitalisticheskikh Stranakh* [The Local Organs of State Power in the USSR and 'Self-Government' in the Capitalist Countries]. Moskva, 1940.

——. *Velikoe Sodruzhestvo Narodov SSSR* [The Great Companionship of the Peoples of the USSR]. Moskva, 1945.

Trotsky, Leon. *The Third International After Lenin*. New York, 1936.

Turubiner, A. M. *Ocherki Gosudarstvennogo Ustroistva S.S.S.R.* [Outlines of the State Structure of the U.S.S.R.]. Moskva, 1925.

Vakhmistrov, A. *Agitatsionno-Massovaia Rabota na Izbiratelnom Uchastke* [The Mass-Agitational Work in the Electoral Precinct]. Moskva, 1945.

Vaksberg, M. A. *Pravovoe Polozhenie Soiuznykh Respublik — Chlenov S.S.S.R.* [The Legal Status of the Union Republics — Members of the U.S.S.R.]. Irkutsk, 1925.

Volin, B. *Velikii Russkii Narod* [The Great Russian People]. [Moskva], 1938.

Vseslavianskii Miting v Moskve [The All-Slav Meeting in Moscow]. Moskva, 1941.

Vyshinsky, A. (ed.). *Sovetskoe Gosudarstvennoe Pravo* [Soviet Public Law]. Moskva, 1938.

——. *Sovetskoe Gosudarstvo v Otechestvennoi Voine* [The Soviet State in the Patriotic War]. Moskva, 1944.

Webb, Sidney and Beatrice. *Soviet Communism: A New Civilization?* 2 vols. New York, 1936.

White, D. Fedotoff. The Growth of the Red Army. Princeton, 1944.

Williams, A. R. *The Soviets.* New York, 1937.

Wright, Quincy. *The Control of American Foreign Relations.* New York, 1922.

Yaroslavsky, E. *O Roli Intelligentsii v S.S.S.R.* [About the Role of the Intelligentsia in the U.S.S.R.]. Moskva, 1939.

2. DOCUMENTARY SOURCES

Bol'shaia Sovetskaia Entsiklopedia [The Great Soviet Encyclopedia]. Vols. 1–46, 50–65. Moskva, 1926–39.

Entsiklopedia Gosudarstva i Prava (*E. G. i P.*) [Encyclopedia of State and Law]. 3 vols. Moskva, 1925–7.

Gorkin, A. *Izbiratel'nyi Zakon Sovetskogo Gosudarstva* [The Electoral Law of the Soviet State]. Moskovskii Rabochii, 1945.

History of the Communist Party of the Soviet Union (*Bolsheviks*). *Short Course.* Edited by a Commission of the Central Committee of the C.P.S.U.(B). New York, 1939.

Istoria Diplomatii [History of Diplomacy]. 3 vols. Moskva, 1945.

Istoria Sovetskoi Konstitutsii v Dekretakh i Postanovleniakh Sovetskago Pravitel'stva 1917–1936 [The History of the Soviet Constitution in Decrees and Decisions of the Soviet Government 1917–36]. Moskva, 1936.

Kalinin, M. I. *Stat'i i Rechi, 1919–1935* [Articles and Speeches, 1919–35]. [Moskva], 1936.

Kommunisticheskii Internatsional v Dokumentakh. Resheniia, tezisy i vozzvaniia kongressov Kominterna i plenumov IKKI. 1919–1932. [Communist International in documents. Resolutions, theses, and appeals of the congresses of the Comintern and plenary sessions of ECCI (Executive Committee of the Communist International.)] Moskva, 1933.

Konstitutsia Soiuza S.S.R. i Konstitutsii Sovetskikh Sotsialisticheskikh Respublik [The Constitution of the Union S.S.R. and the Constitutions of the Soviet Socialist Republics]. Moskva, 1937.

Lenin i Stalin o Sovetskoi Konstitutsii [Lenin and Stalin on the Soviet Constitution]. Moskva, 1936.

Malaia Sovetskaia Entsiklopedia [The Small Soviet Encyclopedia]. Vols. 1–7, 9–10. Moskva, 1933–40.

Manuil'sky, D. *Doklad Delegatsii VKP(b) v IKKI na XVIII S'ezde VKP(b)* (The Report of the CPSU(B) Delegation to the ECCI at the 18th Congress of the CPSU(B). [Moskva], 1939.

Molotov on the New Soviet Constitution. New York, 1937.

Molotov, V. M. *O Vneshnei Politike Sovetskogo Soiuza* [The Foreign Policy of the Soviet Union]. [Moskva], 1939.

Novyi Zakon o Sudoustroistve [The New Law on the Judiciary]. Moskva, 1938.

Report of Court Proceedings in the Case of the Anti-Soviet 'Bloc of Rights and Trotskyites,' Verbatim Report. Moscow, 1938.

Sbornik deistvuiushchikh dogovorov, soglashenii i konventsii zakliuchennykh s inostrannymi gosudarstvami [A collection of treaties, agreements, and conventions in force with foreign states], vyp. I-VII. Moskva, 1924–33.

Seventh World Congress of the Communist International. Resolutions and Decisions. Moscow-Leningrad, 1935.

S'ezdy Sovetov RSFSR v Postanovleniakh i Rezoliutsiakh [The Congresses of Soviets of the RSFSR in Decisions and Resolutions]. Moskva, 1939.

S'ezdy Sovetov RSFSR. Stenograficheskie Otchety [Congresses of Soviets of the RSFSR. Verbatim reports].

(2 *V.S.S.*) *Vtoroi Vserossiiskii S'ezd Sovetov . . . 7–8 Noiabria (25–26 Oktiabria) 1917 g.* [Second All-Russian Congress of Soviets, 7–8 November (25–6 October) 1917]. Moskva-Leningrad, 1928.

(3 *V.S.S.*) *Tretii Vserossiiskii S'ezd Sovetov . . . 10–18 Ianvaria 1918 g.* [Third All-Russian Congress of Soviets, 10–18 January 1918]. Petrograd, 1918.

(4 *V.S.S.*) *Chetvertyi Chrezvychainyi S'ezd Sovetov . . . 15–16 Marta 1918 g.* [Fourth Extraordinary Congress of Soviets, 15–16 March 1918]. Moskva, 1920.

(5 *V.S.S.*) *Piatyi Vserossiiskii S'ezd Sovetov . . . 4–10 Iulia 1918 g.* [Fifth Congress of Soviets, 4–10 July 1918]. Moskva, 1918.

(6 *V.S.S.*) *Shestoi Vserossiiskii Chrezvychainyi S'ezd Sovetov . . . 6–9 Noiabria 1918 g.* [Sixth All-Russian Extraordinary Congress of Soviets, 6–9 November 1918]. Moskva, 1919.

(7 *V.S.S.*) *7-i Vserossiiskii S'ezd Sovetov . . . 5–9 Dekabria 1919 g.* [7th All-Russian Congress of Soviets, 5–9 December 1919]. Gosizdat, 1920.

(8 *V.S.S.*) *Vos'moi Vserossiiskii S'ezd Sovetov . . . 22–29 Dekabria 1920 g.* [Eighth All-Russian Congress of Soviets, 22–9 December 1920]. Gosizdat, 1921.

(9 *V.S.S.*) *Deviatyi Vserossiiskii S'ezd Sovetov . . . 22–27 Dekabria 1921 g.* [Ninth All-Russian Congress of Soviets, 22–7 December 1921]. Moskva, 1922.

(10 *V.S.S.*) *Desiatyi Vserossiiskii S'ezd Sovetov . . . 23–27 Dekabria 1922 g.* [Tenth All-Russian Congress of Soviets, 23–7 December 1922]. Moskva, 1923.

S'ezdy Sovetov SSSR. Stenograficheskie Otchety [Congresses of Soviets of the USSR. Verbatim reports].

(*I S'ezd Sovetov SSSR*) *1-i S'ezd Sovetov Souiza Sovetskikh Sotsialisticheskikh Respublik. 30 Dekabria 1922 g.* [1st Congress of Soviets of the USSR, 30 December 1922]. Moskva, 1923.

(*II S'ezd Sovetov SSSR*) *Vtoroi S'ezd Sovetov . . . 26 Ianvaria-2 Fevralia 1924 g.* [Second Congress of Soviets, 26 January-2 February 1924]. Moskva, 1924.

(*III S'ezd Sovetov SSSR*) *Tretii S'ezd Sovetov . . . 13–20 Maia 1925 g.* [Third Congress of Soviets, 13–20 May 1925]. Moskva, 1925.

(*IV S'ezd Sovetov SSSR*) *4 S'ezd Sovetov . . . 18–26 Aprelia, 1927 g.* [4th Congress of Soviets, 18–26 April 1927]. Moskva, 1927.

(*V S'ezd Sovetov SSSR*) *5 S'ezd Sovetov . . . 20–28 Maia 1929 g.* [5th Congress of Soviets, 20–28 May 1929]. Moskva, 1929.

(*VI S'ezd Sovetov SSSR*) *6 S'ezd Sovetov . . . 8–17 Marta 1931 g.* [6th Congress of Soviets, 8–17 March 1931]. Moskva, 1931.

(*VII S'ezd Sovetov SSSR*) *7 S'ezd Sovetov . . . 28 Ianvaria-6 Fevralia 1935 g.* [7th Congress of Soviets, 28 January-6 February 1935]. Moskva, 1935.

S'ezdy Sovetov SSSR v Postanovleniakh i Rezoliutsiakh [The Congresses of Soviets of the U.S.S.R. in Decisions and Resolutions]. Moskva, 1939.

Sistematicheskoe Sobranie Deistvuiushchikh Zakonov Soiuza Sovetskikh Sotsialisticheskikh

Respublik [A Systematic Collection of the Laws of the U.S.S.R. in Force]. Knigi 1-v. Moskva, 1927.

Sobranie Postanovlenii i Rasporiazhenii Pravitel'stva SSSR [A Collection of Decisions and Ordinances of the Government of the U.S.S.R.]. Moskva, 1938 (Began publication on 19 March 1938).

Sobranie Uzakonenii i Rasporiazhenii Rabochego i Krestianskogo Pravital'stva R.S.F.S.R. [A Collection of Laws and Ordinances of the Workers and Peasants Government of the R.S.F.S.R.]. Moskva, 1917—.

Sobranie Zakonov i Rasporiazhenii Raboche-Krestianskogo Pravitel'stva SSSR [A Collection of Laws and Ordinances of the Worker-Peasant Government of the USSR]. Moskva, 1923–38.

Source Book on European Governments. New York, 1937.

Tsentral'nyi Ispolnitel'nyi Komitet [Central Executive Committee] *RSFSR. Vserossiiskii Tsentral'nyi Ispolnitel'nyi Komitet. Sozyv . . . Stenograficheskii Otchet* [RSFSR All-Russian Central Executive Committee, Convocation . . . stenographic report]. Moskva, 1918–22.

    (2 *VTsIK*) Sozyv II [2nd Convocation]. Sessions between 27 October and 29 December, 1917.

    (4 *VTsIK*) Sozyv IV. [4th Convocation]. Sessions between 20 March and 14 June, 1918.

    (5 *VTsIK*) Sozyv V. [5th Convocation]. Sessions between 15 July and 4 November, 1918.

    (7 *VTsIK*) Sozyv VII [7th Convocation]. Sessions between 2 February and 23 October, 1920.

    (8 *VTsIK*) Sozyv VIII [8th Convocation]. Sessions between 31 December 1920 and 7 October, 1921.

    (9 *VTsIK*) Sozyv IX [9th Convocation]. Sessions between 29 December 1921 and 31 October 1922.

    (10 *VTsIK*) Sozyv X [10th Convocation]. Sessions between 28 December, 1922 and 3 November 1923.

Tsentral'nyi Ispolnitel'nyi Komitet. SSSR. Sozyv . . . Stenograficheskii Otchet [Central Executive Committee USSR. Convocation . . . stenographic report]. Moskva, 1923–37.

    (1 *TsIK*) Sozyv I [1st Convocation]. Sessions of 6 July, 6–12 November, 1923.

    (2 *TsIK*) Sozyv II [2nd Convocation]. Sessions of 2 February, 17–29 October, 1924; 3–7 March 1925.

    (3 *TsIK*) Sozyv III [3rd Convocation]. Sessions of 21 May 1925; 12–25 April, 1926; 14–25 February, 1927.

    (4 *TsIK*) Sozyv IV [4th Convocation]. Sessions of 27 April, 15–20 October, 1927; 11–21 April, 3–15 December, 1928.

    (5 *TsIK*) Sozyv V [5th Convocation]. Sessions of 29 May, 29 November–8 December, 1929; 4–10 January, 1931.

    (6 *TsIK*) Sozyv VI [6th Convocation]. Sessions of 18 March, 22–8 December, 1931; 23–30 January, 28–31 December, 1933; 1 January 1934.

    (7 *TsIK*) Sozyv VII [7th Convocation]. Sessions of 7 February, 1935; 10–17 January, 1936; 11–13 January, 1937.

Stalin, I. [sic]. *O Proekte Konstitutsii Soiuza SSR* [On the Draft of the Constitution of the Union SSR]. [Moskva], 1936.

——.*O Konstitutsii Soiuza SSR* [About the Constitution of the Union SSR]. [Moskva], 1937.

Stalin, Joseph. *Report on the Work of the Central Committee to the Eighteenth Congress of the C.P.S.U.B.* Moscow, 1939.

——. *The Great Patriotic War of the Soviet Union.* New York, 1945.

Stalin on the New Soviet Constitution. New York, 1937.

10 *Let Verkhovnogo Suda Soiuza SSR,* 1924–1934 [10 Years of the Supreme Court of the Union SSR, 1924–34]. Moskva, 1934.

20 *Let Sovetskoi Vlasti, Statisticheskii sbornik* [20 Years of Soviet Power, A Collection of Statistics]. Moskva, 1937.

Vedomosti Verkhovnogo Soveta [Supreme Soviet Gazette]. Began publication on 7 April, 1938.

Verkhovnyi Sovet SSSR. Stenograficheskie Otchety [Supreme Soviet of the USSR. Verbatim reports]. (First Convocation, 1938–46.)

(1 *Sessia V. S.*) *Pervaia Sessia Verkhovnogo Soveta SSSR,* 12–19 *Ianvaria* 1938 g. [First session of the Supreme Soviet USSR, 12–19 January, 1938]. Izdanie Verkhovnogo Soveta SSSR, 1938.

(2 *Sessia V. S.*) *Vtoraia Sessia Verkhovnogo Soveta SSSR* 10–21 *Avgusta* 1938 g. [Second session, 10–21 August, 1938]. Izdanie Verkhovnogo Soveta SSSR, 1938.

(3 *Sessia V. S.*) *Tretia Sessia Verkhovnogo Soveta SSSR* 25–31 *Maia* 1939 g. [Third session, 25–31 May, 1939]. Izdanie Verkhovnogo Soveta SSSR, 1939.

(4 *Sessia V. S.*) *Vneocherednaia Chetvertaia Sessia Verkhovnogo Soveta SSSR* 28 *Avgusta–1 Sentiabria* 1939 g. [Extraordinary fourth session, 28 August–1 September, 1939). Izdanie Verkhovnogo Soveta SSSR, 1939.

(5 *Sessia V. S.*) *Vneocherednaia Piataia Sessia Verkhovnogo Soveta SSSR* 31 *Oktiabria–2 Noiabria* 1939 g. [Extraordinary fifth session, 31 October–2 November 1939]. Izdanie Verkhovnogo Soveta SSSR, 1939.

(6 *Sessia V. S.*) *Shestaia Sessia Verkhovnogo Soveta SSSR* 29 *Marta–4 Aprelia* 1940 g. [Sixth session, 29 March–4 April, 1940]. Izdanie Verkhovnogo Soveta SSSR, 1940.

(7 *Sessia V. S.*) *Sed'maia Sessia Verkhovnogo Soveta SSSR* 1 *Avgusta–7 Avgusta* 1940 g. [Seventh session, 1–7 August 1940]. Izdanie Verkhovnogo Soveta SSSR, 1940.

(8 *Sessia V. S.*) *Vos'maia Sessia Verkhovnogo Soveta SSSR.* 25 *Fevralia–1 Marta* 1941 g. [Eighth session, 25 February–1 March, 1941]. Izdanie Verkhovnogo Soveta SSSR, 1942.

(9 *Sessia V. S.*) *Stenograficheskii Otchet Zasedania Verkhovnogo Soveta SSSR,* 18 *Iunia* 1942 g. [Stenographic report of the session of the Supreme Soviet of the U.S.S.R., 18 June, 1942]. Izdanie Verkhovnogo Soveta S.S.S.R., 1942.

(10 *Sessia V. S.*) *Desiataia Sessia Verkhovnogo Soveta S.S.S.R.* 28 *Ianvaria–1 Fevralia* 1944 g. [Tenth session, 28 January–1 February, 1944]. Izdanie Verkhovnogo Soveta S.S.S.R., 1944.

Voroshilov, K. E. *Stat'i i Rechi* [Articles and Speeches]. Moskva, 1936.

Vsesoiuznaia Kommunisticheskaia Partia(b): VKP(b) [All-Union Communist Party (Bolsheviks): CPSU(B)]. Up to the Fourteenth Congress the Party bore the name of Rossiiskaia Kommunisticheskaia Partia(b): RKP(b) [Russian Communist Party (Bolsheviks): RCP(b)]. Congresses of the Party: verbatim reports.

(*IX S'ezd RKP[b]*) *Protokoly Deviatogo S'ezda RKP(b),* 29 *Marta-4 Aprelia* 1920 g. [Minutes of the Ninth Congress of the RCP(b), 29 March–4 April, 1920]. Moskva, 1920.

(*X S'ezd RKP[b]*) *Protokoly Desiatago S'ezda RKP(b),* 8–16 *Marta* 1921 g. [Minutes of the Tenth Congress of the RCP(b), 8–16 March, 1921]. Moskva, 1921.

(*XI S'ezd RKP[b]*) *Odinadtsatyi S'ezd RKP(b),* Mart-Aprel' 1922 g. [Eleventh Congress of the RCP(b), March–April 1922]. Partizdat, 1936.

(*XII S'ezd RKP[b]*) *Dvenadtsatyi S'ezd Rossiiskoi Kommunisticheskoi Partii (b)* 17–25 *Aprelia* 1923 g. *Stenograficheskii Otchet* [Twelfth Congress of the Russian Communist Party (B), 17–25 April, 1923, stenographic report]. Moskva, 1923.

(*XIII S'ezd RKP[b]*) *Trinadtsatyi S'ezd Rossiiskoi Kommunisticheskoi Partii (Bolshevikov), Stenograficheskii Otchet* 23–31 *Maia* 1924 g. [Thirteenth Congress of the Russian Communist Party (Bolsheviks), stenographic report, 23–31 May, 1924]. Moskva, 1924.

(*XIV S'ezd VKP[b]*) *XIV S'ezd Vsesoiuznoi Kommunisticheskoi Partii* (*b*). 18–31 *Dekabria* 1925 g. *Stenograficheskii Otchet* [Fourteenth Congress of the All-Union Communist Party (B), 18–31 December, 1925 stenographic report]. Moskva-Leningrad, 1926.

(*XV S'ezd VKP[b]*)*XV S'ezd Vsesoiuznoi Kommunisticheskoi Partii* (*b*), 2–19 *Dekabria* 1927 g. *Stenograficheskii Otchet* [15th Congress of the All-Union Communist Party (B), 2–19 December, 1927, stenographic report]. Moskva-Leningrad, 1928.

(*XVI S'ezd VKP[b]*) *XVI S'ezd Vsesoiuznoi Kommunisticheskoi Partii* (*b*), 26 *Iunia*–13 *Iulia* 1930 g. [16th Congress of the All-Union Communist Party (B), 26 June–13 July, 1930]. Moskva-Leningrad, 1931.

(*XVII S'ezd VKP[b]*) *XVII S'ezd Vsesouiznoi Kommunisticheskoi Partii* (*b*), 26 *Ianvaria*–10 *Fevralia* 1934 g. *Stenograficheskii Otchet* [17th Congress of the All-Union Communist Party (B), 26 January–10 February, 1934, stenographic report]. Moskva, 1934.

Vsesoiuznaia Kommunisticheskaia Partia (*b*) *v rezoliutsiakh i resheniakh s'ezdov, konferentsii i plenumov Ts K.* 1898–1935 [The All-Union Communist Party (B) in resolutions and decisions of the congresses, conferences, and plenums of the C. C. 1898–1935]. 2 vols. 5–e izd., 1936.

3. ARTICLES

Aleksandrov, E. 'The Army of the Soviet People and the Capitalist Encirclement,' *Bol'shevik*, No. 5 (1938), pp. 49–59.

Aleksandrov, G. 'Some Tasks of the Social Sciences in the Contemporary Conditions,' *Bol'shevik*, No. 14 (1945), pp. 12–29.

Alekseev, B. 'The Monolithic Unity of the Soviet People,' *Vlast' Sovetov*, No. 10 (1939), pp. 22–5.

Alymov, A. 'In regard to the history of the Soviet constitution,' *Ob Izmeneniakh Sovetskoi Konstitutsii*. Moskva, 1935.

Antipov, N. 'The Work of the Commission of Soviet Control,' *Bol'shevik*, No. 17 (1935), pp. 9–16.

Azizian, A. 'The Successes of the Lenin-Stalin Nationality Policy,' *Bol'shevik*, No. 2 (1945), pp. 36–47.

Bazilevich, B. 'Peter I — Founder of the Russian Military Art,' *Bol'shevik*, No. 11–12 (June 1945), pp. 35–48.

Bazilevich, K. 'Documents Concerning the Prowess and Heroism of Russian Soldiers and Officers;' *Bol'shevik*, No. 5 (March 1945), pp. 59–64.

Bertsinsky, S. 'The Lenin Road of Development of the R.K.I.,' *Sov. Gos.*, No. 1–2 (1933), pp. 40–53.

Cheliapov, N. 'Sovetkaia Konstitutsia' [The Soviet Constitution], *E. G. i P.*, III, p. 916.

Dean, Vera Micheles. 'Russia's Foreign Economic Policy,' *Foreign Policy Reports*, 1 February, 1947.

Denisov, A. 'Constitutional Questions at the Session of the Supreme Soviet of the U.S.S.R.,' *A.R.S.U.*, May 1946, pp. 58–60.

Diablo, V. 'Immunitet' [Immunity], *E.G. i P.*, II, pp. 140–41.

Editorial. 'About the Marxist-Leninist Education of the Personnel of the Soviet Intelligentsia,' *Bol'shevik*, No. 9 (1944), pp. 1–8.

——. 'Create an Abundance of Basic Consumers' Goods,' *Izvestia*, 14 April 1946.

——. 'The Education of the Young Communists — One of the Fundamental Tasks of the Party Organizations,' *Bol'shevik*, No. 6 (1944), pp. 1–6.

——. 'The Fighting Reserve of the Bolshevik Party,' *Bol'shevik*, No. 20 (15 October, 1938), pp. 5–15.

Editorial. 'The Friendship of the Peoples of the U.S.S.R. — Mighty Factor of the Victory Over the Enemy,' *Bol'shevik*, No. 23–4 (December 1944), pp. 1–9.

——. 'The Great Strength of the Soviet Order,' *Bol'shevik*, No. 16 (August 1944), pp. 1–7.

——. 'The Great Desert of the Soviet People Before the History of Humanity,' *Bol'shevik*, No. 5 (March 1945), pp. 1–8.

——. 'The Glorious Working Class of the U.S.S.R.,' *Izvestia*, 26 December, 1945.

——. 'Intensify the Ideological-Political Work of the Party Organizations,' *Bol'shevik*, No. 17–18 (1944), pp. 1–8.

——. 'Leninism — the Most Advanced World View,' *Bol'shevik*, No. 1 (1944), pp. 3–10.

——. 'The Living Truth of Marxism,' *Bol'shevik*, No. 10–11 (1938), pp. 23–35.

——. 'Master Tirelessly Contemporary Technology, Science, and Culture,' *Komsomol'skii Rabotnik*, 21 November, 1945, pp. 19–24.

——. 'The Patriotism of the Soviet Peasantry,' *Izvestia*, 27 December, 1945.

——. 'The Russian People — Leading Force Among the Peoples of Our Country,' *Bol'shevik*, No. 10 (May 1945), pp. 3–12.

——. 'Tirelessly Raise the Ideological-Theoretical Level of the Party-Soviet Cadres,' *Bol'shevik*, No. 22 (1944), pp. 1–7.

——. 'Young Patriots of the Motherland,' *Bol'shevik*, No. 18 (September 1943), pp. 11–18.

Egolin, A. 'The Universal Significance of the Russian Literature,' *Pravda*, 26 December, 1945.

Fairchild, Mildred, 'Social-Economic Classes in Soviet Russia,' *A.S.R.*, June 1944, pp. 263–91.

Florinsky, Michael T. 'The Soviet Union and International Agreements,' *Political Science Quarterly*, March 1946, pp. 61–9.

Gak, G. 'Concerning the Role of the Personality and the Popular Masses in History,' *Bol'shevik*, No. 14 (1945), pp. 45–56.

——. 'Socialist Society and Personality,' *Bol'shevik*, No. 21 (1945), pp. 51–66.

Gatovskii, L. 'The Industrial Foundation of the Military Might of the U.S.S.R.,' *Bol'shevik*, No. 17–18 (September 1944), pp. 43–54.

Golunsky, S. 'The Supreme Soviet U.S.S.R. and the Organs of Justice,' *Sov. Gos.*, No. 3 (1938), pp. 87–93.

Gorshenin, P. 'Strengthen the Defense Organization Osoaviakhim,' *Bol'shevik*, No. 15 (1938), pp. 31–9.

Granovskii, E. 'The Strength and Viability of the Economic Base of the Soviet State,' *Bol'shevik*, No. 22 (November 1944), pp. 19–29.

Gribanov, M. 'Regarding the History of the Development of the Single-Manager and Collegiality Principles in the People's Commissariats,'' *Sov. Gos. i Pr.*, No. 11 (1940), pp. 61–9.

Hazard, John N. 'Housecleaning in Soviet Law,' *A.Q.S.U.*, April 1938, pp. 5–16.

——. 'Cleansing Soviet International Law of Anti-Marxist Theories,' *A. J. I. L.*, vol. 32, No. 2 (April 1938), pp. 244–52.

Iovchuk, M. 'Leninism and the Advanced Russian Culture of the XIX Century,' *Bol'shevik*, No. 21 (November 1945), pp. 35–50.

Iudin, P. 'The Teachings of Leninism about the Victory of Socialism in One Country,' *Bol'shevik*, No. 10–11 (1938), pp. 35–47.

Kaftanov, S. 'The Soviet Intelligentsia in the Great Patriotic War,' *Bol'shevik*, No. 5 (1944), pp. 16–31.

Kalinin, M. 'The Might of the Soviet State,' *Bol'shevik*, No. 7–8 (April, 1944), pp. 20–37.

——. 'About the Moral Face of Our People,' *Bol'shevik*, No. 1 (January 1945), pp. 11–30.

Kareva, M. 'The Composition of the Congresses of Soviets, Executive Committees, and Soviets,' *Sov. Gos.*, No. 6 (1934), pp. 29–37.

Kirpotin, V. 'Socialism and Personality,' *Bol'shevik,* No. 3 (1938) pp. 54–66.

——. 'Russian Culture,' *Bol'shevik,* No. 12 (15 June, 1938), pp. 47–63.

Kohn, Hans. 'Pan-Movements,' *Enc. Soc. Sci.,* vol. 11, pp. 545–7.

Konstantinov, F. 'Concerning the Marxist Understanding of the Role of Personality in History,' *Bol'shevik,* No. 10–11 (1938), pp. 47–61.

Korobkov, N. ' "The Heroic Past of the Russian People," ' [a review], *Bol'shevik,* No. 18 (September 1943), pp. 59–64.

——. 'Russian Military-Naval Traditions,' *Bol'shevik,* No. 5 (March 1944), pp. 50–64.

Kuzmin, L. 'The Marxist-Leninist Dialectics — Mighty Ideological Weapon of Our Party,' *Bol'shevik,* No. 3–4 (1945), pp. 12–23.

Kuz'minov, I. 'The Working Class of the U.S.S.R. in the Great Patriotic War,' *Bol'shevik,* No. 23–4 (1943), pp. 10–19.

Kuznetsov, I. 'The Victory of the Slavic Peoples in the External Struggle Against German Aggressors,' *Bol'shevik,* No. 10 (1945), pp. 25–37.

Laptev, I. 'The Strength of the Kolkhoz Order,' *Izvestia,* 16 December, 1945.

Lassalle, Ferdinand. 'Über Verfassungswesen' (1862), *Gesammelte Reden Und Schriften,* 11, Berlin, 1919.

Libman, Kh. 'About the First Soviet Constitution', *Ob Izmeneniakh Sovetskoi Konstitusii.* Moskva, 1935.

Lorimer, Frank. 'Recent Population Trends in the Soviet Union,' A.S.R., June 1944, pp. 219–22.

Matiushkin, N. 'The Great Strength of the Soviet Multinational State,' *Bol'shevik,* No. 5 (March 1946), pp. 18–29.

McBain, H. L. 'Constitutions,' *Enc. Soc. Sci.,* IV, p. 259.

Medynsky, Eugene. 'Schools and Education in the U.S.S.R.,' *A.S.R.,* June 1944, pp. 287–95.

Melish, William Howard. 'Religious Developments in the Soviet Union,' *A.S.R.,* June, 1944, pp. 279–86.

Mikhailov, N. 'XXV Years of the Leninist-Stalinist Komsomol,' *Bol'shevik,* No. 19–20 (October 1943), pp. 45–55.

Mitin, M. 'The Marxist-Leninist Theory is not a Dogma, but a Guide to Action,' *Bol'shevik,* No. 21–2 (1938), pp. 64–81.

——. 'The Victory of the Ideology of Friendship among Peoples over the Ideology of the Beastly Nationalism of the Fascists,' *Bol'shevik,* No. 21 (November 1944), pp. 22–32.

Moore, B., Jr., 'The Communist Party of the Soviet Union,' 1928–44, A.S.R., June 1944, pp. 267–78.

Morrison, J. A. 'The Evolution of the Territorial-Administrative System of the U.S.S.R.,' *A.Q.S.U.,* October 1938, pp. 35–46.

Plotkin, M. 'International Law Questions at the Second Session of the Supreme Soviet U.S.S.R.,' *Sots. Zak.,* No. 9 (1938), pp. 81–4.

Poliansky, N. 'The Stalin Constitution on the Judiciary and the Procurator's Office,' *Sov. Gos.,* No. 3 (1938), pp. 77–86.

Rabinowitch, Germina. 'Soviet Trade-Union Functions and Activities,' *A.R.S.U.,* February 1946, pp. 3–16.

R. S. M. 'Red Army "Morale Builders," ' *A.R.S.U.,* October–November 1941, pp. 11–24.

Rychkov, N. 'The Soviet Court — Fighting Organ of the Dictatorship of the Working Class, *Bol'shevik,* No. 7 (1938), pp. 23–33.

Seleznev, K. 'About the New Socialist Intelligentsia,' *Partiinoie Stroitel'stvo,* No. 13 (1939), pp. 39–40.

Shabad, Theodore. 'Recent Changes in the Political Geography of the Soviet Union,' *A.R.S.U.,* February 1946.

Shabad, Theodore. 'Political-Administrative Divisions of the U.S.S.R., 1945,' *The Geographical Review*, April 1946.

Shchebletsov, L. 'The Soviets — Conductors of the General Line of the Party,' *Vlast' Sovetov*, No. 1 (1938), pp. 21–4.

Shlifer, B. 'The Presidium of the Supreme Soviet U.S.S.R.' *Vlast' Sovetov*, No. 2 (1938), pp. 36–40.

Shnaidman, B. 'The Presidium of the Supreme Soviet of the Union S.S.R. — a Collective President,' *Sots. Zak.*, No. 8 (1938), pp. 38–46.

Shostak, G. 'About the Recall of Deputies by the Electors,' *Ob Izmeneniakh Sovetskoi Konstitutsii*, pp. 96–110. Moskva, 1935.

Shotwell, James T. 'The Idea of Human Rights,' *International Conciliation*, No. 426 (December 1946), pp. 551–61.

Simonzhenkova, M. 'About the Work of a Deputy of the Supreme Soviet of the Union S.S.R.,' *Vlast' Sovetov*, No. 8 (1938), pp. 27–31.

Speransky, N. 'Ten Years of the Rabkrin,' *Sov. Gos.*, No. 1–2 (1933), pp. 21–40.

Svetlov, V. 'Marriage and the Family under Capitalism and Socialism,' *Bol'shevik*, No. 16 (1938), pp. 44–58.

Talenskii, N. 'The Great Victorious Army of the Soviet Union,' *Bol'shevik*, No. 3 (February 1946), pp. 19–33.

Tikhomirov, P. 'Indestructible Is the Might of the Stalinist Bloc of Communists and Non-Party Men,' *Vlast' Sovetov*, No. 11–12 (1939), pp. 27–31.

Timasheff, N. S. 'Vertical Social Mobility in Communist Society,' *The American Journal of Sociology*, July 1944, pp. 9–21.

——. 'The Soviet School Experiment,' *The Russian Review*, Spring 1945, pp. 72–87.

Timiriazev, A. 'The Founders of Russian Physics,' *Bol'shevik*, No. 16 (August 1944), pp. 32–42.

Trainin, I. 'The Question of Sovereignty,' *Sov. Gos.*, No. 2 (1938), pp. 75–108.

——. 'Communism and the State,' *Sov. Gos. i Pr.*, No. 2 (1939), pp. 109–25.

——. 'The Content and System of Public Law,' *Sov. Gos. i Pr.*, No. 3 (1939), pp. 36–46.

——. 'Nation and Multinational State in the Works of Comrade Stalin,' *Sov. Gos. i Pr.*, No. 6 (1939), pp. 25–47.

——. 'Questions of Sovereignty in the Soviet Federal State,' *Bol'shevik*, No. 15 (1945), pp. 12–23.

Turubiner, A. M. 'The Organization of the Presidium of the Union C.E.C.,' *Sovetskoe Pravo*, No. 2 (1924), pp. 126–8.

Vasil'ev, V. 'About the Composition of Deputies [the Membership] of the Local Soviets of Toilers,' *V.V.S.*, No. 28 (25 June, 1941), p. 4.

Vasiliev, A. 'The Permanent Commissions of the Supreme Soviet of the U.S.S.R.,' *Sov. Gos. i Pr.*, No. 4 (1940), pp. 137–53.

Velikovsky, M. 'Marx and Engels on the National Question,' *Sov. Gos.*, No. 3 (1933), pp. 43–51.

Voznesensky, A. A. 'Temper Our Students Ideologically,' *Pravda*, 14 October, 1946.

Vyshinsky, A. 'Stalin's Constitution,' *Sots. Zak.*, No. 8 (1936), pp. 9–12.

——. 'The Marxian Teaching Concerning Law and State,' *Bol'shevik*, No. 12 (1938), pp. 11–33.

——. 'Lenin and Stalin on State and Law,' *Sov. Gos. i Pr.*, No. 1 (1939), pp. 41–69.

——. 'Stalin's Teaching Concerning the Socialist State,' *Sov. Gos. i Pr.*, No. 2 (1939), pp. 99–109.

——. 'The XVIII Congress of the C.P.S.U.(B) and the Tasks of the Science of Socialist Law,' *Sov. Gos. i Pr.*, No. 3 (1939), pp. 1–25.

Vyshinsky, A. 'Questions of State and Law in the Works of Comrade Stalin,' *Sov. Gos. i Pr.*, No. 6 (1939), pp. 1–25.

——. 'The Triumph of the Constitutional Principles of the Soviet State,' *Sov. Gos. i Pr.*, No. 5 (1939), pp. 12–28.

——. 'The Chief of the Soviet Government,' *Sov. Gos. i Pr.*, No. 2 (1940), pp. 3–23.

Werth, Alexander, 'The Outlook in the U.S.S.R.,' *International Affairs*, XXII, No. 1 (1946), pp. 28–40.

Wright, Quincy, 'Human Rights and the World Order,' *International Conciliation*, No. 389 (April 1943), pp. 238–62.

Zhdanov, A. A. 'Speech at the Festive Plenum of the C.C. of the A.L.C.L.U., *Bol'shevik*, No. 21–2 (15 November, 1938), pp. 38–46.

4. PERIODICALS

Abbreviation	*Name*
A.J.I.L.	The American Journal of International Law
A.J.S.	The American Journal of Sociology
A.P.S.R.	The American Political Science Review
A.R.S.U.	The American Review on the Soviet Union
A.Q.S.U.	(formerly The American Quarterly on the Soviet Union)
A.S.R.	American Sociological Review
	Bol'shevik [The Bolshevik]
B.S.U.	Bulletin on the Soviet Union
	Komsomol'skii Rabotnik [The Komsomol Worker]
	Partiinoe Stroitel'stvo [Party Construction]
	Pod Znamenem Marksizma [Under the Banner of Marxism]
	Political Science Quarterly
P.S.P.	Problemy Sotsialisticheskogo Prava [Problems of Socialist Law]
	Slaviane [The Slavs]
Sots. Zak.	Sotsialisticheskaia Zakonnost' [Socialist Legality]
	Sovetskaia Iiustitsia [Soviet Justice]
Sov. Gos. i Pr.	Sovetskoe Gosudarstvo i Pravo [The Soviet State and Law]
Sov. Gos.	(formerly Sovetskoe Gosudarstvo)
	Sputnik Agitatora [The Agitator's Companion]
	Vlast' Sovetov [The Rule of the Soviets]
	Zhurnal Moskovskoi Patriarkhii [The Journal of the Moscow Patriarchate]

Index